NATURAL
LANGUAGE
UNDERSTANDING

BENJAMIN/CUMMINGS SERIES IN COMPUTER SCIENCE

NATURAL LANGUAGE UNDERSTANDING

JAMES ALLEN
UNIVERSITY OF ROCHESTER

The Benjamin/Cummings Publishing Company, Inc.

Menlo Park, California • Reading, Massachusetts
Don Mills, Ontario • Wokingham, U.K. • Amsterdam
Sydney • Singapore • Tokyo • Madrid • Bogota
Santiago • San Juan

Sponsoring Editor: **Alan Apt**
Production Supervisors: **Mary Picklum / Sharon Montooth**
Cover Designer: **John Edeen**
Copy Editor: **Jonas Weisel**

Library of Congress Cataloging-in-Publication Data

```
Allen, James.
    Natural language understanding.

    Includes index.
    1. Programming languages (Electronic computers)--
Semantics. 2. Language and logic. 3. Artificial
intelligence. I. Title.
QA76.7.A44 1988        005.13        87-24224
ISBN 0-8053-0330-8
```

THE BENJAMIN/CUMMINGS PUBLISHING COMPANY, INC.
2727 Sand Hill Road
Menlo Park, California 94025

Preface

I started work on this book over four years ago for a course I teach at the University of Rochester on natural language understanding. At that time, there was no source for such a course except for collections of research papers, with each paper using a different notation. So much time was spent learning the notations that there was little time to appreciate the general principles underlying the field. Today this situation has changed little. While books on natural language understanding are now available, they either cover only one aspect of the area (say, syntactic processing) or they cover the entire field but not in enough depth.

As a result the primary goal in writing this book was to produce a comprehensive, in-depth description of the entire area of natural language understanding. To do this in a single book, I had to eliminate all the complexity not inherent in the process of understanding language. Most of all, the number of different notations introduced had to be kept to a minimum. This was accomplished by developing adaptations of a few select representations in the area that then could be used to present the range of problems and solutions from a wide range of sources. In addition, I made a deliberate effort not to assume a great deal of programming expertise. The essence of most algorithms in the literature is fairly simple and becomes complex only when the details of a particular implementation are considered. As a result, any reader having some familiarity with the basic notions of programming can obtain an understanding of the fundamental techniques without becoming lost in programming details. There is enough detail in this book, however, that a sophisticated programmer can take the abstract algorithms and produce useful working systems.

The book is intended both as a textbook and as a general reference for researchers in artificial intelligence and other areas related to language. As a text, it is suitable for an advanced undergraduate or beginning graduate level course in computer science or a graduate level course in linguistics. As a reference text, it is suitable for many advanced courses concerning language, for any research and development projects involving natural language processing, or for any individual interested in learning more about the area.

The Organization

Natural language understanding requires background in many different areas--most importantly, programming, linguistics, and logic. Very few people have all this background, however, so the book introduces whatever material is needed. In particular, there is an appendix on the first-order predicate calculus and another on basic programming techniques. Background material from linguistics is introduced as needed throughout the book. This should make the material accessible to all. The more background a reader has, however, the more he or she should be able to get from the book.

The book is organized by problem area, rather than by technique. As a result, much of the duplication found in a set of papers on a particular area is eliminated. It also makes the comparison of different techniques much easier. For example, rather than have a chapter on augmented transition networks, then another on context-free grammars, and another on logic-based grammars, the book is organized by linguistic problem. There is a chapter on basic context-free parsing that shows that the parsing techniques underlying all three of these representations are essentially the same. Then there is a chapter on simple augmented systems, again showing the similarities between each of the approaches. Finally, there is a chapter on how long-distance dependencies are handled.

While three different representations are presented for syntactic processing, the remainder of the book develops a single set of representations and translates all work in the area into these formalisms. In particular, the representations used are based on semantic networks, logical form, Horn clause logic systems, and frame-based systems.

How to Use This Book

To cover the entire book in detail would require a two-semester sequence in natural language processing. However, the book is organized so that it is easy to custom tailor a one-semester course concentrating on the topics that the instructor wants to cover. In particular, it is divided into three main parts: syntactic processing, semantic processing, and the use of context and general world knowledge. Each of these parts contains some introductory chapters that provide enough background that the material in the following parts can be understood. I have taught two different courses from the manuscript. One was a syntax and semantics course, with an emphasis on syntax, which covered Chapters 1-6 and the basic issues in semantics, consisting of Chapters 7 and 8 and selections from Chapter 9. Another was a course emphasizing the contextual aspects of language, which included Chapter 1, Chapters 7 and 8, and then Chapters 11-16 on world knowledge and discourse structure. Many other organizations are possible, either as a first course in the area or as a second--say, following a course that covers mainly syntactic aspects. The following chart outlines the main dependencies between the chapters.

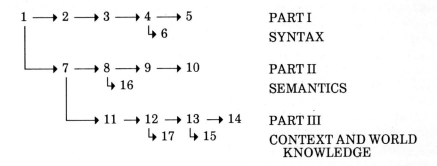

Part IV, Response Generation, contains two chapters. Chapter 16 examines question-answering techniques for database queries and relies only on the work in Part II. It includes two case studies of actual natural language interfaces to databases. Chapter 17 examines the issues in natural language generation and draws on the basic material from all of the first three parts.

References

The book contains extensive pointers into the literature so that the particular details of any one approach can easily be found. Each chapter also contains boxes, which contain optional material examining various issues in detail. Some boxes give additional background material from linguistics or philosophy, while other boxes examine some particular computational work that is related to the chapter. With the references the emphasis has been to identify the most readily available sources rather than the original papers in which ideas appeared. Thus I've cited journal articles, books, and papers in the major conferences in AI. I have tried to avoid technical reports and unpublished notes that are hard to find ten years after the fact. In general, most work in the area is published in technical reports several years before appearing elsewhere, so the dates of the references are often not a good indicator of when the work was actually done. While I've tried to be comprehensive and give credit for all the ideas in the book, I am sure that I've omitted key papers that I will regret immensely when I remember them. To these authors, please accept my apologies.

Acknowledgements

I first want to thank the Computer Science Department at the University of Rochester for their support over the last four years. I was given without question all the time and extra resources I needed to complete this project. I also want to thank Peggy Meeker for the preparation of many different drafts that were actually rewrites and her endless patience and assistance during the final revision and preparation of camera-ready copy. I do not have much of an eye for consistency of notation and style, and much of the continuity of this book is due to her corrections. Thanks also to Gail Cassell for her help in preparing the final draft.

Parts of this book would not have been possible without the support of the Office of Naval Research and the National Science Foundation, who have supported my natural language research for the last eight years. Also, the production of the book itself was greatly aided by the Xerox Corporation, who provided the facilities for producing the camera-ready copy through their University Grants Program.

I also thank the reviewers of the earlier drafts who provided many excellent comments on the presentation and content of the book. Eugene Charniak, Michal Ephratt, Ray Perrault, Bonnie Webber, Natalie Dehn, and Elaine Rich all made specific comments that helped the overall organization of the book, and Glenn Blank, Robin Clark, David Evans, Jim Hendler, Graeme Hirst, and Mike Swain all made detailed comments chapter by chapter that contributed much to the book's overall coherence and organization. This level of feedback would not have been manageable without my editor, Alan Apt, who actively participated in the reviewing process and who provided me with much valuable feedback and support during the final revisions.

Finally, I want to thank my wife, Judith Hook, and Jeffrey, Daniel, and Michael for keeping life interesting when I was trying my antisocial, tedious best to be totally obsessed with the task of completing this book.

Rochester, New York
July 1987

Brief Contents

Contents

Contents

Contents

Chapter 8
Semantic Interpretation 222

Chapter 9
Strategies for Semantic Interpretation 244

Chapter 10
Issues in Semantic Interpretation 282

PART III
CONTEXT AND WORLD KNOWLEDGE 313

Chapter 11
Knowledge Representation 314

Contents

Marcus Parser has limited input buffer

monotonic — logically consistent

prolog not.

Morphological Paradigm
— category which covers many instances
discontinuous - non local
in FSA w/z routes to avoid loop.
center embedding - shallow depth of 1
right embedding - is definite

Chapter 1

Introduction to Natural Language Understanding

1.1 What is Natural Language Understanding?

This book describes the basic techniques that are used in building computer models of natural language production and comprehension. In particular, the book describes the work in the interdisciplinary field called **computational linguistics** that arises from research in artificial intelligence (AI). There are two primary motivations for this type of research. First, the technological motivation is to build intelligent computer systems, such as natural language interfaces to databases, automatic machine-translation systems, text analysis systems, speech understanding systems, or computer-aided instruction systems. Second, the linguistic, or cognitive science, motivation is to gain a better understanding of how humans communicate by using natural language. This second motivation is not unique to computational linguistics, but is shared with theoretical linguistics and psycholinguistics.

The tools that the work in computational linguistics uses are those of artificial intelligence: algorithms, data structures, formal models for representing knowledge, models of reasoning processes, and so on. The goal of this computational approach is to specify a theory of language comprehension and production to such a level of detail that a person could write a computer program that can understand and produce natural language. Typical subareas of the field include the specification of parsing algorithms and the study of their computational properties, the construction of knowledge representation formalisms that can support the semantic analysis of sentences, and the modeling of reasoning processes that account for the way that context affects the interpretation of sentences.

While the goals of the computational approach overlap those of theoretical linguistics and psycholinguistics, the tools that are used in each of these fields differ markedly. Before you examine the computational methods, consider briefly the related disciplines.

Theoretical linguists are primarily interested in producing a structural description of natural language. They usually do not consider the details of the way that actual sentences are processed (the **parsing process**) or the way that actual sentences might be generated from structural descriptions. A major constraint on linguistic theories is that the theories should hold true in general across different languages; thus, theoretical linguists attempt to characterize the general organizing principles that underlie all human languages, and spend less time and effort examining any particular language. The goal of theoretical linguists is a formal specification of linguistic structure, both in the form of constructive rules that define the range of possible structures and in the form of constraints on the possible allowable structures.

Psycholinguists, like the computational linguists, are interested in the way that people actually produce and comprehend natural language. A linguistic theory is only useful to the extent that it explains actual behavior. As a result, psycholinguists are interested in both the representations of linguistic structures and the processes by which a person can produce such structures from actual sentences. The primary tool that is used is experimentation--that is, actual measurements made on people as they produce and understand language, including how much time a person needs to read each word in a sentence, how much time a person needs to decide whether a given item is a legal word or not, what types of errors people make as they perform various linguistic tasks, and so on. Experimental data is used to attempt to validate or reject specific hypotheses about language, which are often taken from the theories that linguists or computational linguists propose.

As mentioned earlier, there can be two underlying motivations for building a computational theory. The technological goal is simply to build better computers, and any solution that works would be acceptable. The cognitive goal is to build a computational analog of the human-language-processing mechanism; such a theory would be acceptable only after it had been verified by experiment. By necessity, this book takes a middle ground between these two criteria. On one hand, this reflects a belief that natural language is so complex that an *ad hoc* approach that a well-specified underlying theory does not support is not possible. Thus, the technological goal cannot be realized without using sophisticated underlying theories that are on the level being developed by theoretical linguists. On the other hand, the present state of knowledge about natural language processing is so preliminary that attempting to build a cognitively correct model is not feasible. Before researchers can begin a project to build such a model, there would have to be simultaneous major advances in both computational linguistics and the experimental techniques used by psycholinguistics. As a result, this book will assume that the current goal of computational linguistics is to produce a comprehensive, computational theory of language understanding and production that is well-defined and linguistically motivated. Constructing such a computational theory would be an important first step in producing a cognitively correct theory, as a computational theory could serve as a starting point for experimental testing and lead to modified theories that account for the experimental evidence.

1.2 Evaluating Computational Models of Language

One obvious method to evaluate a computational theory would be to run the program and see how well it performs. For instance, if the program is meant to answer questions about a database of facts, you might ask it questions to see how good it is at producing the correct answers. If the system is designed to

User:	ELIZA:
Men are all alike.	In what way?
They're always bugging us about something or other.	Can you think of a specific example?
Well, my boyfriend made me come here.	Your boyfriend made you come here.
He says I'm depressed much of the time.	I am sorry to hear you are depressed.
It's true, I am unhappy.	Do you think coming here will help you not to be unhappy?
I need some help; that much seems certain.	What would it mean to you if you got some help?
Perhaps I could learn to get along with my mother.	Tell me more about your family.
My mother takes care of me.	Who else in your family takes care of you?
My father.	Your father.
You are like my father in some ways.	What resemblance do you see?

Figure 1.1 A dialogue with ELIZA

participate in simple conversations on a certain topic, then you might run it and try conversing with it. While ultimately this method of evaluation may be the best test of a theory, at the present stage of the field, it can be misleading. For example, given that most systems only exist in complete working order for a brief time, you usually do not get to interact with the program yourself but must depend on transcripts of others' interactions. These transcripts can easily mislead you: the underlying theory of a program that seems to produce impressive results may prove to be much less interesting and important than another system that seems limited in its abilities. You can attribute much more intelligence to the program than is actually present.

Consider a concrete example--the ELIZA program that was developed in the mid-1960s at MIT. This program must be one of the most popular artificial intelligence programs of all time, and versions of it exist for most machines, including most micros. ELIZA was never claimed to embody a theory of language comprehension and production, and yet its behavior seems impressive. The system plays the role of a therapist and, to obtain the best results, the user should correspondingly play the role of a patient. Figure 1.1 presents a transcript of this system in operation.

Here is a simple description of the basic mechanism of ELIZA. There is a database of particular words that are called **keywords**. For each keyword, the system stores an integer, a pattern to match against the input, and a specification of the output. The algorithm is as follows: given a sentence S, find a keyword in S whose pattern matches S. If there is more than one keyword, pick the one with the highest integer value. Use the output specification that is associated with this keyword to generate the next sentence. If there are no keywords, generate an innocuous continuation statement, such as *Tell me more* or *Go on*.

Figure 1.2 shows a fragment of a database of keywords. In this database, a pattern consists of words and variables. The prefix "?" before a letter indicates a variable, which can match any sequence of words. For example, the pattern

?X are you ?Y

would match the sentence *Why are you looking at me?*, where the variable ?X matches *Why* and ?Y matches *looking at me*. The output specification may also use the same variables. In this case, ELIZA inserts the words that match the variables in the input into the output after making some minor changes in the pronouns (for example, ELIZA would replace *me* with *you*). Thus, for the pattern given earlier, the output specification

Would you prefer it if I weren't ?Y?

would generate a response *Would you prefer it if I weren't looking at you?* When the database lists multiple output specifications for a given pattern, ELIZA selects a different one each time that a keyword rule is used, thereby preventing unnatural repetition in the conversation. Using these rules, you can see the way that ELIZA generated the first two exchanges in the conversation in Figure 1.1. ELIZA generated the first response from the first output of the keyword *alike*, while generating the second response from the first output of the keyword *always*.

This description covers all of the essential points of the program! You will probably agree that this program does not understand the conversation that it is participating in. Rather, it is a simple collection of tricks. Given this, why does ELIZA appear to function so well? There are several reasons. Perhaps the most important reason is that, when people hear or read a sequence of words that they understand as a sentence, they attribute meaning to the sentence and assume that the person (or machine) that produced the sentence actually intended that meaning. People are extremely good at distinguishing word meanings and interpreting sentences to fit the context. As a result, ELIZA appears to be intelligent because you use your own intelligence to make sense of what it says.

Word	Rank	Pattern	Outputs
alike	10	?X	In what way?
			What resemblance do you see?
are	3	?X are you ?Y	Would you prefer it if I weren't ?Y?
	3	?X are ?Y	What if they were not ?Y?
always	5	?X	Can you think of a specific example?
			When?
			Really, always?
what	2	?X	Why do you ask?
			Does that interest you?

Figure 1.2 Sample data from ELIZA

There are other crucial characteristics of the conversational setting that also aid in sustaining the illusion of intelligence. For instance, the system does not need any world knowledge because it never has to make a claim, support an argument, or answer a question. Rather, ELIZA simply asks a series of questions. Except in a patient-therapist situation, this characteristic would be unacceptable. ELIZA evades all direct questions by responding with another question, such as *Why do you ask?* Thus, there is no way to force the program to say something concrete about any topic.

However, even in such a restricted situation, it is relatively easy to show that the program does not understand. For example, since ELIZA has no knowledge about the structure of language, it accepts gibberish just as readily as valid sentences. Thus, if you entered *Green the adzabak are the a ran four*, ELIZA would respond with something like *What if they were not the a ran four?* Furthermore, as a conversation progresses, it becomes obvious that the program does not retain any of the content in the conversation. It begins to ask questions that are inappropriate in light of the earlier exchanges, and its responses in general begin to show a lack of any focus. Of course, if you are not able to play with the program and must depend only on transcripts of conversations by others, you would have no way of detecting these flaws unless they were explicitly mentioned.

Thus, in addition to studying examples of system performance, computational linguistics needs a method to evaluate work. In general, there must be some underlying theory that researchers can describe precisely enough so that they can test new examples against the theory. In addition, generalizations about language in theoretical linguistics should be reflected in the computational theory.

1.3 Knowledge and Language

A language-comprehension program must have considerable knowledge about the structure of the language itself, including what the words are, how to combine the words into sentences, what the words mean, how these word meanings contribute to the sentence meaning, and so on. However, a program cannot completely simulate linguistic behavior without first taking into account an important aspect of what makes humans intelligent--their general world knowledge and their reasoning ability. For example, to answer questions or to participate in a conversation, a person not only must know a lot about the structure of the language being used, but also must know about the world in general and the conversational setting in particular. Thus, a natural language system would need methods of encoding and using this knowledge in ways that will produce the appropriate behavior. Furthermore, the knowledge of the current situation (or **context**) plays a crucial role in determining how the system interprets a particular sentence. This factor comes so naturally to people that researchers overlook it.

The different forms of knowledge have traditionally been defined as follows:

- **Phonetic and phonological knowledge** concerns how words are realized as sounds. While this type of knowledge is an important concern for automatic speech-understanding systems, there is not the space to examine these issues in this book.

- **Morphological knowledge** concerns how words are constructed out of more basic meaning units called **morphemes**. For example, you can construct the word *friendly* from a root form *friend* and the suffix *-ly*.

- **Syntactic knowledge** concerns how words can be put together to form sentences that look correct in the language. This form of knowledge identifies how one word relates to another (for example, whether one word modifies another, or is unrelated).

- **Semantic knowledge** concerns what words mean and how these meanings combine in sentences to form sentence meanings.

- **Pragmatic knowledge** concerns how sentences are used in different contexts and how context affects the interpretation of the sentence.

- **World knowledge** includes the general knowledge about the structure of the world that language users must have in order to, for example, maintain a conversation, and must include what

BOX 1.1 Syntax, Semantics, and Pragmatics

The following examples may help you understand the distinction between syntax, semantics, and pragmatics. Consider each example as the initial sentence of this book, which you know discusses natural language processing:

1. This book describes the basic techniques that are used in building computer models of natural language comprehension.

This sentence appears to be a reasonable start (I hope!). It agrees with all that is known about syntax, semantics, and pragmatics. However, each of the following examples violates one or more of these levels. Sentence 2 is well-formed syntactically and semantically, but not pragmatically:

2. Green frogs have large noses.

This sentence fares poorly as the first sentence of this book simply because the reader would find no reason for starting the book with this sentence. However bad sentence 2 would be as a start, sentence 3 is much worse:

3. Green ideas have large noses.

While sentence 3 is obviously pragmatically ill-formed, it is also semantically ill-formed. To see this, consider that you and I could argue about whether sentence 2 is true or not, but cannot do so with sentence 3. I cannot affirm or deny sentence 3 in coherent conversation. However, the sentence does have some structure for we can discuss what is wrong with it. In particular, ideas cannot be green and, even if they could be green, they certainly cannot have large noses. Sentence 4 is even worse:

4. Large have green ideas nose.

In fact, this sentence is unintelligible, even though it contains the same words as sentence 3. It does not even have enough of a structure so that you can say what is wrong with it. Thus, it is syntactically ill-formed.

Incidentally, there are cases in which a sentence may be pragmatically well-formed even though it is not syntactically well-formed. For example, if I ask you where you are going and you reply "I go store," the response would be understandable even though it is syntactically ill-formed. Thus, this sentence is at least pragmatically well-formed, and may even be semantically well-formed.

each language user must know about the other user's beliefs and
goals.

These definitions are imprecise, and probably cannot be made completely
definite because they are more characteristic of knowledge than actual classes
of knowledge. For instance, any particular fact might include aspects from
several different levels. However, this book will divide the problems into three
large phases of processing that are based on the computational techniques used
in each phase. The **parsing phase** covers those steps that affect the processing
of sentences into structural descriptions by using a grammatical description of
linguistic structure. This phase uses the syntactic and the morphological
knowledge. The **semantic interpretation phase** consists of the mapping of
the structural description of the sentence into a **logical form**, which represents
the meaning of the sentence independent of the context. This phase uses the
semantic knowledge plus parts of the pragmatic knowledge. Finally, the
contextual interpretation phase maps the syntactic and logical forms into a
final representation of the effects of understanding the sentence. This final
meaning is represented using a language that supports an inference component
to model natural reasoning. This phase includes the remainder of the
pragmatic knowledge and general world knowledge.

1.4 Representations and Ambiguity

A quick look at a dictionary will convince you that most words have multiple
meanings, which this book will call **senses**. For example, the word *cook* has a
sense as a verb and a sense as a noun; *dish* has multiple senses as a noun as
well as a sense as a verb; and *still* has senses as a noun, verb, adjective, or
adverb! Yet in most conversations, most people do not notice those senses that
are not appropriate. This fact makes the language comprehension problem
appear much easier that it actually is. While a person does not seem to
consider each of the possible senses of a word when understanding a sentence, a
program must explicitly eliminate them one by one!

Ambiguity occurs at all levels of analysis and not just at the word level. For
instance, even if you determine the right sense of each word in the sentence
Jack cooked Sue's dinner, the sentence could mean that Jack made dinner for
Sue or that Jack cooked the dinner that Sue had bought (either for himself or
someone else). Without knowing the context of the sentence, you cannot
identify the appropriate reading. Other sentences may appear to have only one
meaning, yet you can use them to convey something else. For example, if you
are in the lobby of a theater and the person next to you says, "Excuse me--
you're standing on my foot," it would be inappropriate for you to treat this as a
simple assertion of a fact and respond, "Yes, I agree." In this context, the
sentence obviously is meant as a request that you get off the person's foot.

There are two related subproblems at each of the three phases of analysis. The first subproblem is the **representation problem**: how the different interpretations possible at a given level are represented. The second subproblem is the **interpretation problem**: how the appropriate representations at each level are produced from the input to that level. Before you can examine the specific representations that are used in this book, first consider some essential properties of a representation:

- The representation must be precise and well-defined. In particular, while you may need to represent ambiguity concisely in a representation, it is fundamentally important that you can express every distinct reading of a sentence unambiguously in the representation. In other words, an ambiguous natural sentence may have several distinct, possible representations, with each representation identifying a different reading.

- The representation should capture the intuitive structure of the natural language sentences that it represents. For example, sentences that appear to be structurally similar will have similar structural representations. This property occurs at all levels. For example, at the final-meaning level, the meanings of sentences that are paraphrases of each other should be closely related to each other in some way. (For example, they might be represented by the same form, or they might be similar with respect to the inferences that you can make from them.)

Syntax: Representing Sentence Structure

The syntactic structure of a sentence indicates the way that words in the sentence are related to each other. This structure indicates how the words are grouped together into phrases, what words modify what other words, and what words are of central importance in the sentence. In addition, this structure may identify the types of relationships that exist between phrases, and can store other information about the particular sentence structure that may be needed for later processing. For example, consider the following sentences:

1.   John sold the book to Mary.

2.   The book was sold to Mary by John.

Each of these sentences share certain structural properties. In each, the noun phrases are *John*, *Mary*, and *the book*, and the act described is some selling action. In other respects, these sentences are significantly different. For instance, even though sentence 1 and sentence 2 are always either true or false in the exact same situations, you could only give sentence 1 as an answer to the question *What did John do for Mary?* Sentence 2 is a much better continuation of a sentence beginning with the phrase *After it fell in the river*, as sentences 3 and 4 show. Following the standard convention in linguistics, this book will use an asterisk (*) before any example of an ill-formed or questionable sentence.

3.   *After it fell in the river, John sold Mary the book.

4.   After it fell in the river, the book was sold to Mary by John.

You will recognize other structural properties of sentences by considering sentences that are not well-formed.   As shown next, sentence 5 is ill-formed because the subject and the verb do not agree in number (the subject is singular and the verb is plural), while sentence 6 is ill-formed because the verb *put* requires some modifier that describes where John put the object.

5.   *John are in the corner.

6.   *John put the book.

A parsing process extracts the structural properties of sentences and produces a syntactic representation that assigns a structure name (such as S for sentence or NP for noun phrase) to each major grouping of words. It identifies the properties of each structure as a set of **values**. A **slot name** distinguishes each value and indicates the role that the value plays in the structure. For example, the structural descriptions of sentences 1 and 2 are shown in Figure 1.3. Slot names are in boldface (such as **MAIN-V**), while values are either words (such as John), sets of feature values (such as {3s}), or other structures (such as an NP structure in an S structure).

While you do not need to consider the details of the representation now, certain observations are worth making. In addition to providing an organization for words, each syntactic structure includes other important features that are not explicit in the sentence. For instance, each NP has a **NUM** slot that indicates information about the person and number for that NP. In all of the examples in Figure 1.3, the feature value is {3s}, which indicates third person singular. You can then use this information to check agreement requirements such as subject-verb agreement. Other features shown in Figure 1.3 include **TENSE**, the tense of the sentence, and **VOICE**, the voice of the sentence, which indicates whether the sentence is active or passive.

It is important to realize that you do not store features and make agreement checks just so that you can detect illegal sentences. Making judgments on grammar is not a goal of computational linguistics. Rather, the agreement checks are essential for eliminating potential ambiguities that would arise if they were not used. For example, sentences 7 and 8 that follow are identical

```
(S  SUBJ (NP  NAME John            (S  SUBJ (NP  DET the
              NUM {3s})                          HEAD book
    MAIN-V sold                                  NUM {3s})
    TENSE {PAST}                       MAIN-V sold
    VOICE {ACTIVE}                     TENSE {PAST}
    OBJ  (NP  DET the                  VOICE {PASSIVE}
              HEAD book                AUX was
              NUM {3s})                MODS ((PP PREP to
    MODS (PP  PREP to                            POBJ (NP  NAME Mary
              POBJ (NP  NAME Mary                          NUM {3s}))
                        NUM {3s}))          (PP PREP by
                                                 POBJ (NP  NAME John
                                                           NUM {3s})))
```

Figure 1.3 The structural descriptions of sentence 1 and sentence 2

except for the number feature of the main verb, and represent two quite distinct interpretations:

7.   Flying planes are dangerous.

8.   Flying planes is dangerous.

If you did not check subject-verb agreement, then these two sentences would be indistinguishable and ambiguous. You would be able to find similar examples for every syntactic feature that this book introduces and uses.

Even using a wide range of agreement checks, you will find that many sentences are still structurally ambiguous and, thus, have multiple syntactic forms. When you can recognize this ambiguity by using different feature values, you can list in your representations the possible features by using curly brackets--{ and }--to indicate a list of options. For example, the NP *the fish* is ambiguous between being a single fish and being many fish. A single NP structure

```
(NP DET the
    HEAD fish
    NUM {3s 3p})
```

can represent this ambiguity. In other cases, where the ambiguity involves structures, the output of the syntactic phase may include a list of possible syntactic representations.

The Logical Form

After extracting the structural properties of a sentence, a program must consider the individual meanings of the words and use them to construct an overall sentence meaning. This task is dependent on the context of the discourse. A program may use the context to identify the appropriate sense of a word, the appropriate sentence meaning, or the way that the sentence is being used. For example, the thing that a speaker is referring to when saying the NP *the catch* would depend on whether the speaker is talking about a baseball game or a fishing expedition. Similarly, the question *Do you know the time?* is a request for the time in some situations, an offer to tell someone the time in others, and a simple yes-no question in others.

The question arises as to whether any part of semantic processing is independent of context. This book bases its idea of logical form on the assumption that a lot of semantic processing is independent of context; hence it is worthwhile to use this information to produce a representation of the sentence that the program can then use as input to a contextual processor. By dividing the problem up in this way, each part is correspondingly simpler and easier to understand.

What type of information can the logical form represent? First, there is an abstract set of semantic relationships that can hold between the verb and its NPs. In particular, in both sentences 1 and 2 above, the action described is a selling event, where *John* is the seller, *the book* is the object being sold, and *Mary* is the buyer of the book. These roles are instances of the abstract semantic roles AGENT, THEME and TO-POSS (for final possessor), respectively. Similar semantic roles appear in sentence 9, in which *Jack* is the AGENT, *Mary* is the THEME, and *the Halloween ball* is the TO-LOC (for final location) role:

9.   Jack took Mary to the Halloween ball.

In sentence 9, you also see that the word *ball*, which is ambiguous between the plaything (this book will call this the semantic type SPHERE) and the social event (this book will call this type PARTY), can only take its PARTY interpretation because of the context of the surrounding words. The logical form of the sentence is as follows:

```
(PAST i1 TAKE-ACTION  [AGENT (NAME p1 PERSON "Jack")]
                      [THEME (NAME p2 PERSON "Mary")]
                      [TO-LOC (DEF/SING b1 PARTY
                             (CELEBRATES b1 HALLOWEEN))])
```

You can read this form as follows: i1 is a TAKE-ACTION; its semantic role AGENT is filled with a person named *Jack*, its role THEME is filled with a person named *Mary*, and its role TO-LOC is filled with a particular object **b1** that is a party that celebrates Halloween. As with the syntactic form, the logical form can represent local ambiguities by listing options in curly brackets, whereas more complicated ambiguities will require enumerating separate logical forms for each interpretation. For example, the sentence *Jack left the ball* might have a single syntactic interpretation, but would have these two possible logical forms:

(PAST l1 LEAVE-OBJ [AGENT (NAME j1 PERSON "Jack")]
                    [THEME (DEF/SING **b3** SPHERE])

(PAST l1 LEAVE-LOC [AGENT (NAME j1 PERSON "Jack")]
                    [FROM-LOC (DEF/SING **b3** PARTY)])

The other important method of capturing ambiguity in the logical form is the use of abstract semantic relations. You have seen this already with the semantic roles for verbs. For example, the notion of THEME only captures the relationship between the NP and the verb at a very abstract level; it is the NP that the action described affects or acts upon. This general relation might be realized in the later semantic representation in many different ways. For example, the THEME role in the sentence *Jack invited Mary to the ball* might be realized in the final meaning representation if you use a relation such as INVITEE, which entails that Mary will have to accept or decline the invitation. In the first of the logical forms just given, the THEME role might map to some location relation (for example, the ball is at the same place where Jack was before he left). Similarly, the logical form might contain an abstract possessor relation, POSS, that you can use in NPs such as *Jack's coat*. This abstract relation would then map to more specific relations in the final meaning, such as *the coat owned by Jack, the coat Jack is wearing*, and so on. This concept should become clearer in the next section on the final meaning representation.

The Final Meaning Representation

The final meaning representation is not so easily characterized as the two representations just described, since it is not realized solely from the sentence itself. Rather, it is the result of the sentence, the context of the previous sentences in the conversation, and general background knowledge about the world. Later, this book will present several different formalisms for representing this level. However, for the purposes of this section, assume that the first-order predicate calculus (FOPC) is the final representation language because it is relatively well known, well studied, and is precisely defined. While this book will examine inadequacies of FOPC later, for most of the book these inadequacies are not relevant to the issues being discussed.

Appendix A provides an introduction to logic that you should read next if
you are unacquainted with logic. This section only introduces the notation used
throughout the book, and assumes you are already familiar with FOPC.
Statements in FOPC will always be expressed in italics. Constants will be
uppercase words followed by one or more digits (such as *JOHN1* and *FIDO33*),
functions will be in lowercase (such as *father(JACK44)*), and predicates will be
in uppercase without any digits, although subscripts will be allowed if you need
to represent different senses of a single verb (such as *HAPPY(JACK1)* and
POSSESS₁(JACK1, FIDO55)). The logical operators used will be **and (&)**, **or
(∨)**, **exclusive-or (⊕)**, **not (¬)**, **implication (⊃)**, and **equivalence (⇔)**. The
universal quantifier is ∀ and the existential is ∃. The dot notation is used to
indicate scope; for example, the formula

$$\forall x . P(x) \,\&\, \exists y . Q(x, y) \lor R(y)$$

is equivalent to the formula

$$\forall x \,(P(x) \,\&\, \exists y \,(Q(x, y) \lor R(y)))$$

While this description tells you what the language is, it does not tell you
what the particular predicates are that you should use for representing the
meanings of sentences. Here, you have considerable choice. For example,
consider a classic case of two sentences that are paraphrases of each other:

1.   John sold the book to Mary.

10.   Mary bought the book from John.

Assume that these two sentences map logical forms that involve different
abstract relations for the verb, as shown here:

(PAST **s1** SELL-EVENT [AGENT (NAME **p1** PERSON "John")]
                        [THEME (DEF/SING **b1** BOOK)]
                        [TO-POSS (NAME **p2** PERSON "Mary")])

(PAST **b2** BUY-EVENT [AGENT (NAME **p3** PERSON "Mary")]
                        [THEME (DEF/SING **b2** BOOK)]
                        [FROM-POSS (NAME **p4** PERSON "John")])

In mapping these logical forms to FOPC, you need to do several tasks. First,
you must identify the referents of the NPs. Assume that, in the context that
these sentences are given, a constant *JOHN22* represents *John*, a constant
MARY1 represents *Mary*, and a constant *BOOK67* represents *the book*. Next,
you need to map the abstract relations to predicates; here, the choices arise.
The first choice is whether verb relations map directly to FOPC predicates or to

an expanded form that involves many predicates. For example, analyses 11 and 12 can represent sentence 1:

11.   *SELL(JOHN22, BOOK67, MARY1)*

12.   *SELL-EVENT(E1) & SELLER(E1, JOHN22) &*
      OBJECT(E1, BOOK22) & SELLEE(E1, MARY1)

Typically, you find analyses like 11 in systems that base their representation on logic or on database relations, whereas you usually use analyses like 12 in systems that are based on semantic networks or frames. Both analyses are useful notations, each being more convenient than the other in certain situations. The first is more concise in many settings, whereas the second is more flexible and general.

Another important issue that is relevant to paraphrase examples concerns the selection of predicate names. In particular, given sentences 1 and 10, you could use a single neutral predicate--say *TRANSFER-FOR-MONEY*--to represent both, or have two closely related predicates--say *SELL* and *BUY*. Since you make this decision independent of the first choice made earlier, you should examine it by using only the more concise notation, which was used in analysis 11. The identical argument also works for the extended notation. The neutral representation allows you to represent both sentences 1 and 10 by the same formula:

13.   *TRANSFER-FOR-MONEY(JOHN22, BOOK67, MARY1)*

However, the nonneutral representation uses analysis 11 for the meaning of sentence 1 and the following analysis for sentence 10:

14.   *BUY(MARY1, BOOK67, JOHN22)*

You can see the consequences of this decision when you consider question answering. With the neutral representation, it would be trivial to answer the question *Did Mary buy the book from John?* given sentence 1, since the representation of the question (using *buy*) and the representation of the initial assertion (using *sell*) would be identical. In the nonneutral representation, you could only answer such a question if the two predications were related by an axiom that you could use during question answering. Such an axiom might be as follows:

15. $\forall x, y, z . BUY(x, y, z) \Leftrightarrow SELL(z, y, x)$

Thus, answering the question in the neutral representation is a simple data retrieval, while answering the question in the other is a theorem-proving process. Obviously, if it is possible, the neutral representation is the best. While you can use this technique successfully for simple examples, it does not seem possible to eliminate the need for an inference component in general. This book will examine these issues in detail later. For now, use an informal strategy of using neutral representations where they are applicable, and otherwise depending on there being an inference component to give you the appropriate semantic relationships.

1.5 A Warning about Names in Representations

As is common practice in the literature, the names that are used for formal terms in the representations will be highly suggestive of the natural language words that they represent. For example, the representation may call the semantic category used for the class of birds BIRD, the category for animals ANIMAL, and so on. The relation name used to depict the concept of liking will be LIKES, and the relation name used for the ability to fly will be CAN-FLY. This practice makes it easy for you to keep track of what each object and relation is supposed to represent, and makes descriptions of reasoning processes easier to understand. However, the practice is highly misleading in one crucial respect. The formal system has no knowledge about the intended meaning of terms; it can only use the facts and inference rules that are specified for it. The danger is the same as you saw earlier with the ELIZA program. When presented with a line of reasoning using English terms, you, as a reader, tend to attribute more meaning to the process than is actually present. In fact, the reasoner uses no meaning as you know it. Rather, the reasoner uses a set of formal rules that manipulates symbols totally independently of the way they are written. For example, consider the following application of an inference rule:

$$BIRD(TWEETY1)$$
$$\forall x . BIRD(x) \supset CAN\text{-}FLY(x)$$
$$CAN\text{-}FLY(TWEETY1)$$

You can read this as follows: given that Tweety is a bird and that all birds can fly, you can justifiably conclude that Tweety can fly. You might then believe that this shows that the system knows about birds, and about Tweety in particular. In fact, all of this is misleading; the line of reasoning shows nothing more about birds than the following:

$$HOUSE(WATER33)$$
$$\forall x . HOUSE(x) \supset BURNS(x)$$
$$BURNS(WATER33)$$

Either line of reasoning is as acceptable as the other. Imagine that the semantic interpreter mapped the NP *Tweety* to *WATER33*, the notion of being a bird to the predicate *HOUSE*, and the notion of being able to fly to the predicate *BURNS*. Then this second representation would behave identically to the representation implicit in the naming of the first.

Why is this process dangerous? The representation issues can easily be trivialized and overlooked. By mapping the concept of being a bird to the predicate name *BIRD*, it is often assumed that that step solves the semantic problem--that somehow the objects that satisfy the predicate *BIRD* will have all of the appropriate properties of birds. In actual fact, the only properties of such objects are those that are explicitly derivable from the axioms that involve the predicate *BIRD*. To avoid this confusion, some researchers deliberately use nonsense words for their predicates and constants. Unfortunately, this practice makes the formulas significantly harder to understand. Thus, this book will continue to use the obvious names at the risk of misleading you into overestimating the power of the representation.

It should be pointed out that, while the example just given was created by using FOPC formulas and proofs, the same argument holds for any representation used in AI. Unfortunately, the less defined the formalism, the more likely that this confusion can arise. In fact, this confusion led many people who developed early AI representations to believe that they could represent a wider range of situations than possible by using FOPC. However, when researchers finally defined the notations precisely, the apparent extra power disappeared.

1.6 The Organization of Actual Systems

This book is committed to using a specific organization for a natural language comprehension system, as shown in Figure 1.4. Under this organization, the system processes a sentence by passing it through each of the three phases in sequence. However, the system does not have to process the sentence entirely at one level before analyzing at the next level. In fact, one of the organizations considered is **incremental processing**, where the system passes the partial results from one level onto the next before analyzing the entire sentence. This structure also allows information to flow backwards through the system. For instance, it may be that a partial result passed on by syntax is semantically anomalous. The semantic interpreter could then send this information back to the parser, which could use this information to eliminate parts of the syntactic structure that used the anomalous phrase. For example, consider the following two sentences:

16.   Visiting relatives can be trying.

17.   Visiting museums can be trying.

These two sentences are identical in structure, and so you could consider both to be syntactically ambiguous. In sentence 16, the subject of the sentence might be relatives who are visiting you, or the event of you visiting relatives. Both of these alternatives are semantically valid, and you would need to

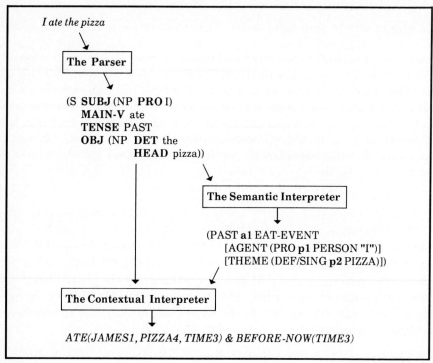

Figure 1.4 The flow of information

determine the appropriate sense by using the contextual mechanism. However, sentence 17 only has one possible semantic interpretation, since museums are not objects that can visit other people; rather they must be visited. In a system with fully separate syntactic and semantic processing, there would be two syntactic interpretations of sentence 17, one of which the semantic interpreter would eliminate. With an incremental organization, however, the system would detect the semantic anomaly as soon as it interprets the phrase *visiting museums*. If this information were sent back to the parser, then it would build only the correct analysis.

Thus, the division into phases is more a conceptual division than one of sequencing. While this book concentrates on each phase independently so that the various techniques in each can be considered in detail, you do not need to organize actual systems along the same lines. In fact, most current systems combine at least two of these phases into a single phase. Some combine the syntactic-interpretation and semantic-interpretation phases to produce a semantically driven parser, whereas others maintain a separate syntactic phase and combine the semantic- and contextual-processing phases.

Summary

This book describes computational theories of natural language processing. These theories are divided into three main subareas that this book will examine in detail. Syntactic processing involves the analysis of a natural language sentence and produces a representation of its structure. A system then uses this structure as input to the semantic interpretation phase, which produces a logical form. Next, the system uses the logical form as input to the contextual interpretation phase, which develops a final representation of the sentence.

Related Work and Further Readings

A good idea of work in the field can be obtained by reading two articles in Shapiro (1987) under the headings Computational Linguistics and Natural Language Understanding. There are also articles on specialized subareas such as Machine Translation, Natural Language Interfaces, Natural Language Generation, and so on. Longer surveys on certain areas are also available. Slocum (1985) gives a survey of machine translation, and Perrault and Grosz (1986) give a survey of natural language interfaces.

You can find a description of the ELIZA program that includes the transcript of the dialog in Figure 1.1 in Weizenbaum (1966). The basic technique of using template matching was developed further in the PARRY system, as described in the paper by Colby in Schank and Colby (1973). That same book also contains descriptions of early natural language systems, including those by Winograd and by Schank. Another important early system is the LUNAR system, an overview of which can be found in Woods (1977). For another perspective on the AI approach to natural language, refer to the introduction in Winograd (1983).

Exercises for Chapter 1

1. *(easy)* Define a set of data rules for ELIZA that would generate the first ten exchanges in the conversation in Figure 1.1.

2. *(easy)* Discover all of the possible meanings of the following sentences by giving a paraphrase of each interpretation. For each sentence, identify whether the different meanings arise from structural ambiguity, semantic ambiguity, or pragmatic ambiguity.

   a) Time flies like an arrow.
   b) He drew one card.
   c) Mr. Spock was charged with illegal alien recruitment.
   d) He crushed the key to my heart.

3. *(easy)* Classify these sentences as being any combination of the following (perhaps none), given that the person uttering the sentence is responding to a complaint that the car is too cold: (*i*) syntactically incorrect; (*ii*) semantically incorrect; (*iii*) pragmatically incorrect.

   a) The heater are on.
   b) The tires are brand new.
   c) Too many windows eat the stew.

4. *(medium)* Implement an ELIZA program that can use the rules that you developed in Exercise 1 and run it for that dialog. Without adding any more rules, what does your program do on the next few utterances in the conversation in Figure 1.1? How does the program do if you run it in a different context--say, a casual conversation at a bar?

PART I

SYNTACTIC PROCESSING

Chapter 2

Linguistic Background: An Outline of English

Chapter 3

Basic Parsing Techniques

Chapter 4

Features and Augmented Grammars

Chapter 5

Grammars for Natural Language: Handling Movement

Chapter 6

Toward Deterministic Parsing

Chapter 2

Linguistic Background:
An Outline of English

This chapter provides background material on the basic structure of English for those who have not taken any linguistics courses. It reviews the major phrase categories and identifies their most important subparts. Along the way, all the basic word categories used in the book are introduced. While the only structures discussed are those for English, much of what is said here applies to nearly all other European languages as well. The reader who has some background in linguistics can quickly skim this chapter, as it does not address any computational issues.

2.1 Words

At first glance the most basic unit of linguistic structure appears to be the word. The word, though, is far from the fundamental element of study in linguistics; it is already the result of a complex set of more primitive parts. Indeed the science of **phonology** analyzes the basic sound units of which words are composed. Unfortunately, this book will not have the time to consider these aspects.

An area of study that will be useful at times throughout the book is **morphology**, which is the study of the construction of words from more basic components corresponding roughly to meaning units. In particular, a word may consist of a **root** form plus additional affixes. For example, the word *friend* can be considered to be a root form from which the adjective *friendly* is constructed by adding a **suffix** *-ly*. This form can then be used to derive the adjective *unfriendly* by adding a **prefix** *un-*. A more complex derivation would allow you to derive the noun *friendliness* from the adjective form. While many interesting and complex issues are concerned with how such words are derived, and how the choice of word form is affected by the syntactic structure of the sentence that constrains it, this book again will not have time to examine such issues in detail.

Two related areas of evidence are used to divide words into categories. The first area concerns the word's contribution to the meaning of the phrase that contains it, and the second area concerns the actual syntactic structures in which the word may play a role. For example, you might posit the class **noun** as those words that can be used to identify the basic type of object, concept, or place being discussed, and **adjective** as those words that further qualify the object, concept, or place. Thus *green* would be an adjective, and *book* would be a noun, as shown in the phrases *the green book* and *green books*. But things are not so simple: *green* might play the role of a noun, as in *That green is lighter than the other*, and *book* might play the role of a modifier, as in *the book worm*. In fact, any noun seems to be able to be used as a modifier in some situation.

Perhaps the classes should be combined, since they overlap a great deal. But other forms of evidence exist. For example, consider what words could complete the sentence *It's so ....* You might say *It's so green*, *It's so hot*, *It's so true*, and so on. Note that even though *book* can be a modifier in *the book worm*, you cannot say *It's so book* about anything. Thus there are apparently two classes of modifiers: adjective modifiers and noun modifiers. In Section 2.2 the description of legal noun phrases will have to include this fact. For now, the examples present evidence for two distinct classes of words.

Consider again the case where adjectives can be used as nouns, as in *the green*. Not all adjectives can be used in such a way. For example, *the hot* or *the angry*, if written in a sentence, would refer to a set of hot things or angry people. They cannot refer to hotness or anger in the same way the phrase *the green* refers to green. With this evidence you could subdivide adjectives into two subclasses--those that can also be used to describe a concept or quality directly, and those that cannot. Alternately, however, you could also simply say that *green* is ambiguous between being an adjective or a noun and, therefore, falls in both classes. Since *green* can behave like any other noun, the second solution seems the most direct.

Similar arguments could be made for all the word classes outlined in the following sections, but this book will not go into them in such detail. It is important to realize, however, that even if you are careful you will always find cases where it is not clear whether to subdivide the classes further, and you will always find particular words that do not fit easily into any but the most general classes and, therefore, need idiosyncratic treatment.

2.2 The Elements of Simple Noun Phrases

Noun phrases (abbreviated here as NPs) are used to refer to things: objects, concepts, places, events, qualities, and so on. The simplest noun phrases consist of a single pronoun, such as *he, she, they, you, me, it, I*, and so on. For example, pronouns can refer to physical objects, as in sentence 1:

1.   *It* hid under the rug.

to events, as in sentence 2:

2.   Once I opened the door, I regretted *it* for months.

and to qualities, as in sentence 3:

3.   He was so angry, but he didn't show *it*.

Pronouns do not take any modifiers, except in rare forms, such as in sentence 4:

4.   *He who hesitates* is lost.

Another basic form of noun phrase consists of a **name** or **proper noun** such as *John* or *Rochester*. These nouns appear in capitalized form in carefully written English. Names may also consist of multiple words, as in *The New York Times* and *Stratford on Avon*.

The remaining forms of noun phrases consist of a main word, called the **head**, and other words that qualify the head and identify the nature of the item being referred to.

The head of a noun phrase is always a noun. Nouns divide into two main classes:

> **count nouns**--nouns used to describe some specific object or set of objects.

> **mass nouns**--nouns used to describe composites or substances.

Count nouns acquired their name because they could be counted. There may be one *dog* or many *dogs*, one *book* or several *books*, one *crowd* or several *crowds*. If a single count noun is used to describe a whole class of objects, it must be in its plural form. Thus you can say *Dogs are friendly* but not *Dog is friendly*.

Mass nouns cannot be counted. There may be *some water, some wheat,* or *some sand*. If you try to count with a mass noun, you change the meaning. For example, *some wheat* refers to a portion of some quantity of wheat, whereas *all wheats* refers to all types of wheat, and *one wheat* is a single type of wheat rather than a single grain of wheat. Mass nouns may be used to describe a whole class of material without using a plural form. Thus you say *Water is necessary for life*, not *Waters are necessary for life*.

In addition to a head, noun phrases may contain **specifiers** and **qualifiers** preceding the head. The qualifiers further describe the general class of objects identified by the head, while the specifiers indicate how many such objects are being described, as well as how the objects being described relate to the speaker and hearer. Specifiers are constructed using words from the following classes:

> **quantifiers**--words indicating how many objects are being referred to. Examples include *each, every, any, all, no, many, few, some, neither, both, half*, and so on.

> **demonstratives**--words indicating how the object is related to the speaker (for example, *this* vs. *that*), whether the object is uniquely identifiable from the situation (for example, *the* vs. *a*), and whether the object needs to be identified by the hearer (for example, *what, which*).

> **possessives**--words constructed from other noun phrases and indicating possession in some sense of the object described in the noun phrase.

> **ordinals**--words identifying an object by its ordering in a set, such as *first*, *second*, and so on.

> **cardinals**--words indicating the number of objects being described, such as *one*, *two*, and so on.

Possessives are formed by adding the suffix *-'s* to nouns or names, as in *John's folly* or *the toad's hole*. Possessive pronouns have their own separate forms, including *my*, *your*, *our*, *their*, and so on.

With few exceptions, a simple noun phrase may contain one demonstrative, one possessive, or one quantifier, but not more than one. In addition, a simple noun phrase may contain at most one ordinal and one cardinal. Thus you can say *each boy* and *this boy* but not *each the boy* or *this each boy*. A significant exception to this rule exists with a few quantifiers such as *many*, *few*, *several*, and *little*. These words can be preceded by a determiner, yielding noun phrases such as *the few songs we knew*. Using this evidence, you could subcategorize the quantifiers, but the present coarse categorization is fine for our present purposes.

Most other apparent contradictions to this rule involve embedded prepositional phrases that will be considered in the next section. Thus a noun phrase such as *some of every class* is not an exception because it is not a simple noun phrase. Rather it is a noun phrase constructed from a quantifier and a prepositional phrase, which itself consists of another noun phrase--namely, *every class*.

A small number of quantifiers, including *all*, *half*, and *both*, appear to contradict the rule explicitly. For example, you can say *all the horses*. Such a phrase, however, can be considered a variant of the noun phrase *all of the horses*. This type of analysis will be discussed at length later in the book.

The qualifiers in a noun phrase occur after the specifiers (if any) and before the head. They consist of adjectives and nouns being used as modifiers. More precise definitions would be as follows:

> **adjectives**--words that attribute qualities to objects yet do not refer to the quality itself (for example, *angry* is an adjective that attributes the quality of anger to something).

> **noun modifiers**--mass or count nouns used to modify another noun, as in *the cook book*.

	Person		
Number	First	Second	Third
singular	I	you	he (masculine) she (feminine) it (neuter)
plural	we	you	they

Figure 2.1 Pronoun system (as subject)

	Person		
Number	First	Second	Third
singular	my	your	his her its
plural	our	your	their

Figure 2.2 Pronoun system (possessives)

	Person		
Number	First	Second	Third
singular	me	you	him her it
plural	us	you	them

Figure 2.3 Pronoun system (as object)

Before moving on to other structures, consider the different forms that nouns take and how they are realized in English. Two forms of nouns--the singular and plural forms--have already been mentioned. Pronouns take forms based on **person** (first, second, and third) and **gender** (masculine, feminine, and neuter). Each one of these distinctions reflects a systematic analysis that is almost wholly explicit in some languages, such as Latin, while implicit in others. In French, for example, nouns are classified by their gender. In English, many of these distinctions are not explicitly marked except in a few cases. The pronouns provide the best example of this. They distinguish **number, person, gender**, and **case** (that is, whether they are used as possessive, subject, or object), as shown in Figures 2.1 through 2.3.

2.3 The Elements of Simple Sentences

While noun phrases are used to refer to things, sentences (abbreviated here as Ss) are used to assert, query, or bring about some partial description of the world. Thus you may assert that some sentence is true, ask whether a sentence is true, or command someone to do something described in the sentence. The way a sentence is used will be called its **mood**. Four basic moods for sentences are shown in Figure 2.4.

The Verb Group

For the moment, consider assertions, which are sentences in the declarative mood. The simplest assertions consist of a single noun phrase, called the **subject**, and a **verb group**. Note that a pronoun in the subject position must be of the proper form (that is, one of the subject forms rather than one of the object or possessive forms). The verb group consists of a **head verb** plus optional **auxiliary verbs**. The head verb may be in one of five distinct forms, as shown in Figure 2.5.

Auxiliary verbs consist of the various forms of *be*, *do*, and *have*, plus a set of **modal** auxiliaries such as *will*, *can*, *could*, and so on. Auxiliary verbs and the forms of the head verb combine in certain ways to form different **tenses**. The tense system refers to when the proposition described in the sentence is said to be true. The tense system is complex; only the basic forms are outlined in Figure 2.6. In addition, verbs may be in the **progressive aspect**. Corresponding to the tenses in Figure 2.6 are the progressive tenses shown in Figure 2.7. Each progressive tense is formed by the normal tense construction of the verb *be*, followed by a present participle.

Verb groups are also encoded by person and number information in the first word (verb or auxiliary) in the verb group. The person and number must agree with the noun phrase preceding the verb. Some verbs distinguish nearly all the possibilities, but most verbs distinguish only the third person singular (by adding an *s* suffix). Some examples are shown in Figure 2.8.

Transitivity and Passives

As explained earlier, a simple form of sentence consists of a noun phrase followed by a verb group. Examples include *Jack laughed*, *He will have been running*, and *The three largest balloons were rising*. Many main verbs, however, cannot be used in such simple sentences, because they require a second noun phrase immediately following the verb group. For example, you cannot say *Jack found*, but you can say *Jack found a key*. Equally, other verbs cannot take a second noun phrase; thus you cannot say *Jack laughed a key*.

Mood	Example
declarative (or assertion)	The cat is sleeping.
yes/no question	Is the cat sleeping?
wh-question	What is sleeping? or Which cat is sleeping?
imperative (or command)	Shoot the cat!

Figure 2.4 Basic moods of sentences

Form	Examples	Example Uses
infinitive	hit, cry, go, be	*Hit* the ball! I want to *go*.
simple present	hit, cries, go, am	The dog *cries* every day. I *am* thirsty.
simple past	hit, cried, went, was	I *was* thirsty. I went to the store.
present participle	hitting, crying, going, being	I'm *going* to the store. *Being* the last in line aggravates me.
past participle	hit, cried, gone, been	I've *been* there before. The cake was *gone*.

Figure 2.5 The five verb forms

Tense	Structure of Verb Group	Example
simple present	simple present	He walks to the store.
simple past	simple past	He walked to the store.
simple future	*will* + infinitive	He will walk to the store.
past perfect (or present/past)	*have* in present + past participle	He has walked to the store.
future perfect	*will* + *have* in infinitive + past participle	I will have walked to the store.
pluperfect (or past/past)	*have* in past + past participle	I had walked to the store.

Figure 2.6 The basic tenses

Tense	Structure	Example
present progressive	*be* in present + present participle	He is walking.
past progressive	*be* in past + present participle	He was walking.
future progressive	*will* + *be* in infinitive + present participle	He will be walking.
past perfect progressive	*have* in present + *be* in past participle + present participle	He has been walking.
future perfect progressive	*will* + *have* in present + *be* as past participle + present participle	He will have been walking.
pluperfect progressive	*have* in past + *be* in past participle + present participle	He had been walking.

Figure 2.7 The progressive aspect

	First	Second	Third
singular	I *am* I *walk*	you *are* you *walk*	he *is* she *walks*
plural	we *are* we *walk*	you *are* you *walk*	they *are* they *walk*

Figure 2.8 Person/number forms of verbs

Verbs that allow an initial noun phrase only, which is the **subject**, are called **intransitive verbs**. Verbs that require a second noun phrase, known as the **object**, are referred to as **transitive verbs**. As an exercise, consider some simple sentences that have transitive verbs and pronouns as their noun phrases. You will see that the subject/object distinction indicated by the pronouns agrees with the preceding description of the noun phrase positions.

Transitive verbs allow another form of verb group called the **passive** form, which is constructed using a *be* auxiliary followed by the past participle. In the passive form the noun phrase that would usually be in the object position is used in the subject position, as can be seen by the examples in Figure 2.9.

Active Sentence	Passive Sentence
Jack saw the ball.	The ball was seen by Jack.
I will find the clue.	The clue will be found by me.
Jack hit me.	I was hit by Jack.

Figure 2.9 Active sentences with corresponding passive sentences

Sentence with Indirect Object	Equivalent Form
Jack gave *Sue* a book.	Jack gave a book *to Sue*.
Jack found *me* a book.	Jack found a book *for me*.

Figure 2.10 Indirect object forms

There are some important things to note about the passive construct. As usual the tense is still carried by the initial verbs in the verb group. Also, even though the first noun phrase semantically seems to be the object of the verb in passive sentences, it is syntactically the subject. This can be seen by checking the pronoun forms. For example, *I was hit*, not *Me was hit*, is correct. Furthermore, the tense and number agreement is between the verb and the syntactic subject. Thus you say *I was hit by them*, rather than *I were hit by them*.

Passive sentences optionally indicate the noun phrase that would be in the subject position in the active counterpart using a prepositional phrase with the preposition *by*. This is the only way that such a noun phrase can explicitly be mentioned in a passive sentence.

Some verbs allow two noun phrases to follow them in a sentence--for example, *Jack gave Sue a book* or *Jack found me a key*. In these cases, there is usually an equivalent sentence that contains the noun phrase immediately following the verb group (called the **indirect object**) preceded by a preposition. In such sentences the second noun phrase corresponds to the object noun phrase outlined earlier. To distinguish this phrase from the indirect object, it is sometimes called the **direct object** rather than the object.

The most common uses of indirect objects indicate the recipient of some transfer of possession named by the verb or indicate the person for whom the action described by the verb is done. These uses can be seen by considering the equivalent sentences using prepositions as shown in Figure 2.10.

Particles

Some verb forms are constructed from a verb and an additional word called a **particle**. Particles generally overlap with the class of prepositions considered in the next section. Some examples are *up*, *out*, *over*, and *in*. With verbs such as *look*, *take*, or *put*, you can construct many different verbs by combining the verb with a particle (for example, *look up*, *look out*, *look over*, and so on). In some sentences the difference between a particle and a preposition results in two different readings for the same sentence. For example, *look over the paper* would mean reading the paper, if you consider *over* a particle (verb is *look over*). The same sentence would mean, not reading the paper, but simply looking at something else behind or above it, if you consider *over* a preposition (verb is *look*).

You can make a sharp distinction between particles and prepositions when the object of the verb is a pronoun. With a verb particle sentence, the pronoun must precede the particle, as in *I looked it up*. With the prepositional reading, the pronoun follows the preposition, as in *I looked up it*.

Particles must immediately follow the verb or immediately follow the object NP. Thus you can say *I gave up the game to Mary* or *I gave the game up to Mary*, but not *I gave the game to Mary up*.

2.4 Prepositional Phrases

The most common form of prepositional phrase consists of a preposition (*on*, *from*, *to*, *by*, *through*) followed by a noun phrase, which is called the **object of the preposition**. You can test the consistency of this naming again by considering the form of pronoun allowed. Thus you can say *by me* but not *by I*.

Prepositional phrases (PPs) may be used to qualify different parts of sentences. A prepositional phrase is said to be attached to the phrase it qualifies. For example, in *I gave the book to Sue*, the PP is attached to the verb structure *give* because it specifies one of the participants in the giving event. In *I gave the book from Sue*, however, the PP qualifies the noun phrase *the book*. It does not make sense to consider it modifying the giving event. Thus each verb identifies a set of PPs that could be used to qualify the verb. For the verb *give*, phrases beginning with *to* can be attached to the verb, while phrases beginning with *from* cannot.

There are more complex prepositional phrases as well. For example, some PPs, such as *out of the oven*, appear to have two introductory prepositions. In other cases the preposition appears to be separated from its object noun phrase, as in *We saw the river that Sam Patch died in*. Sentences like this last one will be considered in the next section.

Finally, you can make good arguments for considering the class of words including *here*, *there*, *afterward*, *later*, *upstairs*, *today*, and *home* to be prepositional phrases without a preposition! The reason is that they can be used wherever a preposition can be used--often in places where a noun phrase is explicitly not allowed. For example, consider the intransitive verb *come*. You can say *I came* or *He came by the back roads*, but you cannot say *I came the rock*. Thus *come* allows a PP, but not an NP, to follow it. Notice that the words just listed are also acceptable--*I came later*, *Come home*, and so on.

2.5 Embedded Sentences

You can build more complex sentences from smaller sentences by allowing one sentence to include another as a subclause. Two common uses of embedded sentences are as noun phrases and as relative clauses in noun phrases.

Several forms of sentences can be used as noun phrases. These forms involve slight modifications to the sentence structure to mark the phrase as a noun phrase, but otherwise the phrases are identical in structure to a sentence phrase. The simplest form involves introducing the word *that* as a signal, as in *That George had the ring was surprising*. Other forms include

> To own a car would be delightful.
> It's impossible for us to finish the job by noon.
> Giving the game up is cowardly.
> John's giving the game up caused many of us to leave the tournament.
> The game being given up by John disappointed the crowd.

In the last two embedded sentences the same sentence appears in active mood and then passive mood. The fact that certain forms, such as the passive mood, hold for these NPs is strong evidence that they should be considered to be sentence structures even though they are being used as NPs.

Relative clauses involve a sentence form used as a modifier in a noun phrase. These clauses are often introduced by a **relative pronoun** such as *who*, *which*, *that*, and so on, as in

> The man who gave Bill the money ...
> The rug that George gave to Ernest ...
> The man who(m) George gave the money to ...

In each of these relative clauses the embedded sentence is the same structure as a regular sentence except that one noun phrase is missing. If this missing NP is filled in with the NP that the sentence modifies, the result is a complete sentence that captures the same meaning as what was conveyed by the relative clause. The missing NPs in the preceding three sentences occur in the subject position, object position, and as object to a preposition, respectively. Deleting

the relative pronoun and filling in the missing NP in each produces the
following:

> The man gave Bill the money.
> George gave the rug to Ernest.
> George gave the money to the man.

As was true earlier, relative clauses can be modified in the same ways that
regular sentences can. In particular, passive forms of the preceding sentences
would be as follows:

> Bill was given the money by the man.
> The rug was given to Ernest by George.
> The money was given to the man by George.

Correspondingly, these sentences could have relative clauses in the passive
form, as follows:

> The man Bill was given the money by ...
> The rug that was given to Ernest by George ...
> The man the money was given to by George ...

Notice that some relative clauses need not be introduced by a relative pronoun.
Often the relative pronoun can be omitted, producing what is called a **reduced
relative clause**.

2.6 Complements

One usual definition of complement refers to it as the phrases that follow the
head word of any of the three major structures studied thus far--namely, S, NP,
and PP. This definition includes the NPs that follow a verb as well as the NP
that follows a preposition. Because these NPs have been dealt with explicitly,
they will be excluded from the present discussion of complement, which
considers only non-NP complements--that is, the sentences and PPs that follow
the head word in NPs, PPs, and Ss.

The discussion has already included several examples of non-NP
complements--for instance, relative clauses, which are complements in an NP
structure, and prepositional phrases, which are complements to the verb in an
S structure. Many of the embedded sentence forms shown earlier can be used as
sentence complements to verbs such as *want, like, decide,* and *believe.* Each
verb, however, may allow only a few specific forms. For example, you can say *I
want to own a car,* but you cannot easily say *I want that I own a car,* even
though the two sentences might appear to mean the same thing. Conversely,
you can say *I believe that I own a car,* but you cannot say *I believe to own a car.*
As yet another example, *decide* allows both forms, as in

I decided to own a car.
I decided that I would own a car.

Notice, however, the difference in meaning between these two forms. Other verbs require the sentential complement to be in the **subjunctive form**. In these cases the verb is in its infinitive form, as in *I insist that we go to the party.*

As with relative clauses, some verb complement sentences have a deleted NP, specifically in the subject position. Sometimes this missing NP is the subject of the main verb, while at other times it is presented in what appears to be the object of the verb. For example, you can say *I want to own a car*, as well as *I believe John to own a car.*

This last example reveals some of the complexities regarding how the main sentence and the embedded sentence are related. Each sentence can be passivized, changing the position of *John*. Passivizing the main S produces *John is believed to own a car (by me)*, whereas passivizing the embedded S produces *I believe a car to be owned by John*. Passivizing both Ss is possible if the embedded sentence is passivized first, producing *A car was believed to be owned by John (by me!)*. This phenomenon will be examined in greater detail in Chapter 5.

2.7 Adjective Phrases

Adjectives can occur singly in NPs, as in *the heavy book*, or multiply in NPs, such as in *the (heavy) (red) book*. In the latter case each adjective modifies the head noun. Adjective phrases also occur as the complement to certain verbs, including *be*, *look*, and *seem*, as in *The book is red* or *The book looks heavy*.

More complex forms of adjective phrases can include qualifiers preceding the adjective as well as complements after the adjective. Qualifiers include other adjectives, such as the phrase *bright red* in *the (bright red) book*, and adverbs, such as *completely red* and *terribly heavy*, and the negative form *not red*.

Adjective complements include PPs, as in *hungry for learning* and *yellow with age*, and Ss, as in *careful to step on every crack*, *afraid that Jack would lose*, *easy to get along with*, and *proud to be a frog*.

Finally, some adjectival forms, called degree clauses, take a qualifier form that requires a complement of a certain form. These include phrases such as *as slow as a dead horse* and *so tired that he passed out*.

Summary

The major phrase structures of English have been introduced--namely, the noun phrases, sentences, prepositional phrases, and adjective phrases. These will serve as the building blocks for the syntactic structures introduced in the following chapters.

Related Work and Further Readings

Another brief survey of the structure of English can be found in Winograd (1983). More extensive discussions can be found in any introductory textbook in linguistics (such as Radford (1981)). The most comprehensive sources are books that attempt to describe the entire structure of English. A good example of one of these books is Quirk et al. (1972). A good source from a computational viewpoint is Sager (1981).

Exercises for Chapter 2

1. *(easy)* Explain in detail, using the terminology of this chapter, why each of the following sentences is ill formed. In particular, state what rule (given in this chapter) has been violated.

   a) He barked the wrong tree up.
   b) She turned waters into wine.
   c) Don't take many all the cookies!
   d) I feel floor today.
   e) They all laughed the boy.

2. *(easy)* Classify the following verbs as being intransitive, transitive, or bitransitive (that is, it takes a two-NP complement). If the verb can be used in more than one of these forms, give each possible classification. Give an example of each to demonstrate your analysis.

   a) cry
   b) sing
   c) donate
   d) put

3. *(easy)* Using the verb *to be*, give example sentences that use the six basic tenses in Figure 2.6 and the six progressive tenses in Figure 2.7.

4. *(easy)* Using the verb *donate*, give examples of the passive form for each of the six basic tenses in Figure 2.6.

5. *(easy)* Give two structurally distinct sentences that involve a double nesting of embedded sentences.

6. *(easy)* Find five verbs not discussed in this chapter that take an indirect object and, for each one, give a paraphrase of the same sentence using a prepositional phrase instead of the indirect object. Try for as wide a range as possible.

7. *(medium)* Wh-questions are questions that use a class of words that includes *what, where, who, when, whose, which,* and *how.* For each of these words, give the syntactic categories (for example, verb, noun, noun group, adjective, quantifier, prepositional phrase, and so on) in which the words can be used. Justify each classification with some examples that demonstrate it. Use both positive and negative arguments as necessary (such as "it is one of these because . . .," or "it can't be one of these even though it looks like it might, because . . .").

Imitation of FS grammars
   strengths - better pattern matchers
      - can generate finite sentences
   weaknesses - don't reflect true structure
      - not good at modeling embedding
         or discontinuous constraints

   top down - goal driven
   bottom up - data driven

Chapter 3

Basic Parsing Techniques

ambiguity 2-terms
- more than one category for some word
- more than one choice from a transaction

To examine how the syntactic structure of a sentence can be computed, you must consider two things: the **grammar**, which is a formal specification of the structures allowable in the language, and the **parsing technique**, which is the method of analyzing a sentence to determine its structure according to the grammar. This chapter examines different ways to specify simple grammars and considers three fundamental parsing techniques. Chapter 4 then describes the methods for constructing syntactic representations that are useful for later semantic interpretation.

The discussion begins by introducing and comparing two grammatical formalisms: context-free grammars and recursive transition networks. The second section describes the characteristics of a good grammar. With this background the text turns to parsing techniques, introducing the top-down parsing technique, a bottom-up parsing method, and finally a mixed-mode strategy.

3.1 Grammars and Sentence Structure

Representing Sentence Structure

In this section you will consider methods of describing the structure of sentences and explore ways of characterizing all the legal structures in a language. The most common way of representing a sentence structure is to use a treelike representation that outlines how a sentence is broken into its major subparts, and how those subparts are broken up in turn. For example, the tree representation for the sentence *John ate the cat* is shown in Figure 3.1. This illustration can be read as follows: The sentence (S) consists of an initial noun phrase (NP) and a verb phrase (VP). The noun phrase is made of the simple NAME *John*. The verb phrase is composed of a verb (VERB) *ate* and an NP, which consists of an article (ART) *the* and a common noun (NOUN) *cat*. In list notation this same structure could be represented as

         (S (NP (NAME John))
             (VP (VERB ate)
                 (NP (ART the)
                     (NOUN cat))))

Context-Free Grammars

To construct such descriptions, you must know what structures are legal for English. A set of rules, called **rewrite rules**, describes what tree structures are allowable. These rules say that a certain symbol may be expanded in the tree by a sequence of other symbols. For instance, a set of rules that would allow the tree structure in Figure 3.1 is the following grammar:

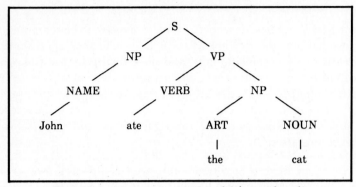

Figure 3.1 A tree representation of *John ate the cat.*

S ← NP VP
VP ← VERB NP
NP ← NAME
NP ← ART NOUN

These rules state the following: An S may consist of an NP followed by a VP; a VP may consist of a VERB followed by an NP; an NP may consist of a NAME, or may consist of an ART followed by a NOUN. Grammars consisting entirely of rules of the form "<symbol> ← <symbol>$_1$ ... <symbol>$_n$," for n≥1, are called context-free grammars (CFGs). CFGs are a very important class of grammars for two reasons. The formalism is powerful enough to be able to describe most of the structure in natural languages, and yet it is restricted enough so that efficient parsers can be built to analyze sentences. Symbols that cannot be further decomposed in a grammar, such as NOUN, ART, and VERB in the preceding example, are called **terminal symbols**. The other symbols, such as NP, VP, and S, are called **nonterminal symbols**. The terminal symbols are actually word categories, and a structure called the **lexicon** maintains a list of all words that fall in each category. Of course, many words will be listed under multiple categories. For example, *can* would be listed under VERB and NOUN.

Two common and simple parsing techniques for CFGs are known as **top-down** and **bottom-up parsing**. Top-down parsing begins by starting with the symbol S and rewriting it--say, to NP VP. These symbols may then themselves be rewritten as per the rewrite rules. Finally, terminal symbols such as NOUN may be rewritten by a word, such as *cat*, which is marked as a noun in the lexicon. Thus in top-down parsing you use the rules of the grammar in such a way that the right-hand side of the rule is always used to rewrite the symbol on the left-hand side. In bottom-up parsing, you start with the individual words and replace them with their syntactic categories. Using the rewrite rules, you may replace the current analysis by one of the same size or smaller. If you rewrite the sentence to S in this way, you have succeeded. In this case the

```
1. S ← NP VP          5. VP ← VERB
2. NP ← ART NOUN      6. VP ← VERB NP
3. NP ← NAME          7. VP ← VERB NP PP
4. PP ← PREP NP       8. VP ← VERB PP
```

Grammar 3.2

left-hand side of the rule is used to rewrite the sequence of symbols on the right-hand side.

A possible top-down parse for *John ate the cat* would be

S → NP VP	
→ NAME VP	(rewriting NP)
→ John VP	(rewriting NAME)
→ John VERB NP	(rewriting VP)
→ John ate NP	(rewriting VERB)
→ John ate ART NOUN	(rewriting NP)
→ John ate the NOUN	(rewriting ART)
→ John ate the cat	(rewriting NOUN)

A possible bottom-up parse of the sentence *John ate the cat* might be

→ NAME ate the cat	(rewriting John)
→ NAME VERB the cat	(rewriting ate)
→ NAME VERB ART cat	(rewriting the)
→ NAME VERB ART NOUN	(rewriting cat)
→ NP VERB ART NOUN	(rewriting NAME)
→ NP VERB NP	(rewriting ART NOUN)
→ NP VP	(rewriting VERB NP)
→ S	(rewriting NP VP)

A slightly larger grammar for a simple class of declarative English sentences, not including embedded sentences, is shown as Grammar 3.2. Some sentences that would be acceptable according to this grammar and a suitable lexicon are

John saw the cat by the pond.
The dog barked in the house.

Also, since this grammar does not encode any information as to what verbs may take objects, and what prepositions are appropriate for each verb, it would also accept the following sentences:

The dog allow the house.
John barked the cat by the pond.

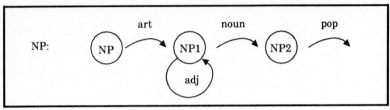

Grammar 3.3

A tree representation, such as Figure 3.1, can be viewed as a record of the CFG rules that account for the structure of the sentence. In other words, if you kept a record of the parsing process, it would be something similar to the parse tree representation. Record keeping will be examined in detail in Chapter 4.

Simple Transition Networks

Another grammar representation is often more convenient for visualizing the grammar. This formalism is based on the notion of a **transition network consisting of nodes and labeled arcs.** Consider the network named NP in Grammar 3.3. Each arc is labeled with a word category. Starting at a given node, you can traverse an arc if the current word in the sentence is in the category on the arc. If the arc is followed, the current word is updated to the next word. A phrase is a legal NP if there is a path from the node NP to a **pop arc** (an arc labeled pop) accounting for every word in the phrase. This network recognizes the same set of sentences as the following context-free grammar:

NP ← ART NP1
NP1 ← ADJ NP1
NP1 ← NOUN

Consider parsing the noun phrase *a purple cow* with the preceding network. Starting at the node NP, you can follow the arc labeled art, since the current word is an article--namely, *a*. From node NP1 you can follow the arc labeled adj using the adjective *purple*, and finally, again from NP1, you can follow the arc labeled noun using the noun *cow*. Since you have reached a pop arc, *a purple cow* is a legal noun phrase.

Recursive Transition Networks

The simple transition network formalism is not powerful enough to describe all languages that can be described by a CFG. To get the descriptive power of CFGs, you need a notion of recursion in the network grammar. **A recursive transition network** (RTN) is like a simple transition network, except that it allows arc labels that refer to other networks rather than word categories. Thus, given the NP network in Grammar 3.3, a network for simple English sentences

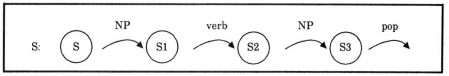

Grammar 3.4

Arc Type	Example	How Used
CAT	noun	succeeds only if current word is of the named category
WRD	of	succeeds only if current word is identical to the label
PUSH	NP	succeeds only if the named network can be successfully traversed
JUMP	jump	always succeeds
POP	pop	succeeds and signals the successful end of the network

Figure 3.5 The arc labels for RTNs

can be expressed as shown in Grammar 3.4. Uppercase labels refer to networks. The arc from S to S1 can be followed only if the NP network can be successfully traversed to a pop arc. Although not shown in this example, RTNs allow true recursion--that is, a network might have an arc labeled with its own name.

Consider finding a path through the S network for the sentence *The purple cow ate the grass*. Starting at node S, to follow the arc labeled NP, you need to traverse the NP network. Starting at node NP, traverse the network as before for the input *the purple cow*. Following the pop arc in the NP network, return to the S network and traverse the arc to node S1. From node S1 you follow the arc labeled verb using the word *ate*. Finally, the arc labeled NP can be followed if you can traverse the NP network again. This time the remaining input consists of the words *the grass*. You follow the arc labeled art, and then the arc labeled noun in the NP network, and take the pop arc from node NP2, and then another pop from node S3. Since you have traversed the network and used all the words in the sentence, *The purple cow ate the grass* is accepted as a legal sentence.

In practice, RTN systems incorporate some additional arc types that are useful but not formally necessary. Figure 3.5 summarizes the arc types, together with the notation that will be used in this book to indicate these arc types. According to this terminology, arcs that are labeled with networks are called **push arcs**, and arcs labeled with word categories are called **cat arcs**. In addition, an arc that can always be followed is called a **jump arc**.

BOX 3.1 Generative Capacity

The three grammatical formalisms discussed here are simple transition networks, recursive transition networks, and context-free grammars. These formalisms can be compared according to their **generative capacity**, which is the range of languages that each formalism can describe. This book is concerned with natural languages, but it turns out that no natural language can be characterized precisely enough to define generative capacity. Formal languages, however, allow a precise mathematical characterization.

For example, consider a formal language consisting of the symbols a, b, c, and d (think of these as words). Then define a particular language L1, where the only legal sentences consist of strings of letters in alphabetical order. For example, abd, ad, bcd, b, and $abcd$ are all legal sentences. Can each of the grammatical formalisms describe this language? In fact, all three can. For example, a transition network to generate this language would be as follows:

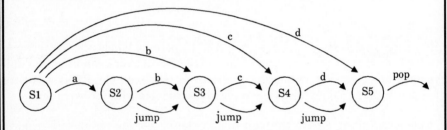

Consider another language, L2, that consists only of sentences that have a sequence of a's followed by an equal number of b's--that is, ab, $aabb$, $aaabbb$, and so on. You cannot write a simple transition network grammar that can generate exactly L2. A CFG to generate L2, however, is simple:

$$S \leftarrow a\,b$$
$$S \leftarrow a\,S\,b$$

Similarly, an RTN is simple:

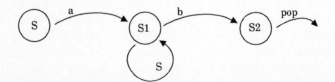

Any language generated by a CFG can be generated by an RTN, and vice versa. Thus they are equivalent in their generative capacity.

Some languages are not generatable by a CFG. One example is the language that consists of a sequence of *a*'s, followed by the same number of *b*'s, followed by the same number of *c*'s--that is, *abc, aabbcc, aaabbbccc,* and so on. Similarly, no context-free grammar can generate the language that consists of any sequence of letters repeated in the same order twice, such as *abab, abcabc, acdabacdab,* and so on. A grammatical formalism, called **context-sensitive grammar,** can generate such sequences, however. A context-sensitive grammar may have more than one symbol on the left-hand side, as long as the number of symbols on that side is less than or equal to the number on the right-hand side. For example,

X Y ← Y X

is a legal context-sensitive rule that would change the order of constituents X and Y.

Work in formal language theory began with Chomsky (1956), who besides defining context-free and context-sensitive grammars, also defined the **regular grammars,** which are a subset of context-free and consist of rules of the form:

<symbol> ← <terminal symbol> <symbol>

Regular grammars are equivalent in generative capacity to the simple transition networks introduced earlier. Since the languages generated by regular grammars are a subset of those generated by context-free grammars, which in turn are a subset of those generated by context-sensitive grammars, these languages are often described as forming a hierarchy of languages called the **Chomsky Hierarchy.**

3.2 What Makes a Good Grammar

When constructing a grammar for a language, you are interested in generality, the range of sentences the grammar analyzes correctly; selectivity, the range of nonsentences that it identifies as problematic; and understandability, the simplicity of the grammar itself.

In small grammars, such as those that describe only a few types of sentences, one structural analysis of a sentence may appear as understandable as another, and little can be said as to why one is superior to the other. As you attempt to extend a grammar to cover a wide range of sentences, however, you often find that one analysis is easily extendable while the other requires complex modification. The analysis that retains its simplicity and generality as it is extended is more desirable.

Unfortunately, here you will mostly be working with small grammars and so will have only a few opportunities to evaluate an analysis as it is extended. You can attempt to make your solutions generalizable, however, by keeping in mind certain properties that any solution should have. In particular, pay close attention to the way the sentence is divided into its subparts, called constituents. Besides using your intuition, you can apply a few specific tests, which will be discussed here.

Anytime you decide that a group of words forms a particular constituent, try to construct a new sentence that involves that group of words in a conjunction with another group of words classified as the same constituent. This is a good test, because apparently only constituents of the same type can be conjoined. For example, the sentences in Figure 3.6 are acceptable.

On the other hand, the following sentences are not acceptable.

*I ate a hamburger and on the stove.
*I ate a cold hotdog and well burned.
*I ate the hotdog slowly and a hamburger.

To summarize, if the proposed constituent doesn't conjoin in some sentence with a constituent of the same class, it is probably incorrect.

Another test involves inserting the proposed constituent into other sentences that take the same category of constituent. For example, if you say that *John's hitting of Mary* is an NP in *John's hitting of Mary alarmed Sue*, then it should be usable as an NP in other sentences as well. In fact this proposition is true--the NP can be the object of a verb as in *I cannot explain John's hitting of Mary*, as well as in the passive form of the initial sentence, *Sue was alarmed by John's hitting of Mary*. Given this evidence, you can conclude that the proposed constituent appears to behave just like other NPs.

As another example of applying these principles, consider the two sentences *I looked up John's phone number* and *I looked up John's chimney*. Should these sentences have the identical structure? If so, you would presumably analyze both as subject-verb-complement sentences with the complement in both cases being a PP. That is, *up John's phone number* would be a PP.

When you try the conjunction test, you should become suspicious of the preceding analysis. Conjoining *up John's phone number* with another PP, as in *I*

NP-NP: I ate <u>a hamburger</u> and <u>a hotdog</u>.

VP-VP: I will <u>eat the hamburger</u> and <u>throw away the hotdog</u>.

S-S: <u>I ate a hamburger</u> and <u>John ate a hotdog</u>.

PP-PP: I saw the hotdog <u>in the bag</u> and <u>on the stove</u>.

ADJP-ADJP: I ate a <u>cold</u> and <u>well burned</u> hotdog.

ADVP-ADVP: I ate the hotdog <u>slowly</u> and <u>carefully</u>.

NOUN-NOUN: I ate a <u>hamburger</u> and <u>hotdog</u>.

VERB-VERB: I will <u>cook</u> and <u>burn</u> a hamburger.

AUX-AUX: I <u>can</u> and <u>will</u> eat the hotdog.

ADJ-ADJ: I ate the very <u>cold</u> and <u>burned</u> hotdog (that is, very cold and very burned).

Figure 3.6 Various forms of conjunctions

looked up John's phone number and in his cupboards, is certainly bizarre. Note that *I looked up John's chimney and in his cupboards* is perfectly acceptable. Thus apparently the analysis of *up John's phone number* as a PP is incorrect.

You will see further evidence against the PP analysis by observing that *up John's phone number* does not seem to be usable as a PP in any sentences other than ones involving a few verbs such as *look* or *thought*. Even with the verb *look*, an alternative sentence such as *Up John's phone number, I looked* is quite implausible compared to *Up John's chimney, I looked*.

This type of test can be taken further by considering changing the PP in a manner that usually is allowed. In particular, you should be able to replace the NP *John's phone number* by the pronoun *it*. But the resulting sentence, *I looked up it*, could not be used with the same meaning as *I looked up John's phone number*. In fact, the only way to use a pronoun in this sentence, retaining the original meaning, is to use *I looked it up*, corresponding to the form *I looked John's phone number up*.

Thus a different analysis is needed for each of the two sentences. If *up John's phone number* is not a PP, then two remaining analyses may be possible for the VP. The VP could be a VERB structure consisting of *looked up*, followed by an NP, or the VP could consist of three components: the VERB *looked*, a **particle** *up*, and an NP. Either one of these is a better solution. What types of tests might you do to decide between these two?

As you develop a grammar, you must specify more and more as to how each constituent can be used. Thus when a new analysis is proposed, you have a large set of tests that can be performed to see if the analysis is reasonable given the grammar that already exists. Of course, sometimes the analysis of a new form of sentence might cause you to go back and modify the existing grammar so that it can be extended to account for the new form. This backward step is unavoidable given the current state of linguistic knowledge. The important point to remember here, though, is that when a new rule is proposed for a grammar, you must carefully consider its interaction with existing rules.

Occasionally, you will confront problems that do not appear to have any reasonable analysis within the grammatical framework. In a few cases these problems will lead to extensions to the grammar's notational system itself.

3.3 Top-Down Parsing Methods

Top-down parsing methods all involve starting from the representation of a sentence and decomposing this representation into its subconstituents, and then decomposing the subconstituents until you derive specific word classes that can be checked against the actual input sentence. This section discusses three top-down parsers: an RTN parser and two CFG parsers. All of them use essentially the same algorithm with minor details changed to account for the differences in the grammatical formalisms.

Top-Down Parsing with Recursive Transition Networks

To consider parsing with RTNs, think about what information you need to precisely define the informal top-down parse procedure outlined earlier. The state of the parse at any moment can be represented by the following:

> **current position**--record of what part of the sentence has not yet been parsed.

> **current node**--the node at which you are located in the network.

> **return points**--if you are in a network because of a call from another network, you need to record the node in the other network where you will continue if you **pop** from the current network.

First, consider a simple algorithm for searching an RTN. Assume that if you can follow an arc, it will be the correct one in the final parse. Also consider only cat, push, and pop arcs as defined in Figure 3.5. It will then be simple to modify this algorithm to a full search for the entire set of arcs using a technique called **backtracking**.

Consider the situation where you are in the middle of a parse and know the three pieces of information just cited. Try to follow an arc, leaving the current node, that can be traversed successfully as one of the cases in the following algorithm:

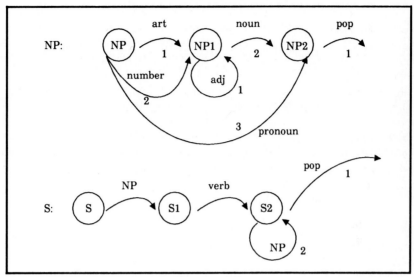

Grammar 3.7

Case 1: If arc names a word category and next word in sentence is in that category,
         Then (1) update *current position* to start at the next word;
                 (2) update *current node* to the destination of the arc.

Case 2: If arc is a push arc to a network N,
         Then (1) add the destination of the arc onto *return points*;
                 (2) update *current node* to the starting node in network N.

Case 3: If arc is a pop arc and *return points* list is not empty,
         Then (1) remove the first return point and make it *current node*.

Case 4: If arc is a pop arc and the *return points* list is empty and there are no words left,
         Then (1) parse completes successfully.

Assume Grammar 3.7 and the following lexicon:

art:	the, a
number:	one
pronoun:	one
adj:	wild, green
noun:	dogs, man, saw, green
verb:	cried, saw, broke, faded, man

The numbers on the arcs simply indicate the order in which arcs will be tried when more than one arc leaves a node. The sentence

1 The 2 wild 3 dogs 4 cried. 5

would be parsed as traced in Figure 3.8, using the algorithm just defined. The number between each word is used to identify the current position of the parser. If you start at node S, the only possible arc to follow is the push arc NP. As specified in case 2 of the preceding algorithm, the new parse state is computed by setting the current node to NP, and putting node S1 on the return points list. From node NP, arc 1 is followed and, as specified in case 1 of the algorithm, the input is checked for a word in category art. Since this check succeeds, the arc is followed and the current position is updated (step 3). The parse continues in this manner to step 5, when a pop arc is followed, causing the current node to be reset to S1 (that is, the NP arc succeeded). The parse succeeds after finding a verb in step 6 and following the pop arc from the S network in step 7.

In this example the parse succeeded because the first arc that was tried succeeded in every case. However, if you gave the sentence *The green faded* to this algorithm, it would fail, because it would initially classify *green* as an adjective and then not be able to find a noun following. To be able to recover from such failures, you need to remember positions in the network where you made a decision that could be wrong. Since you can capture the entire state of a parse with the three pieces of information (current position, current node, and return points), you should have an easy time remembering the positions. When you follow an arc, and there are other arcs leaving the current node that you have not yet tried, you save the positions that would have resulted from following each of these arcs. If the parse ever reaches a point where it cannot continue, it simply takes one of the saved backup points and restarts the parse.

Consider this technique in operation on the following sentence:

1 One 2 saw 3 the 4 man. 5

The parser initially attempts to parse the sentence as beginning with the NP *one saw*, but after failing to find a verb, it backtracks and finds a successful parse starting with the NP *one*. The trace of the parse is shown in Figure 3.9, where at each stage the current parse state is shown in the form of a triple (current node, current position, return points), together with possible states for backtracking. The figure also shows the arcs used to generate the new state and the backup states. Each arc is identified by the name of the node that it leaves plus the number identifier. Thus arc S/1 is the arc labeled 1 leaving the S node. (If only one arc leaves a node, the label 1 is omitted from the figure.)

This trace behaves identically to the previous example except in two places. In step 2, two arcs leaving node NP could accept the word *one*. Arc NP/1 classifies *one* as a number and produces the next current state. Arc NP/3 classifies it as a pronoun and produces a backup state. This backup state is

Step	Current Node	Current Position	Return Points	Arc Followed	Comments
1.	(S,	1,	NIL)	S/1	initial position
2.	(NP,	1,	(S1))	NP/1	followed push arc to NP network, to return ultimately to S1
3.	(NP1,	2,	(S1))	NP1/1	followed arc 1
4.	(NP1,	3,	(S1))	NP1/2	followed arc 4 to NP1 again
5.	(NP2,	4,	(S1))	NP2/2	followed arc 5 since arc 4 was not applicable
6.	(S1,	4,	NIL)	S1/1	the pop arc gets us back to S1
7.	(S2,	5,	NIL)	S2/1	followed arc 7
8.					parse succeeds on pop arc from S2

Figure 3.8 A trace of a top-down parse

Step	Current State	Arc Followed	Backup States
1.	(S, 1, NIL)	S/1	NIL
2.	(NP, 1, (S1))	NP/1 (& NP/3 for backup)	NIL
3.	(NP1, 2, (S1))	NP1/2	(NP2, 2, (S1))
4.	(NP2, 3, (S1))	NP2/1	(NP2, 2, (S1))
5.	(S1, 3, NIL)	no arc can be followed	(NP2, 2, (S1))
6.	(NP2, 2, (S1))	NP2/1	NIL
7.	(S1, 2, NIL)	S1/1	NIL
8.	(S2, 3, NIL)	S2/2	NIL
9.	(NP, 3, (S2))	NP/1	NIL
10.	(NP1, 4, (S2))	NP1/2	NIL
11.	(NP2, 5, (S2))	NP2/1	NIL
12.	(S2, 5, NIL)	S2/1	NIL
13.	the parse succeeds		NIL

Figure 3.9 A top-down RTN parse with backtracking

actually used later in step 6 when it is found that none of the arcs leaving node
S1 can accept the input word *the*.

Of course, in general, many more backup states are generated than in this
simple example. In these cases there will be a list of possible backup states.
Depending on how this list is organized, you can produce different orderings on
when the states are examined (see Box 3.2).

Top-Down Parsers for Context-Free Grammars

You can construct top-down parsers for CFGs by using the techniques just
described, but the relevant information to describe a state of a CFG parse
includes only two items: the current position, as before, and a string of
grammatical symbols that have been derived by the rewrite rules but not yet
matched to the input. At each stage consider the leftmost symbol in the list. If it
names the category of the next word, remove the symbol and update the current
position appropriately. Otherwise, you can construct new possibilities by
rewriting the leftmost symbol according to the grammar. Using the eight-rule
CFG in Grammar 3.2, repeated here as Grammar 3.10, the top-down parse of the
sentence

$_1$ The $_2$ dogs $_3$ cried. $_4$

is shown in Figure 3.11.

In Figure 3.11, the initial S symbol is rewritten using rule 1 to produce a new
current state of (NP VP) in step 2. The NP is rewritten in turn, but since
there are two possible rules for NP in the grammar, two possible states are
generated: the new current state involves (ART NOUN VP) at position 1,
whereas the backup state involves (NAME VP) at position 1. In step 4, a word in
category ART is found at position 1 of the sentence, and the new current state
becomes (NOUN VP). The backup state generated in step 3 remains untouched.
The parse continues in this fashion to step 5, where four different rules can
rewrite VP. The first rule generates the new current state, while the other three
rules are pushed onto the stack of backup states. The parse completes
successfully in step 7, since the current state is empty and all the words in the
input sentence have been accounted for.

Implementing a Parser in a Horn Clause Theorem Prover

One of the more popular methods of building a top-down parser for CFGs is to
encode the rules of the grammar as axioms in a Horn clause theorem prover (see
Appendix B for definition) that uses a top-down proof method, such as in
PROLOG. When you see this technique here, you will realize that it can be used
to implement exactly the same top-down parser for CFG as described in the
preceding section.

```
1.  S  ← NP VP          5.  VP ← VERB
2.  NP ← ART NOUN       6.  VP ← VERB NP
3.  NP ← NAME           7.  VP ← VERB NP PP
4.  PP ← PREP NP        8.  VP ← VERB PP
```

Grammar 3.10

Step	Current State	Backup States	Position	Comment
1.	(S)		1	initial position
2.	(NP VP)		1	rewriting S by rule 1
3.	(ART NOUN VP)		1	rewriting NP by rules 2 & 3
		(NAME VP)	1	
4.	(NOUN VP)		2	matching ART with *the*
		(NAME VP)	1	
5.	(VP)		3	matching NOUN with *dogs*
		(NAME VP)	1	
6.	(VERB)		3	rewriting VP by rules 5-8
		(VERB NP)	3	
		(VERB NP PP)	3	
		(VERB PP)	3	
		(NAME VP)	1	
7.				the parse succeeds as VERB is matched to *cried*, leaving an empty grammatical symbol list with an empty sentence

Figure 3.11 Top-down depth-first parse of a CFG

Consider the following CFG rule:

S ← NP VP

This rule can be reformulated as an axiom that says, "A sequence of words is a legal S if it begins with a legal NP that is followed by a legal VP." If you number each word in a sentence by its position, you can restate this rule as: "there is an S between position p1 and p3, if there is a position p2 such that there is an NP between p1 and p2 and a VP between p2 and p3." This rule can be stated formally by the axiom

(S ?p1 ?p3) < (NP ?p1 ?p2) (VP ?p2 ?p3)

BOX 3.2 Parsing as a Search Process

You can think of parsing as a special case of a **search problem** as defined in artificial intelligence. In particular, the top-down parsers described in this section could be described in terms of the following generalized search procedure. Let the current state and the backup states be considered as one list of possible states called the **possibilities list**. It is initially set to the start state of the parse. Then you repeat the following steps until you have success or failure:

1. select the first state from the possibilities (and remove it from the list);

2. generate the new states from trying every possible option from the selected state (there may be none if we are on a bad path);

3. add the states generated in step 2 to the possibilities list.

For a depth-first strategy, the possibilities list is a stack. Thus, step 3 adds the generated positions onto the top of the stack. Step 2 considers all the arcs leaving the node and, for each one that can be followed, creates the position that would result from following it according to the algorithm at the beginning of this section. These decisions produce the algorithm used in the top-down parses shown in Section 3.3.

In contrast, in a **breadth-first strategy** the possibilities list is manipulated as a queue. Step 3 adds the new positions onto the end, rather than the beginning, of the list.

We can compare these search strategies using the following tree format, which shows the entire space of states for the RTN example (Figure 3.9). Each node in the tree represents a state, and the sons of a node are the possible moves from that state. The number beside each node records the step in the parse where the node was selected in step 1. On the left side is the depth-first order, and on the right side is the breadth-first order.

The only difference between depth-first and breadth-first in this simple example is the order in which the two possible interpretations of the NP are examined. With depth-first strategy, one interpretation is considered and expanded until it fails; only then is the second one considered. With breadth-first strategy, both interpretations are considered alternately, each being expanded one step at a time.

The Search Tree for Two Parse Strategies

Depth-First Order on Left Breadth-First Order on Right

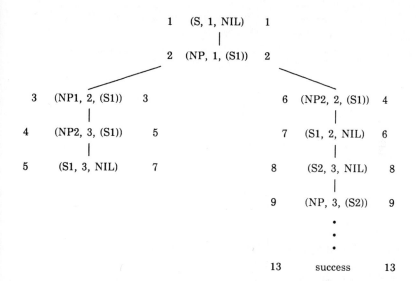

In actual systems based on RTNs the most common search strategy for top-down parsing is the depth-first approach, which generally is more efficient, because the possibilities list remains much smaller than in the breadth-first case. Some grammars, however, could put a pure depth-first strategy into an infinite loop. In such cases the depth-first strategy would never find a solution, whereas a breadth-first would still succeed. In practice, grammar writers must avoid such situations in their grammars. A simple example would be the following network.

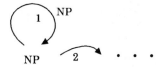

Since arc 1 can always be followed, initiating a recursive call to the NP network, the parser would never stop recursively calling the NP network. In a CFG, we find similar problems with rules involving **left recursion**, such as ADJS ← ADJS ADJ, which, as in the RTN example, could apply to itself indefinitely without ever checking the input sentence.

```
1.  (S ?p1 ?p3) < (NP ?p1 ?p2) (VP ?p2 ?p3)
2.  (NP ?p1 ?p3) < (ART ?p1 ?p2) (NOUN ?p2 ?p3)
3.  (NP ?p1 ?p3) < (NAME ?p1 ?p3)
4.  (PP ?p1 ?p3) < (PREP ?p1 ?p2) (NP ?p2 ?p3)
5.  (VP ?p1 ?p2) < (VERB ?p1 ?p2)
6.  (VP ?p1 ?p3) < (VERB ?p1 ?p2) (NP ?p2 ?p3)
7.  (VP ?p1 ?p4) < (VERB ?p1 ?p2) (NP ?p2 ?p3) (PP ?p3 ?p4)
8.  (VP ?p1 ?p3) < (VERB ?p1 ?p2) (PP ?p2 ?p3)
```

Figure 3.12 A Horn clause representation of Grammar 3.10

To set up the process, you need to add axioms listing the words in the sentence by their position. For example, the sentence *John ate the cat* is described by

(WORD John 1 2)
(WORD ate 2 3)
(WORD the 3 4)
(WORD cat 4 5)

The lexicon is defined by a set of predicates such as the following:

(ISART the)
(ISNAME John)
(ISVERB ate)
(ISNOUN cat)

For each syntactic category, you can define a predicate that is true only if the word between the two specified positions is of that category, as follows:

(NOUN ?i ?o) < (WORD ?word ?i ?o) (ISNOUN ?word)
(ART ?i ?o) < (WORD ?word ?i ?o) (ISART ?word)
(VERB ?i ? o) < (WORD ?word ?i ?o) (ISVERB ?word)
(NAME ?i ?o) < (WORD ?word ?i ?o) (ISNAME ?word)

Ambiguous words would produce multiple assertions--one for each syntactic category to which they belong.

Using the axioms in Figure 3.12, you can prove that *John ate the cat* is a legal sentence by proving (S 1 5) with the axioms listed earlier, as shown in Figure 3.13. In that figure, when there is a possibility of confusing different variables that happen to have the same name, a prime (') is appended to the variable name to make it unique.

This proof trace is in the same format as the trace for the top-down CFG parser as follows. The state of the proof at any time is the list of subgoals

Step	Current State	Backup States	Comments
1.	(S 1 5)		
2.	(NP 1 ?p2) (VP ?p2 5)		
3.	(ART 1 ?p2') (NOUN ?p2' ?p2) (VP ?p2 5)		fails since
		(NAME 1 ?p2) (VP ?p2 5)	there is no
			ART at
			position 1
4.	(NAME 1 ?p2) (VP ?p2 5)		
5.	(VP 2 5)		(NAME 1 2)
			was proven
6.	(VERB 2 5)		fails as no
		(VERB 2 ?p2) (NP ?p2 5)	verb spans
		(VERB 2 ?p2) (NP ?p2 ?p3)	positions 2
		(PP ?p3 ?p4)	to 5!
		(VERB 2 ?p2) (PP ?p2 ?p3)	
7.	(VERB 2 ?p2) (NP ?p2 5)		
		(VERB 2 ?p2) (NP ?p2 ?p3)	
		(PP ?p3 ?p4)	
		(VERB 2 ?p2) (PP ?p2 ?p3)	
8.	(NP 3 5)		(VERB 2 3)
		(VERB 2 ?p2) (NP ?p2 ?p3)	was proven
		(PP ?p3 ?p4)	
		(VERB 2 ?p2) (PP ?p2 ?p3)	
9.	(ART 3 ?p2) (NOUN ?p2 5)		
		(NAME 3 5)	
		(VERB 2 ?p2) (NP ?p2 ?p3)	
		(PP ?p3 ?p4)	
		(VERB 2 ?p2) (PP ?p2 ?p3)	
10.	(NOUN 4 5)		(ART 3 4)
		(NAME 3 5)	was proven
		(VERB 2 ?p2) (NP ?p2 ?p3)	
		(PP ?p3 ?p4)	
		(VERB 2 ?p2) (PP ?p2 ?p3)	
11.	√ proof succeeds		(NOUN 4 5)
		(NAME 3 5)	was proven
		(VERB 2 ?p2) (NP ?p2 ?p3)	
		(PP ?p3 ?p4)	
		(VERB 2 ?p2) (PP ?p2 ?p3)	

Figure 3.13 A trace of a Horn-clause-based parse

remaining to be proven. Since the word positions are included in the goal description, no separate position column needs to be traced. The backup states are also lists of subgoals, which are maintained automatically by a system like PROLOG to implement backtracking. A typical trace of a proof in such a system shows only the current state at any particular time.

3.4 Bottom-Up Parsing Methods

Bottom-up parsing methods are considered only for context-free grammars, because a pure bottom-up approach for transition networks becomes very complex. The main difference between top-down and bottom-up parsers for CFG is the way the rules are used. For example, consider the rule

NP ← ART ADJ NOUN

In a top-down system you use the rule to find an NP by looking for the sequence ART ADJ NOUN. In a bottom-up parser you use the rule to take a sequence ART ADJ NOUN that you have found and identify it as an NP. The basic tool for bottom-up parsing then is to take a sequence of symbols and match it to the right-hand side of our rules. Matches are always considered from the point of view of one symbol, called the **key**. To find rules that match a string involving the key, look for rules that start with the key, or for rules that have already been started by earlier keys and require the present key either to complete the rule or to extend the rule. For instance, consider Grammar 3.14.

If you start with ART in the input as the key, then rules 2 and 3 are matched, since they start with ART. To record this for analyzing the next key, you need to record that rules 2 and 3 could be continued at the point after the ART. You denote this fact by writing the rule with a dot (∘), indicating what has been seen so far. Thus you record

2′.   NP ← ART ∘ ADJ NOUN

3′.   NP ← ART ∘ NOUN

If the next input key is an ADJ, then rule 4 may be started, and the modified rule 2′ may be extended to give

2″.   NP ← ART ADJ ∘ NOUN

You keep a record of the state of a bottom-up parse in a structure called a **chart**. This structure is a record of the positions of the words and the new structures derived from the sentence. The chart also maintains the record of rules that have matched previously but are not complete. You record these rules as **active arcs** on the chart. For example, after seeing an initial ART followed by an ADJ in the preceding example, you would have the chart shown in Figure 3.15. There are two completed constituents--namely, ART1 and ADJ1--and four active arcs: two possible NPs beginning with an ART from 1 to 2, an NP beginning with an ART and ADJ from 1 to 3, and an NP beginning with an ADJ from 2 to 3.

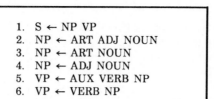

1. S ← NP VP
2. NP ← ART ADJ NOUN
3. NP ← ART NOUN
4. NP ← ADJ NOUN
5. VP ← AUX VERB NP
6. VP ← VERB NP

Grammar 3.14 A simple context-free grammar

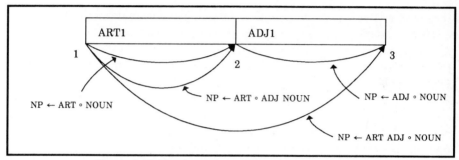

Figure 3.15 The chart after seeing an ADJ in position 2

The parsing algorithm is stated more precisely as follows. There are two data structures: the chart, which maintains all the information about completed constituents and active arcs; and the **key list**, which maintains a stack of completed constituents yet to be entered onto the chart. Whenever the key list is empty, the next word is read in the sentence and all its possible categories are placed on the key list.

Entering a constituent C between positions p_1 and p_2 on the chart involves the following steps:

1. add C between p_1 and p_2;

2. if C begins a rule r in the grammar, add an active arc for rule r from p_1 to p_2;

3. for any active arc A, beginning at p_0 and ending at p_1 (the beginning of C), if C is the next subconstituent in A, then add a new active arc from p_0 to p_2 with the updated rule in A;

4. if any of the active arcs added in steps 2 or 3 are completed rules, add the new constituents, which are named by the left-hand side of the rules, to the key list.

For example, consider using the algorithm on the sentence *The large can can hold the water* with the following lexicon:

    the: ART
    large: ADJ
    can: AUX, NOUN, VERB
    hold: NOUN, VERB
    water: NOUN, VERB

Since the key list is a stack, new keys derived by rules matched by the entry of one of these words will be processed before the next word entry is considered.

Consider a trace of the parse. The key list is initially empty, so the word *the* is read and a constituent ART1 placed on the key list.

     Entering ART1: (*the* from 1 to 2)
        Adds active arc NP ← ART ∘ ADJ NOUN from 1 to 2
        Adds active arc NP ← ART ∘ NOUN from 1 to 2

Both these active arcs were added by step 2 of the algorithm and were derived from rules 2 and 3 in the grammar, respectively. Next the word *large* is read and a constituent ADJ1 is created.

     Entering ADJ1: (*large* from 2 to 3)
        Adds arc NP ← ADJ ∘ NOUN from 2 to 3 (step 2)
        Adds arc NP ← ART ADJ ∘ NOUN from 1 to 3 (step 3)

The second arc added here is an extension of the first active arc added with ART1 and results from step 3 of the algorithm.

The chart at this point has already been shown in Figure 3.15. Notice that active arcs are never removed from the chart. Even when the arc from rule 2 from 1 to 2 was extended, producing the arc from 1 to 3, both arcs remained on the chart. This is necessary because the arcs could be used again in a different way by another interpretation. For the next word, *can*, three constituents, NOUN1, AUX1, and VERB1 are created for its three interpretations.

     Entering NOUN1: (*can* from 3 to 4)

No active arcs are added in step 2, but two are completed in step 3 by NOUN1, producing two NPs, which are added to the key list in step 4. The first, an NP from 1 to 4, is constructed from rule 2, while the second, an NP from 2 to 4, is constructed from rule 4. These NPs are now at the top of the stack of keys.

     Entering NP1: an NP from 1 to 4
        Adding active arc S ← NP ∘ VP from 1 to 4

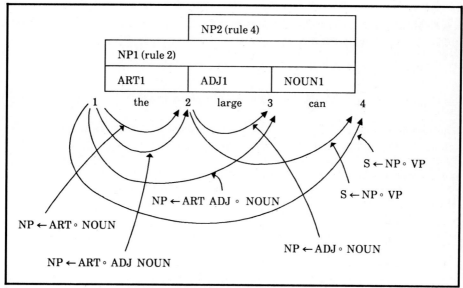

Figure 3.16 After parsing *can* as a NOUN

Entering NP2: an NP from 2 to 4
      Adding arc S ← NP ∘ VP from 2 to 4

The chart is shown in Figure 3.16. This chart illustrates all the completed constituents and all the uncompleted active arcs entered so far. Now the other senses of *can* are considered.

Entering AUX1: (*can* from 3 to 4)
      Adding Arc VP ← AUX ∘ VERB NP from 3 to 4

Entering VERB1: (*can* from 3 to 4)
      Adding Arc VP ← VERB ∘ NP from 3 to 4

The next word read is *can* again, and NOUN2, AUX2, and VERB2 are created.

Entering NOUN2: (*can* from 4 to 5, the second *can*)
      Adds no active arcs

Entering AUX2: (*can* from 4 to 5)
      Adds arc VP ← AUX ∘ VERB NP from 4 to 5

Entering VERB2: (*can* from 4 to 5)
      Adds arc VP ← VERB ∘ NP from 4 to 5
      Adds arc VP ← AUX VERB ∘ NP from 3 to 5

The next word is *hold*, and NOUN3 and VERB3 are created.

Entering NOUN3: (*hold* from 5 to 6)
    Adds no active arcs

Entering VERB3: (*hold* from 5 to 6)
    Adds arc VP ← VERB ∘ NP from 5 to 6
    Adds arc VP ← AUX VERB ∘ NP from 4 to 6

The chart in Figure 3.17 shows all the completed constituents built so far, together with all the active arcs, except for those that cover a single position.

Entering ART2: (*the* from 6 to 7)
    Adding arc NP ← ART ∘ ADJ NOUN from 6 to 7
    Adding arc NP ← ART ∘ NOUN from 6 to 7

Entering NOUN4: (*water* from 7 to 8)
    No active arcs added in step 2
    An NP, NP3, from 6 to 8 is pushed onto the key list, by completing
       arc NP ← ART ∘ NOUN from 6 to 7

Entering NP3: (*the water* from 6 to 8)
    A VP, VP1, from 4 to 8 is pushed onto the key list, by completing
       VP ← AUX VERB ∘ NP from 4 to 6
    A VP, VP2, from 5 to 8 is pushed onto the key list, by completing
       VP ← VERB ∘ NP from 5 to 6

At this stage the chart is shown in Figure 3.18, but only the active arcs to be used in the remainder of the parse are shown.

Entering VP2 (*hold the water* from 5 to 8)
    No active arcs added

Entering VP1 (*can hold the water* from 4 to 8)
    An S, S1, is added from 1 to 8, by completing
       arc S ← NP ∘ VP from 1 to 4
    An S, S2, is added from 2 to 8, by completing
       arc S ← NP ∘ VP from 2 to 4

Since you have derived an S covering the entire sentence, you can stop successfully. If you wanted to find all possible interpretations for the sentence, you would continue parsing until the key list became empty. The chart would then contain as many S structures covering the entire set of positions as there were different structural interpretations. In addition, this representation of the entire set of structures would be more efficient than a list of interpretations, since the different S structures might share common subparts represented in the chart only once. The final chart is shown in Figure 3.19.

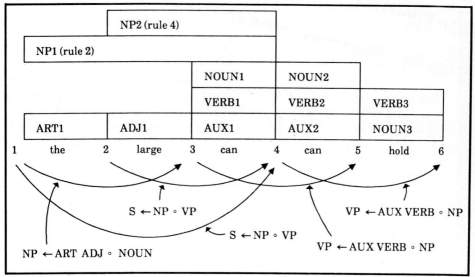

Figure 3.17 The chart after adding *hold*, omitting all active arcs covering only one position

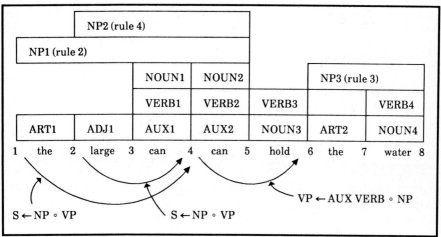

Figure 3.18 The chart after all the NPs are found,
omitting all but the crucial active arcs

Note that in an implementation each chart entry would need to record the syntactic type and the starting and the ending position. As you will see in Chapter 4, many other things can be recorded in the chart entries as well.

3.5 Mixed-Mode Methods

Top-down methods and bottom-up methods both have their advantages and disadvantages. Top-down methods, for instance, have the advantage that they

S1 (rule 1)						
	S2 (rule 1)					
	NP2 (rule 4)		VP1 (rule 5)			
NP1 (rule 2)				VP2 (rule 6)		
		NOUN1	NOUN2		NP3 (rule 3)	
		VERB1	VERB2	VERB3		VERB4
ART1	ADJ1	AUX1	AUX2	NOUN3	ART2	NOUN4
1 the 2	large 3	can 4	can 5	hold 6	the 7	water

Figure 3.19 The final chart position

will never consider word categories in positions where they could not occur in a legal sentence. This advantage stems from the fact that the parser works from a syntactic category and checks that the word fits that category. For example, if you use Grammar 3.20, a top-down parse of the sentence *The can fell* will expect an S to start with an NP, which starts with an ART, followed by an ADJ or NOUN. Since *can* is a NOUN, it finds an NP as expected. The AUX and VERB senses of *can* are never considered.

On the other hand, top-down parsers may operate for quite some time, rewriting rules from a complex grammar before the actual words in the sentence are ever considered. Even more important, the same piece of work may be repeated many times in searching for a solution. For example, consider parsing *The bird sang* with Grammar 3.20. The parser, using rule 1, would find an NP, *the bird*, and then, using rule 8 for the VP, would find the necessary VERB but not the following NP. Thus it backtracks and tries another way to find an S. Rule 2 is tried and the NP *the bird* is parsed (again!), but no AUX is found, so it backs up again and tries rule 3. This succeeds after parsing *the bird* as an NP for the third time.

Such problems are avoided with a bottom-up parser. In the preceding example the NP *the bird* would be constructed only once, and only rule 3 would match to give an S. On the other hand, a bottom-up parser must consider all senses of each word and construct structures that could never lead to a legal sentence. For example, in the previous section, in parsing *The large can can hold the water*, the final chart was shown in Figure 3.19. There are many impossible structures here. An S was considered from position 2 to 7, even though there is no possible legal sentence of form ART S.

```
┌─────────────────────────────────────────────────────────┐
│  1.  S ← NP VP              5.  NP ← ART ADJ NOUN         │
│  2.  S ← NP AUX VERB        6.  NP ← ADJ NOUN             │
│  3.  S ← NP VERB            7.  VP ← AUX VERB NP          │
│  4.  NP ← ART NOUN          8.  VP ← VERB NP              │
└─────────────────────────────────────────────────────────┘
```

Grammar 3.20   A simple context-free grammar

It is possible to design systems that use varying degrees of both top-down and bottom-up methods and gain the advantages of both approaches without the disadvantages. One such approach is to construct a top-down parser that adds each constituent to a chart as it is constructed. As the parse continues, before you rewrite a symbol to find a new constituent, you first check to see if that constituent is already on the chart. If so, you use it rather than applying the grammar to construct the constituent all over again. This can be done with very little modification to your original top-down algorithm.

A Top-Down CFG Parser with a Chart

This section explores how to modify a top-down CFG parser in the manner just described. To motivate the new algorithm, consider how the old one would start to parse the sentence

> $_1$ The $_2$ green $_3$ water $_4$ evaporated. $_5$

(where *green* may be an ADJ or a NOUN, and *water* may be a NOUN or VERB as before). The starting state is as follows:

Current State	Backup States	Position
(S)	NIL	1

Remember that a state generates new parse states by operating on its leftmost symbol. If it names a word category, the next word in the sentence is checked; otherwise the grammar is used to rewrite the first symbol. Replacing S using rules 1, 2, and 3 (in Grammar 3.20), respectively, you get the following situation:

Current State	Backup States	Position
(NP VP)		1
	(NP AUX VERB)	1
	(NP VERB)	1

Rewriting the NP in the current state using rules 4, 5, and 6 produces the following:

Current State	Backup States	Position
(ART NOUN VP)		1
	(ART ADJ NOUN VP)	1
	(ADJ NOUN VP)	1
	(NP AUX VERB)	1
	(NP VERB)	1

The sentence is checked for an ART and then a NOUN successfully, finding the first NP to be constructed. Given the preceding discussion, you would like to record the NP on the chart. Unfortunately, there is no information in the representation here that records that the ART NOUN sequence produced an NP!

To record the NP, the system should be extended to keep each symbol on the list even after it has been rewritten. The system marks the symbol as being rewritten and records the starting position of the phrase. For example, if NP is rewritten at position 1, as earlier, it will put a new structure <NP 1>, called a **construction flag**, on the list when NP is rewritten. When it arrives back at <NP 1> in the parse later, it will be able to tell that it has just completed an NP structure that began at position 1.

The revised algorithm for processing a single position is as follows:

1. If the leftmost symbol in the current state names an entry on the chart, then generate the new state(s) by removing the symbol and updating the sentence position to the position(s) after the chart entry(ies). For example, given the following position and chart,

Current State	Backup States	Position
(NP VP)	NIL	1

two NPs are found on the chart and two new states are generated. One becomes the new current state, and the other a backup. That is, the resulting situation is

Current State	Backup States	Position
(VP)		2
	(VP)	4

2. If the leftmost symbol is a construction flag, such as <NP 1>, add a constituent onto the chart for the symbol (NP) range from the starting position (1) to the current position. For example, given a current state of (<NP 2> VP) at position 5, you would add an NP to the chart from position 2 to 5.

3. Otherwise, if the symbol is a terminal symbol, check the next word in the sentence for inclusion in that category, and add to the chart if successful.

4. Otherwise, if the symbol is a nonterminal symbol, add a construction flag to the position and rewrite the symbol according to the grammar rules. For example, given the state (NP VP) at position 1 and an empty chart, you would produce three new states using Grammar 3.20: (ART NOUN <NP 1> VP), (ART ADJ NOUN <NP 1> VP), and (ADJ NOUN <NP 1> VP), all at position 1.

5. Otherwise, this state is rejected and a backup state is moved to be the current state.

Now, using this algorithm, reconsider parsing the sentence *The green water evaporated.* If you start with the symbol S and position 1, you would rewrite the S symbol, yielding

Current State	Backup States	Position
(NP VP <S 1>)		1
	(NP AUX VERB <S 1>)	1
	(NP VERB <S 1>)	1

Rewriting the NP according to step 4 produces

Current State	Backup States	Position
(ART NOUN <NP 1> VP <S 1>)		1
	(ART ADJ NOUN <NP 1> VP <S 1>)	1
	(ADJ NOUN <NP 1> VP <S 1>)	1
	(NP AUX VERB <S 1>)	1
	(NP VERB <S 1>)	1

The sentence is checked for an ART and NOUN successfully. The current state after these operations is ($<$NP 1$>$ VP $<$S 1$>$) at position 3. The construction flag $<$NP 1$>$ is processed, according to step 2, by adding to the chart an NP structure, NP1, from position 1 to position 3. You then have the following parser state and the chart shown in Figure 3.21.

Current State	Backup States	Position
(VP $<$S 1$>$)		3
	(ART ADJ NOUN $<$NP 1$>$ VP $<$S 1$>$)	1
	(ADJ NOUN $<$NP 1$>$ VP $<$S 1$>$)	1
	(NP AUX VERB $<$S 1$>$)	1
	(NP VERB $<$S 1$>$)	1

Rewriting the VP produces the following situation:

Current State	Backup States	Position
(AUX VERB NP $<$VP 4$>$ $<$S 1$>$)		3
	(VERB NP $<$VP 4$>$ $<$S 1$>$)	3
	(ART ADJ NOUN $<$NP 1$>$ VP $<$S 1$>$)	1
	(ADJ NOUN $<$NP 1$>$ VP $<$S 1$>$)	1
	(NP AUX VERB $<$S 1$>$)	1
	(NP VERB $<$S 1$>$)	1

The current state is rejected, since *water* cannot be classified as an AUX. The top backup state becomes the current state and *water* is classified as a VERB, but then this state is also rejected because there is no NP following the verb. The next backup state succeeds, since an ART can be found at position 1, an ADJ (*green*) at position 2, and a NOUN (*water*) at position 3, creating a second NP. You now have the following situation and the chart in Figure 3.22.

Current State	Backup States	Position
(VP $<$S 1$>$)		4
	(ADJ NOUN $<$NP 1$>$ VP $<$S 1$>$)	1
	(NP AUX VERB $<$S 1$>$)	1
	(NP VERB $<$S 1$>$)	1

Rewriting the VP at position 4 in the current state creates the following new situation:

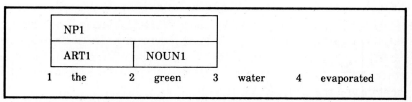

Figure 3.21 The chart after parsing the first NP

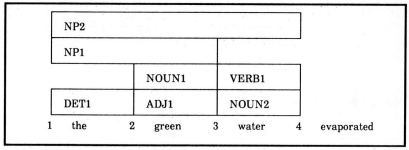

Figure 3.22 After parsing the second candidate for the first NP

Figure 3.23 After failing to find an S using rule 1

Current State	Backup States	Position
(AUX VERB NP <VP 3> <S 1>)		4
	(VERB NP <VP 3> <S 1>)	4
	(ADJ NOUN <NP 1> VP <S 1>)	1
	(NP AUX VERB <S 1>)	1
	(NP VERB <S 1>)	1

You find no AUX at position 4, so the current state is rejected. You do find a
VERB at position 4, but trying for an NP after the verb fails. The next state
(ADJ NOUN <NP 1> VP <S 1>) also fails since *the* cannot be an ADJ. You
are left with the following two states and the chart in Figure 3.23.

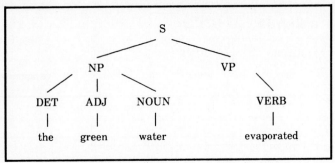

Figure 3.24 The structure of the sentence parsed

Current State	Backup States	Position
(NP AUX VERB <S 1>)		1
	(NP VERB <S 1>)	1

Note that you have now just finished trying every possible parse, starting with S being rewritten by rule 1. Now you are at the point where the use of the chart saves considerable effort. Rather than applying the rules for NP at position 1 next, the parser uses the two NPs already found there, producing

Current State	Backup States	Position
(AUX VERB <S 1>)		3
	(AUX VERB <S 1>)	4
	(NP VERB <S 1>)	1

The current state is rejected, since there is no AUX at position 3. Similarly, the first backup state is rejected, because no AUX can be found at position 4. The correct interpretation is found by continuing from the state (NP VERB <S 1>). Again, the two NPs are found on the chart, producing the following states:

Current State	Backup States	Position
(VERB <S 1>)		3
	(VERB <S 1>)	4

The current state produces an S structure from position 1 to 4 but cannot account for the word *evaporated*. The remaining backup state produces the desired analysis, recognizing a sentence of the form shown in Figure 3.24.

This combination of a top-down/bottom-up parsing strategy is considerably better than either pure strategy. Its only disadvantage in comparison to pure top-down techniques is the extra space needed for the chart. In most cases this added space is negligible compared to the efficiency gained on the parsing time.

BOX 3.3 A Mixed-Mode RTN Parser

An RTN parser can be constructed to use a chart in the same manner as the CFG parser. Each time a pop is followed, the constituent is placed on the chart, and every time a push is found, the chart is checked before the subnetwork is invoked. If the chart contains constituent(s) of the type being pushed for, these are used and the subnetwork is not reinvoked.

You can handle some bookkeeping details by modifying the return points list. In particular, when a push arc is followed, the parser should record where the constituent started with the return point. For example, the return point of the current state of the parser at step 2 in Figure 3.9 would be (NP, 1, <S1 1>). Now, in step 5, in which the pop arc from the NP network is followed, the return point information <S1 1> is used for two purposes. First, it tells you that the continuation point in the S network is node S1 as before, but it also tells you that the NP constituent found started at position 1. With this information you can add an NP entry from 1 to 3 to the chart.

Finally, the algorithm must be modified so that whenever the parser backtracks to a node that begins a network, the chart is checked first for that constituent before the state is processed. If the constituent is found, the parser can immediately pop from this node in the usual way. For example, given an S network starting as follows,

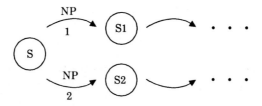

the second step of the parse will be

Step	Current State	Backup States
2	(NP, 1, <S1 1>)	(NP, 1, <S2 1>)

Now, if an NP is found at the beginning of the sentence, it will eventually be added to the chart. If, later on, all possible parses started from arc S/1 are explored and rejected, the parser will eventually consider the backup state shown. At that time the chart is checked for an NP. If an NP from positions 1 to 4 is found, the parser does not search again for an NP but immediately updates its current state to parse from node S2 at position 4.

Summary

The two basic grammatical formalisms are context-free grammars and recursive transition networks. A variety of parsing algorithms may be used for each formalism. For instance, a simple top-down backtracking algorithm can be used for both CFGs and RTNs and, in fact, the same algorithm is used in the standard logic-programming-based grammars as well. Bottom-up algorithms are most commonly used only for context-free grammars. The most effective parsing strategy, however, is the mixed-mode parser, which is built using a modified top-down algorithm in conjunction with the chart structure for the bottom-up method. Since the main algorithm is top-down, this mixed-mode strategy can be used equally well for CFGs or RTNs and can also be used with the logic grammar approach.

Related Work and Further Readings

There is a vast literature on syntactic formalisms and parsing algorithms. The notion of context-free grammars was introduced by Chomsky (1956) and has been studied extensively since in linguistics and in computer science. Some of this work will be discussed in detail later, because it is more relevant to the material in the following chapters.

Transition network grammars and parsers are described in Woods (1970; 1973), chart-based parsers are described in Kay (1973), and Horn-clause-based parsers are described and compared with transition network systems in Pereira and Warren (1980). Winograd (1983) also discusses from a slightly different perspective most of the approaches described here, which could be useful if a certain technique is difficult to understand.

In addition, descriptions of transition network parsers are to be found in many introductory AI texts, such as Rich (1983), Winston (1984), and Charniak and McDermott (1985). These books also contain descriptions of the search techniques underlying many of the parsing algorithms.

Much work on efficient context-free parsing has been done for programming language applications. A classic reference for a mixed-mode parser in this setting is Early (1970). A good general reference for this area is Aho and Ullman (1972).

Exercises for Chapter 3

1. (*easy*) Given Grammar 3.7 and the lexicon defined in Section 3.3, show a trace in the format of Figure 3.9 of a top-down RTN parse of the sentence *The green faded.*

2. *(easy)* Given Grammar 3.10, define an appropriate lexicon and show a trace
    in the format of Figure 3.11 of a top-down CFG parse of the sentence *John
    lived in a closet.*

3. *(easy)* Given the Horn clauses defined in Figure 3.12, show a trace in the
    format of Figure 3.13 of the proof that the following is a legal sentence: *The
    cat ate John.*

4. *(medium)* Extend the RTN interpretation algorithm to handle WRD and
    JUMP arcs.

5. *(medium)*

    a) Express the following tree in the list notation described in Section 3.1.

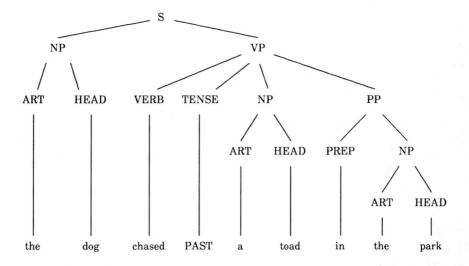

    b) Is there a tree structure that could not be expressed as a list structure?
        How about a list structure that could not be expressed as a tree?

    c) How is the slot-value notation different from the simple list notation for
        syntactic trees?

6. *(medium)* Map the following context-free grammar into an equivalent
    recursive transition network that uses three networks only--an S, NP, and
    PP network.

$$S \leftarrow NP\ VP \qquad\qquad NP3 \leftarrow NOUN$$
$$S \leftarrow NP\ VP\ PREPS \qquad PREPS \leftarrow PP$$
$$NP \leftarrow ART\ NP2 \qquad\quad PREPS \leftarrow PP\ PREPS$$

$$NP \leftarrow NP2 \qquad\qquad PP \leftarrow PREPOSITION \ NP$$
$$NP2 \leftarrow NOUN \qquad\qquad VP \leftarrow VERB$$
$$NP2 \leftarrow ADJ \ NP2 \qquad\quad VP \leftarrow VERB \ NP$$
$$NP2 \leftarrow NP3 \ PREPS \qquad VP \leftarrow VERB \ PREPS$$

7. *(medium)* Given the CFG in Exercise 6 and the following lexicon, construct a trace of a pure top-down parse and a pure bottom-up parse of the sentence *Green herons fly in groups*. Make your traces as clear as possible, select the rules in the order given in Exercise 6, and indicate all parts of the search. The lexicon entries for each word are

> Green: ADJ NOUN
> herons: NOUN
> fly: NOUN VERB ADJ
> in: PREP
> groups: NOUN VERB

8. *(medium)* Read Box 3.2, and then consider the following grammar rules:

> S ← ADJS
> S ← NOUN
> ADJS ← ADJS ADJ
> ADJS ← ADJ

Lexicon: ADJ: red, NOUN: house

a) What happens to the top-down depth-first parser operating on this grammar trying to parse the sentence *red red*? In particular, state whether the parser succeeds, fails, or never stops.

b) How about a top-down breadth-first parser operating on the same sentence *red red*?

c) How about a top-down breadth-first parser operating on the sentence *red house*?

d) How about a bottom-up depth-first parser on *red house*?

e) For the cases where the parser fails to stop, give a grammar that is equivalent to the one shown in this exercise and that is parsed correctly. (Note that correct behavior includes failing on unacceptable sentences as well as succeeding on acceptable ones.)

f) With the new grammar in Exercise 8e, do all the preceding parsers now operate correctly on the two sentences *red red* and *red house*?

9. *(medium)* Consider the following CFG:

> S ← NP VERB
> S ← NP AUX VERB
> NP ← ART NOUN

Trace the mixed-method parser (top-down with chart) in processing the sentence

> 1 The 2 man 3 is 4 laughing. 5

with the lexicon entries:

> ART: the
> NOUN: man
> AUX: is
> VERB: laughing

Show every step of the parse, giving the parse stack, and drawing the chart each time a nonterminal constituent is constructed.

10. *(medium)*

a) Transform Grammar 3.14 into an equivalent recursive transition network and Horn clause parser.

b) Transform the recursive transition network that is Grammar 3.7 into an equivalent context-free grammar.

11. *(medium)* Consider the following CFG that generates sequences of letters:

> s ← a x c
> s ← b x c
> s ← b x d
> s ← b x e
> s ← c x e
> x ← f x
> x ← g

a) If you had to write a parser for this grammar, would it be better to use a pure top-down or a pure bottom-up approach? Why?

b) Trace the parser of your choice operating on the input "bffge."

12. *(hard)* Specify precisely an algorithm that could automatically generate a recursive transition network from an arbitrary CFG. Give some sample

Kleppe says You Cheater!

grammar fragments that are translated poorly, given your algorithm, and show a more elegant transition network equivalent to the fragment.

13. (*hard*) Consider the following sentences:

List A:

i)   Joe is reading the book to the man.
ii) Joe had won a letter.
iii) Joe has to win.
iv) Joe will have the letter.
v)   The letter in the book was read.
vi) The letter must have been in the book by Joe.
vii) The man could have had one.

List B:

i)   Joe has reading the book.
ii) Joe had win.
iii) Joe winning.
iv) Joe will had the letter.
v)   The book was read a man Joe.
vi) Joe will can be mad.
vii) The man could have having one.

a) Write a context-free grammar that accepts all the sentences in list A while rejecting the sentences in list B. You may find it useful to make reference to the grammatical forms of verbs discussed in the notes.

b) Implement one of the parsing strategies and, using the grammar specified in Exercise 7a, demonstrate that your parser correctly accepts all the sentences in A and rejects those in B. You should maintain enough information in each entry on the chart so that you can reconstruct the parse tree for each possible interpretation. Make sure your method of recording the structure is well documented and clearly demonstrated.

c) List three (distinct!) grammatical forms that would not be recognized by a parser implementing the grammar in Exercise 7a. Provide an example of your own for each of these grammatical forms.

CAT recognizes a word from input as a lexical entry and creates a lexical register for it.

cat (verb, Sentin, Sentout, Form, Regsin, Regsout) where verb is category name and Form is lexry ("verb", "love").

Push - starts a new transition network for a non-terminal transition

Pop - exits the current transition network.

Build - produces a non-term from register of a completed subnetwork

Setr - appends a new register to the front of reg list

getr - returns a register from the current reg. list.

golf - returns a feature value, in reg from lexicon.

member - determines whether a token is a member of a list of tokens

appendr - appends a reg. to the children of a non-term reg.

intersect - given two lists - returns the elements they held in common - if none return [].

agree - checks for feature agreement between 2 registers. given feature name and 2 regs. it returns a list of values that they have in common for that feature.

addhold - adds a constituent to the hold list

vif - implements the VIR arc - searches the hold list for a constituent of the correct type, removes it from the hold list, and returns it.

Chapter 4

Features and Augmented Grammars

The mechanisms discussed in Chapter 3 were limited in a number of ways. The most obvious deficiency was that they could only accept or reject a sentence, rather than produce an analysis of the structure of the sentence. More importantly, however, they were limited in characterizing certain forms of dependencies between constituents, such as subject-verb agreement, verb transitivity, and a host of other phenomena. This chapter looks at extended, or **augmented**, grammatical formalisms that can deal with these issues.

All of the grammatical formalisms described in the previous chapter can be augmented in much the same way. The present chapter examines an augmented RTN formalism in detail and then shows how similar extensions can be made to the CFG and logic grammar approaches.

Section 4.1 describes the mechanisms for augmenting the RTN formalism, which involves both generalizing the network notation and introducing more information about words in a structure called the **lexicon**. Section 4.2 then examines some of the important aspects of English that are best described as local dependencies. This information is then used in Section 4.3, which presents an augmented RTN grammar of simple English assertions, and in Section 4.4, which extends this grammar to describe embedded sentences.

The remainder of the chapter looks at the issues of augmenting logic grammars (Section 4.5) and context-free grammars (Section 4.6). While the mechanisms are slightly different between each grammatical formalism, the essential features of augmentation remain constant over them all.

Section 4.7 provides an introduction to recent work that has pushed augmentation techniques to their logical conclusion. This work, often called **unification grammar**, is starting to have a major influence across disciplines, both in computational linguistics and in theoretical linguistics.

4.1 Augmented Transition Networks

The following section introduces the basic mechanisms for collecting information and testing features while parsing using an extension of the RTN framework called an **augmented transition network (ATN)**.

Recording the Sentence Structure While Parsing

Suppose you want to collect the structure of legal sentences in order to further analyze them. One structure seen earlier was the syntactic parse tree that motivated context-free grammars. It is more convenient, though, to represent structure using a slot-filler representation, which reflects more the functional role of phrases in a sentence. For instance, you could identify one particular noun phrase as the syntactic subject (**SUBJ**) of a sentence and another as the syntactic object of the verb (**OBJ**). Within noun phrases you might identify the determiner structure, adjectives, the head noun, and so on. Thus the sentence *Jack found a dime* might be represented by the structure:

> (S **SUBJ** (NP **NAME** Jack)
>   **MAIN-V** found
>   **TENSE** PAST
>   **OBJ** (NP **DET** a
>   **HEAD** dime))

Such a structure is created by the RTN parser by allowing each network to have a set of **registers**. Registers are local to each network. Thus each time a new network is pushed, a new set of empty registers is created. When the network is popped, the registers disappear. Registers can be set to values, and values can be retrieved from registers. In this case, the registers will have the names of the slots used for each of the preceding syntactic structures. Thus the NP network has registers named **DET**, **ADJS**, **HEAD**, and **NUM**. Registers are set by **actions** that can be specified on the arcs. When an arc is followed, the actions associated with it are executed. The most common action involves setting a register to a certain value. Other actions will be introduced as necessary. When a pop arc is followed, all the registers set in the current network are automatically collected to form a structure consisting of the network name followed by a list of the registers with their values. An RTN with registers, and tests and actions on those registers, is an augmented transition network.

The question arises as to how an action gets a value with which to set a register. Certain mechanisms make this reasonably easy. When a cat arc, such as verb, is followed, the word in the input is put in to a special variable named "*". Thus a plausible action on the arc from S1 to S2 in Figure 4.1 would be to set the **VERB** register to the current word, or written more concisely:

> **VERB** ← *

The push arcs, such as NP, must be treated differently. Typically many words have been used by the network called by the push arc. In addition, the network that was used in the push would have set registers that capture the structure of the constituent that was parsed. To make this accessible to the network that contained the push arc, the structure built by the pushed network is returned in the value "*". Thus the action on the arc from S to S1 in Figure 4.1 might be:

> **SUBJ** ← *

If the sentence started with *The purple cow . . .*, this action would result in the register **SUBJ** being set to the structure returned by the NP network, such as

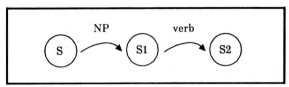

Figure 4.1 A simple transition net

> (NP **ART** the
>   **ADJS** (purple)
>   **HEAD** cow)

Checking Features with Tests

Besides collecting structures, the registers can be used to make the grammar more selective without unnecessarily complicating the network. For instance, in English, the number of the first noun phrase must correspond to the number of the verb. Thus you cannot have a singular first NP and a plural verb, as in *The dog are sick*. More importantly, number agreement is crucial in disambiguating some sentences. Consider the contrast between *Flying planes is dangerous*, where the subject is the activity of flying planes, and *Flying planes are dangerous*, where the subject is a set of planes that are flying. Without checking subject-verb agreement, the grammar could not distinguish between these two readings. You could encode number information by classifying all words as to whether they are singular or plural; then you could build up a grammar for singular sentences and for plural sentences. In an RTN this approach would be as shown in Figure 4.2. But such a method doubles the size of the grammar. In addition, to check some other feature, you would need to double the size of the grammar again. Besides the problems of size, this approach also forces you to make the singular-plural distinction even when it is not necessary to check it.

A better solution is to allow words (and syntactic structures) to have **features** as well as a basic category. You can do so by using the slot value list notation introduced earlier for syntactic structures. This notation allows you to store number information as well as other useful information about the word in a data structure called the **lexicon**. Figure 4.3 shows a lexicon with the root and number information for each word, in which "3s" means singular and "3p" means plural.

Now extend the RTN formalism by adding a **test** to each arc in the network. A test is simply a function that is said to **succeed** if it returns a nonempty value, such as a set or atom, and to **fail** if it returns the empty set or nil. If a test fails, its arc is not traversed. These tests are attempted only after the arc would otherwise succeed. In other words tests are applied after the input word is found to be in the correct category on cat arcs, or after the recursive call has

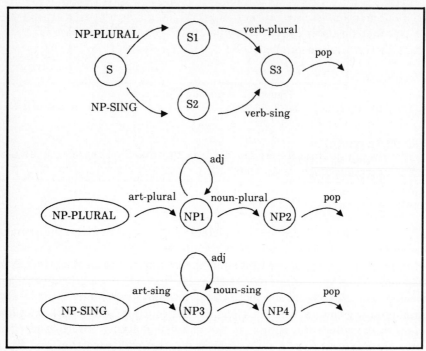

Figure 4.2 A simple RTN distinguishing singular and plural forms

Word	Representation
dogs	(NOUN **ROOT** DOG **NUM** {3p})
dog	(NOUN **ROOT** DOG **NUM** {3s})
the	(ART **ROOT** THE **NUM** {3s 3p})
a	(ART **ROOT** A **NUM** {3s})
cried	(VERB **ROOT** CRY **NUM** {3s 3p})
loves	(VERB **ROOT** LOVE **NUM** {3s})
love	(VERB **ROOT** LOVE **NUM** {3p})
wild	(ADJ **ROOT** WILD)
John	(NAME **ROOT** JOHN)

Figure 4.3 A simple lexicon (assuming third person only)

been made and has succeeded on push arcs. In actual systems facilities are often provided for testing prior to pushes as well for efficiency reasons. For the present, you can ignore such issues.

An Example

You now have enough mechanism to describe an ATN parser for a limited English subset. Grammar 4.4, with its annotation, accepts sentences involving intransitive or transitive verbs and simple noun phrases consisting of a proper name or simple definite descriptions with adjectives. The grammar enforces number agreement and, with the lexicon in Figure 4.3, would accept the following sentences:

> The wild dog cried.
> The dogs love John.
> John loves the wild dogs.

It would not accept sentences such as:

> *A wild dogs cried.   (no number agreement in NP)
> *John love a dog.   (no number agreement in SUBJ/VERB)

The language for expressing actions consists of an assignment statement and a small collection of operators for accessing and combining register values. Registers containing structures that themselves are the value of another register can be accessed using a subscript notation. Thus NUM_{SUBJ} is the NUM register of the structure in the SUBJ register, and NUM_* is the NUM register of the structure in *--that is, the structure created by following the arc. The values of registers are often viewed as sets, and the intersection ($\cap$) and union ($\cup$) of sets is allowed to combine the values of different registers. Finally, for registers that may take a list of values, an **append** function is permitted. For example, Append(**ADJS**, *) returns the list that is the list in the register **ADJS** with the value of * appended on the end. A register without subscripts refers to a register of the current network.

The tests allowed include checking for a particular value in a register (for example, $NUM_{SUBJ} = 3s$) and for the nonnull intersection of two registers containing sets of features ($NUM \cap NUM_*$).

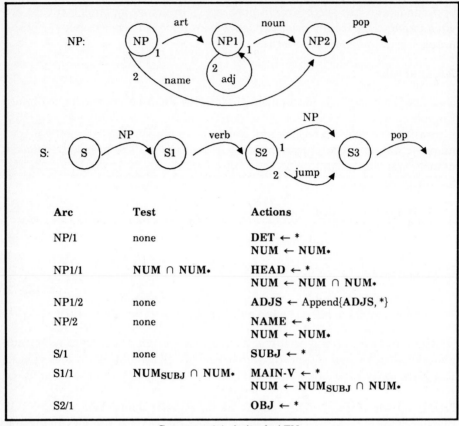

Arc	Test	Actions
NP/1	none	**DET ← *** **NUM ← NUM.**
NP1/1	**NUM ∩ NUM.**	**HEAD ← *** **NUM ← NUM ∩ NUM.**
NP1/2	none	**ADJS ← Append{ADJS, *}**
NP/2	none	**NAME ← *** **NUM ← NUM.**
S/1	none	**SUBJ ← ***
S1/1	**NUM$_{SUBJ}$ ∩ NUM.**	**MAIN-V ← *** **NUM ← NUM$_{SUBJ}$ ∩ NUM.**
S2/1		**OBJ ← ***

Grammar 4.4 A simple ATN

Consider one example. While processing the sentence *The dogs love John*, the ATN in Grammar 4.4 will first check agreement between *the* and *dogs*. *The* can be either singular or plural, but *dogs* must be plural, so the noun phrase constructed will have the **NUM** feature plural (as a result of the action on arc NP1/1). This NP is assigned to the **SUBJ** register and then checked for agreement with the verb. The detailed trace in Figure 4.5 indicates the current node in the network, the current word position, the arc that is followed from the node, and the register manipulations that are performed for the successful parse. Each arc name consists of the node that it leaves plus a number to make it unique. Thus S/1 is the first arc leaving the S node. The sentence, with the word positions indicated, is as follows:

1 The 2 dogs 3 love 4 John 5 .

Trace of S Network

Step	Node	Position	Arc Followed	Registers
1.	S	1	S/1 attempted (for recursive call see trace below)	
5.		3	S/1 succeeds	**SUBJ** ← (NP **DET** the **HEAD** dogs **NUM** {3p})
	S1	3	S1/1 (tests whether {3p} ∩ {3p} not empty)	**MAIN-V** ← love **NUM** ← {3p}
6.	S2	4	S2/1 (for recursive call trace, see below)	**OBJ** ← (NP **NAME** John **NUM** {3s})
9.	S3	5	S3/1 succeeds since no words left	returns (S **SUBJ** (NP **DET** the **HEAD** dogs **NUM** {3p}) **VERB** love **NUM** {3p} **OBJ** (NP **NAME** John **NUM** {3s}))

Trace of First NP Call: Arc 6

Step	Node	Position	Arc Followed	Registers
2.	NP	1	NP/1	**DET** ← the **NUM** ← {3s 3p}
3.	NP1	2	NP/1 (check if {3s 3p} ∩ {3p} not empty)	**HEAD** ← dogs **NUM** ← {3p}
4.	NP2	3	NP2/1	returns (NP **DET** the **HEAD** dogs **NUM** {3p})

Trace of Second NP Call: Arc 8

Step	Node	Position	Arc Followed	Registers
7.	NP	4	NP/2	**NAME** ← John **NUM** ← {3s}
8.	NP2	5	NP2/1	returns (NP **NAME** John) **NUM** {3s})

Figure 4.5 Trace tests and actions used with *The dogs love John.*

BOX 4.1 ATNs as LISP Structures

Actual ATN grammars are usually specified as LISP expressions that closely mirror the data structure in LISP that represents the network. To give an idea of what this is like, here is how a small network would be specified in Woods's original ATN paper (Woods, 1970). The network was represented as a list of node structures, each of the form

$(nodename\ arc_1\ ...\ arc_n)$

Each arc is represented by a list of the form

$(type\ arg\ test\ act_1\ ...\ act_n\ destination)$

The *type* is CAT, WRD, PUSH, or POP, all of which were defined earlier. The *arg* then depends on the type of arc it is. For CAT arcs, it's the lexical category, for PUSH arcs it's the network, for WRD arcs it's the word, and for POP arcs it's an expression that computes the structure to be returned.

The test can be an arbitrary LISP function call. To get the values of registers, the LISP function (*GETR register*) returns the value of the specified register in the current network, and (*GETF structure register*) returns the value of the specified register in the specified structure. Similarly, the actions are arbitrary LISP expressions. The one needed to mirror the capabilities of our ATN notation is

(*SETR register value*) -- sets the indicated register to the
specified value

The destination is a list of the form (*TO nodename*); it indicates to which node the arc points.

Finally, unlike in our ATN system, no structure is built automatically on the pop arcs. Rather, a LISP function *BUILDQ* allows the programmer to construct whatever structure is desired. For example,

(BUILDQ (NP (DET +) (HEAD +)) DET NOUN)

would build an NP structure with a DET slot filled with the value of the DET register, and a HEAD slot filled with the value of the NOUN register.

Given this notation, the NP network in Grammar 4.4 would be represented as follows:

```
(NP (CAT ART T (SETR DET *) (SETR NUM (GETF * NUM))
          (TO NP1))
    (CAT NAME T (SETR NAME *)
                (SETR NUM (GETF * NUM)) (TO NP3))
(NP1 (CAT ADJ T (SETR ADJS (APPEND(GETR ADJS) *))
          (TO NP1))
     (CAT NOUN (AGR (GETF * NUM) (GETR NUM))
               (SETR HEAD *)
               (SETR NUM (AGR (GETF * NUM) (GETR NUM)))
          (TO NP2))
(NP2 (POP (BUILDQ (NP (DET +) (ADJS +) (HEAD +) (NUM +))
          DET ADJS HEAD NUM)))
(NP3 (POP (BUILDQ (NP (NAME +) (NUM +)) NAME NUM)))
```

Note that you had to use an extra node, NP3, in order to build a different structure, depending on what path was followed through the network. The automatic structure building used in the formulation in this book simplifies this.

4.2 Useful Feature Systems

Now that you have seen the augmentation mechanism, consider how it can be used in the analysis of English sentences. This section examines several areas of English syntax where features prove to be very useful in capturing the right generalities. These will provide the basis for most of the feature tests in the augmented grammars that follow.

Subject-Verb Agreement

You have already seen a simple analysis of number agreement between the subject and verb. The other dimension along which a subject and verb must agree is the **person**. Person is explicitly indicated in English in the pronoun system, consisting of first person (I, we), second person (you), and third person (he, she, it, they). All nonpronominal subjects are considered to be the third person.

Because person and number distinctions are made in only a few instances with verbs, it is best to combine these features rather than treat them independently. For example, a large number of verbs distinguish only the third person singular form from the rest. This distinction is seen in the following conjugation:

I love	we love
you love	you love
he/she <u>loves</u>	they love

Rather than have the entry for *love* be five ways ambiguous, a single entry is given listing all the possibilities. The notation for indicating person and number features for verbs will consist of listing all the possible forms for singular and plural. Thus, *love* will be classified as {1s 2s 1p 2p 3p}, indicating it can agree with a first and second person singular subject, or any person plural subject. The entry for *loves*, on the other hand, would be {3s}, indicating it can agree with only a third person singular subject. Other combinations are possible. For example, *saw* has the feature {1s 2s 3s 1p 2p 3p}, indicating it agrees with any subject, *is* has {3s}, *are* has {2s 1p 2p 3p}, and *am* has {1s}. All nonpronominal noun phrases will be either {3s}, {3p}, or {3s 3p}, depending on whether they are singular, plural, or ambiguous between the two. Pronouns have their obvious analysis: *he* is {3s}, *you* is {2s 2p}, *me* is {1s}, and so on.

With this feature system you can easily define a test called **Agr(feature1, feature2)**, which takes two feature sets and computes their intersection. If this intersection is null, the test fails. Otherwise the test succeeds and returns the value of intersection. Thus Agr({3s 3p}, {1s 2s 1p 2p 3p}) succeeds with {3p}, and Agr({2s 2p}, {1s 2s 1p 2p 3p}) succeeds with {2s 2p}, while Agr({3s}, {2s 1p 2p 3p}) fails.

As seen in the previous section, number agreement tests are usable for determiner-head number agreement within NPs as well. The article *a* would have the feature {3s}, while *the* would have the feature {3s 3p}. Number agreement also occurs in sentences involving the verb *be*. For instance, you can say *I am the walrus* but not

    *I am the walruses.

Auxiliary-Verb Agreement

Another area where features provide a significantly cleaner analysis than the alternative of encoding the distinctions in the grammar is the verb group. Specifically, this is the sequence of verbs consisting of zero or more auxiliaries followed by the main verb, such as the following:

I <u>can see</u> the house.
I <u>will have seen</u> the house.
I <u>was watching</u> the movie.
I <u>should have been watching</u> the movie.
I <u>will be seen</u> at the house.

Form	Feature Name	Examples
infinitive	inf	go, be, say, decide
present	pres	go, goes, am, is, say, says, decide
present participle	ing	going, being, saying, deciding
past participle	en	gone, been, said, decided
past	past	went, was, said, decided

Figure 4.6 The verb forms

These may at first appear to be arbitrary sequences of verbs, including *have*, *be*, *do*, *can*, *will*, and so on, but in fact there is a rich structure. Each verb used as an auxiliary places a restriction on the form of the verb that follows it. To review, the verb forms are as shown in Figure 4.6.

Verbs usable as auxiliaries can be divided into types depending on how they restrict the verb following them. The verbs *be*, *do*, and *have* are treated individually. All the rest, such as *can*, *could*, *should*, *might*, and so on, will be considered together as a category called **modal**.

Consider how the auxiliaries constrain the verb that follows them. In particular, the auxiliary *have* must be followed by a past participle form (either another auxiliary or the main verb), and the auxiliary *be* must be followed by a present participle form, or, in the case of passive sentences, by the past participle form. The auxiliary *do* usually occurs alone, but it can accept an infinitive form following it (*I did eat my carrots!*). The modals must always be followed by an infinitive form. Finally, note that the first auxiliary (or verb) in the sequence cannot be in a participle or infinitive form. It must be either the simple past or present. For example, *I going*, *we gone*, and *they be* are all unacceptable. These rules can be encoded as a procedure **AuxAgree(verb, aux-list)** that takes the next verb (auxiliary or main) in a sequence and checks that it satisfies the restrictions of the last auxiliary seen (the last element of aux-list). This procedure is defined in Figure 4.7.

The procedure would operate on the aux-verb sequence *can be seen* as follows:

AuxAgree(*can*, nil) returns T
AuxAgree(*be*, (*can*)) returns MODAL
AuxAgree(*seen*, (*can be*)) returns PASSIVE

Similarly, the phrases *will have been going*, *should have gone*, and *have had* will all be accepted, whereas the phrases *will have being*, *should had gone*, and *have have* would not be allowed.

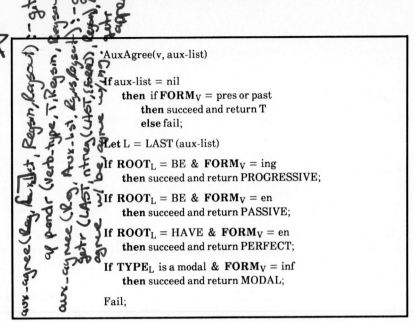

```
AuxAgree(v, aux-list)

If aux-list = nil
    then if FORMᵥ = pres or past
        then succeed and return T
        else fail;

Let L = LAST (aux-list)

If ROOT_L = BE & FORMᵥ = ing
    then succeed and return PROGRESSIVE;

If ROOT_L = BE & FORMᵥ = en
    then succeed and return PASSIVE;

If ROOT_L = HAVE & FORMᵥ = en
    then succeed and return PERFECT;

If TYPE_L is a modal & FORMᵥ = inf
    then succeed and return MODAL;

Fail;
```

Figure 4.7 A simple algorithm for checking auxiliary verbs

These tests do not fully capture all the restrictions by any means, but they will be sufficient for the present purposes. Ordering constraints exist between the auxiliaries as well. For example, the use of *have* forms in the auxiliary must precede the use of *be* forms. The only way a *have* form may follow a *be* form occurs if the *have* form is the main verb. Thus *was having* is a valid aux-verb sequence, but *was having been gone* is not acceptable, even though it passes all the earlier AuxAgree tests. These ordering constraints will be enforced in the grammar itself (see Section 4.3).

The information returned by AuxAgree, together with information on each auxiliary indicating whether it is a past or present form, is necessary for computing the tense and aspect features of the verb group. For example, the phrase *have been going* would be analyzed by AuxAgree, returning the values T, PERFECT, PROGRESSIVE, respectively. The verbs would also be classified as pres, past, and inf, respectively. From this, you should be able to derive that the verb group is in the past perfect progressive form. This analysis can be very complicated, however, and cannot be considered in detail in this book.

Verb Complements

The complement structure of a verb includes the NPs and clauses that immediately follow the verbs. This section will outline a single feature system to handle the most common forms of verb complements. In essence the verb determines what subcategories can be in the VP structure that contains it. The information about the complement structure is often called the **subcategorization** of the verb.

You have already seen that verbs can be categorized by how many NPs they allow to follow them immediately without the use of prepositions. **Intransitive** verbs allow no NPs, **transitive** verbs allow one NP to follow (the object), and **bitransitive** verbs allow two NPs to follow (indirect-object, object). The indirect object is optional for all bitransitive verbs, since it can always be expressed using a prepositional phrase. The object NP, however, is considered obligatory in most uses of transitive or bitransitive verbs.

This would be all quite straightforward except that many verbs that you would think to classify as transitive actually do allow a second NP to follow the verb. These verbs will be classified as **benefactive**, because they can be followed by an NP that indicates for whom the action is done. You see this with transitive verbs, as in *Sing me a song*, *Did you find me a job?*, and so on. At the syntactic level, since there is no advantage to distinguishing between bitransitive and benefactive verbs, you can consider all these verbs to be bitransitive. The effect is that there are a lot less transitive verbs than you might think.

You can classify most verbs by outlining one or two constituents that can follow the verb. These components will be encoded in a **SUBCAT** slot in the definition of each verb. So far you have seen the features:

NONE	no complements allowed (intransitive)
OBJ	single NP allowed to follow verb (transitive)
IOBJ + OBJ	two NPs allowed to follow verb (bitransitive)

Some verbs, such as *seem* and *be*, can take an adjective phrase as a complement, as in *Jack seemed angry*. Others allow an object and an adjective, such as *Jack makes me angry*. To account for these verbs, there are two new features:

ADJ	takes an adjective complement
OBJ + ADJ	takes an object followed by an adjective phrase

Another class of verbs involves those that subcategorize for PPs. For example, the usual sense of the verb *put* must take an object NP plus a PP, as in *Jack put the money on the counter*. Thus its feature is

OBJ + PP

A more sophisticated feature set might restrict the PP to be a location term, but this feature will be left for the semantic analysis phase.

Now consider the complements that are clauses. The most common forms of complements are those involving infinitives, those involving tensed verbs, and those involving wh-terms. The following discussion will consider each in turn.

The infinitive complements all involve the use of the infinitive as the first verb in the verb group. They may or may not include a *to* preceding the verb and may or may not allow the entire complement to begin with a phrase of the form "for NP." The possibilities allowed will be FOR-TO-INF, as in *for the doctor to come in time*; TO-INF, as in *to fry the bacon*; and INF, as in *fry the bacon*. You can combine these with the NP complement features to obtain new subcategorizations, such as the following:

FOR-TO-INF	-	as in *I prayed for the doctor to come in time*.
OBJ + TO-INF	-	as in *I persuaded him to do it*.
TO-INF	-	as in *I tried to do it*.
OBJ + INF	-	as in *I saw him do it*.
INF	-	as in *I helped do it*.

Of course, many verbs accept multiple forms. The verb *help*, for example, allows the forms OBJ, OBJ + TO-INF, OBJ + INF, and INF, while *want* allows the forms OBJ, OBJ + TO-INF, and TO-INF.

The tensed complements all involve a clause with the normal tense information of a regular sentence. These clauses are often introduced by the complementizer *that*. It is difficult to find a verb that allows tensed complements yet does not allow optional use of the *that* complementizer, so one feature will be used throughout the text for both cases. Combining this feature with the NP complement, you find the following two combinations:

THAT	-	as in *I know that Jack left*.
		I know Jack left.
OBJ + THAT	-	as in *Jack told Mary that he had lost his bicycle*.

Another common complement form involves the use of wh-words, such as *what*, *why*, *when*, and *how*, as complementizers, as in *I know what Jack said* and *I know how many times I tried to fly*. These forms are obviously strongly related to wh-questions. Complements, such as *Harold knows whether Jack lied*, may be treated in the same class, although they are treated differently in many analyses. This book uses the following features:

WH-COMP   -   as in *We doubt what John said*.

OBJ + WH-COMP -   as in *They asked Jack whether it was raining*.

This covers the most common forms of subcategorizations. There are others, such as complements involving gerunds--for instance, *refusing*, as in *I don't understand Jack's refusing the prize*--but they will not be considered here.

Note that there is a large class of sentence forms that allow complements yet are not easily analyzable in terms of the main verb. For example, earlier you saw a class of sentences involving the verb *be* plus an adjective. Many of these forms allow complements, as in *It is impossible for me to get those clothes clean*, *Jack was sad that my canary died*, and *I was destined to face my insecurities*. A wide range of complement types is not added for verbs such as *be* and *seem*. Rather the range of allowable complements is determined by the adjective. For instance, you cannot say

> *Jack was sad *for me to get my clothes clean*.
> *I was destined *that my canary died*.

To handle such cases, you need to allow complement features on adjectives for when they are used in this way. In addition, certain nouns in noun phrases subcategorize for complex complements as well, such as in the NP *The fact that I lied*.

Unlike number agreement and the auxiliary features, the SUBCAT features are used more to select arcs (or rules) in the grammar than to perform agreement checks. For example, the grammar should not try to parse for an NP following a verb unless the verb allows an object--that is, has one or more of the features OBJ, OBJ + TO-INF, OBJ + INF, and so on.

To represent tests concisely in the following grammars, consider these functions, where f is an arbitrary subcategorization feature set:

Intrans(f)   =   f ∩ {NONE ADJ FOR-TO-INF TO-INF INF
                            THAT WH-COMP}

Trans(f)   =   f ∩ {OBJ IOBJ + OBJ OBJ + TO-INF
                         OBJ + INF OBJ + ADJ OBJ + PP
                         OBJ + THAT OBJ + WH-COMP}

4.3 A Sample ATN Grammar for Assertions

This section specifies a grammar for simple assertions in English that uses the lexicon in Figure 4.8. This excludes the question and command forms, as well

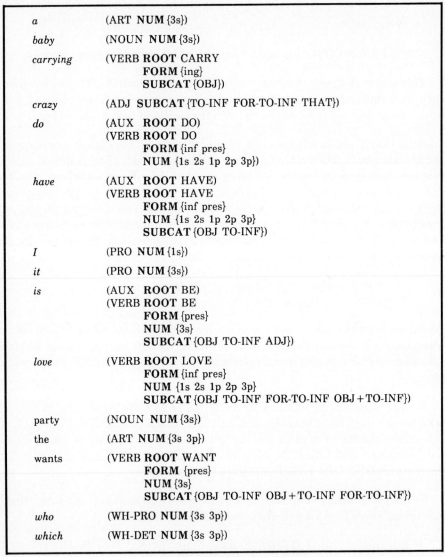

a	(ART **NUM** {3s})
baby	(NOUN **NUM** {3s})

carrying	(VERB **ROOT** CARRY
	    FORM {ing}
	    SUBCAT {OBJ})

crazy	(ADJ **SUBCAT** {TO-INF FOR-TO-INF THAT})

do	(AUX **ROOT** DO)
	(VERB **ROOT** DO
	    FORM {inf pres}
	    NUM {1s 2s 1p 2p 3p})

have	(AUX **ROOT** HAVE)
	(VERB **ROOT** HAVE
	    FORM {inf pres}
	    NUM {1s 2s 1p 2p 3p}
	    SUBCAT {OBJ TO-INF})

I	(PRO **NUM** {1s})
it	(PRO **NUM** {3s})

is	(AUX **ROOT** BE)
	(VERB **ROOT** BE
	    FORM {pres}
	    NUM {3s}
	    SUBCAT {OBJ TO-INF ADJ})

love	(VERB **ROOT** LOVE
	    FORM {inf pres}
	    NUM {1s 2s 1p 2p 3p}
	    SUBCAT {OBJ TO-INF FOR-TO-INF OBJ + TO-INF})

party	(NOUN **NUM** {3s})
the	(ART **NUM** {3s 3p})

wants	(VERB **ROOT** WANT
	    FORM {pres}
	    NUM {3s}
	    SUBCAT {OBJ TO-INF OBJ + TO-INF FOR-TO-INF})

who	(WH-PRO **NUM** {3s 3p})
which	(WH-DET **NUM** {3s 3p})

Figure 4.8 Sample lexicon entries

as other complexities such as the passive, relative clauses, and so on. These will be dealt with in later chapters.

The sentence structure consists of an initial NP, followed by the auxiliaries and the main verb, which may then be followed by a maximum of two NPs and many PPs, depending on the verb. By using the feature system extensively, you can create a grammar that accepts any or all of the preceding complement

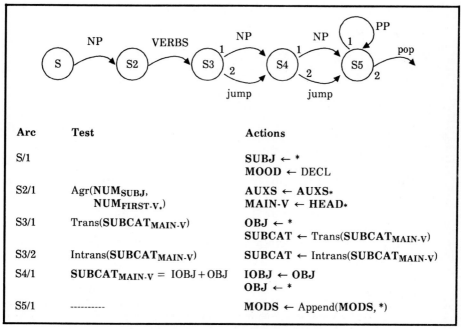

Arc	Test	Actions
S/1		SUBJ ← * MOOD ← DECL
S2/1	Agr(NUM$_{SUBJ}$, NUM$_{FIRST-V*}$)	AUXS ← AUXS* MAIN-V ← HEAD*
S3/1	Trans(SUBCAT$_{MAIN-V}$)	OBJ ← * SUBCAT ← Trans(SUBCAT$_{MAIN-V}$)
S3/2	Intrans(SUBCAT$_{MAIN-V}$)	SUBCAT ← Intrans(SUBCAT$_{MAIN-V}$)
S4/1	SUBCAT$_{MAIN-V}$ = IOBJ + OBJ	IOBJ ← OBJ OBJ ← *
S5/1	----------	MODS ← Append(MODS, *)

Grammar 4.9 An S network for assertions

forms, and leaves the actual verb-complement agreement to the augmentation. A simple S network is shown in Grammar 4.9.

The auxiliary and main verb network (see Grammar 4.10) is a simple ordering on the type of optional auxiliaries. In particular, any modal auxiliary must come first, followed by any auxiliary with root *have*, followed by any auxiliary with root *be*, followed by the main verb. The feature tests outlined in Section 4.2 enforce the appropriate forms, depending on what auxiliaries are present. This network does not include the passive form, which allows a second *be* auxiliary. The passive will be discussed in Section 4.7.

The NP network (Grammar 4.11) allows simple names, bare plural nouns (such as *Lions are dangerous*), pronouns, and the standard sequence of a determiner followed by an adjective and a head noun. The noun complements allowed include an optional number of prepositional phrases. Note that both the determiner structure and the adjective structure could be considerably more complex and justify a network in their own right. For example, a determiner structure not covered here is *None but the finest diamonds*, while an adjective structure not covered here is *The very pale green sky*.

The prepositional phrase network (Grammar 4.12) is straightforward, except that it includes a class of words called PP-NOUNS, such as *yesterday*, *now*, *here*, *home*, and so on. These words are classed as PPs since they may be

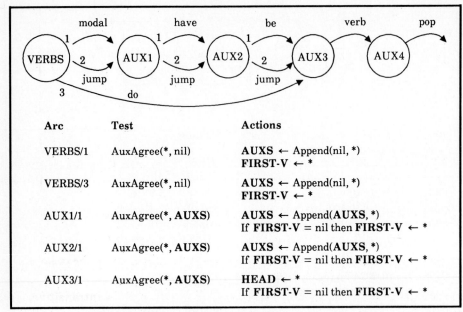

Grammar 4.10 The network of auxiliaries with main verb

Arc	Test	Actions
VERBS/1	AuxAgree(*, nil)	**AUXS** ← Append(nil, *) **FIRST-V** ← *
VERBS/3	AuxAgree(*, nil)	**AUXS** ← Append(nil, *) **FIRST-V** ← *
AUX1/1	AuxAgree(*, **AUXS**)	**AUXS** ← Append(**AUXS**, *) If **FIRST-V** = nil then **FIRST-V** ← *
AUX2/1	AuxAgree(*, **AUXS**)	**AUXS** ← Append(**AUXS**, *) If **FIRST-V** = nil then **FIRST-V** ← *
AUX3/1	AuxAgree(*, **AUXS**)	**HEAD** ← * If **FIRST-V** = nil then **FIRST-V** ← *

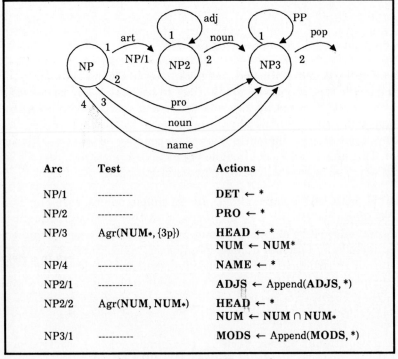

Arc	Test	Actions
NP/1	----------	**DET** ← *
NP/2	----------	**PRO** ← *
NP/3	Agr(**NUM***, {3p})	**HEAD** ← * **NUM** ← **NUM***
NP/4	----------	**NAME** ← *
NP2/1	----------	**ADJS** ← Append(**ADJS**, *)
NP2/2	Agr(**NUM, NUM***)	**HEAD** ← * **NUM** ← **NUM** ∩ **NUM***
NP3/1	----------	**MODS** ← Append(**MODS**, *)

Grammar 4.11 The NP network

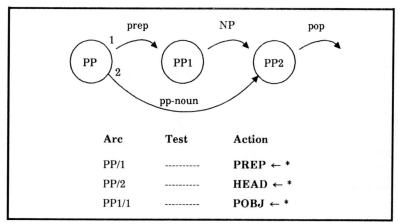

Arc	Test	Action
PP/1	----------	**PREP** ← *
PP/2	----------	**HEAD** ← *
PP1/1	----------	**POBJ** ← *

Grammar 4.12 The PP network

freely used wherever a normal PP could be used. For example, if they were classified as NPs, the transitivity constraints on verbs would become considerably more complicated. For example, the verb *come* is intransitive, as seen by the sentences

John came to our party.
*John came the party.

Thus, *come* does not allow an NP to follow but does allow a PP. Sentences such as *John came home* and *John came here*, however, are perfectly acceptable. When you consider semantic analysis of sentences, this classification of these words as PPs will also appear to be the best match with your intuitive ideas of what the sentences mean. This network does not include more complex PPs, where the object of the initial preposition might be another PP itself, as in *in out of the rain*.

Examples of parsing sentences with this grammar are left for the exercises.

4.4 Verb Complements and Presetting Registers

One further extension to the feature manipulation facilities in ATNs will be considered before generalized feature systems in other frameworks are examined. This extension involves the ability to preset registers in a network as that network is being called, much like parameter passing in a programming language. This facility, called the **SENDR** action in the original ATN systems, is useful to pass information to the network that aids in analyzing the new constituent.

Consider a class of verbs, including *want* and *pray*, that accepts complements using the infinitive form of verbs, which are usually introduced by the word *to*. According to the classification of verb complements in Section 4.2, this includes the following variants:

TO-INF	Mary wants <u>to have a party</u>.
OBJ+TO-INF	Mary wants John <u>to have a party</u>.
FOR-TO-INF	I prayed <u>for John to leave the party</u>.

As you may have noticed, the complements in this form appear to be identical in structure to sentences except that the subject NP and the auxiliaries are missing, and the verb must be in the infinitive form. It would be more elegant to reuse the already existing S network rather than writing a new network to handle such complements. All the feature checking incorporated into the S network can be reused as is with infinitive complements.

To do this, you need to be able to start in the S network at a different node than the usual. (While you could feasibly start at the S node and use jump arcs to get to the appropriate starting point, it would be messy.) Thus the desirable starting point is node S2.

So far, so good. But now consider the difference between *Mary wants to have a party* and *Mary wants John to have a party*. In the first case it is Mary who would be the host; in the other case it would be John. Apparently there is a different "understood" subject in each of these embedded sentences. The understood subject could be retrieved later during semantic analysis, but this would make the semantic interpreter more complex. Furthermore, there are other good reasons for actually inserting the understood subject at the syntactic level. For example, consider the sentences

> Mary wants to dress herself in the closet.
> Mary wants John to dress himself in the closet.
> *Mary wants to dress himself in the closet.
> *Mary wants John to dress herself in the closet.

The last two sentences are unacceptable because the gender of the reflexive pronoun does not agree with that of the understood subject in the complement. To enforce such a restriction the grammar needs to access the gender of the SUBJ in the complement.

Thus it would be useful to be able to preset the **SUBJ** register in the new S network when it is called. An extended push arc of the following form allows presetting:

> PUSH (N, <register in N> ⇐ <register in current network>)

For example,

> PUSH (S2, **SUBJ** ⇐ **SUBJ**)

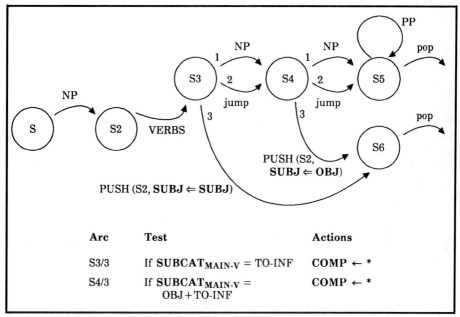

Grammar 4.13 The final S network for TO-INF complements

will push to the node S2 in the S network and preset the **SUBJ** register in the new S network to the value of the **SUBJ** register in the current S network. This is just what is needed for _Mary wants to have a party._ For the second case, _Mary wants John to have a party,_ you need a call of the form

PUSH (S2, SUBJ ← OBJ)

The last problem to consider is how to deal with the word _to_. The first auxiliary or verb found following the word _to_ must be in the infinitive form. You could add an arc that accepts the _to_ before calling the VERBS network, but the call to the VERBS network from arc S2/1 would fail, because it requires the first verb to be in either the simple present or past form. An elegant solution to this problem is to consider the word _to_ to be an auxiliary modal verb. If this is done, the verb following it will have to be in its infinitive form (as it must be for all modals). The final network to handle these cases is shown in Grammar 4.13.

Consider a trace of the parse of _Mary wants John to have a party_, starting at node S4 in Grammar 4.13, with _to have a party_ remaining to be parsed. The set of registers for the outer S network at this stage is

SUBJ (NP1 **NAME** Mary)
MAIN-V wants
OBJ (NP2 **NAME** John)

Following arc S4/3, do the push for the complement that is traced in Figure 4.14. The **SUBJ** register in the embedded S is initialized to the value of the **OBJ** register--namely, NP2. To indicate that this is a copy, use the notation →NP2 as the value of the **SUBJ** register. Figure 4.14 traces the path through the S network for the verb complement. In the second step in this trace a push to the VERBS network picks up *to* and then *have* as the main verb in infinitive form, as required. The third step involves a simple push to the NP network to parse *a party*.

The final analysis of this sentence is

(S **SUBJ** (NP1 **NAME** Mary)
    MAIN-V wants
    OBJ (NP2 **NAME** John)
    COMP (S **SUBJ** →NP2
             AUXS (to)
             MAIN-V have
             OBJ (NP **DET** a
                        HEAD party)))

4.5 Augmenting Chart Parsers

Chart-based parsers can be augmented in much the same way as ATNs. Each CFG rule has tests and actions associated with it that manipulate registers maintained on the chart. The test associated with a rule may examine the chart entries for the constituents matching the right-hand side of the rule, and the action builds a slot-value structure to add onto the chart. During the parse, whenever a rule is completed, its test is tried. If it succeeds, a new constituent is constructed using the actions associated with the rule and then is added to the chart. For example, consider the rule

NP ← ART NOUN

with the test

$NUM_{ART} \cap NUM_{NOUN}$

and the actions

DET ← ART
NUM ← $NUM_{ART} \cap NUM_{NOUN}$
HEAD ← NOUN

Node	Arc Followed	Registers
S2	S2/1	**AUXS** = (to) **MAIN-V** ← have
S3	S3/1	**OBJ** ← (NP **DET** a **HEAD** party)
S4	S4/2	----------
S5	S5/1	returns (S **SUBJ** →NP2 **AUXS** (to) **MAIN-V** have **OBJ** (NP **DET** a **HEAD** party))

Figure 4.14 Trace of parse of embedded S

At the time this rule is completed successfully during a parse there will be an entry on the chart for the ART and the NOUN. Rather than automatically adding an NP constituent to the chart and continuing the parse as seen in Chapter 3, the parser for the augmented grammar would apply the test (that is, $\text{NUM}_{\text{ART}} \cap \text{NUM}_{\text{NOUN}}$). If this succeeds, then the actions are performed to build a slot-value structure for the new NP to be added to the chart. If the test fails, the parser rejects the rule as though it never completed. Assuming the test succeeds, the new NP constituent would have the chart entry built for the ART as the value of its **DET** register, the entry for the NOUN as the value of its **HEAD** register, and the intersection of the **NUM** register of the ART and NOUN as the value of its **NUM** register. An augmented CFG is shown in Grammar 4.15.

When making an entry into the chart, the parser needs to know not only the starting and ending point of the new constituent but also its subconstituents. For example, there might be two NPs that cover positions 1 to 3 but that have different structures and therefore must be distinguished. With the nonaugmented parser there was no need to be able to distinguish this case, since all that was needed in the chart was the syntactic category and position of each constituent. The system maintains this information by adding a third position to the construction flag (such as <NP 1 r3>), which means an NP was started at position 1 using grammar rule 3. The system also uses the rule to identify the constituents that make up the NP when it is completed.

Consider a trace of a mixed-mode parse of *The dog cried*, using the lexicon in Section 4.2. Start with a parse state of an S at position 1. Rewriting the S symbol with rule 6 produces the state (NP VP <S 1 r6>) at position 1. Rewriting the NP symbol with rules 1, 2, and 5 creates the following states:

Rule	Test	Actions
1. NP ← ART ADJS NOUN	$\text{NUM}_{ART} \cap \text{NUM}_{NOUN}$	DET ← ART MODS ← ADJS HEAD ← NOUN NUM ← NUM_{ART} $\cap \text{NUM}_{NOUN}$
2. NP ← ART NOUN	$\text{NUM}_{ART} \cap \text{NUM}_{NOUN}$	DET ← ART HEAD ← NOUN NUM ← NUM_{ART} $\cap \text{NUM}_{NOUN}$
3. ADJS ← ADJ ADJS	----------	HEAD ← ADJ OTHERS ← ADJS
4. ADJS ← ADJ	----------	HEAD ← ADJ
5. NP ← NAME	----------	NAME ← NAME NUM ← NUM_{NAME}
6. S ← NP VP	$\text{NUM}_{NP} \cap \text{NUM MAIN-V}_{VP}$	NUM ← NUM_{NP} $\cap \text{NUM}_{VERB}$ SUBJ ← NP PRED ← VP
7. VP ← VERB		MAIN-V ← VERB NUM ← NUM_{VERB}
8. VP ← VERB NP		MAIN-V ← VERB OBJ ← NP NUM ← NUM_{VERB}

Grammar 4.15 An augmented CFG

Current State	Backup States	Position
(ART ADJS NOUN <NP 1 r1> VP <S 1 r6>)		1
	(ART NOUN <NP 1 r2> VP <S 1 r6>)	1
	(NAME <NP 1 r5> VP <S 1 r6>)	1

In processing ART next, the system first checks the chart, but it is empty. It then checks the input sentence at position 1 and succeeds. After adding the entry onto the chart, it has the following possibilities and the position shown in Figure 4.16.

Current State	Backup States	Position
(ADJS NOUN <NP 1 r1> VP <S 1 r6>)		2
	(ART NOUN <NP 1 r2> VP <S 1 r6>)	1
	(NAME <NP 1 r5> VP <S 1 r6>)	1

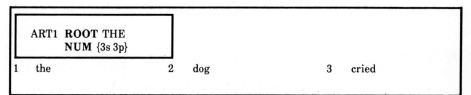

Figure 4.16 After parsing the first word

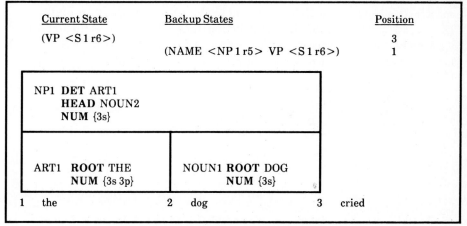

Figure 4.17 After parsing the first NP

ADJS is rewritten, and the first possibility generated from rule 3 fails, since *dog* is not an adjective, as does the possibility generated from rule 4. Thus the top backup state becomes the current state

(ART NOUN <NP 1 r2> VP <S 1 r6>) at position 1

ART1 is already on the chart, so the current state is updated to

(NOUN <NP 1 r2> VP <S 1 r6>) at position 2

Checking for a NOUN on the chart fails. Checking the input sentence succeeds, the parser finding the word *dog*, and a constituent NOUN1 is added to the chart. Next is the constructor flag <NP 1 r2>. The system checks the tests on rule 2--that is, it checks that the **NUM** of ART1 agrees with the **NUM** of NOUN1. If this succeeds, it then adds a constituent NP1 to the chart, producing the parser situation shown in Figure 4.17. The symbol VP is rewritten according to the grammar rules, producing the following situation:

Current State	Backup States	Position
(VERB <VP 3 r7> <S 1 r6>)		3
	(VERB NP <VP 3 r8> <S 1 r6>)	3
	(NAME <NP 1 r5> VP <S 1 r6>)	1

Checking the sentence for a VERB succeeds, and a constituent VERB1 for *cried* is added to the chart. Processing the construction flag <VP 3 r7>, the system constructs a constituent VP1, resulting in the situation shown in Figure 4.18. During the processing of the construction flag <S 1 r6>, the subject-verb agreement is checked, according to the annotation on rule 6, and an S entry, S1, is made from positions 1 to 4 of the form:

```
S  SUBJ (NP DET ART1
              HEAD NOUN1
              NUM {3s})
       PRED (VP MAIN-V VERB1
              NUM {3s 3p})
       NUM {3s}
```

Thus the system has constructed an analysis of *The dog cried* and checked for number agreement.

Note that the values of the registers in existing chart entries are never changed in this process. New registers and constituents are always created to store new values. For example, even though NP1 was computed to be singular, the chart entries for ART1 and VP1 remain ambiguous between singular and plural. This is important because these structures might also be used by other structures to form different interpretations. Thus, in a sentence with two different structures, there might be two references to VP1--one requiring it to be singular, and the other requiring it to be plural.

4.6 Augmenting Logic Grammars

You can augment a logic grammar by adding extra arguments to each predicate to encode register values. As a very simple example, you could modify the grammar in Section 3.3 to enforce number agreement by adding an argument for the number on every predicate for which the number is relevant. Thus you would have rules such as

```
a)     (NP ?p1 ?number ?p3) <  (ART ?p1 ?number1 ?p2)
                                (NOUN ?p2 ?number2 ?p3)
                                (AGREE ?number1 ?number2 ?number)
```

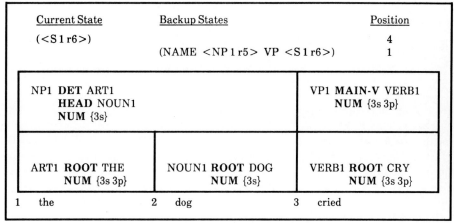

Figure 4.18 After parsing the VP

where the predicate AGREE is defined elsewhere to succeed only if the third argument is the nonnull intersection of the first two arguments. This definition of AGREE would be defined by a set of Horn clauses that calculated the intersection and checked that it was not empty. The lexicon values would be modified to include number information as follows:

b)   (ART ?i ?number ?o) < (WORD ?word ?i ?o) (ISART ?word ?number)
c)   (ISART a {3s})
d)   (ISART the {3s 3p})
e)   (NOUN ?i ?number ?o) < (WORD ?word ?i ?o) (ISNOUN ?word ?number)
f)   (ISNOUN dog {3s})
g)   (ISNOUN dogs {3p})
h)   (ISNOUN fish {3s 3p})

As before, a sentence is declared by listing the words. For example, *the dog cried* would be captured by the assertions

        (WORD the 1 2)
        (WORD dog 2 3)
        (WORD cried 3 4)

With the preceding axioms, when a word such as *the* is checked to be an article by ISART, the number feature for the word is returned. You can see this in the trace of the simple proof of

        (NP 1 ?number 3)

Using rule (a), you have the following subgoals:

```
(ART 1 ?number1 ?p2)
(NOUN ?p2 ?number2 3)
(AGREE ?number1 ?number2 ?number)
```

The first subgoal succeeds by using rule (b) and proving

```
(WORD the 1 2) (ISART the {3s 3p})
```

with the following bindings:

```
?number 1 ← {3s 3p}
?p2 ← 2
```

The second subgoal now is

```
(NOUN 2 ?number2 3)
```

By using rule (e) you succeed, binding

```
?number2 ← {3s}
```

The final subgoal now is

```
(AGREE {3s 3p} {3s} ?number)
```

which should succeed when defined appropriately, binding

```
?number ← {3s}
```

Thus the parse succeeds and the number agreement was enforced.

The grammar can also be extended to record the structure of the parse by adding another argument to the rules. For example, to construct a parse tree, you could use the following rules:

1.   (S ?p1 ?number (S ?np ?vp) ?p3) <
          (NP ?p1 ?number1 ?np ?p2)
          (VP ?p2 ?number2 ?vp ?p3)
          (AGREE ?number1 ?number2 ?number)

2.   (NP ?p1 ?number (NP ?art ?head) ?p3) <
          (ART ?p1 ?number1 ?art ?p2)
          (NOUN ?p2 ?number2 ?head ?p3)
          (AGREE ?number1 ?number2 ?number)

3.   (VP ?p1 ?number (VP ?verb) ?p2) <
          (VERB ?p1 ?verb ?p2)

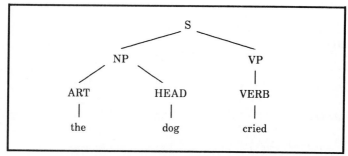

Figure 4.19 A tree representation of the structure

4.   (ART ?i ?number (ART ?word) ?o) <
        (WORD ?word ?i ?o) (ISART ?word ?number)

5.   (NOUN ?i ?number (NOUN ?word) ?o) <
        (WORD ?word ?i ?o) (ISNOUN ?word ?number)

6.   (VERB ?i ?number (VERB ?word) ?o) <
        (WORD ?word ?i ?o) (ISVERB ?word ?number)

These rules would allow you to prove the following on the sentence *The dog cried*.

(S 1 {3s} (S (NP (ART the) (HEAD dog)) (VP (VERB cried))) 4)

In other words, between positions 1 and 4 there is a sentence with number feature {3s} and the structure (rewritten as a tree) shown in Figure 4.19.

Of course, different structure building specifications could produce a slot-value representation identical to that with the ATN in the previous section, and you could make additional agreement checks by adding additional argument positions.

For specifying grammars, most logic-based grammar systems provide a more convenient format that is automatically converted into Horn clauses. For example, since the word position arguments are on every predicate, they could be omitted by the user and inserted by the system. Similarly, since all the predicates representing terminal symbols (for example, ART, NOUN, VERB) are defined systematically, the system could automatically generate these rules.

For example, you could write the preceding grammar by specifying just three rules, where the square brackets indicate a predicate with the position arguments deleted:

$$S [?number (S ?np ?vp)] \leftarrow NP [?n1\ ?np]$$
$$VP [?n2\ ?vp]$$
$$(AGREE\ ?n1\ ?n2\ ?number)$$

$$NP [?number (NP ?art ?head)] \leftarrow ART [?n1\ ?art]$$
$$NOUN [?n2\ ?head]$$
$$(AGREE\ ?n1\ ?n2\ ?number)$$

$$VP [?number (VP ?verb)] \leftarrow VERB [?number\ ?verb]$$

It is simple to write a preprocessor that would convert these rules in the new notation back into the rules 1, 2, and 3.

4.7 Generalized Feature Manipulation

In the last few sections you saw two different ways of recording and manipulating features. The one method considered in most detail was the use of register tests and actions in the ATN and augmented chart systems. The other method, of course, was the use of extra parameters in the logic grammar. While these two frameworks overlap in abilities substantially, they also have some significant differences.

For instance, in the ATN system, you could specify the augmented grammar shown in Grammar 4.20, demonstrating a technique often used to deal with the passive construct.

In this case the first NP is initially assigned to the SUBJ register, but if the sentence is found to be passive, it is reassigned to the OBJ register, and the SUBJ is reassigned to nil. This cannot be done in the logic grammar systems. For example, consider the rule

$$S [(Sentence ?subj ?aux ?verb ?obj)] \leftarrow NP [?subj]$$
$$AUX [?aux]$$
$$VERB [?verb]$$
$$(PASSIVE\ ?aux\ ?verb\ ?obj\ ?subj)$$

Once ?subj is bound to a value--say, (NP (ART the) (HEAD book))--it cannot be bound to another value, no matter how the PASSIVE predicate was defined, since variables are bound only by the unification process.

The passive construct can be handled in logic grammars by using another variable for the first NP and then deciding later whether to assign it to the variable representing the subject or object. For example, the rules in Grammar 4.21 have the same effect as the ATN in Grammar 4.20. Rule 2 first checks that the auxiliary and verb forms indicate the passive, and then unifies the variable ?first with the variable for the object. Rule 3 covers the active

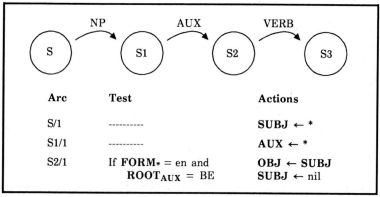

Arc	Test	Actions
S/1	----------	SUBJ ← *
S1/1	----------	AUX ← *
S2/1	If **FORM**$_*$ = en and **ROOT**$_{AUX}$ = BE	OBJ ← SUBJ SUBJ ← nil

Grammar 4.20 One approach to passives

---

1. S [(Sentence ?first ?subj ?aux ?verb ?obj)] < NP [?first]
                                                      AUX [?aux]
                                                      VERB [?verb]
                                                      (PASSIVE ?first ?aux ?verb ?subj ?obj)

2. (PASSIVE ?first (WORD ROOT BE FORM ?f) (WORD ROOT ?v FORM en) ?subj ?first)

3. (PASSIVE ?first ?aux ?verb ?first ?obj)

Grammar 4.21 An equivalent logic grammar for passives

sentences and unifies ?first with the variable in the position for the subject. You could modify the ATN in Grammar 4.20 to use a new register **FIRST-NP**, and thus have an ATN that doesn't reassign registers either.

Although such reassignment might seem to be a minor issue, it has major implications. If you allow registers to be reassigned during a parse, you are limiting the parsing strategies that can be used with that grammar. For instance, with the ATN framework, you looked only at top-down parsing. In fact, it is very difficult to consider bottom-up parsing techniques if variables can be reassigned, because the tests on arcs check conditions on variable values. If a variable value can be changed, at one stage of the parse a test may appear to succeed, but later the variable might be reassigned such that the test fails. If registers cannot be reassigned, this problem doesn't arise.

Thus there are advantages to restricting the grammar so that registers may not be reassigned but only made more specific using unification rather than assignment. Another key advantage, as you will see, is that unification-based approaches allow partial information to be stored easily.

A simple system can be based on generalized unification by slightly modifying the augmented context-free grammar formalism. In particular, all tests and actions are replaced by the unification equations described in the following text. The unification process used in logic grammars is not convenient for manipulating grammatical structures, so a variant is derived here based on the same general ideas. Specifically, suppose that two register-value structures unify if each of the register values specified is consistent with that same register's value in the other structure. Any register specified in one but not the other is simply copied to the resulting structure. For example, the structures

> (S **VERB** (VERB **ROOT** LOVE))

and

> (S **VERB** (VERB **FORM** en)
>   **NUM** {3s})

unify to produce a new structure

> (S **VERB** (VERB **ROOT** LOVE
>   **FORM** en)
>   **NUM** {3s})

Registers that take a set of disjunctive features are unified in the obvious way by intersecting their sets. If the intersection is empty, the unification of the structures fails. This is the way that agreement restrictions can be enforced. Thus

> (VP **TRANS** {IOBJ TO-INF})

and

> (VP **TRANS** {TO-INF FOR-TO-INF})

would unify to produce

> (VP **TRANS** {TO-INF})

Unification equations are all of the form *structure = structure*, as in

> (NP **NUM** {1s 2p 3p}) = (NP **NUM** {1s 2s 3s})

which has the result (NP **NUM** {1s}). To be useful as a rule annotation, equations may specify registers in the current constituent being built and in the subconstituents (that is, the right-hand side of the rule), just as in the augmented CFG formalism. Thus the following are legal unification equations for the rule NP ← ART ADJS NOUN:

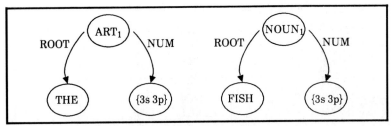

Figure 4.22 Lexical entries for *the* and *fish*

DET = ART

> This equation unifies the **DET** register with the structure built as the ART. Note that if the **DET** register is empty prior to this unification, this situation is identical to the register assignment (**DET** ← ART) in the old formalism. If the **DET** register is set to some value before the unification, the two values are unified, and both the **DET** register and the ART constituent are changed to the resulting structure.

NUM = NUM$_{ART}$ = NUM$_{NOUN}$

> This equation, which unifies three structures, is equivalent to the old test on rule 1 plus the register assignment action to the **NUM** register. The values of **NUM** register in the constituents ART and NOUN are unified, and if this is not empty, the result is unified with the **NUM** register in the new NP. If the result of the unification is empty, the entire rule is rejected.

The power of a unification-based formalism is that it can easily maintain partial information about structures and the results are completely independent of the order in which rules of the grammar are applied. Thus it is an ideal framework in which to investigate different parsing strategies, such as mixtures of top-down and bottom-up and so on.

The formalism can be defined precisely by defining each slot name as a function from a constituent to a value. You can see this by using a representation based on directed, acyclic graphs. In particular, each constituent and value is represented as a node, and the slots are represented as labeled arcs. Thus the constituents

(ART$_1$ **ROOT** THE   (NOUN$_1$ **ROOT** FISH
    NUM {3s 3p})   **NUM** {3s 3p})

would be represented by the graphs in Figure 4.22.

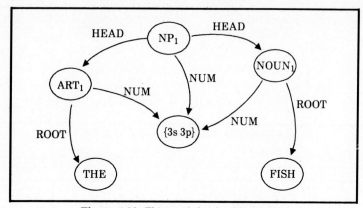

Figure 4.23 The graph for the NP *the fish*

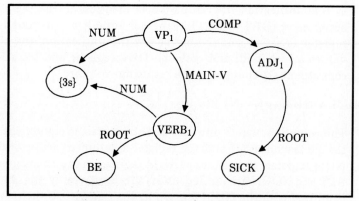

Figure 4.24 The analysis of the VP *is sick*

The unification equations on a rule state how to construct a new constituent out of the subconstituent graphs. Most importantly, nodes may be collapsed together as the result of a unification (assuming the intersection of their values is nonempty, of course). For example, if ART_1 and $NOUN_1$ represent the entries for a noun phrase *the fish*, the rule

NP ← ART NOUN

DET = ART
HEAD = NOUN
NUM = NUM$_{ART}$ = NUM$_{NOUN}$

specifies how to construct the graph defining an NP constituent, shown in Figure 4.23.

Assume that the verb phrase *is sick* has been analyzed in a similar fashion and is represented as in Figure 4.24. Given these initial analyses, the analysis of the sentence *The fish is sick* constructed by the rule

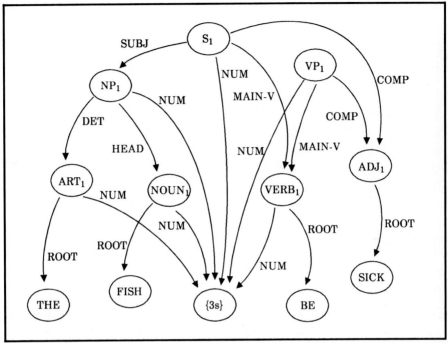

Figure 4.25 An analysis of *The fish is sick.*

S ← NP VP

SUBJ = NP
MAIN-V = MAIN-V$_{VP}$
COMP = COMP$_{VP}$
NUM = NUM$_{NP}$ **= NUM**$_{VP}$

is shown in Figure 4.25.

Note that the value of the NUM slot is now the same node for S_1, NP_1, ART_1, $NOUN_1$, VP_1, and $VERB_1$! Thus the value of the NUM slot of ART_1, for instance, changed when the NUM slots of NP_1 and VP_1 were unified.

The ability to maintain partial information allows you to represent constraints between constituents easily. For example, to handle infinitive complements in the ATN system, a new mechanism was introduced to preset registers. This is not necessary in the unification grammar, because the notation already allows such manipulations. For example, a unification-based CFG similar in capability to the part of the ATN grammar in Figure 4.7 dealing with infinitive complements is shown in Figure 4.26. Consider the first unification equation on rule 1--that is, **SUBJ = SUBJ**$_{S\text{-INF}}$ **= NP**. This equation unifies the **SUBJ** register in the new S being built, the **SUBJ** register in the infinitive complement (S-INF), and the NP constituent. In particular, if

1.	S ← NP VERB S-INF	$\textbf{SUBJ} = \textbf{SUBJ}_{\text{S-INF}} = \text{NP}$ $\textbf{MAIN-V} = \text{VERB}$ $\textbf{SUBCAT}_{\text{VERB}} = \{\text{TO-INF}\}$ $\textbf{COMP} = \text{S-INF}$
2.	S ← NP$_1$ VERB NP$_2$ S-INF	$\textbf{SUBJ} = \text{NP}_1$ $\textbf{MAIN-V} = \text{VERB}$ $\textbf{SUBCAT}_{\text{VERB}} = \{\text{OBJ} + \text{TO-INF}\}$ $\textbf{OBJ} = \textbf{SUBJ}_{\text{S-INF}} = \text{NP}_2$ $\textbf{COMP} = \text{S-INF}$
3.	S-INF ← AUX VERB NP	$\textbf{AUXS} = (\text{AUX ROOT TO}) = \text{AUX}$ $\textbf{MAIN-V} = \text{VERB}$ $\textbf{OBJ} = \text{NP}$

Figure 4.26 A unification-based grammar for infinitive complements

both **SUBJ** registers are initially unset, both will be assigned the NP constituent as desired. As another example, the equation $\textbf{SUBCAT}_{\text{VERB}} = \{\text{TO-INF}\}$ simply checks that the verb in the sentence allows this form of complement.

Because the **SUBJ** register of S-INF is always set from outside rule 3, there is no mention of the **SUBJ** register in rule 3. The structure built when this rule is successfully applied, however, will always have its **SUBJ** register set as appropriate.

Summary

This chapter has extended the simple grammatical formalisms introduced in Chapter 3 by adding an augmentation to each rule or arc. Thus RTNs become ATNs, and CFGs become augmented CFGs. Two basic methods of augmentation may be used. The first method, which draws on an analogy with programming languages, allows a set of tests and actions to be performed on the registers defined for each constituent. It can be used in the ATNs and augmented chart-based CFGs. The second method enforces restrictions and collects structure by unifying syntactic structures. It can be used for logic grammars, where the information is stored in extra argument positions on the predicates. A more complicated version of this method can be used in the unification grammars, which can be seen as an extension of the chart-based augmented CFG formalism.

Related Work and Further Readings

The ATN framework described here is drawn from the work described in Woods (1973) and Kaplan (1973). A good survey of ATNs is Bates (1978). Logic programming approaches to natural language parsing originated in the early 1970s with work by Colmerauer, which is discussed in Colmerauer (1978). This approach is perhaps best described in a paper by Periera and Warren (1980).

BOX 4.2   Unification Is a Destructive Operation and Requires Copying Chart Entries

During a parse you may need to make new copies of structures to store the results of unifications so that the original structures remain available for use in alternate interpretations. For example, consider a simple analysis of *give* with two complement forms OBJ and IOBJ + OBJ. In a sentence starting with *We gave the boy ...*, it is not definite which complement form is in use, since the sentence could be completed as

> We gave the boy to the orphanage.
> We gave the boy an ice cream cone.

If your grammar had rules

a)   VP ← V NP   **SUBCAT** = {OBJ}
b)   VP ← V NP NP   **SUBCAT** = {IOBJ + OBJ}

then the initial chart entry for *give*--namely,

> (VERB **ROOT** give
>   **FORM** pres
>   **SUBCAT** {OBJ IOBJ + OBJ})

is consistent with each rule. Unifying with rule (a) would produce a VERB structure with **SUBCAT** = {OBJ}. Because unification is a destructive operation, this would change the chart entry for *give*, which means that rule (b) could not succeed later in the parse. The solution is to add on the chart a new entry that is a copy of the VERB structure with **SUBCAT** = {OBJ}, leaving the original entry for use later by other rules. Efforts to reduce the proliferation of copies by extensive structure sharing are discussed by Pereira (1985b).

More recent developments can be found in McCord (1980) and Pereira (1981). An excellent source on logic programming techniques in general and its use in artificial intelligence is Kowalski (1979).

Augmented CFGs have been used in computational models since the introduction of **attribute grammars** by Knuth (1968), who employed them for parsing programming languages. Since then many systems have utilized annotated rules of one form or another. A good number of such systems have relied on arbitrary LISP code for annotations, although the types of operations commonly implemented are simple feature tests and structure building along the lines discussed in this chapter. Examples of such systems are in Sager (1981) and Robinson (1982).

The discussion of unification-based grammars is based loosely on work by Kay (1985) and the PATR-II system (Shieber, 1984; 1986). There is a considerable amount of active research in this area. An excellent survey of the area is found in Shieber (1986).

A linguistic theory that has been influential in the development of recent augmented formalisms is **lexical functional grammar** (Kaplan and Bresnan, 1982), usually abbreviated as LFG. LFG can be viewed as a type of unification-based grammar with additional features added for phenomena like unbounded movement (to be discussed in the next chapter). For example, a typical LFG rule is as follows:

$$S \leftarrow NP \qquad\qquad VP$$
$$(\uparrow SUBJ) = \downarrow \qquad \uparrow = \downarrow$$

The up-arrow ($\uparrow$) indicates the constituent named on the left-hand side of the rule (the S constituent), while the down-arrow ($\downarrow$) indicates the constituent to which the annotation is attached. Thus this rule is equivalent to the following in the notation:

$$S \leftarrow NP\ VP \qquad\qquad \textbf{SUBJ} = NP$$
$$S = VP$$

Note the unification of the entire S and VP structure, making them the same constituent. Computationally, this can be viewed as an efficient way to transfer all the registers from the VP to the S, but it has linguistic implications as well, as discussed in Kaplan and Bresnan (1982). The effect is that any further modification to the S or VP structure will affect both, since they are now the same constituent.

LFG also differs from our formalism by encoding more information in the lexicon. In particular, lexical entries may indicate which slots they will fill in the constituent that contains them. For example, the entries for *a*, *the*, and *bird* might be as follows:

a   ART $(\uparrow SPEC) = INDEF$
                        $(\uparrow NUM) = \{3s\}$

the   ART $(\uparrow SPEC) = DEF$

bird   NOUN $(\uparrow NUM) = \{3s\}$
                        $(\uparrow HEAD) = BIRD$

The up-arrow annotations actually fill in slots in the NP structure. Thus using the rule

NP ← ART NOUN

on the phrase *a bird* would result in the **NUM** register of the NP being set to {3s} when the word *a* is parsed, and then this value is unified with {3s} to check number agreement when the noun *bird* is parsed. With the article *the*, no number agreement is checked, since the word *the* does not set the **NUM** register of its NP.

Exercises for Chapter 4

1. (*medium*) Consider the following CFG and RTN:

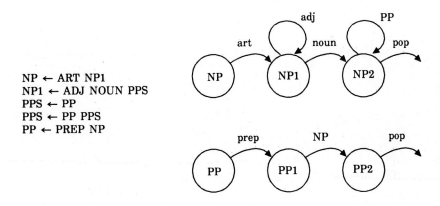

NP ← ART NP1
NP1 ← ADJ NOUN PPS
PPS ← PP
PPS ← PP PPS
PP ← PREP NP

a) State two ways in which the languages described by these two grammars differ. For each, give a sample sentence that is recognized by one grammar but not the other and that demonstrates the difference.

b) Write a new CFG equivalent to the RTN shown here.

c) Write a new RTN equivalent to the CFG shown here.

2. (*medium*)

a) Write an ATN fragment that will successfully allow the following phrases:

three o'clock	ten minutes to six
half past four	quarter after eight
seven thirty five	

but does not permit the following:

> half to eight
> ten forty five after six
> three twenty o'clock

For each, specify in the notation defined in this chapter the tests and actions that are necessary so that once the parse is completed, two registers, HOUR and MINUTES, are set.

b) Choose two other forms of grammatical phrases accepted by the ATN. Find an acceptable phrase not accepted by the ATN. If any nongrammatical phrases are allowed, give one example.

3. *(medium)* Consider the following simple ATN.

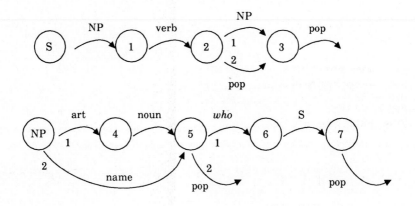

a) Specify some words by category and give four structurally different sentences accepted by this network.

b) Specify an augmentation for this network in the notation defined in this chapter so that sentences with the main verb *give* are allowed only if the subject is animate, and sentences with the main verb *be* may take either an animate or inanimate subject. Show a lexicon containing a few words that can be used to demonstrate the network's selectivity.

4. *(medium)* English pronouns distinguish case. Thus *I* can be used as a subject, and *me* can be used as an object. Similarly, there is a difference between *he* and *him*, *we* and *us*, and *they* and *them*. The distinction is not made for the pronoun *you*.

Specify an augmented context-free grammar for simple subject-verb-object sentences that allows only appropriate pronouns in the subject and object positions and does number agreement between the subject and verb. Thus, it should accept *I hit him*, but not *me love you*. Your grammar should account for all the preceding pronouns, but it need have only one verb entry and need cover no other noun phrases but pronouns.

5. *(hard)*

   a) The grammar for parsing the auxiliary verb structure in English shown in Section 4.3 cannot handle phrases of the following form:

   > Jack <u>has to see</u> a doctor.
   > The cat <u>had to be found</u>.
   > Joe <u>has to be winning</u> the race.
   > The book <u>would have had to have been found</u> by Jack.

   Extend the grammar such that it accepts the preceding auxiliary sequences yet does not accept unacceptable sentences such as

   > Jack <u>has to have to see</u> a doctor.
   > Janet <u>had to played</u> the violin.
   > Will <u>would to go</u> to the movies.

   b) Perform a similar analysis, showing examples and counterexamples, of the use of phrases of the form *be going to* within the auxiliary system.

6. *(hard)* Section 4.5 said that if registers can be reassigned during a parse, then problems can occur using bottom-up parse strategies. Specifically, two problems were mentioned:

   i) At one stage of the parse a parse appears to succeed, but later the variable is reassigned such that the test fails.

   ii) The parse makes a test involving a register that hasn't been set yet.

   Construct some examples in which these problems occur, and give a trace showing the difficulty.

Chapter 5

Grammars for Natural Language: Handling Movement

This chapter extends the grammar developed in the last section to cover a much wider range of English sentences. Many of the new structures will appear to be simple variants on the basic sentence structure you have already seen. In some cases simple words or phrases may be locally reordered; in others a phrase apparently can be moved arbitrarily far from its expected position in a basic sentence. Also included are examples of the simple addition and deletion of phrases.

For example, consider the structure of yes-no questions and how they relate to their assertional counterpart. In particular, consider the following examples:

John went to the store.   He will run in the marathon next year.
Did John go to the store?   Will he run in the marathon next year?

Jack is giving Sue a back rub.   Henry goes to school every day.
Is Jack giving Sue a back rub?   Does Henry go to school every day?

As you can readily see, yes-no questions are identical in structure to their assertional counterpart except that the subject NP and the first auxiliary have swapped positions. If there is no auxiliary in the assertional sentence, an auxiliary of root *do*, in the appropriate tense, is used. Taking a term from linguistics, this rearranging of the subject and the auxiliary is called **subject-aux inversion**.

Informally, you can think of deriving yes-no questions from assertions by moving the constituents in the manner just described as an example of local (or bounded) movement. The movement is considered local in that the rearranging of the constituents is specified precisely. This type is in contrast to **unbounded movement**, which occurs in wh-questions. In cases of unbounded movement, constituents may be moved arbitrarily far from their original position.

For example, consider the wh-questions that are related to the assertion:

The fat man will angrily put the book in the corner.

If you are interested in who did the action, you might ask one of the following questions:

Which man will angrily put the book in the corner?
Who will angrily put the book in the corner?

On the other hand, if you are interested in how it is done, you might ask one of the following questions:

How will the fat man put the book in the corner?

In what way will the fat man put the book in the corner?

Similarly, if you are interested in other aspects, you may ask one of these questions:

What will the fat man angrily put in the corner?
Where will the fat man angrily put the book?
In what corner will the fat man angrily put the book?
What will the fat man angrily put the book in?

Each question has the same form as the original assertion except that the part being questioned is removed and replaced by a wh-phrase at the beginning of the sentence.

Examples like wh-questions have provided the main motivation to linguists for investigating grammatical formalisms that are more powerful than context-free grammars (and RTNs). The augmented grammars provide a formalism that can handle many of these cases, but it is not clear how the unbounded movement can be accommodated. This chapter examines further extensions that provide a computational analysis of the unbounded movement cases. At the end of the chapter, however, the discussion reexamines the problem in the light of recent work that suggests that the simple augmented grammars may be adequate after all.

5.1 Local Movement

This section looks at two cases of local movement--namely, yes-no questions and passive sentences--and shows how the existing augmented frameworks can provide reasonable analyses of them. These cases will be developed using the ATN grammar. Similar analyses can be easily done in the other augmented formalisms.

Yes-No Questions

The goal is to extend the ATN grammar of assertions minimally so that it can handle yes-no questions. In other words, you want to reuse as much of the original grammar as possible. This is easily done. You simply extend the grammar to allow an auxiliary before the first NP and then reuse the existing network following the first NP. To capture the similarity, you assign the registers so that the resulting analysis is the same as the analysis of the assertional counterpart. If you also set some register--say, **MOOD**--to a value like YES-NO-Q in one case and ASSERTION in the other, you retain the information about the form of the sentence.

Consider this approach in more detail. Grammar 5.1 gives a fragment of an ATN grammar for sentences and presents additions to handle yes-no questions. The sentences *I love you* and *Do I love you* would have the analyses shown in

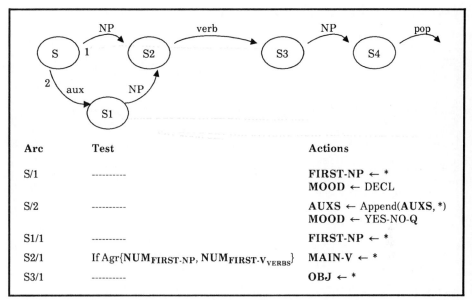

Arc	Test	Actions
S/1	----------	**FIRST-NP** ← * **MOOD** ← DECL
S/2	----------	**AUXS** ← Append(**AUXS**, *) **MOOD** ← YES-NO-Q
S1/1	----------	**FIRST-NP** ← *
S2/1	If Agr{**NUM**$_{FIRST\text{-}NP}$, **NUM**$_{FIRST\text{-}V_{VERBS}}$}	**MAIN-V** ← *
S3/1	----------	**OBJ** ← *

Grammar 5.1 An S network for very simple yes-no questions

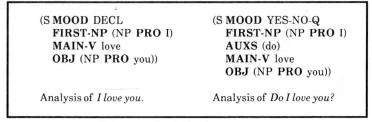

(S **MOOD** DECL
  FIRST-NP (NP **PRO** I)
  MAIN-V love
  OBJ (NP **PRO** you))

Analysis of *I love you.*

(S **MOOD** YES-NO-Q
  FIRST-NP (NP **PRO** I)
  AUXS (do)
  MAIN-V love
  OBJ (NP **PRO** you))

Analysis of *Do I love you?*

Figure 5.2 Analysis of two sentences

Figure 5.2. Note several important things here. First, the structures constructed for assertions and yes-no questions are identical, except for the **MOOD** register and the **AUXS** register, which may contain an extra *do*. Thus the similarity between the sentences is captured well. Second, all the tests for subject-verb agreement, tense, and transitivity are identical in both sentences. Thus you have been able to use to a great extent the original grammar for declarative sentences.

Passives

Most verbs, except the intransitive verbs, may take the passive form. This form involves using the normal object position NP as the first NP in the sentence, where the subject normally goes, and either omitting the NP usually in the subject position or putting it in a PP with the preposition *by*. The passive form is indicated by adding an auxiliary verb with root *be*, followed by a past

BOX 5.1   Movement in Linguistics

The term *movement* arose in transformational grammar (TG) because of the way sentences such as wh-questions were derived. TG posited two distinct levels of structural representation for a sentence. One level, which corresponds the closest to the actual sentence structure, is called the **surface structure**, while the other level is called the **deep structure**. The deep structure plays much the same role as the slot-value structures that the augmented grammars have been constructing. In particular, many generalities across different surface forms can be captured by abstracting away from the actual surface structure.

In TG, a context-free grammar generates the deep structure, and then a set of **transformations** map the deep structure into the surface structure. For example, the sentence *Will the cat scratch John?* might be derived as follows. The deep structure for the sentence looks like a structure for an assertional counterpart of the question--roughly as follows:

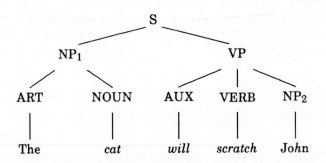

The yes-no question is then generated from this deep structure by a transformation expressed schematically as follows:

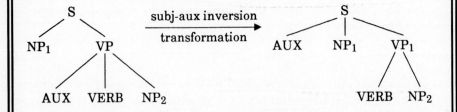

With this transformation the surface form will be

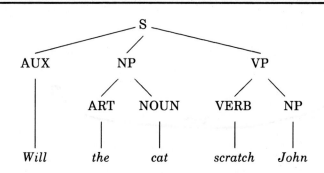

In early TG, as described in Chomsky (1965), transformations could do many operations on trees, including moving constituents (as shown here) and putting features into constituents, as well as adding and deleting constituents. Besides subj-aux inversion, there were transformational accounts of passives, wh-questions, embedded sentences, and most other phenomena described in this chapter.

The modern descendants of TG do not use transformations in the same way. In fact, in the immediate successor to TG--namely, **government-binding (GB) theory**--there is a single transformation rule called Move-α that allows any constituent to be moved anywhere! The main enterprise in GB theory is then to discover linguistic constraints on movement that prohibit the generation of illegal surface structures.

participle. The tense information in passives is encoded entirely in the auxiliary verbs. For example, the active voice sentences

> I will hide my hat in the drawer.
> I hid my hat in the drawer.
> I had hid my hat in the drawer.
> I was hiding my hat in the drawer.
> I had been hiding my hat in the drawer.

can be rephrased as the following passive voice sentences:

> My hat will be hidden (by me) in the drawer.
> My hat was hidden (by me) in the drawer.
> My hat had been hidden (by me) in the drawer.
> My hat was being hidden (by me) in the drawer.
> My hat had been being hidden (by me) in the drawer.

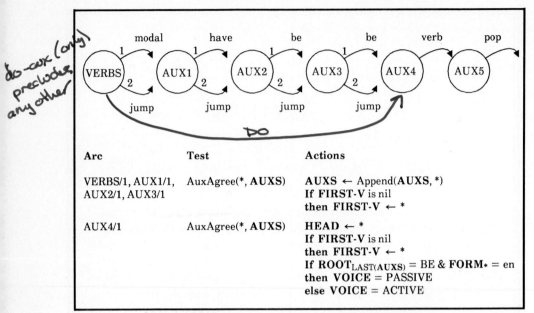

do-aux (only) precludes any other

Arc	Test	Actions
VERBS/1, AUX1/1, AUX2/1, AUX3/1	AuxAgree(*, **AUXS**)	**AUXS** ← Append(**AUXS**, *) If **FIRST-V** is nil then **FIRST-V** ← *
AUX4/1	AuxAgree(*, **AUXS**)	**HEAD** ← * If **FIRST-V** is nil then **FIRST-V** ← * If $\text{ROOT}_{\text{LAST(AUXS)}}$ = BE & **FORM**$_*$ = en then **VOICE** = PASSIVE else **VOICE** = ACTIVE

Grammar 5.3 The new VERBS network including passives

You can deal with passives by setting a new register **VOICE** to the value ACTIVE or PASSIVE accordingly, and by assigning the first noun phrase in the sentence to a register **FIRST-NP**, and then assigning it to the register **SUBJ** or **OBJ** as appropriate, after the verb group is analyzed. This treatment of passives interacts well with other solutions examined thus far. In particular, remember that in dealing with TO complements in the last chapter the sentence *Mary believes John to be a fool* was analyzed by calling the S network starting at S2 and presetting the **SUBJ** register in the embedded sentence to the value of the **OBJ** register--that is, *John*. Consider what happens with the passive form, *John is believed to be a fool (by Mary)*. In this case the understood subject of the embedded sentence is *John*. This is exactly the analysis that is found, since *John* is assigned to the **OBJ** register when the outer sentence is found to be in the passive voice and is subsequently passed in as the subject of the embedded sentence.

The new VERBS network that would be needed to handle the passive forms is shown in Grammar 5.3. Grammar 5.4 shows the S network to handle passives using a simplified auxiliary analysis so as better to show the analysis of the passive. The initial NP is stored into a register **FIRST-NP** and later assigned to the **SUBJ** register or **OBJ** register as appropriate. This is accomplished in the annotation on arc S2/2. After checking auxiliary-verb agreement and subject-verb agreement in the tests, the actions check for the passive form and assign the **VOICE**, **SUBJ**, and **OBJ** registers as appropriate.

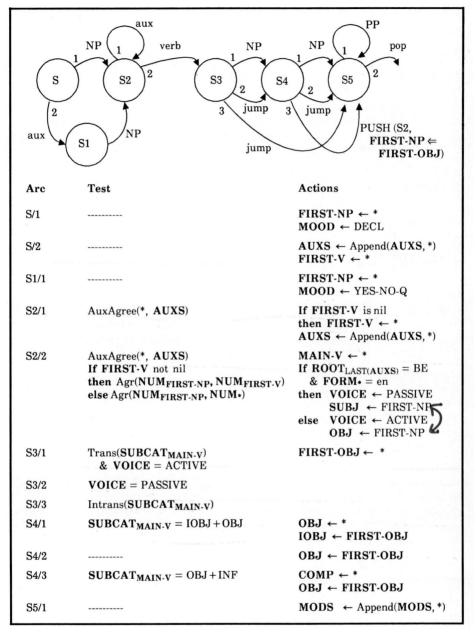

Arc	Test	Actions
S/1	----------	**FIRST-NP** ← * **MOOD** ← DECL
S/2	----------	**AUXS** ← Append(**AUXS**, *) **FIRST-V** ← *
S1/1	----------	**FIRST-NP** ← * **MOOD** ← YES-NO-Q
S2/1	AuxAgree(*, **AUXS**)	If **FIRST-V** is nil then **FIRST-V** ← * **AUXS** ← Append(**AUXS**, *)

S2/2	AuxAgree(*, **AUXS**)
	If **FIRST-V** not nil
	then Agr($\text{NUM}_{\text{FIRST-NP}}$, $\text{NUM}_{\text{FIRST-V}}$)
	else Agr($\text{NUM}_{\text{FIRST-NP}}$, NUM_*)
		MAIN-V ← *
		If $\text{ROOT}_{\text{LAST(AUXS)}}$ = BE
		    & FORM_* = en
		then **VOICE** ← PASSIVE
		       SUBJ ← FIRST-NP
		else **VOICE** ← ACTIVE
		       OBJ ← FIRST-NP

S3/1	Trans($\text{SUBCAT}_{\text{MAIN-V}}$) & **VOICE** = ACTIVE	**FIRST-OBJ** ← *
S3/2	**VOICE** = PASSIVE	
S3/3	Intrans($\text{SUBCAT}_{\text{MAIN-V}}$)	
S4/1	$\text{SUBCAT}_{\text{MAIN-V}}$ = IOBJ + OBJ	**OBJ** ← * **IOBJ** ← FIRST-OBJ
S4/2	----------	**OBJ** ← FIRST-OBJ
S4/3	$\text{SUBCAT}_{\text{MAIN-V}}$ = OBJ + INF	**COMP** ← * **OBJ** ← FIRST-OBJ
S5/1	----------	**MODS** ← Append(**MODS**, *)

Grammar 5.4 An S network with passives

This grammar does not set **SUBJ** when a PP is found with the preposition *by* because it cannot be certain that the subject is being indicated without semantic information about the type of the NP. If the NP describes an animate being, it probably should be the subject. Otherwise, it probably is just a simple modifier, as in *The hat was hidden by three o'clock*.

Consider how well this solution works in other sentence forms. For example, you know the grammar handles simple sentences with complements such as *Jack wants Sue to kiss George*, and the solution for passives was devised so that it would correctly analyze sentences such as *Sue was wanted to kiss George (by Jack)*. But will the solution correctly analyze sentences where the embedded S is in the passive form, as in *Jack wants George to be kissed by Sue*? In fact, it works. *George* is initially picked up as the **OBJ** of the outer S and passed in an arc S4/1 as the **FIRST-NP** of the embedded S. The passive voice of the embedded S is detected on arc S2/1, and the NP analysis of *George* is assigned to the **OBJ** register of the embedded S. It is left as an exercise to the reader to show that the analysis also works if both the embedded and outer S's are in the passive voice.

5.2 Wh-Questions and the Hold Mechanism

In the introduction to this chapter you saw that wh-questions had the same structure as assertions except that the wh-term was moved to the initial position in the sentence. In addition, except when the part being queried is the subject NP, the subject and the auxiliary are apparently inverted, as in yes-no questions. You can further explore this similarity with yes-no questions by considering sentences without an auxiliary. If the analysis is correct, then a *do* auxiliary should be inserted. In fact, this is the case, as seen by the sentences:

> I found a bookcase.
> Who found a bookcase?
> What <u>did</u> I find?

Thus you may be able to reuse Grammar 5.1 for wh-questions. A serious problem remains, however, concerning how to handle the fact that a constituent is missing from someplace later in the sentence. For example, consider the VP in the sentence:

> What will the fat man <u>angrily put in the corner</u>?

While this is an acceptable sentence, *angrily put in the corner* should not be acceptable as a VP in your grammar because you cannot allow sentences such as *I angrily put in the corner*. Only in wh-questions can such a VP be allowed, and then it can be allowed only if the wh-constituent is of the right form to make a legal VP if it were inserted in the sentence. For example,

> What will the fat man angrily put in the corner?

is acceptable, but not

*Where will the fat man angrily put in the corner?

If you constructed a special grammar for VPs in wh-questions, you would need a separate grammar for VPs that allows the constituent being queried to be missing. Thus apparently the existing grammar cannot be reused elegantly without extending the grammatical notation.

The extension discussed here involves introducing a mechanism to store constituents that can be used later to fill **gaps** in another constituent. Then you allow your grammar to check for a stored constituent if it fails to find the appropriate constituent later in the sentence. If a stored constituent is found in the right category, the grammar continues as though that constituent had been in the gap all along. Thus the analysis of the VP in a sentence such as

What will the fat man angrily put in the corner?

is parsed as though it were *angrily put <u>what</u> in the corner*, and the VP in the sentence

What will the fat man angrily put the book in?

is parsed as though the VP were *angrily put the book in <u>what</u>*.

There is further evidence for the correctness of this analysis--other than that it seems to work in the cases you've seen so far. In particular, all the well-formedness tests like subject-verb agreement, the case of pronouns (who, whom), and verb transitivity operate as though the wh-term were actually filling the gap. For example, consider verb transitivity. The question *What did you put in the cupboard?* is acceptable even though *put* is a transitive verb and thus requires an object. The object is filled by the wh-term, satisfying the transitivity constraint. Furthermore, a sentence where the object is explicitly filled is unacceptable:

*What did you put the bottle in the cupboard?

This sentence is unacceptable, just as any sentence with two objects for the verb *put* would be unacceptable. In effect it is equivalent to

*You put what the bottle in the cupboard?

Thus the standard transitivity tests will work if you assume the initial wh- can be inserted or moved to the standard object NP position.

BOX 5.2 Different Types of Movement

While the discussion will be concentrating on wh-questions throughout this chapter, and thus be examining the movement of wh-terms extensively, the techniques discussed are also needed for other forms of movement as well. Here are some of the most common forms of movement discussed in the linguistics literature. For more details, see a textbook in transformational grammar, such as Radford (1981).

Wh-Movement

Move a wh-term to the front of the sentence to form a wh-question.

Topicalization

Move a constituent to the beginning of the sentence for emphasis:

I never liked this picture.
This picture, I never liked.

Adverb Preposing

Move an adverb to the beginning of the sentence:

I will see you tomorrow.
Tomorrow, I will see you.

Extraposition

Move certain NP complements to the sentence final position:

A book discussing evolution was written.
A book was written discussing evolution.

The Hold Mechanism in ATNs

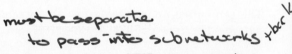
(handwritten: must be separate to pass into subnetworks + back)

The ability to store constituents for later use in an ATN system requires several modifications to the simple ATN described in Chapter 4. First, you need a data structure, called the **hold list**, to maintain the constituents that are stored. You will use this mechanism later for other phenomena besides wh-questions, so more than one constituent may be on the hold list at a single time. For the simple questions considered in this section, however, only one constituent will ever be on the hold list. Constituents are added to the hold list by a new action allowable on arcs, the **hold action**, which takes a constituent and places it on the hold list.

The hold action can store a constituent currently in a register (for example, HOLD SUBJ holds the constituent in the **SUBJ** register), or it can store the current constituent being built (for example, HOLD without an argument holds the constituent under construction by the current network).

To obtain the correct analysis of some sentences, and to reject others as anomalous, you must always use a held constituent to fill a gap. Otherwise, sentences such as *What did you put the bottle in the cupboard?* would be accepted by simply not using the held wh-term during the rest of the sentence. This constraint is enforced by not allowing a pop arc to succeed from a network until any constituent held by an action on an arc in that network has been used. In other words, the held constituent must have been used to fill a gap in the current constituent being accepted or in some subconstituent.

Finally, you need a mechanism to detect and fill gaps. The ATN mechanism uses a new arc called VIR (short for virtual), which takes a constituent name as an argument. This arc can be followed if such a constituent is present on the hold list. If the arc is followed successfully, the constituent is removed from the hold list and returned as the value of the arc in the identical form that a PUSH returns a constituent.

The ATN grammar that handles yes-no questions can be expanded to deal with wh-questions as well. The hold mechanism will be used for every case of wh-question, even when the subject is being queried, as in *Who won the race?* This instance could be handled separately, since it is the only case that does not require subj-aux inversion, but the grammar is simpler with the uniform treatment.

Grammar 5.5 extends Grammar 5.4 to handle wh-questions beginning with NPs, such as *who*, *what*, and *which boy*, by parsing an initial NP containing the wh-word, and then analyzing the remainder of the sentence as a sentence with a gap in it. VIR arcs are added whenever a gap can occur.

The extended NP network that accepts wh-terms is shown as Grammar 5.6. The arcs from S basically divide the sentence into the three categories: DECL, YES-NO-Q, and WH-Q, depending on whether the sentence starts with a non-wh-NP, an auxiliary, or a wh-NP, respectively. For the WH-Q sentences, the wh-NP is stored on the hold list for use in filling a gap. Note that three gaps are allowed in this simple grammar: one for the subject position, and one for each of the object positions. This grammar would correctly analyze

Who is carrying the baby?
Who is the baby carrying?

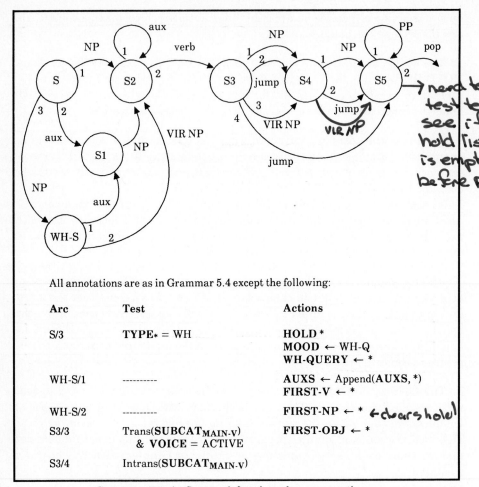

(handwritten annotations on figure:) → need to test to see if hold list is empty. before POP?

All annotations are as in Grammar 5.4 except the following:

Arc	Test	Actions
S/3	**TYPE**$_*$ = WH	**HOLD** * **MOOD** ← WH-Q **WH-QUERY** ← *
WH-S/1	----------	**AUXS** ← Append(**AUXS**, *) **FIRST-V** ← *
WH-S/2	----------	**FIRST-NP** ← * *←clears hold*
S3/3	Trans(**SUBCAT**$_{\text{MAIN-V}}$) & **VOICE** = ACTIVE	**FIRST-OBJ** ← *
S3/4	Intrans(**SUBCAT**$_{\text{MAIN-V}}$)	

Grammar 5.5 An S network for wh- and yes-no questions

Who is the baby?

Note that in order to handle the last two sentences, one of them must be initially misanalyzed, and backtracking must occur to find the correct analysis. Which one requires backtracking given the ATN in Grammar 5.5?

The analysis produced for the three preceding sentences is shown in Figure 5.7. The notation →NP$_1$ indicates a pointer to a constituent constructed earlier. For now you can think of it as a shorthand for copying the structure.

A more general grammar would have to handle gaps of prepositional phrases, verb phrases, and adverbial phrases as well, allowing wh-terms such as in

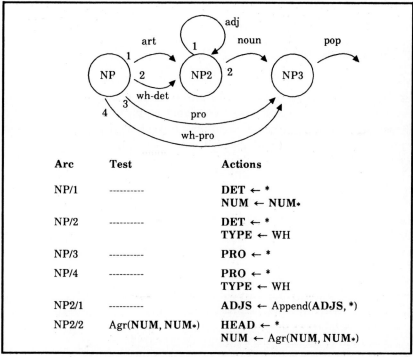

Arc	Test	Actions
NP/1	----------	DET ← * NUM ← NUM*
NP/2	----------	DET ← * TYPE ← WH
NP/3	----------	PRO ← *
NP/4	----------	PRO ← * TYPE ← WH
NP2/1	----------	ADJS ← Append(ADJS, *)
NP2/2	Agr(NUM, NUM*)	HEAD ← * NUM ← Agr(NUM, NUM*)

Grammar 5.6 An NP network including wh-words

(S **WH-QUERY** (NP₁ **PRO** who
                              TYPE WH)
              MOOD WH-Q
              SUBJ →NP₁
              AUXS (is)
              VERB carrying
              OBJ (NP **DET** the
                          HEAD baby))

Analysis of *Who is carrying the baby?*

(S **WH-QUERY** (NP₁ **PRO** who   (S **WH-QUERY** (NP₁ **PRO** who
                            TYPE WH)   **TYPE** WH)
        MOOD WH-Q   **MOOD** WH-Q
        AUXS (is)   **SUBJ** →NP₁
        SUBJ (NP **DET** the   **VERB** is
                    HEAD baby)   **OBJ** (NP **DET** the
        VERB carrying   **HEAD** baby)
        OBJ →NP₁)

Analysis of *Who is the baby carrying?*   Analysis of *Who is the baby?*

Figure 5.7 Analyses of simple wh-questions

<u>In which town</u> were you born?
<u>How fast</u> did you run?
<u>What</u> did you do?

In the first case the PP *in which town* is held and later inserted to fill the gap after the verb, yielding an analysis similar to the sentence *You were born in which town?* In the second case the adverbial phrase *how fast* is held and inserted in a position where an adverb is allowed, as in *You ran how fast?* In the third case *what* is held and inserted as the rest of the verb phrase, as in *You did what?*

5.3 Relative Clauses

Relative clauses are often (but not necessarily) introduced by function words such as *who*, *which*, and *that*. They are used to further specify a noun phrase. Consider the following relative clauses modifying *the man*.

The man <u>who hit Mary with a book</u> has disappeared.
The man <u>who(m) Mary hit with a book</u> has disappeared.
The man <u>hitting Mary with a book</u> is angry.
The man <u>Mary is hitting with a book</u> is angry.
The man <u>Mary hit John with</u> has disappeared.
The man <u>whose book was used to hit John</u> has disappeared.
The man <u>with whom Mary disappeared</u> wore a red hat.

As before, you would like to be able to capture these clauses using as much as possible of the regular sentence grammar that you already have.

Considering the same arguments as were used with wh-questions, you can see that relative clauses should be thought of as complete sentences but with a constituent missing. You will be able to handle this type of problem using the hold mechanism discussed earlier. Thus the analysis of *The man who hit Mary with a book has disappeared* should be something like:

```
(S MAIN-V disappear
   SUBJ (NP₁ DET the
         HEAD man
         MOD (S MAIN-V hit
              SUBJ →NP₁
              OBJ (NP NAME Mary)
              MODS (PP PREP with
                    POBJ (NP DET a
                          HEAD book))))
   TENSE PAST)
```

First consider relative clauses introduced with an explicit relative pronoun or determiner. The idea is to add to the NP network an arc that accepts a

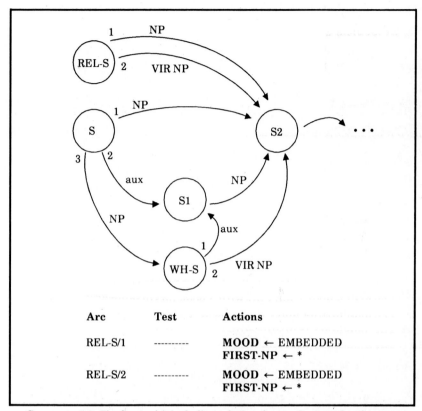

Arc	Test	Actions
REL-S/1	----------	**MOOD** ← EMBEDDED **FIRST-NP** ← *
REL-S/2	----------	**MOOD** ← EMBEDDED **FIRST-NP** ← *

Grammar 5.8 The S network including relative clauses (tests and actions on arcs are the same as in Grammar 5.5, with these additions)

wh-term after the head noun is found and puts the simple NP constructed so far on the hold list. The next arc calls the S network recursively to parse the relative clause (with the held constituent). But not all paths through the S network are usable in relative clauses. For example, you can't allow subject-aux inversion, as is used in a wh-question such as *Who will Mary hit with a book?* This path does not produce a corresponding embedded form, such as

*The man who will Mary hit with a book.

Grammar 5.8 uses a new start node for relative clauses--namely, REL-S. The arcs leaving REL-S allow an NP or a virtual NP and then continue in the regular S network at node S2.

The NP network is extended by adding additional arcs from node NP3, as shown in Grammar 5.9. Note that this grammar handles relative clauses introduced by a wh-word, as well as the related relative clauses that have the

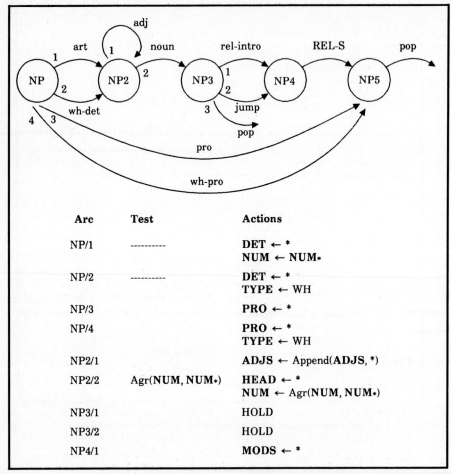

Grammar 5.9 An NP grammar with relative clauses

wh-term omitted, which can be called **reduced relatives**. Thus the grammar will handle both *The dog that John loved* and *The dog John loved*. It does not handle relative clauses beginning with prepositional phrases or possessives involving a wh-term. Note that this is the first time you have used the hold action without an argument. This puts the current constituent under construction (in this case the NP) onto the hold list.

The category REL-INTRO should include the words that can be used to introduce relative clauses, such as *that, which, who,* and *whom*. With this grammar you now would obtain the following analysis of *The dog that John loved*:

```
(NP₁ DET the
     HEAD dog)
     MODS ((S MOOD EMBEDDED
               SUBJ (NP NAME John)
               VERB love
               OBJ →NP₁)))
```

You need to check that the analysis of relative clauses just presented interacts properly with solutions to other problems, such as the analysis of passives. For example, consider a relative clause involving a passive such as *The dog that was loved by John*. When the REL-S network is called from arc NP3/1, the hold list will contain the current NP--say, NP₁--with the structure

```
(NP₁ DET the
     HEAD dog
     NUM {3s})
```

In the S network (Grammar 5.8), arc REL-S/1 involves a virtual NP that succeeds, removing NP₁ from the hold list and putting it in register **FIRST-NP**. The parse continues as usual, and in taking arc S2/1, NP₁ is moved to the register **FIRST-OBJ**, as desired.

5.4 Using a Hold List in the Mixed-Mode Parser

You can augment the top-down and the mixed-mode parser for context-free grammars in much the same way as was done with ATNs by extending the parser to maintain a hold stack and recognize the HOLD and VIR operations. Here you can use a notation that allows two new complex symbols on the right-hand side of rules:

HOLD(C) -- signifies that a constituent C must be found and should be placed on the hold stack;

VIR(C) -- succeeds if there is a constituent C on the hold stack.

Here is an example of such a grammar to handle the simplest cases of **topicalization**. Topicalization describes sentences in which a constituent appears at the start of the sentence rather than in its usual position. This format is typically used for emphasis. Thus you might write a sentence such as *Mary, John saw at the party* instead of *John saw Mary at the party*. Similarly, in some circumstances, you can say both of the following:

To John I gave the book.
John I gave the book to.

A grammar for such sentences is shown in Grammar 5.10.

Rule	Actions
1. S ← HOLD(NP) S′	**TOPIC** ← NP **SENTENCE** ← S′
2. S ← HOLD(PP) S′	**TOPIC** ← PP **SENTENCE** ← S′
3. S′ ← NP VP	**SUBJ** ← NP **MAIN-V** ← VERB$_{VP}$ **OBJ** ← OBJ$_{VP}$ **MODS** ← MODS$_{VP}$
4. VP ← VERB NP PP	**VERB** ← VERB **OBJ** ← NP **MODS** ← PP
5. PP ← PREP NP	**PREP** ← PREP **POBJ** ← NP
6. NP ← NAME	**NAME** ← NAME
7. NP ← ART NOUN	**DET** ← ART **HEAD** ← NOUN
8. NP ← VIR(NP)	
9. PP ← VIR(NP)	

Grammar 5.10 A CFG using hold lists for topicalization

The mixed-mode parser defined in Chapter 3 can be used if you extend it to handle the new constructs as follows. A rule containing HOLD(C) for some constituent symbol C causes the parse to try to build a C constituent and place it on the hold stack. You can successfully apply a rule containing VIR(C) if a constituent of type C is on the hold list. If so, you remove that constituent from the hold list and add its registers to the chart at the appropriate position. Note that since this chart entry uses no input, its beginning position and ending position are identical.

The restriction that a held constituent must be used was enforced on the pop arc in ATNs. In the CFG you can enforce this restriction when you encounter the construction flag. Here you simply fail if something was held during the parse of the constituent being constructed that has not yet been used. Otherwise, the constituent is built and added to the chart as usual.

Trace the parse for the sentence *Mary John saw at the party*. Rule 1 is applied, and after the initial NP *Mary* is constructed, it is placed on the hold stack. Then the parse proceeds as usual, parsing *John* and *saw* using rules 3 and 4, creating the state shown in Figure 5.11. Now rules 6 and 7 fail, but rule 8 succeeds, since NP1 is on the hold list. This state is shown in Figure 5.12, with the moved constituent indicated by a triangle. The parse now continues as

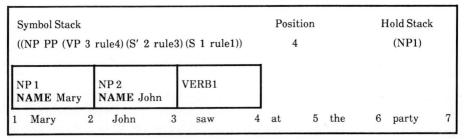

Figure 5.11 Before rule 8 is applied

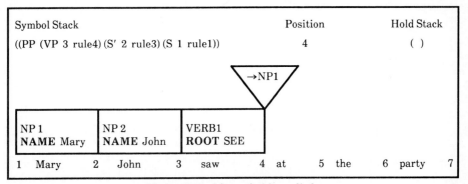

Figure 5.12 After rule 8 is applied

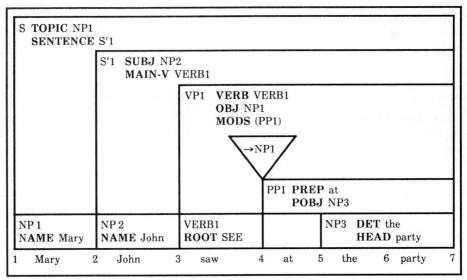

Figure 5.13 The final analysis

usual, the PP *at the party* is found, and the VP, S′, and S entries are constructed. The final analysis is shown in Figure 5.13.

BOX 5.3 Other Forms of Reduced Relatives

Noun phrases of the form *The man hitting Mary with a book* must be treated by another mechanism. In such cases more than the simple NP is missing in the embedded sentence. In fact this sentence seems equivalent to the sentence *The man who is hitting Mary with a book*, but the *who is* is deleted. This construct can be accepted by presetting the **AUXS** register to have a constituent with the ROOT register set to *be* in the embedded S network--that is

$$\text{PUSH (REL-S, } \mathbf{AUXS} \Leftarrow ((\text{AUX } \mathbf{ROOT} \text{ BE})))$$

During a parse of the sentence *The man hitting Mary*, the REL-S network would be invoked with the NP *the man*--say, NP_1--on the hold list and the **AUXS** register preset to ((AUX **ROOT** BE)). The relative clause *hitting Mary* would then be parsed as follows:

1) Arc REL-S/2: **FIRST-NP** is set to $\rightarrow NP_1$;

2) Arc S2/1 (in call to VERBS network): auxiliary-verb agreement between *be* and *hitting* succeeds, **SUBJ** set to $\rightarrow NP_1$;

3) Arc S3/1: picks up the NP *Mary*, and assigns it to **FIRST-OBJ** slot;

4) Arc S4/3: assigns NP *Mary* to register **OBJ**.

This solution also works with relatives in the passive voice, such as in the NP *The sand blown by the wind*. The noun phrase NP_3 for *the sand* will be on the hold list, and the **AUXS** register is preset to ((AUX **ROOT** BE)). The **FIRST-NP** register is set to NP_3 appropriately when arc REL-S/2 (that is, VIR NP) is followed. Now when arc AUX4/1 picks up the verb *blown*, the value of preset **AUXS** register allows the passive test to succeed as desired. Thus NP_3 is later assigned to **OBJ** as desired.

One other possible form is also passive but does not use the preset **AUXS** value in the passive test. An example is *The man being sent to the store*. Here again the preset *be* allows the progressive auxiliary verb *being*, which, in turn, is used in the passive test on arc AUX4/1. Thus the presetting of the **AUXS** register appears to handle this phenomenon as well.

BOX 5.4 Bottom-Up Parsing and Movement

You may have noticed that all the examples of parsing grammars that handle movement have involved top-down algorithms, or the mixed-mode algorithm driven by a top-down predictor. This is for a good reason. If you allow gaps in a grammar, a pure bottom-up parsing strategy may have no choice but to suggest a gap at every position in the sentence. For example, if you have a rule such as

1.   NP ← VIR(NP)

then this rule would always match the input at any location, since it uses no input. Of course, most of the time this rule will not be able to combine with higher-level constituents to form a complete analysis, so this effort is all wasted. To understand the extent of this problem, consider that if rule 1 matches at every position, then any rule starting with an NP will also match at every position. In addition, any rule in progress and needing an NP next--say,

VP ← V ∘ NP

would automatically match whenever such rules are present. Thus the number of erroneous alternatives added to the chart is tremendous.

Any parser that uses bottom-up parsing techniques with a grammar that allows an empty constituent (that is, the VIR category) will, therefore, need some top-down component to control the proliferation of false gaps at every position. The mixed-mode parser does just this by trying to build only constituents suggested by the top-down prediction algorithm.

5.5 Handling Movement in Logic Grammars

The hold list mechanism can be introduced into logic grammars by adding extra argument positions to each predicate--one argument for the value of the hold list coming in, and one for the resulting hold list after the constituent is parsed. Thus the predicate

(S *position-in position-out hold-list-in hold-list-out*)

is true only if there is a legal S constituent between *position-in* and *position-out* of the input. If a held constituent was used to build the S, it was present in *hold-list-in*, not in *hold-list-out*. On the other hand, if the S constituent is to be

1. (S ?i ?o ?hold-i ?hold-o) < (NP ?i ?i1 ?hold-i ?hold1)
                                  (VP ?i1 ?o ?hold1 ?hold-o)

2. (VP ?i ?o ?hold-i ?hold-o) < (VERB ?i ?i1)
                                  (PP ?i1 ?o ?hold-i ?hold-o)

3. (VP ?i ?o ?hold-i ?hold-o) < (VERB ?i ?i1)
                                  (NP ?i1 ?o ?hold-i ?hold-o)

4. (NP ?i ?o ?h ?h) < (NP-HEAD ?i ?i1)
                        (NP-COMP ?i1 ?out)

5. (NP ?i ?o ?h ?h) < (PRO ?i ?o)

6. (NP-HEAD ?i ?o) < (DET ?i ?i1)
                       (NOUN ?i1 ?o)

7. (NP-COMP ?i ?i) <

   (This covers the case where there is no NP complement.)

8. (NP-COMP ?i ?o) < (REL-INTRO ?i ?i1 nil ?hold-o)
                       (S ?i1 ?o ?hold-o nil)

   (Here we hold the Rel-Intro constituent, and must use it in
   the following S.)

9. (REL-INTRO ?i ?o ?hold-i (HELD NP ?hold-i))
        < (REL-INTRO-WORD ?i ?o)

   (If a word such as *that* or *who* is found, hold an NP.)

10. (REL-INTRO ?i ?o ?hold-i (HELD PP ?hold-i))
        < (PREP ?i ?i1)
           (WH-PRO ?i1 ?o)

11. (NP ?i ?i (HELD NP ?h) ?h) <

12. (PP ?i ?i (HELD PP ?h) ?h) <

(Rules 11 and 12 remove elements of the hold list.)

Figure 5.14 A logic grammar to parse relative clauses

held itself, it is present in *hold-list-out*. In cases where the hold list happens not to be used, *hold-list-in* and *hold-list-out* will be identical.

Consider an example dealing with relative clauses, including clauses that begin with prepositions, as in the NP *The man of whom we spoke*. The rules required are as shown in Grammar 5.14.

To see these rules in use, consider the parse of the noun phrase

1 The 2 man 3 of 4 whom 5 we 6 spoke. 7

The proof that this is a legal noun phrase is shown in Figure 5.15. The held PP is created in step 7, when rule 10 is applied, binding ?hold-o to (HELD PP nil). This constituent is then passed successively to the NP predicate in step 10, and then to the VP predicate in step 11, since it was not used in rule 5. From the VP

Step	State	Comments
1.	(NP 1 7 nil nil)	the initial goal
2.	(NP-HEAD 1 ?i1) (NP-COMP ?i1 7)	applied rule 4
3.	(DET 1 ?i1') (NOUN ?i1' ?i1) (NP-COMP ?i1 7)	applied rule 6
4.	(NOUN 2 ?i1) (NP-COMP ?i1 7)	proved (DET 1 2)
5.	(NP-COMP 3 7)	proved (NOUN 2 3)
6.	(REL-INTRO 3 ?i2 nil ?hold-o) (S ?i2 7 ?hold-o nil)	rule 8
7.	(PREP 3 ?i1'') (WH-PRO ?i1'' ?i2) (S ?i2 7 (HELD PP nil) nil)	rule 10 (note that ?hold-o is bound to (HELD PP nil))
8.	(WH-PRO 4 ?i2) (S ?i2 7 (HELD PP nil) nil)	proved (PREP 3 4)
9.	(S 5 7 (HELD PP nil) nil)	proved (WH-PRO 4 5)
10.	(NP 5 ?i1 (HELD PP nil) ?hold1) (VP ?i1 7 ?hold1 nil)	rule 1
11.	(PRO 5 ?i1) (VP ?i1 7 (HELD PP nil) nil)	rule 5 (note that ?hold1 is bound to (HELD PP nil))
12.	(VP 6 7 (HELD PP nil) nil)	proved (PRO 5 6)
13.	(VERB 6 ?i1''') (PP ?i1''' 7 (HELD PP nil) nil)	rule 2
14.	(PP 7 7 (HELD PP nil) nil)	proved (VERB 6 7)
15.	nil	rule 12

Figure 5.15 The proof that *The man of whom we spoke* is a legal NP

predicate, it is finally passed to the PP predicate in step 15, which is provable using rule 12.

5.6 Slashed Categories: An Alternative to Hold Lists

A very different approach to unbounded movement has been developed recently. Rather than extend the parser and grammatical formalism to include hold lists, this approach involves directly writing a grammar that explicitly allows the appropriate gaps. The result is a conventional context-free grammar that may be considerably larger than the equivalent grammar using hold lists. The essential idea is to allow into the grammar complex symbols such as

S/NP

which signifies an S constituent with one NP missing. For example, given the grammar

1.   S ← NP VP

2.   VP ← VERB NP

3.   NP ← ART NOUN

you could extend the grammar to handle relative clauses by adding the rule

4.   NP ← NP REL-INTRO S/NP

(that is, a noun phrase is a noun phrase followed by a relative clause
introductory word, followed by an S with an NP missing). To complete the
grammar, you must derive the rules for S/NP from the preceding rules by
taking each nonterminal on the right-hand side and producing a new slashed
rule, as follows:

1a.   S/NP ← NP/NP VP

1b.   S/NP ← NP VP/NP

2a.   VP/NP ← VERB NP/NP

Assuming that NP/NP must be the null symbol--that is, not using any
input--you have a grammar to recognize simple relative clauses. It is a simple
exercise to design an algorithm to generate these slashed rules from an
arbitrary grammar.

The use of slashed categories does not necessarily change the form of the
final syntactic analysis, since the augmentation on these rules could be built to
set the same register structures as was done using the hold stack technique, as
long as the analysis of the constituent that fills the gap can be passed along
through the parse.

For example, Grammar 5.16 contains a simple CFG with unification of
features. To handle relative clauses, a slashed category S/NP is introduced in
rule 4.

The unifications for S/NP are derived as follows. A register **HELD** is
assigned to the "missing" NP. Thus, if a rule is derived by deleting an NP from
the right-hand side, the unifications involving that NP structure would be
changed to involve the **HELD** register. If the rule passes on the deleted NP, it
simply sets the **HELD** register in the appropriate subconstituent. The derived
rules are shown in Grammar 5.17.

Consider a trace of the mixed-mode parser on the NP *The fish that saw the
worm*. Trace the top parse state only, the sentence position, and each
unification as it is made. Part of the trace is shown in Figure 5.18.

Rule	Unifications
1. S ← NP VP	**SUBJ** = NP **MAIN-V** = **VERB**$_{VP}$ **OBJ** = **OBJ**$_{VP}$
2. VP ← VERB NP	**VERB** = **VERB** **OBJ** = NP
3. NP ← ART NOUN	**DET** = ART **HEAD** = NOUN
4. NP ← NP′ REL-INTRO S/NP	**DET** = **DET**$_{NP′}$ **HEAD** = **HEAD**$_{NP′}$ **MODS** = S/NP **HELD**$_{S/NP}$ = NP′

Figure 5.16 A simple CFG

Rule	Unifications
5. S/NP ← VP	**SUBJ** = **HELD** **MAIN-V** = **VERB**$_{VP}$ **OBJ** = **OBJ**$_{VP}$
6. S/NP ← NP VP/NP	**SUBJ** = NP **MAIN-V** = **VERB**$_{VP/NP}$ **OBJ** = **OBJ**$_{VP/NP}$ **HELD**$_{VP/NP}$ = **HELD**$_{S/NP}$
7. VP/NP ← VERB	**VERB** = **VERB** **OBJ** = **HELD**

Figure 5.17 Slashed rules derived from Grammar 5.16

The crucial part of this trace is in step 1, when the register **HELD**$_{S/NP_1}$ is unified with NP$_2$, and in step 7, when **HELD**$_{S/NP_1}$ is used to set the register **SUBJ**$_{S/NP_1}$ to fill the gap in the subject position of the relative clause. Of course, if the NP had been *The fish that the worm saw* instead, step 9 would not have been possible and the parser would have had to backtrack to step 6 and try rule 7 instead (thereby "undoing" the unification of **SUBJ**$_{S/NP_1}$ and **HELD**$_{S/NP_1}$).

5.7 A Comparison of the Methods Using Constraints

While the hold list is an important extension to the grammatical formalisms that seem needed in order to preserve the simplicity of grammars, it can be shown to be overly general in many cases. In fact you can contrast the hold

Step	Current State	Position	New Unifications
1.	NP_2 REL-INTRO$_1$ S/NP$_1$	1	$DET_{NP_1} = DET_{NP_2}$ $HEAD_{NP_1} = HEAD_{NP_2}$ $MODS_{NP_1} = S/NP_1$ $HELD_{S/NP_1} = NP_2$
2.	ART_2 $NOUN_2$ REL-INTRO$_1$ S/NP$_1$	1	$DET_{NP_2} = ART_2$ $HEAD_{NP_2} = NOUN_2$
3.	$NOUN_2$ REL-INTRO$_1$ S/NP$_1$	2	$ART_2 = the \ (= DET_{NP_1})$
4.	REL-INTRO$_1$ S/NP$_1$	3	$NOUN_2 = fish \ (= HEAD_{NP_1})$
5.	REL-INTRO$_1$ S/NP$_1$	3	
6.	S/NP$_1$	4	*that* is parsed
7.	VP_3	4	$SUBJ_{S/NP_1} = HELD_{S/NP_1}$ $\qquad = NP_2$ $MAIN\text{-}V_{S/NP_1} = VERB_{VP_3}$ $OBJ_{S/NP_1} = OBJ_{VP_3}$
8.	$VERB_4$ NP_4	4	$VERB_{VP_3} = VERB_4$ $OBJ_{VP_3} = NP_4$
9.	NP_4	5	$VERB_4 = saw$

Figure 5.18 Partial trace of parse of *The fish that saw the worm.*

mechanism with the slashed category approach by examining the different forms of movement they allow.

For instance, one of the assumptions made in deriving rules for slashed categories was that a symbol such as NP/NP cannot be realized except as the empty string. In other words, it could not be that you have an NP with an NP gap in it. On the other hand, such a structure could be parsable using a hold list. In particular a sentence such as

*Who did the man who saw hit the boy?

while not comprehensible, would be accepted by Grammar 5.8. This is because the hold list would contain both an NP for *the man* and another for *who* when the relative clause *who saw* is parsed. The first NP would be taken as the subject and the second NP would be taken as the object, and the following structure would be built:

(S **MOOD** WH-Q
    WH-QUERY (NP$_1$ **PRO** who
                     TYPE WH)
    AUXS (did)
    SUBJ (NP$_2$ **DET** the
               HEAD man
               MODS (S **SUBJ** →NP$_2$
                         MAIN-V see
                         OBJ →NP$_1$))
    MAIN-V hit
    OBJ (NP$_3$ **DET** the
               HEAD boy))

This sentence is not acceptable by any grammar using slashed categories, because it would require the constituent NP/NP to be nonempty and would need double slashed rules for the relative clause (that is, S/NP/NP). As such, the slashed mechanism explains the movement phenomena more precisely. In particular if you have the rule

NP ← ART NOUN REL-INTRO S/NP

for simple noun phrases with relative clauses, there is no way that a second constituent of any type could also be missing from the constituent S/NP. The formalism simply can't express it.

The hold list mechanism in the ATN framework must be extended to capture these constraints since there is no obvious way to prevent held constituents from being used anytime they are available. The only possible way to restrict it using the existing mechanism would be to use feature values to keep track somehow of what held constituents are available in each context. This could become quite messy. You can, however, make a simple extension. You can introduce a new action--say, called HIDE--that temporarily hides the existing constituents on the hold list until either an explicit action--say, UNHIDE--is executed, or the present constituent is completed. With this extension the ATN grammar to handle relative clauses could be modified to execute a HIDE action just before the hold action that holds the current constituent is performed.

The technique for maintaining the hold list in the logic grammars provides a direct way to capture the constraints. In particular, since the hold list is explicitly passed from predicate to predicate during a parse, you can write the grammar so that in the cases where the constraints apply, the hold list is simply not passed in. An example of this is rule 4 in Grammar 5.10. The rule was defined so that the hold list was unchanged by any part of the NP subproof. In fact the list was not handed to NP-COMP at all.

BOX 5.5 The Movement Constraints

In linguistics the principles that govern where gaps may occur are called **island constraints**. This term draws on the metaphor of constituent movement. An island is defined to be a constituent from which no subconstituent can move out (just as a person cannot walk off an island).

The A over A Constraint: *no constituent of category A can be moved out of a constituent of type A*. This means you cannot have an NP gap within an NP, a PP gap within a PP, and so on, and provides justification for not allowing nonnull constituents of the form NP/NP, PP/PP, and so on. This constraint disallows sentences such as

*Who did the man who saw hit the boy?

Complex-NP Constraint: *no constituent may be moved out of a relative clause or noun complement*. This constraint disallows sentences like

*To whom did the man who gave the book sing?

where the PP *to whom* would have been part of the relative clause *who gave the book to whom*.

Sentential Subject Constraint: *no constituent can be moved out of a constituent serving as the subject of a sentence*. This overlaps with the other constraints when the subject is an NP, but non-NP subjects are possible as well, as in the sentence *For me to learn these constraints is impossible*. This constraint eliminates the possibility of a question like

*What for me to learn is impossible?

Wh-Island Constraint: *no constituent can be moved from an embedded sentence with a wh-complementizer*. For example, while *Did they wonder whether I took the book?* is an acceptable sentence, you cannot ask

*What did they wonder whether I took?

Coordinate Structure Constraint: *a constituent cannot be moved out of a coordinate structure*. For example, while *Did you see John and Sam?* is an acceptable sentence, you cannot ask

*Who did you see John and?

Note that these constraints apply to all forms of movement, not just wh-questions. For example, they constrain topicalization and adverb preposing as well.

In both these cases, however, it is not the formalism itself that expresses the constraints. Rather, the formalism is used to state the constraints; it could just as easily describe a language that violates the constraints.

While a true account of all the movement constraints is considerably more complicated, this simple analysis makes an important point. If a formalism is too weak, you cannot describe the language at all. If it is too strong, the grammar may become overly complicated in order to eliminate sentence structures that it can describe but that are not possible. The best solution, then, is a formalism that is just powerful enough to describe natural language. In such a language many of the constraints that first appear to be arbitrary restrictions might turn out to be a consequence of the formalism itself and need no further consideration.

Summary

Different techniques can be used to handle those aspects of language often classified as movement. Examples of bounded movement include yes-no questions and passives. In these cases, through careful use of augmented tests and actions, much of the original grammar for assertions could be reused without change. Unbounded movement includes wh-questions and relative clauses. To reuse the original grammar effectively with this format, you need to extend the grammatical formalism with a hold list and take appropriate actions to save constituents and reuse them later. Finally, an alternate technique involves automatically deriving an expanded grammar using slashed categories that handle unbounded movement without a hold list mechanism.

Related Work and Further Readings

The first reasonably comprehensive computational study of movement phenomena was in the ATN framework by Woods (1970). He went to some length to show that much of the phenomena accounted for by transformational grammar (Chomsky, 1965) could be parsed in ATNs using register testing and setting together with a hold list mechanism. Much of this chapter is a simplified and cleaned-up account of that paper, incorporating later work by Kaplan (1973). Alternate presentations of ATNs can also be found in Bates (1978) and Winograd (1983).

Similar augmentation techniques have been adapted to systems based on CFGs, although in practice many of these systems have been overly lax and have accepted many structures that are not reasonable sentences. This is because the grammars are built so that constituents are optional even in contexts where there could be no movement. The parser then depends on some ad hoc feature manipulation to eliminate some of these false positives or depends on semantic interpretation to reject the ill-formed sentences that were accepted. A good example of how much can be done with this approach is provided by Robinson (1982).

Still other systems deal with the problem by essentially producing an explicit subgrammar for wh-questions by hand--producing a grammar that is similar to that generated by using slashed categories.

The technique of storing the held constituent as an argument in a logic grammar, which is then later used to allow an empty constituent, is described in Pereira (1981). In that same paper Pereira introduces a new grammatical formalism called **extraposition grammar**, which, besides allowing normal context-free rules, allows rules of the form:

REL-MARK ... TRACE → REL-PRO

which essentially says that the constituent REL-MARK, plus the constituent TRACE later in the sentence, can be rewritten as a REL-PRO. Such a rule violates the tree structure of syntactic forms and allows the analysis shown in Figure 5.19 of the NP *the mouse that the cat ate*. Although such a grammar seems hard to grasp at first, Pereira shows how such rules can be compiled into a logic grammar using additional arguments to the predicates.

The phenomena of unbounded dependencies has motivated a significant amount of research into grammatical formalisms. These fall roughly into several categories, depending on how close the grammar remains to the context-free grammars. Theories such as transformational grammar (Chomsky, 1965; Radford, 1981), for example, propose to handle unbounded dependencies completely outside the CFG framework. Theories such as lexical functional grammar (Kaplan and Bresnan, 1982) retain a context-free base yet add other mechanisms similar to the hold list. Finally, theories such as generalized phrase structure grammar (GPSG) (Gazdar, 1982; Gazdar et al., 1985), on which the section on slash categories is based, propose a method of capturing the dependencies with the CFG formalism at the expense of considerably increasing the size of the grammar.

GPSG is aimed at providing a grammar for English that remains within the context-free class of formalisms. The resulting CF grammars, however, can become much larger than desirable. In particular, many of the arguments for introducing features and the hold list were based on the objective of keeping the basic grammar as simple as possible. GPSG adopts this stance in a different way. It introduces methods to generate the actual grammar of the language automatically from a much more concise grammar of the sort used in this book. The slashed categories, introduced in Section 5.6, are a good example of these. Once you have created a basic grammar that does not handle unbounded movement, you can automatically generate another grammar that

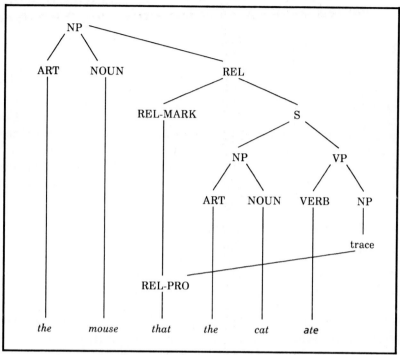

Figure 5.19 A parse tree in extraposition grammar

does handle unbounded movement by deriving the rules for the slashed categories.

In addition, GPSG allows a finite set of features to be attached to any grammatical symbol. These features play much the same role as the features in the annotations of our rules. In GPSG there are no slot names. Rather, all feature values are unique so that there is no confusion. For example, a plural noun phrase in the third person with gender female could be written as

NP[PL, 3, F]

Many of the generalities underlying local movement are captured by a set of metarules that, given a simple grammar, will generate a new grammar extended according to the rules. The passive metarule, for instance, takes a grammar for active sentences and produces a set of new rules to add so that passive sentences are also handled. In this respect metarules play much the same role as transformations, but they are limited to act on only a single rule at a time, whereas transformations may operate on arbitrary trees. There is not the space here to introduce many complexities of the actual notation, but the passive metarule looks something like this:

Sentinel Subject Constraint — no constituent can be moved out of constituent serving as subject

VP ← VERB[TRANSITIVE] NP X ⇒
VP[PASSIVE] ← VERB X (PP[by])

Here the symbol X stands for any sequence of constituents, and the constituents in parentheses are optional. Thus, this metarule says that if there is a rule for a VP consisting of a transitive verb, an NP, and possibly some other constituents, then there is another rule for a passive VP consisting of the same verb and constituents, except for the NP, possibly also with a PP with head *by*. As long as there is an upper limit to the number of symbols the variable X can match, you can show that the language described by the grammar expanded by all possible metarule applications remains a context-free language.

A descendant of GPSG, more oriented toward computational issues, is **head-driven phrase structure grammar** (Pollard, forthcoming; Pollard and Sag, forthcoming). This theory uses subcategorization information on the heads of phrases extensively and, by doing so, greatly simplifies the context-free grammar (at the expense of a more complex lexicon). In this way it is similar to LFG (see discussion in Chapter 4).

Yet another approach to handling unbounded dependencies is to use a more powerful grammatical formalism. The trick is to stay close to the power of a context-free grammar and add just enough extra power to handle the linguistic phenomena. A good example of this approach is the **tree adjoining grammars** (TAGs) of Joshi (1985). There are no grammar rules in this formalism. Rather, there is a set of initial tree structures that describe the simplest sentences of the language, and a tree operation, called **adjoining**, that inserts one tree into another to create a more complex structure. In this theory there is no movement. Instead the constituents start off being close to each other, and then additional structure is inserted between them by the adjoining operation. The result is a formalism of slightly greater power than CFG but definitely weaker than context-sensitive grammar.

Exercises for Chapter 5

1. *(easy)* Distinguish between bounded (local) movement and unbounded (nonlocal) movement. What extensions were added to the augmentation system to enable it to handle unbounded movement?

2. *(easy)* Why is wh-movement called unbounded movement? Give examples to support your claim.

3. *(easy)* State the Complex-NP Constraint. Write a sentence that violates the constraint, and explain why it does.

4. *(medium)* Give a full detailed trace of the ATN parse of the NP *The dog that was loved by John* using the NP Grammar 5.9 and the S Grammar 5.8.

5. *(medium)* Consider the following ATN grammar for sentences. On arc

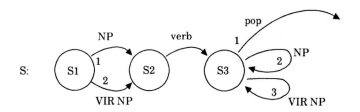

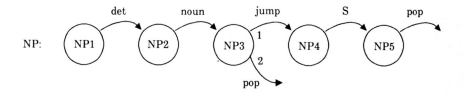

NP3/1, there is the action of holding the current noun phrase.

a) Give a sequence of legal sentences that can be made arbitrarily long and still be accepted by this ATN.

b) Which of the following sentences would be accepted by this ATN (assuming appropriate word categories for words)? For those that are accepted, outline the structure of the sentence as parsed by the network (that is, a plausible register value structure).

   i)   The man Mary hit hit the ball.
   ii)   The man the man hit the man hit.
   iii) The man hit hit.
   iv)   Hit the man hit the man.

6. *(hard)* Extend the grammar in Grammars 5.5 and 5.6 to handle questions involving PPs, such as

   In which town were you born?
   Where were you born?
   When did they leave?
   What town were you born in?

Where is the best place to account for the wh-words *where* and *when* in the grammar? Defend your choice by comparing it to another possible solution.

7. (*hard*) The following noun phrases arise in some dialogs between a computer operator and various users of the computer system.

   Could you mount <u>a magtape</u> for me?

   <u>No ring</u> please.

   I am not exactly sure of <u>the reason</u>, but we were given <u>a list of</u> <u>users we are not supposed to mount magtapes for</u> and you are on it.

   Could you possibly retrieve <u>the following two files</u>. I think <u>they</u> were on <u>our directory</u> last night.

   Any chance I can recover from <u>the most recent system dump</u>?

   Write a grammar in the formalism of your choice that accepts these noun phrases. Construct the grammar as though it were to be used in a complete system, and structure it around the major syntactic units (S, NP, PP). For example, the third sentence involves calls to a PP network, which calls the NP network, which then calls the S network.

8. (*hard*) Consider the following ATN of a little-known English dialect:

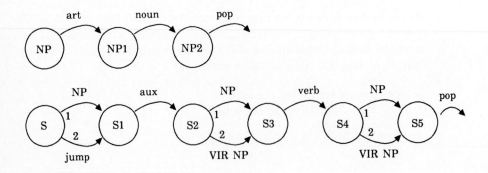

Arc	Actions
NP/1	DET ← *
NP1/1	HEAD ← *
S/1	FIRST ← *
	HOLD *
	MOOD ← TYPE1
S/2	MOOD ← TYPE2
S1/1	AUX ← *
S2/1	SECOND ← *
S2/2	SECOND ← *
S3/1	MAIN-V ← *
S4/1	THIRD ← *
S4/2	THIRD ← *

a) Characterize the entire set of structurally different sentences that can be recognized by this grammar (for example, give all sequences of terminal symbols that can be accepted). One such sentence structure is

ART NOUN AUX VERB ART NOUN

b) Assuming appropriate lexicon, draw the final structure produced by this grammar for the sentence *The man is eating the cake.*

c) Give a CFG that *uses slashed categories* and that is equivalent to this ATN. In other words the parts of the ATN that use VIR arcs should be handled using the slashed-rule mechanism.

d) Augment the grammar in (c) using the unification-based grammar formalism so as to compute structures equivalent to the structures built by the ATN.

9. *(hard)* Read Box 5.3 on other forms of reduced relatives in Section 5.3. Modify the NP Grammar 5.6 so that these forms are accepted. Make sure your grammar does not accept forms such as *The man who holding the book* and *The man having seen the movie* as legal NPs. Give a detailed trace of your grammar on these ill-formed NPs, showing why it fails, and give a trace of your grammar successfully parsing the NP *The man being sent to the store.*

10. *(hard)* The following grammar is an attempt to account for the following sentences:

   i)   I put the box in the corner.
   ii) I saw Jack put the box in the corner.
   iii) I saw Jack put the box in the corner from the roof.
   iv) I saw Jack.

v)   I saw Jack from the roof.

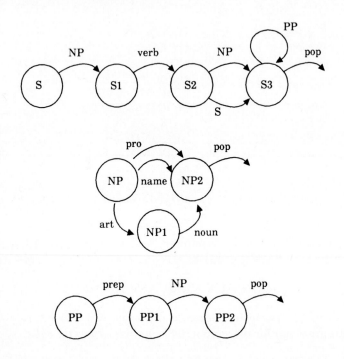

a) By using the necessary verb subcategorizations, modify and augment this grammar so that the preceding sentences are accepted but the following are not:

    *I put Jack saw the box.
    *I put Jack.
    *I saw Jack runs the mile.

Be sure to show the lexical entries for the verbs *saw*, *put*, *run*, and *runs*.

b) Extend this grammar to interpret the following wh-questions correctly:

    vi)   Where did I put the box?
    vii) Where did I see Jack put the box?
    viii) Where did I see Jack run the mile?

Give the syntactic structure generated by your grammar for the sentence:

    Where did I put the box in the corner?

Chapter 6

Toward Deterministic Parsing

All of the parsing frameworks discussed so far have depended on search techniques to find possible interpretations of a sentence. To many, such search processes do not correspond well with their intuitions about human processing of language. In particular, human parsing seems close to a deterministic process--that is, a process that doesn't search alternatives but rather uses the information it has at the time to choose the correct interpretation. While intuitions about such psychological matters are known to be highly unreliable, some experimental evidence suggests that people do not perform a complete search of a grammar while parsing. This chapter examines the computational models of deterministic, or near-deterministic, parsing.

Section 6.1 briefly explores some of the psycholinguistic theories concerning the human parsing process. In particular, the discussion identifies several parsing preferences that predict that certain sentences should be difficult to parse at all, even though there is a reasonable grammatical structure that could be found in a search.

Section 6.2 then presents a new class of parsers, the shift-reduce parsers, that are used for deterministic grammars such as those employed for programming languages. These techniques are then generalized in Section 6.3 to handle ambiguous grammars. The parsing preferences described in Section 6.1 can then be used to suggest appropriate strategies for choosing when multiple rules are applicable.

Section 6.4 introduces a mechanism that can extend all the parsing frameworks discussed thus far. Essentially, it allows the parse to look ahead at the next few words in the input, rather than just the next word. Such lookahead tests can be used effectively to choose between multiple paths that could be searched. These techniques can be used either to build a deterministic parser or to reduce dramatically the search in a nondeterministic parser.

The final section describes Mitch Marcus's deterministic parsing framework, which attempts to limit the grammar in such a way that the sentences that people misparse will be misparsed by the system as well. In light of this parser the parsing preferences discussed in Section 6.1 are reexamined.

6.1 Human Preferences in Parsing

So far this book has discussed parsing in the abstract without regard to any psychological evidence concerning the type of parsing process that people use. This section considers a few recent results from psycholinguistic research and tries to relate them to the parsing models described thus far.

One area where there have been some results concerns the parsing of sentences with ambiguous syntactic structure. The fact that people don't usually recognize an ambiguity but pick a single interpretation suggests that some analyses are favored over others. Researchers in the field have suggested a few general principles.

Minimal Attachment

The first principle is called the **minimal attachment** strategy, which involves a preference for the syntactic analysis that creates the least number of nodes in the parse tree. Thus, given Grammar 6.1, the sentence *The man kept the dog in the house* would be interpreted with the PP *in the house* modifying the verb rather than the NP *the dog*.

The interpretation with the PP attached to the VP is derived using rules 1.1, 1.2, and 1.6 and three applications of rule 1.4 for the NPs. The parse tree has a total of 14 nodes. The interpretation with the PP attached to the NP is derived using rules 1.1, 1.3, 1.5, and 1.6 and three applications of rule 1.4, producing a total of 15 nodes in the parse tree. Thus this principle predicts that the first interpretation is preferred, which probably agrees with your intuition. These two interpretations are shown in Figure 6.2.

This principle may be so strong that it can cause certain sentences to be almost impossible to parse correctly. One example is the sentence

> We painted all the walls with cracks.

which, against all common sense, is often read as meaning that cracks were painted onto the walls, or that cracks were somehow used as an instrument to paint the walls. Both these anomalous readings arise from the PP being attached to the VP (*paint*) rather than the NP (*the walls*). Another classic example is the sentence

> The horse raced past the barn fell.

which has a reasonable interpretation corresponding to the meaning of the sentence *The horse that was raced past the barn fell*. In the initial sentence, however, creating a reduced relative clause when the word *raced* is encountered introduces many more nodes than the simple analysis where *raced* is the main verb of the sentence. Of course, this second interpretation renders the sentence unanalyzable when the word *fell* is encountered. Such sentences are often called **garden path sentences**, because they "lead the reader up the garden path."

Right Association

The second principle is called **right association** or **late closure**. This principle states that, all other things being equal, new constituents tend to be interpreted as being part of the current constituent under construction (rather than part of some constituent higher on the parse stack). Thus, given the sentence

1.1	S ← NP VP
1.2	VP ← VERB NP PP
1.3	VP ← VERB NP
1.4	NP ← ART NOUN
1.5	NP ← NP PP
1.6	PP ← PREP NP

Grammar 6.1 A simple CFG

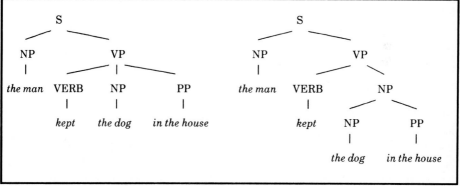

Figure 6.2 The interpretation on the left is preferred by the minimal attachment principle

George said that Henry left in his car.

the preferred interpretation is that Henry left in the car, rather than the interpretation that George spoke in the car. Both interpretations are, of course, syntactically acceptable analyses. The former attaches the PP to the VP immediately preceding it, whereas the second attaches the PP to the VP higher up the stack. Thus the right association principle prefers the former. The two interpretations are shown in Figure 6.3. Similarly, the preferred interpretation for the sentence *I thought it would rain yesterday* is that yesterday was when it was thought to rain, rather than the time of the thinking.

Lexical Preferences

In certain cases these principles seem to conflict with each other. In fact, in the first example, *The man kept the dog in the house*, the principle of right association appears to favor the interpretation in which the PP modifies the dog, while the minimal attachment principle appears to favor the PP modifying the VP. You might then suggest that minimal attachment takes priority over right association in such cases; however, the relationship appears to be more complex than that. Consider the sentences

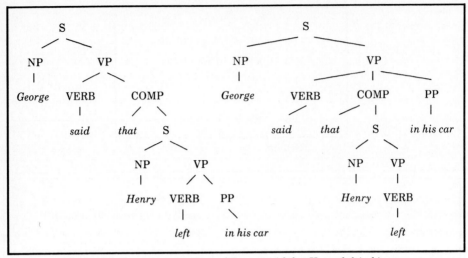

Figure 6.3 Two interpretations of *George said that Henry left in his car.*

1.   I wanted the dog in the house.

2.   I kept the dog in the house.

3.   I put the dog in the house.

The PP *in the house* in sentence 1 seems most likely as modifying *dog* (although the other interpretation is possible, as in the sense *I wanted the dog put/kept/left in the house.*). In sentence 2, the PP seems to be most likely as modifying the VP (again, modifying the NP is possible, as in *I kept the dog that was in the house.*). Finally, in sentence 3, the PP is definitely attached to the VP, and no alternative reading is possible.

These examples demonstrate that the verb affects the attachment preferences. A new strategy, called **lexical preference**, may be able to handle these cases. Each verb is classified by which prepositions indicate the PP must be attached to the VP and which ones are preferred to be attached to the VP. If neither of these cases holds, the PP will be attached to the NP, using the right association principle as a default.

Thus, for the preceding verbs, *want* has no preference for any PPs, whereas *keep* prefers PPs with prepositions *in*, *on*, or *by* to be attached to the VP. Finally, the verb *put* requires a PP beginning with *in*, *on*, *by*, and so on, to be attached to the VP.

Embodying the Preferences in Parsers

Various attempts have been tried to incorporate these strategies into the well-known parsing frameworks. For instance, researchers have suggested that in ATNs, the principles of right association and minimal attachment can be captured by imposing constraints on the order that arcs are tried. In particular the right association preference is captured by ordering arcs so that the pop arcs are always tried last. This way, any possible interpretation that includes the next constituent as a subpart of the current network will be tried before the pop is used to complete the current constituent. Similarly, theorists have suggested that minimal attachment can be captured by ordering the cat and wrd arcs before any push arcs. That way, if the next input can be recognized as a direct part of the current constituent, rather than part of a subconstituent built by a push arc, it will be recognized as such (resulting in a simpler analysis). While these strategies make some computational sense as well, there are difficulties in arguing that they truly account for the phenomena. The primary problem is that the arc-ordering approach works only on certain grammars, whereas with other equivalent grammars it does not produce the desired results. Furthermore, any fixed arc-ordering strategy cannot account for lexical preferences, as will be seen in the following discussion.

You may have difficulty devising a strategy for top-down parsing using CFGs that captures the same preferences. One possibility is to order the rules in the grammar so that the longest rules are always tried first, and if two rules are the same length, the one that starts with the most number of terminals is tried first. If you are careful about constructing the grammar, you may be able to generate a strategy comparable to the ATN strategy. Of course, this approach still does not account for lexical preference. Bottom-up parsing strategies with preferences will be examined in a later section after a new parsing algorithm has been introduced in Section 6.2.

You cannot encode lexical preference into the parsing frameworks described so far without giving up some ability to recover from trying a wrong path through the grammar. To see this, consider encoding lexical preferences for verbs and using them in a CFG parser. The entries for the verbs *want*, *keep*, and *put*, as described earlier, are shown in Grammar 6.4.

Here for each verb are listed the prepositions that signal a preference to attach to the VP in the **PREFS** register. A fragment of a grammar for VPs is shown in Grammar 6.5.

These three rules may appear to do the trick. In particular, the verb *want* would enable rule 2.2, *keep* would enable rules 2.2 and 2.3, and the longest rule preference would try 2.3 first, and *put* would enable only rule 2.1. The problem is that you now cannot parse *I want the sofa in that corner*, as said to the movers

```
┌─────────────────────────────────────────────────────────┐
│                                                         │
│        (VERB ROOT WANT                                  │
│              PREFS nil                                  │
│              SUBCAT {OBJ OBJ + TO-INF TO-INF})          │
│                                                         │
│        (VERB ROOT KEEP                                  │
│              PREFS (in on by)                           │
│              SUBCAT {OBJ})                              │
│                                                         │
│        (VERB ROOT PUT                                   │
│              PREFS nil                                  │
│              SUBCAT {OBJ + PP})                         │
│                                                         │
└─────────────────────────────────────────────────────────┘
```

Grammar 6.4 Sample lexicon with preference information

	Rule	Annotation
2.1	VP ← VERB NP PP	$\text{SUBCAT}_{\text{VERB}} = \text{OBJ} + \text{PP}$
2.2	VP ← VERB NP	$\text{SUBCAT}_{\text{VERB}} = \text{OBJ}$
2.3	VP ← VERB NP PP	$\text{PREFS}_{\text{VERB}} = \text{PREP}_{\text{PP}}$

Grammar 6.5 A CFG fragment attempting to encode lexical preference

when they carry in the sofa. The restrictions on rules 2.1 and 2.3 are not satisfied by *want*. If you generalized them in some way to allow this sense of *want*--say, by adding OBJ + PP to the **SUBCAT** of *want*--then this rule will be tried first since it is longer than rule 2.2. Unfortunately, you can't encode preferences into the feature tests, since preferences can be violated, while feature tests cannot. An extension to the parsing frameworks that allows this type of preference will be discussed in Section 6.4, which describes lookahead in parsing.

6.2 Shift-Reduce Parsers

There is a fair-sized subset of the context-free grammars for which deterministic parsing algorithms can be built. While natural language is certainly not one of these because of its ambiguous nature, these techniques may be able to be extended in various ways that may make them applicable to natural language parsing. Furthermore, many of these techniques could be used to reduce the search in other parsing frameworks as well.

Consider a simple example. You could attempt to specify a deterministic parser by keeping track of all possible parses briefly when an uncertainty arises, and hoping that the input seen later eliminates all but one of these parses. If you did this explicitly at parse time, you would have an algorithm similar to the breadth-first parser described earlier. The efficiency in the technique described in this section is that all the possibilities are considered in advance, and the

3.1	S ← NP VP
3.2	VP ← VERB NP
3.3	NP ← NAME
3.4	NP ← ART NOUN

Grammar 6.6 A small grammar

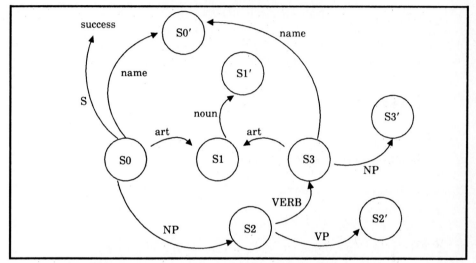

Figure 6.7 A transition network derived from Grammar 6.6

information is stored in a table that controls the parser, resulting in parsing algorithms that are much faster than described thus far.

Specifying the Parser State

Consider how this process is done on a small grammar in Grammar 6.6. The following discussion derives all possible states that the parser could be in, and determines the transitions from one state to another, as shown in Figure 6.7.

What terminal symbols could start a legal sentence according to this grammar? You can find out by looking at all possible derivations for the first terminal that could derive S. Using the dotted rule notation from the bottom-up parser, you start with

S ← ∘ NP VP

This says an S may start with an NP. Adding the rules for NP, you find

NP ← ∘ NAME

NP ← ∘ ART NOUN

Checking these, you see that an NP may start with a NAME or an ART. So you know that all legal sentences must begin with a word in category NAME or ART. A state of the parse can be described by the set of dotted rules applicable in that state. Thus the initial state is as follows:

Initial State S0:   S ← ∘ NP VP
                     NP ← ∘ NAME
                     NP ← ∘ ART NOUN

What states could follow the initial state? To calculate this, consider advancing the dot over a terminal or a nonterminal and deriving a new state. If you pick the symbol NAME, the resulting state consists solely of the rule

State S0′:   NP ← NAME ∘

If you pick the symbol ART, the resulting state is

State S1:   NP ← ART ∘ NOUN

If you pick the symbol NP, the rule is

S ← NP ∘ VP

in the new state. Now if you expand out the VP to find all its possible starting symbols, you get the following by considering how VP could be derived:

State S2:   S ← NP ∘ VP
             VP ← ∘ VERB NP

The only terminal symbol allowed from state S2 is a VERB, resulting in the state

State S3:   VP ← VERB ∘ NP
             NP ← ∘ NAME
             NP ← ∘ ART NOUN

Continuing with a VP from S2, you arrive at the following state:

State S2′ :   S ← NP VP ∘

Continuing with state S3 with a NAME, you find yourself back in state S0′; continuing with an ART, you get state S1; continuing with an NP, you get the following state:

State S3':   VP ← VERB NP ∘

When this process is completed, you can derive a transition network that can be used to control the parsing of sentences. This is shown in Figure 6.7.

A Shift-Reduce Parser

These states can be used to control a parser that maintains two stacks: the **parse stack**, which contains parse states (that is, the nodes in Figure 6.7) and grammar symbols; and the **input stack**, which contains the input and some grammar symbols. At any time the parser operates using the information specified for the top state on the parse stack.

The states are interpreted as follows. The states that consist of a single rule with the dot at the far right-hand side, such as

S ← NP VP ∘

indicate that the parser should rewrite the top symbols on the parse stack according to this rule. This is called a **reduce action**. The newly derived symbol (such as S, given the preceding rule) is pushed onto the top of the input stack.

Any other state, not containing any completed rules, is interpreted by the transition diagram. If the top input symbol matches an arc, then it and the new state (at the end of the arc) are pushed onto the parse stack. This movement is called the **shift action**. Using this information, you can construct a table that indicates what to do in each state. Because this information can be used to "tell the parser what to do" in all situations, it is sometimes called the **oracle**. The oracle for Grammar 6.6 is shown in Figure 6.8.

Consider parsing the sentence *Jack ate the carrot*. The initial state of the parser is

Parse Stack	Input Stack
(S0)	(Jack ate the carrot)

Looking up the entry in the table in Figure 6.8 for state S0 for the input NAME, you see a shift action and a move to state S0':

Parse Stack	Input Stack
(S0' NAME S0)	(ate the carrot)

Looking up the entry in the table for this state, you then reduce by rule 3.3, producing the state:

State	Top Input Symbol	Action	GoTo
S0	NAME	Shift	S0'
S0'	----------	Reduce by rule 3.3	-----
S0	ART	Shift	S1
S0	NP	Shift	S2
S1	NOUN	Shift	S1'
S1'	----------	Reduce by rule 3.4	-----
S2	VERB	Shift	S3
S2	VP	Shift	S2'
S2'	----------	Reduce by rule 3.1	-----
S3	ART	Shift	S1
S3	NAME	Shift	S0'
S3	NP	Shift	S3'
S3'	----------	Reduce by rule 3.2	-----

Figure 6.8 The oracle for Grammar 6.6

Parse Stack	Input Stack
(S0)	(NP ate the carrot)

Again, consulting the table, you now do a shift and move to state S2:

Parse Stack	Input Stack
(S2 NP S0)	(ate the carrot)

Next, the three remaining words all cause shifts and a move to a new state, ending up with the parse state:

Parse Stack	Input Stack
(S1' NOUN S1 ART S3 VERB S2 NP S0)	( )

The reduce by rule 3.4 specified in state S1' pops the NOUN and ART from the stack (thereby popping S1 and S1' as well), and the resulting NP is placed on the input stack:

Parse Stack	Input Stack
(S3 VERB S2 NP S0)	(NP)

You are now back at state S3, with an NP in the input, and after a shift to state S3′, you reduce by rule 3.2, producing:

Parse Stack	Input Stack
(S2 NP S0)	(VP)

Finally, from state S2, you shift to state S2′ and reduce by rule 3.1, producing:

Parse Stack	Input Stack
(S0)	(S)

From this state you are in a position to accept the sentence.

Thus you have parsed the sentence without ever trying a rule in the grammar incorrectly and without ever constructing a constituent that is not part of the final analysis. Thus this is a deterministic parsing process for CFGs with no ambiguity.

6.3 Shift-Reduce Parsers and Ambiguity

Shift-reduce parsers can be successfully applied for many grammars because the algorithm allows decisions about which rule to apply to be delayed until further on in the parse. For example, if you had the following rules for parsing an NP,

1.   NP ← ART NOUN REL-PRO VP

2.   NP ← ART NOUN PP

a top-down parser would have to pick a rule and try it. A bottom-up parser, on the other hand, would wait until all the constituents in the phrase have been recognized. The shift-reduce parser is like the bottom-up parser in this respect.

Consider some of the parse states:

      NP1:   NP ← ∘ ART NOUN REL-PRO VP
             NP ← ∘ ART NOUN PP

If an ART is found, the next state will be

      NP2:   NP ← ART ∘ NOUN REL-PRO VP
             NP ← ART ∘ NOUN PP

Thus the ART can be recognized and shifted onto the parse stack without committing to which rule it is used in. Similarly, if a NOUN is seen at state NP2, the state is

NP3:   NP ← ART NOUN ∘ REL-PRO VP
        NP ← ART NOUN ∘ PP
        PP ← ∘ PREP NP

Now from NP3, you finally can distinguish the cases. If a REL-PRO is found next, the state is

NP4:   NP ← ART NOUN REL-PRO ∘ VP
        VP ← ∘ VERB NP

which leads eventually to a reduction by rule 1. If a PREP is found, you move to a different state, which eventually builds a PP that is used in the reduction by rule 2. Thus the parser delays the decision until sufficient information is available to choose between the rules.

The shift-reduce parser, however, cannot be thought of as a simple bottom-up parser either, since it never applies rules that do not contribute to the final analysis. Thus it is best classified as a bottom-up parser with top-down prediction.

Lexical Ambiguity

This ability to postpone decisions can be used to deal with some lexical ambiguity by a simple extension to the parsing process. Whereas earlier you classified a lexical entry when it was shifted (that is, *carrot* was converted to NOUN during the shift), you now allow ambiguous words to be shifted onto the parse stack as is, and you delay their categorization until a reduction involving them is made.

To accomplish this extension, you must expand the number of states to include states that deal with ambiguities. For instance, given Grammar 6.9 and a lexicon that recognizes the ambiguity of *can* between an AUX and a VERB, you will originally have states such as are shown in Figure 6.10.

If *can* could be an AUX or a VERB, you need to generate a new state from VP1 to cover both possibilities simultaneously. This new state will be the union of states VP2 and VP3. In this case the next input will resolve the ambiguity. To see this, consider the union of VP2 and VP3:

VP2&3:   VP ← AUX ∘ VERB NP
          VP ← VERB ∘ NP
          NP ← ∘ DET NOUN

If you see a VERB next, you would move to a new state, which happens to be VP4! If you see a DET next, you would move to VP5. If you see an NP next, you will move to VP3! Thus the new state maintains the ambiguity long enough for

4.1   S ← NP VP

4.2   NP ← DET NOUN

4.3   VP ← AUX VERB NP

4.4   VP ← VERB NP

Grammar 6.9 A simple grammar with an AUX/VERB ambiguity

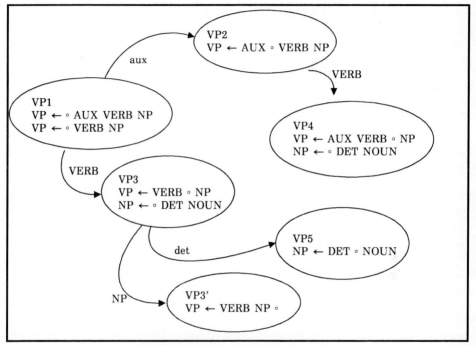

Figure 6.10 The states for Grammar 6.9

succeeding words to resolve the problem. Of course, in general, the next word might also be ambiguous as well, so the number of new states could be quite large. But if the grammar is unambiguous--that is, there is only one possible interpretation of the sentence once it is completely parsed--this technique can be used to delay the decisions as long as necessary. (In fact, for those who know automata theory, this process is simply the construction of a deterministic simulation of a nondeterministic finite automata.)

Ambiguous Parse States

There are, however, other forms of ambiguity that this parser, as it now stands, is not able to handle. The simplest examples involve the ambiguity that arises

when one rule is a proper prefix of another. For instance, consider Grammar
6.11.

The problem arises because the parser can arrive at a state containing the
rules:

NP ← ART ∘ NOUN
NP ← ART ∘ NOUN PP

If the next input is a NOUN, you move to a state consisting of

NP5:   NP ← ART NOUN ∘
       NP ← ART NOUN ∘ PP
       PP ← ∘ PREP PP

But now there is a problem. If the next input is a PREP, eventually a PP will be
built and you return to state NP5. But the parser cannot decide whether to
reduce by rule 5.4, leaving the PP to be attached later, or to shift the PP (and
then reduce by rule 5.5). With the present grammar, both choices would lead to
acceptable parses of the sentence.

There are two other ways to deal with this problem. The first strategy
maintains a deterministic parser and accepts the fact that it may misparse
certain sentences. The goal here is to model human parsing performance and fail
on only those that would give people trouble. The second strategy is to
reincorporate search strategy on top of the shift-reduce parser that can deal with
each possibility separately. This discussion will consider each briefly.

One recent suggestion following the first approach is that the human
preferences in parsing described in the previous section could be used to choose
the rule. In particular, this approach claims that

i) the right association strategy corresponds to favoring shift
   operations over reduce operations; and

ii) the minimal attachment strategy corresponds to resolving all
    reduce-reduce conflicts in favor of the longest rule (that is, the one
    that uses the most symbols from the stack).

Using these strategies you could build a deterministic parser that picks the most
favored rule and ignores the others. In particular, given the preceding situation
at state NP5, if the input contains a PP, then the parser would choose to shift the
PP, thereby leading to a reduction by rule 5.5. Thus the PP is attached to the
rightmost constituent as required by the principle of right association.

5.1	S ← NP VP
5.2	VP ← VERB NP
5.3	VP ← VERB NP PP
5.4	NP ← ART NOUN
5.5	NP ← ART NOUN PP
5.6	PP ← PREP NP

Grammar 6.11 A grammar with one rule by the prefix of another

Another form of conflict can arise between two reduce actions. For example, there is a parse state that contains the following dotted rules (to find it, trace from the initial state through inputs NP, VERB, and NP):

VP ← VERB NP ∘
VP ← VERB NP ∘ PP
NP ← ART NOUN ∘ PP

From this state, if the input is a PP, the principle will favor a shift over the reduce by rule 5.2, producing the state:

VP ← VERB NP PP ∘
NP ← ART NOUN PP ∘

If one of these rules were longer than the other, the minimal attachment strategy would favor the longer. In this case you must simply choose at random if you can't consider both interpretations. This example reveals a problem with these strategies: they are highly dependent on the grammar. For example, if rule 5.5 were instead

5.5′   NP ← NP PP

the preceding conflict would be between rules

VP ← VERB NP PP ∘
NP ← NP PP ∘

and the PP would be attached to the VP by reducing with rule 5.2. On the other hand, if 5.2 were rewritten as

5.2′   VP ← VP ∘ PP

and 5.5 were as originally stated, then the conflict would be between

VP ← VP PP ∘
NP ← ART NOUN PP ∘

and the PP would be attached to the noun phrase by reducing with rule 5.5!

The second approach to dealing with the ambiguous states is to abandon the deterministic requirement and reintroduce search. In this case you could consider each alternative by either a depth-first search with backtracking or a breadth-first search maintaining several interpretations in parallel. Both of these approaches can yield efficient parsers. The depth-first approach can be integrated with the preference strategies so that the preferred interpretations are tried first.

6.4 Lookahead in Parsers

Clearly many choice points in a parse can be resolved more effectively if the parser is allowed to inspect words further down the input stream. If you were to take this principle to its absurd limit, a parser might look ahead at the entire sentence in order to decide which grammar rule to apply as the first step of the parse. This approach, of course, would make the lookahead analyzer as complex as the parser of which it was intended to be a part. Thus lookahead is typically restricted to a fixed (small) number of words and/or completed constituents. A lookahead of one or two can be extremely useful, and while a lookahead of four or five would definitely yield a more powerful parser, managing such a long lookahead is often difficult.

Suppose you want to add a lookahead capability to a selection of the parsing frameworks discussed thus far. In all of these frameworks you will use the same notation, as follows. The lookahead consists of a sequence of feature tests on the input enclosed in angle brackets, such as

$$< = NOUN > \quad < = AUX, TYPE = MODAL > \quad < = VERB, FORM = inf >$$

The first is a test on the current input symbol, the next for the word following it, and so on. Thus this lookahead succeeds if the current input is a noun, followed by a modal auxiliary and an infinitive verb form.

At any point in the parse where a choice has to be made, you allow a set of lookahead tests that can identify the best choice given the input. For instance, in an ATN each node might have a set of lookahead tests to identify which arc to try first. In a top-down CFG parser each nonterminal symbol could have a set of lookahead tests that identify which rule to use to rewrite the symbol. In the shift-reduce parser each state could have a set of lookahead rules that identify which one of the possible shifts and reductions should be selected.

Consider some examples. Start by considering the problem of determining the end of noun phrases, especially those that involve noun-noun modification, such as *fire truck*, *water channel*, *soup pot cover*, and so on. With this type of

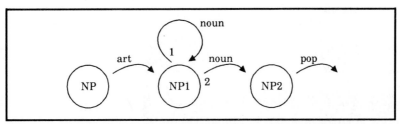

Grammar 6.12 A simple NP network with noun-noun modification

structure it is difficult to find examples where the modifying noun is a plural noun. Thus you cannot use NPs such as *The soups pot cover* or *The soup pots cover*. The last case must be distinguished from the possessive form *The soup pot's cover*, which is a perfectly acceptable NP. Can you go beyond this? In general it is difficult, but in some cases you can. For instance, if the NP in question is the first NP in the sentence it must agree with the verb following. Since many words are ambiguous between nouns and verbs, this check can be useful. For example, both *pot* and *cover* are ambiguous between being a singular NOUN or a plural VERB. But if you tried a shorter NP, given the input *The soup pot cover*, you would violate subject-verb agreement. Thus, if the NP were *The soup pot*, the verb following would have to be *covers*, not *cover*.

In other cases, where the NP is not followed by a verb, there may still be problems that are not resolved by simple checks. The best heuristic in these cases is to extend the NP as far as possible until a non-NOUN is found. Typically, this would be a preposition, a relative pronoun, or a determiner. Even so, there are some sentences, such as *We gave the man fish at dinner*, where this strategy fails. It is improbable, therefore, that you can design a lookahead that is infallible. But lookahead can be very useful in deciding the best alternatives to try first within a search.

Encode the following strategy on the NP network shown in Grammar 6.12. The strategy has two heuristics:

a) if the current word is a plural noun, then try NP1/2 first (that is, interpret it as the head noun);

b) otherwise, if the next two words can be NOUNs, try NP1/1 first (that is, interpret the current word as a modifier);

c) otherwise, try NP1/2 first.

In our lookahead language, you would express these as follows. For node NP1

If < =NOUN, NUM=3p> then try NP1/2, NP1/1
If < =NOUN> < =NOUN> then try NP1/1, NP1/2
If < =NOUN> then try NP1/2, NP1/1

This strategy would choose the correct path on the first try for NPs such as:

1.   The soup pot cover broke.

2.   The soup pot covers are missing.

3.   The soup pots cover the marbles.

4.   We gave the men fish for dinner.

The strategy would not, however, choose correctly with the following sentences (the first NP hypothesized is underlined; the actual NP is in italics):

5.   *The soup pot* covers the marbles.

6.   We saw *the soup pot* cover the marble.

7.   We gave *the man* fish for dinner.

8.   *The sales* slip was lost.

While these tests leave something to be desired for NPs in the subject position, they work quite effectively for NPs elsewhere in sentences.

Note that these lookahead tests could not be encoded in the normal arc tests, even if you didn't mind them being tested after the arc was tried. This is because lookahead tests are simply heuristics for ordering the arcs and are not required to be true in the final interpretation. In particular, if the preceding tests were included in the tests on arc NP1/1 and NP1/2, the sentences initially misparsed would become unacceptable by the network.

6.5 The Marcus Parser

A quite different approach to parsing natural language was proposed in the late 1970s by Mitch Marcus. This parser, named PARSIFAL, is not based on search but depends entirely on lookahead tests to direct its operation. In the terms introduced in the previous sections, it is built directly from the notions of the parser state and the lookahead rules. Instead of allowing only shift and reduce actions, however, Marcus allows a richer set of actions that operate on an input stack called the **buffer**. Rather than shifting constituents onto the parse stack to be later consumed by a reduce operation, the parser builds constituents incrementally by **attaching** buffer elements into their parent constituent, which is an operation similar to register assignment. Thus, rather than shifting an NP onto the stack, later to be used in a reduction S ← NP VP, Marcus creates an S constituent on the parse stack and attaches the NP to the S. Thus there is no reduce operation. To summarize, rather than a shift and reduce operation, Marcus has the operations

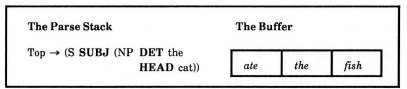

Figure 6.13 A situation during a parse

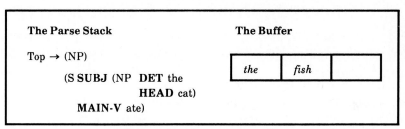

Figure 6.14 After creating an NP

a) **Create** a new node on parse stack (pushes the symbol onto the stack);

b) **Attach** an input constituent to the top node on the parse stack; and

c) **Drop** top node in the parse stack into the buffer.

The drop action allows a completed constituent to be reexamined by the parser, which will then assign it a role in a higher constituent still on the parse stack. This technique makes the limited lookahead technique surprisingly powerful.

To get a feeling for these operations, consider the situation in Figure 6.13, which might occur in parsing the sentence *The cat ate the fish*. The first NP has been parsed and assigned to the **SUBJ** register of the S constituent on the parse stack. The operations introduced earlier can be used to complete the analysis. Note that the actual mechanism for deciding what operations to do has not yet been discussed, but the effect of the operations is shown here to provide intuition about the data structure. The operation

Attach to **MAIN-V**

would remove the lexical entry for *ate* from the buffer and assign it to the **MAIN-V** register in the S. Next the operation

Create NP

would push an empty NP constituent onto the parse stack, creating the situation in Figure 6.14.

Next the two operations

> Attach to **DET**
> Attach to **HEAD**

would successfully build the NP from the lexical entries for *the* and *fish*. The input buffer would now be empty. The operation

> Drop

pops the NP from the parse stack and pushes it back onto the buffer, creating the situation in Figure 6.15.

The parser is now in a situation to build the final structure with the operation

> Attach to **OBJ**

which takes the NP from the buffer and assigns it to the **OBJ** slot in the S constituent.

Marcus also allows other operations that prove very useful in capturing generalizations in natural languages. In particular, he allows actions to

d) **Switch** the nodes in the first two buffer positions;

e) **Insert** a specific lexical item into a specified buffer slot; and

f) **Insert** an empty NP into the first buffer slot.

Examples of each of these actions are shown later in this section.

A **packet** consists of a set of lookahead rules that identify the appropriate parser action for a given situation. Additional actions are available for changing the parser state by selecting which packets to use. In particular, there are actions to

g) **Activate** a packet (that is, all its rules are to be used to interpret the next input); and

h) **Deactivate** a packet.

As with the states in the shift-reduce parser, the active packets are associated with the symbols on the parse stack. If a new constituent is created (that is, pushed on the stack), all the active packets associated with the previous top of the stack become inactive until that constituent is again on the top of the stack. Consequently, the drop action will always deactivate the rules associated with the top node. Unlike the states in the shift-reduce parser, more than one packet

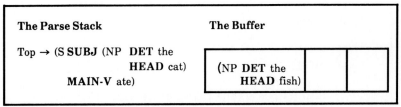

The Parse Stack	The Buffer
Top → (S **SUBJ** (NP **DET** the **HEAD** cat) **MAIN-V** ate)	(NP **DET** the **HEAD** fish)

Figure 6.15 After the drop action

Pattern	Actions	Priority
Packet BUILD-AUX:		
1. < =AUX, **ROOT**=HAVE> < =VERB, **FORM**=en>	Attach to **PERF TENSE** ← Append(**TENSE**, perf)	10
2. < =AUX, **ROOT**=BE> < =VERB, **FORM**=ing>	Attach to **PROG TENSE** ← Append(**TENSE**, prog)	10
3. < =AUX, **ROOT**=BE> < =VERB, **FORM**=en>	Attach to **PASSIVE VOICE** ← PASSIVE	10
4. < =AUX, **TYPE**=modal> < =VERB, **FORM**=inf>	Attach to **MODAL TENSE** ← Append(**TENSE**, modal)	10
5. < =AUX, **ROOT**=DO> < =VERB, **FORM**=inf>	Attach to **DO**	10
6. <true>	Drop	15

Grammar 6.16 The rules for packet BUILD-AUX

may be active at a time. Thus there would be no need to create packets consisting of the union of packets to deal with word ambiguity, since both can be active simultaneously anyway.

Consider the example rules shown in Grammar 6.16, which deals with parsing the auxiliary structure (as described by the VERBS network in Chapter 4, except the HEAD verb is not parsed here). The priority associated with each rule is used to decide between conflicting rules. The lower the number, the higher the priority. In particular, rule 6, with the pattern <true>, will always match, but since its priority is low, it will never be used if another one of the rules also matches. It simply covers the case when none of the rules match, and it completes the parsing of the auxiliary and verb structure.

Figure 6.17 shows a parse state in which the state BUILD-AUX is active. It contains an AUXS structure on the top of the stack with packet BUILD-AUX active and an S structure below with packets PARSE-AUX and CPOOL that will become active once the AUXS constituent is dropped into the buffer.

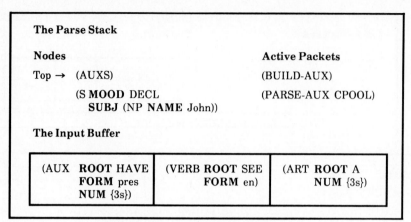

Figure 6.17 A typical state of the parser

Given this situation, and the rules in Figure 6.16, the next action of the parser is determined by seeing which rules match. Rules 1 and 6 succeed, and 1 is chosen because of its higher priority. Applying the actions of rule 1 produces the new parse state shown in Figure 6.18. Now the rules in BUILD-AUX are applied again. This time only rule 6 succeeds, so the next action is a drop, creating the state in Figure 6.19.

At this stage the rules in packets PARSE-AUX and CPOOL are active; they compete to determine the next move of the parser (which would be to attach the AUXS structure into the S structure).

The lookahead rules are restricted to examining at most the first three buffer elements, with one exception that occurs when an NP subconstituent needs to be constructed. If the NP starts in the second or third buffer position, then while it is being parsed, that position is used as though it were the first buffer. Called **attention shifting**, this circumstance is the only exception to the three-buffer restriction. With this qualification, a rule may still inspect only three buffer positions, but the starting position may be shifted. Attention shifting is restricted so that under no circumstances can a rule inspect a position beyond the first five.

One of the more interesting things about this parser is the way it captures many linguistic generalizations in an elegant fashion by manipulating the input buffer. For example, consider what is needed to extend a grammar that parses assertions into one that parses yes-no questions as well. In Chapter 5, you handled yes-no questions by adding a few rules to the grammar that handled the initial AUX and NP, and then connecting back into the grammar for assertions. This present parser actually reuses the rules for the initial subject and auxiliary as well. Consider this example in detail. The rules to analyze the start of a

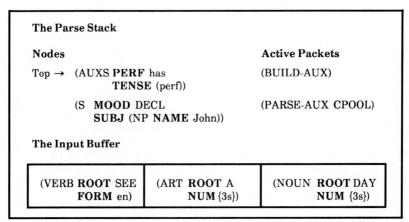

Figure 6.18 After rule 1 is applied

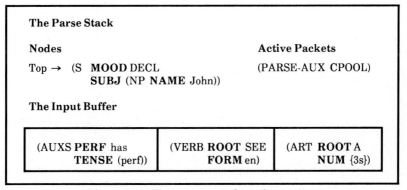

Figure 6.19 The parse state after a drop action

declarative sentence and the rule for yes-no questions are shown in Grammar 6.20. These rules operate after the NP has been built by other rules in the network. Note that in the yes-no question case, an NP has been built in the second buffer position by using the attention-shifting mechanism. Rule 9 recognizes the **FIRST-NP** in the sentence for both declarative sentences and yes-no questions. It can do this since rule 8, in recognizing a yes-no question, switched the first two buffer positions. Rule 8 is the only addition to the grammar necessary to account for yes-no questions. Thus the switch action provides as concise a description of auxiliary inversion as you could hope for.

Another of the special actions allowed is the insertion of an empty NP into the first buffer position. This is useful in analyzing imperative sentences. In fact, if you add the rule

Pattern	Action
Packet SET-MOOD:	
7. < =NP> < =VERB>	**MOOD** ← DECL Deactivate SET-MOOD Activate PARSE-SUBJ
8. < =VERB> < =NP>	Switch **MOOD** ← YN/Q Deactivate SET-MOOD Activate PARSE-SUBJ
Packet PARSE-SUBJ:	
9. < =NP> < =VERB> Agr(**NUM**$_1$, **NUM**$_2$)	Attach to **FIRST-NP** Deactivate PARSE-SUBJ Activate PARSE-AUX

Grammar 6.20 Rules for yes-no questions and declaratives

Pattern	Action
10. < =VERB, **FORM**=inf>	**MOOD** ← Imperative Insert NP Deactivate SET-MOOD Activate PARSE-SUBJ

to the packet SET-MOOD, the grammar will handle imperatives as well. Rule 10 inserts a dummy NP to be used as the subject by rule 9.

Finally, the other special action was to insert specific lexical items into the buffer. This is useful to handle a range of phenomena where words can be deleted. For example, the reduced relative clause can be handled by inserting a *that* into the first buffer and using the grammar for the full relative clause. A phrase such as *all the boys* can be analyzed by the grammar that accepts *all of the boys* by inserting an *of* into the second buffer.

Because these actions are available, the core grammar that needs to be captured can be considerably simpler than it would be if all these alternatives needed to be accounted for explicitly.

Psychological Validity

Because of the limits on the lookahead and the deterministic nature of this parser, you can examine in detail its limitations as well as its coverage. Some researchers have argued that the limitations of the mechanism itself account for various constraints on the form of language, such as the complex-NP constraint described in Chapter 5. Rather than having to impose such a constraint on the grammar--as was done with the logic grammar approach, for instance--this parser, because of its limitations, could not operate in any other way.

Because of the limited lookahead, this mechanism must commit to certain structural analyses before the entire sentence has been examined. In certain cases a sentence may begin in such a way that the wrong decision is made and the sentence becomes unparsable. These examples were referred to earlier as garden path sentences. The interesting thing about this phenomena is that it provides a concrete proposal that can be experimentally validated. In particular, you might ask if the sentence structures with which this parser has difficulty are the same as the ones with which people have trouble. While the answer to this question is not yet clear, the fact that the question can be asked means that this framework can be investigated experimentally.

In essence, the theory is that sentences that retain an ambiguity over more than a three-constituent window may cause trouble with a reader, while those that do not remain ambiguous as long as this should be invariably parsed correctly. Note that the lookahead is three constituents, not words; thus an ambiguity might be retained for quite some time without causing difficulty. For example, the following two sentences are identical for the first seven words:

> Have the students who missed the exam take it today.
> Have the students who missed the exam taken it today?

The ambiguity between being an imperative or a sentence versus a yes-no question, however, never extends beyond three constituents, because six of the words are in a single noun phrase. Thus the parser will reach a state where the following two tests can easily distinguish the cases:

> $<\,=\text{have}>\ <\,=\text{NP}>\ <\,=\text{VERB},\ \textbf{FORM}=\text{inf}> \rightarrow$ imperative

> $<\,=\text{have}>\ <\,=\text{NP}>\ <\,=\text{VERB},\ \textbf{FORM}=\text{en}> \rightarrow$ yes-no question

On the other hand, a sentence such as

> Have the soldiers given their medals by their sweethearts.

cannot be disambiguated using only three constituents, and this parser, like most people, will initially misinterpret the sentence as a yes-no question that is ill formed, rather than recognize the appropriate imperative reading corresponding to *Have their sweethearts give the soldiers their medals.*

Summary

Several techniques can be used for building deterministic parsers. Such techniques can increase the efficiency of search-based parsing models and specify an entirely new model of parsing that is inherently deterministic. The methods work by using a parse state that can encode temporary ambiguities until more of the sentence is parsed, and by using a mechanism called a lookahead. Simple lookahead allows the parser to inspect a fixed number of input words before deciding what to do. A more general form of lookahead works in terms of constituents, not just the input words. This form permits lookahead over entire constituents, such as NPs, and greatly increases the power of the technique.

Related Work and Further Readings

Much of the literature on parsing preferences starts from the work by Kimball (1973), who suggested the principles of minimal attachment and right association. Interest in incorporating these principles into parsers has inspired work in new parsing strategies (Frazier and Fodor, 1978), as well as work incorporating the principles into existing formalisms such as ATNS (Wanner, 1980), shift-reduce parsers (Shieber, 1984; Pereira, 1985a), and more traditional CFG parsers (Schubert, 1986). Lexical preference principles were introduced by Ford, Bresnan, and Kaplan (1982).

As mentioned in the text, shift-reduce parsers have traditionally been used for parsing programming languages with unambiguous grammars. A good text discussing this work is Aho, Sethi, and Ullman (1986). These techniques have been generalized to handle ambiguity in natural language by various techniques. Shieber (1984) introduces the techniques, described in Section 6.3, which generalize the treatment of terminal symbols to delay lexical classification of words, and which use parsing preferences to select between rules when more than one rule appears to be applicable. Tomita (1986) reincorporates a full search with an optimized parse-tree representation while taking advantage of the speed of the oracle-driven shift-reduce parsing.

The use of lookahead in grammars for programming languages has been well studied. In fact, the shift-reduce parser can be extended to handle an arbitrary symbol lookahead at the cost of large amounts of space for the oracle (Aho, Sethi, and Ullman, 1986). More informal uses of lookahead have been incorporated into natural language parsers, such as in the RUS system (Bobrow and Webber, 1980), which uses an ATN-like grammar.

Lookahead in terms of constituents was popularized by the work of Marcus (1980). This work has been extended in several ways since its initial development. Milne (1986) examined a variety of techniques for dealing with lexical ambiguity, and Charniak (1983a) developed a variant where the parse states were automatically generated from a context-free grammar. Berwick (1985) used this framework in an investigation of language learning.

There are several good papers by psycholinguists investigating the psychological reality of various parsing mechanisms in Dowty et al. (1985).

Exercises for Chapter 6

1. *(easy)* Give a trace of the shift-reduce parser using the oracle in Figure 6.8 as it parses the sentence *The dog saw the bone.*

2. *(easy)* Given the rules in Figures 6.16 and 6.20 and the rule specified here for the Marcus parser, trace the parser in detail operating on the following sentence fragment, assuming the initial packet activated is SET-MOOD:

    Can NP be given

    Assume that the NP constituent was already constructed, so the preceding might be the initial input for a sentence such as *Can the rabbit be given a carrot?* The additional rule defines the packet PARSE-AUX:

    State PARSE-AUX:

    11. <true>   Create AUXS
                        Activate BUILD-AUX

3. *(medium)* List and define the three parsing strategies that the text says people use. Discuss how the following sentences are ambiguous and state which reading is preferred in the framework of these parsing strategies.

    a) It flew past the geese over the field.
    b) The artist paints the scene in the park.
    c) He feels the pain in his heart.

4. *(medium)* Consider the following sentences:

    The green can be distressing.
    The green can is distressing.
    The factory can can the tomatoes.

    a) Give an ATN grammar that can parse these sentences correctly.

    b) Specify lookahead tests on some of the nodes so that each of these sentences can now be parsed without using backtracking. Your lookahead tests should not be specific to individual words, such as *can*, *be*, and so on, but should be in terms of general categories and feature tests.

    c) Find a sentence that is parsable by your ATN but still requires backtracking.

5. *(medium)* Extend and modify the rules in Figures 6.16 and 6.20 so that the parser will accept and build reasonable structures for sentences in the following simple active and passive forms. You do not need to provide rules for the NP analyses and may assume they appear in the input fully processed.

> NP likes NP
> NP is liked by NP
> NP gave NP to NP
> NP was given to NP

6. *(medium)* Design a deterministic grammar that can successfully parse both

> I know that boy is   lazy.
> | | |
>   NP   VERB ADJ

and

> I know that boys are   lazy.
> | | | |
> | NP   VERB   ADJ
>   COMPLEMENTIZER

You may use as much of the grammar presented in this chapter as you wish. Trace the parser on each of these sentences in the style found in this chapter. Describe the important points of your analysis. Discuss how general your solution is in dealing with the various uses of the word *that*. Show at least one further example of a sentence involving *that* and outline how your grammar accounts for it (them).

7. *(hard)*

a) Construct the oracle for the following VP grammar involving to-infinitives and prepositions:

> VP ← VERB NP   PP ← PREP NP
> VP ← VERB INF   NP ← DET N
> VP ← VERB PP   NP ← NAME
> INF ← to VP

b) Can the oracle correctly analyze both the following VPs without resorting to guessing? Trace the parse for each sentence starting at the word *walked*.

> Jack walked to raise the money.
> Jack walked to the store.

c) Consider allowing word ambiguity in the grammar. In particular, the word *sand* can be either a noun or a verb. What does your parser do with the VPs

> Jack turned to sand.
> Jack turned to sand the board.

8. *(hard)*

a) Consider a depth-first, top-down parsing strategy for CFG that always tries the longest rules first. Trace the parser carefully, and find the first analysis produced using the following grammar on the sentence

> Jack hoped Mary hit the dog by the door.

1. S ← NP VP
2. NP ← NAME
3. NP ← ART NOUN
4. NP ← ART NOUN PP
5. VP ← VERB NP
6. VP ← VERB S
7. VP ← VERB NP PP
8. VP ← VERB S PP
9. PP ← PREP NP

b) What happens if you replace rules 7 and 8 with the more general rule:

10. VP ← VP PP

RVG algorithm

- initialize state reg.
  repeat
   look up next word - return categories
   find a production label in the table where
    label = a lexical prod. label
     condition vector matches state reg.
   perform actions
   change state reg. w/results
  until no more words and state regs match
    or No Match (failure). $^{Final\ Stat}$

Sem Roles

 INTR - intrinsic vector - property define lex.cal env
 FIGURE - head or object of prep.
 Grand - obj. of prep.
 Oblique - associated to ditransitive
  relation roles - frompos s, to pos s, to loc

PART II

SEMANTIC INTERPRETATION

Chapter 7

Semantics and a Logical Form

Deriving the syntactic structure of a sentence is just one step toward the goal of building a model of the language understanding process. As important as a sentence's structure is its meaning. While it is difficult to define precisely, sentence meaning allows you to conclude that the following two sentences are saying much the same thing:

I gave a contribution to the boy scouts.
The boy scouts received a donation from me.

Sentence meaning, coupled with general world knowledge, is also used in question answering. Thus, if it is asserted that *John drove to the store*, then the answer to the question *Did John get into a car?* is *yes*. To answer such a question, you need to know that the action described by the verb *driving* is an activity that must be done in a car.

As stated in the introduction, the approach taken here divides the problems of semantic interpretation into two stages. In the first stage the appropriate meaning of each word is determined, and these meanings are combined to form a **logical form** (LF). The logical form is then interpreted with respect to contextual knowledge, resulting in a set of conclusions that can be made from the sentence.

This chapter examines only the first of these issues. Sections 7.1 through 7.5 deal with word meanings and the way one word may constrain the interpretation of other words in a sentence. Section 7.6 then considers semantic networks, a representation for encoding word meanings and sentence meanings. The final section introduces the logical form to be used throughout the rest of the book.

7.1 Why Derive a Logical Form?

An intermediate semantic representation is desirable because it provides a natural division between two separate, but not totally independent, problems. The first problem concerns word sense and sentence ambiguity. Just as many words fall into multiple syntactic categories, each word within each syntactic class may have several different meanings, or **senses**. The verb *go*, for instance, has over 50 distinct meanings. Even though most words in a sentence have multiple senses, a combination of words in a phrase often has only a single sense, since the words mutually constrain each others' possible interpretations. Encoding and enforcing these constraints, which is a complex process worth study in its own right, is essentially the process of deriving the logical form.

The second problem involves using knowledge of the world and the present context to identify the particular consequences of a certain sentence. For instance, if you hear the sentence *The president has resigned*, you must use knowledge of the situation to identify who the president is (and what organization he or she heads) and to conclude that that person no longer holds that office. Depending on the circumstances, you might also infer other consequences, such as the need for a replacement president. In fact, the consequences of a given sentence could have far-reaching effects. Most attempts to formalize this process involve encoding final sentence meaning in some form of logic and modeling the derivation of consequences as a form of logical deduction.

The first process just described, which is known as word sense disambiguation, is not easily modeled as a deductive process. The components of meaning--word meanings, phrase meanings, and so on--often correspond at best to fragments of a logic, such as predicate names, types, and so on, over which deduction is not defined. For example, when analyzing the meaning of the following sentences, you might use the predicate BREAK to model the verb meaning.

1.   John broke the window with a hammer.
2.   The hammer broke the window.
3.   John broke the window.
4.   The window broke.

Furthermore, assume that BREAK takes three arguments: the breaker, the thing broken, and the instrument used for the breaking. To analyze these sentences, you must utilize information about the semantics of the NPs *John*, *the hammer*, and *the window*, together with the syntactic form of the sentence, to decide that the subject NP corresponds to the third argument in sentence 2, the first argument in sentences 1 and 3, and the second argument in sentence 4. It is not clear how this could be modeled as a deductive process.

The logical form is the intermediate representation between the syntactic form of the sentence and a logical representation of the sentence. It resembles a logic in many ways but has a syntax closer to that of syntactic structure. Any decisions that require contextual knowledge will not be made in deriving the logical form. Rather the information from the sentence structure is recorded in the logical form for use later by the contextual analyzer.

7.2 Types and Features

Before you can specify the meanings of words and sentences, you need some methods of expressing knowledge about the structure of the world. The most important aspect of this knowledge is the way that objects in the world are classified into groups by their properties. One of the most fundamental properties of any object is its **type**, which identifies what kind of object it is. For example, some objects can be classified as dogs and others as cats. More

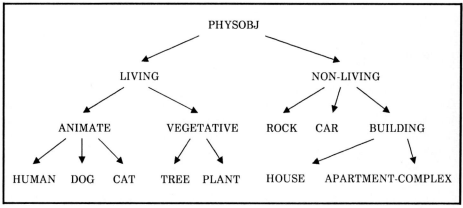

Figure 7.1 A type hierarchy of physical objects

generally, these same objects can be classified as examples of animals or living creatures.

You can construct **type hierarchies** describing the physical world, as shown in the simple example in Figure 7.1. Note a few things with this simple hierarchy. Some decompositions are exhaustive; for example, every physical object (PHYSOBJ) must be either living or nonliving. Similarly, every LIVING thing is either ANIMATE or VEGETATIVE. Others are not exhaustive; there are more classes of ANIMATE objects than HUMAN, CAT, and DOG.

An important issue concerns what a type may represent. For instance, you might want to distinguish between objects that can be carried by one person and objects that cannot. Clearly if you place no restriction on what can or cannot be a type, the type hierarchies will get extremely complicated, and you will lose the advantages of a conceptually simple mechanism. Also, given a new problem in semantic interpretation, you will tend to make up a new type that solves exactly that one problem in that sentence. To avoid these difficulties, only types that correspond to single English words will be allowed. Thus DOG is an acceptable type, whereas "carryable by one person" is not, since the closest you can get is something like "carryable," which is not specific to whether it is carryable by 1 person, 10 people, or a construction crane!

This definition, however, does not exclude a type such as KID, which includes baby goats and human children, which appear to be distinct classes. A few concrete linguistic tests have been suggested to define the notion of typehood. For example, certain constructs require references to identical classes of objects. The sentence *I have two kids, and George has three* could mean that George and I are goat farmers, or that we have children, but it can't mean a combination of both (I have goats and George has children). The same constraint applies to verb senses as well. Thus the sentence *I ran last year, and George did too* could mean that we both were candidates in an election, or that we both ran some race, but it cannot be a mixture of the two. Thus, if a proposed type corresponds to a word that fails these tests, the word is ambiguous and must be represented as having several senses--each one identified by a type.

By the preceding definition, any type that has subtypes may appear to be ambiguous, but this is not the case. For example, the type HORSE might be subdivided into MARE, COLT, TROTTER, and so on. Even so, it is perfectly acceptable to say *I have one horse and George has two*, even when I have a colt and George has mares. Thus HORSE is a reasonable type.

Other things besides physical objects may correspond to types. In fact, all verb senses will be identified as types as well. In these cases the types will be roughly divided into events and states. The class EVENT includes verb senses such as WALK, DONATE, FALL, SLEEP, and so on, while the class STATE involves verb senses such as BE (for example, be happy), BELIEVE, WANT, and OWN. These verb classes can be distinguished by certain linguistic tests. In particular, **stative verbs**, which describe states, cannot be freely used in the progressive aspect. For instance, you would not typically say the following:

> *I am believing that Jack caught a rabbit.
> *I am owning a car.

Nonstative verbs, which describe events, do take the progressive aspect readily but can be used only in the simple present if a repetitive activity is being described. For example, except in unusual circumstances, *I walk to the store* can mean only that I walk to the store regularly. An important subclass of events are those describing actions by agents--events caused (possibly intentionally) by some agent.

It is not hard to find examples to show that types cannot all be organized into a simple hierarchy. For instance, the word *pet* might correspond to a type PET, but it is not clear where this would fit into the hierarchy shown in Figure 7.1. For example, most dogs are pets, but some dogs, such as stray dogs and wild dogs, are not. Thus PET could not be put either above or below DOG in the hierarchy. In general, arbitrary relationships may hold between types: they may intersect (as do PET and DOG), or be disjoint (LIVING and NON-LIVING), or some types may be the intersection of other types. For instance, if you allow the types BABY and ADULT, then one sense of *kid* would be the intersection of BABY and HUMAN, while the other would be the intersection of BABY and GOAT. Designing a representation that explicitly maintains such information is possible but not necessary for the work that follows. What is important here is that some set of types exists and that large subsets of this set can be arranged hierarchically.

BOX 7.1 Early Type Hierarchies

The earliest formal classifications of objects arise in the writings of Aristotle (384-322 B.C.). He made the fundamental distinction that is maintained in logic: the difference between propositions (that are true or false) and functions (that denote some entity). The major classes that Aristotle suggested were substance (closest to our PHYSOBJ), quantity (such as numbers), quality (such as bright red), relation, place, time, position, state, action, and affection. In a modern account of language these classes would still be close to a complete enumeration of the topmost types in the type hierarchy. For a brief history of logic in ancient times, see Edwards (1967).

An example of a quite complex type that will be useful throughout is the type ORG, which includes any object capable of agency. Thus this type includes objects of type ANIMATE, objects of type LEGAL-ENTITY, such as companies, and objects of type AUTOMATA, such as vending machines.

Some large classes of abstract objects that have not been mentioned so far are also modeled as types. These abstractions, which include notions of COLOR, TIME, LOCATION, IDEAS, GROUPS, and so on, will be introduced freely as they are needed.

7.3 Selectional Restrictions

Besides classifying the different senses of words, you need to specify how words and phrases interact with other words and phrases to produce a semantic interpretation of the larger phrase. This will be the task of the semantic interpretation rules defined in the next chapter.

For the moment, consider the simpler task of trying to eliminate semantically anomalous word senses by considering how one word sense constrains the senses of the words near it. These restrictions, which are often called **selectional restrictions**, will be represented here as a set of patterns that are matched against syntactic structures.

For example, consider the adjective *green*. If *green* is used as an adjective, it must modify a physical object. *The green cow* is a well-formed NP, but *the green belief* is not. This restriction could be encoded in the lexical entry for *green* by extending it to maintain a set of patterns that describe constraints on the semantic types of phrases containing the word. For instance, the restriction might be expressed as the pattern

(NP **ADJS** (green)
    HEAD +physobj)

This pattern will match any structure that contains the word *green* in the list in the **ADJS** slot with a word that has a sense compatible with the type PHYSOBJ in the **HEAD** slot. More complex type restrictions are allowed in such patterns; in particular, the restriction *+physobj −animate* would allow any sense that is a PHYSOBJ but is not ANIMATE.

Another sense of *green* is "naive," as in *the green recruits*. This sense, which would also be listed in the lexicon, would have a different selectional restriction that forces the head noun to be a person, such as

(NP **ADJS** (green)
    HEAD +human))

A selectional restriction on a verb might restrict the type of the subject NP. To allow this, you need some mechanism to derive a type for constituents larger than single words. For the present, assume the type of a constituent to be the type of its head word (that is, the **HEAD** slot for NPs, the **PREP** slot for PPs, and the **MAIN-V** slot for S's). Using this mechanism, you can express as follows a selectional restriction on the verb *die* that its subject must be animate:

(S **SUBJ** +animate
    MAIN-V die)

This rule, together with the rule for *green*, would allow the sentence *The green sole died* to be analyzed and the appropriate word senses identified. In particular, the noun *sole* has an inanimate sense (the sole of a shoe) and an animate sense (the fish). The analysis of the NP *The green sole* would not distinguish between these senses, because both are physical objects. But the verb restriction would force the NP (and thus its **HEAD**) to be animate, and the fish sense is identified.

Not only adjectives and verbs have selectional restrictions; nouns and prepositions may have them as well. For example, the noun *president* would require the **POBJ** of a prepositional phrase modifier with preposition *of* to be of type +legal-entity. On the other hand, the preposition *in*, if used in its sense involving containment, requires its **POBJ** to be +physobj.

7.4 Case Relations

Significant generalizations can be made concerning how noun phrases are semantically related to the verbs and adjectives in a sentence. The most influential work for computational approaches has been **case grammar** and its successors and modifications. For present purposes, case grammar outlines the range of semantic roles, called **cases**, that a noun phrase may play with a verb or adjective. One of the most interesting claims of case grammar is that the number of possible semantic relationships is quite small, although there has been little agreement on what this small set consists of. The approach discussed here assumes that the set of possible semantic cases forms a well-defined hierarchy and that the number of immediate subcases for any case is limited to a small quantity. Given this framework, many of the different sets of cases proposed by different researchers can be explained by the fact that they base their semantic analysis at differing levels in the hierarchy.

Since the ultimate goal of this analysis is to extract the meaning of a sentence, the analysis of sentences with different meanings should lead to different results. Similarly, sentences with different syntactic structures but the same meaning should get mapped to similar structures. For example, consider the group of sentences:

> John broke the window with a hammer.
> The hammer broke the window.
> The window broke.

John, *the hammer*, and *the window* play the same semantic roles in each of these sentences. *John* is the actor, *the window* is the object, and *the hammer* is an instrument used in the act "breaking of the window."

To make this more precise, this section defines some particular cases that will be useful throughout the rest of the book. Perhaps the easiest to identify is the AGENT case. A noun phrase fills the AGENT case if it describes the instigator of the action described by the sentence. Furthermore, this case may attribute intention, violation, or responsibility for the action to the agent described. One test for AGENT-hood involves adding phrases like *intentionally* or *in order to* to active voice sentences. If the resulting sentence is well formed, the subject NP can fill the AGENT case. For example, the following sentences are acceptable

> John intentionally broke the window.
> John broke the window in order to let in some air.

but these are not

> *The hammer intentionally broke the window.
> *The window broke in order to let in some air.

Thus the NP *John* fills the AGENT case in the first two preceding sentences.

Not all animate NPs, even in the subject position, fill the AGENT case. For instance, you cannot normally say

*John intentionally died.
*Mary remembered her birthday in order to get some presents.

Of course, by adding the phrase *intentionally* in these sentences, you may construct some plausible reading of the sentences (*John killed himself*), but this is a result of modifying the initial meaning of the sentence *John died*.

NPs that describe something undergoing some change or being acted upon will fill a new case called THEME. This usually corresponds to the syntactic OBJECT and, for any transitive verb X, is the answer to the question "What was Xed?" For example, given the sentence *The grey eagle saw the mouse*, the NP *the mouse* is the THEME and is the answer to the question "What was seen?" For intransitive verbs, the THEME case is used for the subject NPs that are not AGENTs. Thus in *The clouds appeared over the horizon*, the NP *the clouds* fills the THEME case. More examples follow, with the THEME NP underlined.

> The rock broke.
> John broke the rock.
> I gave John the book.

The next three cases (AT, TO, and FROM) have to do with descriptions of states of objects and changes of state. Consider these first using the concrete example of location. You can assert the location of some object or activity using prepositional phrases, as in

> Harry walked along the road.
> We stayed by the door.

Here is a case of describing where the walking took place and where we stayed. These all will be taken as filling the AT-LOC (or LOCATION) case.

Other sentences describe a change in location, such as

> I walked from here to school yesterday.
> It fell to the ground.
> The birds flew from the lake along the river gorge.

The PPs that describe where something came from fill the FROM-LOC (or SOURCE) case, while those that describe where something went fill the TO-LOC (or DESTINATION) case. A sentence may also contain all three of these location cases, as in

> They drove from the farm to the lake on route 71.

These three location cases can be generalized into cases over arbitrary state values, called the AT case, and cases for arbitrary state change (the FROM and

TO cases). Thus, AT-LOC is a specialization of the AT case, FROM-LOC a specialization of the FROM case, and TO-LOC a specialization of the TO case. You can see other specializations of these cases when you consider possession, as in

I threw the ball <u>to John</u>.	(the TO-LOC case)
I gave a book <u>to John</u>.	(the TO-POSS case)
I caught the ball <u>from John</u>.	(the FROM-LOC case)
I borrowed a book <u>from John</u>.	(the FROM-POSS case)
<u>The box</u> contains a ball.	(the AT-LOC case)
<u>John</u> owns a book.	(the AT-POSS case)

Similarly, you might define AT-TIME, TO-TIME, and FROM-TIME cases, as well as general state and state change cases, as with temperature in

The temperature remains <u>at zero</u>.	(AT-VALUE)
The temperature rose <u>from zero</u>.	(FROM-VALUE)

Thus the notion of general value and change of value along many dimensions seems to be supported by the similarity of the ways of realizing these cases in sentences.

Given the present taxonomy, you cannot easily classify the NP case in a sentence such as

<u>John</u> believed that it was raining.

The THEME case is filled with the clause *that it was raining*, since this is what is believed. *John* cannot be an AGENT here because there is no intentionality in believing something. Thus you must introduce a new case, called EXPERIENCER, which is filled by animate objects that are in a described psychological state, or that undergo some psychological process such as perception, as in the preceding sentence and as in

<u>John</u> saw the unicorn.

Another case that has not been explored is the BENEFICIARY case, which is filled by the animate person for whom a certain event is performed, as in

I rolled on the floor <u>for Lucy</u>.
Find <u>me</u> the papers!
I gave the book to Jack <u>for Susan</u>.

The last example demonstrates the need to distinguish the TO-POSS case (that is, *to Jack*) from the BENEFICIARY case.

The INSTRUMENT case describes a tool, material, or force used to perform some event.

Jack saw the ship <u>with the telescope</u>.
Jack used <u>the telescope</u> to see the ship.
Harry broke the glass <u>with the telescope</u>.
<u>The telescope</u> broke the glass.
I used <u>some flour</u> to make a cake.
I made a cake <u>with some flour</u>.

Depending on the verb, the INSTRUMENT case sometimes can be used as the surface subject when the AGENT case is not specified. Natural forces will also be included in the INSTRUMENT category here, although you could argue for a different analysis. Thus the following are also examples of the INSTRUMENT case:

<u>The sun</u> dried the apples.
Jack used <u>the sun</u> to dry the apples.

The AGENT and INSTRUMENT cases could be combined into a more general case named CAUSAL-AGENT.

Other cases need to be identified before certain sentences can be analyzed. For example, some sentences describe situations where two people perform an act together, as in

Henry lifted the piano with Jack.

To handle such sentences, you must introduce a case CO-AGENT to account for the PP *with Jack*.

A more complicated case occurs in sentences involving exchanges or other complex interactions. For example, consider the sentences

Jack paid $1 to the man for the book.
Jack bought the book from the man for $1.

These sentences both describe a situation where Jack gives the man $1 and receives the book in exchange. In the first sentence, however, the *$1* is the THEME and there is no case to account for *the book*. In the second sentence the situation is reversed: *the book* is the THEME and *$1* is unaccounted for. To handle these cases you must add a case CO-THEME for the second object in an exchange.

A more general solution to this problem would be to analyze such sentences as describing two events. The **primary event** is the one you have been considering so far, but a **secondary event** may be present. In this analysis you might analyze the first sentence as follows (the primary event being Jack paying the dollar, and the secondary being Jack receiving the book):

Case	Sub-Cases	Common Names	Definition
CAUSAL-AGENT			-- the object that caused the event to happen
	AGENT		-- intentional causation
	INSTRUMENT		-- force or tool used in causing the event
THEME			-- the thing that was affected by the event; with a transitive verb X, it is the thing in answer to the question "What was Xed?"
EXPERIENCER			-- the person who is involved in perception or in a psycho-logical state
BENEFICIARY			-- the person for whom some act is done
AT			-- the state/value on some dimension where the event occurred
	AT-LOC	LOCATION	
	AT-POSS	POSSESSOR	
	AT-VALUE		
TO			-- final value in a state change
	TO-LOC	DESTINATION	-- final location
	TO-POSS	RECIPIENT	-- final possessor
	TO-VALUE		-- final temperature
FROM			-- original value in a state change
	FROM-LOC	SOURCE	-- original location
	FROM-POSS		-- original possessor
	FROM-VALUE		-- original temperature
CO-AGENT			-- a secondary agent in an action
CO-THEME			-- a secondary theme in an exchange

Figure 7.2 Some possible semantic roles

Jack	-	AGENT of both PRIMARY and SECONDARY event
$1	-	THEME of PRIMARY event
the man	-	TO-POSS of PRIMARY, FROM-POSS of SECONDARY
the book	-	THEME of SECONDARY event

This possibility will not be pursued further at the present time, however, since it leads into many issues not relevant to the remainder of this chapter.

Figure 7.2 provides a summary of most of the cases distinguished thus far and the hierarchical relationships between them.

7.5 The Structure of Verbs

As you've seen, verbs can be classified by the semantic cases that they require.
To classify them precisely, however, you must make a distinction between those
cases that are "intimately" related to the verb and those that are not. For
example, almost any past tense verb allows an AT-TIME case realized by the
adverb *yesterday*. Thus this case is apparently more a property of verb phrases
in general than a property of any individual verb. However, other
cases--namely, those realized by constituents for which the verb
subcategorizes--seem to be properties of the verb. For example, the verb *put*
subcategorizes for a PP, and, furthermore, this PP must realize the TO-LOC
semantic case. In verb classification this latter type of case is important, and
these cases are called the **inner cases** of the verb.

The preceding examples suggest one test for determining whether a given
case is an inner case for a given verb: if the case is obligatory, it is an inner case.
Other inner cases, however, appear to be optional, so other tests are also needed.

Another test is based on the observation that all verbs may take at most one
NP in any given inner case. If multiple NPs are needed, they must be related by
a conjunction. Thus you can say

> John and I ran to the store.

but not

> *John I ran to the store.

Similarly, you can say

> I ran to the store and to the bank.

but not

> *I ran to the store to the bank.

Thus the AGENT and TO-LOC cases for the verb *run* are inner cases. Contrast
this with the sentence

> I saw the play in Rochester at the Eastman Theater.

where two AT-LOC cases are used acceptably.

Verbs typically specify up to three inner cases, at least one of which must
always be realized in any sentence using the verb. Sometimes a particular case
must always be present (for example, TO-LOC with *put*). Typically, the THEME
case is also obligatory as well, whereas the AGENT case is always optional for

Case	Realization
AGENT	-- as SUBJECT in active sentences -- preposition *by* in passive sentences
INSTRUMENT	-- as SUBJECT in active sentences with no AGENT -- preposition *with*
EXPERIENCER	-- as SUBJECT in active sentences with no AGENT
BENEFICIARY	-- as IOBJ with transitive verbs -- preposition *for*
AT-LOC	-- prepositions *in, on, beyond*, etc.
AT-POSS	-- possessive NP -- SUBJECT of sentence if no AGENT
TO-LOC	-- prepositions *to, into*
TO-POSS	-- preposition *to*, IOBJ with certain verbs
FROM-LOC	-- prepositions *from, out of*, etc.
FROM-POSS	-- preposition *from*

Figure 7.3 Common realizations of the major cases

any verb that allows the passive form. The details of how to encode all these constraints for particular verbs will be considered in the next chapter.

There are syntactic restrictions on how various cases can be realized as well. Figure 7.3 shows a sample of ways in which cases can be realized in different sentences.

The following are some sample sentences with each NP, PP, and embedded S classified by its case in order of occurrence.

Jack ran.	AGENT only
Jack ran with a crutch.	AGENT + INSTRUMENT
Jack ran with a crutch for Susan.	AGENT + INSTRUMENT + BENEFICIARY
Jack destroyed the car.	AGENT + THEME
Jack put the car through the wall.	AGENT + THEME + TO-LOC
Jack sold Henry the car.	AGENT + TO-POSS + THEME
Henry pushed the car from Jack's house to the junkyard.	AGENT + THEME + FROM-LOC + TO-LOC

BOX 7.2 Case Grammar and Thematic Roles

Most work in case grammar originates from work described by Fillmore (1968), who introduced six cases. Three of these correspond directly to cases discussed here already: Fillmore's AGENTIVE is the AGENT case; his INSTRUMENTAL is the INSTRUMENT, and his OBJECTIVE is the THEME. Other cases he introduced are the DATIVE case, which covers the EXPERIENCER case and some parts of the TO and FROM cases that involve animate objects (TO-POSS, FROM-POSS); the FACTITIVE case, which covers part of the THEME case when it is the result of an action being described, and is considered to be part of the verb; and the LOCATIVE case, which includes the AT-LOC, TO-LOC, and FROM-LOC cases. In Fillmore's formulation each NP must fill exactly one case (that is, it can't fill two simultaneously).

An alternate approach is by Gruber (see discussion in Jackendoff (1972)), who actually allows an NP to fill multiple cases simultaneously. His cases, which he calls **thematic relations**, include AGENT and THEME, more or less as defined in this chapter, as well as relations corresponding to the abstract cases AT (called LOCATION by Gruber), TO (called GOAL), and FROM (called SOURCE). In a sentence such as *The boy rolled over the hill*, the subject NP would simultaneously fill the case of AGENT (as the actor intentionally causing the act) and the case of THEME (as the object undergoing the rolling).

Jack is tall.	THEME
Henry believes that Jack is tall.	EXPERIENCER + THEME
Susan owns a car.	AT-POSS + THEME
I am in the closet.	THEME + AT-LOC
The ice melted.	THEME
Jack enjoyed the play.	EXPERIENCER + THEME
The ball rolled down the hill to the water.	THEME + AT-LOC + TO-LOC

7.6 Semantic Networks

The term **semantic networks** is used for many different representations and for many different purposes. The formalism is introduced here as a means to represent the semantic information discussed so far in this chapter--namely, to represent word senses and the selectional restrictions between senses, especially

BOX 7.3 Subcategorization, Inner Cases, and Syntactic Structure

In most linguistic theories the subcategorization information for verbs actually determines what constituents appear as subconstituents of the verb phrase and what constituents are outside the verb phrase. You can see this by comparing the syntactic trees for the sentences *I put the box in the corner* and *I saw the box from the roof*, as shown here.

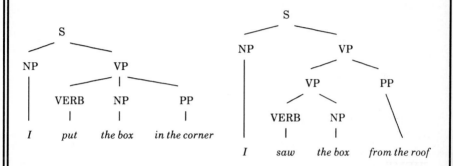

If you assume a compositional semantics, it makes sense that the inner cases are best specified by the main verb since they are parts of the same VP. The outer cases, however, are realized by PPs outside of the VP containing the verb and are best analyzed in terms of the preposition.

those based on case relations. First the notation is defined for expressing general information, and then it is extended to represent specific sentences.

Representing General Information about Word Senses

A semantic network is a graph structure with labeled links between labeled nodes. The nodes represent word senses, and the links represent semantic relationships between the senses. For example, a type hierarchy is easily defined in a semantic network using a link labeled "s" to represent the subtype relationship. Figure 7.4 defines a fragment of a type hierarchy including a division into physical objects and abstract objects.

The case frame information can also be stored in a network form using arcs. Thus you might say that all actions have an agent case filled by an animate object using the network in Figure 7.5. Introduced here is a new node type, called an **existential node** and depicted by a square, which represents a case value. In this case the agent case is restricted to be an object of type ANIMATE. Many such representations allow other information to be stored about case

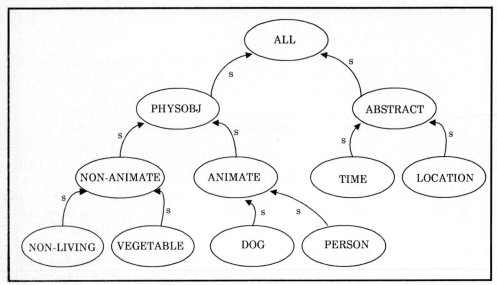

Figure 7.4 Part of a type hierarchy

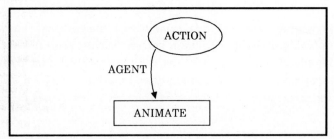

Figure 7.5 All actions have an animate agent

values as well, such as whether they are obligatory or not, and whether they represent a single filler or a group of fillers.

A formal semantics can be given to the semantic network fragments presented so far by mapping each structure to an equivalent axiom in FOPC. For instance, type nodes can be mapped to unary predicates, and then the subtype link between two nodes--say, ANIMATE and PHYSOBJ--would be equivalent to the assertion that all animate objects are physical objects. That is,

$$\forall x . ANIMATE(x) \supset PHYSOBJ(x)$$

Similarly, case value nodes can be mapped to existentially quantified variables and case links to binary predicates. For example, the network in Figure 7.5 might map to an assertion that all actions have animate agents and that all agents of actions are animate:

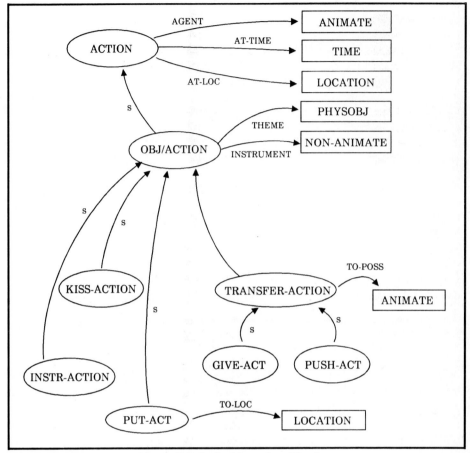

Figure 7.6 Action hierarchy with roles

$$\forall x \ . \ ACTION(x) \supset \exists \ a \ . \ AGENT(x, a) \ \& \ ANIMATE(a)$$
$$\forall a, x \ . \ ACTION(x) \ \& \ AGENT(x, a) \supset ANIMATE(a)$$

Given this semantics, you can define an operation called **inheritance**, where a subtype inherits all the properties of its supertype. With the mappings to FOPC, this simple form of inheritance can be seen to be a specialized form of logical implication. Figure 7.6 summarizes the case information for a set of verb senses that are all subclasses of actions. Using the inheritance mechanism, you can see the action class TRANSFER-ACTION allows the cases AGENT, AT-TIME, and AT-LOC, inherited from the class ACTION; the cases THEME and INSTRUMENT, inherited from the class OBJ/ACTION; and the case TO-POSS, which is explicitly defined for TRANSFER-ACTION. Note that this representation is attempting to define all the allowable cases, not just the inner ones. Verb specific information of this sort will be examined in the next chapter.

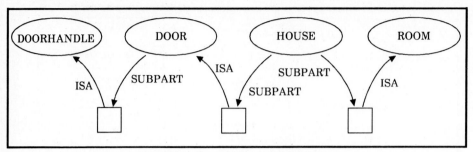

Figure 7.7 Some subpart relationships

Semantic networks are also used to represent other forms of general knowledge about the structure of the world besides type hierarchies. Another important hierarchy is the **part-of** hierarchy, in which objects are related to their subparts. To exploit the similarity between subparts and cases, you can encode the subparts using the "existential" square nodes that were used with cases. This example, however, expresses the type information for the existential node using a new link **ISA**. This is equivalent to the notation where the type is enclosed in the box, and the two notations will be used interchangeably. Thus you can represent that a house has rooms and doors as subparts, and that doors have handles, as in Figure 7.7.

A complete representation system would need to be able to indicate whether a subpart is a unique object (the handle on a door) or a set of objects (the rooms in a house). In addition, it would need to be able to represent the spatial and other relationships that would hold between subparts. For instance, if a person's body has the subparts head, body, arms, and legs, then you need to represent that the head is unique and is connected to the body, that there are two arms connected to the body, and so on. All this would be part of the subpart classification of BODY. Further details on these issues, though, would lead this book too far afield into knowledge representation.

Representing Sentence Meanings: Tokens

The semantic network formalism developed so far suggests a way of representing the meaning of particular sentences--namely, allowing networks of a structure similar to the earlier ones but specific to particular instances rather than types. A new class of nodes, called **tokens**, are introduced to represent particular objects and particular actions. For example, a representation of the content of the sentence *Jack kissed Jill* is shown in Figure 7.8. Paraphrasing this network, it says there is a KISS-ACTION, s1, that has an AGENT case filled with j1, a person, and a THEME case filled with j2, a person. Furthermore, j1 is named by "Jack" and j2 is named by "Jill." Networks can be used to

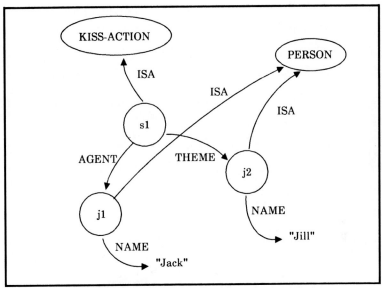

Figure 7.8 A semantic network for *Jack kissed Jill.*

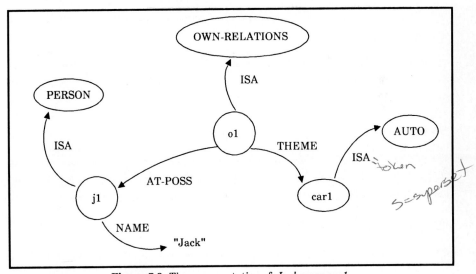

Figure 7.9 The representation of *Jack owns car1*

represent sentences describing states as well. Figure 7.9 shows a representation of the fact that Jack owns a particular car (here represented by node **car1**).

Many semantic network formalisms have offered only a limited ability to represent quantified formulas and formulas involving disjunction and negation. This limitation, however, is not inherent in the formalism itself, and several modern semantic network representations offer a representational power greater than or equal to FOPC. However, since many of these details are not crucial to the points in this course, only a minimal system has been described here.

7.7 The Logical Form

The semantic network in the last section can be used as a starting point for deriving a logical form. It does not quite meet the criteria set for the LF at the beginning of the section, however, because context would be needed to map noun phrases into the nodes that represent the object to which they refer. In addition, the token network as defined had no ability to represent quantified noun phrases such as *Every boy owned a dog*. The representation based on the cases is attractive, however, and will be adopted in the new LF. In particular, the network seen earlier as Figure 7.8 would correspond to an LF such as:

> (PAST s1 KISS-ACTION (AGENT s1 (NAME j1 PERSON "Jack"))
> (THEME s1 (NAME j2 PERSON "Jill")))

Each LF statement is made up of the following components:

-- an **operator** indicating the type of structure; here PAST means that this represents an assertion of some event occurring in the past;

-- a **name** for the object being described--in this case the instance of KISS-ACTION called s1;

-- the **type** of the object--that is, KISS-ACTION;

-- the **modifiers** of the object, which may be a list of LF structures; in this case the modifiers consist of two cases, AGENT and THEME.

Other operators for sentence structures will include PRES (simple present tense), FUT (simple future), and INF (for infinitive clauses).

The Logical Form of NPs

This language is extended to represent noun phrases as follows. The operator for simple noun phrases will be used to indicate the determiner information so that it can be used by later processing. The possible combinations for unquantified NPs are then

DEF/SING	-	definite singular reference (*the boy*)
DEF/PL	-	definite plural reference (*the boys*)
INDEF/SING	-	indefinite singular reference (*a boy*)
INDEF/PL	-	indefinite plural reference (*boys*)

BOX 7.4 Representing Assertions about Actions

There are two distinct ways of representing assertions of actions. The method taught informally in introductory logic courses usually involves introducing a predicate that is defined to be true whenever the action occurs. That is, the predicate

$HIT(a, b, t)$

would be true whenever agent a hit agent b at time t. The representation implicit in the encoding in semantic networks is quite different, however. The same situation, if mapped to FOPC, would be described in the following way:

$$\exists h \,.\, HIT\text{-}EVENT(h) \,\&\, AGENT(h, a) \,\&\, THEME(h, b)$$
$$\&\, AT\text{-}TIME(h, t)$$

As first pointed out by Davidson (1967), there are several advantages to the latter representation. In particular, additional qualifiers can be represented easily. For instance, the situation where a hit b slowly with a wrench w would be represented as just shown but with the additional qualifications:

$$\dots \,\&\, INSTRUMENT(h, w) \,\&\, SLOW(h) \,\&\, ISA(w, WRENCH)$$

With the first style of representation you would have had to add extra argument positions to the predicate for every possible modifier. Since there seems to be no limit to the number of ways a situation could be qualified, the technique of adding arguments would rapidly become impractical.

The name and type for simple NPs will be as expected, and the modifiers will consist of any qualifications produced by adjectives or other modifying phrases. Thus the LF for the NP *The large boy* would be

(DEF/SING **b1** BOY (LARGE **b1**))

The quantified NPs map to similar structures using different markers as appropriate. Thus the sentence *Each boy ate a large pizza* would be represented as

BOX 7.5 Conceptual Dependency

One influential semantic-network-based representation is **conceptual dependency** (CD) (Schank, 1973; Schank and Riesbeck, 1981). This theory posits not only a limited number of cases but also a limited number of action types. These action types are called **primitives**, since many other action verbs are reduced to combinations of the primitive types. This technique of reduction to a set of primitives will be examined in more detail in Chapter 12.

CD has three primitives based on the abstract notion of transfer: ATRANS, abstract transfer (such as of possession of an object); PTRANS, physical transfer; and MTRANS, mental transfer (such as talking). It also includes primitive actions of bodily activity such as PROPEL (apply force), MOVE (move a body part), GRASP, INGEST, and EXPEL, as well as a few mental actions such as CONC (conceptualize or think) and MBUILD (perform inference). The cases include ACTOR (AGENT plus some uses of the THEME case), OBJECTIVE (mostly THEME), and two complex cases that include two parts related to the TO and FROM cases. The RECIPIENT case combines the TO-POSS and FROM-POSS cases, while the DIRECTIVE combines the TO-LOC and FROM-LOC cases.

Primitive acts are linked together by temporal connectives and, most importantly, by the INSTRUMENTAL relation. Most action verbs decompose into a group of primitive acts related by instrumentality. For example, using the notation of semantic networks, you would represent the sentence *John threw a rock at Sam* as the following, which could be paraphrased as *John physically transferred a rock from himself to Sam by propelling it.*

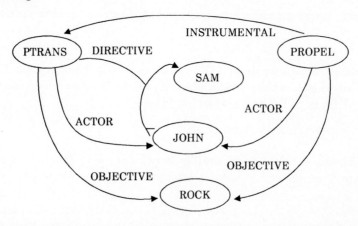

```
(PAST a1 EAT-EVENT
    (AGENT a1 (EACH b2 BOY))
    (THEME p1 (INDEF/SING p1 PIZZA (LARGE p1))))
```

For wh-questions, the wh-terms need a special marker in the LF. You can use three forms--WH, WH/PL, and WH/SING--depending on whether the number is unspecified, plural, or singular, respectively. For example, the NP *who* has the LF

```
(WH p1 PERSON)
```

whereas the NP *which dogs* has the LF

```
(WH/PL d1 DOG)
```

Two special forms are used for NPs that consist of proper names and pronouns. You've already seen the first form--the operator NAME identifies an NP consisting of a proper name, and the name is listed in the position directly after the type. Modifiers can be added if needed. For instance, the NP *Big bad John* might map to

```
(NAME j3 PERSON "John" (BIG j3) (BAD j3))
```

For pronouns a similar form with the marker PRO is defined. Thus the NP *he* is represented as

```
(PRO h1 MALE "he")
```

The logical form for NPs that describe events is virtually identical to the representation of event sentences, except that the marker will indicate a determiner rather than a tense marker. For example, the NP *The arrival of George at the station* would be represented as

```
(DEF/SING a1 ARRIVE-EVENT
    (AGENT a1 (NAME g1 PERSON "George"))
    (TO-LOC a1 (DEF s4 STATION)))
```

whereas the sentence *George arrived at the station* would be represented by the logical form:

```
(PAST a2 ARRIVE-EVENT
    (AGENT a2 (NAME g1 PERSON "George"))
    (TO-LOC a2 (DEF s6 STATION)))
```

For the restrictions on events that are inner case specifications, you can drop the relation form and use an abbreviation using square brackets. With this, the logical form of the S *George arrived at the station* would be rewritten as

(PAST **a2** ARRIVE-EVENT [AGENT (NAME **g1** PERSON "George")]
                         [TO-LOC (DEF **s6** STATION)])

If simple ambiguities are present in a logical form, they can be represented by listing the alternatives in curly brackets. For example, the NP *the ball* is ambiguous between the round sphere and the social dance. This could be represented by one form with the ambiguity indicated as follows:

(DEF/SING **b1** {SPHERE, DANCE})

The Logical Form of Sentences

A few details remain in dealing with sentences. In particular, nothing in the LF so far distinguishes between declarative, imperative, or interrogative sentences, and nothing has been said about embedded sentences and compound sentences.

Each of the four major sentence types has a corresponding logical form that takes the sentence interpretation as an argument. These are as follows. For declarative sentences, such as *The man ate a peach*, the complete LF is

(ASSERT (PAST **e1** EAT [AGENT (DEF/SING **m1** MAN)]
                        [THEME (INDEF/SING **p1** PEACH)]))

For yes-no questions, such as *Did the man eat a peach?*, the LF is

(Y/N-QUERY (PAST **e1** EAT [AGENT (DEF/SING **m1** MAN)]
                           [THEME (INDEF/SING **p1** PEACH)]))

For wh-questions, such as *What did the man eat?*, the LF is

(WH-QUERY **w1** (PAST **e1** EAT [AGENT (DEF/SING **m1** MAN)]
                                 [THEME (WH **w1** PHYSOBJ)]))

Finally, for commands, such as *Eat the peach*, the LF is

(COMMAND (INF **e1** EAT [THEME (DEF/SING **p1** PEACH)]))

Embedded sentences, such as relative clauses, can be handled in the same way as other sentences. Any pointers in an embedded structure are analyzed simply by inserting the name of the structure built for the constituent that is referenced. Thus the sentence *I want to leave*, with the syntactic form

(S **SUBJ** (NP$_1$ **PRO** I)
   MAIN-V want
   TENSE pres
   COMP (S **SUBJ** →NP$_1$
             MAIN-V leave))

> **BOX 7.6 Scope Ambiguities and the Logical Form**
>
> The logical form encodes quantifier information within the representation of the NP, as opposed to outside the predicate structure as is traditional in FOPC. As a result, the current LF cannot represent scoping distinctions. For example, the sentence *A large boy ate each pizza* is ambiguous between the interpretation where there is one boy, and the interpretation where there is one boy per pizza. These interpretations could be represented in FOPC by the following two formulas:
>
> $\forall x . PIZZA(x) \supset \exists b . LARGE(b) \& BOY(b) ATE(b, x)$
> $\exists b . BOY(b) \& LARGE (b) \& \forall x . PIZZA(x) \supset ATE(b, x)$
>
> The LF cannot make this distinction. In fact, that is desirable, because the selection of the appropriate reading depends on context. Thus this sentence has a single LF that does not commit to either one of these interpretations--namely:
>
> (PAST e1 EAT-EVENT [AGENT
>   (INDEF/SING b1 BOY (LARGE b1))]
>   [THEME (EACH p1 PIZZA)])
>
> Quantifier scoping will discussed in Chapter 9.

has an LF of

(ASSERT (PRES **w1** WANT [EXPERIENCER (PRO i1 PERSON "I")]
                         [THEME (INF l1 LEAVE [AGENT i1])])))

The final issue--namely, dealing with compound sentences--leads to many complex issues that will be considered later. When needed, sentence operators such as conjunction (*and, or, but*) will be introduced in a fairly ad hoc way. For example, the sentence *I wanted to leave but I lost the keys* would have the LF

(ASSERT (BUT (PAST **w1** WANT [EXPERIENCER
                         (PRO i1 PERSON "I")]
                     [THEME (INF l1 LEAVE
                         [AGENT i1])])
          (PAST l1 LOSE [AGENT (PRO i2 PERSON "I")]
                         [THEME (DEF/PL k1 KEY)])))

Summary

A semantic theory has a number of basic building blocks. For instance, the notion of type can be used to represent word senses; selectional restrictions and case grammar indicate interword constraints. Semantic networks are a mechanism for defining this information. This representation allows the definition of type hierarchies, type restrictions on case values, and general information on part-whole relationships. Using a generalization of the semantic network formalism to particular instances, or tokens, as motivation, you can define a logical form language to represent the context-independent meaning of a sentence.

Related Work and Further Readings

The issues of semantics are studied in many disciplines, and the work described here is based on work originally done in philosophy and linguistics. For general references into the area, see Fodor (1977) and Lyons (1977). The idea of selectional restrictions and semantic features on words was first formalized by Katz and Foder (1963; 1984). Variations on selectional restrictions have been used in virtually every computational theory as one of the key ways of reducing potential ambiguity.

The form of case grammar discussed here is a descendant of the work by Fillmore (1968; 1977), with influences from Gruber (1967), Jackendoff (1972), and Schank (Schank and Riesbeck, 1981). The idea of cases has been incorporated into many AI representations used for natural language analysis, such as semantic networks (see Bruce (1975a) for a survey of early work). Since frame-based systems use a slot-value type of representation, there has been some speculation that the slots in frame systems and the cases in case grammar could be one and the same thing. This issue is discussed by Charniak (1981). In practice, some frame-based representations stay quite close to a case grammar representation, while others bear almost no relation to them.

Semantic networks for natural language were introduced by Quillian (1968) as a means of representing word meanings and the associations between words. While this work produced a considerable amount of work in network representations, it was not until Woods (1975) that there was a significant attempt at formally defining the semantics of the representation. A good example of a recent semantic network system is found in Sowa (1984). An excellent collection of work in knowledge representation is an edited volume by Brachman and Levesque (1985).

The need for an intermediate representation between syntax and the final meaning has been recognized for quite some time, most often in the context of dealing with quantifier scoping. Several theories (Woods, 1978; Cooper, 1983) have used a two-part representation of logical form: one part for the predicate-argument structure and the other for the quantifier information. The logical form developed here, which is equivalent to these two-part representations, has the advantage of retaining the information in one uniform notation by allowing the unscoped quantifiers. Similar approaches to this can be found in Schubert and Pelletier (1982) and in Hobbs and Shieber (1987). McCord (1985) examines the relationship between scoping and logical form in depth.

Exercises for Chapter 7

1. (*easy*) Identify the cases of each NP and PP in the following sentences using the definitions outlined in the notes. Where there is some ambiguity about the interpretation, discuss the possibilities and justify your answer.

   The wind tore the sheet from the clothesline.
   Jack left the money for his mother.
   Jack left his wife for another woman.
   The river ran through the forest, over some rocks, and disappeared
       into a gorge.
   We reached the summit within an hour.

2. (*easy*) Give examples (not in the chapter) of the use of the TO case, both as an inner case and as an outer case.

3. (*easy*) Specify a plausible logical form for the following sentences:

   We returned the ring to the store.
   We returned to the party.
   We found the large dog in the corner.
   The boys leaving the house locked the door.
   The owner of each car on the street received a ticket.

4. (*medium*) Define a data structure to represent simple type networks with case value restrictions. Write a program that, given such a hierarchy, computes the complete set of case value restrictions for any given type in the hierarchy. Test this on the network shown in Figure 7.6 and retrieve the case value restrictions for PUT-ACT.

5. (*medium*) One technique for assigning cases to various phrases in sentences is to consider syntactic variants of the sentence as well. Since the case assignment is based on the semantic relation between a phrase and the verb, the case assignments should not change. For example, consider the following sentence:

   The box contains a ball.

What case should be assigned to *the box*? The semantic relationship here is the same as in the sentence

> A ball is contained in the box.

In this sentence *in the box* would presumably be best analyzed as the AT-LOC case, with *the ball* as the THEME. Thus in the first sentence *the box* also should be analyzed as the AT-LOC case.

Identify a plausible assignment of cases to the NPs and PPs in the following sentences, justifying your decisions for each case on semantic grounds, or by considering syntactic variants. If the sentence is ambiguous, analyze each possibility.

> I gave John the book.
> I found John the book.
> I showed John the book.
> John owns the book.
> John sold the book.
> John remembered the book.

6. (*medium*) For each of the following sentences, give their syntactic forms and their logical forms. If sentences are ambiguous, handle each distinct interpretation separately if necessary. If there are difficulties in representing the sentence at some level, discuss the problems and describe your approximation to a solution.

> Every boy loves a dog.
> One of the boys wearing a hat dropped a brown bag.
> We saw the ship on the rocks.

7. (*medium*) Implement a system that maintains a type hierarchy and allows you to test whether two types are compatible. In particular your system should allow type information to be added with the following function:

> (Add-Subtype T1 T2) - asserts that T1 is a proper subtype of T2

This information can then be used in the function

> (Test-Intersection T1 T2)

which returns nil if the two types are not known to intersect, and the name of the intersection if the types do intersect. In particular, if T1 is a subtype of T2, then T1 would be returned; if T3 is a subtype of both T1 and T2, then T3 is assumed to be the intersection and T3 is returned. Document your data structures and demonstrate the range of i/o that your system can handle.

Canonical form — define meaning of lex entry

maprelation — handles predicate to predicate relations
map into canonical forms

Chapter 8

Semantic Interpretation

This chapter specifies a method of using the semantic information described in the preceding chapter to generate a logical form. This particular interpreter is completely separate from the syntactic processing--that is, it takes complete syntactic descriptions as its input. More flexible and interactive organizations using these same basic techniques will be considered in detail in Chapter 9.

8.1 The Basic Operations for Semantic Interpretation

Semantic interpretation is accomplished by the application of interpretation rules that consist of a pattern in the format of the selectional restrictions introduced in Chapter 7 and a specification of a partial logical form to be constructed. These partial logical forms will be called **partial descriptions** (or PDs). The PDs are constructed using the following functions:

*   - signifies a new unique name to represent the object described by the logical form

$T(slotname)$ - returns the semantic type of the constituent in the indicated slot

$V(slotname)$ - returns the entire semantic interpretation of the constituent in the indicated slot

For example, the semantic interpretation rules for the adjective *green* might be as shown in Figure 8.1.

Rule (green.1) matches any NP with an **ADJS** slot containing the word *green* and a **HEAD** slot that has a semantic type of PHYSOBJ; this rule produces a partial logical form consisting of an unspecified marker, a new name, the semantic type of the constituent in the **HEAD** slot, and a modifier (*COLOR* * *GR137*) (*GR137* is assumed to be the constant used to represent the color of green). In any particular circumstance where the rule is used, a unique name is created for the constituent being interpreted and is used to replace all the occurrences of "*". For example, given the NP

        (NP DET a
             ADJ (green)
             HEAD apple)

rule (green.1) would produce the PD

        (? c1 APPLE (COLOR c1 GR137)

whereas rule (green.2) would produce the PD

        (? c1 APPLE (UNRIPE c1))

(green.1)	(NP **ADJS** (green) **HEAD** + physobj)	→	(? * T(**HEAD**) (COLOR * GR137))
(green.2)	(NP **ADJS** (green) **HEAD** + fruit)	→	(? * T(**HEAD**) (UNRIPE *))
(green.3)	(NP **ADJS** (green) **HEAD** + person)	→	(? * T(**HEAD**) (NOVICE *))

Figure 8.1 The interpretation rules for *green*

Rule (green.3) fails to match this NP, since the lexicon entry for *apple* would not classify it as PERSON.

For constituents that have complex subconstituents, the V function is used to obtain the semantic analysis of that constituent. This value is stored in a new slot in the constituent called **SEM**. For example, after the semantic processing of the NP *the man* is completed, the structure for the sentence *The man laughed* will be

```
(S  SUBJ (NP DET the
              HEAD man
              NUM {3s}
              SEM (DEF/SING m1 MAN))
     MAIN-V laugh
     TENSE PAST)
```

Now consider interpreting this using the following rule for *laugh*:

(laugh.1)   (S **SUBJ** + animate
                MAIN-V laugh) → (? * LAUGH [AGENT V(**SUBJ**)])

The rule will match since the type of the **SUBJ** register (that is, MAN) is a subtype of ANIMATE, and the following PD will be constructed:

(? l1 LAUGH [AGENT (DEF/SING **m1** MAN)])

Merging

To construct a complete logical form, you must combine the partial descriptions generated. This process, called **merging**, can be viewed as a variant of unification. In the simplest cases two PDs merge if they agree on each subpart, or one of them has no value specified for the subpart. For example, the rule for the article *a* is

(a.1) (NP **DET** a) → (INDEF/SING * ? ?)

When applied to the syntactic structure for the NP *a green apple*, it will produce the PD

    (INDEF/SING c1 ? ?)

This PD can be merged with either of the PDs derived from the rules for *green* earlier to produce two possible complete interpretations of the entire NP--namely

    (INDEF/SING c1 APPLE (COLOR c1 GR137))
    (INDEF/SING c1 APPLE (UNRIPE c1))

The complexities in merging arise in dealing with the modifiers. At its most general, deciding whether two PDs can merge would involve checking if all the modifiers of both, taken together, are logically consistent. This book will take a considerably more limited approach: two PDs merge if the modifiers that correspond to the inner cases are consistent. As discussed in Chapter 7, there can be at most one value for any inner case. In situations where two PDs contain a modifier specifying the value of a particular inner case, these two values must be successfully merged. For example, the following two PDs

    (? r1 RUN1 [THEME (NAME j1 PERSON "John")])
    (? r1 RUN1 [THEME (DEF/SING p1 PRINT-PRESS)])

are not mergeable since the THEME cases are not mergeable. On the other hand, the PDs

    (? r1 RUN1 [AGENT (NAME j1 PERSON "John")])
    (? r1 RUN1 [THEME (DEF/SING p1 PRINT-PRESS)])

are mergeable and produce the PD

    (? r1 RUN1 [AGENT (NAME j1 PERSON "John")]
           [THEME (DEF/SING p1 PRINT-PRESS)])

which might be a PD produced while processing the sentence *John ran the printing press*.

If a PD contains an ambiguous value (that is, a list in curly brackets), then such values are merged by intersecting the values in both PDs. An example of a simple type ambiguity is introduced by the interpretation rule for *ball* that includes both the physical object sense (called the type SPHERE) and the social event sense (called the type DANCE). The interpretation rule for *ball* might be

    (NP **HEAD** ball) → (? * {SPHERE, DANCE} ?)

which would generate the following PD, given a syntactic analysis of the NP *a colorful ball*:

> (? **b2** {SPHERE, DANCE} ?)

When lexical items have multiple senses, only one of the senses might satisfy the type restrictions in an interpretation rule. In these cases if the type of that item is used to construct a PD, only those senses that match the pattern are used. For example, even though *ball* can be of type SPHERE or DANCE, in the NP *the green ball*, rule (green.1) will match only the SPHERE sense, since it requires PHYSOBJ. Thus (green.1) would produce the PD

> (? **b3** SPHERE (COLOR **b3** GR137))

More complex cases occur when the interpretation of an entire constituent is ambiguous. For example, the NP *the white dishwasher* could mean a person hired as a dishwasher whose race is white, or it could mean a white appliance. Thus the semantic interpretation of this NP would result in two interpretations, both of which are stored in the **SEM** slot. Given this, an intermediate stage of the analysis of the sentence *The white dishwasher laughed* could be

> (S **SUBJ** (NP **DET** the
>   **ADJS** (white)
>   **HEAD** dishwasher
>   **SEM** {(DEF/SING **d1** PERSON-TYPE-43
>   (RACE **d1** WHITE)),
>   (DEF/SING **d1** APPLIANCE-TYPE-3
>   (COLOR **d1** WHITE))})
>   **MAIN-V** laugh
>   **TENSE** PAST)

When rule (laugh.1) is applied to this, only the first sense of the NP is compatible with the type restriction +animate, so the resulting PD would be

> (? **l3** LAUGH [AGENT (DEF/SING **d1** PERSON-TYPE-43
>   (RACE **d1** WHITE))])

With other verbs an ambiguity might continue to be retained in the S structure. For example, a rule for *wash* might produce the following PD when matching the syntactic structure of the sentence *The pot was washed by the white dishwasher*:

> (? **w1** WASH [AGENT {(DEF/SING **d1** PERSON-TYPE-43
>   (RACE **d1** WHITE)),
>   (DEF/SING **d1** APPLIANCE-TYPE-3
>   (COLOR **d1** WHITE))}]
>   [THEME (DEF/SING **p1** POT)])

```
(past.1)        (S TENSE PAST)          →        (PAST ? ? ?)

(laugh.1)       (S SUBJ +animate
                MAIN-V laugh)           →        (? * LAUGH [AGENT V(SUBJ)])

(dishwasher.1)  (NP HEAD dishwasher)    →        (? * {PERSON-TYPE-43,
                                                    APPLIANCE-TYPE-3} ?)

(the.1)         (NP DET the
                NUM {3s})               →        (DEF/SING * ? ?)

(white.1)       (NP ADJS (white)
                HEAD +physobj−human)    → (? * T(HEAD) (COLOR * WHITE))

(white.2)       (NP ADJS (white)
                HEAD +human)            →        (? * T(HEAD) (RACE * WHITE))
```

Figure 8.2 Some semantic interpretation rules

This ambiguity might later be resolved by a merge with another PD, or it might be retained in the final interpretation and left for the contextual analyzer to resolve.

8.2 The Interpretation Algorithm

The semantic interpretation algorithm traverses the syntactic structure by first attempting to interpret the outermost S and then recursively interpreting its subconstituents as needed to satisfy the semantic tests made in the patterns used. To get an idea of this in a very simple situation, consider interpreting the sentence *The dishwasher laughed* using the interpretation rules in Figure 8.2.

The initial syntactic structure is

```
(S SUBJ (NP DET the
            NUM {3s}
            HEAD dishwasher)
    MAIN-V laugh
    TENSE PAST)
```

For rule (laugh.1) to succeed, the **SUBJ** slot must be of type ANIMATE. To make this check, however, the NP must first be analyzed recursively. Rules (the.1) and (dishwasher.1) match successfully and produce two PDs

```
(DEF/SING d1 ? ?)
(? d1 {PERSON-TYPE-43, APPLIANCE-TYPE-3} ?)
```

which when merged produce a full logical form for the NP that is put in its **SEM** slot. The structure now is as follows:

```
(S  SUBJ (NP DET the
            NUM {3s}
            HEAD dishwasher
            SEM (DEF/SING d1 {PERSON-TYPE-43,
                                APPLIANCE-TYPE-3}))
     MAIN-V laugh
     TENSE PAST)
```

Rule (laugh.1) can now perform its semantic test on the subject and, succeeding, builds the following PD in which the semantic type of the subject NP is now resolved:

(? l1 LAUGH [AGENT (DEF/SING d1 PERSON-TYPE-3)])

Once rule (past.1) is used to generate the PD (PAST ? ? ?), the final interpretation is produced by merging these two PDs--that is,

(PAST l1 LAUGH [AGENT (DEF/SING d1 PERSON-TYPE-3)])

Interpreting a Single Constituent

Given the preceding organization, where subconstituents are interpreted as needed, you can examine in detail the algorithm for a single constituent. It consists of two major phases: **head analysis** and **modifier analysis**. Head analysis consists of interpreting the head word of the phrase (that is, the MAIN-V in S, HEAD in NP, or PREP in PP) together with the subconstituents for which it subcategorizes. The modifier analysis then interprets all the remaining parts of the constituent.

You perform head analysis by retrieving all the interpretation rules for the lexical entry in the head position and using them to produce a set of PDs. You then merge these PDs to produce one or more interpretations of the head and its subcategorized constituents. In cases where multiple interpretations are found, each one may account for a slightly different set of subconstituents.

Next you perform the second phase, modifier analysis, for each of the head interpretations found in the first phase. In this phase you find the subconstituents not accounted for in the head analysis, and you recursively analyze each to produce the PDs to merge with the head analysis. The following sections examine these two phases more closely.

Head Analysis

The head analysis phase must produce a set of PDs that comprise the different interpretations of the head word and its subcategorized phrases, and a list of the constituents that have been accounted for (to pass on to the modifier analyzer).

This list of constituents can simply be a list of the constituents that were used in the patterns of the rules used to interpret the head. You can identify a constituent by its slot name, except in the case where the value is a list of elements. In this case the particular item on that list that was accounted for must also be explicitly mentioned.

Consider a very simple example. The output of the head analysis for the NP *the white dishwasher* would be a single PD (derived from rule (dishwasher.1)), (? **d1** {PERSON-TYPE-43, APPLIANCE-TYPE-3} ?), and the list of constituents accounted for is simply the head word (that is, the **HEAD** slot). This means that the constituents in the slots **DET**, **NUM**, and **ADJS** must be accounted for by the modifier analysis.

As another example, with the S analysis of the sentence *The dishwasher laughed,* the head analysis would interpret almost the entire constituent, since rule (laugh.1) accounts for the constituents in both the **SUBJ** and **MAIN-V** slots. Only the **TENSE** slot needs to be accounted for in the modifier analysis.

Modifier Analysis

You generate the PDs for the modifier analysis by finding the interpretation rules for each of the subconstituents that still need to be accounted for. If the subconstituent is a lexical item or a simple value (PAST), you can directly access the rules for that item. If it is a constituent, such as a PP, you use the rules for the head of that constituent (the PREP in this case).

Once you have generated the PDs, you construct the set of final interpretations by merging each head interpretation with one of the possible interpretations of each of the modifiers.

For example, with the NP *the white dishwasher,* you need to account for the slots **DET**, **NUM**, and **ADJS**. Thus you generate the following PDs in the modifier analysis:

    for **DET** and **NUM**: (DEF/SING **d1** ? ?)
    for **ADJS**:   (? **d1** APPLIANCE-TYPE-43 (COLOR **d1** WHITE))
                    (? **d1** PERSON-TYPE-3 (RACE **d1** WHITE))

You can generate two final interpretations, each using the head interpretation of *dishwasher* generated earlier, the PD generated from the **DET** slots, and one of the PDs generated from the **ADJS** slot:

    (DEF/SING **d1** APPLIANCE TYPE-43 (COLOR **d1** WHITE))
    (DEF/SING **d1** PERSON-TYPE-3 (RACE **d1** WHITE))

In general, you generate the set of final interpretations by searching through all possible sets of merged PDs. You generate an acceptable final interpretation

by merging a set of PDs (call this the PD-SET) if and only if the following
conditions hold:

1. all subconstituents are accounted for by at least one rule used to
   generate PD-SET; and

2. PD-SET is as small as possible--that is, there is no PD in the
   PD-SET that could be removed and have PD-SET still account for
   all the constituents.

Compositionality

Since you typically build up the interpretation of a constituent by using the
interpretations of its subconstituents, this form of interpretation can be said to
be **compositional**. In principle, you could build the semantic interpretation
bottom-up; in this case you would analyze the subconstituents in isolation from
the larger constituent that contains it. While compositionality is desirable, it
must be weakened in certain cases. For example, an idiomatic phrase may be
assigned an interpretation that is independent of the interpretation of its
apparent subconstituents. For instance, the sentence *John is having a ball*
means that John is enjoying himself; it has nothing to do with the meaning of a
ball as in the SPHERE or DANCE sense. You can capture this distinction in the
present framework by a rule such as:

        (S **SUBJ** +animate
            MAIN-V have
            OBJ (NP **ART** a
                     HEAD ball)) → (? * ENJOY [EXPERIENCER V(SUBJ)])

Note that since there was no semantic test on the object NP, the interpreter
was never recursively called to interpret the NP phrase.

As a result, this interpreter is not compositional in the strongest sense of the
term. It is compositional in a weaker sense of the term, however, given that it is
only in cases like the preceding, where the syntactic form of a subconstituent is
matched directly within a rule, that the subconstituent does not receive
semantic interpretation independently.

8.3 An Example: Assigning Case Roles

Consider how you can use this interpreter to analyze the cases of verbs. As
mentioned earlier, the inner cases will be analyzed in the head analysis phase
by rules defined for the verb, while the outer cases will be analyzed in the
modifier analysis by rules defined for the prepositions. For example, the
AT-LOC case, which can modify almost any verb, is produced by a rule for (at.1):

BOX 8.1 The Interpretation Algorithm

This algorithm assumes that each subconstituent is interpreted automatically when the first semantic type check is made on it.

1. Create a new name for use in replacing the "*".

2. Head Analysis:

   a) apply all interpretation rules indexed by the head word;

   b) merge the PDs produced in (a) to give one or more possible head interpretations.

3. For each head interpretation, do the following until all modifiers are accounted for:

   a) select a modifier (that is, a syntactic slot not yet interpreted);

   b) apply all interpretation rules indexed for the head of the modifier;

   c) merge the PDs generated in (b) to produce one or more possible modifier interpretations.

4. Produce the final LFs by finding all successful merges consisting of one head interpretation and one modifier interpretation for each of the modifiers.

(at.1) (S **MODS** (PP **PREP** at

  POBJ + location)) → (? * ? (AT-LOC * $\underline{V}$(**MODS POBJ**)))

This rule introduces a slight generalization on the notation: in rules with patterns that extend over more than one constituent, the $\underline{V}$ and $\underline{T}$ functions may take a chain of slot names as arguments. Thus $\underline{V}$(**MODS POBJ**) is the semantic value of the **POBJ** slot of the **MODS** slot that matched the pattern.

The inner cases are defined for each verb. For example, part of the set of interpretation rules for *give* is defined in Figure 8.3.

Consider the interpretation of the sentence *The man gave the company a car at the fairgrounds*. The initial syntactic structure (with the details of NP analysis suppressed) is as follows:

(give.1)	(S **MAIN-V** give	
	SUBJ +animate)	→ (? * GIVE1 [AGENT <u>V</u>(**SUBJ**)])
(give.2)	(S **MAIN-V** give	
	OBJ +physobj)	→ (? * GIVE1 [THEME <u>V</u>(**OBJ**)])
(give.3)	(S **MAIN-V** give	
	IOBJ +org)	→ (? * GIVE1 [TO-POSS <u>V</u>(**IOBJ**)])
(give.4)	(S **MAIN-V** give	
	MODS (PP **PREP** to	
	POBJ +org)) →	(? * GIVE1 [TO-POSS <u>V</u>(**MODS POBJ**)])

Figure 8.3 Some interpretation rules for *give*

```
(S SUBJ (NP "the man")
   MAIN-V give
   TENSE PAST
   OBJ (NP "a car")
   IOBJ (NP "the company")
   MODS ([PP PREP at
            POBJ (NP "the fairground")]))
```

In the head analysis phase the rules for *give* are used to produce three PDs (from rules (give.1), (give.2), and (give.3)) that, when merged together, form a single head analysis.

```
(? g1 GIVE1 [AGENT (DEF/SING m1 MAN)]
            [THEME (INDEF/SING c1 AUTO)]
            [TO-POSS (DEF/SING c2 COMPANY-ORG)])
```

The slots not accounted for in this phase are **TENSE** and **MODS**. You generate one PD for each of these slots, from rules (past.1) and (at.1):

```
(PAST ? ? ?)
(? g1 ? (AT-LOC g1 (DEF/SING f1 FAIRGROUND)))
```

When these are merged together, the final interpretation of the sentence is

```
(PAST g1 GIVE1 [AGENT (DEF/SING m1 MAN)]
               [THEME (INDEF/SING c1 AUTO)]
               [TO-POSS (DEF/SING c2 COMPANY-ORG)]
               (AT-LOC g1 (DEF/SING f1 FAIRGROUND)))
```

Remember that the distinction between inner and outer cases is emphasized by using the square brackets only for the inner cases.

```
(break.1)   (S  MAIN-V break
                SUBJ +animate)        →    (? * BREAK[AGENT V(SUBJ)])

(break.2)   (S  MAIN-V break
                OBJ +physobj)         →    (? * BREAK[THEME V(OBJ)])

(break.3)   (S  MAIN-V break
                SUBJ +physobj–animate
                OBJ +physobj)         →    (? * BREAK[INST V(SUBJ)]
                                                    [THEME V(OBJ)])

(break.4)   (S  MAIN-V break
                SUBJ +physobj–animate
                OBJ nil)              →    (? * BREAK [THEME V(SUBJ)])

(break.5)   (S  MAIN-V break
                MODS (PP PREP with
                        POBJ + physobj–animate))
                                      →    (? * BREAK [INST V(MODS POBJ)])
```

Figure 8.4 The interpretation rules for *break*

Consider a slightly more complicated analysis involving the verb *break*, which may be used in the following ways:

> The man broke the window with a hammer.
> The hammer broke the window.
> The window broke.

The rules for *break* are shown in Figure 8.4.

These rules successfully interpret the three preceding sentences. For example, the analysis of *The hammer broke the window* would involve PDs generated from rules (break.2) and (break.3) and would produce the following head analysis:

> (? **b1** BREAK [INST (DEF/SING **h1** HAMMER)]
>   [THEME (DEF/SING **w1** WINDOW)])

Note that rule (break.4) fails to match this sentence since the **OBJ** slot is not empty. The analysis of *The window broke*, on the other hand, would produce the following from rule (break.4):

> (? **b2** BREAK [THEME (DEF/SING **w1** WINDOW)])

Rule (break.1) fails on this sentence since the subject is not ANIMATE, and rules (break.2) and (break.3) fail because there is no value in the **OBJ** slot. The NP *the window* is assigned to the THEME case in each instance, as desired.

(inf.1)	(S **MOOD** EMBEDDED		
	TENSE INF)	→	(INF ? ? ?)
(want.1)	(S **MAIN-V** want		
	SUBJ +animate)	→	(? * WANT [EXPERIENCER $\underline{V}$(**SUBJ**)])
(want.2)	(S **MAIN-V** want		
	COMP +action)	→	(? * WANT [THEME $\underline{V}$(**COMP**)])

Figure 8.5 Semantic interpretation rules for *want* and infinitive complements

8.4 Embedded and Nonembedded Sentences

Embedded Sentences

Nothing said thus far has been specific to nonembedded sentences, so extending the interpreter to embedded sentences is trivial. Only one detail has not yet been considered: a slot may be filled with a pointer to constituent as the result of some movement analysis. In this case the interpreter simply inserts the same name as the name used in the interpretation of the original constituent. For example, the sentence *John wants to break the window* has the following analysis:

```
(S SUBJ (NP₁ NAME John)
   TENSE PRES
   MAIN-V want
   COMP (S MOOD EMBEDDED
           SUBJ →NP₁
           MAIN-V break
           TENSE inf
           OBJ (NP₂ ART the
                    HEAD window
                    NUM {3s})))
```

Using the rules defined previously plus the new rules shown in Figure 8.5, this sentence is interpreted as follows. The head analysis of the outer S, using rule (want.1), initiates the recursive interpretation of the subject NP, which produces the result (NAME j1 PERSON "John"). Rule (want.2) initiates the interpretation of the embedded S. The head analysis of the embedded S uses the rules for *break* to produce the following partial descriptions after merging:

```
(? b1 BREAK  [AGENT j1]
             [THEME (DEF/SING w1 WINDOW)])
```

Note that **j1**, the name generated when the subject of the outer S was interpreted, is reused as the interpretation of the pointer in the **SUBJ** slot of the embedded S. After the modifier analysis of the embedded S, the state of the interpretation is as follows:

```
(S SUBJ (NP₁ NAME John
                SEM (NAME j1 PERSON "John"))
    TENSE PRES
    MAIN-V want
    COMP (S MOOD EMBEDDED
             SUBJ →NP₁
             MAIN-V break
             TENSE INF
             OBJ (NP₂ ART the
                      HEAD window
                      NUM {3s}
                      SEM (DEF/SING w1 WINDOW))
             SEM (INF b1 BREAK
                       [AGENT j1]
                       [THEME (DEF/SING w1 WINDOW)])))
```

Once the results of (want.1) and (want.2) are merged and the modifier analysis of the outer S picks up the **TENSE** slot, the final interpretation is

```
(PRES w1 WANT [EXPERIENCER (NAME j1 PERSON "John")]
              [THEME
               (INF b1 BREAK
                    [AGENT j1]
                    [THEME (DEF/SING w1 WINDOW)])])
```

Analysis of Mood

You still need one final phase of analysis--the analysis of the mood of the outermost S. Given the simple formulation of the interpreter introduced here, the simplest treatment of the problem is to assume a special case treatment of each major form. Thus if the **MOOD** of the outermost S is DCL, the results of interpretation are simply embedded in a structure for assertions. Thus the final interpretation of the sentence *John broke the window* will be

```
(ASSERT (PAST b1 BREAK [AGENT (NAME j1 PERSON "John")]
                       [THEME (DEF/SING w2 WINDOW)]))
```

If the **MOOD** of the outermost S is Y/N-Q, on the other hand, the logical form for a yes-no question is generated. Thus the final interpretation of the sentence *Did John break the window?* will be

```
(Y-N-QUERY (PAST b1 BREAK
                 [AGENT (NAME j1 PERSON "John")]
                 [THEME (DEF/SING w2 WINDOW)]))
```

Wh-questions are treated similarly, but in this case you use the analysis of the constituent in the slot **WH-QUERY** to obtain the name of the semantic information being queried. For example, the sentence *Which window did John break?* will have the syntactic form:

        (S **MOOD** WH-Q
            WH-QUERY (NP$_1$ **DET** which
                                HEAD window)
            TENSE PAST
            SUBJ (NP$_2$ **NAME** John)
            MAIN-V break
            OBJ →NP$_1$)

and the final logical form:

        (WH-QUERY (WH/SING **w1** WINDOW)
                    (PAST **b1** BREAK [AGENT (NAME **j1** PERSON "John")]
                                [THEME **w1**]))

8.5 Rule Hierarchies

The semantic interpreter is driven by rules associated with particular lexical items and feature values. Many readers will probably have noticed by now that this could result in huge numbers of rules where no generalities appear to have been captured. You can create a much more satisfactory organization of interpretation rules by allowing rules to be based on entire classes of words. For example, rules (laugh.1), (break.1), and (give.1) all stated the same relationship between the **SUBJ** slot and the **AGENT** case--a relationship, in fact, that is regular across all action verbs. What you would really like here is a single rule that captures the regularity, such as the following:

(action.1)   (S **MAIN-V** + action
                SUBJ + animate) → (? * T(**MAIN-V**) [AGENT V(**SUBJ**)])

You could organize such rules in a semantic network with an inheritance mechanism so that all rules applying to a given type T apply to every subtype and instance of T. For example, you could reexpress the set of rules given for *laugh*, *give*, and *break* using the type hierarchy and the interpretation rules shown in Figure 8.6. While the number of individual rules is not much smaller with this organization than with the rules for each explicit verb, you will see a dramatic benefit as you add new verbs. For example, you obtain the interpretation rules for *cry* simply by classifying it as an instance of ACTION, you obtain the rules for *hit* by classifying it as an OBJ/ACTION, you obtain the rules for *burn* by classifying it as an INST/ACTION, and so on. Thus you can expand the lexicon rapidly by using the hierarchical structure of the existing rules.

One technical problem makes the use of these hierarchies more complicated than it first appears. In particular a problem can arise when a rule is inherited

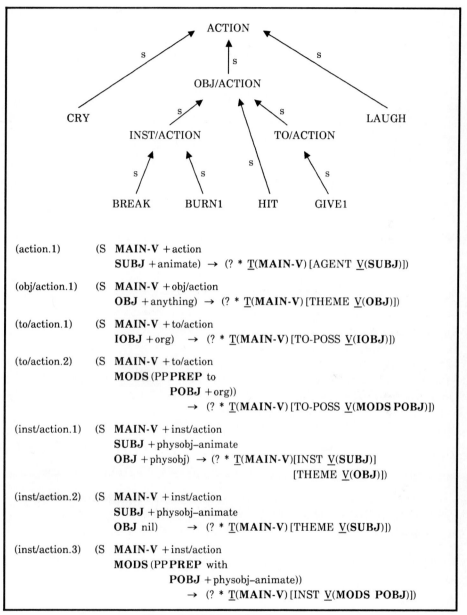

(action.1)	(S **MAIN-V** + action **SUBJ** + animate) → (? * <u>T</u>(**MAIN-V**) [AGENT <u>V</u>(**SUBJ**)])
(obj/action.1)	(S **MAIN-V** + obj/action **OBJ** + anything) → (? * <u>T</u>(**MAIN-V**) [THEME <u>V</u>(**OBJ**)])
(to/action.1)	(S **MAIN-V** + to/action **IOBJ** + org) → (? * <u>T</u>(**MAIN-V**) [TO-POSS <u>V</u>(**IOBJ**)])
(to/action.2)	(S **MAIN-V** + to/action **MODS** (PP **PREP** to **POBJ** + org)) → (? * <u>T</u>(**MAIN-V**) [TO-POSS <u>V</u>(**MODS POBJ**)])
(inst/action.1)	(S **MAIN-V** + inst/action **SUBJ** + physobj–animate **OBJ** + physobj) → (? * <u>T</u>(**MAIN-V**)[INST <u>V</u>(**SUBJ**)] [THEME <u>V</u>(**OBJ**)])
(inst/action.2)	(S **MAIN-V** + inst/action **SUBJ** + physobj–animate **OBJ** nil) → (? * <u>T</u>(**MAIN-V**) [THEME <u>V</u>(**SUBJ**)])
(inst/action.3)	(S **MAIN-V** + inst/action **MODS** (PP **PREP** with **POBJ** + physobj–animate)) → (? * <u>T</u>(**MAIN-V**) [INST <u>V</u>(**MODS POBJ**)])

Figure 8.6 A hierarchical rule base

but is too general. For example, the verb sense BURN1 inherits appropriate rules from INST/ACTION so that sentences such as *Jack burned the meat with a blowtorch* would receive the appropriate interpretation:

```
(PAST b1 BURN1 [AGENT (NAME j1 PERSON "Jack")]
               [THEME (DEF/SING m1 MEAT)]
               [INSTRUMENT (INDEF/SING b2 TOOL-TYPE-7)])
```

But the rules used are overly general for *burn*; they don't capture the constraints that the THEME must be a burnable object and the instrument must be a source of heat. Thus a sentence such as *Jack burned the rock with some water* would currently be semantically acceptable.

As a result, you cannot express the semantics of words completely by the inheritance of interpretation rules; you still need some other mechanism that is specific to the word. With the semantic network formalism, you could use the selectional restriction information to do this, as shown in Figure 8.7.

With this extension the application of an interpretation rule will consist of two parts: the matching and generation of a PD; and then the application of the case restrictions to check if the PD is semantically acceptable. In particular the sentence *Jack burned the rock with the water* would have the syntactic form:

```
(S SUBJ (NP NAME John)
   MAIN-V burn
   TENSE PAST
   OBJ (NP DET the
           HEAD rock)
   MODS (PP PREP with
            POBJ (NP DET the
                     HEAD water)))
```

Using rules (action.1), (obj/action.1), and (inst/action.3), which are all inherited rules for *burn*, the head analysis would generate the following PDs:

```
(? b1 BURN [AGENT (NAME j1 PERSON "John")])
(? b1 BURN [THEME (DEF/SING s1 STONE)])
(? b1 BURN [INST (DEF/SING w1 WATER)])
```

It would then check these PDs against the selectional restrictions for BURN and reject the second two as anomalous.

Summary

A semantic interpreter can be created by using a set of pattern-action interpretation rules that match parts of the syntactic structure of sentences and produce partial descriptions. By merging partial descriptions together, you get a final logical form for the sentence. The interpreter attempts to build the logical form top-down but interprets each subconstituent recursively before the semantic value of that subconstituent is used as part of the analysis of the main

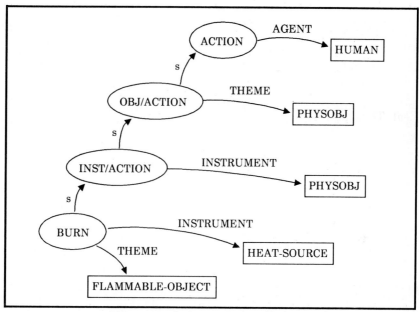

Figure 8.7 The role restrictions for *burn*

constituent. Finally, a method of hierarchically organizing the interpretation rules can capture semantic generalities and dramatically reduce the number of interpretation rules needed.

Related Work and Further Readings

The technique of using a rule base to match syntactic structures to produce a logical form was used extensively in the LUNAR system (Woods, 1977). In this system the rules did not produce partial descriptions but rather produced a mixture of the logical form and LISP code that when evaluated would produce the remainder of the logical form. The interpreter was organized into three phases, two of which correspond to the head analysis and modifier analysis. The other was a specific phase to deal explicitly with governing operators, such as determiners and modal operators, which was here incorporated into the modifier analysis. The ability to use arbitrary LISP code on the right-hand side of the rule makes it difficult to characterize the power of the LUNAR interpreter, because in theory any manipulation is possible.

Recent work in semantic interpretation has used more restrictive formalisms closer to the type specified here, and these are typically purely compositional systems. Perhaps the closest to the system described here is that by Hirst (1987), who uses case information and selectional restrictions to build a case-frame-based logical form in a purely compositional way from the syntactic form. His framework is compositional in the strongest sense, and besides interpreting S and NP constituents, it performs finer-grained analyses as well. For example, prepositions map to slot names, and a single rule can be used for analyzing prepositional phrases. That is, prepositions map to slot-value pairs where the slot is the interpretation of the preposition and the value is the interpretation of the object of the preposition.

The technique of using a hierarchical organization of rules is described in Bobrow and Webber (1980). More recently, hierarchical lexicons have been used to encode both syntactic features and semantic information (Flickinger et al., 1985; Shieber, 1986).

Exercises for Chapter 8

1. (*medium*) Consider the following modifiers of the noun *shoe*:

>   brown shoes
>   brake shoes
>   alligator shoes
>   horse shoes

Assume that these modifiers refer to objects in a domain with the types SHOE, BRAKE-SHOE, and HORSE-SHOE, and the predicates

>   (*COLOR* object color)
>   (*MADE-OF* object material)
>   (*WORN-BY* object user)

Give a set of semantic interpretation rules that correctly analyzes each of these noun phrases. Try to capture generalities whenever possible.

2. (*medium*) This question involves specifying the semantic interpretation rules to analyze the different senses of the verb *roll*, as in

>   We rolled the log into the river.
>   The log rolled by the house.
>   The cook rolled the pastry with a large jar.
>   The ball rolled around the room.
>   We rolled the piano to the house on a dolly.

a) Identify the different senses of the verb *roll* in the preceding sentences, and give an informal definition of each meaning. (You may use a dictionary if you wish.) Try to identify how each different sense allows different conclusions to be made from each sentence. For example, consider whether the THEME case in each of the preceding sentences describes the object that is actually undergoing some rolling motion. Classify each sense into the verb hierarchy given in Figure 8.6.

b) List the interpretation rules in the chapter that apply to the different senses of each verb, and add any new rules necessary to build the appropriate analysis for each sense. If one of these new rules is strictly more specific than a rule from the chapter, explicitly point this out. Finally, for each verb sense, identify which rules named in this chapter will be used to analyze sentences using that sense.

c) Given the set of rules outlined in Exercise 2b, generate all the possible partial descriptions for each of the preceding sentences, and show the final merged interpretation(s) of each sentence.

3. (*medium*) Consider the range of sentence forms for the verb *dry*:

    i)   The prunes dried in the sun.
    ii) The sun dried the prunes.
    iii) The prunes dried by the rocks.
    iv) John dried the prunes in the sun.
    v)   John dried the prunes in a bucket.
    vi) The prunes were dried by the sun.
    vii) The prunes were dried in the sun by John.
    *viii)*The prunes were dried.

a) Specify a reasonable syntactic analysis that you assume for sentences *i, ii, vi,* and *vii.*

b) Define a set of semantic interpretation rules that can interpret all the preceding sentences correctly without generating any spurious interpretations. Explicitly identify any particular problems in this task, and outline the assumptions you made to solve (or get around) them. Identify and define each case you use and the type hierarchy you assume.

c) Give all logical forms produced by your rules for sentences *i, ii, vi,* and *vii.*

4. (*medium*) Using the interpretation rules defined in this chapter, and defining any others that you need, give a detailed trace of the semantic interpretation of the sentence *The man gave the green apple to Bill.* In particular, trace the analysis of each constituent and show all PDs generated and the results of each phase of the analysis.

5. (*medium*) Suppose you opened a random page in the dictionary and found the verb *pay* in its following senses (among others):

    i)   to give someone what is due for goods or services, as in *Jack paid the company $10 for those boots.*

    ii) to yield, as in *The job pays George $10 a week.*

iii) to be profitable or beneficial, as in *It pays to be on time.*

iv) to settle, as in *We paid our bill at the store.*

Analyze each of these senses in detail and design a set of semantic interpretation rules to account for the different uses of the verb. You may integrate rules into the verb hierarchies described in this chapter if you want to inherit general rules for the verb classes.

6. (*medium*) Give the semantic interpretation rules necessary to generate partial descriptions for the elements of the following sentences:

a) Jack drove to the store in a hurry.
b) John bought a car with money from Jane.
c) He jumped with help from the springboard.
d) Mary drew the line from one mark to the other.

You may use the hierarchy of verbs as defined in this chapter and give only the additional rules that are necessary to analyze the sentences.

7. (*medium*) Implement a simple version of the semantic interpreter described in the chapter. Your system should support the full range of pattern-matching abilities described, but it does not need to deal with the recursive calling of the interpreter or the final merging of partial descriptions. Thus, given a set of semantic interpretation rules, your program will take a syntactic structure with the NPs already interpreted and output a complete list of partial descriptions generated by the rules. For example, your system should be able to take an input such as

```
(S SUBJ (NP ART the
          HEAD man
          SEM (DEF/SING m1 MAN))
   MAIN-V give
   OBJ (NP ART the
          HEAD company
          SEM (DEF/SING c1 COMPANY))
   MODS (PP PREP to
          POBJ (NP NAME Bill
                   SEM (NAME b1 PERSON "Bill")))))
```

8. (*hard*) Extend the system built for Exercise 7 in the following way. Implement a simple merging algorithm and extend the system to handle the recursive analysis of subconstituents and to produce a set of complete logical forms for the sentence. Document your merging algorithm and discuss its limitations as well as its abilities. Make sure you test your system on some ambiguous examples.

Chapter 9

Strategies for Semantic Interpretation

The last chapter outlined a particular method of semantic interpretation that involved a complete separation of syntactic and semantic processing. This chapter considers other ways of organizing semantic interpretation that are found in the literature. These approaches include techniques that completely encode semantic information into a syntactic grammar (the semantic grammars in Section 9.2), techniques that have separate modules but run in an incremental fashion (Sections 9.3 and 9.4), techniques of semantic interpretation as an annotation on the grammatical rules (Sections 9.5 and 9.6), and techniques that are essentially semantically driven and use minimal syntactic information (Section 9.7).

All of these frameworks have particular advantages and disadvantages. They vary in the ease of constructing the grammar and semantic interpretation information, as well as in the generality of the approach as the grammars become large. To facilitate comparison, Section 9.1 presents a simple example in the framework discussed in Chapter 8. Whenever possible, this same example will be reused when considering the alternate frameworks.

The main technical reason for bringing semantic information to bear as early as possible is to reduce ambiguity. You've already seen some examples of syntactically ambiguous sentences that actually are not ambiguous when semantic information is considered. For example, the sentence *We broke the window with a hammer* is syntactically ambiguous as to whether the final prepositional phrase modifies the NP *the window* or the main verb. Using semantic information, however, you would not be able to find an analysis of the NP *the window with a hammer*. You would be able to analyze *breaking with a hammer* easily, though, since here the hammer fills the INSTRUMENT case of the breaking event. Similarly, the sentence *The sun rose from behind the toolbox with a hammer*, while syntactically ambiguous in the same way as the preceding example, can only be semantically interpreted with the PP modifying the NP. In sentences with multiple ambiguities, since the number of syntactically possible interpretations could easily grow quite large, early semantic interpretation becomes even more crucial.

9.1 A Sample Domain

This section describes a small grammar and a set of semantic interpretation rules that will be used for comparison throughout the chapter. The grammar deals with a set of questions that could be asked about airline schedules. In particular the grammar and semantic interpretation rules will handle sentences such as the following:

> When does the flight from Boston to Chicago leave?
> At what time does the flight to Chicago leave Boston?
> Can you book a flight to Chicago for me?

Rules		Equation
1.	S ← AUX NP VP	
2.	S ← PP AUX NP VP/PP	$\text{TYPE}_{PP} = \text{WH}$
		$\text{HELD}_{VP/PP} = \text{PP}$
		$\text{ROOT}_{AUX} = \text{DO}$
3.	VP ← SIMPLE-VP	
4.	VP ← SIMPLE-VP PPS	
5.	VP/PP ← SIMPLE-VP PPS/PP	$\text{HELD}_{PPS/PP} = \text{HELD}$
6.	SIMPLE-VP ← VERB	$\text{SUBCAT}_V = \text{NONE}$
7.	SIMPLE-VP ← VERB NP	$\text{SUBCAT}_V = \text{OBJ}$
8.	NP ← ART NOUN	$\text{TYPE} = \text{TYPE}_{ART}$
9.	NP ← ART NOUN PPS	$\text{TYPE} = \text{TYPE}_{ART}$
10.	NP ← PROPER-NAME	
11.	NP ← PRO	
12.	NP/PP ← ART NOUN PPS/PP	$\text{HELD}_{PPS/PP} = \text{HELD}$
13.	PPS ← PP	
14.	PPS ← PP PPS	
15.	PPS/PP ←	
16.	PPS/PP ← PPS	
17.	PP ← PREP NP	$\text{TYPE} = \text{TYPE}_{NP}$
18.	PP ← WH-WORD	$\text{TYPE} = \text{WH}$
		$\text{HEAD} = \text{WH-WORD}$

Grammar 9.1 A grammar for simple questions

Grammar 9.1 presents a grammar for these questions in the CFG format using the techniques described in Chapter 5 to deal with questions. The only annotations shown are those dealing with wh-movement and verb subcategorization. With appropriate structure-building annotation this grammar would produce the following interpretations. The first sentence, *When does the flight from Boston to Chicago leave?*, would have the structure:

```
(S TYPE WH-Q
   WH-QUERY (PP₁ TYPE WH HEAD when)
   SUBJ (NP DET the
            HEAD flight
            MODS ((PP PREP from
                       POBJ (NP NAME Boston))
                  (PP PREP to
                       POBJ (NP NAME Chicago))))
   MAIN-V leave
   MODS (→PP₁))
```

1. (S **TYPE** Y-N-Q
        SUBJ (NP **PRO** you)
        AUXS (can)
        MAIN-V book
        OBJ (NP **DET** a
                HEAD flight
                MODS ((PP **PREP** to
                                POBJ (NP **NAME** Chicago))
                        (PP **PREP** for
                                POBJ (NP **PRO** me)))))

2. (S **TYPE** Y-N-Q
        SUBJ (NP **PRO** you)
        AUXS (can)
        MAIN-V book
        OBJ (NP **DET** a
                HEAD flight)
        MODS ((PP **PREP** to
                POBJ (NP **NAME** Chicago))
            (PP **PREP** for
                POBJ (NP **PRO** me))))

3. (S **TYPE** Y-N-Q
        SUBJ (NP **PRO** you)
        AUXS (can)
        MAIN-V book
        OBJ (NP **DET** a
                HEAD flight
                MODS ((PP **PREP** to
                                POBJ (NP **NAME** Chicago))))
        MODS ((PP **PREP** for
                POBJ (NP **PRO** me))))

Figure 9.2 Three interpretations of *Can you book a flight to Chicago for me?*

The second sentence, *At what time does the flight to Chicago leave Boston?*, has a similar structure except that there is an object *Boston* in the S structure. The third sentence, *Can you book a flight to Chicago for me?*, is syntactically ambiguous, because the two PPs at the end of the sentence may be attached to the verb or to the last NP. These possibilities lead to three interpretations, shown in Figure 9.2.

The semantic interpretation rules needed for this domain include the rules shown in Figure 9.3. The fragment of the verb hierarchy relevent for these examples is shown in Figure 9.4. While the higher parts of the hierarchy represent general classes of verbs, such as ACTION and EVENT, the lower parts of the hierarchy are specific to the verb uses in this domain. For instance, the sense of *depart* defined here is for flights only, and the TO and FROM

```
(action.1)        (S VERB +action
                     SUBJ +human) → (? * T(VERB) [AGENT V(SUBJ)])

(obj/action.1)    (S VERB +obj/action
                     OBJ +anything) → (? * T(VERB) [THEME V(OBJ)])

(event.1)         (S VERB +event
                     SUBJ +physobj−human) → (? * T(VERB) [THEME V(SUBJ)])

(leave.1)         (S VERB +departing
                     OBJ +location) → (? * T(VERB) [FROM-LOC V(OBJ)])

(to.1)            (S MAIN-V +move
                     MODS (PP PREP to
                              POBJ +location)) →(? * T(MAIN-V)
                                            (TO-LOC * V(MODS POBJ)))

(to.2)            (NP HEAD +vehicle
                      MODS (PP PREP to
                              POBJ +location)) →(? * T(HEAD)
                                            (TO-LOC * V(MODS POBJ)))

(from.1)          (S MAIN-V +move
                     MODS (PP PREP from
                              POBJ +location)) →(? * T(MAIN-V)
                                            (FROM-LOC * V(MODS POBJ)))

(from.2)          (NP HEAD +vehicle
                      MODS (PP PREP from
                               POBJ +location))
                         →  (? * T(HEAD)
                                 (FROM-LOC * V(MODS POBJ)))

(for.1)           (S MAIN-V +ben/action
                     MODS (PP PREP for
                               POBJ +org))
                         →  (? * T(MAIN-V)
                                 (BENEFICIARY * V(MODS POBJ)))
```

Figure 9.3 The rules for the verbs and prepositions

locations must be cities. The rules for interpreting the NPs and the wh-terms are shown in Figure 9.5. The nouns are assumed to be organized in a hierarchy similar to the verb hierarchy. In these examples the only general rule is (anything.1), which applies to any noun.

Applying these rules to the syntactic structures produced for the first two sentences results in the following analyses:

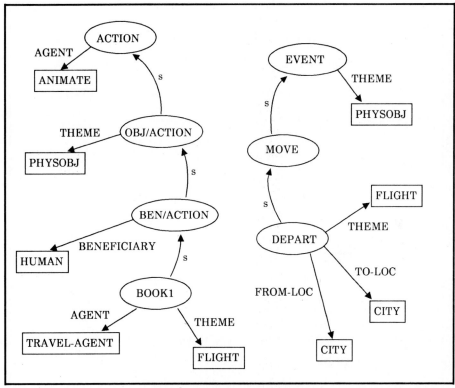

Figure 9.4 The verb hierarchy

When does the flight from Boston to Chicago leave?

(PRES d1 DEPARTING
          [THEME (DEF/SING f1 FLIGHT
                         (FROM-LOC f1 (NAME b1 CITY "Boston"))
                         (TO-LOC f1 (NAME c1 CITY "Chicago")))]
          [AT-TIME (WH/SING t1 TIME)])

At what time does the flight to Chicago leave Boston?

(PRES l2 DEPARTING
          [THEME (DEF/SING f2 FLIGHT
                         (TO-LOC f2 (NAME c1 CITY "Chicago")))]
          [FROM-LOC (NAME b1 CITY "Boston")]
          [AT-TIME (WH/SING t2 TIME)])

In the third sentence, *Can you book a flight to Chicago for me?*, there were three possible syntactic analyses, as shown in Figure 9.2. Of these, only one is semantically interpretable. Interpretation 1 cannot be analyzed since the only

(when.1)	(S MODS (PP **HEAD** when)) → (? * ? (AT-TIME * (WH/SING ** TIME)))

(at.1)	(S MODS
	    (PP **PREP** at
	        POBJ +time)) → (? * ? (AT-TIME * <u>V</u>(POBJ)))

(wh.1)	(NP **DET** +wh
	    NUM {3p}
	    HEAD +anything) → (WH/PL * <u>T</u>(HEAD))

(wh.2)	(NP **DET** +wh
	    NUM {3s}
	    HEAD +anything) → (WH/SING * <u>T</u>(HEAD))

(name.1)	(NP **NAME** +name) → (NAME * <u>T</u>(NAME) <u>V</u>(NAME))
(anything.1)	(NP **HEAD** +anything) → (? * <u>T</u>(HEAD))
(the.1)	(NP **DET** the **NUM** {3s}) → (DEF/SING * ?)
(the.2)	(NP **DET** the **NUM** {3p}) → (DEF/PL * ?)
(pro.1)	(NP **PRO** +pro) → (PRO * <u>T</u>(PRO) <u>V</u>(PRO))
(a.1)	(NP **DET** a) → (INDEF/SING * ?)

Figure 9.5 The rules for wh-terms and the NPs

rule for a PP with PREP *for* requires it to modify a BEN/ACTION verb, not a flight. Similarly, the rule for a PP with PREP *to* can modify a MOTION/VERB or a VEHICLE but not a RESERVING action, so interpretation 2 is eliminated as well. Interpretation 3 is analyzed to produce:

    (PRES **b1** RESERVING
                [AGENT (PRO **y1** HUMAN "you")]
                [THEME (DEF/SING **f3** FLIGHT
                          (TO-LOC **f3** (NAME **c1** CITY "Chicago")))]
                [BENEFICIARY (PRO **m1** HUMAN "me")])

The reason for examining combined syntax and semantic analyses is, of course, to eliminate the semantically anomalous syntactic interpretation as soon as possible and thereby reduce much of the ambiguity during parsing.

9.2 Semantic Grammars

The first technique for combining syntactic and semantic processing involves collapsing them into a single uniform framework--either a context-free grammar or an ATN. This result, called a **semantic grammar**, looks like a regular grammar, except that it uses semantic categories for terminal symbols. For example, rather than having a rule such as

VP ← SIMPLE-VP PPS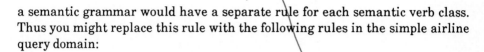

a semantic grammar would have a separate rule for each semantic verb class. Thus you might replace this rule with the following rules in the simple airline query domain:

(sem.1)   RES-VP ← RESERVING RES-MODS
(sem.2)   DEP-VP ← DEPARTING DEP-MODS

Rule (sem.1), which might be realized by the phrase *book a flight for me*, involves verbs of reserving, such as *book*, plus their allowable complements. Rule (sem.2), on the other hand, is for verbs of departure and might be realized by the phrase *leaves for Chicago*.

Similarly, the rules for SIMPLE-VP and PPS are replaced by their semantic grammar equivalents. For the RESERVING verbs, you need the rules:

(sem.3)   RESERVING ← RESERVE-VERB FLIGHT
(sem.4)   RES-MODS ← for PERSON
(sem.5)   RES-MODS ←

Notice that only those PP modifiers that are semantically interpretable are now allowed by this grammar fragment. In particular, a modifying PP such as *for me* is acceptable, as in *book it for me*, whereas the PP *to Boston* is not acceptable.

For the DEPARTING verbs, you need the rules:

(sem.6)   DEPARTING ← DEPART-VERB
(sem.7)   DEPARTING ← DEPART-VERB SOURCE-LOCATION
(sem.8)   DEP-MODS ← DEP-MOD DEP-MODS
(sem.9)   DEP-MODS ←
(sem.10)   DEP-MOD ← to DEST-LOCATION
(sem.11)   DEP-MOD ← from SOURCE-LOCATION

Again, only the modifying PPs that are semantically acceptable are now accepted by this grammar.

So far, 6 syntactic rules (3, 4, 6, 7, 13, and 14) have been replaced with 11 semantic grammar rules to cover 2 verb categories. Adding more verb categories could continue to expand the semantic grammar at approximately this same rate of about 6 new rules per verb category. Thus semantic grammars will tend to be much larger than their corresponding syntactic grammars, and hence the efficiency of the parser might be expected to degrade considerably. In fact, this doesn't happen in most cases, since the number of words in each terminal category is much smaller. (For example, compare the number of words in category DEPART-VERB with the number in the syntactic category VERB.) This means that for any given sentence only a small subset of the grammar will ever be applicable.

The main difficulty with the semantic grammar approach is in achieving generality. One of the reasons that the grammars are so large is that many linguistic generalizations that were captured elegantly in the syntactic grammar now need to be handled by brute force. For example, to deal with passive form sentences, you need to add in a rule for the passive form of every semantic verb category used (one for DEPARTING, one for RESERVING, and so on). As you try to find more elegant solutions, you move the grammar back toward a syntactic solution and start to lose the semantic categories.

For example, consider what happens if you want to retain the hold list solution for wh-questions. The brute force approach duplicates rule 2 for each verb category. If you consider only the DEPARTING category, you need the following rules:

(sem.12)   S ← WH-DEP-MOD AUX FLIGHT   **HELD = WH-DEP-MOD**
                DEP-VP/DEP-MOD

(sem.13)   WH-DEP-MOD ← when

(sem.14)   WH-DEP-MOD ← to what DEST-LOCATION

(sem.15)   WH-DEP-MOD ← from what SOURCE-LOCATION

(sem.16)   WH-DEP-MOD ← at what TIME

(sem.17)   DEP-VP/DEP-MOD ← DEPARTING   **HELD = HELD$_{\text{DEP-VP/DEP-MOD}}$**
                DEP-MODS/DEP-MOD

(sem.18)   DEP-MODS/DEP-MOD ←   **FIRST = HELD**

(sem.19)   DEP-MODS/DEP-MOD ← DEP-MODS   **FIRST = HELD**

You would need a similar number of rules to handle the RESERVING verbs.

If you want to capture this concept in a more general way, you have to relax the goal that only semantically interpretable sentences can be parsed by the grammar. In particular, rule (sem.12) and the definition of WH-DEP-MOD in rules (sem.13) to (sem.16) are necessary to enforce that the queried term can be a legal modifier of the verb. This guarantees that when the held constituent is used (by rule (sem.18) or (sem.19)), a semantically interpretable structure is built. If you had used a general rule to hold any wh-term at the beginning of wh-questions, you would have no guarantee that the HELD constituent could be inserted as a DEP-MOD and produce a legal sentence.

In practice, semantic grammars are extremely useful for producing a quite robust natural language interface in limited domains where it is feasible to analyze the range of all possible questions by hand. For more general systems, the task of constructing such a grammar seems to be unacceptably difficult, unless you rely on some sort of automatic generation of the grammar from user-specified syntactic and semantic information.

As a final comment, if you want to construct a logical form for the sentence as it is being parsed, you can do so quite directly from a semantic grammar using the augmentation on the rules. Since each rule in the grammar is specific to a single semantic situation, all that is left to do is to specify the appropriate logical form built by each rule.

9.3 A Simple Interleaved Syntactic and Semantic Analyzer

The advantage of having separate syntactic and semantic processing stages is that it allows for more sophisticated parsing models because the syntactic portion of the system is relatively domain independent. Thus each new application can build on the previous work in other applications. On the other hand, a single stage combining syntactic and semantic processing, such as in a semantic grammar, is able to use semantic information early on to eliminate many syntactic interpretations that are semantically anomalous. This section describes a simple system that gains many of the advantages of both these approaches. The syntactic and semantic processing is separate, yet semantic information is brought to bear early in the syntactic analysis.

Consider the semantic analysis of NP structures. In nearly all of the examples so far the interpretation of an NP has proceeded independently of the context (the S or PP structure) in which it is found. This situation suggests that you could call the semantic interpreter immediately when an NP structure is proposed by syntax. If the NP is successfully interpreted, the interpretation is saved and the syntactic parse continued as usual. If a semantic interpretation cannot be found, however, the syntactic processor fails on the NP (that is, it will backtrack, or fail to add the NP to the chart for use later, depending on the parsing algorithm being used). Thus many syntactically possible yet semantically anomalous NPs will be eliminated as soon as they are proposed. Of course, there is no reason to limit this technique to NP analysis. The same technique could be used for analyzing embedded S structures, as well as PP and ADJP structures.

Consider a specific example of this technique in a chart-based mixed-mode parser. The top-down component could be a CFG or an ATN system that suggests constituents to add to the chart. Before the entry is added, however, the semantic interpreter is called. If one or more semantic interpretations can be found, the entry is augmented with these interpretations and added to the

Step # in Syntactic Parse	Proposed Constituent
1.	(NP1 **PRO** you)
2.	(NP2 **DET** a **HEAD** flight)

3.	(NP3 **DET** a
	    HEAD flight
	    MODS ((PP "to Chicago")))

4.	(NP4 **DET** a
	    HEAD flight
	    MODS ((PP "to Chicago")
	         (PP "for me")))

5.	(S1 **TYPE** YES-NO-Q
	    AUXS (can)
	    SUBJ NP1
	    MAIN-V book
	    OBJ NP4)

6.	(S2 **TYPE** YES-NO-Q
	    AUXS (can)
	    SUBJ NP1
	    MAIN-V book
	    OBJ NP2
	    MODS ((PP "to Chicago")
	         (PP "for me")))

7.	(S3 **TYPE** YES-NO-Q
	    AUXS (can)
	    SUBJ NP1
	    MAIN-V book
	    OBJ NP3
	    MODS ((PP "for me")))

Figure 9.6 A trace of the constituents added by a pure syntactic parse

chart. If no interpretation can be found, the constituent is not added to the chart, and the top-down component is signalled to backtrack. Consider the parse of the sentence *Can you book a flight to Chicago for me?* using the grammar and interpretation rules outlined in Section 9.1. Tracing the top-down component will be left as an exercise for you. Here, though, consider the NP and S constituents that are proposed for adding to the chart. Figure 9.6 shows the constituents that would be proposed by the syntactic component if no semantic filtering were done. Figure 9.7 shows a trace of the same sentence parsed with semantic filtering. Notice that some constituents are proposed and rejected, and still others that arise in the pure syntactic parse are never even considered since they were built from constituents that were rejected earlier. In other cases a constituent may be semantically acceptable, but it would never

Step	Proposed Constituent	Result of Semantic Filter
1.	(NP1 **PRO** you)	(PRO **h1** HUMAN "you")
2.	(NP2 **DET** a **HEAD** flight)	(INDEF/SING **f1** FLIGHT)
3.	(NP3 **DET** a **HEAD** flight **MODS** ((PP "to Chicago")))	(INDEF/SING **f2** FLIGHT (TO-LOC **f2** (NAME **c1** CITY "Chicago")))
4.	(NP4 **DET** a **HEAD** flight **MODS** ((PP "to Chicago") (PP "for me")))	rejected since *for me* cannot modify *flights*
5.	(S2 **TYPE** YES-NO-Q **AUXS** (can) **SUBJ** NP1 **MAIN-V** book **OBJ** NP2 **MODS** ((PP "to Chicago") (PP "for me")))	rejected since *to Chicago* cannot modify *book*
6.	(S3 **TYPE** YES-NO-Q **AUXS** (can) **SUBJ** NP1 **MAIN-V** book **OBJ** NP3 **MODS** ((PP "for me")))	(PRES **b1** RESERVING [AGENT (PRO **h1** HUMAN "you")] [THEME (INDEF/SING **f2** FLIGHT (TO-LOC **f2** (NAME **c1** CITY "Chicago")))] [BENEFICIARY (PRO **h2** HUMAN "me") 1])

Figure 9.7 A trace of constituents filtered by semantics

be proposed by syntax. For example, after step 3 in Figure 9.6, an S constituent could be built covering the words *Can you book a flight*. This is never added to the chart because this top level S constituent does not cover the complete sentence.

Here the semantic filtering eliminated two of the possible interpretations of this sentence: one was proposed by syntax and rejected (step 5 in Figure 9.7), and the other was never even proposed because the rejection of NP4 eliminated an entire part of the normal syntactic search for sentences using this NP. As grammars get larger and ambiguity grows, the savings from such early filtering can be impressive.

There are problems with this method, however. In particular, an NP may appear anomalous in isolation but can participate in a legal sentence. For instance, the NP *the moon in our car* makes no sense in isolation, yet it could be used in a sentence such as *It's impossible for you to have seen the moon in our car, because it wouldn't fit.* On the other hand, if you relax the semantic filtering so that this NP is acceptable, the semantic filter will be of no use in disambiguating a sentence such as *We saw the moon in our car*, which has a good interpretation corresponding to *We saw the moon while we were in our car.* Since the bad interpretation involving the NP *the moon in our car* would be acceptable in order to handle the first sentence, this second sentence would remain ambiguous. The problem, of course, is that the semantic filter is an all-or-nothing filter. It can only accept or reject, and as you find various strange sentences, the boundary of acceptance must keep moving closer and closer to accepting everything. What is needed is a way of rating semantic interpretations so that some are preferred over others. The job of the parser then would be to find the best interpretation. Some techniques for designing such a system are discussed in the next section.

9.4 Semantic Interpretation Based on Preferences

The strategy of having the semantic interpreter simply accept or reject a proposed   syntactic constituent can be shown to be too rigid for many situations. In particular, it either eliminates many sentences that should be interpretable or weakens the mechanism of case-value restrictions on verbs to the point that they do not reduce ambiguity at all. This section considers a generalization of the interleaved parser in which the semantic interpreter assigns a well-formedness rating to each constituent and thereby avoids this dilemma.

Before looking at the mechanism in detail, however, consider an example of the problem. The verb *give* can be defined by classifying it as an IOBJ/ACTION and using the case-value restrictions that the THEME case is nonhuman and the TO-POSS case is a human or an organization. This information could be used to avoid backtracking in the sentences

> We gave the man the money.
> We gave the money to the man.

With the former, since the NP immediately following the verb is of type HUMAN, it could be immediately classified as the TO-POSS (and hence the IOBJ slot). With the latter, the NP immediately following the verb is nonhuman and so could be immediately classified as the THEME (and hence parsed as the OBJ).

While these restrictions seem reasonable, they can easily be violated, as in the sentence *We gave the man to the police.* To handle this sentence in the present framework, the case restriction on the THEME case would have to be revised to simply be a PHYSOBJ. But even this is too restrictive, because there are contexts where nonphysical objects might fill the THEME case, as in *The*

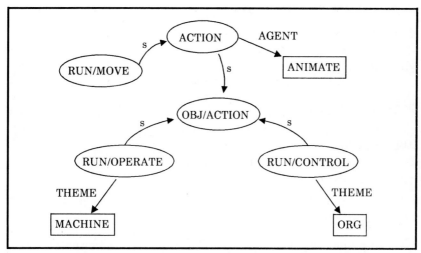

Figure 9.8 Case-value restrictions for three senses of *run*

water gave the plant a new lease on life. Similar examples could be formed to nullify virtually all the case-value restrictions. If there were no case-value restrictions, however, the number of spurious readings of sentences would grow dramatically.

The solution to this dilemma is to allow the semantic interpreter to return some rating of semantic well-formedness rather than a simple accept or reject. The parser can than be modified to find the best rated interpretations. Thus in the usual cases the case-value restrictions eliminate many spurious readings (that are not as semantically well rated), but in the exceptional cases an interpretation can still be found. The idea is that if a case-value restriction is violated, the interpreter still returns a semantic interpretation but reflects the violation in a measure of well-formedness. One simple measure might be just to count the number of violations that occurred in an interpretation. A perfectly acceptable sentence would have a reading of 0 (no violations), whereas as a sentence with a single violation would have a rating of 1, and so on.

Consider a concrete example. Besides the intransitive sense of *run* (*Jack ran in the race*), there are two transitive senses of *run*: one takes a THEME case that typically is a machine (*Jack ran the printing press*), and the other takes a THEME that is an organization (*Jack runs the company*). Thus the semantic interpretation information for these senses of *run* can be defined as shown in Figure 9.8.

There are more creative uses of *run*, however. For example, you might say *I'm running the money,* meaning that you are in charge of keeping track of the funds collected at some event. You would like a semantic interpretation to be

Rules		Equation
2.5	S ← NP VP	
2.6	S/NP ← VP	**SUBJ** = HELD
7.5	SIMPLE-VP ← VERB NP NP	**SUBCAT** = IOBJ + OBJ
9.5	NP ← SIMPLE-NP S/NP	**HELD** = SIMPLE-NP
		FORM$_{\text{MAIN-V}}$ = ing

Grammar 9.9   Additional rules for Grammar 9.1

constructed even though money does not satisfy the case-value restrictions specified for the senses of *run*.

You can implement such a parsing algorithm by a minor extension to the bottom-up chart parser described in Chapter 3. Remember that the algorithm is driven by the key list of completed constituents, which you implemented as a stack to obtain a depth-first control strategy. To incorporate semantic preferences, you will change the stack into a more general **priority stack**. Each constituent will have an associated rating for semantic well-formedness, and when a new entry with a rating of X is added to the key list, it is placed after all the constituents that have a lower score than X. If all the constituents ever proposed have the same rating, you have a simple stack as before. Otherwise, you have many stacks--one for each rating--and the lower-rating stacks are emptied first. Consider parsing the sentence *We gave the man running the money the check*, using Grammar 9.1 with the additional rules shown in Grammar 9.9 that allow simple declarative sentences and relative clauses. As before, the equations that build the structures are not specified but are assumed to be present. The numbers are chosen to indicate the ordering of rules when combined with those in Grammar 9.1.

Omitting unnecessary detail, the parser quickly builds up the initial NP constituent, the verb, and starts processing the NP following the verb. The NPs *the man* and *the man running* are also found as expected, resulting in the situation shown in Figure 9.10. The rating for each constituent is given in the top right corner of each entry on the chart. Since no violations have been detected, every constituent has a rating of 0.

When the parser adds the NP *the money* to the chart, several possibilities arise. First, the active arc starting from position 2 to 6 is completed, suggesting a new constituent, SIMPLE-VP1 (*gave the man running the money*). Second, the active arc starting at position 5 also completes, suggesting the constituent SIMPLE-VP2 (*running the money*). Both of these are put on the key list. Assuming the parser next adds SIMPLE-VP1 to the chart, it in turn creates a completed VP *gave the man running the money*, which when added next creates

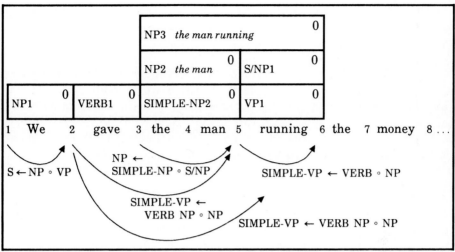

Figure 9.10 Important details of parse state after parsing *We gave the man running*

a completed S (*We gave the man running the money*). Since this S does not cover the entire sentence, however, it is not an acceptable analysis.

Next the parser adds SIMPLE-VP2, resulting in a new VP (rule 3) and a new S/NP (rule 2.6), which has the structure

> (S **SUBJ** →NP$_1$ (that is, *the man*)
>   **VERB** run
>   **OBJ** (NP$_2$ **DET** the
>   **HEAD** money))

The semantic analyzer is called and returns an analysis only after relaxing one slot-value restriction on either the RUN/OPERATE sense or the RUN/CONTROL sense. Hence this new S/NP constituent is given a score of 1, and is placed at the *bottom* of the key list (after the remaining entries for the rest of the words in the sentence). The key list now consists of

Score	Constituent
0	ART3 (*the* at position 8)
0	NOUN5 (*check* at position 9)
1	S/NP2 (*running the money* at position 5)

In effect this forces the parser to consider all other alternative parsings of the sentence before the S/NP2 is allowed to be used in the analysis.

The parse continues, eventually building NP5, *the check*, which in turn creates no new constituents when added. This exhausts all the score 0 constituents and would signify a failure if the semantic filter had rejected S/NP2 outright. The important details of the current parse state are shown in Figure 9.11.

The key list contains one constituent, S/NP2 with score 1. When it is added to the chart at position 5, it completes an active arc to create NP6, *the man running the money*, with score 1, since the rating of each constituent counts all the violations of all its subconstituents as well. Next NP6 is added, resulting in the extension of the active arc at position 2, which finds both NPs required and builds SIMPLE-VP3 *gave (the man running the money) (the check)* with score 1. This is added next, creating the constituent S1 with score 1 that is the desired analysis of the sentence.

Thus the best interpretation of the sentence is found even though it involved the relaxation of a semantic case restriction. If there had been an analysis of the sentence with score 0, the parser would have stopped before the score 1 constituents were added, and the interpretation built in this example would never have been constructed.

A system based on preferences gives more leeway in designing rules to deal with relative semantic plausibility, since a semantic interpretation rule does not have to be general enough to accept any possible sentence. In fact, you can use the rules to express expected type restrictions and let the exceptional cases be analyzed by the rule relaxation. Thus the rules now express a preference for certain semantic structures rather than a rejection criteria for semantic structures (hence the name of this section).

Of course, you could devise more sophisticated rating schemes. Rather than simply counting violations, for instance, the semantic interpreter could return some score based on how bad the violation is. Such a measure might be calculated from the distance in the type hierarchy between the type in the case-value restriction and the type of the actual constituent filling that case. Techniques based on this measure are discussed in the next chapter, where word ambiguity is considered further.

9.5 Rule-by-Rule Semantic Interpretation Based on the λ-Calculus

One of the unsatisfying characteristics of the interleaved parser involves the size of the constituents that are built before the semantic filter is called. In particular, whole NP and S structures were constructed without any semantic guidance and were verified only after the fact. This section pushes the interleaved approach to its logical conclusion and examines methods of calling the semantic interpreter each time a syntactic rule is applied. This technique is called the rule-by-rule approach, because there is a pairing of syntactic and semantic rules.

advantages
– semantic guidance more immediate
– preserves syntax
disadvantages
– tuned on many rules

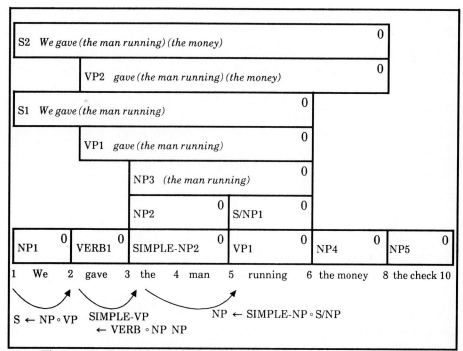

Figure 9.11 The parse state after all constituents with score 0 have been added

To accomplish this approach, you have to have a valid logical form corresponding to each syntactic category. For example, many grammars have rules such as

1.   S ← NP VP

2.   VP ← VERB NP

If you perform semantic interpretation whenever a rule is used, you must have for rule 2 an interpretation of the VP (built from the interpretation of the VERB and the NP), which is then later combinable with an NP interpretation to produce an S interpretation. Presumably, the VP analysis would look like the S analysis except that the subject would be missing. One way to allow such forms is to use a version of the **lambda calculus**. The lambda (λ-) calculus provides a general mechanism for specifying functional expressions. For instance, if the final logical form for the sentence *The man kissed the dog* is

(PAST **k1** KISS   [AGENT (DEF/SING **m1** MAN)]
                [THEME (DEF/SING **d1** DOG)])

then the SEM of the VP *kissed the dog* would be the function

λ (x) (PAST **k1** KISS [AGENT x]
                           [THEME (DEF/SING **d1** DOG)])

In general the form of these expressions is

λ (x) Px

which denotes a function of one variable (x), which takes an argument and produces an expression that is the result of substituting the argument for x in the expression Px. An operator **Apply** is defined to compute the value of the function. Thus Apply (λ (x) (PAST **k1** KISS [AGENT x]), (DEF/SING **m1** MAN)) would produce (PAST **k1** KISS [AGENT (DEF/SING **m1** MAN)]).

How would the VP interpretation be constructed from the VERB and NP interpretations when rule 2 is used? One way is for the lexicon entry for each transitive verb to specify a function that maps an NP interpretation into a VP interpretation. In our example the meaning for *kiss* would be

λ (o) (λ (x) (PAST * KISS [AGENT x] [THEME o]))

The nesting of lambda operators will usually be abbreviated by using multiple arguments. Thus the meaning for *kiss* could be rewritten as

λ (o, x) (PAST * KISS [AGENT x] [THEME o])

Applying this to the NP interpretation (DEF/SING **d1** DOG) would produce a VP interpretation as shown earlier. The "*" notation is used as before--that is, when the rule is instantiated, a new name is created to replace the "*".

This using of a lambda variable for each required case handles the obligatory parts of the verb's case structure but cannot be used easily for optional restrictions, such as a time qualifications. To handle these, you allow the SEM of certain structures to be a restriction for use in some other SEM structure. For example, the meaning of the adjective *green* might be

λ (x) (COLOR x GREEN)

which is a function that produces a restriction. To ensure the correct operation of this, you introduce a new operation called **R-Apply** (for restriction apply). This takes a logical form expression as an argument, binds the lambda variable to the name in the logical form, and inserts the resulting expression as a restriction in that form. If the meaning of *green* is R-Applied to the PD (? **b1** SPHERE), it will produce the PD (? **b1** SPHERE (COLOR **b1** GREEN)).

Similarly, you can define a function **O-Apply** that applies a lambda function to a logical form and places the result in the operator position in that

$$
\begin{array}{ll}
\text{NP} \leftarrow \text{ART N1} & \mathbf{DET} = \text{ART} \\
& \mathbf{ADJ} = \text{ADJ}_{N1} \\
& \mathbf{HEAD} = \text{HEAD}_{N1} \\
\\
\text{N1} \leftarrow \text{ADJ NOUN} & \mathbf{ADJ} = \text{ADJ} \\
& \mathbf{HEAD} = \text{NOUN} \\
\\
\text{N1} \leftarrow \text{NOUN} & \mathbf{HEAD} = \text{NOUN}
\end{array}
$$

Grammar 9.12 A simple NP grammar

(NP **ADJ** green
   HEAD + physobj − human) → (? * T(HEAD) (COLOR * GREEN))

(NP **ADJ** green
   HEAD + human) → (? * T (HEAD) (INEXPERIENCED *))

(NP **DET** a) → (INDEF/SING * ?)

Figure 9.13 Simple semantic interpretation rules

form. The most trivial use of O-Apply would be with a determiner such as *a*, which has the lexicon entry INDEF/SING (that is, a function that has the constant value INDEF/SING). Using O-Apply with this value on the form

(? **b1** SPHERE (COLOR b1 GREEN))

would simply insert the value as the operator, producing

(INDEF/SING b1 SPHERE (COLOR b1 GREEN))

Consider a simple situation with the separate syntactic and semantic processing stages and see how it can be reformulated into the rule-by-rule analysis. Grammar 9.12 contains a grammar for simple noun phrases, and Figure 9.13 contains the associated semantic interpretation rules.

To enforce the selectional restriction information, you need to use a typed λ-calculus notation. The entry for the first sense of *green* would be

λ (x: physobj − human) (COLOR x GREEN)

This function takes an object of type + physobj − human and builds the appropriate COLOR predication. The entry for the second sense is

λ (x: human) (INEXPERIENCED x)

Figure 9.14 contains the lexicon entries for a few selected words.

Word	SEM
ADJ: green	λ (x: physobj − human) (COLOR x GREEN)
	λ (x: human) (INEXPERIENCED x)
HEAD: ball	(? * {SPHERE, DANCE})
HEAD: man	(? * HUMAN (MALE x))
ART: a	INDEF/SING

Figure 9.14 Lexicon

1. NP ← ART N1   **SEM** = O-Apply (**SEM**$_{ART}$, **SEM**$_{N1}$)

2. N1 ← ADJ NOUN   **SEM** = R-Apply (**SEM**$_{ADJ}$, **SEM**$_{NOUN}$)

3. N1 ← NOUN   **SEM** = **SEM**$_{NOUN}$

Grammar 9.15 An NP grammar computing the semantic interpretation

The grammar that computes the semantic interpretation in a rule-by-rule manner is shown in Grammar 9.15. While the syntactic structure is not collected in this grammar, the annotations to do this could be simply added.

Consider parsing the NP *a green ball*. You would add the constituents to the chart in the following order: Rule 2 would apply to *green ball*, and the SEM for the N1 structure is computed as

R-Apply (**SEM**$_{ADJ}$, **SEM**$_{NOUN}$)

Considering the possible values for **SEM**$_{ADJ}$ (that is, the lexicon entries for *green*), and those for **SEM**$_{NOUN}$ (that is, *ball*), you can see that only one combination satisfies the type restrictions, which is as follows:

R-Apply (λ (x: physobj − human) (COLOR x GREEN),
            (? s1 {SPHERE, DANCE}))

With the definition of R-Apply, this expression simplifies to the expression

(? s1 SPHERE (COLOR s1 GREEN))

This is the value of **SEM**$_{N1}$. Next, rule 1 applies and **SEM**$_{NP}$ is computed using the operation

O-Apply (**SEM**$_{ART}$, **SEM**$_{N1}$)

Applying the SEM of *a* yields

(rul.1)	S ← AUX NP VP	**TYPE** = YES-NO-Q **SEM** = Apply (**SEM**$_{VP}$, **SEM**$_{NP}$)
(rul.3)	VP ← SIMPLE-VP	**SEM** = **SEM**$_{SIMPLE-VP}$
(rul.4)	VP ← SIMPLE-VP PPS	**SEM** = R-Apply (**SEM**$_{PPS}$, **SEM**$_{SIMPLE-VP}$)
(rul.6)	SIMPLE-VP ← VERB	**SEM** = **SEM**$_{VERB}$ **SUBCAT**$_{VERB}$ = NONE
(rul.7)	SIMPLE-VP ← VERB NP	**SEM** = Apply (**SEM**$_{VERB}$, **SEM**$_{NP}$) **SUBCAT**$_{VERB}$ = OBJ
(rul.8)	NP ← SIMPLE-NP	**SEM** = **SEM**$_{SIMPLE-NP}$ **NUM** = **NUM**$_{SIMPLE-NP}$
(rul.9)	NP ← SIMPLE-NP PPS	**SEM** = R-Apply (**SEM**$_{PPS}$, **SEM**$_{SIMPLE-NP}$) **NUM** = **NUM**$_{SIMPLE-NP}$
(rul.10)	NP ← NAME	**SEM** = **SEM**$_{NAME}$
(rul.11)	NP ← PRO	**SEM** = **SEM**$_{PRO}$
(rul.12)	SIMPLE-NP ← ART NOUN	**NUM** = **NUM**$_{ART}$ = **NUM**$_{NOUN}$ **SEM** = O-Apply (**SEM**$_{ART}$, **SEM**$_{NOUN}$)
(rul.14)	PPS ← PP	**SEM** = Insert (**SEM**$_{PP}$, nil)]
(rul.15)	PPS ← PP PPS	**SEM** = Insert (**SEM**$_{PP}$, **SEM**$_{PPS}$)]
(rul.18)	PP ← PREP NP	**SEM** = Apply (**SEM**$_{PREP}$, **SEM**$_{NP}$)]

Grammar 9.16 A grammar that computes the semantic
interpretation on a rule-by-rule basis

final

(INDEF/SING s1 SPHERE (COLOR s1 GREEN))

as desired.

A Detailed Example

Consider constructing a grammar equivalent to a subset of the original
grammar and semantic interpretation rules described in Section 9.1. Grammar
9.16 shows this grammar with an annotation that directly computes the
semantic interpretation for each rule. To make it simpler, most registers
collecting syntactic information are not shown. Each rule is labeled with a
number that corresponds to the number of the syntactic rule in the original
grammar. Figure 9.17 defines the lexicon in the format already outlined with
the addition of syntactic restrictions that must be satisfied before an entry can
be used.

Word	Features	SEM
HEAD: flight		(? * FLIGHT)
NAME: Chicago		(NAME * c1 CITY "Chicago")
MAIN-V: leave	SUBCAT = NONE	λ (o: physobj − human) (? * DEPARTING [THEME o])
	SUBCAT = OBJ	λ (x: location) λ (o: physobj − human) (? * DEPARTING [THEME o] [FROM-LOC x])
MAIN-V: book	SUBCAT = OBJ	λ (x: flight) λ (a: human) (? * RESERVING [AGENT a] [THEME x])
PRO: me		(PRO * HUMAN me)
PRO: you		(PRO * HUMAN you)
PREP: to		λ (l: location) λ (x: {motion/act, vehicle}) (TO-LOC x l)
PREP: for		λ (o: organization) λ (b: ben/action) (BENEFICIARY b o)
PREP: at		λ (t: time) λ (x) (AT-TIME x t)
HEAD: when		λ (x) (AT-TIME x (WH/SING * TIME))
DET: a		INDEF/SING
DET: the	NUM = 3s	DEF/SING
DET: the	NUM = 3p	DEF/PL

Figure 9.17 Lexicon

Suppose you are parsing the sentence *Can you book a flight to Chicago for me?* again and you are using the rule-by-rule interleaved parser. As with the simple interleaved parser, the constituents will be traced as they are suggested for entry onto the chart. Whereas with the original interleaved parser, only NP and S constituents were filtered, here you will see all constituents being filtered. As before each constituent that would be suggested by the syntactic parse without filtering will be listed, and then the result of the filter on the right-hand side will be indicated. The simple system used a call to the semantic interpreter after the syntactic constituent was built, but this system directly computes the semantic interpretation as part of the annotation of the grammar. If a semantic interpretation cannot be constructed, the constituent is not completed, and the top-down predictor of the parser must backtrack. The initial part of the trace is shown in Figure 9.18.

This first part is straightforward. The NPs *you* and *a flight* are analyzed. The latter analysis takes place in two stages: first a SIMPLE-NP constituent is built using the lexicon entries for *flight* and *a* (step 2); second, the noun phrase NP2 is built using the SIMPLE-NP analysis (step 3). This NP is then used to

Step	Proposed Constituent	Comments
1.	(NP **SEM** (PRO **h1** HUMAN "you"))	(rul.11) and a lexicon entry for *you*
2.	(SIMPLE-NP2 **NUM** {3s} **SEM** (INDEF/SING **f1** FLIGHT))	(rul.12) and entries for *a* and *flight*
3.	(NP2 **SEM** (INDEF/SING **f1** FLIGHT) **NUM** {3s})	(rul.8) and SIMPLE-NP2
4.	(SIMPLE-VP1 **SEM** λ (a: human) (? **b1** RESERVING [AGENT a] [THEME (INDEF/SING **f1** FLIGHT)]))	(rul.7) and an entry for *book*
5.	(VP1 **SEM** λ (a: human) (? **b1** RESERVING [AGENT a] [THEME (INDEF/SING **f1** FLIGHT)]))	(rul.3)

Figure 9.18 Part I of the trace

Step	Proposed Constituent	Comments
6.	(NP3 **SEM** (NAME **n1** CITY "Chicago"))	(rul.10) and a lexicon entry for *Chicago*
7.	(PP1 **SEM** λ (x: {motion/act, vehicle}) (TO-LOC x (NAME **n1** CITY "Chicago")))	(rul.18) and a lexicon entry for *to*
8.	(PPS1 **SEM** (λ (x: {motion/act, vehicle}) (TO-LOC x (NAME **n1** CITY "Chicago"))))	(rul.14)
9.	(NP4 **NUM** {3s} **SEM** (INDEF/SING **f2** FLIGHT (TO-LOC **f2** (NAME **n1** CITY "Chicago"))))	(rul.9) with PPS1 and SIMPLE-NP2

Figure 9.19 Part II of the trace

build the constituent SIMPLE-VP1, which is used to build VP1. The parser next tries to build an S (corresponding to *Can you book a flight*), but it fails since it has not reached the end of the sentence. The parser backtracks and continues as shown in Figure 9.19.

In the next stage (part II) the PP *to Chicago* is analyzed as a restriction. Next a PPS structure is built consisting of this one PP structure, and an NP *a flight to Chicago* is built in step 9. The parser will go on to build a VP and then try to build an S covering *Can you book a flight to Chicago*. As before, this attempt fails, since it is not at the end of the sentence, and the parser backtracks and continues as shown in Figure 9.20.

The attempt in step 13 to combine both PPs with the SIMPLE-NP *a flight* fails because FLIGHT cannot unify with BEN/ACTION. Since NP6 cannot be constructed, the S interpretation that would have used NP6 is not even proposed. After backtracking, the next constituent proposed is VP2, a VP constructed from SIMPLE-VP1 modified by the two PPs in PPS2. This constituent fails since the type RESERVING (*book*) is incompatible with the type constraint +MOTION/ACT (that is, *to Chicago* cannot modify *book*). Thus VP2 is rejected; consequently, the second possible syntactic interpretation of the sentence, which is as follows:

```
(S2 TYPE  YES-NO-Q
    FIRST-NP NP1
    VERB book
    OBJ NP2
    MODS PPS2)
```

is never proposed. This is the main difference between the simple interleaved parser and the rule-by-rule parser on this sentence. Whereas the simple version built this second S interpretation only to reject it, the rule-by-rule parser rejected the VP earlier on and never constructed the S. The parser backtracks once more and finally produces the last constituent:

```
(S3 TYPE  YES-NO-Q
    FIRST-NP NP1
    VERB book
    SEM (PRES b1 RESERVING
         [AGENT (PRO h1 HUMAN "you")]
         [THEME (INDEF/SING f1 FLIGHT
             (TO-LOC f1 (NAME n1 CITY "Chicago")))]
         [BENEFICIARY (PRO h2 HUMAN "me")]))
```

Of course, with a more complex grammar, the savings using a rule-by-rule analysis could be considerably greater. This savings is balanced, however, against the extra cost of computing semantic interpretations of subconstituents that could be eliminated on syntactic grounds alone. The rule-by-rule interleaving gives the maximum amount of semantic guidance to a syntactically driven parse.

This current version is not, however, without some problems, many of which have been discussed previously with the simple interleaved parser. In addition, the present framework needs to be extended to deal with ambiguity at each level of semantic analysis. The techniques described for the separate semantic interpreter in the last chapter could be reused here. In particular, each constituent could maintain a list of possible semantic interpretations,

Step	Proposed Constituent	Comments
10.	(NP5 **SEM** (PRO **h1** HUMAN "me"))	the NP *me* using (rul.11)
11.	(PP2 **SEM** λ (b: ben/action) (BENEFICIARY b (PRO **h1** HUMAN "me")))	using (rul.14) and a lexicon entry for *for*
12.	(PPS2 **SEM** (λ (x: {motion/act, vehicle}) (TO-LOC x (NAME **n1** CITY "Chicago"))) λ (b: ben/action) (BENEFICIARY b (PRO **h1** HUMAN "me")))	combining PP1 and PP2 using (rul.15)
13.	(NP6 **SEM** XXX)	the attempt to build an NP out of SIMPLE-NP2 and PPS2 fails because of incompatible types

Figure 9.20 Part III of the trace

each of which is combined with the analyses of other constituents when they are combined.

9.6 Rule-by-Rule Interpretation Using Variables

Rule-by-rule semantic interpreters can be built without using the λ-calculus by taking advantage of the power of unification to leave parts of a structure unspecified until a later date. This section briefly considers an example of this technique drawn from the logic-grammar approach.

Semantic interpretation in logic grammars can be accomplished by adding additional argument positions that directly build the logical form. For example, the following rules (ignoring the arguments for word position and syntactic structure) can construct an interpretation of *A cat ate a mouse*:

(S ?LF) < (NP ?subj) (VP ?subj ?LF)

(VP ?subj ?LF) < (TransV ?subj ?obj ?LF) (NP ?obj)

(NP ?nlf) < (ART ?n ?nlf) (NOUN ?n)

(NOUN CAT1) < [cat]

(NOUN MOUSE1) < [mouse]

(ART ?type (INDEF ?name ?type)) < [a]

(TransV ?subj ?obj (PAST ?e EAT [AGENT ?subj] [THEME ?obj])) < [ate]

Figure 9.21 shows the trace of the parse of the sentence with the construction of the logical form. Note in step 7 that the variable ?LF is bound to

Step of Proof	Comments
1. (S ?LF)	
2. (NP ?subj) (VP ?subj ?LF)	
3. (ART ?n ?subj) (NOUN ?n) (VP ?subj ?LF)	
4. (NOUN ?type) 　　(VP (INDEF ?name ?type) ?LF)	(ART ?type (INDEF ?name ?type)) proven from input *a*
5. (VP (INDEF ?name CAT1) ?LF)	(NOUN CAT) proven from input *cat*
6. (TransV (INDEF ?name CAT1) ?obj ?LF) (NP ?obj)	
7. (NP ?obj)	(TransV (INDEF ?name CAT1) ?obj 　　(PAST ?e EAT 　　　[AGENT (INDEF ?name CAT1)] 　　　[THEME ?obj])) proven from input *ate*
8. (ART ?n ?obj) (NOUN ?n)	
9. (NOUN ?type1)	(ART ?type1 (INDEF ?name1 ?type1)) proven from input *a*
10. ----------	(NOUN MOUSE1) proven from input *mouse*

Figure 9.21 Constructing a logical form using a logic grammar

$$\text{(PAST ?e EAT [AGENT (INDEF ?name CAT1)]}$$
$$\text{[THEME ?obj])}$$

and then in step 9, ?obj is bound to (INDEF ?name1 ?type1). Once ?type1 is bound in step 10 to MOUSE1, ?LF is bound to the following complete logical form:

$$\text{(PAST ?e EAT [AGENT (INDEF ?name CAT1)]}$$
$$\text{[THEME (INDEF ?name1 MOUSE1)])}$$

In actual practice, logic-based grammars do not usually generate a case-based logical form but generate an FOPC representation directly. The same techniques are used as described in this section, but the manipulations are more complicated in order to obtain the quantifier scoping.

9.7 Semantically Directed Parsing Techniques

Since at the syntactic level of analysis there may be considerable ambiguity that can be resolved by semantic interpretation, researchers have done a fair

BOOK.1   [+animate][=booked] → [(PAST * RESERVING [AGENT V(1)])]

BOOK.2   [+reserving][+physobj] → [V(1) ∧ (? * RESERVING [THEME V(2)])]

BOOK.3   [+reserving][+animate] → [V(1) ∧ (? * RESERVING
                                                                        [BENEFICIARY V(2)])]

BOOK.4   [+reserving][=for][+animate] → [V(1) ∧ (? * RESERVING
                                                                        [BENEFICIARY V(2)])]

S.end   [+anything][= "."] → pop

Figure 9.22 Sample lexicon

amount of work to design parsers that primarily perform semantic interpretation directly on the input and use syntactic information only when necessary. Typically, these systems do not construct a syntactic representation of the sentence, and thus only local syntactic information about the sentence is available to the parser. This section considers a lexically based parser that uses only minimal syntactic information.

While the actual representation details vary, these systems all perform a case analysis of sentences directly from the input words. The grammatical and semantic information is stored in the lexicon entries for the words. In particular the lexicon will contain essential information such as the different senses possible for the word, including case-frame information for verbs and adjectives, and a specification of a procedure for disambiguating the word and integrating it into larger semantic structures by combining it with other words. Here you will consider a system where this information is stored as a set of pattern-action rules similar to the framework you developed for the deterministic parser. In particular, remember that the deterministic parser maintained a buffer for the input constituents and used pattern-action rules to manipulate this buffer. This system will also have a buffer, but it will contain semantic constituents. Where the deterministic parser used a set of states to organize its rules, this interpreter maintains a list of active rules. Whenever you enter a new word, the rules in that word's lexicon entry are made active. Individual rules also may be activated or deactivated in the action part of other rules.

For example, the rules associated with the word *booked* would include those shown in Figure 9.22. Each rule contains a pattern that tests for semantic categories and individual words in the buffer. When a pattern matches, the buffer elements involved in the match are removed and replaced by the structures specified in the action part. In addition, the action part of the rule may activate and deactivate additional rules. For example, rule BOOK.1 in Figure 9.22 will match a buffer with an entry of type ANIMATE followed by a buffer containing the word *booked*, and it will replace these two buffers with an entry of form (PAST * RESERVING [AGENT V(1)]). As you can see, the semantic form specified in the action part of a rule looks much like the specifications in the semantic interpretation rules described previously. Numbers are used to refer to the buffer entries that matched the pattern. Thus V(1) refers to the value of the first buffer involved in the match. An explicit merge operator ($\wedge$) is used to construct a new interpretation from two partial descriptions, which is identical to the merging operation outlined in Chapter 7.

Consider a simple example of parsing the sentence *John booked me a flight to Chicago* using the preceding rules. For the moment, assume that all NPs have been preprocessed before this parse commences. The parser starts with the single rule S.end active (which checks for the end of the sentence) and with the first two buffers filled with the terms (NAME j1 HUMAN "John") and *booked*, respectively. The rules for *booked* are made active, and BOOK.1 succeeds. This replaces the first two buffer elements with a single buffer containing

(PAST r1 RESERVING [AGENT (NAME j1 HUMAN "John")])

Rules BOOK.2 to BOOK.4 remain active as the next buffer is filled with the structure (PRO m1 HUMAN me). Rules BOOK.2, BOOK.3, and BOOK.4 are tried, and BOOK.2 and BOOK.3 succeed. Using a heuristic to favor the rule with the most specific pattern, the interpreter favors rule BOOK.3. Its action merges a new structure with the value of the first buffer--that is, V(1)--producing the following structure that becomes the new value of buffer 1:

(PAST r1 RESERVING [AGENT (NAME j1 HUMAN "John")]
                    [BENEFICIARY (PRO m1 HUMAN "me")])

The next input is the analysis of the noun phrase *a flight to Chicago* (INDEF/SING f1 FLIGHT (TO-LOC f1 (NAME c1 CITY "Chicago"))). When you try the remaining rules (BOOK.2 and BOOK.4), BOOK.2 matches, and the result is again merged with the first buffer, producing the following analysis in buffer 1:

(PAST r1 RESERVING [AGENT (NAME j1 HUMAN "John")]
                    [BENEFICIARY (PRO m1 HUMAN "me")]
                    [THEME (INDEF/SING f1 FLIGHT
                            (TO-LOC f1 (NAME c1 CITY "Chicago")))])

When the final period is read in, rule S.end fires and signals the completion of the parse with the preceding analysis.

To extend this interpreter to handle the analysis of noun phrases, you need to introduce a mechanism similar to the attention-shifting mechanism in the deterministic parser. In particular the rule for *a* is

ART.1	[=a] → (INDEF/SING * ?)
	Activate rules NP.end1 and NP.end2
FLIGHT.1	[+empty/np] [=flight] → [V(1) ∧ (? * FLIGHT)]
FLIGHT.2	[+flight] [=to] [+location] → [V(1) ∧ (? * ? (TO-LOC * V(3))])]
MAN.1	[+empty/np] [=man] → [V(1) ∧ (? * MAN)]
CHICAGO.1	[=chicago] → (NAME c1 CITY "Chicago")
ME.1	[=me] → (PRO * HUMAN "me")
NP.end1	[=.] → pop (a period signals the end of an NP)
NP.end2	[+verb] → pop (a verb signals the end of the subject NP)

Figure 9.23 Some rules for noun phrase analysis

ART.1 [=a] → (INDEF/SING * ?)

In the preceding example, if the noun phrase *a flight to Chicago* had not been preprocessed, the parser would have reached the following position:

Buffer 1: (PAST **r1** RESERVING [AGENT (NAME **j1** HUMAN "John")]
[BENEFICIARY
(PRO **m1** HUMAN "me")])

Buffer 2: *a*

None of the currently active rules (BOOK.2, BOOK.4, and ART.1) would match this configuration. However, rule ART.1 could match if patterns could start matching at positions other than the first. As in the deterministic parser, you allow such matches to occur and create an attention shift. The rules that were active are temporarily removed from the active list, and the parse continues as though buffer 2 were the first buffer. The parser is now in a position to use the rules for *flight*, *to*, and *Chicago* shown in Figure 9.23 to construct the noun phrase analysis. When the NP is completed, the original state of the parser is restored by a new action called **pop**.

Trace the parse continuing from the point shown earlier where the word *a* enters the second buffer. Rule ART.1 fires and an attention shift is made, resulting in rules BOOK.2 and BOOK.4 being deactivated temporarily, and buffer 2 is set up as the first buffer for matching. When you enter the word *flight*, you have the following situation:

Buffer 1: (PAST **r1** RESERVING [AGENT (NAME **j1** HUMAN "John")]
[BENEFICIARY
(PRO **m1** HUMAN "me")])

Buffer 2: (INDEF/SING **obj1** ?) **patterns start matching here**

Buffer 3: *flight*

The active rules are FLIGHT.1 and FLIGHT.2. FLIGHT.1 matches and replaces the contents of buffer 3 with (INDEF/SING **obj1** FLIGHT). Next the word *to* is entered into buffer 4. No patterns match, however. Next *Chicago* is entered and rule CHICAGO.1 fires, immediately replacing the word with the term (NAME **c1** CITY "Chicago"). Now the buffer looks as follows:

Buffer 1: (PAST **r1** RESERVING [AGENT (NAME **j1** HUMAN "John")]
[BENEFICIARY
(PRO **m1** HUMAN "me")])

Buffer 2: (INDEF/SING **obj1** FLIGHT) **patterns start matching here**

Buffer 3: *to*

Buffer 4: (NAME **c1** CITY "Chicago")

Now rule FLIGHT.2 matches and replaces buffer 2 with the value (INDEF/SING **obj1** FLIGHT (TO-LOC **obj1** (NAME **c1** CITY "Chicago"))). Next a period is entered into buffer 3 and rule NP.end1 fires and executes a pop, resetting the parser to the state before the NP was begun. Rules BOOK.2 and BOOK.4 are reactivated and the parse continues as shown earlier.

While parsers can be built quickly in such a framework to handle some specific set of sentences, problems arise in viewing these systems as a general model of parsing. In particular, since all the rules are indexed by individual words, there is no opportunity to capture linguistic generalizations in a convenient way. For example, rule BOOK.1 identifies the first noun phrase found as the AGENT of the action RESERVING, one sense of *booked*. But this seems to be an instance of a general rule that applies for all action verbs. When the rules are accessed solely through lexical entries, however, you have no choice but to specify such a rule with each action verb. Consequently, the extensive grammars are cumbersome to construct.

More importantly, these systems can use only local syntactic information, since the only state they maintain consists of the current case-frame structure being specified and the current input. Thus, to disambiguate a word, you can at best inspect one word or so before it and a few words after. In practice, as these rules become more complex, they apply to fewer and fewer situations, and more

BOOK.5   [+flight] [+be] [=booked] → [(PAST * RESERVING [THEME V(1)])]
remove rules BOOK.1, BOOK.6
add rule B.1

BOOK.6   [+flight] [=booked] [=by] → [V(1) ∧ (? * FLIGHT V(2))]
[(PAST * RESERVING [THEME V(1)])] [=by]
remove rules BOOK.1 to BOOK.3 and BOOK.5
add rule B.2

B.1   [+reserving] [by] [+animate] → [V(1) ∧ (? * RESERVING
[AGENT V(3)])]

B.2   [+verb] → pop

Figure 9.24 Additional rules

equally complex rules need to be added to handle simple syntactic variants. For example, the definition of the verb *booked* earlier considered only its use as the main verb of a sentence in the simple past. In fact, *booked* is also a past participle and thus can be used in a passive sentence and can introduce a relative clause, as in *The flight booked by the travel agent leaves at three*. To handle these cases, the rules in Figure 9.22 would need to be augmented with rules such as those in Figure 9.24.

Rule BOOK.5 recognizes the simple passive construct, assigns the THEME case appropriately to the subject noun phrase, removes two rules that are now not applicable (that is, BOOK.1 is for active sentences, BOOK.6 is for the reduced relative clause), and adds one rule to recognize the agent from a prepositional phrase using *by*. The intention in rule BOOK.6 is that you would push for a sentence (the relative clause) with the flight (V(1)) being the moved constituent, and the embedded sentence itself (the new contents of buffer 2) being a modifier of the flight. Some rules are removed that will not be applicable in this construction, and rule BOOK.6 is added to recognize the end of the relative clause when a new verb is found.

Even with all this complexity, rule BOOK.6 is certainly not general enough. Rule B.2, which completes the relative clause when a verb is found, for instance, can easily be fooled by a verb in another embedded relative clause, as in the noun phrase *The flight booked by the man sitting at the door*. Furthermore, for noun phrases not in the subject position, it will not work at all. Thus you would have to modify the rule to signal termination of the relative clause in other situations as well. But even a more generalized rule is unlikely to work correctly, because there is simply too little syntactic information being retained to handle this construct properly.

BOX 9.1 Conceptual Analysis: A Semantically Driven Parser

The most influential semantically driven parsers have been developed by the Yale natural language understanding group. The analyzer described in (Birnbaum and Selfridge, 1981) is probably the best reference for an introduction to the work. The analyzer is driven by a case-based representation called **conceptual dependency** (see Box 7.5). The key idea is that certain words, especially verbs, identify meaning structures that have cases, and the parser's main job is to identify these words and use the rest of the sentence to fill in the values of these cases. While the details of the parser are different in style from the semantically driven parser described in this section, the type of operations performed are similar. The system is organized as a set of pattern-action rules called **requests** that are associated with lexical items. When a word is read, its requests become active. In general, a request may test for two types of information: it may check for a particular word or phrase in the input, or it may check for certain semantic properties on the structures in the buffer, which is called the C-LIST. The actions allowed include the actions implicit in our presentation. In particular, they may add a new item to the C-LIST, fill in a slot in some structure on the C-LIST (a function performed by merging structures), and activate or deactivate other requests.

Recent work has aimed at remedying these deficiencies by reinstating a syntactic component that can be used to aid the interpretation in complex sentences. You can maintain syntactic context by running a syntactic parser in tandem with this interpreter. The actions of the parser, however, will be suggested by the semantic analyzer. The syntactic parser can simply return whether the syntactic operation identified by the semantic analyzer is a possible next move or not. If it isn't, the semantic interpreter attempts to find a different analysis.

It is not clear, however, whether the semantic analyzer can handle complex sentences involving movement in a clean way. When the syntactic analyzer is controlling the processing, the syntactic component can be used to eliminate these complexities before the semantic analyzer is invoked. With the control scheme suggested here, the semantic analyzer itself would have to be able to handle the complexities, and only then would it have the analysis verified by the syntactic component.

Summary

Many different strategies for semantic interpretation bring semantic information to bear while the syntactic parsing of the sentence is in progress. These methods range from encoding the semantic information directly into the grammar (that is, the semantic grammar approach) through various degrees of interaction between syntactic and semantic processing. The interleaved parsers perform semantic interpretation when each major constituent is completed, while the rule-by-rule interpretation does the semantic interpretation incrementally as each syntactic rule is used.

There are advantages to each of these approaches. Semantic grammars tend to be easily built for small domains and can be very efficient. They are not easily transportable to new domains, however. The interleaved strategies are generally more domain-independent because of the syntactic grammar. Most of the work in moving to a new domain involves changes to the semantic interpreter. The rule-by-rule analysis offers the strongest form of interaction and can be used to eliminate syntactically valid but semantically anomalous interpretations as early as possible. These methods, however, do incur a hidden cost over the completely separate syntactic and semantic processing. In particular, syntactic analysis is quite efficient compared to semantic interpretation. Because of this, much time could be wasted building semantic interpretations of fragments that turn out later not to be syntactically possible.

A semantic interpreter may also assign ratings to constituents rather than return a simple decision of accept or reject. Finally, there is a semantically driven parser in which syntactic information plays a minimal role. While this technique does surprisingly well in many situations, it has to reintroduce syntactic information to capture complex sentences in a reasonable manner.

Related Work and Further Readings

Semantic grammars have been used effectively in many systems. The technique was first used in the SOPHIE system (Brown and Burton, 1975), which was a tutorial system for debugging electronic circuits. It used a simple top-down parser on a semantic grammar that had terminal symbols such as REQUEST, TRANSISTOR, JUNCTION/TYPE, and so on. Each rule was associated with a function that could take the analysis of the subconstituents and produce LISP code that would perform the appropriate query. Semantic grammars have also been used successfully in constructing natural language interfaces to databases. For example, the LIFER system (Hendrix et al., 1978) has been used for query databases storing naval command and control information, and the PLANES system (Waltz and Goodman, 1977) provided an interface to a database of maintenance and flight records for naval aircraft.

The LSP project (Sager, 1981) combines an extensive syntactic grammar with the techniques of semantic grammar to introduce semantic constraints appropriate to the particular sublanguage that arises in the domain of application. Semantic templates, similar to semantic grammar rules, are applied to the output of the syntactic parser rather than directly onto the input.

Interleaved syntactic and semantic analysis was used extensively in the SHRDLU system (Winograd, 1972). This system performed semantic analysis of a constituent incrementally as each subconstituent was constructed. For example, when a simple NP (determiner, adjectives, head) has been constructed, its semantic interpretation is constructed, and then as each postmodifier is parsed, the semantic interpretation of the NP is extended with the interpretation of the modifier. In actual fact at times it is difficult to separate out a syntactic and semantic phase in SHRDLU, because both are implemented as a set of procedures. There is no notion of a separate grammar and semantic interpreter, and thus it is hard to compare this in any detail with the techniques described in this chapter. Other features of this system will be described in later chapters in dealing with context.

The RUS system (Bobrow and Webber, 1980) is an interleaved parser based on the ATN framework. It allows actions on the arcs that invoke a semantic interpreter that incrementally constructs an extended case frame semantic description for the constituents parsed so far. In particular the parser suggests that some specific functional relation holds between a previously interpreted constituent and the constituent that is currently being constructed. The semantic analyzer can either reject the proposal from syntax, in which case the arc is not followed, or accept the proposal and return a pointer to the partial semantic interpretation constructed for the current constituent. This pointer is not used by the syntactic component except in other messages to the semantic analyzer. Woods (1980) provides a more formal analysis of such interleaved parsers using a formalism he calls "Cascaded ATN Grammars." Another ATN-based system with interleaved semantic processing as each constituent is built is described in detail in Ritchie (1980).

One of the most influential works in incorporating preferences into semantic interpretation is the work by Wilks (1975). The semantic information in this system consists of a set of semantic templates defining the possible semantic relationships in the system and a semantic formula for each lexical entry. An example of a template is "<animate> <own> <physobj>." The essential operation in this system is matching these templates to a representation of the sentence where the basic phrase structure has been extracted. The unique feature of this approach is that partial matches are allowed, and the system produces a group of templates, each partially matching some portion of the input sentence. It then selects the combination of templates that matches the input with the least number of type violations. Other work related to preference-based systems involves systems that address the general issue of handling ill-formed input. Several approaches are described in a special issue of *Computational Linguistics* (1983) devoted to this topic. These methods deal with syntactic, as well as semantic, ill-formedness. Approaches that suggest semantic relaxation similar to those in this chapter are Weischedel and Sondheimer (1983) and Fass and Wilks (1983). Jensen and Binot (1987) describe a system for determining prepositional phrase attachment using a semantic rating scheme based on the word definitions in on-line dictionaries.

Rule-by-rule semantic interpretation is used in many systems. For example, the DIAGRAM system (Robinson, 1982) uses an extended context-free grammar, allowing optional constituents in rules, together with an augmentation on each rule that is a set of LISP procedures. These procedures, which are executed when the rule is applied, construct a syntactic structure, as well as building a semantic interpretation for the constituent. Other systems encode a semantic analysis into a specialized interpretation language used to augment the grammar (Thompson and Thompson, 1975).

The logic grammar approach can be used to encode all the preceding strategies. The rule-by-rule interpretation described in Section 9.6 is based on Pereira and Warren (1980). McCord (1985) describes an excellent example of an interleaved approach using logic grammars. Generalized unification-based grammars, such as described by Kay (1985) and Kaplan and Bresnan (1982) also use a rule-by-rule approach to semantics. For example, in LFG the semantic form is constructed using equations in the lexicon. The lexical entry for *hates* might be

$$hates \text{ VERB } (\uparrow \text{ TENSE}) = \text{PRES}$$
$$(\uparrow \text{ SEM}) = \text{'DISLIKE} < (\uparrow \text{ SUBJ}), (\uparrow \text{ OBJ}) >'$$

This entry indicates that anytime the word *hates* is used in a constituent (a VP), the TENSE slot of that VP must be set to PRES, and the SEM slot must be set to a formula of the form DISLIKE $<x, y>$, where x is the value of the SUBJ slot and y is the value of the OBJ slot. This rule results in the correct result even if the value of the OBJ slot is not yet known. Because of the way unification works, when the OBJ slot is set later, the SEM structure will be automatically filled in as well.

A major influence on the rule-by-rule systems was the work by Montague (see text on Montague by Dowty, Wall, and Peters (1981)). Montague's primary claim was that natural languages can be viewed as formal languages and offer a compositional, albeit complicated, syntax and semantics. Key to this approach is the notion of function application--that is, the meaning of one constituent is often a function that takes the meaning of another constituent and produces the meaning of the constituent that contains them both. For example, given a rule S ← NP VP, the interpretation of the NP is a function that takes a VP interpretation and produces an S interpretation. To make this work requires a very complex formalism including the λ-calculus embedded in an intensional logic with explicit intension and extension operators. This work has had a significant influence on modern work in semantics in linguistics, and many of the ideas, in simplified form, have been adapted to computational systems (Rosenschein and Shieber, 1982; Schubert and Pelletier, 1982).

The semantically driven parser in Section 9.7 is modeled after the conceptual analyzer of Birnbaum and Selfridge (1981) (see Box 9.1), which itself is a descendant of the earlier parsers (Schank, 1975; Riesbeck and Schank, 1978). An interesting semantically driven parser that drives a syntactic component to verify the analysis is described by Lytinen (1986).

Exercises for Chapter 9

1. *(easy)* List the different methods of semantic interpretation used in this chapter, and give an overview of how they work and a brief analysis of their strengths and weaknesses.

2. *(medium)* Show the derivation of the logical forms of the three sentences shown in Section 9.1 from the syntactic analyses given in the same section. For each, list all the partial descriptions generated as well as the final forms.

3. *(medium)* Describe the type of semantic interpretation you would use in the following situations and briefly explain why.

   a) The simplest possible natural language understanding system designed to answer questions about which floor articles could be found in a department store.

   b) A language translation system.

4. *(medium)* Show how the syntactically driven parser with rule-by-rule semantic interpretation would analyze the following sentence. Give a trace as is done in Figures 9.18, 9.19, and 9.20.

   Do you know the time of the flight from Boston to Chicago?

5. *(hard)* Write a semantic grammar that accepts the following sentences:

   Flight thirty-three arrives in Atlanta at seven.
   Flight seven connects with flight sixty-three at Chicago.
   The next Atlanta-bound flight connects with flight seven in Atlanta.
   The next Chicago flight arrives in six minutes.

Your grammar should identify the appropriate semantic cases of each phrase and word. For example, *seven* in the first sentence is a time, whereas *seven* in the second sentence is a flight number; and *at seven* in the first sentence is the time that the arrival is occurring, whereas *at Chicago* is the place where the connection is made. For each sentence, show the parse tree that would be constructed by your grammar.

6. (*hard*) Write a grammar using rule-by-rule semantic interpretation that accepts assertions and questions about a simple microworld containing blocks. Blocks may be blue, green, or red and large or small. Blocks may be on other blocks. Your grammar should at least accept the following sentences:

> Is a red block on the small blue block?
> Are all blocks to the right of the large block?
> Is a small block green?
> Are all green blocks small?
> The red block is on the small green block.
> The block that is on the red block is green.

Construct four other sentences relevant in this domain and modify your grammar to accept them. Show the final analysis for each sentence. Your grammar should check for number agreement, but it need not do any tense analysis. You may use any parts of the grammars defined in the book that you find useful.

Chapter 10

Issues in
Semantic Interpretation

The logical form and semantic interpretation strategies discussed in the last three chapters, while reflecting the current abilities of existing systems, still fall far short of a comprehensive semantic theory of language. This chapter briefly considers a set of problems that either are or must become areas of active research. The major issues are interpretation of modifiers in noun phrases, the treatment of quantifiers, the resolution of ambiguity, and tense analysis.

10.1 Scoping Phenomena

This section discusses the syntactic and semantic issues that affect the scoping of quantifiers and operators in sentences. While not all scoping can be determined independently of context, certain sentences have strong preferences toward a particular scoping.

Quantifier Scoping in Sentences with Simple NPs

The current logical form allows quantifiers to be expressed without any information about the relative scope of each quantifier. This is very useful for representing ambiguity. For example, the sentence *Every man loves a dog* is ambiguous between the *every* taking the wide scope, which could be expressed in FOPC as:

1. $\forall m . TYPE (m, MAN) \supset$
      $(\exists d . TYPE (d, DOG) \& LOVES (m,d))$

and the *a* taking the widest scope, which could be expressed as:

2. $\exists d . TYPE (d, DOG) \& (\forall m . TYPE (m, MAN) \supset LOVES (m,d))$

In interpretation 1, there may be many different dogs, each one loved by a man, whereas in interpretation 2 there is one dog--say, Lassie--who is loved by all men. The following logical form expresses this ambiguity exactly:

   (PRES l1 LOVING [AGENT (EVERY m1 MAN)]
                    [THEME (INDEF/SING d1 DOG)])

   Certain syntactic considerations do affect quantifier scoping, and hence you may want to be able to express scope information in the logical form if it is available. For instance, the sentence *There is a dog that is loved by every man* only has interpretation 2. To be able to express scoping in these situations, yet remain uncommitted in others, the logical form is extended with an optional index on each specifier that can indicate a dependency on another term in the form. Interpretation 2 could then be represented as

(PRES 11 LOVING [AGENT (ALL$_{d1}$ **m1** MAN)]
[THEME (INDEF/SING **d1** DOG)])

The subscript indicates that the variable **d1** should be defined outside the scope of the variable **m1**. Interpretation 1 can be expressed similarly by putting a subscript of **m1** on the INDEF/SING specifier. The structure where ALL is subscripted by **d1** and INDEF/SING is subscripted by **m1** is illegal since the ordering dependencies cannot be satisfied.

Scoping dependencies are created by the use of different quantifiers, as well as various syntactic structures. For example, the quantifiers *all*, *every*, and *each* all seem to map to the universal quantifier but differ in the scoping dependencies they create (among other things). For instance, the sentence *A man saw every dog* tends to be read as meaning there is one man who saw all the dogs. But the sentence *A man saw each dog* is not so clear--it may be that there was a different man for each dog. Thus the quantifier *each* tends to indicate a wider scope than the quantifier *every*.

You can compare other quantifiers in sentences in a similar way, but you have to be careful of the effect of syntactic position as well. For example, there seems to be a strong preference for wide scope of the first NP in the sentence. This preference is evident in the sentences:

3.   A man saw every dog.

4.   Every dog saw a man.

In sentence 3 you see the indefinite NP taking the widest scope, but in sentence 4 you don't. In fact, the interpretation with *every* taking the widest scope may be preferable. Because of this phenomenon, a passive may differ in scoping from its active counterpart. For instance, the passive counterpart of sentence 4, *A man was seen by every dog*, strongly favors the interpretation in which there is a single man.

Noun phrases involving the definite article provide the best example of a scoping restriction. In sentences 5, 6, and 7, you can produce an interpretation only where there is a single man:

5.   Every dog saw the man.

6.   The man saw every dog.

7.   Each dog saw the man.

Thus the definite article takes the widest scope, irrespective of its position in these simple sentences. (Later you will see that this is not always the case in

Sentence	Interpretation
Who saw every dog?	(PAST **s1** [AGENT (WH **x1** PERSON)] [THEME (ALL$_{x1}$ **d1** DOG)])
Who saw each dog?	(PAST **s1** [AGENT (WH **x1** PERSON)] [THEME (ALL **d1** DOG)])
Each dog was seen by the man.	(PAST **s1** [AGENT (DEF/SING **m1** MAN)] [THEME (ALL$_{m1}$ **d1** DOG)])
Each dog was seen by a man.	(PAST **s1** [AGENT (INDEF/SING$_{d1}$ **m1** MAN)] [THEME (ALL **d1** DOG)])

Figure 10.1 Examples of the scoping algorithm

complex NPs.) So far, NPs with *the* take the widest scope, followed by NPs with *each*, followed by NPs with *every* and *a*.

Finally, consider wh-noun phrases that occur in questions. Wh-phrases seem to fall between *each* and *every*, as shown by sentences 8 and 9:

8.   Who saw every dog?

9.   Who saw each dog?

In sentence 8 you are asking for a single person, but in sentence 9 you may be asking for a list of people--one or more for each dog. Using similar tests, the following initial list of preference strengths for wide scope seems plausible:

> *the* > *each* > wh-terms > *every, all, some, a*

Using the syntactic position and the preference inherent in the quantifiers, the following is a conservative algorithm for simple sentences:

1. Give all definite NPs the widest scope.

2. In sentences in the form "There is Q X that ...," give the term X the next widest scope. (The Q could be *a, some, a few, ...*)

3. Given two quantifiers Q1 and Q2 whose relative scoping is not yet determined by the previous steps, if Q1 > Q2 in the strength ordering, make Q2 dependent on Q1 unless Q1 is in the first constituent in the sentence.

This algorithm will add scoping constraints where there is strong evidence for a particular scoping and will remain uncommitted where there is conflicting evidence between syntactic position and specifier scoping strength. Examples of the analyses produced for certain sentences are shown in Figure 10.1. You could extend the algorithm to make more assignments. For instance, you could create a dependency between two equally strong quantified terms when one is in the initial position. But the more decisions made here, the higher the chance that they will have to be undone when context is considered.

PP Modifiers

There are constructions where even a term introduced by a definite noun phrase can become dependent on another term. The simplest cases of this occur in PP modifiers, as in *The kitchen in every house had a stove*, where in the preferred reading there are many different kitchens. This case turns out to be an instance of a quite strong scoping preference with PP modifiers. Consider other examples, such as *We saw a man on every street corner*, where there seem to be many different men, and *Each representative from some countries spoke at the meeting*, where not all representatives at the meeting spoke (that is, there's probably a country with a representative who didn't speak). Thus to handle PP modifiers, another step would be added to the earlier algorithm, to the effect that if a term X is modified by a PP with a term Y, then X is dependent on Y. The final logical form of *The kitchen in every house had a stove* would be

$$\begin{array}{l} \text{(PAST c1 CONTAIN} \\ \quad \text{[THEME (INDEF/SING d1 STOVE)]} \\ \quad \text{[AT-LOC (DEF/SING}_{h1} \text{ k1 KITCHEN} \\ \qquad \text{(IN-LOC k1 (EVERY h1 HOUSE)))])} \end{array}$$

A similar situation occurs with PP modifers to the sentence, as in *The kitchen was painted yellow in every house*. This can be complicated, however, since every term in the sentence need not be dependent on the the term in the PP modifier, although something must. Thus in the earlier sentence, both *the owner* and *the kitchen* may be dependent on *every house*. In other words, there was a different owner in every house or there was one owner of all the houses who moved around a lot. Because of the complications, the scoping order here will be left to the contextual processing.

Relative Clauses

Relative clauses seem to affect the scoping in exactly the opposite way. For example, the sentence *The kitchen that was in every house had a stove* seems very awkward, presumably because our world knowledge contradicts the scoping indicated by the sentence (that there is one kitchen that somehow is in every house). If you change the sentence so that it agrees with your intuition, you find no problem with sentences of this form, as in *The bed that I made every day broke*. Here it is plausible that there is one bed and the sentence seems fine. One way to view the origin of this scoping preference is to consider the semantic interpretation of the relative clause as a separate process from the interpretation of the outer sentence. In particular the quantifiers in the

---

BOX 10.1 Generating a Fully-Scoped Logical Form

Current question-answering systems must commit to a definite ordering of quantifiers and thus employ a less conservative ordering strategy than outlined in this chapter. In general, this is done by using the quantifier strength information alone to resolve any remaining ambiguities after whatever structural preferences are used. In practice, this means that definite NPs always take widest scope, followed by *each*, then the wh-terms, then *all* and *every*, and lastly the indefinite and existential NPs.

While some work has aimed at generating the set of possible scopings (Hobbs and Shieber, 1987), there currently are few general techniques for using context to select the most appropriate ordering from such a set.

---

relative clause usually do not have wider scope than the relative clause itself. Thus the final interpretation of the sentence *The bed that I made every day broke* is

(PAST b1 BREAK
    [THEME (DEF/SING b1 BED
        (PAST m1 MAKE
           [AGENT (PRO h1 HUMAN "I")]
           [THEME b1]
           [AT-TIME (EVERY$_{b1}$ d1 DAY)]))]

The Final Algorithm

The following is an algorithm for assigning scope that incorporates the information on PP and relative clauses.

1. Recursively consider all relative clauses, and then make each Q introduced in the relative clause dependent on the variable of the NP that the relative clause modifies.

2. Given two specifiers Q_{np} and Q_{pp}, where Q_{pp} is in a PP modifier of the NP of Q_{np}, make Q_{np} dependent on Q_{pp}.

3. Unless contradicted by steps 1 or 2, give all definite NPs the widest scope.

4. Unless contradicted by a previous step, with sentences of the form "There is Q X that ...," give the term X the next widest scope. (The Q could be *a, some, a few, ...*)

5. Given two specifiers Q1 and Q2 whose relative scoping is not yet considered by the previous steps, if Q1 > Q2 in the strength ordering, make Q2 dependent on Q1 unless Q1 is in the first constituent in the sentence.

Negation

Negation interacts with quantifiers in a way that is best analyzed as a scoping problem. In particular, changing the scope of the negation operator changes the possible interpretation of a sentence. By introducing some constraints on the scope, you can exactly capture the range of possible interpretations. For instance, to many speakers the sentence *Every boy does not like Mary* is ambiguous between the case where no boy likes Mary:

$$\forall b \, . \, TYPE(b, BOY) \supset \neg \, LOVES(b, MARY1)$$

and the case where some boys do not like her, but some might:

$$\neg \, (\forall b \, . \, TYPE(b, BOY) \supset LOVES(b, MARY))$$

If you treat the NOT operator in a way similar to the quantifiers and make it subject to scoping, the logical form will capture this ambiguity. In particular, allow NOT to modify any logical form structure. For the preceding sentence the logical form would be

```
(NOT n1 (PRES l1 LOVE
         [AGENT (EVERY b1 BOY)]
         [THEME (NAME m1 MARY)]))
```

The name for the negated predication can be used to indicate scoping constraints if necessary. Thus, if you wish to force the first interpretation just shown, you would use the form

```
(NOT_{b1} n1 (PRES l1 LOVE
         [AGENT (EVERY b1 BOY)]
         [THEME (NAME m1 MARY)]))
```

If you want to force the second interpretation, you would use the form

```
(NOT n1 (PRES l1 LOVE
         [AGENT (EVERY_{n1} b1 BOY)]
         [THEME (NAME m1 MARY)]))
```

If the negation does not modify the sentence, however, the number of possible interpretations may be fewer. For instance, the sentence *Not every boy likes Mary* allows only the second reading. The logical form for this sentence then might be

(PRES l1 LOVE [AGENT (NOT n1 (EVERY$_{n1}$ b1 BOY))]
                      [THEME (NAME m1 MARY)]))

This forces the negation to have wider scope than the other quantifier but doesn't yet capture the phenomenon with multiple quantifiers, as in the sentence *Not every boy loves some girl.* As before, the negation would have wider scope than the universal, but there would be multiple interpretations depending on the scope of the existential. Thus you have the interpretation that there is a boy who doesn't love any girl (final nesting order: NOT every some), and possibly the interpretation where there is a particular girl whom not every boy loves (final nesting order: some NOT every), but you can't have the interpretation that it's not the case that a particular girl is loved by every boy (final nesting order: NOT some every). In other words, not only is the nesting order for the negation and the quantifier determined, but also no other quantifier can come between them in the nesting order.

Other Operators Involving Scoping

There are many other constructs that also may involve scoping issues. In particular, verbs such as *believe* and *want* often introduce scoping ambiguities with their complements. For example, the sentence *Jack believes a man found the ring* is ambiguous between the case where Jack knows of a particular man who he believes found the ring, or the case where all Jack believes is that the ring was found by some man. These ambiguities are often captured by scoping differences. To see this, you must examine the logical form of such sentences in more detail.

Verbs like *believe* and *want* are quite different from the verbs you've seen so far, such as *loves*, in that they take a sentence as an argument. Because of this, they cannot be modeled as simple predicates in the first-order predicate calculus, which restricts the arguments of predicates to be terms (that is, NPs). These verbs, which are closer in form to the logical operators such as AND, OR, and NOT, are called **sentential operators**. These operators are different from both logical operators and predicates because they do not support the normal inference rule of substituting of equals. In other words, if John is that tallest man, then if you are given the fact that *John kissed Sue*, you can conclude that *the tallest man kissed Sue*. The similar inference, however, does not work for belief sentences. If you are given *Sam believes John kissed Sue*, you cannot conclude that *Sam believes the tallest man kissed Sue*, since Sam may not know that John is the tallest man. Worse yet, Sam may believe that George is the tallest! Because equal terms cannot be substituted for each other in the scope of such operators, they are often called **referentially opaque**. In contrast, normal predicates are said to be **referentially transparent**. These issues will be examined in detail in Chapter 15. All you need to know here is that *believe* and *want* are fundamentally different types of verbs from standard predicates.

Opaque operators introduce a new form of scoping ambiguity. In particular a quantifier can be inside the scope of the operator as well as being outside its scope. This can be used to capture the ambiguities in *John believes a man found the ring*. The first reading involves John knowing who the man is; it could be paraphrased by *There is a particular man who John believes found the ring*. Its form is

    (PRES$_{m1}$ b1 BELIEVE
        [EXPERIENCER (NAME j1 JOHN)]
        [THEME (PAST f1 FIND
                    [AGENT (INDEF/SING m1 MAN)]
                    [THEME (DEF/SING r1 RING)])])

The second case involves John simply believing that some man found the ring, though he doesn't know who. It would have the following form:

    (PRES b1 BELIEVE
        [EXPERIENCER (NAME j1 JOHN)]
        [THEME (PAST f1 FIND
                    [AGENT (INDEF/SING$_{b1}$ m1 MAN)]
                    [THEME (DEF/SING r1 RING)])])

The logical form without any scoping constraints is ambiguous between these two interpretations.

There are many other examples of this phenomenon, some of which can be quite complicated. For example, some time ago I was at a party and someone walked into the kitchen and said *I'm waiting for a phone call*. This expression later lead to some confusion because I had understood it in the usual interpretation that he was waiting for a call from someone in particular. It turned out, however, that the speaker simply wanted to hear the phone ring, so any call would do! Interestingly enough, the intent of the original sentence could have been conveyed unambiguously by the rather unusual sentence *I'm waiting for any phone call*. But this sentence is unusual simply because the contexts in which it is appropriate are very rare.

10.2 Modifiers and Noun Phrases

This section describes the semantic interpretation of noun phrase modifiers in considerably more detail than in previous chapters. Much of the discussion provides background information on the linguistic phenomenon itself, rather then a fully worked out solution within the framework.

```
1.   (NP ART the
        NUM {3s}) → (DEF/SING * ? ?)

2.   (NP HEAD +physobj) → (? * T(HEAD) ?)

3.   (NP ADJS alleged) → (? * ? (ALLEGED *))
```

Figure 10.2 Some incorrect interpretation rules for *the alleged murderer*

Adjectives

Adjectives generally introduce restrictions on the object referred to in the NP, but in many cases the analysis becomes more complex. Adjectives can be classified into two classes: **intersective** adjectives and **nonintersective** adjectives. Intersective adjectives are so called because they can be analyzed in terms of set intersection. For example, to generate the set of *green balls*, you could intersect the set of *balls* with the set of *green objects*. Because of this, such adjectives can be handled as you have seen in the previous chapters--that is, interpretation rules for the adjective add a restriction to the NP.

There are several classes of nonintersective adjectives. Examples of the first class are *large*, *slow*, and *bright*, which in all but the most simplified domains are relative to the noun phrase being modified. For instance, a slow dolphin travels considerably faster than a fast snail. Similarly, viewed as a college professor, a person might be considered a fast runner, but when viewed as an athlete, he or she might not be considered fast. These examples show that you cannot simply model *fast* as a one-place predicate true of all objects that are fast. At the very least, the predicate must be relative to the type to which the object is being compared.

Examples of the second class of nonintersective adjectives include *average*, *toy*, and *alleged*. Thus *average grade* may not be an actual grade, *a toy gun* is not really a gun, and *an alleged murderer* is not necessarily guilty of murder. You cannot analyze these adjectives as simple restrictions. For instance, consider the rules in Figure 10.2 that might be suggested for analyzing the NP *the alleged murderer*. Applying these rules to the NP would produce the analysis

(DEF/SING m1 MURDERER (ALLEGED m1))

This analysis classifies the referent of this NP as a murderer, so the object **m1** will have all the characteristics of being a murderer, including committing the crime! Thus the adjective *alleged* seems to have no effect. To remedy this, you need to perform something like the following analysis. Any NP with an adjective *alleged* does not take its type from the head noun alone. Rather, the type is some more neutral set (HUMAN, for instance), and a restriction is added that this object is accused of some action that must be derived from the head noun (MURDERING in this case). Thus you would like a final analysis along the lines of

(DEF/SING m1 HUMAN (ACCUSED-OF m1
                    (DEF/SING m2 MURDER [AGENT m1])))

Thus *the alleged murderer* would be analyzed in the same way as the NP *the person accused of the murder*. To construct such an analysis, you would have to extend the head interpretation phase to detect when such adjectives are used. Before this example can be discussed in detail, you need to examine how nouns such as *murderer* should be analyzed.

Role Nouns

Words like *murderer*, *actor*, and *thief*, typically ending in the suffixes *-er* or *-or*, all classify agents by the acts they perform. Thus a murderer performs one or more murders, an actor acts, and a thief steals things. There are other nouns that also identify cases other than the AGENT case. For instance, *recipient* indicates the TO case in transfer acts, *donation* identifies the THEME case in a donating act, and general words with the suffix *-ee*, such as *addressee* and *rentee*, indicate cases filled by animate objects that are not the AGENT in two-person interactions. While these words could be analyzed independently of the events they suggest by introducing types such as MURDERER, DONOR, and so on, many generalities will be lost. For example, the handling of phrases like *alleged murderer* would require a mechanism completely separate from the analysis of *murder*. In addition, such nouns may subcategorize for constituents that identify other cases in the action. For example, in *the murderer of John*, the NP *John* intuitively fills the THEME case of the murder act. Thus an analysis of *murderer* in terms of the action of murdering seems to capture many generalities.

Specifically, the following rules might be used for the head analysis of NPs with the head *murderer*:

(NP HEAD murderer) → (? * HUMAN (? ** MURDER [AGENT *]))

(NP HEAD murderer
     MODS (PP PREP of
               POBJ +animate))
               → (? * HUMAN (? ** MURDER
                                 [AGENT *]
                                 [THEME V̲(MODS POBJ)])))

Similar techniques could be used to define the words *donor* and *donation* as the AGENT and THEME cases of an act DONATE:

(NP HEAD donor) → (? * HUMAN (? ** DONATE [AGENT *]))

(NP HEAD donation) → (? * PHYSOBJ (? ** DONATE [THEME *]))

With this treatment you can now examine how *alleged* might be handled. What would be needed is an extension to the mechanism to allow the head analysis of the NP without the *alleged* to be transformed into another analysis where the act is only claimed to have occurred. While there is no mechanism in the current framework for this, it would have to transform the head analysis for the NP *the alleged murderer of John* as follows:

(? **h1** HUMAN (? **m1** MURDER
                 [AGENT **h1**]
                 [THEME (NAME **j1** PERSON "John")]))

and produce a new head analysis:

(? **h1** HUMAN (CLAIMED-TO-BE-TRUE
                 (? **m1** MURDER
                    [AGENT **h1**]
                    [THEME (NAME **j1** PERSON "John")])))

Other nonintersective adjectives would modify the basic type. For example, the adjective *toy* would need to take the normal head analysis and transform it to a new type. For example, if the usual sense of *gun* is FIREARM1, *toy gun* might produce some type like (TOY FIREARM1).

PP Modifiers

Earlier you saw that some head nouns may subcategorize for PPs. In particular, the same inner case/outer case distinction can be made. There is a simple test for distinguishing between inner and outer cases: If the PP modifier can be paraphrased as a relative clause, it is an outer case, and its meaning is derived from the meaning of the preposition. If it cannot be paraphrased in this way, it is an inner case. For example, in the NP *the destruction of the city*, the PP cannot be paraphrased using a relative clause. You may, therefore, infer an inner case associated with the definition of the noun *destruction*. To point out the similarities of this noun to the verb *destroy*, you would call this the THEME case. Similarly, an AGENT case can be introduced using the preposition *by*, as in *the destruction by the Huns*, with the analysis

(DEF/SING **d1** DESTROYING [AGENT (DEF/PL **h1** HUN)])

As with the cases for verbs, there are syntactic regularities that identify the particular cases. For instance, a PP with preposition *of* usually signifies the THEME case, while *by* signifies the AGENT case (as with verbs). The possessive form can signify either the AGENT case (*the Huns' destruction*) or the THEME case (*the city's destruction*). The rules for the outer cases seem to be the same for both verb phrases and noun phrases.

Other nouns seem related to verbs but don't refer to an event. For example, the NP *the weight of the cow* appears to refer to a case and could be represented by an analysis that is related to the sentence *The cow weighed a hundred pounds*. For instance, if the verb *weigh* takes the cases THEME (*the cow*) and AT (*a hundred pounds*), you could define the type WEIGHT (that is, values of weights) as being the AT case of the *weigh* relation. In other words, it could be viewed as a function that takes an argument and produces the appropriate value by considering that argument as the THEME case in the WEIGHING relation. The logical form could thus be

        (DEF/SING w1 WEIGHT (PAST w2 WEIGHS
                          [THEME (DEF/SING c1 COW)]
                          [AT w1]))

or more simply, you could allow the type WEIGHT to take a THEME case:

        (DEF/SING w1 WEIGHT [THEME (DEF/SING c1 COW)])

A similar analysis could be used for other nouns that are not related directly to verb forms, such as *area*, *height*, and *head*. For example, while *head* is in many ways ambiguous, it always refers to a part of some larger object or organization, such as *head of the committee*, *the head of the hammer*, and so on. In these cases you can either make the analysis relative to a relation name, such as

        (DEF/SING p1 PERSON (LEADER-OF p1
                          (DEF/SING c1 COMMITTEE))

or else introduce cases for the noun, as in the second form of the preceding analysis:

        (DEF/SING h1 HEAD [THEME (DEF/SING c1 COMMITTEE)])

In any case, whether here in the logical form, or later in the final semantic representation, the relationship of such nouns to the appropriate relations will have to be made explicit.

10.3 Adjective Phrases

Multiple Adjective Ambiguity

When several adjectives are present in an NP, new forms of ambiguity arise. In particular, with two adjectives, the first may modify the second, or they both might independently modify the head noun. Thus an NP such as *the light red block* may describe a block that is light red in color, or it may describe a red block that does not weigh much. The latter possibility may be identified syntactically by using a comma (as in *light, red block*). In general, however, the clustering of adjectives must be made on semantic grounds.

You could extend the semantic interpreter in a way to handle a list of adjectives, but this would involve significant changes to the way the interpreter is constructed. It is easier to build the ambiguity into the syntactic portion of the grammar and then use the semantic analyzer as a filter.

To analyze ADJ-ADJ modification, you need richer theories concerning the properties that objects can take. For example, a simple theory of the color of objects should allow objects to take a certain basic color value (RED, GREEN, PURPLE, and so on) that then can be qualified by its intensity (LIGHT, MEDIUM, DARK). A full theory of color would, of course, have to concern itself with blends of colors, such as *bluish-green*, as well as multicolored objects, but this simple theory will suffice to make the necessary points. The color of an object will be asserted using a predicate COLOR that takes an object and a color value. For example, (COLOR BLOCK1 RED) will assert that BLOCK1 is red, while (COLOR BLOCK1 (LIGHT RED)) will assert that BLOCK1 is light red. The qualities LIGHT and DARK can also be used independently; thus a dark block might be asserted with the form (COLOR BLOCK2 DARK). You could think of this as being nonspecific about the color (for example, between (DARK RED), (DARK BLUE), and so on).

A theory of weight is also complex, because there is no interpretation of a heavy object independent of context. For example, a heavy cat is much lighter than a very light cow! For the sake of simplicity, ignore this complication and assume that two predicates, (LIGHT-MASS x) and (HEAVY x), will suffice.

With these two simple treatments of color and weight, a lexicon is shown in Figure 10.3 and a grammar for adjectives in Grammar 10.4. Note that there are three entries for the word *light*: one as a modifier of color adjectives, one as a color modifier of physical objects, and one as a weight modifier of physical objects. To allow complex color values, the SEM for an adjective such as *red* anticipates a modifier (such as *light*).

Note that in the Grammar 10.4, rule 4 applies the SEM of an adjective to the identity function (IDENTITY-FUNCTION), which is defined simply to return the value of its argument. This, in effect, removes the unnecessary parameter for a qualifier from the logical form. In other words the value of the expression

$$\text{Apply } (\lambda (q) \lambda (x) (\text{COLOR x Apply } (\text{SEM}_q, \text{RED})),$$
$$\text{IDENTITY-FUNCTION})$$

Word	Type	SEM
ADJ: red	COLOR	λ (q: color-qualifier) λ (x: physobj) (COLOR x Apply (SEM_q, RED))
ADJ-QUAL: light	COLOR-QUALIFIER	λ (x: color) (LIGHT x)
ADJ: light	COLOR	λ (x: physobj) (COLOR x LIGHT)
ADJ: light	WEIGHT	λ (x: physobj) (LIGHT-MASS x)
ADJ-QUAL: dark	COLOR-QUALIFIER	λ (x: color) (DARK x)
ADJ: dark	COLOR	λ (x: physobj) (COLOR x DARK)
ADJ: heavy	WEIGHT	λ (x: physobj) (HEAVY x)

Figure 10.3 Sample lexicon for some adjectives

1.	ADJS $\leftarrow$ ADJP ADJS	SEM = Append (SEM_{ADJP}, SEM_{ADJS})
2.	ADJS $\leftarrow$ ADJP	SEM = SEM_{ADJP}
3.	ADJP $\leftarrow$ ADJ-QUAL ADJ	TYPE = $\underline{T}$(ADJ) SEM = Apply (SEM_{ADJ}, $SEM_{ADJ\text{-}QUAL}$)
4.	ADJP $\leftarrow$ ADJ	TYPE = $\underline{T}$(ADJ) SEM = Apply (SEM_{ADJ}, IDENTITY-FUNCTION)
5.	NP1 $\leftarrow$ ADJS NOUN	**ADJS** = ADJS **HEAD** = NOUN **SEM** = R-Apply (SEM_{ADJS}, SEM_{NOUN})]

Grammar 10.4 Grammar fragment for adjective phrases

is simply λ (x) (COLOR x RED), since Apply ($SEM_{IDENTITY\text{-}FUNCTION}$, RED) = RED.

Consider the resulting charts from parsing the NP fragments *heavy red car* and *light red car*, as shown in Figures 10.5 and 10.6. The NP fragment *heavy red car* has only one interpretation, since *heavy* cannot modify *red* (its lexicon entry restricts it to being an ADJ, not an ADJ-QUAL).

The fragment *light red car*, on the other hand, has three interpretations according to this grammar. Rule 3 can apply to combine *light* and *red*, yielding interpretation NP1. Alternatively, both *light* and *red* can be treated independently and produce interpretations NP2 and NP3. Two interpretations arise because of the lexical ambiguity of the word *light*. A more complex grammar might eliminate NP3 since it is subsumed by NP1.

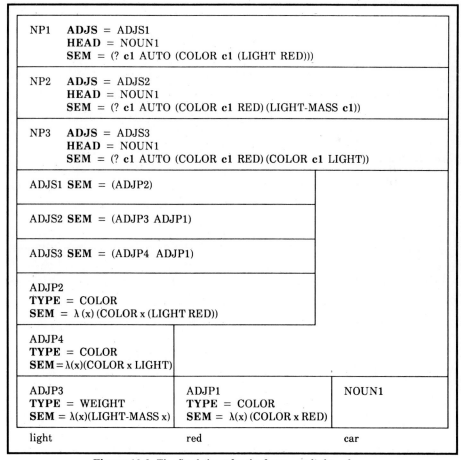

Figure 10.5 The final chart for the fragment *heavy red car*

Figure 10.6 The final chart for the fragment *light red car*

Predicate Adjectives

Now that you have seen this analysis of adjective phrases and constructed semantic analyses for them in terms of λ-expressions, you can see that this analysis easily extends to sentences involving the verb *be* and an adjective phrase, as in *The car is light red.* A simple grammar for such sentences is

$$S \leftarrow NP\ VP \qquad\qquad SEM = Apply\ (SEM_{VP},\ SEM_{NP})$$

$$VP \leftarrow VERB\ ADJP \qquad ROOT_{VERB} = BE$$
$$SEM_{VP} = SEM_{ADJP}$$

You can easily see that the existing grammar for ADJP applies directly for these forms. In particular, the **SEM** of the ADJP *light red* would be λ (x) (COLOR x (LIGHT RED)), which becomes the **SEM** of the VP and, when applied to the **SEM** of the NP *the car,* produces the final interpretation:

(COLOR (DEF/SING c1 AUTO) (LIGHT RED))

Note that this is a substantially different form of analysis from what you've seen for all other verbs, which have received a case-based analysis. This should not be too surprising, since the verb *be* seems to be a spec   ial case throughout, and it is not clear how a case-based analysis could apply to it.

Comparatives and Superlatives

Two other classes of adjectives are the **comparatives** and the **superlatives**. The comparatives appear to fall into the intersective class of adjectives and include *larger, heavier,* and *faster,* as well as complex adjectives such as *more colorful, more aggravating,* and so on. These do not affect the type of the NP and can be analyzed as adding additional restrictions onto the NP. When a comparative is used as an adjective, there is an another understood object to which the current object is being compared. Thus *the larger deer* might be analyzed to a logical form such as

(DEF/SING d1 DEER (LARGER d1
                               (DEF/SING d2 DEER (NOT (EQ d1 d2)))))

This could be paraphrased as *the deer larger than the other deer* or something like that. This paraphrase suggests the other way comparative adjectives can be used--to introduce a complement to the NP. In this form the object being compared to is made explicit; thus *all rabbits heavier than the dog* would be analyzed as

(ALL r1 RABBIT (HEAVIER r1 (DEF/SING d1 DOG)))

6. NP0 ← SUPERL NP1	$\text{SEM} = (? * \underline{T}(\text{SEM}_{\text{NP1}})$
	$(\underline{V}(\text{SUPERL}) *$
	$\text{O-Apply }(\text{DEF/PL}, \text{SEM}_{\text{NP1}})))$
7. NP0 ← SUPERL of NP	$\text{SEM} = (? * \underline{T}(\text{SEM}_{\text{NP}}) (\underline{V}(\text{SUPERL}) * \underline{V}(\text{NP})))$
8. NP0 ← NP1	$\text{SEM} = \text{SEM}_{\text{NP1}}$

Figure 10.7 Rules for the superlative

The superlative class of adjectives are nonintersective. A word such as *largest* cannot be treated as a simple adjectival modifier. Rather it looks more like an operator on the entire NP, with a logical form such as the following for the sentence *the largest dog in the pound*:

(DEF/SING **d1** DOG (LARGEST **d1** (DEF/PL **d2** DOG
(IN **d2** (DEF/SING **p1** POUND))))

That is, **d1** is the largest dog in the set of dogs (**d2**) consisting of all dogs in the pound. Constructing such an interpretation rule in the present interpreter is not straightforward. For example, the obvious interpretation rule for *largest* might be

(NP **ADJS** largest
HEAD +physobj) → (? * $\underline{T}$(**HEAD**)
(LARGEST * (DEF/PL ** $\underline{T}$(**HEAD**))))

But applying this to an NP such as *the largest dog in the pound* would produce (assuming you have the other rules required):

(DEF/SING **d1** DOG (LARGEST **d1** (DEF/PL **d2** DOG))
(IN **d1** (DEF/SING **p1** POUND)))

This is the largest dog (in the world) that happens also to be in the pound! The problem is that the superlative adjective modifies the entire NP, rather than simply modifying the head noun. This indicates that you might best treat superlatives as a special case and modify the grammar to capture the desired structure. For example, you might use rules such as in Figure 10.7, where NP1 is defined as in Grammar 10.4.

Rule 6 handles cases such as in the fragment *largest dog in the pound* by using the semantic interpretation of the NP1 fragment *dog in the pound*, which would have a value like

(? **d1** DOG (IN **d1** (DEF/SING **p1** POUND)))

The O-Apply operation inserts the specifier DEF/PL into this logical form, and
the final analysis is

> (? **d2** DOG (LARGEST **d2** (DEF/PL **d1** DOG
> (IN **d1** (DEF/SING **p1** POUND)))))

Rule 7 handles phrases such as *largest of the dogs in the pound* in a
straightforward way, while rule 8 covers the cases where no superlative is
present.

10.4 Noun-Noun Modifiers

NPs with noun-noun modifiers such as *car paint, soup pot handle, water glass,*
and *computer evaluation* are notoriously difficult to analyze. The syntactic form
provides little guidance, and general semantic constraints like those used for
analyzing multiple adjectives do not seem to be present. There are two main
problems. One is determining what modifies what, which is similar to the
problem with multiple adjectives. The other problem is detecting the semantic
relationship between the modifying noun and the modified noun.

Most computational work on this second problem generally falls into two
techniques:

-- identifying a set of general semantic relationships that commonly
   underlie the noun-noun modification

-- using cases for nouns that have an associated verb sense

The first technique involves identifying common semantic relationships.
Some possible relationships for an NP consisting of a sequence of two nouns, X
and Y, are

-- Y is a subpart of X (*pot handles*)

-- Y is used for some activity involving X (*car paint*)

-- Y is made out of material X (*stone wall*)

Thus a *pot handle* is a handle that is part of a pot, *car paint* is paint used to
paint cars, and a *stone wall* is a wall made out of stone.

Given a noun-noun modification, each of these relationships could be
checked one by one and retained as a possible reading, if not eliminated on the
basis of general world knowledge. Thus to analyze the NP *a water glass,* a
system might check the following:

1.   Could a glass be a subpart of water?   NO

2.   Could a glass be used in an activity involving water?   YES, drinking.

3.   Could a glass be made out of water?   NO

Assuming these questions can be answered as shown, the final interpretation of *a water glass* would be paraphrased as *a glass used for drinking water.*

Note that simple forms of the preceding questions could be represented and answered in the semantic network representation introduced in Chapter 7. For instance, general subpart information can be represented to answer the first question. The second question could be answered by looking for a subtype of ACTION that involves a glass and water. Presumably an action such as DRINK will satisfy this. To answer the third and final question, the representation would have to be extended to represent knowledge about substances and what substances things are made of.

Nouns that have associated cases, or that identify the case of a particular verb, can be analyzed in terms of those cases. For example, with the NP *the contest winner*, the noun *winner* identifies the AGENT case of a WIN action, and *contest* can be seen to fit the THEME case. Thus this NP might be analyzed as

> (DEF/SING **p1** PERSON (INF **w1** WIN
> [AGENT **p1**]
> [THEME (DEF/SING **c1** CONTEST)]))

The NP *the car evaluation*, on the other hand, refers to an evaluation event directly, and the car is seen to fit the THEME case. If the modifier can fill more than one case, the NP will be ambiguous. For example, *the computer evaluation* could be either *the evaluation of the computer* or *the evaluation by the computer.*

Finally, other noun-noun modifications appear not to be resolvable by simple strategies. Either they are learned directly, or they involve quite general forms of association between the objects in a certain context.

10.5 Lexical Ambiguity

Thus far in this text you have seen several techniques for dealing with lexical ambiguity--that is, words that have multiple senses. This section will quickly review the techniques developed so far and discuss some remaining problems. Then the discussion will consider some additional techniques that can be useful in attacking this problem.

Constraints Imposed by Syntax and Semantics

You can often disambiguate words that are ambiguous between syntactic classes by syntactically analyzing the sentence that contains them. For example, given the sentence *We forgot to book our flight to Europe before the deadline*, the word *book* here can only be a verb, because the readings in which it is a noun do not allow a syntactic analysis to be constructed. With only syntactic knowledge, however, the word is still ambiguous between its "reserve" sense and the "charge with a crime" sense.

This ambiguity can be resolved by semantic information. By combining knowledge about the case structure of verbs with selectional restrictions on what types of objects can fill those cases, the interpreter picks the "reserve" sense, since reserving a flight makes sense. The "charge" sense of the verb would take a person, as in *They wanted to book him with murder*.

The semantic interpretation rules, however, cannot disambiguate all sentences. For instance, in a culture where baseball is played, a person hearing the sentence *The batter hit the ball past the pitcher and ran for first base* has no trouble identifying the correct sense of *batter*, *pitcher*, *ball*, or *base*, although all these words have other senses. For example, the word *pitcher* has a sense as a household item, as in *a pitcher of water*. Selectional restrictions on the verb *hit*, however, would not eliminate this sense. Rather, it seems to be eliminated because all the words identify a baseball setting and hence the appropriate sense of *pitcher*. The semantic interpretation rules have no mechanism for capturing such word-word interaction. As another example, consider the sentence *We found the book, but the page had disappeared*. There is no selectional restriction that eliminates the "page boy" sense of *the page*. In fact, in some contexts, such as in describing a mystery involving a stolen book in the House of Congress, where a page boy was suspected, this could be a reasonable interpretation. But without this strong setting, there is a definite strong preference for the reading where the page was part of the book.

Lexical Association

The associations between words can sometimes be so strong as to cause sentences to be interpreted anomalously even though there is an appropriate reading. For example, the sentence *The astronomer married a star* is best interpreted as the astronomer marrying a famous person, but many peoples' first reading interprets *star* as a celestial object and may construct a metaphorical reading of the sentence to account for this meaning (that is, the astronomer spends all his time working). One explanation for this interpretation is that the words *astronomer* and *star* are closely related semantically and reinforce the related senses. This explanation has in fact been confirmed by psycholinguists in numerous experiments. When a person hears a particular word, he or she can recognize semantically related words significantly faster than nonrelated words.

A simple computational measure of semantic closeness between two word senses is their distance from each other in the type hierarchy. For instance, assume that you are given the hierarchy of professions in Figure 10.8. You could then compute a semantic closeness measure of two professions by tracing up the type hierarchy from each until you find an intersection, and keeping count of how many steps were taken. Presumably, the smaller the number of steps, the more closely related the two professions.

For example, assume the word *manager* is ambiguous between a bank manager and a business manager. Then given the sentence *The teller left the manager the keys*, you would need to identify the most likely sense of *manager*. The bank manager node (MANAGER2) and the TELLER node intersect at the BANKING node (path length of 2), whereas the MANAGER1 node and the TELLER node intersect at PROFESSION (a path length of 5). Thus MANAGER1 is semantically closer to TELLER than MANAGER2 and, in the absence of any other evidence to the contrary, would be the preferred interpretation of the word *manager*.

To handle cases such as the sentence *We found the book, but the page had disappeared*, you can use a technique similar to the preceding based on the part-of relationship. Figure 10.9 shows such a hierarchy concerning libraries and the House of Congress. Given the example, you could find the appropriate sense of *page* by activating both senses, PAGE1 and PAGE2, as well as the sense for *book* (and the other words). You find a direct subpart relationship between BOOK and PAGE1, and at best a very indirect relationship between BOOK and PAGE2 (through ORGANIZATION). Thus the appropriate reading is preferred.

Other relationships can also play an important role in determining lexical associations. Two objects might be related by the fact that they both play roles in some common action or relation. An action is semantically related to other actions that are part of the way in which the action is commonly performed (that is, an action-subaction hierarchy). In other words any relationship that is representable in a semantic network might contribute the evaluation of how closely word senses are semantically related.

Computational models of this process have been called **spreading activation** models. In these frameworks each word sense is represented by a node in a semantic network. When a word is recognized, all the nodes representing its senses are made **active**, and these nodes then activate the other nodes to which it is linked. When a node is activated from two different links, a chain of links has been detected connecting two of the initial activated

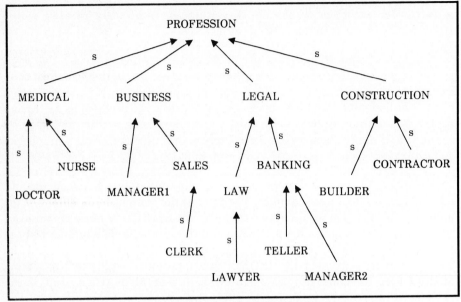

Figure 10.8 A hierarchy of professions

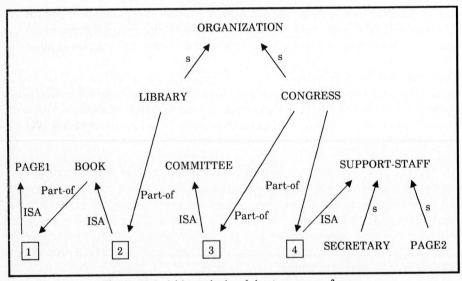

Figure 10.9 A hierarchy involving two senses of *page*

nodes. If the system keeps track of the activation paths, this chain can be easily retrieved.

While this scheme will find all the possible connections in the network, unless it is constrained it will also find even more intersections that are not relevant to the word senses. For instance, if you allow activation to spread both up and down subtype links, then this scheme will rapidly activate every type node in the network! To avoid this, you can place a restriction that activation only spread up subtype links (that is, from subtype to supertype). For example, with the type network in Figure 10.8, if the nodes MANAGER1, MANAGER2, and TELLER are activated, the following nodes are then activated up the hierarchy:

BUSINESS   -   from MANAGER1
BANKING   -   from MANAGER2 and TELLER

If you stop at the first intersection, you have found the best path between two of the nodes--namely, from TELLER to BANKING to MANAGER2. If you allowed the activation to continue spreading, you would also activate

LEGAL   -   from BANKING
PROFESSION   -   from BUSINESS, and then from LEGAL

Thus one other path that would be possible is from TELLER to BANKING to LEGAL to PROFESSION to BUSINESS to MANAGER1.

Activation through the part-of hierarchy might similarly be restricted to only pass activation up (from part to whole). Thus from node PAGE2 in Figure 10.9, the node SUPPORT-STAFF would be activated, which in turn would activate existential node 4, via the ISA arc, then activating CONGRESS up the subpart arc, and ultimately activating ORGANIZATION. Given the constraints on passing activation down the subpart of subtype hierarchies, that would be the extent of the activation from PAGE2.

Such a restriction cannot be made, however, to limit activation from case values to the object with that case, or vice versa. This is because certain objects are semantically related only because they share an object that they are both related to via some relation. For example, in the sentence *That guitarist owns a lovely instrument*, the "guitar" (or "musical instrument") sense of *instrument* (vs. a stage light, or a medical instrument) is semantically related only because *guitarist* is related to *guitar* via some relation, say "play." The relevant part of the semantic network in shown in Figure 10.10.

As you can see, the path between the appropriate word senses of *guitarist* and *instrument* consists of the isa link from GUITARIST to the case value g1, the agent link to PLAY-ACTION, the theme link to the case value g2, the isa link to GUITAR, and the subtype link to MUSICAL-INSTRUMENT. Because of the restriction on not passing activation down the s link, GUITAR would not be activated from the sense *instrument*, so the connection could be found only by the path from GUITARIST.

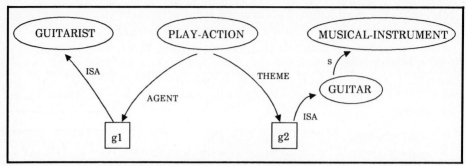

Figure 10.10 The relationship between GUITARIST and MUSICAL-INSTRUMENT

There are other ways to limit the spreading of activation through a semantic network. One common way involves using levels of activation rather than a simple active-nonactive distinction. For example, you could give each word a certain weight--say, *n* units. It would then divide this weight equally among its word sense nodes. At each stage of activation a node then distributes its weight equally among all the links along which activation can pass. Once an activation level diminishes below a certain threshold, the node does not become activated. Alternately, nodes might be able to pass their full weight along each link, but different link types might have a multiplicative factor that might diminish the level of activation passed along that type of link. Either way, the activation levels tend to diminish the longer the path from the originating nodes.

Needless to say, there are many problems remaining in disambiguating words that are not addressed by the simple models here. You will have an opportunity to reexamine this issue extensively when you consider the integration of sentences into context in the following chapters.

10.6 Tense and Aspect

The logical form presented here deals with only the simplest forms of tense. In particular the operators you've used for sentence structures have included only PAST (for simple past) and PRES (for simple present). Of course, you could easily add an operator FUT for future, and PASTPERF for past perfect, and so on, but there are definite limits to how far this approach can be extended.

For instance, the progressive aspect can be used with any of the preceding simple tenses. To capture this in our current LF, you would need to introduce a new set of operators PASTPROG, PRESPROG, and so on. Then the modal verbs (*can*, *would*, *might*) need to be handled as well, introducing many new dimensions. To handle such complexities in a way that captures generalities requires extending the expressive power of the formalism.

One possible solution might be to allow the nesting of simple tense operators. Thus a tense like the future perfect, as in *Jack will have left the store*, might be represented as

> (FUT (PAST s1 LEAVE [AGENT (NAME **j1** PERSON "Jack")]
> [FROM-LOC (DEF/SING s1 STORE)]))

To paraphrase this, in the future it will be true in the past that Jack left the store. Similarly the past perfect might be represented as a nesting of one PAST operator inside another. To make this truly work, additional constraints would have to be added. For instance, with the future perfect tense, the constraint would be that the event occurs in the future. As it stands, if John left the store yesterday, that would satisfy the intuitive reading given earlier. Similarly, what is the difference between an event that occurred in the past (simple past) and one that occurred in the past of some past time (past perfect)? The generally accepted answer, arising from Reichenbach (1947), is that besides encoding the time of the event, tense also encodes a time of reference. This is the time with respect to which the event is being considered. Thus there are three times relevant in the analysis of tense: the time that the sentence is spoken (S), the time of the event described (E), and the reference time (R). If you use Reichenbach's notation, the ordering between these three times is indicated using a comma (,) for cotemporal and an underscore (_) for preceding. With this notation the situation described by the simple past has the reference and event times identical, and preceding the speech time, which is written as

> E , R _ S

The past perfect, on the other hand, has the event time preceding the reference time:

> E _ R _ S

The future and future perfect are related in a similar way. The simple future, as *I will find the ring*, has the structure

> S , R _ E

whereas *I will have found the ring* would be

> S _ E _ R

The generality to observe is that the perfect forms force the E time to precede the R time.

The progressive aspect, on the other hand, seems to indicate whether the event described has completed or not. Thus, given *I walked to the store,* you know that I arrived there sometime in the past, whereas given *I was walking to the store,* you do not know whether the event was completed. In particular the next event described is likely to be something that happened while I was walking.

You cannot weigh the significance of all this analysis until you have considered multisentence discourse in the chapters to come. What is important as far as the logical form is concerned, however, is that the simple tenses, the perfective, and the progressive seem to be orthogonal, and all need to be retained. This suggests a complex tense operator consisting of a triple whose elements are selected from the values PAST/FUT/PRES, PERF/NON-PERF, and PROG/NON-PROG. With this, the LF of *Jack will have been running* would be

((FUT, PERF, PROG) **r1** RUN [AGENT (NAME **j1** PERSON "Jack")])

The modal auxiliaries each seem to indicate a different semantic analysis and would be modeled as operators on the logical form the same way as negation and conjunction.

Summary

One important issue in semantic interpretation concerns the complexities of interpreting noun phrases, including the interpretation of adjectives, noun-noun modification, and determining quantifier scope. Another issue has to do with the treatment of word ambiguity that remains once the syntactic and semantic restrictions are applied. A simple spreading activation technique can model the semantic associations between words. Finally, some problems remain in representing tense and aspect information. All these issues are areas of active research where good computational analyses remain to be developed.

Related Work and Further Readings

Determining the scoping of quantifiers has been a central concern for those building natural language database query systems, and many of the heuristics described in this book have been used in work by Woods (1978), Pereira (1983), and Grosz et al. (1987). Hobbs and Shieber (1987) described an algorithm for generating all possible scopings, eliminating only those that are linguistically unacceptable in any context. More general treatments of scoping including adverbs and sentential operators have been examined by McCord (1987).

The discussion of modifiers draws from Woods (1978) and Pereira (1983). A satisfactory account of complex adjectival phrases remains for future work, but some interesting work has been done on color terms (Schubert et al., 1986). Work on noun-noun modification testing for a relationship from a fixed set of choices is examined in detail by Finin (1980).

Spreading activation techniques were the first motivation for semantic network representations (Quillian, 1968). After a period of disillusionment, when the technique was abandoned since it could not be extended to solve all the language representation problems, such models have recently become the object of much study. Charniak (1983b) gives a good motivation for the use of these models in conjunction with other processing techniques, and they have been examined in detail in Hirst (1987) and Hendler (1987).

Another related area attracting considerable attention involves **connectionist models**, where the entire computational process is described in terms of the interactions between thousands of limited processors. Useful examples of the application of these models to natural language comprehension are Cottrell and Small (1983) and Pollack and Waltz (1985). A good introduction to the framework is Feldman and Ballard (1982), and a recent book describing distributed connectionist models is Rumelhart and McClelland (1986).

The theories of tense are drawn from philosophy and linguistics. A classic early work describing operators for past and future is Prior (1967). The introduction of a reference time to provide a model for natural language tenses was suggested by Reichenbach (1947). Issues of tense analysis in multisentence text will be considered in Chapters 13 and 14.

Another important area of semantic interpretation not discussed here is the interpretation of phrases (mainly prepositional phrases) describing locations. A good reference for this area is Herskovits (1986).

Exercises for Chapter 10

1. *(medium)* Modify the existing semantic interpreter so that it can analyze a particular, but common, form of relative clause of the form "RELPRO BE PP" and "RELPRO BE ADJ." The goal is to have a single rule for each use of adjective and preposition that can be used both for *the green ball* and *the ball that was green*, and *the man in the corner* and *the man who was in the corner*. Outline in detail the modifications that need to be made to the interpreter and any extensions that need to be made to the lexicon and the form of semantic interpretation rules. Demonstrate your solution by giving rules that correctly analyze the preceding four NPs.

2. *(medium)* Give an analysis of NPs that use the adjective *average*. Specify what extensions need to be made to the lexicon, the logical form, and the semantic interpretation rule format to handle NPs such as *the average grade in my class* and *the average of the grades in my class*. Give the interpretation rules needed to handle the preceding two NPs.

3. *(medium)* Design a data structure to represent logical forms including quantifier dependency information. Write a program that, given such a logical form, generates all possible quantifier scopings consistent with the dependency information. Thus, given a representation of the following as input:

```
(PRED s1 SIT  (AGENT (INDEF/SING m1 MAN))
              (AT-LOC (DEF/SING h1 k1 KITCHEN
                              (IN k1 (EVERY h1 HOUSE)))))
```

the program would output

```
(FOR INDEF/SING m1 MAN;
   (FOR EVERY h1 HOUSE;
      (FOR DEF/SING k1 KITCHEN (IN k1 h1);
         (PRED s1 SIT (AGENT m1) (THEME k1)))))
```

and

```
(FOR EVERY h1 HOUSE;
   (FOR DEF/SING k1 KITCHEN (IN k1 h1);
      (FOR INDEF/SING m1 MAN;
         (PRED s1 SIT (AGENT m1) (THEME k1)))))
```

Construct a sentence that is 6 ways ambiguous due to quantifier scoping and test your program using its logical form as input. As usual, your program should be well documented and fully tested.

neats - use logic, want well defined formal notation. (FOPC)
         McCarthy, Nillson
scruffies - concerned w/ how knowledge structured
         and retrieved - Schank, Minsky, Wilks
both - try to formalize scruffy schemes
         Sowa, Allen.

PART III

CONTEXT AND WORLD KNOWLEDGE

Chapter 11

Knowledge Representation

Chapter 12

Reference

Chapter 13

Using World Knowledge About Actions

Chapter 14

Discourse Structure

Chapter 15

Belief Models and Speech Acts

Chapter 11

Knowledge Representation

In its most general sense a knowledge representation is any framework in which information about language and the world can be stored and retrieved. In this sense, you have already seen several such knowledge representations in this book. The syntactic knowledge about sentences was represented in various grammatical formalisms, and word sense information was represented using semantic networks and semantic interpretation rules. This chapter turns to a third type of representation--representing world knowledge. This category includes knowledge of a general nature (birds can fly, a person needs a key to drive a car, and so on) as well as knowledge of the specific situation at a certain time (I currently own a car, I believe it is raining outside, and so on).

World knowledge is essential for solving many language interpretation problems--one of the most important being disambiguation. For example, the proper attachment of the final PP in the following two sentences depends solely on the reader's background knowledge of the appropriate time taken for reading and evolution:

> I read a story about evolution in ten minutes.
> I read a story about evolution in the last million years.

World knowledge is also important for determining the reference of noun phrases. In particular, knowledge of the specific situation may suggest relevant objects, and knowledge of causality may be needed to identify the connections of the objects within the sentences. For example, given the sentence *As I swung the hammer at the nail, the head flew off,* your knowledge of causality helps you identify *the head* as the head of the hammer, not the head of the nail.

The other important use of world knowledge is in answering questions. If a system is to demonstrate its understanding of a set of sentences by answering questions, it must be able to draw on world knowledge to provide information that is only implicit in the sentences given. Ideally, the knowledge representation should support all inferences that a person would find as obvious conclusions given a sentence.

This chapter examines the basic issues underlying knowledge representation. Section 11.1 reviews some of the basic distinctions that you can use to classify representations. Then the chapter offers two examples of representations. Section 11.2 looks at a logic-based framework, and Section 11.3 considers structured-object representations. Finally, Section 11.4 discusses knowledge about actions, one of the most important forms of knowledge.

11.1 The Major Issues in Knowledge Representation

While there are a wide range of different knowledge representation formalisms, all share some common properties. All make the distinction between propositions--those things that can be said to be true or false--and terms--those things that represent (or **denote**) objects, be they concrete physical objects (such as a chair) or more illusive objects (such as events, ideas, or time). Given this similarity, the representations then diverge in several major ways, including what types of predicates they support, what types of inferential behavior are definable, and the method by which inference is accomplished.

Knowledge representation systems can be thought of as being made up of two distinct parts: the **knowledge base** (KB), which is the set of data structures that store the information, and the **inference engine**, which provides a set of operations on the knowledge base. As you will see, the emphasis on which part encodes the knowledge differs significantly from representation to representation.

What Are the Predicates?

Although FOPC does not commit to a particular set of predicates, logic-based representations do in practice use a level of predicates different from other representations such as semantic nets. For instance, the sentence *Jack hit Jill* would map to a predicate *HIT* in a typical logic-based system, producing a representation such as

$$HIT(JACK1, JILL1)$$

In semantic net representation, however, the sentence would map to a graph structure that asserts that an event occurred with certain roles. A paraphrase of this in FOPC is

$$HIT\text{-}EVENT(H1) \,\&\, AGENT(H1, JACK1) \,\&\, THEME(H1, JILL1)$$

While in many cases the same style of inference could be done for either of these representations, the latter also directly supports reasoning involving roles. For instance, to answer the query *What did Jack do?* in the latter representation, you should find an action A such that $AGENT(A, JACK1)$. It is not clear how to express such a query in the first representation.

You can make yet another distinction between representations that keep their predicates close to the word senses and those that use a much reduced set of predicates. For example, you can define the word *father* as a *male parent*:

$$\forall x \,.\, FATHER(x) \equiv PARENT(x) \,\&\, MALE(x)$$

Indeed you could replace all occurrences of the predicate $FATHER$ in the knowledge base with its definition.

If you can characterize most word meanings by such definitions, you have opened up a new way of organizing the knowledge. If the system reduces predicates to their definitions and then reduces the terms in that definition to their definitions, it will eventually end up with a formula in terms of a set of predicates that are not further decomposable. These predicates would be the **primitives** of the semantic representation.

The advantage of primitive-based representations is that commonalities between terms can be captured by the overlap in their semantic decomposition. For example, if *FATHER* is decomposed into *PARENT* and *MALE*, and *MAN* decomposes into *MALE* and *PERSON*, the common semantic properties between them would result from them both having *MALE* in their definition.

The problem with representations based purely on primitives is that many words cannot be precisely defined, especially if you are using a relatively small set of primitives. For example, the verbs of moving, such as *walk, run, saunter, hop, skip, hobble,* and so on, all presumably would involve some primitive predicate of motion, together with primitives about qualities of movement. For example, you would need a set of primitives *P1, P2, ..., Pn* such that *WALKING* was defined by a formula of the form

$$MOVING(w) \ \& \ P1 \ \& \ P2 \ \& \ ... \ \& \ Pn$$

P1, P2, ..., Pn would probably include information about the normal speed of walking to distinguish it from sauntering and information about leg contact to the ground to distinguish it from hopping or skipping. Of course, most of the time you don't need this level of information, and the fact that the person is moving may be the most salient part. But in other circumstances much might be implied about a person's state of mind from the fact that he or she is sauntering. All this would need to be derivable from the decomposition.

Types of Inference

Many different forms of inference are necessary to understand natural language. The major distinction, however, is between those that are **deductive** and those that are **nondeductive**.

Deductive forms of inference are all justified by the logical notion of entailment. Given a set of facts, a deductive inference process will make only conclusions that logically follow from those facts. If a representation uses only pure deductive inference, it is a **monotonic representation**. Thus, if new consistent facts are added to the knowledge base, all the things that were inferred to be true previously are still true. Adding facts can only increase the number of propositions that hold.

Nondeductive inference falls into several classes. Examples include inference involving the learning of generalities from examples (inductive inference) and inference involving finding the most plausible interpretation for a sentence given its context.

An important class of nondeductive inference concerns the use of **default information**. A default rule is an inference rule to which there may be exceptions; thus it is **defeasible**. If you write default information using the notation A ⇒ B, then the default inference rule could be stated as follows. If A ⇒ B, A is true, and ¬B is not provable, then conclude B. For example, the sentence *Birds fly* could have the following as its meaning:

$$\forall x \; BIRD(x) \Rightarrow FLIES(x)$$

This has the effect that whenever there is a bird B for which it is not provable that ¬*FLIES(B)*, then it can be inferred that *FLIES(B)*. In other words, all birds fly unless it is explicitly stated that they do not.

You can see that any system with default rules must be nonmonotonic. In particular, given the facts that birds fly, penguins do not fly, and Penny is a bird:

$$\forall x . BIRD(x) \; \Rightarrow \; FLIES(x)$$
$$\forall x . PENGUIN(x) \; \Rightarrow \; \neg FLIES(x)$$
$$BIRD(PENNY1)$$

then you can conclude that Penny can fly (since Penny is a bird, birds fly, and it is not provable that Penny does not fly). If it is then asserted that Penny is a penguin:

$$PENGUIN(PENNY1)$$

then the system should now be able to conclude that Penny does not fly. A problem has arisen here: since both *PENGUIN(PENNY1)* and *BIRD(PENNY1)* are true, either default rule could be used, leading to one result or the other. The systems that allow such rules all encode the same strategy for these situations--the most specific type information takes priority. Thus they would now conclude ¬*FLIES(PENNY1)*, based on the fact the *PENNY1* is a *PENGUIN*.

Inference Techniques

The two main classes of inference techniques are **procedural** and **declarative**. The prototypical declarative technique is a logic theorem prover. The knowledge is represented as a set of FOPC axioms, and inference is performed using a deductive theorem-proving algorithm. In a strongly declarative system the emphasis is on assigning a formal semantics to the expressions of the representation independent of the inference component.

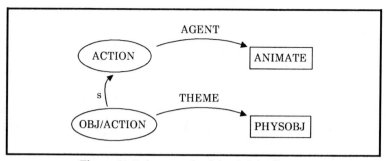

Figure 11.1 An example of simple inheritance

Procedural inference systems, on the other hand, emphasize the inferential aspects of the representation, and in extreme cases the expressions in the KB may be given no meaning independent of how they are manipulated by the program. An example of a procedural representation might be a system that represents arithmetic expressions and uses the computer's own built-in arithmetic procedures to manipulate these expressions without representing any knowlege about mathematics. In practice, procedural systems can be very effective at specific inference tasks in well-defined domains but are often hard to analyze and lack generality. All usable knowledge representation systems, however, use some procedural techniques either for efficiency or to implement nondeductive inference strategies that are not otherwise analyzable.

Consider an example. In Chapter 7, the technique of inheritance was introduced for semantic networks. This inference process can be realized procedurally or declaratively. The purely declarative approach is to model each fact as an axiom carefully defined so that inheritance is simply a form of logical deduction. For example, given the simple network in Figure 11.1, the following axioms might be defined to be equivalent:

$$\forall x \,.\, ACTION(x) \supset \exists a \,.\, AGENT(x, a) \,\&\, ANIMATE(a)$$
$$\forall x \,.\, OBJ/ACTION(x) \supset ACTION(x)$$
$$\forall x \,.\, OBJ/ACTION(x) \supset \exists a \,.\, THEME(x, a) \,\&\, PHYSOBJ(a)$$

Using these axioms, you can prove that the class OBJ/ACTION inherits the AGENT role. For any object A such that *OBJ/ACTION(A)* is true, then

$$\exists a \,.\, AGENT(A, a) \,\&\, ANIMATE(a)$$

That is, A has an animate AGENT role.

A procedural version of this would be a program that starts at the specified node OBJ/ACTION, finds all roles attached at that node, and then follows the S arc up to the supertype ACTION and finds all the roles attached there. The complete set of roles gathered by this procedure is the answer. Thus any OBJ/ACTION has an AGENT role inherited from the class ACTION.

Both these techniques compute the same result, but the first does it by giving an interpretation to the data structure and using deduction, while the other is a program doing graph traversal. The first technique seems more rigorously defined, but the second is probably more efficient. In cases like this you can have the best of both approaches: a rigorously defined notation and an efficient procedure to perform that form of inference.

Consider a more complex case, however. You can extend the procedural approach to handle simple defaults as follows: The algorithm is modified so that once a type restriction is found for a particular role R, all other information about R on the higher nodes is simply ignored. It is considerably more complex to provide axioms that do the same thing. In particular, you must introduce default rules to the logic and define nonmonotonic inference. While you can do this, current work in this area is mostly of theoretical interest and has yet to be introduced into practical knowledge representation systems.

11.2 Logic-Based Representations

Logic-based representations consist of a knowledge base of axioms and a collection of theorem-proving strategies for its inference component. As such, these representations emphasize the role of deductive inference and say little about nondeductive inference. An interesting approach to defaults, however, can be defined in frameworks where the inference process is reasonably efficient.

Most modern logic-based systems are derived from the resolution method. This method uses two important techniques: you convert all formulas to a normal form, called **clause form**, and you define a single inference rule, called the **resolution rule**. The resolution rule is sufficient to allow a proof of any provable formula. You have already seen a representation framework based on these principles--the Horn clause prover. Viewed as a knowledge representation, the knowledge base consists of the Horn clause formulas, and the inference engine is the backward-chaining proof procedure outlined in Appendix B. Since this framework has already been introduced, it can be used here as a prototypical logic-based representation.

One key technique needed in all representations is the treatment of quantifiers. In Horn clause systems there are variables that correspond to universally quantified variables in FOPC, but what is the equivalent of existentially quantified variables? The answer involves a technique called **skolemization**. This technique basically involves replacing all existential variables by function terms that represent the objects asserted to exist. For each new existential variable, you must introduce a completely new function name to avoid undesired identification with previously used terms. Quantifier scoping information is maintained by using any universally quantified variables outside the scope of the existential as arguments to the skolem function. For example, the formula $\exists x \forall y P(x, y)$ would map to the skolemized formula (P sk1 ?y), where sk1 is a skolem representing the object asserted to exist. The formula $\forall y \exists x P(x, y)$, on the other hand, would map to (P (sk2 ?y) ?y). In this, (sk2 ?y) is a skolem function whose value varies with the value of the universal variable ?y. Thus the appropriate scoping information is retained, and you can prove that the skolemized version is formally equivalent to the original version.

Several other features are necessary to make this framework a reasonable representation. Since skolems may be introduced often, and a large part of the language understanding task is dealing with reference, the representation should be able to support equality reasoning. Thus if the fact (P sk1) is in the knowledge base, and it is asserted that sk1 = A, then (P A) should be provable.

Another important ability involves default reasoning. Practical logic-based systems use an extension called **proof by failure** for such purposes. This extension essentially allows a formula to be proven if another formula cannot be proven. If you call this special predicate UNLESS, then the formula (UNLESS P) is true only if the prover recursively attempts to prove P and fails. Using this formula, you can express the defeasible rule that all birds except penguins fly with

(FLIES ?x) < (BIRD ?x) (UNLESS (PENGUIN ?x))

With this extension the language ceases to be a monotonic, fully declarative representation, because the success of a proof may now depend on the particular proof strategy used and the ordering of the facts in the knowledge base. Furthermore, you can prove a formula that you later find to be false when you add new information. With the addition of this feature the pure theorem prover starts to become a programming language (in this case, PROLOG).

11.3 Frame-Based Systems *— generalization of ideas from semantic networks - inheritance hierarchy*

Most of the more procedurally-oriented representations use a representation technique based on the notion of **frames**. In its most abstract formulation a frame is simply a cluster of facts and objects that describe some typical situation, together with specific inference strategies for reasoning about the situation. The situations represented could range from visual scenes, to the structure of complex physical objects, to the typical method by which some action is performed. Frame-based systems usually offer facilities such as default reasoning, automatic inheritance of properties through hierarchies, and procedural attachment. In some systems all reasoning is accomplished by specialized inference procedures attached to the frame, whereas in others the

General Knowledge rep. formalism for bundling together knowledge about a concept, especially stereotyped knowledge.

frames are mostly declarative in nature and are interpreted by a more uniform inference procedure. The representation examined here will be of the latter type.

The principal objects in a frame are assigned names, called **roles.** For instance, the frame for a house may have roles such as kitchen, living room, hallway, front door, and so on. The frame also specifies the relationships between the roles and the object represented by the frame. For example, the kitchen role of the house frame has to be physically located within the house, and it must contain the various appliances needed for preparing meals. You can view each of these roles as a function that takes an object described by the frame (an **instance** of the frame) and produces the appropriate role value. Thus a particular instance of the house frame--say, H1--consists of a particular instance of a kitchen, which can be referred to as "the kitchen-role of H1," or kitchen(H1), plus particular instances of all the other roles as well. Conversely, if you specified a set of role values--a particular kitchen, living room, and so on--such that all the required relationships held between them, that cluster of objects would completely define a particular instance of the house frame.

There is a strong similarity between the notion of frames and roles as described here and the case-grammar-based notion of verb type and cases used in the logical form notation. The definition of a frame for the class of objects that are personal computers might look as follows:

```
(Define-Class PC with
    [Keyb + keyboard]
    [Disk1 + diskdrive]
    [MainBox + cpu])
```

This structure is defined to mean that all objects of type PC have roles of type keyboard, disk-drive, and cpu (which are identified by the functions Keyb, Disk1, and MainBox, respectively). As with the semantic networks, you can define the meaning of this structure by mapping it to an equivalent FOPC representation. In fact, you could easily represent this structure in a semantic network notation as well, as shown in Figure 11.2. An instance of the type PC--say, PC3--having the subparts KEYS13, DD11, and CPU00023 would be represented in the frame notation as:

```
(PC3 isa PC with
    [Keyb KEY13]
    [Disk1 DD11]
    [MainBox CPU00023])
```

To facilitate referring to instances a functional form is defined. In particular, you could also refer to PC3, as defined earlier, as PC(KEY13, DD11, CPU00023). Roles can be identified using a functional form as well. For instance, Keyb(PC3) represents the keyboard of PC3--namely, KEY13.

list of slot-filler pairs (attribute, value)
look like records

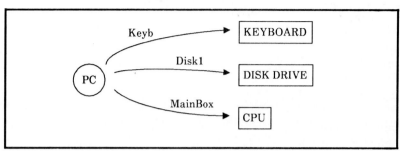

Figure 11.2 A semantic network defining the roles of PC

Roles with Restrictions

In general, you need more than a superficial knowledge of the structural components of a PC. For instance, in the setting up of a PC, the frame would need considerably more information about how the role values interrelate. For example, you might want to assert that each role is a subpart and indicate how the parts are connected: The keyboard, as well as the disk drive, plugs into the CPU box at the appropriate connector. To assert this, you would have to define the CPU itself as a frame structure that had roles such as "KeyboardPlug," "DiskPort," "PowerPlug," and so on. The notation is extended as in the following example that redefines the class of PCs so that the keyboard and disk are subparts and are connected to the CPU.

```
(Define-Class PC with
    [Keyb + keyboard PART-OF(Keyb, Self) &
        CONNECTED-TO(Keyb, KeyboardPlug(MainBox))]
    [Disk1 + diskdrive PART-OF(Disk1, Self) &
        CONNECTED-TO(Disk1, DiskPort(MainBox))]
    [MainBox + CPU PART-OF(MainBox, Self)])
```

You refer to roles of the frame being defined simply by name, whereas you refer to roles of other frames by using functional form. You refer to the object defined by the frame as Self. Thus the KeyB slot is restricted to be of type KEYBOARD, it is a subpart of the PC, and its value must be connected to the KeyboardPlug role of the value of the role MainBox. An instance of PC--say, PC4--with roles KEY14, DD12, and CPU07 would have the following structure:

```
(PC4 isa PC with
    [Keyb KEY14 PART-OF(KEY14, PC4) &
        CONNECTED-TO(KEY14, KeyboardPlug(CPU07))]
    [Disk1 DD12 PART-OF(DD12, PC4) &
        CONNECTED-TO(DD12, DiskPort(CPU07))]
    [MainBox CPU07 PART-OF(CPU07, PC4)])
```

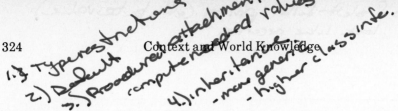

As you can see, the instance immediately acquires all the properties defined for the class.

Since frames are a way of encoding knowledge about classes of objects, it makes sense that frame information should be inherited through the type hierarchy. For example, if you define a subtype of PCs called PC-With-Second-Disk, this type should inherit all the roles of PC. If you define a new role for this type--say, Disk2--then all instances will have four roles: Keyb, Disk1, MainBox, and Disk2.

Defaults

In a frame-based system default information is allowed as a default value for slots. For example, you might define a frame for the type FLIGHT in a knowledge base representing airline schedules as follows:

```
(Define-Class FLIGHT with
     [ID + flight-number]
     [Destination + city]
     [Source + city default BOS]
     [Dtime + time]
     [Atime + time AFTER(Atime, Dtime)]])
```

The implementation of defaults will be very simple. When you create an instance of a frame, the system attempts to find the values for each of its roles using any specific information given in the knowledge base. For instance, the speaker may have identified several role values in the last few utterances. If the system is then called upon to answer a question that requires knowing the value of a slot that remains unknown, it uses a default value if one is specified. Thus, given the preceding frame for flights, if the system needs to identify a particular flight, such as *the 10:30 flight to New York*, it will use the default value of BOS.

Complications arise very quickly as you try to use defaults in a more extensive manner. For example, what happens if a type is a subtype of two different supertypes, each one specifying a different default value for the same role? What happens if you allow the default value to be used to conclude that some proposition P is true, and then later are given an explicit value for the role that is not the default, from which you could not conclude P? To avoid these issues, this text will use defaults only in the simple manner described earlier.

11.4 Representing Actions

A large percentage of conversation (including story telling) involves human action. As such, the representation of action has been one of the most studied areas in work on knowledge representation. This section examines some of the issues involving representing actions and develops a simple representation that will be used throughout the following chapters.

What Is an Action?

Before you start into the details, consider how you might define an action. This issue has defied philosophers for thousands of years, so you should not expect to find a simple answer. But you can make some distinctions. First, there is a distinction between action by intentional agents and actions that arise from natural laws. The latter form of action is studied in elementary physics, and concepts such as force and inertia provide a reasonable theory. In that framework you might define an action simply as the application of some force. In general this force will induce some change of state in the world; for example, an object might move, change shape, or even change state.

Human actions are considerably more complex. While most human actions still involve change, some examples seem to defy this rule. For instance, you might deliberately stand still in order to block an entryway. This seems to be just as much an action as moving out of the doorway, but no change is occurring in the world.

Actions as State Change

All existing computational models of action make certain simplifying assumptions about the world being modeled. The most common of these assumptions is a constraint that only one action ever happens at a time. Thus you do not have to consider situations where actions occur simultaneously. Given this assumption, you can describe the state of the world at any particular time by a set of facts that are true at that moment. Such a collection of facts describing the world at some instant of time is called a **world state**. Actions can be modeled as functions from one world state to a new state that is the resulting world after the action has occurred.

More specifically, you define these functions for a class of actions by specifying conditions that fall into the following classes that characterize two of the forms of causality outlined earlier:

> **Preconditions**: A set of logical formulas that must be true before the action can successfully be executed (enablement).

> **Effects**: A set of formulas that describe the changes to the present world state to produce the world state after the action has been successfully executed (result).

If the preconditions of an action are not satisfied in the initial world state, you cannot successfully execute the action, and you cannot reason about the

---

BOX 11.1 Defining Causality

There are several common-sense notions concerning how actions relate to each other and the world around them. Many of these fall under the notion of **causality**. One action causes another to occur, or causes some effect, if the performance of that action somehow leads to that effect. Intuitively, you might want to say that the effect would not have arisen if the action had not occurred. While this seems straightforward, it is extremely difficult to define causality in terms of some simpler concepts. For example, you might try to model that the action of dropping the glass caused the glass to break in FOPC by an axiom of the form:

$$DROP(Sam, Glass) \supset BROKEN(Glass)$$

But this formula would be trivially true if the Agent did not drop the glass because, given the definition of logical implication, a false antecedent trivially makes the implication true. If you then augment the definition by saying the preceding, plus the fact that the antecedent is true (that is, Sam did drop the glass), then this is logically equivalent to the conjunction:

$$DROP(Sam, Glass) \,\&\, BROKEN(Glass)$$

which doesn't capture the notion of causality either. You might augment this further by saying that if Sam had not dropped the glass, it would not have broken. This gets closer to a definition but introduces further problems. First, the preceding statement is called a **counterfactual** statement; that is, it makes a claim about how the world would be if something that is actually true were not true. Such statements cannot be modeled in simple FOPC but require the introduction of modal operators and an appropriately more complex semantic model (Lewis, 1973). Even if this were done, however, it still wouldn't precisely define the notion of causality, because if Sam had not dropped the glass, some other event could have occurred causing the glass to break (maybe Sam dropped the glass because someone had thrown a stone at him, and if he had not dropped the glass, it would have been hit by the stone). Given all these difficulties, representations usually take the notion of causality as primitive and do not try to decompose it further.

---

resulting world state. The list of effects is divided into two classes that specify how to construct the resulting world state given the initial state: The **deletions** specify the facts that need to be deleted from the old state, and the **additions** specify the facts that need to be added to the new state. All facts in the old state that are not explicitly deleted remain true in the new state.

Strips

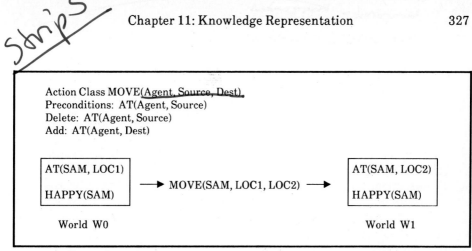

Action Class MOVE(Agent, Source, Dest).
Preconditions: AT(Agent, Source)
Delete: AT(Agent, Source)
Add: AT(Agent, Dest)

| AT(SAM, LOC1) | | AT(SAM, LOC2) |
| HAPPY(SAM) | ⟶ MOVE(SAM, LOC1, LOC2) ⟶ | HAPPY(SAM) |

World W0   World W1

Figure 11.3 Applying the definition of MOVE to produce a resulting world

Consider the simple example in Figure 11.3, in which a class of movement actions is defined, and an instance of this class is applied in a world W0 to produce a resulting world W1. As you can see, the precondition of MOVE(SAM, LOC1, LOC2) is AT(SAM, LOC1), which holds in W0. Thus the function can be applied. Taking the facts in W0, you delete AT(SAM, LOC1) and add AT(SAM, LOC2) to produce the resulting world W1. Notice that the fact that Sam is happy carries through to W1 since the definition of MOVE indicated no effect on this fact.

Action definitions such as these were developed to study a type of reasoning called **planning**, in which the task is to construct a plan, or a sequence of actions, to achieve some goal state. For example, the simplest planners can be viewed as simple search processes. The planner is given an initial state of the world and a **goal state**, which describes the desired resulting world. The plan to be constructed is simply a sequence of actions that transforms the initial state into the goal state. You could accomplish this sequence by searching through all the actions available from the initial state until you find the goal state. In general, a better strategy is **backward chaining**, which is a search starting from the goal state and working backward to the initial state. In particular you select a fact in the goal state that does not hold in the initial state, and then you select an action that has this fact as one of its effects. If the preconditions of this action hold in the initial state, you are done and can go on to consider any other facts in the goal state that are not in the initial state. If one of the preconditions--say, P--does not hold, however, you try to find an action that has P as an effect and introduce it into the plan as well. You repeat this process until you have constructed an action sequence where the first action's preconditions hold in the initial state.

[handwritten notes in top margin: actions involve decomposition / 2 kinds / - temporal - horizontal / - hierarchical - vertical]

Actions as Activities

Another useful form of knowledge about actions is that one action can be performed by performing some other action or set of actions. If you emphasize this sort of knowledge about actions, you get a different model--actions are like programs. An action stands for a sequence of more primitive actions, which, when performed, constitute performing the initial action. Thus the action of turning on a light might consist of flipping the switch, and the action of buying a ticket might consist of going to the ticket booth, giving the clerk some money, and receiving a ticket in return.

More specifically, consider a domain that includes the predicates, functions, and actions to descibe the purchasing action. You need predicates such as

> HAS(agent, object)--the agent owns the object

> AT(agent, location)--the agent is at the location

and the function

> Price(object)--which is the price of the object

The PURCHASE action as described earlier will be formalized as shown in Figure 11.4, which recasts the definitional form for actions into the frame notation, and introduces a graphical depiction of its decomposition. The arrow between subactions indicates temporal ordering. The parameters of the action are roles in the frame that describes the action class. The preconditions and effects are additional roles in the frame but are distinguished from the roles that are parameters by a slightly different notation. Note that this definition assumes a very simplistic view of money: The buyer has the exact amount before buying the ticket and has no money afterward.

Planners that use decomposition information to construct plans are often called **hierarchical planners**. Instead of starting with an initial world state and a goal state, such planners typically start with an initial state and a specific action to perform. The planner then has to find a decomposition of the specified action down to a level of primitive actions, such that the sequence of primitive actions can be executed starting from the initial world state. This might involve selecting between alternative ways of decomposing an action and then further decomposing subactions as necessary. The resulting plan, viewed abstractly, can be represented as a tree of actions.

For example, assume you are in a train station and have the actions summarized in Figure 11.5 in addition to the PURCHASE action defined in Figure 11.4. The planner, SAM, might be given the goal to take some train to Rochester--TAKE-TRIP(SAM, (any train), ROC). In cases where a parameter

The Action Class PURCHASE(Buyer, Seller, Object):
(Define-Class PURCHASE with
    [Buyer + human]
    [Seller + human]
    [Object + physobj]
    Preconditions: HAS(Buyer, Price(Object))
                HAS(Seller, Object)
    Delete: HAS(Buyer, Price(Object))
          HAS(Seller, Object)
    Add: HAS(Buyer, Object)
          HAS(Seller, Price(Object))
    Decomposition:
    GOTO(Buyer, Loc(Seller)) → GIVE(Buyer, Seller, Price(Object))
       → GIVE(Seller, Buyer, Object))

Figure 11.4 The definition of PURCHASE with its decomposition

The Action Class TAKE-TRIP(Actor, Train, Destination)
preconditions: DESTINATION(Train, Destination)
add: IN(Actor, Destination)
decomposition: PURCHASE(Actor, CLERK, Ticket(Train)) →
    GOTO(Actor, Loc(Train)) → GET-ON(Actor, Train)

The Action Class GOTO(Actor, Loc)
preconditions: ¬AT(Actor, Loc)
add: AT(Actor, Loc)

The Action Class GET-ON(Actor, Train)
preconditions: AT(Actor, Train)
              HAS(Actor, Ticket(Train))
add: ON-BOARD(Actor, Train)
decomposition: GIVE(Actor, Conductor(Train), Ticket (Train))
    → FIND-SEAT(Actor, (any SEAT))

The Action Class GIVE(Actor, Recipient, Object)
precondition: HAS(Actor, Object)
delete: HAS(Actor, Object)
add: HAS(Recipient, Object)

The Action Class FIND-SEAT(Actor, Seat)
precondition: EMPTY(Seat)
delete: EMPTY(Seat)
add: SITTING-IN(Actor, Seat)

Figure 11.5 Definition of action classes in train station domain

value is not specified in a goal, a new existential parameter is indicated using the form (any <type>). Such a goal can be satisfied by an action instance with any value of the appropriate type substituted for the form. In this case any train going to ROC could satisfy the goal. Given that the actions defined here each have at most one decomposition, the planning process consists simply of

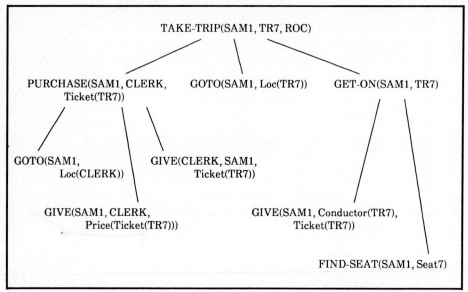

Figure 11.6 A fully-instantiated hierarchical plan to take a trip to Rochester

expanding the decompositions until there are no more actions left to decompose, resulting in a plan summarized as a tree in Figure 11.6.

Using the Action Representation

While this representation of action was developed primarily for planning systems, the same representation is very useful for natural language analysis and for question answering. Chapters 13 and 14 examine its use in natural language analysis in detail. For the moment, consider how such a representation could be used in question answering. If the system were told that some action occurred--say, with the sentence *Jack bought a car*--the final representation of the content in the sentence would be that some instance of a purchasing event, such as B1, occurred. This instance might be defined as follows (note that since no Seller was specified you use a skolem Seller(B1) as the filler of the Seller role):

```
(B1 isa PURCHASE with
    [Buyer JACK1]
    [Seller Seller(B1)]
    [Object CAR1]
    Precondition: HAS(JACK1, Price(CAR1))
    Delete: HAS(JACK1, Price(CAR1))
    Add: HAS(JACK1, CAR1)
    Decomposition: GOTO(JACK1, Loc(Seller(B1))) →
                   GIVE(JACK1, Seller(B1), Price(CAR1)) →
                   GIVE(Seller(B1), JACK1, CAR1))
```

From the fact that B1 occurred, the system can now infer many things. For one, all the preconditions of B1 must have been true in the past, thus HAS(JACK1, Price(CAR1)) was once true. For another, all added effects are true after the action, so the system can infer that Jack now owns the car. Finally, the system can infer that all the actions in the decomposition took place, and it can make conclusions from the definitions of each of them. Thus the system can conclude a large body of information from the fact that a single action occurred. In Chapter 13 there will be many more examples of this type of inference.

Summary

There are many different forms of knowledge representation, depending on what predicates and forms of inference are used. Two example representations are the logic-based system and the frame-based system. The frame representation, extended with the action definitions, allows general world knowledge to be represented in a way that makes it accessible for the specialized inference techniques that will be described in the following chapters.

Related Work and Further Readings

Knowledge representation, which is a highly diverse area in artificial intelligence, and is fundamental to many problems beyond language understanding. Perhaps the best introduction to the field is the collection of papers in Brachman and Levesque (1985). In particular, the article by Brachman (1979) reprinted in that volume provides an excellent discussion of the different levels of representation that have been addressed in previous work.

The strongest proponent of representations based on decompositions into primitives has been Schank (1975), whose conceptual dependency theory reduced all action verbs to approximately 13 primitives. His more recent work, however, while retaining the primitives for some levels of analysis, has also used nondecomposable predicates for representing complex activities and situations (Schank and Riesbeck, 1981).

Although deductive inference strategies are generally found in declarative representations, and nondeductive inference strategies are generally found in procedural representations, a considerable amount of recent work has been aimed at developing formal languages where typically procedural inference techniques, such as defaults, can be given a precise semantics and representation in a declarative framework. Much of the work on default logics stems from work by Reiter (1980). Etherington and Reiter (1983) used this formalism to define inheritance formally with exceptions in type hierarchies. Touretzky (1986) offers another analysis of the same problem in a quite different framework.

Another formal technique being applied to a wide range of nondeductive inference problems is circumscription (McCarthy, 1980). This theory is based on the notion of **minimal models**. A minimal model of a set of formulas makes as few things true as possible while satisfying the formulas.

Horn clause representations have been used in many question-answering systems as a generalization of question answering on standard databases. An example of such a system is presented in Chapter 16. These systems evolved from work in resolution theory proving as introduced by Robinson (1965). Robinson introduced the notions of skolemization and unification and their uses in theorem proving. The technique of proof-by-failure was used in the early AI programming language PLANNER (Hewitt, 1971). It is a key feature in the programming language PROLOG (Clocksin and Mellish, 1981).

The introduction of frames by Minsky (1975) produced a large body of subsequent work in representation. The representation in this chapter is a simplified version of KRL (Bobrow and Winograd, 1977). Hayes (1979) performed an analysis of such frame-based systems in terms of FOPC. Another good reference relating logic, frames, and semantic networks is Nilsson (1980). Most modern representation systems, such as the systems described in Brachman and Levesque (1985), can be seen as a combination of frame systems and semantic networks.

One of the most important theories in AI concerning the representation of action is the situation calculus (McCarthy and Hayes, 1969), in which actions are defined as functions between **situations**, which are instantaneous snapshots of the world. This model led to the development of the STRIPS system (Fikes and Nilsson, 1971), where actions were modeled by their preconditions and their add and delete lists, as described in this chapter. The representation of actions as procedures was explored in detail by Sacerdoti (1977), who built a planner based primarily on the notion of action decomposition. An excellent overview of the work in planning can be found in Nilsson (1980).

Exercises for Chapter 11

1. *(medium)* One of the major problems with default representations arises when a certain object is an instance of more than one type, each one specifying a different default value. Using the notation in this chapter, give a detailed example of a situation where such a problem could naturally arise. Discuss what type of extension to the representation would be needed to handle such situations.

2. *(medium)* Using the formalism for representing actions described in this chapter, define an action class DRIVE that corresponds to a sense of the verb *drive* in

    i)   I drove to school today.

In particular, your definition should contain enough detail so that each of the following statements could be concluded from sentence *i*:

    ii) I was inside the car at some time.
    iii) I had the car keys.
    iv) The car was at school for some time.
    v) I opened the car door.

For each of these sentences, discuss in detail how the necessary knowledge is represented (as a precondition, effect, decomposition, and so on) and what general principle justifies it being a conclusion of sentence *i*.

Identify three other conclusions that can be made from sentence *i*, and discuss how the required knowledge to make that conclusion is encoded. Should any of the definitions be considered to be default knowledge? If so, discuss why. If not, identify one further conclusion that could be made if some default knowledge were used.

3. *(medium)* List the order in which all the actions in Figure 11.6 are completed as the plan to take a trip to Rochester is executed. Does this sequence define the order in which the actions would appear in a script for taking a trip? Identify one key way in which the script representation and the hierarchical plan representation differ.

antecedent – Jack
cenaspher – he

Chapter 12

Reference

The term *reference* is traditionally used to name the study of how phrases in a sentence connect to objects in the real world. An example might be how the NP *the brown cow* actually identifies a particular cow. In computational systems, where there is a knowledge representation, reference generally considers the relationship of phrases to terms in the knowledge representation (which in turn might represent some object in the real world). This chapter, which considers the basic techniques used for this task, concentrates on the analysis of noun phrases.

There are two major forms of noun phrase reference. An **anaphoric reference** involves an NP that refers to an object mentioned earlier in the sentence or in a previous sentence. In **nonanaphoric reference** the NP identifies a particular object that has not been previously mentioned. Examples of anaphoric reference are underlined in the following sentences:

> Jack$_i$ saw himself$_i$ in the mirror.
> Jack$_i$ went to the party and he$_i$ got drunk.
> I found a red pen$_i$ and blue pencil. The pen$_i$ didn't work.

Within an example, phrases marked with same subscript refer to the same object. Thus the phrase *the pen* in the third example refers to the same object as that introduced earlier by the phrase *a red pen*. These two NPs are said to **corefer.**

Examples of nonanaphoric reference can also be seen in the preceding sentences. In particular the NP *Jack* in the first sentence refers to a person not previously mentioned, and the indefinite *a red pen* in the third sentence introduces an object not previously mentioned.

As with most distinctions, some cases are not easily classified. For instance, one NP might introduce a set of objects that are subsequently referred to, such as

> We bought two guitars at the store. The new one was cheap, but the used one was expensive.

Here the underlined NPs do refer back to objects mentioned earlier, but they were not individually mentioned. Another case is seen in the following:

> We bought a new desk. When it was delivered, we found out that the drawer was broken.

Here the NP *the drawer* refers to a subpart of a previously mentioned object--the desk.

Not all reference problems involve noun phrases. For instance, some pronomial forms refer to events introduced by a previous sentence, as in

Jack lost the race. <u>It</u> surprised Sam.

Other forms appear to refer to events introduced by verb phrases, as in

Jack congratulated the winner. After some hesitation, Sam <u>did it too</u>.

The next sections examine these problems in detail. Section 12.1 examines simple nonanaphoric reference, and Section 12.2 introduces the idea of a *history list* and uses it for simple anaphoric reference. Section 12.3 looks at some of the more complicated reference examples and extends the history list mechanism appropriately. Section 12.4 looks at some forms of reference that appear to be based on the syntactic forms of previous sentences, and Section 12.5 describes some of the remaining problems in reference. Finally, Section 12.6 discusses the related issue of ellipsis.

12.1 Simple Reference

The simplest view of reference is that noun phrases either introduce new objects to the context or identify objects already in the context. The determiner structure of the NP identifies which form of reference is being used. In particular, **indefinite reference** (such as *a dog, some people*) introduces new objects into the context (that is, new constant terms in the knowledge representation), and **definite reference** (such as *the dog, these dogs, Jack*) identifies objects that already exist in the context. On another dimension **singular reference** (*a dog, the dog*) identifies a single individual, while **plural reference** (*the dogs*) identifies a set of individuals.

It is easy to handle simple indefinite reference. You create a new term of the appropriate type and use it as the referent. For example, if you assume the knowledge representation is a frame-based system, the NP *a dog*, with the logical form (INDEF/SING d1 DOG) will map to a new term--say, DOG17--that is an instance of the type DOG. From then on, any anaphoric reference back to this term will add further information about DOG17. Once a new term is introduced, it is available for subsequent reference and is identical in form to any other term stored in the knowledge base.

Nonanaphoric definite reference is more complicated than the indefinite case because the referent should be a constant that already exists in the knowledge base. In general the computational techniques for simple definite reference depend on the particular form of the NP. Systems typically handle proper names, such as *Jack*, by mapping them directly to constants in the KB using a simple table lookup. This means that the name always refers to the same term irrespective of context. For example, the logical form (NAME **j1** PERSON "Jack") might always map to a constant PERSON37.

Singular definite descriptions, those singular NPs beginning with *the*, require a more complex analysis, involving a search of the KB for objects that satisfy the description. For example, the NP *the brown cow* might have a logical form (DEF/SING **c1** COW (COLOR **c1** BROWN)). The KB would be searched for all terms of type COW that have the property of being brown. In a frame-based system this might mean a search for any instance that matches the form

        (? isa COW with
            [COLOR BROWN])

In a logic-based representation this might involve a query to find all instantiations of variable ?x such that the formula (COW ?x) & (COLOR ?x BROWN) is provable. In either case if a single answer is found, that term is the referent of the definite description. If more than one constant is found, or if none is found, this technique fails.

If the description is more complex, the procedure may need to interpret subconstituents recursively before the referent of the NP can be identified. For example, a system cannot interpret the NP *the cow in the field,* with a logical form (DEF/SING **c1** COW (AT-LOC **c1** (DEF/SING **f1** FIELD))), until it interprets the subconstituent *the field.* If the system is frame-based, it might first try to find instances of type FIELD; if it found a single one--say, F17--it would then attempt to find an instance of a frame:

        (? isa COW with
            [LOCATION F17])

A more general approach to this problem allows both NPs to be resolved simultaneously. For example, using a logic-based representation, you might try to find all instantiations of the variables ?c and ?f such that

        (COW ?c) & (FIELD ?f) & (IN ?c ?f)

If you find a single answer, the instantiations are the referents.

This latter technique will succeed in situations where the former technique fails. In particular, assume that there are two cows, C1 and C2, and two fields, F1 and F2. Furthermore, cow C1 is in field F1, whereas COW C2 is in a barn B1, and field F2 is empty. In the latter case the query just shown will still succeed, and C1 will be identified as the unique answer. In the frame-based approach described earlier, the NP *the field* will not be analyzable since there are two possible referents, F1 and F2. Thus you would need to specify some additional mechanism to allow for this case.

BOX 12.1 Russell's Treatment of Definite Descriptions

One of the earliest works on representing definite descriptions was by Russell and Whitehead (1925). They suggested that sentences containing definite descriptions were in fact abbreviations for more complex sentences that include the assertion that exactly one object satisfies the description. They introduced the **iota operator** (i) and represented a definite description such as *the brown dog* as:

$$i(x) . DOG(x) \& COLOR(x, BROWN)$$

A formula using the iota operator, such as $BARK\ (i(x)\ .\ DOG(x))$, is defined to be an abbreviation for the standard FOPC formula:

$$\exists x . DOG(x) \& \forall y (DOG(y) \supset x=y) \& BARK(x)$$

If you break up this conjunction, it says

1. (existence) there is a dog, x;

2. (uniqueness) any dog is equal to x;

3. (context) x barks.

While this theory has been very influential, it has obvious defects. Like the analysis in Section 12.1, it has no account for the role of context; furthermore, if there is a reference failure, the sentence turns out to be false rather than ill formed. For example, given that there are two brown cows, you would probably want to say that the sentence *The brown cow died* is faulty, whereas in Russell and Whitehead's analysis:

$$\exists c . COW(c) \& \forall d ((COW\ d) \supset c=d) \& DIED(c)$$

it would be false because the uniqueness condition is false.

Plural definite descriptions can be handled in the same way as singular ones with the exception that you need not find a unique answer to the KB query. In fact, all the answers returned are simply grouped together as a set that represents the referent. Few current knowledge representations handle sets in a general way, so issues in dealing with plural reference usually tend to be ignored.

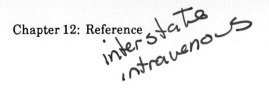

The major weakness of the approach described in this section is the failure to account for context. The next section introduces a model of context for anaphoric reference, and Section 12.3 then adapts the model to nonanaphoric uses.

12.2 Simple Anaphoric Reference

There are significant syntactic constraints on what objects an anaphoric NP may refer to, and this area is currently very active in linguistics. Only some of the simplest and best-known results will be discussed here. In particular, in order for a definite NP, NP2 (called the **anaphor**), to corefer with another NP, NP1 (called the **antecedent**), the following conditions must usually hold:

1. they must agree in number, person, and gender;

2. NP1 should precede NP2; and

3. if NP1 is the subject of the clause that contains NP2, then NP2 must be in the reflexive form; otherwise, NP2 must not be in the reflexive form.

The following ill-formed sentences demonstrate these constraints. As before, the same subscript indicates that the NPs corefer. The number following the sentence indicates what constraint is violated.

> *Jack$_i$ went to the party and she$_i$ got drunk.   1
> * He$_i$ said Jack$_i$ wants to leave.   2
> *Jack$_i$ saw him$_i$ in the mirror.   3

Acceptable versions of these three sentences are

> Jack$_i$ went to the party and he$_i$ got drunk.
> Jack$_i$ said he$_i$ wants to leave.
> Jack$_i$ saw himself$_i$ in the mirror.

You need two different techniques for handling anaphor: one to handle intersentential uses (the antecedent is in the same sentence), and one to handle intrasentential uses. Reflexive pronouns appear only in the intrasentential use, whereas nonreflexive pronouns may appear in either use. The common uses of different NP forms are shown in Figure 12.1.

Intrasentential Reference

The syntactic structure of the sentence is important in accounting for the reflexive use. Although it is a considerable simplification, the following algorithm handles intrasentential anaphoric and nonanaphoric NPs using the three constraints outlined earlier. Each NP is analyzed in turn, in the order that it appears in the sentence, depending on its form.

Form	Intrasentence Anaphor	Intersentence Anaphor	Non-anaphor
reflexive pronoun	yes, to subject	no	no
nonreflexive pronoun	yes, but not to subject	yes	rarely
definite NP	no	yes	yes
indefinite NP	no	no	yes
proper names	no	no	yes

Figure 12.1 The common uses of referring phrases

1. If it is a proper name, indefinite NP, or definite NP, the referent is found as described in Section 12.1 and the answer stored in a new slot **REF**.

2. If it is a reflexive pronoun, the **REF** is set to the value in the NP in the **SUBJ** slot (assuming the number and gender are compatible).

3. If it is a nonreflexive pronoun, all NPs that precede it, except for the subject NP, are tested for number and person agreement. Any of those that are compatible are possible antecedents.

If the system finds no possible antecedent for the nonreflexive pronominal forms, it tries the tests for intersentential anaphora. These tests will be described in the next section. If more than one possible antecedent is found, the system must either pick one (say the most recent) or retain the ambiguity for later processing.

Consider two closely related sentences: *Jack saw himself with the mirror* and *Jack saw him with the mirror*. The first has the semantic and syntactic form:

```
(S SUBJ (NP₁ NAME Jack
              SEM (NAME j1 PERSON "Jack"))
   MAIN-V see
   TENSE PAST
   OBJ (NP₂ PRO himself
            SEM (PRO h1 MALE "himself"))
   MODS (PP PREP in
            POBJ (NP₃ DET the
                      HEAD mirror
                      SEM (DEF/SING m1 MIRROR)))
   SEM (PAST s1 SEE [AGENT (NAME j1 PERSON "Jack")]
                   [THEME (PRO h1 MALE "himself")]
                   [INST (DEF/SING m1 MIRROR)]))
```

BOX 12.2 When Must the Reflexive Be Used?

The discussion has already presented an initial characterization of when the reflexive must be used--namely, when the antecedent is the subject of the simple S structure containing the pronoun. Thus sentence a must use the reflexive, whereas sentence b must use the nonreflexive if both pronouns are to refer to Jack.

    a) Jack likes himself.
    b) When Jack climbed over the fence, Sue saw him.

In b, of course, the subject of the sentence containing *him* is Sue. But there are many cases where this simple heuristic fails, as shown in sentence c, where the nonreflexive must be used even though the pronoun can refer to the subject Jack.

    c) Jack saw his father.

Thus the preceding rule might be modified so that the pronoun must be an immediate constituent of the S. Thus, since *his* is a subpart of the NP *his father*, it cannot be in the reflexive form. But this additional restriction would then prohibit the use of the reflexive in sentence d, so it is obviously wrong.

    d) Jack washed the car by himself.

Finally, sentences e, f, g, and h show complications that arise in using the possessive. The reflexive may appear in contexts even where there is no subject yet defined for a sentence. While a single nesting of the possessive in sentence e requires the reflexive, the double nesting in sentence f requires the nonreflexive form.

    e) Jack's present for himself had been stolen.
    f) Jack's father's present for him had been stolen.
    g) Jack saw Sue's picture of him.
    h) Jack saw a picture of himself.

To explain these facts, a richer framework defining the constraints of the use of the reflexive is needed. One approach is to define the notion of a generalized subject that includes the standard notion of subject in an S structure and the possessive NP in an NP structure. The actual constraints on reflexives can then be stated as follows: The antecedent of a reflexive pronoun must be the closest generalized subject in the NPs and Ss that contain the pronoun.

Given these examples, the following chart identifies the closest subject for each pronominal form in each sentence.

Sentence	Pronoun	Antecedent	Closest Subject	Reflexive Use?
a)	himself	Jack	Jack	YES
b)	him	Jack	Sue	NO
c)	his	Jack	his (the closest subject is itself!)	NO
d)	himself	Jack	Jack	YES
e)	himself	Jack	Jack	YES
f)	him	Jack	Jack's father	NO
g)	him	Jack	Sue	NO
h)	himself	Jack	Jack	YES

In example h the reason that Jack is the closest subject is that the NP *a picture of himself* has no possessive modifier and hence contains no generalized subject.

The algorithm processes this form as follows: NP_1 is first analyzed and mapped to a constant in the knowledge base--say, J1. This is stored in the **REF** slot of NP_1, producing

> (NP₁ **NAME** Jack
>   **SEM** (NAME j1 PERSON "Jack")
>   **REF** J1)

When NP_2 is analyzed, the reflexive pronoun forces the **REF** of NP_2 to be the same as the **SUBJ** NP--namely, NP_1. Thus the **REF** of NP_2 would be set to J1 as well.

In the second sentence the only difference in the syntactic and semantic structure is that NP_2 is not reflexive. Since the **SUBJ** NP is not eligible as a referent, no antecedent can be found. Thus the analysis of *him* is left for the intersentential anaphora stage.

This algorithm fails to handle cases where the pronoun is in a clause modifying the phrase with which it corefers. For example, the NP *the man who dropped his hat* cannot be analyzed in the reading where *his* and *the man* corefer. To see the problem, consider that the referent of the entire NP would need to be determined before the referent of the pronoun *his*, but since the pronoun is part of the whole phrase, it would need to be analyzed before the

Last Sentence

(S   **WH-QUERY** (PP$_1$ **HEAD** when)
     SUBJ (NP$_1$ **DET** the
                    HEAD flight
                    NUM {3p}
                    MODS (PP **PREP** from
                                 POBJ (NP$_2$ **NAME** Boston)))
     MAIN-V arrive
     TENSE PRES
     MODS ((PP **PREP** in
                   POBJ (NP$_3$ **NAME** Chicago))
              →PP1))

History List

Constituent	Object	Type	Other Information
NP$_3$	CHI	CITY	
NP$_1$	FLIGHT0124	FLIGHT	
NP$_2$	BOS	CITY	

Figure 12.2 The record after *When does the flight from Boston arrive in Chicago?*

entire NP is analyzed. In this case the coreference of the two needs to be determined before a referent can be found. If this is done, the query to find the referent might be (MAN ?m) & (DROP ?m ?h) & (HAT ?h) & (OWN ?m ?h).

Intersentential Anaphora

The main technique for handling intersentential anaphora is the maintenance of a record of all objects mentioned in the preceding sentences. This record consists of the syntactic analysis of the immediately preceding sentence, plus an ordered list of all referents mentioned in the last several sentences, called the **history list**. For the moment, assume the history list grows indefinitely.

Given this structure, to find the referent of an anaphoric NP (whose antecedent was not identified in the intrasentence stage), you search the history list, starting from the most recently mentioned objects, until you find one that satisfies the number and person information of the pronoun.

When a constituent a is a subconstituent of another constituent A and both are on the history list, then they are ordered so that A is found first in the search for antecedents. For example, the record after processing the sentence *When does the flight from Boston arrive in Chicago?* would be as shown in Figure 12.2.

Given this record, consider analyzing the first NP in the sentence *Does that flight serve lunch?* Assume that the analysis of *that flight* is as follows:

Box 12.3 How Long Do Objects Stay on the History List?

A difficult question concerns how long an object should remain on the history list. In fact apparently this question cannot be answered in terms of a fixed number of sentences, and the answer can be found only after considering the structure of discourse in more detail (see Chapter 14).

Some statistical studies indicate that most antecedents are actually very close and thus the history list can be quite short. In particular, Hobbs (1978) examined 100 consecutive examples of pronoun use in three very different forms of text and found that 98 percent of the antecedents were either in the current sentence or the immediately preceding sentence. He also found, however, one case where the antecedent was nine sentences before the pronoun. Grosz (1974) reports cases that are even a further distance.

```
(NP DET that
    HEAD flight
    NUM {3s}
    SEM (PRO/SING f1 FLIGHT))
```

Using the information in the **SEM** slot, check the history list for a constituent that describes a single object of type FLIGHT. It cannot be constituent 1, since CHI is a CITY and not a FLIGHT, but it can be constituent 2. Thus the **REF** slot of the constituent for *that flight* is set to the constant FLIGHT0124.

Consider now the case in which the speaker says *Does it serve lunch?* You might think that the pronoun *it* could match any singular object with neutral gender, and thus the proposed referent would be CHI, because it is the first constituent on the history list. In fact the selectional restrictions imposed during semantic interpretation provide the information necessary to handle this case. In particular the restriction on the verb *serve* would require that its subject be either of type PERSON or FLIGHT. Thus, if the initial interpretation of *it* is a logical form such as (PRO/SING x1 ANYTHING − PERSON "it"), after being assigned as the subject of the verb *serve*, it will have been further restricted to be (PRO/SING x1 FLIGHT "it"). Thus, when matched against the history list, the appropriate referent will again be found in exactly the same fashion as the previous example.

The algorithm to handle nonanaphoric NPs, intrasentential anaphora, and intersentential anaphora is as follows:

Object	Type	Other Information
NewPencil34	PENCIL	
NewPen12	PEN	(COLOR NewPen12 RED)

Figure 12.3 The relevant part of the history list after sentence B.2

1. If the NP is a proper name or an indefinite NP, use the techniques of Section 12.1 to identify or create the referent.

2. If the NP is a reflexive pronoun, then apply the techniques for intrasentential reference described previously.

3. If the NP is a nonreflexive pronoun, then apply the techniques for intrasentential anaphora and, if this fails to produce an antecedent, apply the techniques for intersentential anaphora just described.

4. If the NP is a definite NP, then apply the techniques of intersentential anaphora, and only if this fails, apply the techniques of Section 12.1 for nonanaphoric use.

12.3 Extending the History List Mechanism

So far the system has handled definite noun phrases in two ways: checking the history list and searching the knowledge base for a unique object that satisfies the description. In many other cases, however, the NP is related to an object on the history list but is not identical to it. Then you must find this connection to identify the appropriate referent. To see this, consider a new example that is a dialog between two speakers, A and B:

A.1: Do you have a pen I can borrow?
B.2: I have a red pen or a pencil.
A.3: I'll take the pencil.
B.4: Oh, sorry, the lead is broken, so you'll have to take the pen.

The definite NP *the pencil* in sentence A.3 is analyzed successfully as an intersentential anaphora. In particular the relevant part of the history list after sentence B.2 will contain the referents for the NPs *a red pen* and *a pencil*, which are listed with the information stored about them in the knowledge base, as shown in Figure 12.3.

As usual the definite NP *the pencil* in sentence A.3 is mapped to a logical form such as (DEF/SING **p1** PENCIL). The referent for this NP will be found by traversing through the history list, testing each referent in turn to see if it satisfies the description in the logical form. In this case the description is simply that the object is of the type PENCIL. As expected, the object NewPencil34 (the object constructed from the NP *a pencil* in B.2) will be selected as the referent as desired.

Reference to Related Objects

The history list mechanism is inadequate for analyzing the NP *the lead* in sentence B.4, since no lead has been mentioned previously in the conversation. Note also that the word *lead* is ambiguous between being the lead of a pencil, a fishing lead, or a piece of metal. To analyze this word correctly, the system needs to know that a lead is a part of a pencil and recognize that the referent of *the lead* is the appropriate subpart of the previously mentioned pencil--namely, NewPencil34.

You can take one of two general approaches to this problem. The first approach is to extend the history list with objects related to the mentioned objects. In this approach the lead of the pencil would be added to the extended history list when the pencil was added. The second approach is to define certain relationships, such as PART-OF; when matching a description against the history list, you also match against objects that can be related to an object on the history list by these relationships. In either case, whether explicitly or implicitly, you have to identify the set of objects that are closely related to each object mentioned.

It is probably not possible to compute the set of related objects that could be referred to, but some simple cases can be identified. In particular, when an object is added to the history list, its component parts should be accessible for definite reference. The lead/pencil case is an example of this; another is the relationship between kitchen and stove, as in *When we entered the kitchen, we noticed that the stove had been left on.* As with the lead/pencil example, the system needs to identify *the stove* as referring to the stove that is in the kitchen just mentioned. Another class of examples involves events and their roles, as in *The next day after we sold our car, the buyer returned and wanted his money back.*

If the knowledge representation uses a frame representation, one attractive possibility is that the closely related objects are all roles of the objects placed on the history list. This representation certainly could handle the range of examples discussed earlier, since subparts would be roles. Consider how the example with the NP *the lead* could be processed in such a representation. The definition of the classes PENCIL and PEN might be

Object	Derived Object	Type	Other Information
NewPencil34		PENCIL	
	Lead34	PENCIL-LEAD	(PART-OF Lead34 NewPencil34)
	Ersr34	PENCIL-ERASER	(PART-OF Ersr34 NewPencil34)
	Shft34	PENCIL-SHAFT	(PART-OF Shft34 NewPencil34)
NewPen12		PEN	(COLOR NewPen12 RED)
	Ink12	INK	(PART-OF Ink12 NewPen12)
	Tip12	PEN-TIP	(PART-OF Tip12 NewPen12)
	Rfl12	PEN-REFILL	(PART-OF Rfl12 NewPen12)
	Shft12	PEN-SHAFT	(PART-OF Shft12 NewPen12)

Figure 12.4 The extended history list after sentence A.3

(Define-class PENCIL with
    [Lead + pencil-lead]
    [Eraser + pencil-eraser]
    [Shaft + pencil-shaft])

(Define-class PEN with
    [Ink + ink]
    [Tip + pen-tip]
    [Refill + pen-refill]
    [Shaft + pen-shaft])

When an object is added to the history list, the system now automatically adds all its roles in a new list called **derived objects**. Thus, after sentence A.3 is understood, the history list is as shown in Figure 12.4.

The logical form of the NP *the lead* is (DEF/SING l1 {PENCIL-LEAD, FISHING-LEAD, LEAD-METAL}). You match this into the history list by checking each object and subpart one at a time to see if the object could fit the description in the NP. In this case you are searching for an object of type PENCIL-LEAD, FISHING-LEAD, or LEAD-METAL. As desired, you find the object Lead34, a subpart of the previously mentioned object NewPencil34.

While this technique covers many cases, it cannot handle a number of obvious examples. For instance, it could handle the sentence *When we entered the kitchen, we saw that the stove was on*, and it could recognize that the stove referred to is in the kitchen just mentioned. In this case the stove could easily be a role in the kitchen frame. But an equally reasonable sentence is *When we entered the kitchen, we saw that the gas had been left on*. In this case the NP *the gas* is presumably the gas used by the stove that is part of the kitchen. To handle this example, the system would have to add the roles of derived objects to the history list as well!

Another possible approach to this problem would use the spreading activation models discussed in Section 10.5. The system would use spreading activation to find a semantic relationship between the possible interpretations of the current NP and the previously mentioned objects. The strongest semantic connection suggests the relationship between the new referent and a previously introduced object.

Definite Reference and Sets

Plural noun phrases refer to sets of objects and, as a result, introduce new complications into the process of finding the intended referent. In particular a plural NP might refer to a set of objects that have been mentioned only individually, as in

> While diving near the old wreck, we found a gold coin and a rusted knife. We took <u>these objects</u> to the harbor police when we returned.

The NP *these objects* refers to the coin and knife mentioned in the previous sentence. In addition an object introduced in a set by a plural NP may subsequently be referred to, as in

> We found seven coins on the next dive. The <u>oldest</u> was dated 1823.

The NP *the oldest* picks out a particular member of the set of coins. Cases such as these using a superlative in some sense do not introduce new information, since every (finite) set of objects is known to have a largest element. In other examples, however, new information that could not be previously known may be introduced, as in:

> I used two scuba tanks for those dives. The 1600 psi tank was my favorite because it is very compact.

In this case the NP *the 1600 psi tank* refers to one of the tanks mentioned in the previous sentence, even though the reader does not know what the pressure ratings were on the tanks when the set was introduced.

To handle these cases, the history list mechanism needs extending again. Objects on the list may be combined to form sets, and sets may be broken apart into their individual components. On the other hand, it would be a mistake to construct every possible set of objects automatically from the items on the history list, because this would create many sets that could never be referenced. While you can't exactly delimit the cases where sets should be constructed or taken apart, certain cases seem clear.

Before you consider some examples in detail, note that plural descriptions involve two classes of information--information about the set itself and information about the individual members. For example, cardinality information in the specifiers (such as *two, three, several, both*) apply to the set, as do some modifiers, such as in *the two men who met at the corner*, where the meeting is a property of the two men jointly, not a property of one of the men alone. In all the following examples, however, modifiers apply to each element of the set and are not properties of the set itself.

First consider cases of set construction. Again there is a choice in the algorithm. The system can construct sets and add them to the history list when the individual objects are added. Then it can deal with subsequent references to a set by inspecting the history. Alternatively, it might not construct the sets until the subsequent reference is made. Each method has its advantages. If you construct the sets in advance, certain syntactic information (such as the fact that the objects were introduced in a conjunction, making them likely to be combined as a set) can be used to construct the likely sets. If you construct sets only on demand when needed, sets will not be constructed in situations where they are not needed. Consider a mixed strategy:

- if objects are introduced in a conjunction, then explicitly construct the set and add to the history list;

- when given a plural definite NP, first check the history list for a set that matches (this is essentially the same step as for singular NPs); only if that fails, attempt to construct a set from the objects on the history list that satisfy the description given.

This algorithm encodes a preference for explicitly introduced sets and implicit sets introduced by conjunctions for the referent of plural definite NPs. Only if a referent cannot be found is a set built on the basis of semantic information. As a result this algorithm is crucially dependent on the strategy deciding how long an entry stays on the history list. If objects stayed on indefinitely, undesirable consequences would arise, since the algorithm depends on not finding a referent to trigger the set construction process. Obviously, you would not usually want some explicit set mentioned several pages ago in a text to be preferred over a simple set construction out of some recently mentioned objects. To find a better answer to this problem, you must look more at the structure of discourse, as discussed in Chapter 14.

When dealing with examples that involve reference to elements of a previously mentioned set, you may not know anything about the individuals that make up the set until they are referred to. Thus the following strategies will all concern reasoning about contents of a set after the subsequent reference has been made.

The use of the superlative and comparative adjectives explicitly signals a selection from a set. In these cases you can immediately try to identify the set in question. With the comparative form you know you are looking for a set consisting of two elements, as in

> At the zoo we saw a monkey climb out on a tree limb above two elephants. The larger one snorted its disapproval.

To analyze *the larger one*, the system checks the history list for a set of two objects and immediately finds the set of elephants.

The use of the superlative indicates that the object should be identified from a set of more than two elements and can be dealt with in a similar manner as the comparatives. Note that set construction may be needed to construct the set in the first place! For example:

> On our trip to the store we saw one dog on our street, another in the park, and yet another outside the store door. The largest was a German shepherd.

In this example you need to construct the set of dogs seen on the shopping trip so that a referent for the NP *the largest* can be identified. Note that even though the largest dog is one of the three mentioned individually, there is no information as to which of these dogs was identified.

You can make a similar analysis for NPs involving cardinal numbers such as *first* and *second*, except that in these cases you need to be able to represent ordered sets. Once you can do this, you can also handle specifiers such as *next*.

Perhaps the most complex cases occur with singular definite NPs that add new information as they pick out an element of a previously mentioned set, as in the example mentioned earlier:

> I used two scuba tanks for those dives. The 1600 psi tank was my favorite because it is very compact.

To handle such cases, you must modify the algorithm for finding the referent of definite NPs. In particular you have to introduce a new step that involves matching the description against the known properties of elements of any set on the history list. In the usual case this match will not fail unless at least one property mentioned in the description is ignored. For example, with the NP *the 1600 psi tank*, you must ignore the capacity rating of the tank and match solely on the object being a tank. In simple instances like this, where there are few additional restrictions in the NP, the system can usually simply match on the type of the object. In more complex cases the system must try to determine which of the restrictions are important and which can be ignored during the match. These complexities are not addressed in the following algorithm.

The Extended Algorithm for Definite NPs

This algorithm, which is based on the algorithm for intersentential anaphora, is extended to cover the cases discussed in this section. It does not address the issue of how long an object stays on the history list.

1. To Find the Referent

   1.1 Attempt to find an object on the history list that was explicitly introduced in the previous text and that satisfies the description of the current NP exactly (including number agreement). The first one found is the referent.

   1.2 Attempt to find a derived object on the history list, such as a role, that satisfies the description of the current NP exactly. If one is found, that is the referent.

   1.3a If description is singular: attempt to find a set on the history list that contains an object that matches the description of the current NP exactly. If this fails, retry ignoring the modifiers in the current NP. If successful, introduce a new constant as the referent and assert its appropriate set membership.

   1.3b If description is plural: attempt to construct a set by gathering all objects on the history list that match the description, ignoring number information. If successful, introduce a new constant (that is, naming a set) as the referent and assert the appropriate membership relations.

   1.4 Retrieve all objects satisfying the description from the database. If exactly one is found, that is the referent.

2. Update the History List

   2.1 If a referent was successfully found, add the referent onto the history list together with any derived objects retrieved from the database (for example, add all roles of the object). In addition, if the sentence contained a conjunctive construction over NPs, construct and add the set containing the referents of those NPs.

12.4 One-Anaphora and VP-Anaphora

Other forms of anaphora have not yet been considered. This section examines one-anaphora and VP-anaphora.

One-Anaphora

One class of reference involves referring back to a syntactic structure previously mentioned and then reinterpreting it to produce a new semantic interpretation. Typical examples include the use of the pronouns *one* or *some*, or concern prepositional phrase or relative clause modifiers on the pronoun. Sentences involving this form of anaphora often include a modifier such as *too*, *as well*, and *also*. For example, the following sentence sequence involves surface anaphoric reference:

> I saw two bears in the woods. Bill saw <u>some</u> in the parking lot too.

Other cases arise in using numbers. Consider the following two commands that might be given in sequence to an airline database system:

> Reserve a seat for me on the flight to Boston. Reserve one for Jack
> as well.

The *one* in the second sentence refers not to the previously mentioned seat but to a new object in the same class as a previously mentioned object--in this case, a seat on the next flight to Boston. The modifiers of *one* indicate the differences between the previously mentioned phrase and the intended phrase. You can analyze simple cases of this behavior using the syntactic structure of the previous sentence. First, a pattern must be derived from the syntactic analysis of the *one* phrase. In particular, the phrase *one for Jack* would initially be analyzed as

>   (NP PRO one
>   NUM {3s}
>   MODS (PP PREP for
>   POBJ (NP NAME Jack)))

With the representation of patterns used in the semantic interpretation rules, a pattern is generated from the syntactic form to match against the history list. Since the modifiers indicate new information not present in the antecedent, all embedded NPs are replaced by the type of their semantic interpretation. In addition, all number information is ignored, because you can have a singular pronominal form match a plural antecedent, or vice versa. In the preceding example the resulting pattern will be

>   (NP MODS (PP PREP for
>   POBJ +person))

As desired, this pattern will match the entry on the history list that was derived from the phrase *a seat for me on the flight to Boston*. That is,

```
(NP  DET a
     HEAD seat
     MODS (PP PREP for
                POBJ me)
           (PP PREP on
                POBJ (NP DET the
                         HEAD flight
                         MODS (PP PREP to
                                   POBJ Boston))))
```

The final step is to construct a new syntactic structure by using the structure found on the history list with new values substituted from the anaphoric phrase. Thus the final result would be

```
(NP  PRO one
     NUM {3s}
     HEAD seat
     MODS (PP PREP for
                POBJ Jack)
           (PP PREP on
                POBJ (NP DET the
                         HEAD flight
                         MODS (PP PREP to
                                   POBJ Boston))))
```

This structure would then be semantically analyzed and interpreted like an indefinite reference.

The technique also applies to numbers in general. For instance, the preceding sentence could just as well have been *Reserve two on a flight to Chicago for Jack as well.* Thus the number agreement is not enforced between the surface anaphora and its antecedent phrase.

The main weakness of this method is that it is particularly sensitive to the way things are said. For instance, the current algorithm would fail to analyze the NP *one to Chicago for me* correctly, since it would be looking for a previous NP with a PP modifier of the form "to + city," whereas the history list has an NP with the modifier of the form "the flight to + city."

VP- and Sentence Anaphora

The introduction contained some examples of pronominal reference to objects introduced by sentences and verb phrases:

Jack lost the race. It surprised Sam.

Object	Type
LOSE-EVENT23	LOSE-EVENT
R111	RACE
JACK155	PERSON

Figure 12.5 The history list after *Jack lost the race*.

Jack congratulated the winner. After some hesitation, Sam did it too.

In the first example the *it* refers to the event of Jack losing the race, which was introduced by the entire previous sentence. In the second example the *did it* refers to the action of congratulating the winner, which was introduced by the verb phrase of the previous sentence. To handle these types of examples, the history list needs to contain constituents other than just NPs.

Consider the sentence anaphora case first. The sentence *Jack lost the race* intuitively makes an assertion and does not seem to refer to an object, event, or fact. Once the sentence has been said, however, the fact that was asserted can later be referred to--say, by an NP *the fact that Jack lost the race*. It turns out that, because of the way sentences are represented in the logical form, you already have a name that stands for the fact (or event) that is asserted by a sentence. If the final representation uses a similar technique of representation, you have the referent needed to handle S anaphora. If the final representation does not retain this type of analysis, then S anaphora cannot be handled. Assuming the final representation maintains facts and events as objects, a plausible extended history list formed from the sentence *Jack lost the race* is shown in Figure 12.5.

The pronoun *it* in *It surprised Sam* will be analyzed as a reference to a neuter, singular object (the meaning of *it*), which must be a fact or event (from the selectional restriction on subjects to the verb *surprise*). This will match the first item, and the referent will be LOSE-EVENT23, as desired.

The VP-anaphora form *did it* requires a VP constituent to be added to the history list. To do this, the system must allow lambda expressions as values on the history list. In particular, the entry for the VP *lost the race* would be

$$\lambda x \, (PAST \; 11 \; LOSE\text{-}EVENT \; [AGENT \; x] \\ [THEME \; (DEF/SING \; r1 \; RACE)])$$

The resolution of the form *did it* would explicitly check the VPs in the history list and construct an interpretation of the new sentence by applying the lambda expression to the new subject NP.

12.5 Other Problems in Reference

Thus far the chapter has concentrated on definite reference and pronominal reference. There are many other forms of noun phrases whose interpretation depends on reference techniques. This section considers some of these issues, although there are not yet any well-established techniques for handling these problems.

Referential and Attributive Noun Phrases

A basic distinction can be made between **referential** noun phrases, where the NP is used to refer to a particular object, and **attributive** uses of noun phrases, where the NP is used to describe a set of characteristics. In general there is no way to detect the use of a noun phrase from its syntactic form, though the sentential content in which the NP occurs may strongly favor a particular interpretation. For example, the NP *the chairman of the board* is referential in the usual reading of the sentence *I saw the chairman of the board*. In this case the speaker is using the NP to identify a particular person who happens to be the chairman of the board. On the other hand, the same NP is probably used attributively in the sentence *I want to be the chairman of the board*. Even if you know that Joe is currently the chairman of the board, this sentence is not about Joe. The speaker does not mean *I want to be Joe*. Rather the speaker wishes for the position of chairman of the board. If you were to characterize these sentences using the FOPC, you would have an analysis like

SAW(JAMES1, JOE3)

for the first one (that is, *the chairman of the board* is the object JOE3), and

WANT(JAMES1, BOARD-CHAIRMAN(JAMES1))

for the second (that is, *be the chairman of the board* is the predication BOARD-CHAIRMAN).

Indefinite Noun Phrases

In some cases an indefinite NP does not introduce an object available for subsequent reference. For instance, some indefinite NPs within the scope of a negation operator do not create such an object. As a result the usual reading of the following sentences is incoherent: *I don't own a dog. It has brown fur.* It is difficult to determine a strong constraint for such cases, however. If there are multiple NPs within the scope of the negation operator, each one can subsequently be referred to in certain circumstances. For example, the sentence *I didn't see a man leave a bag* could be followed by either *He left a box* or *A woman left it* (but not by *He left it*, of course). There are even examples when a single NP is in the scope of the negation but can still be referred to, as in the sentence sequence *I don't own a dog. It was stolen.*

Quantifiers

The quantifiers *all*, *each*, *every*, and *some* often create a context that complicates subsequent reference. For example, consider the sentences:

> At the party, after each boy receives a present, <u>he</u> has to go to the owner and thank him before <u>he</u> can open <u>it</u>.

> Each boy received a model airplane. They then took <u>the planes</u> out to the field to try them out.

In the first sentence the pronoun *he* remains within the scope of the quantifier *each*. In particular there is no specific referent for *he*; rather it must range over each of the boys receiving a present. Similarly, the pronoun *it* refers to a different present for each boy. In the second set of sentences the NP *the planes* refers to a set never explicitly mentioned. It is the set of airplanes that the boys received.

Generics

Other complications arise with the generic use of descriptions, such as in the sentence *Lions are dangerous*. This sentence can't have the same meaning as the sentence *All lions are dangerous*, since it is perfectly acceptable to assert that lions are dangerous even though one knows of a tame lion that is not dangerous. The NP *lions* does not refer to the set of lions nor to an individual lion, yet it may create objects on the history list to serve as antecedents for later pronouns or other noun phrases. For example, consider the sentences

> Ants are one of our most durable life forms. <u>They</u> can live in highly radioactive areas without problem.

> The ant is one of our most durable life forms. <u>It</u> can live in highly radioactive areas without problem.

In both these cases the subsequent pronoun continues to refer to the generic use introduced in the first sentence.

In addition a speaker can generalize from a specific object mentioned in one sentence to the class of that object and comment on the class in a succeeding sentence. For instance, consider

> Each boy received a model airplane. <u>They</u> are always good presents for 10-year-olds.

The pronoun *they* here refers to model airplanes in general, not to the specific planes mentioned in the first sentence, and thus is a generic use. Recognizing this form can be difficult unless some word such as *always, usually,* or *typically* is present in the sentence. This example would work just as well if the word *always* was deleted, and all existing algorithms would at best classify the antecedent as the set of model planes that the boys received.

Forward Reference

Another class of reference that has not yet been considered in this chapter occurs when the pronoun precedes its referent in the text, as in

> When he returned home, John found his front door was open.

In such cases there is no antecedent for the pronoun at the time it is encountered, and the antecedent appears later in the text! The models presented earlier cannot be adapted to handle such behavior easily. The algorithm would have to allow pronouns where a referent cannot (or should not) be found. This would then be entered on the history list, but then the system needs to know that when *John* is encountered, a previous reference to John may already be on the history list. Adding these extensions would probably drastically reduce the effectiveness of the algorithm on the usual cases.

To deal with such cases a better solution would be to devise a special-purpose mechanism that is signalled by certain syntactic structures (for example, a pronoun appears in a subordinate structure that precedes the main sentence). While there will be some examples that are not detected--for instance, a novel might start using a pronoun and identify the person nonanaphorically several paragraphs into the novel--these cases are rare. In the middle of a text, of course, a system would have to deal with ambiguities between a pronoun being treated in the usual sense and it being used as a forward reference.

12.6 Ellipsis

Ellipsis involves the use of sentences that appear ill-formed because they do not form complete sentences. Typically the parts that are missing can be extracted from the previous sentence. The clearest cases of ellipsis consist of an isolated NP, as in the third exchange in the following dialog:

> A: Where did you find the bananas?
> B: Aisle three.
> A: The peaches?

Speaker A's second utterance can be understood only in the context of A's first question and is understood as an elliptical form of *Where did you find the peaches?*

Syntactic Constraints on Ellipsis

The hypothesis underlying the following analysis of ellipsis is that the phrase given in an elliptical utterance (the **input fragment**) must correspond in structure to a subconstituent in the previous utterance (the **target fragment**) or introduce a modifier to a constituent in the previous utterance. The final syntactic structure of the utterance is constructed by' replacing the target fragment in the previous sentence with the input fragment. There are two qualifications to make. First, in a two-person dialog, the last utterance by each of the speakers must be available for the analysis. For example, in the earlier dialog about the location of bananas, the phrase *the peaches* has as its target phrase *the bananas* in A's previous utterance. Second, the input fragment sometimes may be a sequence of constituents rather than a single constituent, and it may correspond to a sequence in the initial utterance as the target fragment, as in the following example dialog:

A: Did the clerk put the bananas on the shelf?
B: Yes.
A: The ice cream in the refrigerator?

The elliptical phrase here is a sequence of an NP and a PP, both of which will serve as subconstituents of the VP with the verb *put*. Thus the target fragment in the original sentence is *the bananas on the shelf*.

Other cases simply introduce qualifiers on the initial sentence and do not replace a target fragment:

A: How much are the bananas?
B: Fifty cents.
A: By the pound?

The last utterance, which is actually a qualification or clarification of the original question, should be analyzed as a modifier, as in *How much are the bananas by the pound?*

Some constraints simplify the problem. Consider the cases where the input fragment is a single NP. In these cases there are agreement restrictions on the determiners of the input and target NPs. If the input fragment has the definite article, the target fragment will most likely have the definite article as well. Likewise, if the article in the input fragment is indefinite, the article of the target fragment should be indefinite as well. For example, consider the following continuations after the sentence *Did the dog chase a mouse?* With *the cat*, the best interpretation is *Did the cat chase a mouse?* whereas with *a cat*, the best interpretation is *Did the dog chase a cat?* As usual, there are some exceptions to this rule, but they are rare.

```
                (S   WH-QUERY (PP₁ PP-WORD  where)
                     SUBJ (NP₁ PRO  you)
                     VERB  find
                     OBJ (NP₂  DET  the
                              NUM {3p}
                              HEAD  bananas)
                     MODS (→PP₁))


                     The Initial Question



  (NP  DET  the                    (NP  DET  the
       NUM {3p}                          NUM {3p})
       HEAD  peaches)


     The Input Fragment            The Pattern from the Input Fragment
```

Figure 12.6 A simple example of ellipsis

An Algorithm Based on Syntax

To handle ellipsis the system needs to maintain the complete syntactic analysis
of the last sentence (or two sentences, in the case of a dialog). To parse the input
fragment the system needs to maintain a chartlike structure while parsing.
That way, when the parser fails to construct an entire sentence, the
subconstituents will be on the chart. Some systems allow only limited forms of
ellipsis, such as single noun phrases. In these cases they often add a rule that
allows a sentence to be an isolated NP. Thus the parser may initially try to find
an S; if that fails, the system eventually tries the rule looking for a single NP. In
any case the desired output from the parser is a sequence of subconstituents that
forms the input fragment.

Finding potential target fragments in the analysis of the previous sentence is
a simple search using a pattern derived from the input fragment. To find
fragments that are as parallel in structure as possible, you start with a pattern
that contains all the information in the input fragment except for the content
words. In other words nouns and adjectives will be removed, but function words
(such as prepositions and articles) will be retained. If this match fails to produce
any potential target fragments, you can try again using a less specific pattern
(for example, delete the number restriction, remove the specific articles and
prepositions, and so on). Consider a simple example using the dialog about the
bananas. The syntactic analysis of the original question *Where did you find the
bananas?* is shown in Figure 12.6. The initial parse of the phrase *the peaches* is
also shown, together with the pattern produced to search for potential target
phrases.

As expected, if you traverse the syntactic analysis of the initial question looking for constituents that match the pattern, you will successfully find a single constituent--namely, NP$_2$. The intended sentence is then reconstructed by replacing the target fragment in the initial structure with the input fragment, producing the desired result. Sometimes the input fragment will contain modifiers that have no structural correlate in the target fragment. For example, the sentence *Where did you find the bananas?* could be followed by the fragment *The herring in wine sauce?* This constituent contains a modifying PP that has no correlate in the target fragment *the bananas*. Thus modifiers must be deleted when the pattern to search the initial syntactic structure is generated.

To deal with fragment sequences, as would be constructed from the utterance *the ice cream in the refrigerator*, the pattern matcher can search for each fragment individually with the constraint that the order of the constituents in the input fragment should be the same as the order of the target constituents in the initial question. Furthermore, the sequence of target fragments should all be subparts of the same constituent. For example, reconsider the dialog:

A: Did the clerk put the bananas on the shelf?
B: Yes.
A: The ice cream in the refrigerator?

The syntactic forms of A's initial utterance and the input fragment are shown in Figure 12.7, together with the pattern sequence generated from the input fragment.

The NP pattern would successfully match NP$_3$, NP$_4$, and NP$_5$, whereas the PP pattern would initially fail, but after relaxing the constraint that the preposition be *in*, it would successfully match PP$_2$. But only the pair NP$_4$ and PP$_2$ occur within a single constituent (the S), and they appeared in the original sentence in the appropriate order. Thus NP$_6$ replaces NP$_4$, and PP$_3$ replaces PP$_2$ when constructing the new interpretation.

Semantic Preferences

The algorithm given earlier will sometimes not uniquely identify the appropriate target fragment. For example, consider the simple dialog:

A: Did the clerk put the ice cream in the refrigerator?
B: No.
A: The TV dinners?

In this case the pattern generated from the input fragment will match the NPs *the clerk, the ice cream*, and *the refrigerator* equally well. Here semantic information has to be used in order to select *the ice cream* as the appropriate

```
               (S   MOOD Y/N-Q
                    AUX did
                    SUBJ (NP₃ DET the
                                HEAD clerk)
                    VERB put
                    OBJ (NP₄ DET the
                                HEAD banana)
                    MODS (PP₂ PREP on
                                POBJ (NP₅ DET the
                                            HEAD shelf)))


                 The Initial Question


(NP₆  DET the                          (NP  DET the)
      HEAD ice-cream)
(PP₃  PREP in                          (PP  PREP in
      POBJ (NP₇ DET the                      POBJ (NP DET the))
            HEAD refrigerator))

       The Input Fragment Sequence           The Patterns
```

Figure 12.7 An example with multiple constituents

target fragment. Similarly, a continuation of *The manager?* should identify *the clerk* as the appropriate target fragment, and a continuation of *The freezer?* should identify *the refrigerator* as the target fragment.

A technique that can account for each of the preceding examples is to compute a semantic similarity measure between the input fragment and the potential target fragments and to select the closest one. The techniques introduced in Chapter 10 when considering word-sense disambiguity will work well here. For example, assume the system has a taxonomic hierarchy as shown in Figure 12.8.

Now consider the case where the input fragment is *the TV dinners?* and the possible target fragments are *the clerk*, *the ice cream*, and *the refrigerator*. You can compute a semantic closeness measure between these by counting the number of steps between the nodes in the hierarchy. The results are

> TV-DINNER and CLERK: 7 (via PHYSOBJ)
> TV-DINNER and ICE-CREAM: 4 (via FOOD)
> TV-DINNER and REFRIG: 6 (via INANIMATE)

Thus the preferred target fragment is *the ice cream*, and the appropriate analysis is generated.

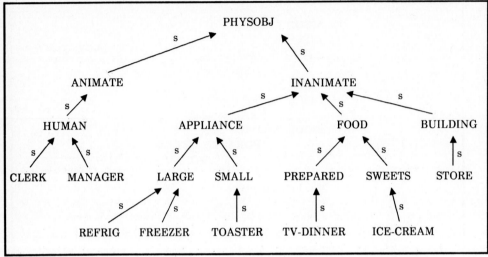

Figure 12.8 A type hierarchy

In still other cases the semantic closeness measure may select a target that turns out to be inappropriate. The semantic interpreter may be unable to analyze the resulting structure successfully. If it fails, then other possible target choices can be attempted. For example, consider the following dialog:

> A: Did you see the clerk in the store?
> B: Yes.
> A: The toaster oven?

This case would have the following semantic closeness checks:

> TOASTER and CLERK: 7 (via PHYSOBJ)
> TOASTER and STORE: 5 (via INANIMATE)

Thus the semantic closeness check would select *the store* as the target fragment and construct a new interpretation corresponding to the sentence *Did you see the clerk in the toaster oven?* Hopefully, the semantic interpretation rules are rich enough to fail on this sentence. The ellipsis algorithm then would suggest the next alternative, with *the clerk* being the target fragment, and construct an interpretation corresponding to the sentence *Did you see the toaster oven in the store?* as desired.

Summary

One of the basic techniques for dealing with the reference problem is the use of history lists to model the local context necessary to handle anaphoric reference and ellipsis. The success of this approach depends strongly on a hypothesis of recency: The referent for an anaphoric NP is the object mentioned most recently that fits all the constraints imposed by the form of the anaphora (that is, number, gender, person, reflexive) and the selectional restrictions imposed by the sentence containing the anaphora. These techniques will be extended in the next chapter on discourse structure.

Related Work and Further Readings

Some form of history list for resolving reference can be found in most natural language systems. Winograd (1972), for instance, maintained a list of previously mentioned objects that was searched to find the referents for pronouns. The history list was also used to identify the referent of singular definite NPs when their description did not specify a unique item in the database. Hobbs (1978) presents a detailed examination of the history list mechanism and presents an algorithm for intrasentential anaphora that generalizes the approach described here. Hirst (1981a) provides an extensive survey of work in the area. Starting with the work of Charniak (1972), much of the computational work in anaphora has emphasized the use of world knowledge and the structure of discourse, which will be addressed in the next two chapters. Many of the techniques described in this chapter for definite reference and for resolving ellipsis can be found in Walker (1978). The technique of using semantic closeness for ellipsis is used in virtually all systems that provide natural language interfaces to databases (Hendrix et al., 1978; Bates et al., 1986; Grosz et al., 1987).

Grosz (1977) describes a generalization of the history list mechanism to include all objects relevant to the particular topic of conversation. She introduces a notion of **focus spaces** in a semantic network representation and organizes the search for referents by searching the representation relative to a focus space. Goodman (1986) looks at techniques for dealing with inaccurate reference where the actual description given does not identify the correct referent.

The LUNAR system (Woods, 1977) maintained the syntactic information from previous NPs as well and could handle a form of surface anaphora involving pronouns with PP modifiers using techniques similar to those described in this chapter. An example of this occurs in the two-sentence sequence:

> Give me all analyses of sample 10046 for hydrogen. Give me <u>them for oxygen</u>.

The LUNAR system also used the semantic interpretation rules to infer further semantic type information for pronouns along the lines described in Section 12.2 (that is, the example *Does it serve lunch?*). An interesting variant of this approach is found in systems based on semantic grammars such as the

SOPHIE system (Brown and Burton, 1978) and LIFER system (Hendrix et al., 1978). In these systems a pronoun such as *it* could be a terminal in a large number of terminal semantic categories (such as NODE, TRANSISTOR, and JUNCTION/TYPE). As a result, when constructing the parse of the sentence containing the pronoun, the system will find the semantic type of the pronoun's antecedent and it will be retrievable from the parse tree. For example, if there was a rule dealing with phrases for the length of a ship, such as

<ATTRIB> ← length of <SHIP>

then in applying this rule to the phrase *length of it*, the antecedent of *it* is constrained to be a SHIP. This information can then be used to select the appropriate referent from the history list. These systems also handle ellipsis in the same way. The parser will construct an analysis of the input fragment that is more specific than simply "NP" or "PP." For example, given the utterance *the length of it*, this would be parsed to be an ATTRIB. The parse tree of the previous sentence could then be inspected for any constituent of the form ATTRIB.

Webber (1983) provides one of the most extensive investigations into the space of possible discourse entities that could serve as an antecedent later in the text. Besides discussing the range of cases mentioned in this chapter, she brings up several other important issues. For instance, she points out that quantifier scoping is more complicated than might first be imagined. In particular, plural noun phrases may arise in three distinct senses. Consider the sentence *Three boys bought five roses*. In the **distributive reading** each of the three boys individually bought five roses; in the **collective reading** the three boys formed a consortium and purchased five roses to share; and, finally, in the **conjunctive reading** a total of five roses were purchased and all three boys were involved in purchasing at least one rose. To represent these possibilities, the logical form must be able to distinguish between them. Webber suggests a notation using an explicit set operator and lambda abstraction that can express each of these possibilities.

One of the most influential works in dealing with definite descriptions is Russell and Whitehead (1925) (see Box 12.1). The referential-attributive distinction was discussed by Donnellan (1977), who argued that Russell's analysis might correspond to an attributive use but said little about how NPs are used by speakers to refer to particular objects. For more information on generics, the reader should see Carlson (1982) and the work on default logics, such as the logic proposed by Reiter (1980), which may provide a reasonable semantics for these constructions.

There is a vast literature in linguistics that considers the different constraints on anaphora. Most of this work involves specifying the conditions under which two NPs cannot corefer. A good survey of this work is by

Perlmutter and Soames (1979). More recent works in this area include Kamp (1984) and Reinhart (1983).

Exercises for Chapter 12

1. *(easy)* Give the syntactic structures for each of these sentences and show in detail how the one-anaphora in the second sentence is resolved.

   I bought a ticket for the early show on Tuesday. Jack bought one for the late show.

2. *(easy)* Using the semantic preference technique with the hierarchy in Figure 12.8, show in detail how the interpretation is constructed for the third sentence.

   A: Did Jack give the toaster to the manager?
   B: No.
   C: The clerk?

3. *(medium)* Using the frame-based system, specify an algorithm that can find the referent of the noun phrase *the cow in the field* given the situation described in Section 12.1. Give a representation of the situation in the frame language, and trace your algorithm through its major steps.

4. *(medium)* Trace the history list as it is constructed through the following sentences. For each noun phrase, classify it as anaphoric or nonanaphoric, and describe in detail how its referent is determined. Discuss any problems that arise, and describe the assumptions you make to avoid them.

   Jack went to a party at the old house.
   He left quickly when he heard that Sam was in the kitchen.
   Sam saw him as he was leaving.

5. *(hard)* In Section 10.2, a treatment of role nouns was suggested for semantic analysis. Discuss how such a representation could then be used with the history list mechanism to identify the referent of NPs involving role nouns. In particular, for each NP in the following text, give a reasonable logical form and the current state of the history list, and discuss the process of identifying the referent.

   The museum received a large grant from a local corporation. The donation will allow the recipient to stay open through the summer.

Chapter 13

Using World Knowledge
About Actions

Much of language cannot be understood without considering the everyday knowledge that all speakers share about the world. This chapter considers one of the major aspects of that knowledge--knowledge about how actions are performed. It examines how such knowledge is used to understand texts consisting of several sentences.

Section 13.1 examines the process of mapping the logical form of sentences to a frame-based knowledge representation. This problem is similar to the reference problem discussed in the last chapter, except that it deals with sentence interpretation rather than noun phrase interpretation. There are several different ways in which knowledge about actions can then be applied in understanding language. In the framework examined in Section 13.2, which is called **script-based processing**, the actions involved are relatively large-scale descriptions with all the details filled in for an entire activity. In such systems language interpretation involves selecting the appropriate script, or action description, and using the information that it encodes to interpret the sentence. The alternative approach, described in Section 13.3, is to represent relatively small-scale actions and use a general reasoning system to group the actions together in a coherent way, such as plan structures, as defined in Chapter 11. In this framework the language interpretation involves constructing a plan that encodes the connections implicit in the language.

Section 13.4 then extends the plan-based analysis by starting to account for the information such as the sentential connectives and the tense. Finally, Section 13.5 examines some of the inadequacies of the simple plan-based models and suggests directions for future work in the area.

The texts examined in this chapter will be simple narrative fragments of a few sentences duration. Such text could be found in simple stories or in conversations where two people are discussing how to perform some simple task.

13.1 Mapping to the Final Representation

Chapter 12 discussed techniques for mapping noun phrases to terms in the knowledge base that represented their referents. All that remains to produce a complete representation of a sentence is to map the propositional parts of the logical form to the knowledge base as well. Consider an example. The sentence *Jack bought a car* has the logical form

> (PAST b1 BUY [AGENT (NAME j1 PERSON "Jack")]
> [THEME (INDEF/SING c1 CAR)])

The techniques described in the preceding chapter might identify a constant JACK1 as the referent for *Jack* and create a new constant, CAR18, for the indefinite NP *a car*. It is still necessary to map the action described in the sentence to an appropriate structure in the KB. Using the definition of the class PURCHASE from Chapter 11, the system could create an instance P1, and set the role Buyer to JACK1 and the role Object to CAR18, resulting in the final representation (ignoring issues of tense until later in the chapter):

> (P1 isa PURCHASE with
>   [Buyer JACK1]
>   [Seller Seller(P1)]
>   [Object CAR18])

Once P1 is created, all the conclusions that result from the definition of PURCHASE are available for further processing.

To define this process precisely, you need further information describing how the cases on word senses map to the roles in the frames. This information can be specified in the notation in Figure 13.1, in which the senses BUY and SELL are mapped to the PURCHASE frame. This mapping indicates that the sense BUY maps to a PURCHASE frame in which the AGENT case maps to the Buyer role, the THEME maps to the Object role, and so on. The sense SELL also maps to the PURCHASE frame, but the case-to-role mappings differ.

In many systems the cases and frame roles are collapsed to the same set and a single representation is used for both lexical knowledge and the final representation. Because of the similarities between the representations, this is a tempting thing to do. It is not clear, however, whether such a conflation of representations is wise, since quite different information is being represented.

For instance, the cases all represent objects that can be syntactically realized in a sentence. If a case is obligatory, it must be realized in every sentence involving that word sense. If it is optional, it may or may not be realized. There are no cases that are not realized in any sentence. The frame roles, on the other hand, refer to the principal components of the object being represented. A frame may have a role that is not realizable syntactically in some word senses.

For example, the frame representing the activity of taking a train trip might have many roles that are essential to the activity: Actor, Train, Ticket, Destination, and so on. A particular word sense that refers to this activity, however, may allow only a subset of these roles to realized. One sense of the verb *take*--say, TAKE7, as in *Jack took the train to Rochester*--requires an obligatory THEME case (in this case, it maps to the Train role) and typically has an AGENT and TO-LOC cases as well. One sense of the verb *go*--say, GO1, as in *Jack went to Rochester by train*--requires an obligatory TO-LOC case (in this case, it maps to the Destination role) and optionally allows an INSTRUMENT case, which is the train. You would have a hard time encoding

Word Sense / Cases		Frame / Roles
BUY	SELL	PURCHASE
AGENT	TO-POSS	Buyer
THEME	THEME	Object
FROM-POSS	AGENT	Seller

Figure 13.1 Mapping word senses BUY and SELL to the PURCHASE frame

all these different verbs sense uses in terms of one frame structure that represents their common meaning.

The frame representation can also be considerably more detailed than the case representation, and a single case might map to different frame roles in different situations. For example, in the following two sentences, the noun phrases *my favorite pen* and *my left hand* may both fill the INSTRUMENT case.

> I wrote the letter with my favorite pen.
> I wrote the letter with my left hand.

The frame representing writing action, however, may have two roles, such as Controller and WritingTool, that distinguish between these two objects. To handle this, the mapping would have to consider the type of the case values as well. For example, the INSTRUMENT case filled with an object that can be used for writing would map to the WritingTool role, whereas an INSTRUMENT case filled with a body part would map to the Controller role.

While a detailed mechanism for handling this mapping could be examined, it is not the focus of this chapter. The rest of the chapter works under the assumption that such a mapping can be done fairly simply.

13.2 Understanding Stereotypical Courses of Action: Scripts

As defined in the introduction, scripts are simply large-scale action descriptions representing a typical course of action that might be described in a story or conversation. For example, a very simple script might involve buying a train ticket, which would include all the information encoded in the definition of PURCHASE in Chapter 11, as well as a set of defaults that specify the typical situation where the buying occurs. The importance of defaults for story understanding is that they will be assumed to hold unless the story indicates otherwise. If the default information were not used, very little could be inferred about a story, since the standard background facts are generally not all stated. For example, you are unlikely to hear a story such as

> Sam wanted to buy a ticket to Rochester from the clerk in the ticket booth. He went to the ticket booth and, because he had

enough money, he was able to give this money to the clerk who then gave him a ticket.

Virtually all this information is redundant. The typical reader would be able to infer all of the preceding from the sentence *Sam bought a ticket to Rochester.* All the rest can be assumed. Only when some part of this knowledge is not satisfied does it arise explicitly in a story. For instance, you might see the following fragment in a more reasonable story:

Sam wanted to buy a ticket to Rochester, but he didn't have enough money.

Here the default assumption that Sam has enough money is not valid, and presumably the story will go on to tell how Sam tried to get around this problem.

Some defaults can be derived using general principles. For example, if you are told that an action was performed, you can assume that its preconditions held, and that at least one of its decompositions was executed. In the simple case where there is only one decomposition, you should assume that the steps in that decomposition were performed. Other defaults, such as default values for parameters, need to be explicitly stated. For instance, you would probably want to encode in the TRAVEL-BY-TRAIN script that the clerk is in the ticket booth. This script is shown in Figure 13.2. It includes the steps of going to the booth and buying the ticket, and then going to the appropriate departure location and boarding the train.

Two main problems arise when you use script-based knowledge in language understanding. The first problem is script selection: How can the system tell which script is relevant? The second problem is maintaining the current state of the relevant script: How does the system keep track of what part of the script is currently being described? You can make a strong analogy between this situation and trying to follow a play using a playwright's script. You would first have to identify which play is in progress; once you have done so, you would have to find the place in the script for that play that corresponds to what is currently being performed. This place will be called the **now point**, since it indicates the present time from the perspective of the script.

Consider the use of scripts in the analysis of very simple narrative stories. In particular all sentences in these stories will be in the simple past tense, and each sentence will describe either:

- a goal that the actor is pursuing;
- an action that just occurred; or
- a state that currently holds.

```
The Script to TRAVEL-BY-TRAIN:

(Define TRAVEL-BY-TRAIN with
     [Actor + animate]
     [Other + ticket-clerk]
     [Source + city default NEWYORK]
     [Destination + city]
     [Train + train FROM-LOC(Train, Source)
          & TO-LOC(Train, Destination)]
     [Ticket + ticket TICKET-TO(Ticket, Destination)]
     [Booth + ticket-booth AT(Other, Booth)])
Preconditions:  HAS(Actor, Price(Ticket))
                HAS(Other, Ticket)
Delete list:  HAS(Actor, Price(Ticket))
Add List:  ON-TRAIN(Actor, Train)
Decomposition:
     GOTO(Actor, Booth) → GIVE(Actor, Other, Price(Ticket)) →
     GIVE(Other, Actor, Ticket) →
     GOTO(Actor, DepartLoc(Train)) → BOARD(Actor, Train)
```

Figure 13.2 A script to buy a ticket at a train station (in New York)

You match sentences into the script structures in different ways depending on what the sentence describes. For instance, sentences describing goals are used to identify the relevant scripts. Sentences delineating actions are used to update the progress of a script, or to select a script containing that action if no script has previously been selected. Sentences describing states are used to update progress of a script to a point where the state holds. There are three ways to introduce a script if none is currently in progress:

1. Describe an action as a goal, as in *Jack wanted to take the train to Rochester*. In these cases the logical form of the action is used to identify possible scripts using the mapping techniques described in the last section.

2. Describe a state as a goal, as in *Jack needed to be in Rochester*. In these cases the logical form of the state is matched against the effects of the scripts to find ones that could achieve the desired state.

3. Describe an action in execution, as in *Jack walked up to the ticket booth*. In these cases the logical form is matched against the decompositions of the scripts to find the ones that could have this action as a step.

Once a script is selected, there are two ways to update it:

1. Describe an action in execution, as in *Jack walked up to the ticket booth*. In these cases the now point of the script is updated to be just after the described action.

2. Describe a state as holding, as in *Jack had his ticket*. In these cases the now point of the story relative to the script is updated to just after the action that has the described state as an effect.

Script and Role Instantiation

Consider how the simple TRAVEL-BY-TRAIN script could be used to analyze the following story fragment:

> Sam wanted to take a train to Rochester. He handed the clerk the money.

The sentences will be integrated into the script one at a time. Assume that the first sentence has the logical form:

```
(PAST w1 WANT
    [AGENT (NAME s1 PERSON "Sam")]
    [THEME (INF b1 TAKE
            [AGENT s1]
            [THEME (INDEF/SING t1 TRAIN
                (TO-LOC t1
                    (NAME r1 CITY "Rochester")))])])
```

The system has to recognize that a sentence of the form "agent wants action" is a statement of a goal to perform an action--in this case, taking the train. The mapping rules for the verb sense TAKE7 can be used to identify the TRAVEL-BY-TRAIN action as the relevant script, and an instantiation of it is created to describe the current situation. Consider this sequence in detail. After processing by the reference component as described in Chapter 12, the names in the logical form would be mapped to the appropriate constants in the database, producing an intermediate form in the THEME case as follows:

```
(INF b1 TAKE
    [AGENT SAM1]
    [THEME TR3])
```

TR3 is a new constant generated as the referent of the indefinite NP *a train to Rochester*. Mapping this to the definition of the TRAVEL-BY-TRAIN action produces the following matches, which are used to specify an instance of this script, which can be called T1. The AGENT case matches the Actor since

```
T1 isa TRAVEL-BY-TRAIN with
    [Agent SAM1]
    [Other Other(T1)]
    [Source NEWYORK1]
    [Destination ROC]
    [Train TR3 FROM-LOC(TR3, Source(T1)) & TO-LOC(TR3, ROC)]
    [Ticket Ticket(T1) TICKET-TO(Ticket(T1), ROC)]
    [Booth Booth(T1) AT(Other(T1), Booth(T1))]
Preconditions: HAS(SAM1, Price(TR3))
Delete list: HAS(SAM1, Price(TR3))
Add List: ON-BOARD(SAM1, TR3)
Decomposition:
    GOTO(SAM1, Booth(T1)) →
    GIVE(SAM1, Other(T1), Price(Ticket(T1))) →
    GIVE(Other(T1), SAM1, Ticket(T1)) →
    GOTO(SAM1, DepartLoc(TR3)) → BOARD(SAM1, TR3)
```

Figure 13.3 The definition of the script instance T1

SAM1 is +animate, and so the role Actor(T1) is set equal to SAM1. The THEME case matches the Train role since TR3 is a train, and thus the role Train(T1) is set to TR3. In addition, in matching the restriction in the logical form with the restriction on the Train role--that is, TO-LOC(TR3, Destination)--the role Destination(T1) is set to ROC. All of the parameters that were not set by matching to the input sentence are existential terms whose value is not yet known. Note that the term for the train, TR3, is also an existential created by the indefinite reference. Thus making Train(T1) equal to TR3 does not really add any information to the script. TR3 is placed on the history list, however, and is available for subsequent anaphoric reference. The final definition of T1 is shown in Figure 13.3. The now point is shown in bold. In this case, since the first sentence states a wish to do the action, and does not state that Sam has begun it, the now point is at the beginning of the decomposition.

The system now uses this instantiated script to interpret the next sentence: *He handed the clerk the money.* The logical form for this sentence is as follows:

(PAST **g1** HAND-OVER [AGENT (PRO **h1** PERSON "he")]
                      [THEME (DEF/SING **m1** MONEY)]
                      [TO-POSS (DEF/SING **c1** CLERK)])

Now you can see the first benefits of having the script. If this logical form is analyzed by the reference mechanism described in Chapter 12, the pronoun *he* will be easily resolved to SAM1, but the definite NPs *the money* and *the clerk* will not have identifiable referents. If the script T1 is used as the context, however, the logical form is matched against the next steps in the script. The exact next step is not required to match, since most stories will not put in all the detail, and so steps will be missed. In fact, this situation is exactly what scripts are designed to address--to fill in the parts of the story that were not explicitly mentioned. Matching the current sentence against the definition of the act GOTO(SAM1, Other(T1)) will fail, because the verb sense HAND-OVER cannot map to a GOTO action. Matching with the second step, GIVE(SAM1, Other(T1), Price(Ticket(T1))), should succeed, if the mapping shown in Figure 13.4 is used.   To successfully match, the referent of (DEF/SING m1 MONEY) must be Price(Ticket(T1)) and the referent of (DEF/SING c1 CLERK) must be Other(T1). The primary assumption made in a script-based system is that if the type constraints are satisfied, and any restrictions stated are not violated, then the referent identification can be made. Thus, since Price(Ticket(T1)) is of type MONEY, and there are no other restrictions specified in the NP, this is assumed to be the referent of the NP. Likewise Other(T1) is identified as the referent of the NP *the clerk*. The updated decomposition of the script T1 is shown in Figure 13.5.

Thus simple knowledge about the typical behavior, represented as scripts, can be used to provide the connection necessary for certain forms of definite reference. This mechanism does not replace the mechanisms for reference discussed in Chapter 12; it augments them, providing new sources for possible referents that have not been explicitly mentioned previously. Scripts also can help select between referents that have been explicitly mentioned and thus can be useful for the resolution of some anaphoric reference. For example, the earlier story could continue with the sentence *The clerk gave him one and he rushed for the train.* Consider only the first conjunct here. Its logical form is

        (PAST g2 GIVE [AGENT (DEF/SING c2 CLERK)]
                       [THEME (PRO/SING o1 ANYTHING "one")]
                       [TO-POSS (PRO/SING h1 PERSON "him")])

The reference component described in Chapter 12 would have no trouble with the pronoun *him* but would find many possible antecedents for *one*, including money and a ticket. Here the script matching can provide the solution. Matching this logical form to the third step of T1 produces the following matches:

        the clerk → Other(T1)
        him → SAM1
        one → Ticket(T1) (that is, the specific ticket that was bought)

Thus in this case the script matching identifies the correct referent for the pronoun *one*.

HAND-OVER	GIVE
AGENT	Actor
THEME	Object
TO-POSS	Recipient

Figure 13.4 The script for GIVE together with its case role mapping

GOTO(SAM1, Booth(T1)) →
GIVE(SAM1, Other(T1), Price(Ticket(T1))) →
GIVE(Other(T1), SAM1, Ticket(T1)) →
GOTO(SAM1, DepartLoc(TR3)) → BOARD(SAM1, TR3)

Figure 13.5 The current decomposition of the script instance T1

Question Answering and Filling in Missing Information

Besides playing a valuable role in connecting the sentences in a story, script structures are also important in providing an ability to answer questions that were not explicitly addressed in the story. In its simplest version every step in the decomposition of a script must have occurred if the script occurred. Thus the steps that were in T1 but were never mentioned are still assumed to have occurred. For instance, given the earlier story, the system should be able to answer the question *Did Sam go to a ticket clerk?* with a *yes*. A simple implementation of such a question answerer could just keep track of all the instantiated scripts that have been used in the story and answer questions by matching into these scripts. To allow for partial execution of a script, or a failure to complete a script, the question-answering mechanism should assume that only the acts in the decomposition up to the last one explicitly mentioned have definitely occurred. These are, of course, the acts that precede the now point in the script instance. Thus, to answer the earlier question, assuming it has the logical form

(QUERY (PAST **g1** GO [AGENT (NAME **s1** PERSON "Sam")]
[TO-LOC (INDEF/SING **c1** TICKET-CLERK)]))

which after reference resolution would have AGENT as SAM1, the system would match into the script T1 and succeed at the first step. The answer, therefore, is *yes, Sam did go to a ticket clerk*. When answering the question, the system also identifies this clerk as Other(T1).

This technique will answer only a limited range of questions that relate to the exact actions done in the script. More complicated methods need to be used to answer questions that deviate even slightly from this. For example, if the earlier question had been *Was Sam at a ticket booth sometime?* the system would not find a direct match in the script. To answer this question, it must match the effects of the actions as well as the actions themselves. Thus the answer *yes* can be found only by matching against the effect of GOTO(SAM1, Booth(T1)), which is AT(SAM1, Booth(T1)). Other questions, however, quickly go beyond any simple matching process and require some sort of theorem-proving process. For example, to answer the question *Was Sam at the ticket booth when he received the ticket?* the system could not simply use the effect of the GOTO step, since it must show that Sam was still there when the clerk gave him the ticket. To check this, it would have to construct the sequence of world states and show that AT(SAM1, Booth(T1)) was still true in the world state immediately preceding the action GIVE(Other(T1), SAM1, Ticket(T1)). This, of course, should be the case in the preceding example since the two GIVE steps do not change any location information.

Scripts can also be used more generally in word sense disambiguation of verbs. The logical form of a sentence might contain several possible senses for the verb consistent with the entire sentence. When the logical form is matched against a script structure, a successful match will identify the verb sense intended. For example, the sentence *The clerk gave him one*, in isolation, could have a wide range of meanings consistent with the verb *give*. It could be physical transfer of something (*He lent Sam his hat*), the transfer of possession (*He gave Sam the ticket that he just bought*), or many forms of violence (*He gave Sam a kick*) or nonviolent acts (*He gave Sam a haircut*). The appropriate sense in the context of the story is obviously the one that matches the scrip--that is, he gave Sam the ticket.

Generalizations of Scripts

Several fairly obvious generalizations of the script structure would be needed to handle examples even in simple situations. The decomposition structure could be extended to allow a partial ordering on the subactions. For example, the TRAVEL-BY-TRAIN script might not enforce an ordering between the traveler giving the clerk the money and the clerk giving the traveler the ticket. This change would not make a big difference in the integration of a new sentence into the story, but it would add complications to question answering. In particular, since the system might not know the exact order of the subactions, it might not be able to construct the sequence of world states that occurred, since two different orderings might produce two different world sequences. In such cases all that could be given would be answers that held in all possible ways that the actions could have been ordered.

Another important extension is to allow some form of choice point in a script. Such an extension would allow a script to follow different paths depending on the state of the world when the actions were executed. Some

[handwritten margin annotations: keywords - might not be used / might not mention / so getting too / select to abstract / to abstract / needs / or / semantic representation / very rigid / don't acct for the unexpected]

stories explicitly refer to choice points in giving explanations of why some action was performed or was successful. For instance, a script for entering a house may have a choice point depending on whether the doors are locked. If they are locked, the agent must have a key and use it to unlock the door. Such information would be necessary to understand a sentence in a story such as *Even though Sam had lost his keys, he got in the house because the door was unlocked*. To make sense of the last phrase, the system must connect the fact that the unlocked door allowed Sam to get in without a key.

Heuristics for Script Selection

Earlier you saw three different ways of selecting scripts. The first two--explicitly naming the script as a goal and explicitly naming an effect of a script as a goal--are fairly straightforward. The third--naming an action that is a step in a script--is the most complicated. For example, a story could start with *Sam walked up to the ticket booth*. In this case the action of walking is not specific enough to identify a single script, because many might involve walking, but the other object involved may provide crucial information. Here the words *ticket booth* give a strong pointer to the TRAVEL-BY-TRAIN script.

A useful technique that takes advantage of this difference is to use a specificity heuristic. If two scripts match the input, but one is a more specific match than the other (its type restrictions are more restrictive), the system selects the most specific one. For example, given the sentence *Sam walked up to the ticket booth*, the system might find a match to the step GOTO(Agent, Booth) in the TRAVEL-BY-TRAIN script, as well as others such as a step GOTO(Agent, Loc) in a general travel script. In this case, since the location of ticket booths is more specific than locations in general, the system would select the TRAVEL-BY-TRAIN script.

Even using such a technique, you will still often find that the first sentence does not uniquely identify a script. In these cases the system would have to wait until further actions are described and continue matching into each of the possible scripts in this set. It can then use a new selection heuristic: Choose the script that explains the greatest number of observed actions. For example, after an action A1 has been observed, three scripts--S1, S2, and S3--are possible. When the next observed action A2 is found, it is matched into each of the three. Say that A2 is found in S1 and S3, but not in S2; then S2 is eliminated. Then, say a third action A3 is observed. It is matched into S1 and S3, and only S3 matches. In this case S3 is chosen as the interpretation.

An abstraction hierarchy of scripts might also be used to reduce the number of possible alternative scripts. In particular a single abstracted script might capture the common parts of all three of S1, S2, and S3. If this were the case, after A1 had been observed, there would be only a single (albeit abstracted) script accounting for the action. The later observations would then specialize this abstract script until the most specific answer, in the preceding example S3, is selected as the interpretation.

All the techniques in this section can be made to work as long as only one script actually is in progress at any one time, but in most cases it will not be possible to capture the essential connections in a story with a single script. For instance, a story about a business lunch might require information from both a restaurant script and a negotiate-contract script to be fully understood. Generalizations that handle such cases are the subject of current research.

13.3 Plan-Based Analysis

Scripts can successfully model the content of a story or a conversation only as long as nothing unusual or unexpected happens. A richer framework is needed to model the content of examples where unexpected connections need to be made between actions. Plan-based models were developed to address this deficiency. Although the action representations used in both models are very similar (in fact, the same representation is used here), the type of processing is different. While script systems essentially perform a matching operation into existing fully specified plans, or scripts, a plan system actually attempts to construct a plan by piecing together the actions, states, and goals that explain the story or conversation. Two pieces of a plan may be put together by adding an explicit causal relationship between them. For instance, a system might put two actions together using a substep-whole relation (one is part of the decomposition of the other), or an action and a state might be put together using a result relation (the state is an effect of the action) or an enable relation (the state is a precondition of the action).

Such a **plan inference system** could abstractly be viewed as a search process over a space of all plans that can be constructed from the known actions and states using the causal relationships. Each plan constructable in this search space could be viewed as a script structure, but, of course, it would be impractical to attempt to construct this collection of scripts explicitly in any nontrivial domain. Thus the plan inference framework has the potential to model much richer and complex stories and conversations.

Decomposition Chaining

You can view the simplest model of plan inference as a modest extension of the script-matching technique outlined previously. It uses the same mapping algorithm to match the logical form to action definitions. Rather than stopping once a match is found, however, the matching process is then repeated on the newly derived action description to see if it is part of the decomposition of yet another action. This process continues until no further actions can be derived, or the system finds a connection to a previous sentence.

The Action Class TAKE-TRIP(Actor, Train, Destination)
preconditions: DESTINATION(Train, Destination)
add: IN(Actor, Destination)
decomposition: PURCHASE(Actor, CLERK, Ticket(Train)) →
    GOTO(Actor, Loc(Train)) → GET-ON(Actor, Train)

The Action Class GOTO(Actor, Loc)
preconditions: ¬AT(Actor, Loc)
add: AT(Actor, Loc)

The Action Class GET-ON(Actor, Train)
preconditions: AT(Actor, Train)
                HAS(Actor, Ticket(Train))
add: ON-BOARD(Actor, Train)
decomposition: GIVE(Actor, Conductor(Train), Ticket(Train))
    → FIND-SEAT(Actor, (any SEAT))

The Action Class GIVE(Actor, Recipient, Object)
precondition: HAS(Actor, Object)
delete: HAS(Actor, Object)
add: HAS(Recipient, Object)

The Action Class FIND-SEAT(Actor, Seat)
precondition: EMPTY(Seat)
delete: EMPTY(Seat)
add: SITTING-IN(Actor, Seat)

The Action Class PURCHASE(Buyer, Seller, Object)
preconditions: HAS(Buyer, Price(Object))
               HAS(Seller, Object)
delete: HAS(Buyer, Price(Object))
        HAS(Seller, Object)
add: HAS(Buyer, Object)
        HAS(Seller, Price(Object))
decomposition: GOTO(Buyer, Loc(Seller)) →
    GIVE(Buyer, Seller, Price(Object)) → GIVE(Seller, Buyer, Object)

Figure 13.6 The actions used for plan inference

For example, assume a story starts with the sentence *Jack went to the ticket clerk* and that the logical form of this sentence maps to an action instance GOTO(JACK1, Loc(CLERK)). The technique of decomposition chaining could make the following inferences, given the set of actions defined in Figure 13.6 (which is simply a copy of the actions defined in Figures 11.4 and 11.5). Two actions have a GOTO action as a step: TAKE-TRIP and PURCHASE. The first possibility is eliminated since the LOC role of the GOTO must be a location of a train. The GOTO step of the PURCHASE action is consistent with the input, and an instance of PURCHASE--say, P1--is created with

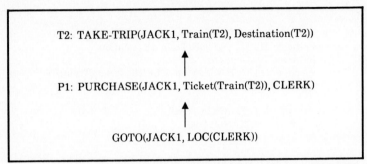

Figure 13.7 The decomposition chain from GOTO(JACK1, Loc(CLERK))

Buyer(P1) = JACK1
Seller(P1) = CLERK

In functional notation, P1 is the act PURCHASE(JACK1, Object(P1), CLERK). Now the process is repeated. Only one action (TAKE-TRIP) has a PURCHASE action as a step. An instance of this action--say, T2--is created with

Actor(T2) = JACK1
Ticket(Train(T2)) = Object(P1)

The second conclusion states that the object being purchased (in P1) is a ticket for whatever train is being taken (in T2). The results of this process can be summarized as shown in Figure 13.7.

In story understanding the importance of such an analysis is the connections that it can make between sentences. To connect sentences, systems must use the analysis of the previous sentences to affect the processing of the next sentence. To do this, plan inference systems maintain a set of **expectations**, which are the plans that it has constructed as possible explanations of the previous sentences. A new sentence is then analyzed using the decomposition chaining technique; however, at each stage the action introduced is matched against the expectations to check for a connection.

For example, a plan inference system might do the following with the input *Jack wanted to take a train to Rochester. He gave the clerk the money.* Assume it starts with no expectations. The logical form would match against the TAKE-TRIP action using a suitably defined mapping from the cases for the verb *take* to the action definition TAKE-TRIP. Trying to find an action that contains TAKE-TRIP in the decomposition would fail, and thus the final analysis is that the sentence describes an action instance TRIP1 of type TAKE-TRIP with roles Actor equal to JACK1, Destination equal to ROC, and Train equal to a skolem--say, TR1.

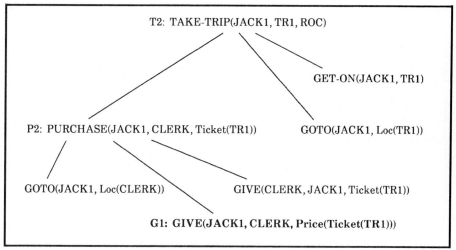

Figure 13.8: The plan constructed from *Jack wanted to take the train to Rochester. He gave the clerk the money.*

To analyze the second sentence, the system first checks if the logical form

(PAST **g1** GIVE7 [AGENT (PRO **j1** PERSON "he")]
                 [THEME (DEF/SING **m1** MONEY)]
                 [TO-POSS (DEF/SING **c1** CLERK)]])

can map to any action that is any part of the decomposition of TRIP1. In this case it fails since the action does not directly match any substep. In particular, matching the substeps involving the actions PURCHASE, GOTO, and GET-ON all fail because there is no mapping from a sense of *give* to these actions.

Given that the current sentence cannot be explained directly by the expected plan, the system attempts decomposition chaining. The logical form can be mapped to a GIVE action, G1, with Actor role JACK1 and as yet undetermined values for the Recipient and Object roles, although the Object must be of type MONEY. G1 will match the GIVE step in the decomposition of a PURCHASE plan, suggesting that the action may be interpreted as a PURCHASE action, P2, with Buyer equal to JACK1. The Seller and Object roles are undetermined, except that you know that Seller(P2) = Recipient(G1) and Object(P2) = Object(G1). You now repeat the whole algorithm using P2 as the input action. This time, when checking the expected actions in the TAKE-TRIP plan, the system finds a plausible match at the "buy ticket" step with Seller(P2) = CLERK and Object(P2) = Ticket(TR1). In constructing this partial plan, the system has identified the appropriate relationship between the two sentences and identified the referents of the definite noun phrases. The final plan fragment that would be used as the expectation for the next utterance is shown in Figure 13.8. As before, the now point is shown in bold.

BOX 13.1   Problems in Computing Matches

Many complications hidden within the matching algorithm were purposely avoided in the examples. Consider the case of matching locations--for instance, when the story fragment is *Jack wanted to take the train to Rochester. He went to the ticket booth.* The first sentence would be processed as shown in Section 13.3. The logical form of the second sentence is:

(PAST g1 GO1 [AGENT (PRO j1 PERSON "he")]
                    [TO-LOC (DEF/SING b1 TICKET-BOOTH)])

This is first matched against each part of the decomposition of the TAKE-TRIP action and fails. In particular the substeps involving the actions PURCHASE and GET-ON fail because the word sense GO1 cannot map to these actions. The match against the substep GOTO(JACK1, Loc(TR1)) appears close yet intuitively should fail as well. The system must know that a ticket booth cannot be the same location as a train. If the second sentence had instead been *He rushed to the platform*, the match should succeed since the train is at the platform. Thus the system needs to be able to reason about locations and have general knowledge about where objects can be located. To behave correctly in the preceding cases, the matcher would have to accept that trains may be at platforms but not at ticket booths. In general, such spatial reasoning could become quite complex.

Action-Effect-Based Reasoning

Other forms of plan reasoning also need to be considered in many situations. The decomposition-based techniques do not go far beyond the power of a simple script system, except that a larger number of situations can be described more succinctly. Stories and conversations often don't just report sequences of actions but also describe why actions were done, what effect they had, what motivated the actors to behave in the way they did, and so on. To recognize and use connections of these sorts, you need additional forms of plan reasoning.

One simple case involves the action-effect relationship. The two sentences in the story fragment *Jack needed to be in Rochester by noon. He bought a ticket at the station* can be connected only if the system realizes that the first sentence describes the effect of performing the action TAKE-TRIP to Rochester, while the second is a substep of that same plan. To handle such examples, goal states

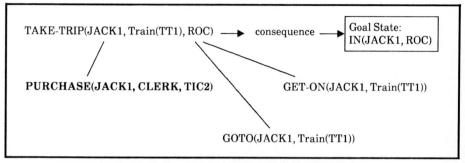

Figure 13.9 The plan linking the state IN(JACK1, ROC)
with the act PURHASE(JACK1, CLERK, TIC2)

must be allowed as expectations, which will be called the **expected goals.** The extended plan inference algorithm must not only search from actions to other actions via decompositions but also search from actions to expected goals via the actions' effects, and vice versa.

For example, the first sentence in the preceding fragment would be analyzed initially as a goal state IN(JACK1, ROC). The logical form of the second sentence, *He bought a ticket at the station,* would not match directly into the expectation. Resorting to decomposition chaining, the system could find a match to the action PURCHASE(JACK1, CLERK, TIC2) in a new instance of the TAKE-TRIP plan--say, TT1. As a result of this match, the system would conclude that Actor(TT1) = JACK1 and Ticket(Train(TT1)) = TIC2. The algorithm, as before, would then recursively try to integrate TT1. Again, a direct match into the expectation fails, but matching the effects of TT1 into the expectations produces a match with IN(JACK1, ROC), so that the system concludes Destination(TT1) = ROC. Thus the connection between the two sentences is found. The plan that would be used as the expectation for the next sentence is shown in Figure 13.9. The fact that an effect of the TAKE-TRIP action matched the goal state IN(JACK1, ROC) is indicated by an arc labeled "consequence."

More complex examples of action-effect-based reasoning arise when two actions are related, not by both being steps of some other action, but by one action enabling the other to occur (that is, one action's effects satisfy the preconditions of the other). For example, consider a domain where the action TAKE-TRIP is not defined but PURCHASE and GET-ON are defined. To understand the relation between the two actions in the story fragment *Jack bought a ticket and boarded the train,* the plan inference algorithm would need to do the following sort of reasoning. The first action would be recognized as an instance (P3) of a PURCHASE action with Buyer(P3) = JACK1 and Object(P3) = TIC55. The next action (Jack boarding the train) would be analyzed initially as an instance, G2, of GET-ON with Actor(G2) = JACK1 and Train(G2) =

TR4. Matching this action against the PURCHASE action in the expectations will fail. To find the connection, the system must match the precondition of GET-ON against the effects of P3. In this case a match can be found between the precondition HAS(JACK1, Ticket(TR4)) of G2 and the effect HAS(JACK1, TIC55) of P3, with the result that the system concludes Ticket(TR4) = TIC55. This plan is summarized in Figure 13.10.

A Plan Inference Algorithm

This section will take the time to formulate a plan inference algorithm in a more precise manner. The algorithm can be stated in three parts: one for dealing with sentences describing an action (*John rushed to the train*), one dealing with sentences describing a state (*John had a ticket*), and one dealing with sentences describing a goal (*John wanted to go to Rochester*). Throughout the plan structure that serves as the expectation will be called the E-plan. In general the system might have to maintain many different E-plans to handle ambiguity. In this case the following algorithm would have to be performed with each one. While this algorithm does involve decomposition chaining, it checks only for immediate action-effect and action-precondition connections. In other words it could not connect two actions, A1 and A3, that required the inference of a chain from A1 to an effect E1 to some new action A2, not previously in the E-plan, to an effect E2 of A2 that then matches a precondition of A3. While this sort of effect chaining would be easy to specify, it would make the search space that needs to be explored considerably larger. The algorithm is also stated assuming that there is only one E-plan. It is a straightforward extension to allow multiple possible E-plans.

To integrate an Action A:

Part 1: Find the possible matches into the E-plan:

1.1 Match A directly against any actions in the E-plan.

1.2 If step 1.1 failed, match the effects of A against any expected goals in the E-plan and the preconditions of A against any states in the E-plan.

1.3 If step 1.2 failed, match A's preconditions against the effects of the actions in the E-plan.

1.4 If step 1.3 failed, match A into the decompositions of all actions known to the system. For each action X for which this succeeds, recursively attempt to integrate X into the E-plan.

Part 2: Integrate the action:

1.5 If one of the steps in part 1 succeeded, add the equality assertions needed to integrate A into the E-plan, and then add all the steps of A's decomposition into the E-plan.

PURCHASE(JACK1, Seller(P3), TIC55) $\longrightarrow$ enables $\longrightarrow$ GET-ON(JACK1, TR4)

Figure 13.10 The integration of two actions by enablement

1.6   If none of the preceding steps succeeded, add A to the E-plan without any connections to other actions in the E-plan.

To integrate a state S:

2.1   Match S against the effects and preconditions of each action in the E-plan.

2.2   If a match was found in step 2.1, add the equalities needed to integrate state S into the E-plan.

2.3   If no matches were found in step 2.1, add S to the E-plan.

To integrate a goal state G:

3.1   Match G against the effects of any actions in the E-plan.

3.2   If a match was found in step 3.1, add the equalities needed to integrate goal G into the E-plan.

3.3   If no matches were found in step 3.1, add G to the E-plan.

13.4 Linguistic Structures and Plan Tracking

The plan inference algorithm just outlined uses the semantic content of the input sentences and ignores issues such as tense and aspect, as well as other linguistic structures that provide clues as to what type of causal connection exists between events, states, and goals. The only information it assumes is that statements of goals can be identified and distinguished from reports of actions occurring or states holding. But many other constructs provide specific information about how things are related. For instance, given the sentence *Sam bought a ticket in order to get on the train*, the connective *in order to* signals some enablement or decomposition relationship between actions. As a result the system should check if buying a ticket can be a substep of getting on a train and if buying a ticket has an effect that matches a precondition of getting on a train. The other possible relationships that the standard algorithm would try should not be attempted. In particular it should not check if getting on a train could be a substep of buying a ticket, or if getting on a train has an effect that enables the buying of a ticket. Thus this information about the meaning of the connective can be used to eliminate steps in the general integration algorithm presented earlier. The connective also gives information as to where to place the now point in the plan. It should be placed immediately following the PURCHASE action, not after the GET-ON action, since that action has not yet completed.

Other constructs besides connectives can provide clues to the relationship as well. For instance, if ability is involved, that suggests some relationship via a precondition of the act involved. For example, the fragment *Jack could get on the train because he had a ticket* explicitly signals that the state of having a ticket should connect somehow with a precondition of getting on the train. Of course, such a direct match may not always arise, and it might be a matter of inference to derive the appropriate connection. But the modal *could* strongly indicates the type of connection that needs to be found. Consider the fragment *Sam had some money, so he could get on the train.* In this case, having money is a precondition not to boarding a train but to buying a ticket, which has an effect that is a precondition to boarding the train.

The point of these examples is that while a general integration algorithm like the one presented earlier is unlikely to be feasible in any moderately sized domain, using linguistic clues can significantly reduce the types of connections being searched for so as to give some hope of developing a reasonably tractable model. Constructing such a system that operates in a reasonable domain, however, is still a matter of current research. Figure 13.11 summarizes some of the linguistic constructs that could be used to provide guidance to a plan inference mechanism. The term ACT refers to any action description, STATE refers to a state description, and GOAL refers to a statement of a goal (using *want, need,* and so on). The causal connection *ACT1 enables ACT2* means that there is an effect-precondition-action chain from ACT1 to ACT2, and *STATE1 is a consequence of ACT1* means that STATE1 is an effect of ACT1, or is derivable from the effect-precondition-action chain from ACT1 to an act ACT2 that has the effect STATE1, or is derivable from a decomposition chain to an act ACT3 that has the effect STATE1.

Tense in Stories

Another important linguistic device that needs be exploited to improve the integration algorithm is tense and aspect. To use tense information effectively, the system needs to use knowledge about the now point, which has already been introduced. The tense system provides information as to whether the plan should be searched for connections before, after, or near the now point. It also gives information on how the now point should be updated. The conventions underlying the use of tense differ according to the type of situation. For instance, in the narrative mode of simple stories, the simple past tense is used whenever the sequence of events described is the same as the sequence in which they occurred. Thus given the fragment *Jack went to the station. He bought the tickets*, you assume that Jack went to the station before he bought the tickets. In a conversation, however, the simple past may actually refer to past events, and the temporal ordering might not be intended. If agents A and B are talking about how busy Jack has been lately and discussing how he

Construct	Connection Suggested
can do ACT, or *able to, could*	via precondition of ACT
ACT1 *in order to* ACT2	ACT1 is a substep of ACT2, or enables ACT2
ACT1 *in order to* STATE1	STATE1 is a consequence of ACT1; STATE1 is an expected goal
ACT1 *by* ACT2, or *by means of*	ACT2 is a substep of ACT1, or enables ACT1
STATE1 *by* ACT1	STATE1 is a consequence of ACT1
ACT1/STATE1 *enabled* ACT2	via precondition of ACT2
ACT1 *because* STATE1	no information
ACT1 *because* GOAL	GOAL is a consequence of ACT1

Figure 13.11 Some connectives and the plan connections they suggest

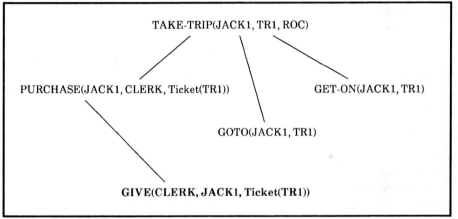

Figure 13.12 The expected future plan given the plan in Figure 13.8

picked someone up at the station yesterday and also bought some theater tickets, A might say *Jack went to the station yesterday, he bought the tickets yesterday, and today he's going to clean the house.*

Consider the case of simple stories. You just saw that a sequence of sentences in the simple past tense indicates a temporal sequence of events. This means that the integration algorithm should attempt to match to actions and states that appear only after the now point in the plan. This set of actions, states, and goals can be called the **expected future plan**. This plan consists of actions that include the now point in their decomposition and actions that are after those actions. For example, given the plan in Figure 13.8, the expected future plan would consist of the plan shown in Figure 13.12. As expected, the actions preceding the now point are not included, but the actions above and to the right of the now point are included. This means that any of these actions could be referred to using the simple past tense. Thus the fragment *Jack* *wanted to take a train to Rochester. He gave the clerk the money* could be continued with sentences such as *The clerk gave him a ticket* or *He rushed for the train* or *He arrived in Rochester by lunchtime.* Albeit these continuations may be somewhat boring, and the final continuation makes the story somewhat abrupt and pointless, but the technique is reasonable, and a richer plan would allow more interesting stories. Once a sentence in the simple past is integrated into the plan, the now point is then updated to that point for the next sentence.

Using other tenses in the story has different effects. Using the perfect past, for instance, indicates that the event should be integrated prior to the now point. Define the **expected past plan** as the set of actions in the original plan but not in the expected future plan. The perfect past would then match into the expected past plan. For example, given an initial story fragment *Jack rushed to catch the train to Rochester. He gave the conductor his ticket*, the expected plan might look as in Figure 13.13. The now point is indicated in bold and is the act of giving the conductor the ticket as part of the GET-ON action. Given this plan, the sentence *He had bought the ticket earlier*, being in the perfect past, indicates matching the expected past plan, which would include the PURCHASE action, possibly its decomposition, and the GOTO action. The logical form would match the PURCHASE action and be integrated into the plan as usual.

A difficult question concerns whether the now point should be updated when the past perfect is used. An argument for not updating it is that if the next sentence were a simple past sentence, such as *He found a seat*, the plan should be searched from the now point as indicated in Figure 13.13. In other cases, however, the story might continue to describe events that occurred while buying the ticket. These issues will be addressed again in the next chapter.

Other uses of tense in simple stories are harder to illustrate using the simple plan structures just outlined. One example is the use of the past progressive, which indicates that an action is in progress. The action in progress may or may not have completed successfully. For instance, consider the sentence *They were making dinner when the tractor exploded.* Here there is a temporal connection between the two events: Making dinner was in progress when the tractor exploded, yet no causal connection is necessarily implied. The present tense can be used to describe situations that are assumed to still hold at the time of the story, as in *Two boys live in the old house at the top of the hill. They are both in their early teens. One day, they went to a movie.* Here you see that the descriptive background can be in the present tense, but as soon as a specific event is described, the simple past is used. The present tense for sentences describing actions can be used only to describe habitual actions, again serving as background to the story, as in *The boys take the bus to town each evening.* Most other tenses are not common in stories, except of course

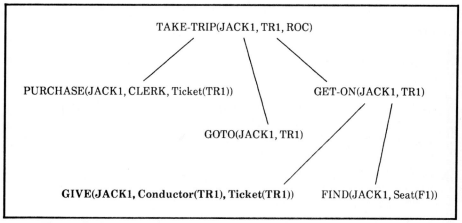

Figure 13.13 The perfect past tense may refer to actions prior to the now point

when dialog is described, where the full richness of the tense system is used freely.

13.5 Complex Goals and Plans

The preceding representation of plans still can represent the content of only quite simple situations. Most actual stories and conversations rapidly move beyond the range of this formalism. This section considers some of the areas in which extensions need to be made to handle more realistic text.

Perhaps the most obvious deficiency is that the stories and conversations that can be modeled still all involve the execution of some plan without running into any difficulty. In actual situations, however, much time is spent dealing with and describing the problem-solving process itself. For example, many stories describe people's attempts at achieving some goal, including how they failed, how they thought they might succeed, what reaction they had to the failure, how they compensated, and ultimately, how they overcame the problem. If you are to model such stories, you need to make the process of planning and acting more explicit. Given the present state of research in this area, no concrete answers can be given. This text will outline a few possible approaches.

One of the simpler examples might involve precondition failure, as in the story fragment *Susan went to the booth to get a ticket for the next train to Rochester but didn't have enough money*. The connective *but* gives a strong clue that the connection should concern some violated precondition. In this case you might be able to connect the state ¬HAVE(SUE2, Money(H1)) with the prerequisite of the first GIVE step in the decomposition of the PURCHASE action. Thus the system could make the appropriate connections that Sue doesn't have the price of a ticket to Rochester. But what expectations can be set

BOX 13.2 Tense in Other Forms of Discourse

The tense system is used differently in other forms of discourse. For example, consider a scenario involving an expert advising a novice on how to construct or repair some machine, such as a lawnmower. As before, the content of the conversation can be represented by a plan and goal structure with a now point. Whereas with stories the now point was simply the current point of the plan under discussion, in this situation the now point may also be the actual place in which the plan is in progress (that is, the step that is currently being executed). A dialog can involve sentences that describe what is happening now, what happened in the past, or what should happen in the future.

For example, consider a situation consisting of one agent reporting progress to another as he or she executes a plan, while the other offers advice on what to do next. In this setting the action currently in execution is referred to using the present progressive, as in *I'm attaching the pull-rope to the engine*; completed actions are reported in the simple past, as in *I attached the pull-rope*; and actions that will be executed (probably soon) are reported in the simple future, as in *I will attach the pull-rope now*. These distinctions, however, do not correspond directly to the now point and the expected past and future plans as one might expect, because activity may occur without being mentioned. Thus an agent may report that some action is completed using the past tense even if it is in the future of the now point. For example, assume that one agent is receiving reports on a walkie-talkie from a friend taking a train trip. He might say *I'm walking to the ticket booth*, putting the now point on the GOTO action in the decomposition of the PURCHASE ticket plan. This might be followed after a brief pause by *I bought the ticket*. This reports that an action in the expected future plan is completed and the now point should be updated appropriately. On the other hand, the past tense can be used to refer to an action prior to the now point, although such uses typically include some modifier such as *already*, *previously*, or *before that*. Thus the sentence *I'm walking to the train* might be followed by *I bought my ticket already*, although it might be better in the past perfect, as in *I've bought my ticket already*.

The present progressive and future use, on the other hand, cannot refer to an action in the expected past, and thus the search may be limited to the expected future plan. The present progressive use will update the now point to the action described, while the future use will not, because the described action has not yet been executed.

up for the next sentence? Obviously the TAKE-TRIP action cannot continue as usual. The story may go on to describe how Sue overcame the problem--for instance, she got some money from the automatic teller in the station--or how she abandoned the goal of taking the train and went to the bus station or simply went home, and so on. One approach to handling this is to classify each type of problem-solving situation that might arise and explicitly outline how to generate a set of expectations for the next sentence. Thus you might have a rule for the precondition failure as follows:

If a precondition failure is detected, then create the following expectations:

1. The agent may try to execute a plan to achieve the precondition and then resume the original plan. For example, Sue may go to the teller machine, get money, and go back to the ticket booth.

2. The agent may abandon the execution of the present action but execute a plan to achieve a goal higher in the hierarchy, possibly reusing the rest of the current plan after this goal is achieved. For example, Sue stands in a corridor and steals a ticket from a passerby, thereby achieving the goal HAVE(SUE2, Ticket(TR44)), and then resumes the original plan at the GOTO train step. Or Sue goes to the bus station and goes by bus, thereby achieving the goal IN(SUE2, ROC).

3. The agent may abandon the top goal altogether and do something else--Sue goes out to the movies.

These strategies describe what E-plans should be used to process the next utterance. Given the preceding example, each new E-plan would consist of a single goal starting from the failed precondition and then moving up the plan hierarchy. Thus the E-plans would include the goals

HAVE(SUE2, Price(Ticket(TR44)))
HAVE(SUE2, Ticket(TR44))
IN(SUE2, ROC)

The next utterance might connect to one of these goals using the usual strategy. If this occurs, the new E-plan could be expanded using the part of the original plan that followed the goal identified. If no connection can be made, you can assume the alternative of abandoning the goal and deleting the three E-plans.

You could devise similar strategies for other problematic cases as well, but this approach is inherently limited. What is really needed is a well-defined theory of problem-solving behavior from which a strategy similar to the earlier strategy for dealing with precondition failure is derivable from general principles. Such a theory would need to be explicitly representable and usable by the plan inference mechanism in order to account for dialogs in which such activities are discussed, such as in the story fragment *Sue had to find a way to get enough money for the ticket. She tried to use the automatic teller machine, but it was broken. She eventually gave up and walked to the bus station and took a bus.* To understand such phrases as *find a way*, *try*, and *give up*, you need to define some sort of explicit structure that has these actions as steps.

Other complications arise from inadequacies in the types of goals and plans that can be represented. For instance, plans that involve repetition of some activity, such as pounding a nail in with a hammer, or cyclic events, such as walking to school each day, cannot be represented in any general fashion. For instance, the system might need to recognize that an agent bought a bus pass so that he or she could take the bus into work each day. The one action of buying the pass serves as an enabling condition for a whole series of bus trips. Important aspects of a story could be missed if the action of buying a bus pass was linked only to a single occurrence of the TAKE-BUS action. Other goals are difficult to represent even though they don't involve repetition. For instance, what is the goal of the action of going to the theater? Intuitively you know it is to see the play and ultimately to enjoy yourself. You would have to represent this goal explicitly to understand a story in which an evening out at the theater was ruined because your wallet was stolen. To handle this, you would need a theory of what makes activities worthwhile and enjoyable.

Complications also arise because people usually don't have a single goal, and when considering situations where multiple goals are described, the system needs to understand situations where these goals conflict or are in concord. For example, a story might describe a person's dilemma in deciding between studying for an exam tomorrow (and thus passing) or going out to see a movie. The system would need to be able to represent this dilemma and reason about such things as why the goals conflict. And it would have to understand descriptions of how the person attempts to avoid the conflict and achieve both goals. Another story might describe a situation where two people have conflicting goals (say both want to own a particular race horse), and you would need to interpret their respective actions in light of this conflict. Similar cases occur where goals complement each other and when people are cooperating toward mutually compatible goals.

Summary

Knowledge about everyday activities is essential for understanding simple narrative stories. Indeed you cannot correctly handle many word ambiguities and many examples of reference without using such knowledge. In addition this knowledge is essential for answering simple questions that demonstrate a basic level of comprehension of the story.

The techniques in this area range from the fairly inflexible large-scale script structures to more flexible plan inference systems that use general knowledge about actions and goals. The script-based techniques are obviously simpler and more efficient when they can be used, but their range of application is limited. Significant work remains to be done before these techniques can be applied to stories of realistic complexity.

Related Work and Further Readings

One of the earliest works that used general world knowledge to identify the connections between sentences was by Schank and Rieger (1974). They identified 16 different classes of connections, most of which have since been reformulated into the plan-based reasoning systems. Rieger's system involved searching through all possible inferences from each sentence and thus was quite inefficient. Much of the work that followed was aimed at removing the inefficiencies by using larger-scale, more specialized representations of knowledge about actions.

Schank and Abelson (1977) introduced scripts, and Cullingford (1981) built the first script-based system. Section 13.2 describes this work in some detail but recasts it in a more conventional action representation. Lehnert (1978) built a script-based question-answering system that handled a wide range of simple questions. A more recent script-based system that uses scripts to extract partial information from newspaper stories is described by DeJong (1979).

The plan-based analysis of stories described in Section 13.3 is a combination of many sources, but the major sources are Wilensky (1983) and Allen and Perrault (1980). Wilensky also analyzes many of the outstanding problems with the plan-based approach discussed in Section 13.5. Other important works in this area are by Carbonell (1978), Schank (1980), and Dyer (1983).

Robinson (1981) describes how a plan-based model can be used to determine the appropriate meanings for verb phrases in natural dialogs, and discusses some ways in which tense and aspect affect the interpretation process. The chapter by Grosz in Walker (1978) describes a dialog system that uses plan tracking techniques to maintain context and determine the referents of noun phrases. Another overview of work in this area can be found in Charniak and McDermott (1985).

Exercises for Chapter 13

1. *(easy)* Give examples of sentences that exemplify each relationship described in Figure 13.11. Make sure you give examples of why the connective *because* does not provide much information. Also, find three counterexamples to the rules given, and suggest how the rules might be corrected.

2. *(medium)* Define the mapping between the cases of the verb sense *rush* and the roles of the action GOTO. Discuss the operations required to understand the following story fragment. In particular, give the logical form for each sentence and, using the TRAVEL-BY-TRAIN script, discuss the matching that takes place. Identify all the conclusions made about the value of roles in the script.

> Jack rushed to the ticket booth.
> The clerk gave him a ticket to Rochester.

Write three questions that can now be answered and that are not explicit in the sentences without the script knowledge.

3. *(medium)* Using the action definitions in Figure 13.6, describe in detail the plan inference process that uses decomposition chaining to recognize the following sentence as part of the action TAKE-TRIP.

> Jack gave the conductor a ticket.

Draw the resulting decomposition chain showing the values of each role.

4. *(medium)* Trace the full plan inference algorithm as it finds the connection between the following two sentences:

> Jack needed to have a ticket.
> He walked to the ticket clerk.

In particular, define the mappings from the word senses of the verbs to the action definitions, and trace each step of the plan inference algorithm that is part of the solution. Draw the final plan constructed to connect the two sentences.

5. *(medium)* Extend the full plan inference algorithm so that it accounts for the simple past and past perfect tenses in simple narrative. Construct a simple story in the train station domain where changing the tense in one of the sentences changes the plan that is recognized. Trace the important steps in your examples and draw the final plans recognized in each case.

6. *(hard)* Implement a system that can produce an explanation of a single sentence using the technique of decomposition chaining. It should use definitions of actions with decompositions (as in Figure 13.6) and information for mapping word senses to these actions. The input should be a logical form for a sentence after it has been processed by the (unimplemented) reference component.

Chapter 14

Discourse Structure

This chapter examines techniques for representing and reasoning about discourse beyond what has been considered so far, which has consisted of finding quite local connections between sentences. To handle larger fragments of discourse, you need to examine more closely the structure of discourse itself.

For example, the history list mechanism in Chapter 12 depends on the notion of recency to identify a referent. Specifically, the most recently mentioned object that fits the restrictions generated from an NP was selected as its referent. In dialogs where the topic may shift and change, however, you can easily see that this principle is inadequate. For instance, consider the following dialog fragment (say over the telephone) between some expert E and an apprentice A while E helps A fix a lawnmower:

1.1   E: Now attach the pull rope to the top of the engine.
1.2   By the way, did you buy gasoline today?

1.3   A: Yes. I got some when I bought the new lawnmower wheel.
1.4   I forgot to take the gas can with me, so I bought a new one.

1.5   E: Did it cost much?

1.6   A: No, and we could use another anyway to keep with the tractor.

1.7   E: OK, how far have you got?
1.8   Did you get it attached?

The referent of *it* in sentence 1.8 was last mentioned seven sentences earlier. In addition, several of the objects mentioned since then would satisfy any of the selectional restrictions that would be derived for *it* from its thematic role with *attach* (for example, the wheel is something that can be attached to the lawnmower). Thus the history list mechanism would fail to find the correct referent in this situation, and no simple generalization of that mechanism that retained its linear ordering of referents can provide a satisfactory solution. Intuitively, you know what is going on. Sentences 1.2 through 1.6 are a subdialog incidental to the other interaction involving attaching the pull rope. In sentence 1.7, E makes it clear that the original topic is being returned to. Thus in the interpretation of sentence 1.8, the relevant previous context consists only of the analysis of sentence 1.1. An account of this structure needs a notion of **discourse segments**, stretches of discourse in which the sentences are addressing the same topic, and requires a generalization of the history list structure that takes the segments into account.

A generalization of the plan inference models derived in the last chapter might be useful for identifying the segments. Using such techniques, the system might be able to recognize that sentence 1.2 is not the expected continuation of the plan to attach the pull rope and thus represents a digression. Once the digression is completed, the plan recognizer could analyze sentence 1.8 as querying the status of the action introduced in sentence 1.1. Of course, trying to do all the work within the plan recognizer would be difficult. In particular, whenever there is a shift of topic, such as at sentences 1.2 and 1.7, the plan reasoner would have to fail to find a connection between the old sentence and the new, and on the basis of this failure, initiate a new topic. This could be quite expensive, and might not be possible in some cases, since there might be an obscure interpretation that would allow a sentence such as 1.2 to be viewed as a continuation of the action described in sentence 1.1 (for instance, the gasoline might be used to clean the engine before attaching the rope).

Intuitively, however, you no doubt recognize that E explicitly told A that the topic had changed in sentence 1.2 by using the phrase *By the way.* Such phrases, known as **cue phrases**, play an important role in signalling topic changes in discourse. There must be some other form of discourse structure beyond the plan reasoner to allow a clean analysis of cue phrases. In addition, in other conversational settings, such as in debates, a plan-based model may not be appropriate, and intersentence relationships such as "sentence X supports the claim in sentence Y" or "sentence X contradicts the claim in sentence Y" may be relevant. Yet the same cue phrases could be used in this setting as well. Thus the theory of discourse structure cannot be explained solely in terms of action reasoning.

This chapter examines a model of discourse structure that allows each of the techniques discussed in the last two chapters to be generalized and integrated with other processing techniques based on the structural properties of discourse. The key idea is that discourses can be broken down into **discourse segments**, each one being a coherent piece of text and analyzable using techniques similar to those presented already. These segments, which are organized hierarchically in any discourse, can be modeled using a stack-based algorithm. Section 14.1 motivates and discusses the idea of discourse segments. The overall architecture of the model is then described in Section 14.2. Each different form of analysis will be modeled as a procedure that encodes specific knowledge about one aspect of discourse structure. The next three sections discuss three of these processes: the tense analysis (14.3), the reference analysis (14.4), and the plan-based analysis (14.5). The final section then discusses some of the important computational models of discourse in the literature that have not been considered earlier.

14.1 Segmentation

While the need for segmentation is almost universally agreed upon, there is little consensus on what the segments of a particular discourse should be or how segmentation could be accomplished. One reason for this lack of consensus is that there is no precise definition of what a segment is beyond the intuition that certain sentences naturally group together. A good model of segmentation is essential to simplify the problem of understanding discourse. In particular, it divides the problem into two major subproblems: what techniques are needed to analyze the sentences within a segment and how segments can be related to each other.

A segment of discourse can be defined as a sequence of sentences that display local coherence. In particular the following properties should hold for a segment:

- some technique based on recency (for example, a history list) should be usable for reference analysis and the handling of ellipsis;

- a simple progression of time and location runs through the segment (as in the simple narratives in Chapter 13);

- a fixed set of speakers and hearers is relevant; and

- a fixed set of background assumptions is relevant.

The last requirement is that the modality of the text remains constant. For example, the text cannot switch from describing a sequence of actual events to a description of a hypothetical event within a single segment.

Note that this definition allows segments that include sentences not adjacent to one another in the text. For example, the dialog given earlier has a segment consisting of sentences 1.1, 1.7, and 1.8 that satisfies the definition. The simple history list generated from this sequence will correctly predict the referent for *it* in sentence 1.8, and sentences 1.1 and 1.8 are describing the same activity.

The rest of this section gives some examples that show that identifying the structural properties of discourse can be very useful for determining reference and for constructing causal analyses of a text.

Chapter 13 briefly considered examples of how tense shift can affect the types of reasoning done by the plan reasoner. For instance, a tense change between two action sentences gave information to the plan reasoner as to how the two actions were related in the plan. If this is modeled as a shift between segments, the theory will have certain desirable properties.

For example, in stories where the simple past is used to indicate a normal temporal progression for the events in the story, a shift to the past perfect signals a new segment and indicates that the new segment describes a situation prior to what was described in the last segment. Now the story could continue discussing more detail at the time in the past (thus continuing the new segment), or it could resume discussing the story where it left off before the tense shift (thus resuming the first segment). By maintaining a now point relative to each segment, the same plan reasoning mechanism can be used for both of these cases. For example, consider the following simple story:

2.1   Jack and Sue went to a hardware store to buy a new lawnmower
2.2   since their old one had been stolen.
2.3   Sue had seen the men who took it
2.4   and had chased them down the street,
2.5   but they'd driven away in a truck.
2.6   After looking in the store, they realized that they couldn't afford
       a new one.

Here, clause 2.1 starts a segment that is then interrupted by a second segment (in the past perfect) that describes what happened to the old lawnmower (clauses 2.2 to 2.5). The initial segment is resumed in sentence 2.6 by resuming the simple past. Identifying this structure is crucial for determining the referent of the pronoun *they* in sentence 2.6, since the most recent candidate using a linear history list would be *the men*. Thus the segmentation is needed to provide the information necessary to eliminate the most recent (but wrong) candidate.

Another major source of information about discourse segments is the use of cue phrases to signal segment boundaries. For example, the preceding story might continue as follows:

2.7   By the way, Jack lost his job last month
2.8   so he's been short on cash recently.
2.9   He has been looking for a new one,
2.10   but so far hasn't had any luck.
2.11   Anyway, they finally found one that met their needs at a garage sale.

The phrase *By the way* explicitly signals that a new segment (which will be some sort of digression) is starting. Thus a new segment is signaled even though the tense remains in the simple past. The digression continues on until sentence 2.11, where another cue phrase is used. The word *Anyway* signals that the current segment is completed and the speaker will be returning to a previous segment. Without the cue phrase in clause 2.7, some direct connection would be searched for between clauses 2.7 and 2.6. If the information in the cue phrase were used, however, such a search could be avoided, because a digression is explicitly signalled.

The structural organization of segments in a discourse can be revealed by considering the three main types of functions that cue phrases can signal:

- those that signal that the clause ends a segment (*OK, fine, that's all*);

- those that signal that the clause resumes a previous segment (*anyway, in any event, so*); and

- those that signal that the clause begins a new segment, not completing the previous segment (*now, by the way, next*).

Given these functions, a stack-based organization of segments, where the top segment is always the one being extended by the next sentence, is exactly what is needed. Newly-created segments are pushed onto the stack, completed segments are popped off the stack, and a segment is resumed by popping off the segments above it on the stack. Most notations for segmentation reflect this stack-based organization. For instance, the structure of a dialog can be represented as a tree, a boxing of text, or a sequence of states of the stack. All of these are shown in Figure 14.1. Since this chapter emphasizes the process of integrating the next sentence of a discourse at a particular time, the stack-based representation is the most convenient.

14.2 The Attentional State and Cue Phrases

This section describes the top-level algorithm for processing discourse. The central data structure is the segment stack, as discussed in the preceding section. At its most general level the algorithm for determining which segment a new sentence S extends consists of a search asking the following two questions:

- Can S extend the top segment?

- Can S begin a new segment to be pushed onto the stack above the current top segment?

You could find a complete set of possible interpretations by successively popping the stack and asking these two questions for each segment on the stack. In practice, however, a system would select the first interpretation and terminate the search. Two preferences on interpretations will be used throughout this chapter:

- a continuation is preferred over a push of a subsegment; and

- the interpretation that involves the least number of pops of the stack is preferred.

Of course, the details of this algorithm are all hidden in the notion of what constitutes reasonable continuations and reasonable introductions of subsegments. These questions will be answered by checking to see that all the properties of a segment mentioned earlier are valid. Each particular aspect will be checked by a separate process called a **filter**. A filter takes a proposal of the form that a sentence S continues a segment, or introduces a new segment, and returns an acceptance or rejection of the proposal. In addition, if the proposal is accepted, it must return a data structure containing all the information this filter needs about the effect of integrating the sentence into the segment.

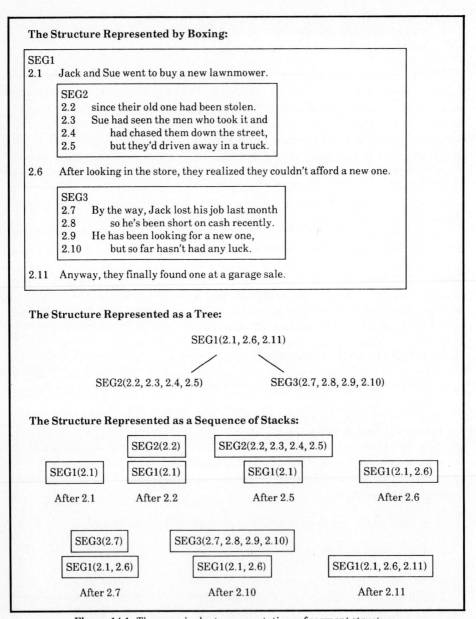

Figure 14.1 Three equivalent representations of segment structure

For example, a reference filter based on the techniques of Chapter 12 would take the history list associated with the segment and allow S as a continuation if the referents of all the referring expressions in S could be identified. If this is the case, it would return a new history list including the objects introduced in S.

Input Parameters: STACK -- the segment stack
                    S -- the new sentence
                    POP, PUSH, CONTINUE -- the flags for cue phrases

1. If POP is set to true, then pop STACK once and continue.

2. If PUSH is not set, then search STACK for a segment SEG such that all the
    filters allow S to be an extension of SEG. The first one found is the answer.

3. If step 2 failed to produce an answer, and CONTINUE is not set to true,
    then search STACK for a segment SEG such that all the filters allow S to
    introduce a subsegment of SEG. The first one found is the answer.

Figure 14.2 An algorithm for incorporating the next sentence into the segment stack

Some examples of filters will be described in detail in the following sections. For now, the algorithm can be specified assuming that the filters exist. This algorithm manipulates the segment stack and provides a preliminary analysis of the role of cue phrases.

A cue phrase is classified by how its presence constrains the interpretation of the new sentence: it may indicate the termination of a segment (a **POP phrase**); it may indicate the start of a new segment (a **PUSH phrase***); or it may indicate the continuation of a segment (a **CONTINUE phrase***). An individual cue phrase may indicate one or more of these functions. The word *anyway,* for instance, signals both a POP and a CONTINUE.

Figure 14.2 incorporates these classifications into a more detailed version of the algorithm. The algorithm takes as input a stack of segments, the analysis of the new sentence, and three variables--POP, PUSH, and CONTINUE--that are set to true if a corresponding cue phrase is present in the sentence. The first step is a check for an explicit POP; if it is found, the top segment is popped. Then the algorithm checks repeatedly for possible continuations of segments on the stack and then for possible pushes of new subsegments onto the stack.

Consider a simple example of the algorithm in operation--in this case, processing the first dialog in this chapter using three filters: a reference filter, which allows continuations only where the referents are appropriately identified; a plan filter, which allows only continuations that can be causally connected to the rest of the segment; and a tense filter, which allows only continuations that indicate a normal temporal progression.

Initially the segment stack is empty and sentence 1.1 must be processed as introducing a new segment, SEG1. Each filter would specify the information it needs in the data structure for SEG1. In sentence 1.2, the input would be the logical form of the sentence plus the analysis of *By the way*, which would set PUSH to true. Thus steps 1 and 2 of the algorithm are not tried, and step 3

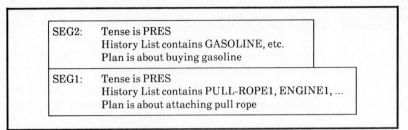

Figure 14.3 A sketch of the information on the segment stack after sentence 1.2

produces an interpretation of the sentence as the beginning of a new segment, SEG2. Again, each of the filters would specify the information it needs to store about SEG2, and the result is shown in Figure 14.3. Note that the information about SEG1 is not affected in the analysis of sentence 1.2.

Sentence 1.3 continues segment SEG2 by addressing the question, and sentence 1.4 goes on to elaborate the plan about how the gas was purchased. Finally, in sentence 1.7, the cue phrase *OK* is used, which signals a pop. The algorithm is called with POP set to true, and SEG2 is popped off the stack. Now the top segment is SEG1, and the history list, as it was after sentence 1.1 was processed, is available to determine the referent of *it* in sentence 1.8.

To examine the process in more detail, you must consider the different filters. The next sections describe simple versions of a tense filter, a reference filter, and a plan filter, and give more detailed examples of the processing using the segment stack.

14.3 The Tense Filter

As described previously, each of the filters must be able to answer two types of questions:

- Can sentence S be a reasonable extension to segment SEG?

- Can sentence S be a reasonable introduction to a new subsegment of segment SEG?

At the present time there are no complete answers to these questions, and the area of tense analysis and temporal representation is very active. What follows are a few simple examples of the types of analysis that the tense filter would need to do for simple narratives.

As discussed in Chapter 13, the simple past is used as the normal continuation in a narrative and thus is the primary tense allowed for extending an existing segment. Other allowable continuations appear when the tense of

Tense of Last Sentence in SEG	Tense of New Sentence	Acceptable Continuation
X	X	YES
X	X/PROG	YES
X	X/PERF	NO
X/PROG	X	NO
X/PERF	X	YES
X is any simple tense: PAST, PRESENT, or FUTURE		

Figure 14.4 The tense constraints on continuing a segment

the new sentence is identical to the tense of the preceding segment. For example, a segment might consist of two sentences in the simple future, as in

> We will be going to the museum this afternoon.
> There we will see the dinosaurs.

The tense filter puts almost no restrictions on the tense of a sentence that introduces a new subsegment. For example, a sentence in the simple past could introduce a new subsegment, as in

> We went to the museum.
> Meanwhile, Jack found the ring in the closet.

The second sentence is explicitly flagged as a new segment by the cue phrase *Meanwhile*. Both sentences, however, are in the simple past. While there are no restrictions, the tense information can be useful in identifying how the current sentence relates to the current segment. In particular, in cases where the subsegment elaborates on something described in the current segment, or remains within the same general topic, the tense shift indicates the temporal relationship. For example, a sentence in the past perfect following a segment in the simple present indicates that the subsegment describes some events prior to the events described in the present segment. In another case a sentence in the simple past following a segment whose last sentence was in the past progressive may describe an event that is during the last mentioned event, as in

> We were climbing the cliff.
> A rock fell down, and just missed us.

The second sentence describes a series of events that occurred during the climbing event.

A rough approximation of the tense constraints for continuation of a segment is given in Figure 14.4 for simple narratives.

A very simple version of the tense filter would involve storing the tense of each segment in the stack (say, in a variable TENSE) and deciding on continuations by comparing each segment's TENSE value with the tense of the new sentence. If there are several segments on the stack, a new sentence might consistently continue more than one of them. For example, after the following sentences had been analyzed:

Jack rushed to the train.
Earlier in the day, Sam had bought him his ticket.

there would be two segments on the stack--SEG1 in the simple past (describing Jack rushing for the train); and SEG2 in the past perfect (describing Sam buying the ticket, prior to Jack rushing). If the next sentence is in the simple past, it could continue either of these segments. For example, the sentence *As a result, he was able to board immediately* would continue SEG1 (causing SEG2 to be popped), while the sentence *He left it at the information booth for Jack to pick up* would continue SEG2. The tense filter cannot distinguish between these cases, and it would be left to the plan analysis to select the appropriate interpretation.

Many other things also affect the temporal analysis of text. For instance, temporal phrases such as *earlier in the day* give a specific setting that affects how the tenses are interpreted. In this case the system should be able to conclude that the sequence of events described in SEG2 all occurred earlier in the day. To model this, the system would need to store more information in the segment structure than the TENSE--namely, a time interval corresponding to *earlier in the day* and the constraint that all events described in this segment will occur within this time interval.

Temporal connectives such as *when, while, before*, and *after* also give explicit temporal information about how events and states are connected. For example, *before* indicates that the event in the subordinate clause precedes the event in the main clause, as in *Before Jack lost his wallet, he bought a ticket.* Analyzing these connectives and their effect on different tenses gets very complex and is beyond the scope of this book.

14.4 The Reference Filter

As a starting point the reference component described in Chapter 12 can be used as the reference filter. This turns out not to be quite strong enough, however, because that model was not set up to evaluate whether a sentence is a reasonable continuation of a segment. In particular the referent of definite noun phrases could be found from different sources not always on the history list. For example, background world knowledge and the plan-based analysis might identify the referent. With pronominal forms, however, there are more constraints, since the form is nearly always anaphoric. This section describes a model of pronominal reference that makes stronger claims than were made in the simple history list model. This technique uses the notion of **focus**.

The term *focus* is used in many different ways in the literature, but here it is used in a quite specific way. A particular object, called the focus, must be referred to using a pronoun if any pronouns are used in a sentence. If there are several pronouns in a sentence, one of them must refer to the focus. In addition the focus can change in only a limited number of ways, to be outlined shortly.

If this claim is correct, the surest way to identify the focus is to find the referent of a pronoun contained in a sentence that has only one pronoun in it. But then the notion of focus would be totally dependent on the phenomena that it is intended to solve--that is, finding the referents of pronouns! Thus it is important to find other independent methods of determining the focus, or at least restricting the range of possibilities for the focus.

One suggestion for constraining focus is based on the thematic roles that each NP plays with the verb. This view claims that the NP in the THEME role is most likely to be the focus of the next sentence. Evidence for this claim consists of examples of pronouns that on semantic grounds do not uniquely identify a referent yet are resolved to the THEME. Thus in

> Sue put the key under the doormat. When she came home, she saw that it was stolen.

the referent of *it* seems to be the key, even though the doormat is a possible referent (and could have been stolen). In practice, however, such influences are quite weak and are easily overridden by the influence of making the story more coherent. For example:

> Sue went to put the key under the doormat. When she lifted it up, a bug quickly scampered across the porch.

While it is semantically possible for the referent of *it* to be the key, the referent is more likely to be the doormat.

A good indicator of focus is the use of certain syntactic constructs that explicitly identify the focus. Examples include sentences in the following forms, where the focused element is underlined:

> It was <u>Jack</u> who took the key from under the doormat.
> It was <u>Jack</u> who Sue saw fall through the barn floor.
> There was <u>an old man</u> who took a key from under a doormat.
> The place where the key was stolen from was <u>the hidden safe</u>.
> <u>Jack</u> is a man who will go far.

In addition, focus can also be indicated by stress in spoken sentences. The following sentences use capital letters for stress and differ only by the resulting focus. Try changing the stress in the examples. In most cases the second sentence then seems somewhat incoherent.

> JACK saw Sam take the key from under the doormat. He quickly went to the police station.

> Jack saw SAM take the key from under the doormat. He quickly hid it in his coat.

> Jack saw Sam take the KEY from under the doormat. It was the last one we had.

The Focus Hypothesis

You can now state a set of hypotheses about how the notion of focus constrains the use of anaphoric reference within a discourse segment. At any time there is an object that has a distinguished status in the segment, called the focus, which is the prime candidate for pronominal reference. In fact every sentence that contains one or more pronouns must have one of its pronouns refer to the focus. Furthermore, the focus changes only when forced. For example, a sentence might contain a single pronoun that is semantically incompatible with the present focus, forcing the focus to shift. If the pronoun is semantically compatible with the present focus, however, it must refer to the focused object. For example, consider the following story segment:

> Jack gave Sam $10. He had $15 left. He hopes to have enough to buy a present for Sue.

The pronoun *he* in the second sentence is contextually constrained to be Jack due to the semantics of *left* and *give*. According to the preceding hypothesis, the next use of *he*, in the third sentence, while semantically not selective between Jack and Sam, must refer to Jack as well. Why? The discourse focus is established unambiguously in the second sentence to be Jack. The third sentence cannot change the focus since it is consistent that the present focus, Jack, could be the referent of the pronoun *he*.

The focus can change only by the use of explicit signals or by the use of a pronoun that cannot possibly refer to the focused element. As a result, if the focus is ambiguous at one stage in the processing and later is uniquely identified, any pronoun that seemed ambiguous before will then be resolved after the fact to the focus. For example, consider the following story fragment:

3.1   Jack gave Sam $10.
3.2   He now has $15.
3.3   He also gave $5 to Sue.

When processing sentence 3.2, you cannot determine whether *he* refers to Jack or to Sam, because both are possible as the segment focus. In sentence 3.3, however, the use of *also* indicates that the referent of *he* in sentence 3.3 must be Jack. Thus the focus must have been Jack all along, and the pronoun *he* in sentence 3.2 also is resolved to Jack. This conclusion is corroborated by the fact that sentence 3.4 could not be used to continue the story:

3.4   Thanks to Jack, he can go to the movies tonight.

This example is anomalous, because the local sentence structure eliminates Jack as the referent for *he*, but *he* is semantically compatible with the focused element--namely, Jack!

Tracking Focus

Here's a simple algorithm for maintaining and tracking focus as it changes throughout a discourse segment. The algorithm operates by maintaining a set of possible candidates for the focus. When the focus is uniquely identified, this set will contain only a single element. The focus may shift when a sentence contains a pronoun that cannot be resolved to the focused element, in which case the pronoun is assumed to refer to an object mentioned in the immediately preceding sentence. Failure to find a referent is treated as a signal for a segment boundary. Note that this algorithm is not foolproof, and counterexamples can be found, but it is a reasonable starting point for developing better algorithms.

The sentence to be incorporated into the segment is called S, the list of elements referred to in the immediately preceding sentence in this segment is called PF (for potential foci), and the complete history list constructed from the sentences in this segment is a list called HISTORY. The set of possible candidates for the focus will be a set called FOCUS, which in the first sentence in the discourse is empty. In all other sentences that start a new segment, it is the focus of a previous segment. Whenever the process of matching a pro-form into a list (either FOCUS, PF, or HISTORY) is mentioned, all the techniques for finding a referent described in Chapter 12 are assumed to be used. For example, derived antecedents, such as set construction for conjoined NPs, are allowable as matches. The procedure either returns a new value (or a list of possible new values) for the focus or it fails.

It turns out that there is little difference to the reference filter whether a segment is being continued or a subsegment is being introduced. The algorithm in Figure 14.5 is used for both. It allows focus shifts to an element that was

Input: the analysis of the sentence S; and information from the active
        segment: FOCUS, the focused element(s); PF, the discourse
        elements mentioned in the last sentence; and HISTORY, the
        history list for the sentences in SEG.

1. If S contains no pronominal forms, then use the techniques from
    Chapter 12 for definite reference using the history list HISTORY.

2. If S contains a pronominal form:

    2.1 If it can refer to any element in FOCUS, these become the
         possible antecedents.

    2.2 If it can't refer to any element in FOCUS, then check if it can
         refer to any elements in PF. If so, these become the possible
         antecedents.

    2.3 If no antecedents were found above, then return FAILURE, for
         this sentence cannot extend SEG.

    2.4 Set FOCUS to the list of possible antecedents found in steps
         2.1 or 2.2.

3. If S contains explicit indicators for a focused element, set FOCUS to
    that element.

4. Return new information for the segment: FOCUS is as set in step 2
    or 3; PF is the list of elements mentioned in S; HISTORY is the old
    history list plus the elements mentioned in S.

Figure 14.5 The algorithm for the reference filter

explicitly mentioned in the previous sentence. For instance, consider the
processing of SEG2 in the story in Section 14.1, repeated here:

2.3   Sue had seen the men who took it
2.4   and had chased them down the street,
2.5   but they'd driven away in a truck.

The value of PF for processing sentence 2.3 will be the objects mentioned in the
previous sentence: the set consisting of Jack and Sue, named SET2; the
lawnmower they want, named L1; and their old lawnmower, named L2. When
sentence 2.3 is processed, the focus would be found to be L2 (from the referent of
it). Thus, when sentence 2.4 is analyzed, FOCUS will be (L1) and PF will be
(SUE1, MEN33). When this sentence is processed, the pronoun *them* cannot
refer to the focus L1; thus the PF list is checked and the set representing the
men (MEN33) is found as a possible referent. Thus FOCUS is set to MEN33,
causing a focus shift. Sentence 2.5 is processed using MEN33 as the FOCUS and
is analyzed without further complication.

Definite Descriptions

Many other issues that make reference complicated can affect the tracking of focus as well. For example, the use of definite descriptions that are only implicitly related to previously mentioned objects, such as a subpart, can provide the information needed to identify the correct focus. For example, consider the following story fragment:

> An old lawnmower is next to a TV set in the garage. Even though the engine stalls frequently, we still hope to sell it.

The initial candidates for focus include the lawnmower, L3, and the TV, TV5. On the surface, *it* in the second sentence could refer to either of these objects (for example, both can be sold). However, the NP *the engine* in the second sentence must relate to the lawnmower, and thus to make the story coherent, L1 should be identified as the referent of *it* and hence as the focus. In general, this example suggests a hypothesis that such reduced definite descriptions should be implicitly related to the focused element.

14.5 Analyzing a Story Using Cue Phrases, Tense, and Reference

Before considering the filter based on plan reasoning, consider processing a dialog using all the mechanisms developed so far. Each segment will maintain the information needed for the tense filter and the reference filter, and you will be able to see how they interact to give a preliminary analysis of the dialog. Since the example does not depend on the use of history lists, the variable HISTORY will be ignored throughout.

The initial sentence

2.1   Jack and Sue went to a hardware store to buy a new lawnmower
2.2   since their old one had been stolen.

creates a segment SEG1, with values FOCUS = (SET2), PF = (JACK1, SUE1, STORE1, L1, L2), and TENSE = PAST, where SET2 is the set consisting of JACK1 and SUE1, STORE1 is the hardware store, L1 is the new lawnmower, and L2 is the old lawnmower. The next sentence is a conjunction, and the system considers each conjunct one at a time. The first conjunct

2.3   Sue had seen the men who took it

contains a tense shift (to past perfect), and thus the proposal that clause 2.3 extends SEG1 is rejected by the tense filter. Next a proposal is made that clause 2.3 starts a new subsegment SEG2. The reference filter is called, with FOCUS set to (SET2) and PF set to (JACK1, SUE1, L1, L2), and it returns the new focus

(L2). SEG2 is created and added to the segment stack, which now looks as shown in Figure 14.6.

The next clause

2.4   and had chased them down the street,

is found to be an acceptable extension of SEG2, and the reference filter in analyzing the pronoun *them* detects a focus shift to MEN33. Thus SEG2 is updated as shown in Figure 14.7. The next conjunct is processed similarly and makes no changes to the focus.

2.5   but they'd driven away in a truck.

In the next sentence

2.6   After looking in the store, they realized that they couldn't afford
          a new one.

the referent of *the store* cannot be identified in SEG2, so the reference filter rejects the sentence as a continuation of SEG2. The sentence can continue SEG1, however, and this interpretation is selected. The segment stack now contains only SEG1, which is updated so that its FOCUS = (SET2) and PF = (STORE1, L3), where L3 is the new lawnmower they couldn't afford.

The next sentence contains an explicit cue phrase that a new segment is being started:

2.7   By the way, Jack lost his job last month
2.8   so he's been short on cash recently.

A segment SEG3 is created with initial values FOCUS = (SET2) and PF = (STORE1, L3). These values are used by the reference filter, which returns as the new focus the list (JACK1, JOB3) from processing clause 2.7, and then selects JACK1 as the focus after processing clause 2.8. The next sentence is as follows:

2.9   He has been looking for a new one,
2.10   but so far hasn't had any luck.

The reference filter finds this to be an acceptable continuation of SEG3, and the segment stack is updated as shown in Figure 14.8, where JOB4 stands for the job Jack is looking for and JOB3 is his old job.

The final sentence is as follows:

2.11   Anyway, they finally found one that met their needs at a garage sale.

SEG2: FOCUS = (L2), PF = (SUE1, MEN33, L1), TENSE = PASTPERF

SEG1: FOCUS = (SET2), PF = (JACK1, SUE1, STORE1, L1, L2), TENSE = PAST

Figure 14.6 The segment stack after clause 2.3

SEG2: FOCUS = (MEN33), PF = (STREET4), TENSE = PASTPERF

SEG1: FOCUS = (SET2), PF = (JACK1, SUE1, STORE1, L1, L2), TENSE = PAST

Figure 14.7 The segment stack after clause 2.4

SEG3: FOCUS = (JACK1), PF = (JOB4, JOB3), TENSE = PASTPROG

SEG1: FOCUS = (SET2), PF = (JACK1, SUE1, L1, L2), TENSE = PAST

Figure 14.8 The segment stack after clause 2.10

The cue phrase *anyway* signals a POP and a CONTINUE, and so SEG3 is popped off the stack, and the sentence is successfully analyzed as a continuation of SEG1 as desired. Consequently, the one-anaphor is appropriately identified as a lawnmower. Note that if SEG3 had not been popped off the stack, the first interpretation considered for *one* would have been a job!

This example showed that if sufficient cue phrases and tense shift signals are used, the segment tracking can be done successfully and allow the pro-forms to be analyzed appropriately. This treatment, however, is not fully general. Obviously more analysis, along the lines of the plan-based analysis in Chapter 13, is needed as well. This will be the topic of the next section.

Definite Reference and Segments

While it has not been explicitly considered so far, an important effect of segmenting a discourse is the structure that it imposes on the history list. Each segment maintains a section of the history list that contains the objects mentioned in that segment. When a segment is popped off the stack, that part of the history list disappears as well. This is crucial in order to determine the appropriate reference of definite descriptions in many cases. Since the mechanism that accomplishes this is essentially the same as that used for anaphora, the text here will just consider a simple example. The first dialog, shown earlier in this chapter, could be continued with sentence 1.9 as follows:

1.1   E: Now attach the pull rope to the top of the engine.
1.2   By the way, did you buy gasoline today?

1.3   A: Yes. I got some when I bought the new lawnmower wheel.
1.4   I forgot to take the gas can with me, so I bought a new one.

1.5   E: Did it cost much?

1.6   A: No, and we could use another anyway to keep with the tractor.

1.7   E: OK, how far have you got?
1.8   Did you get it attached?

1.9   A: No, a little knob that screws onto the side just fell off.

After the system processes sentence 1.6, the segment stack, with the history lists included, might look as shown in Figure 14.9, where SET3 is the set consisting of the agents A and E, and TOP2 is the top of ENGINE5. SEG10 represents the segment from sentence 1.2 to sentence 1.6 (which might in fact be multiple segments, but this is not important for the point of this example).

With sentence 1.7, SEG10 is popped off the stack, and in sentence 1.8 the focus is identified as being ROPE3. As sentence 1.9 is processed, the history list consists of (ENGINE5, TOP2, ROPE3). The definite description *the side* will fail to find a direct referent in this list, but an implicit referent is found by considering the subpart relationship, and *the side* is identified as the side of ENGINE5, as desired.

If the history list was maintained not in the segments but as a global list derived from the entire discourse, the history list going into sentence 1.9 would have begun with (TRACTOR4, SET3, COST4, GASCAN1, WHEEL1, GASOLINE, ENGINE5, TOP2, ROPE3). In this case *the side* would have been identified as the side of the tractor using the recency heuristic. While this interpretation is semantically acceptable for sentence 1.9, it could not have been intended by the speaker. Thus segment structuring is essential for identifying the referents of definite descriptions as well as for anaphora.

SEG10:   FOCUS = (GASCAN2), PF = (SET3, TRACTOR4), HISTORY =
         (TRACTOR4, SET3, COST4, GASCAN1, WHEEL1, GASOLINE)

SEG9:   FOCUS = (ROPE3, TOP2, ENGINE5), PF = ( ),
         HISTORY = (ENGINE5, TOP2, ROPE3)

Figure 14.9 The segment stack after sentence 1.6

Semantic Returns

An important point concerns the nature of resumption of segments. Earlier the discussion referred to what could be called a **discourse return**, in which a topic is suspended at one point in the discourse and then later resumed as though it had not been interrupted. All the focus information for reference is still intact when the topic is resumed. The key constraint here is that a true discourse return is possible only to a segment that is still on the stack. If it had been popped at some earlier time, such a return would not be possible.

Many people immediately feel this is an obvious error in the theory: surely there are lots of cases where a previous topic is resumed even after it has been popped off the stack. For instance, the earlier dialog about the lawnmower and gas can might be continued as follows:

1.10   E: That's OK, you can put it back on later.
1.11   By the way, when you brought the gas can home, where did you put it?

In this continuation sentence 1.10 continues the new segment introduced in sentence 1.9, but then sentence 1.11 appears to resume segment SEG10, which was popped off the stack earlier. In fact this reveals the mistake. It does not continue SEG10; rather it creates a new segment--say, SEG12--that happens to continue the topic introduced in SEG9. Remember that the discourse segments are structural properties of the discourse and do not represent the discourse content. Thus it is fine to have a new segment that in effect continues some old topic. This in fact can be seen by the constraints on how such a topic is resumed. Sentence 1.11 uses a cue phrase *By the way*, which explicitly signals a digression, not a true discourse return. In addition, the objects that were in focus in the earlier segment cannot be pronominalized without explicit reintroduction. For example, E would not have said *By the way, when you brought it home, where did you put it?*

14.6 The Plan-Based Filter

The plan-based filter for narratives is one example of a more general process for finding connections between sentences in different forms of discourse. With a system that followed debates, for instance, this filter would have to analyze the logical connections inherent in arguments as well.

Like the tense filter, the plan filter places no restrictions on what sentences could be classified as introducing a new subsegment (except that the organization of segments would prefer a continuation over a push, so if a sentence can be a continuation, the subsegment alternative would not be pursued). The plan filter, however, can be instrumental in finding how the new subsegment relates to the current top segment. In particular, at least three different types of relationships are common:

1. The subsegment may deal with a subpart of the current activity described in the current segment.

2. The subsegment may describe another part of the same plan as the current segment.

3. The subsegment may be causally independent of the current segment, although it may still be temporally related.

The plan filter could identify the appropriate relationship by trying the first two possibilities and, if it does not succeed in finding a connection, picking the third alternative as the default case. An example of the second class of subsegments is given in the following discussion.

The plan filter places quite strong constraints on what can be a continuation of a segment. It must find a connection between the new sentence and the segment at a point at or after the current now point. To maintain the plan context, each segment must store both the plan that is being tracked throughout the segment and the now point in that plan. As a result, each segment, in addition to storing the FOCUS, PF, HISTORY, and TENSE information, must store a now point, called NOW, and a plan structure, called the PLAN.

The plan reasoner is then called with three pieces of information: an indication of whether this is a continuation or a push; the now point; and the plan for the old segment. It either returns a rejection of the proposal or returns values for NOW and PLAN for the new segment (in a push) or for updating the old segment (in a continuation). Consider how this might work with the following story fragment:

5.1   Jack rushed to the train.
5.2   Earlier in the day Sam had bought him his ticket.

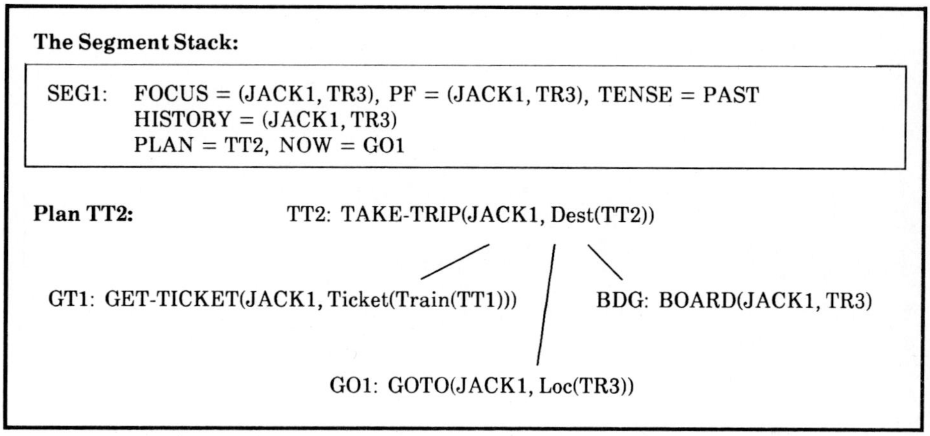

The Segment Stack:

SEG1:   FOCUS = (JACK1, TR3), PF = (JACK1, TR3), TENSE = PAST
             HISTORY = (JACK1, TR3)
             PLAN = TT2, NOW = GO1

Plan TT2:   TT2: TAKE-TRIP(JACK1, Dest(TT2))

GT1: GET-TICKET(JACK1, Ticket(Train(TT1)))   BDG: BOARD(JACK1, TR3)

GO1: GOTO(JACK1, Loc(TR3))

Figure 14.10 The segment stack and plan after sentence 5.1

5.3   He left it at the information booth for Jack to pick up.
5.4   When Jack was at the platform, he found he'd forgotten to pick it up.

Assume that the story prior to sentence 5.1 is sufficient such that the plan reasoner can identify 5.1 as describing a step in a variant of the TAKE-TRIP plan as defined in Chapter 13. A segment, SEG1, is created, with this information in it as well as the information from the other filters. This state of the segment stack and the plan is as shown in Figure 14.10, where GO1 is the name of the GOTO action in the TAKE-TRIP plan TT2.

Sentence 5.2 contains a temporal modifier, *earlier in the day,* and a tense shift to PAST PERFECT, both signalling a PUSH of a new segment--say, SEG2. The reference filter would identify the referent of the pronouns as JACK1, and the plan reasoner would need to reason that a different agent can purchase the ticket for him as a way of getting a ticket. Assuming this can be done, the plan and discourse states would be as shown in Figure 14.11.

Sentence 5.3 is acceptable to the tense filter as a continuation of SEG2, and, assuming the appropriate actions are defined for methods of giving people things, the plan reasoner could connect the action described in sentence 5.3 as a continuation of the GET-TICKET plan. The discourse and plan structures would then be as shown in Figure 14.12.

Sentence 5.4 contains an action in a clause introduced by *when.* A search of the plan for the state described would reveal that being at the platform was an effect of the action GO1. Thus sentence 5.4 is a reasonable continuation of SEG1, and SEG2 must be popped. The plan reasoner would then have to reason about plan failure in order to interpret the remainder of sentence 5.4.

The Segment Stack:

SEG2: FOCUS = (JACK1), PF = (SAM1, TIC3), TENSE = PASTPERF
HISTORY = (JACK1, SAM1, TIC3)
PLAN = TT2, NOW = BUY1

SEG1: FOCUS = (JACK1, TR3), PF = (JACK1, TR3), TENSE = PAST
HISTORY = (JACK1, TR3)
PLAN = TT2, NOW = GO1

Plan TT2:   TT2: TAKE-TRIP(JACK1, Dest(TT2))

GT1: GET-TICKET(JACK1, TIC3)   BDG: BOARD(JACK1, TR3)

GO1: GOTO(JACK1, Loc(TR3))

BUY1: PURCHASE(SAM1,
Clerk(TT2), TIC3)   GIVE(SAM1, JACK1, TIC3)

Figure 14.11 The segment stack and plan after sentence 5.2

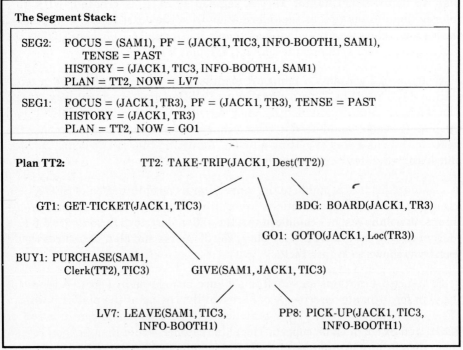

The Segment Stack:

SEG2: FOCUS = (SAM1), PF = (JACK1, TIC3, INFO-BOOTH1, SAM1),
TENSE = PAST
HISTORY = (JACK1, TIC3, INFO-BOOTH1, SAM1)
PLAN = TT2, NOW = LV7

SEG1: FOCUS = (JACK1, TR3), PF = (JACK1, TR3), TENSE = PAST
HISTORY = (JACK1, TR3)
PLAN = TT2, NOW = GO1

Plan TT2:   TT2: TAKE-TRIP(JACK1, Dest(TT2))

GT1: GET-TICKET(JACK1, TIC3)   BDG: BOARD(JACK1, TR3)

GO1: GOTO(JACK1, Loc(TR3))

BUY1: PURCHASE(SAM1,
Clerk(TT2), TIC3)   GIVE(SAM1, JACK1, TIC3)

LV7: LEAVE(SAM1, TIC3,   PP8: PICK-UP(JACK1, TIC3,
INFO-BOOTH1)   INFO-BOOTH1)

Figure 14.12 The segment stack and plan after sentence 5.3

14.7 Explicit Discourse Relations

This chapter has concentrated on a particular approach to analyzing discourse structure, where the discourse model provided a mostly structural role depending on the domain modeling to account for much of the actual flow of topics. An alternate approach involves specifying a set of domain-independent relationships between sentences that define coherent discourse. Proponents of this approach often claim that if you can discover the complete set of relationships underlying the discourse, you would need no additional mechanisms. This is not a necessary claim for the approach, however, and a theory of discourse relations would be useful as part of an overall theory of discourse, where domain reasoning, segmentation, and focus tracking still play an important role.

For example, the plan-based analysis used in the last section could be recast as a theory of discourse relations, albeit an inadequate one, because it can model only a limited range of discourses. The discourse relations would correspond to the different connections that the plan reasoner can find between sentences, such as enablement, causal effect, obstacle, subaction, and so on. Thus a complete theory of discourse relations would subsume the plan-based analysis.

The following section is a sampling of discourse relations suggested in the literature. While there is no agreement as to what the set of relations are, the ones discussed here are found in virtually all theories under one name or another. In addition, this text will consider discourse relations as relations between segments, whereas in some approaches the relations hold only between clauses or sentences.

Discourse Relations

The elaboration relation holds between two segments S0 and S1, if S1 provides additional information about S0, or simply repeats the claim in S0. In any event the overall goal underlying S1 is the same as that underlying S0.

For example, the **instrumental causation** relation, derivable by the plan reasoner using decomposition chaining, provides a clear example of elaboration. Segment S0 states that some action is occurring, and S1 then provides more information on the details of how the action is being executed. Another example, involving states of knowledge rather than actions, occurs in the following discourse fragment:

6.1   I know how to get to your house.
6.2   I go down Main Street, turn left at the light, and it's the third house
       on the left.

Sentence 6.1 makes a claim, and the sequence of clauses in sentence 6.2 gives directions that prove that sentence 6.1 is true. In other cases the second sentence merely provides evidence that the first sentence is the case.

Another important class of discourse relations involves a segment S0 creating a situation with respect to which segment S1 is interpreted. The most obvious case of this occurs when segment S0 describes a place and time, and then S1 describes an event that takes place in that setting. Another common case is the **enablement** relation used by the plan reasoner. Recall that in these cases segment S0 describes some state, or decribes an action that causes some state, in which the action described in S1 is enabled (that is, the state satisfies a precondition). The following example may or may not be considered an enablement relation, depending on how general it is, but it is definitely in the situation-setting class:

7.1   Jack arrived in Rochester at five o'clock by train.
7.2   Mary met him at the station.

In this case there is an implicit temporal ordering between the events described in sentences 7.1 and 7.2. In addition, one of the effects of sentence 7.1 (that Jack is in the station) satisfies a prerequisite for the event described in sentence 7.2 (that to meet someone, both agents must be in the same place). An example of situation setting is seen between the clauses in sentence 6.2. The event of going down Main Street provides both the location and orientation required to interpret the event of turning left at the light, which itself provides the location and orientation for the statement *it's the third house on the left*. A term such as *left* cannot be interpreted without an assumed orientation.

Another important relation in this class is the **causality-effect relation,** which was already implicitly used as part of the analysis of sentences 7.1 and 7.2, where S0 describes some event and S1 is, or could be, one of its effects.

Another way in which two segments may relate is when one segment describes a situation for a class of objects, whereas the other describes the same (or a similar) situation for a particular object in that class. If S0 is the general segment, and S1 is the specific segment, you can say that S1 **exemplifies** S0, and you can use a cue phrase like *for example* to introduce S1. On the other hand, if S0 is specific and S1 is general, you can say that S1 **generalizes** S0, and you can use a cue phrase such as *in general*. You can find examples of these relations in their full generality and complexity throughout this book anywhere you find the phrases *for example* or *in general*.

The **contrast** relation holds between two segments whenever they describe two objects or situations in terms such that some property is true of one, while a mutually exclusive property is true of the other. A **violated expectation** relation holds when S0 implicates some property P that is then explicitly denied by S1. Both of these relations can be realized using the conjunction *but*, as in *A riding lawnmower is faster on the flat stretches, but a push mower is better getting under trees* (a contrast), and *I know you found the stolen money on me, but I didn't steal it!* (a violated expectation relation).

A relation virtually the opposite of the contrast relation is the **parallel** relation. In this case segments S0 and S1 both assert the same (or a similar) property on two different objects or situations. This can be realized using the conjunction *and*, as in *Jack went to the grocery store and Sue went to the liquor store.*

Another relation often suggested is that of simple **sequencing**. For example, two segments might be related simply by a temporal relationship. Some argue that pure temporal ordering is not sufficient to produce coherent discourse, and that some other relation must hold in addition between the segments. For instance, a sequence is allowed if each segment is dominated by the same segment. Thus Jack might list seven reasons why everyone should vote for him. Each of the reasons might take a segment, and these seven segments are related to each other only by being in this sequence. They all, however, are elaborations on the same segment that has the purpose of getting the votes.

Discourse Grammars

One method of organizing the discourse relations is to incorporate them into a grammar of discourse. You then have two possibilities, depending on what the terminals in the grammar are. In the first method, the terminals are the discourse relations themselves, and a separate process then connects each terminal to its realization in the actual discourse. In the second method, the terminals are actually the clauses in the discourse together with the sentence connectives and cue phrases. In the latter scheme each discourse relation is represented by a grammar that states how it is realizable in the actual discourse.

The idea that a discourse grammar is necessary is supported by the intuition that in a discourse situation the preceding discourse constrains what can occur next in ways that are not simply a result of its semantic content. For example, if an agent A asks agent B a question, B's reply should be an answer, a statement indicating that B doesn't know the answer or cannot answer for some other reason, or a request for clarification about what agent A is asking. This knowledge, in fact, might be crucial for properly interpreting B's response. Thus if A asks *Is the hardware store open?* and B responds *It's a holiday today*, then A should not simply interpret B's sentence as making some claim but should attempt to interpret this as an answer to the question. Thus if A doesn't know whether hardware stores are usually open on holidays or not, A might request a clarification as in *Does that mean they're closed?*

BOX 14.1 The Debate about Discourse Relations

You can create classes of relationships as described in the text, but how can you recognize a given relationship in an actual discourse situation? The easy cases occur when you use explicit cue phrases, but in general you need some other mechanism to find the connections between two segments so that you can identify the relationship. But, if such a process is possible, it will be doing all the analysis, and the discourse relations would not need to be an explicit part of the model, since it would work just as well without them. If this is the case, the classes are useful only as a classification of the types of connections that a complete domain reasoner would need to be able to handle.

On the other hand, even if discourse relations may only be summaries of the types of connections that a domain reasoner can find, the presence of discourse relations may be necessary to constrain the search for a connection so that it is computationally possible. Not only can cue phrases be handled gracefully (that is, a cue phrase identifies possible discourse relations, which in turn identify possible types of connections), but there may be a structure that you can impose on a discourse in terms of these relations so that not all relations are possible at any given time.

Some argue that the preceding example can be fully explained by considering the plans of A and B, and that an answer is expected simply because A's plan to ask a question (and receive an answer) is recognized by B and thus is mutually known between them. But other examples are not so easily explained from general principles of rational behavior. For example, in the beginning of a conversation the expression *How are you?* can be interpreted as a simple greeting requiring no literal response. Later in a conversation, however, the same question must be treated literally as a question. This is because the greeting interpretation is simply not allowed in mid-conversation.

Another example occurs when a speaker is comparing two objects. He or she could start by identifying the aspects in common between them (say, by mentioning some class of objects that they both belong to). This would typically be followed by a series of segments discussing some property of the first object and then discussing the contrasting property of the second object. In fact there are explicit linguisitic devices for conveniently referring to the objects involved in a comparison: One may be called *the former*, or *this one*, while the other may be called *the latter*, or *that one*. The simple segment stack structure described earlier cannot account for these cases and would need extending.

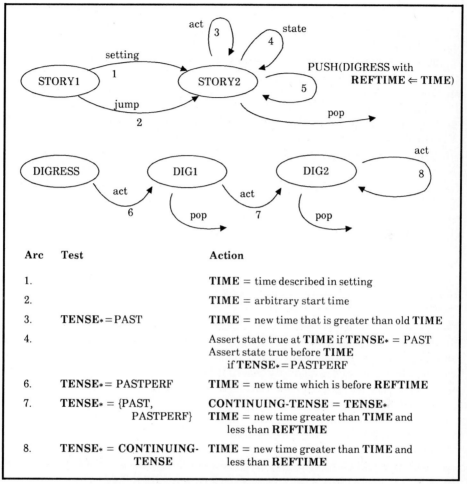

Figure 14.13 An ATN for simple past tense stories

Arc	Test	Action
1.		**TIME** = time described in setting
2.		**TIME** = arbitrary start time
3.	**TENSE**$_*$ = PAST	**TIME** = new time that is greater than old **TIME**
4.		Assert state true at **TIME** if **TENSE**$_*$ = PAST Assert state true before **TIME** if **TENSE**$_*$ = PASTPERF
6.	**TENSE**$_*$ = PASTPERF	**TIME** = new time which is before **REFTIME**

7.	**TENSE**$_*$ = {PAST,
	  PASTPERF}
		CONTINUING-TENSE = **TENSE**$_*$
		TIME = new time greater than **TIME** and
		  less than **REFTIME**

8.	**TENSE**$_*$ = CONTINUING-
	  TENSE
		TIME = new time greater than **TIME** and
		  less than **REFTIME**

While the mechanics for constructing a discourse grammar are quite straightforward, they have to allow for the topic suspension and resumption behavior seen in discourse. Among other things, therefore, the possibility of an interruption must be allowed at virtually every place in the grammar. Consider the more constrained case in which you describe a grammar for modeling simple stories, including the ability to digress into a discussion of previous events. Assume that each terminal and nonterminal maintains a structure similar to the structure of segments discussed earlier, which can be accessed using the notation developed for ATNs. You will not need to maintain a segment stack, however, since this will be managed by the grammar. The grammar for a simple narrative could be as shown in Figure 14.13. This grammar maintains only the temporal relationships between the events in the story, though it could easily be extended to maintain other information, such as focus information, as well. It allows digressions that describe past events. These are signaled by the initial use of the past perfect tense and may be continued using one of the past perfect or the simple past in succeeding utterances. The annotation on the grammar computes time points for each event and relates them to the other events in the story.

This example indicates that the treatment of segment pushes and pops in the ATN model and in the segment stack model are quite similar. In the segment stack model a digression forced the creation of a new segment on the stack. When this segment was popped off the stack later, the discourse could resume at the point where the digression was initiated. In the ATN model each network maintains the information needed for the segment. Here a digression is a push to a new network, and when this network completes, the discourse resumes in the previous network.

Summary

Discourse is hierarchically structured and can be modeled using a mechanism close to a stack structure. The tense and aspect of a sentence can constrain how the sentence may temporally and causally relate to the sentences surrounding it. The notion of a focused element can be used to constrain anaphoric reference and affect the discourse structure. The plan reasoner can be generalized to analyze stories that do not simply describe the actions in the order in which they occur. The discourse stack provides the structure that allows all these processes to interact.

Related Work and Further Readings

The diverse area of discourse analysis has mainly consisted of work that focuses on only one particular aspect, such as focus, plan tracking, and so on. Only recently have attempts been made to specify an overall framework into which all these pieces fit. In particular, Grosz and Sidner (1986) outline a model that motivated the organization of this chapter. They divided the problem into three parts: the segmentation and attentional state, which were discussed in this chapter, and the intentional state, which will be considered in Chapter 15.

The discussion of tense as a discourse phenomenon is based on work by Webber (1987a). She gives a good range of examples of how segment shifts and tense can interact, and she suggests four ways in which a new sentence might get integrated into the previous context. Of these four methods, three are captured by the segment stack mechanism described in Section 14.3. The fourth method deals with embedded narrative, which occurs when a conversation is described in a story. A good paper examining the complexities of analyzing temporal connectives such as *when* and *while* is Steedman (1982). There is a large literature in linguistics and philosophy addressing issues of tense and aspect. Good collections of papers can be found in Dowty (1986) and Tedesci and Zaenen (1981). Work in AI on representing temporal information includes Bruce (1972), Kahn and Gorry (1977), McDermott (1982), and Allen (1984).

The notion of a local focus that is primarily influenced by sentence structure has a long history in linguistics under various names and disguises. The work described in this chapter is derived from work by Sidner (1983) and Grosz, Joshi, and Weinstein (1983). Sidner basically allowed four different types of focus operations that could occur. A sentence might leave the focus the same as the previous sentence, it might shift to an object explicitly mentioned in the previous sentence, it might return to a previous focus, or it might shift to an object implicitly related to the previous focus. Only the last case has not been examined in detail in this chapter, and some techniques for handling that case were presented in Chapter 12 in discussing implicitly defined objects on the history list.

Sidner founded her algorithm on a set of preferences for the focus based on thematic roles. She proposed that the theme role was the top candidate for the focus of a sentence, in apparent conflict to the normal opinion that the subject of a sentence is generally the focus. This dilemma is resolved by realizing that Sidner actually uses the preferences for determining the focus of the next sentence rather than the focus of the present. Given this, her preference for the object reflects that this role is the most likely to be the focus in the next sentence. Sidner's hypothesis was that the focus is selected according to her preference heuristics, and only if a semantic or pragmatic contradiction eliminates the top preference do the other possibilities get considered. In contrast, the algorithm described in this chapter does not commit to a focus until forced to by subsequent sentences.

Grosz, Joshi, and Weinstein (1983) define the notion of a **backward-looking center**. This is the object that links the current sentence to the preceding discourse. They propose a basic constraint relating the center to pronominalization:

> If the center of the current utterance is the same as the center of
> the previous utterance, a pronoun should be used.

There are several implications of this. First, it does not prohibit the use of pronouns for other entities as well if one of them refers to the center. Second, if the center changes, this rule does not have any effect. In cases of change the new center is typically selected from the set of entities mentioned in the previous utterance, which are defined to be the **forward-looking centers** of the utterance.

In linguistics many different terms have been introduced to capture notions similar to focusing behavior, but you can make an important distinction. In computational models the focus is part of a cognitive model--it is the focus of the speaker. In linguistics the same term is used by certain people, but in many cases the focus is a structural property of a sentence. While these may coincide much of the time, they also could be quite different. Good surveys of the work in linguistics can be found in Chafe (1976) and Winograd (1983).

The idea that sentences can be related by some analysis of the speaker's purpose has a long history. In recent times, however, a major influence on the approach comes from Grimes (1975). He identified three general classes of functions that can be used in discourse: A sentence may support or supplement what has come before (elaborate); it may create a setting (identify time and location of an event); and it may identify an object (introduce a new object for discussion or revert to an old object). A fair number of computationally oriented frameworks have since been developed, each one introducing a different set of relations. A good survey of these models and their use in the analysis of anaphora can be found in Hirst (1981b).

A major proponent of the discourse relations approach is Hobbs (1979). He takes the view that independent discourse structure is not needed and that all discourse structure can be accounted for by domain reasoning under the control of discourse relations, which he calls **coherence relations**. Each discourse relation is defined in terms of some inferential connection between the new sentence and the preceding discourse. In addition, each discourse relation can be independently justified in terms of some communicative function. For example, the text

John can open the safe. He knows the combination.

is coherent because the sentences are related by the elaboration relation, which is defined by the condition that both sentences describe essentially the same conditions: The first states that an action can be performed, and the second states why (that is, the prerequisite of knowing the safe is satisfied). The conversational purpose underlying this is to get the listener to infer the entire situation that the speaker is trying to convey. In this case it is simply that John can open the safe because he knows the combination.

In addition this inference process is claimed to account wholly for the treatment of referent determination. For example, in the earlier two sentences, you would determine the referent of *the combination* as the combination of the safe just mentioned as part of the process of finding the connection between the two sentences. This is similar to, but more general than, the type of referential identification that occurred in tracking the topic of a conversation with a plan, as discussed in Chapter 12.

Reichman (1978; 1985) proposes a theory of discourse that is a primary influence on the development in this chapter. Her work pointed out the importance of incorporating the use of cue phrases (called **clue words** in her model). The model uses a grammar of **conversational moves** that correspond to this chapter's discourse relations. This grammar controls the construction of a complex representation of the state of the discourse based on a representation called **context spaces**. A context space (CS) contains the sort of information maintained in segment structures plus additional information that reflects its current status in the discourse. At any time there are up to three CSs relevant to the discourse: the active one, which corresponds to the top of the segment stack in this chapter's model; the controlling one (immediately below on the stack); and the generating space, which has no correlate in the model described in this chapter. The generating space contains some claim by a speaker that has not yet been resolved and may be returned to later, but it does not allow the immediate pronominalization of the focused elements when resumed. By including this space, Reichman can present a good analysis of some forms of dietic reference (for example, the use of *this* and *that*).

Each CS also may identify the rhetorical technique, such as analogy or contrast, used to achieve its discourse purpose, and thus they are more richly structured than the segments defined in this chapter. Reichman chooses to put more structure into the CSs and depend less on independent domain-based reasoning. She also uses a more finely-grained analysis of focus: An element can be in high, medium, or low focus. In addition, a level of zero focus is used to account for implicit reference (ellipsis). These levels are used by four rules constraining reference:

1. Only elements in high focus in the active and controlling CS may be pronominalized.

2. Only elements in the active and controlling space may be referenced by a close deitic reference (*this*, *here*).

3. Full definite descriptions are needed for all other elements in the active and controlling spaces.

4. Far dietic reference (*that*, *there*) and full definite description can be used for objects in the generating space.

One of the major differences in the claims made is that Reichman argues that objects may not be put into high focus by merely being pronominalized. Rather the primary tools for putting an object in high focus are: (1) to use it in the subject position of the sentence; or (2) to refer to it by name after it is introduced by description (that is, the raising of an object from low to medium focus actually raises it to high focus).

As discussed in this chapter, discourse grammars can come in different guises depending on whether the model primarily addresses the semantic connections between sentences or whether it addresses topic flow, interruption, and resumption. A major proponent of the first sort is Rumelhart (1975), who proposes modeling the structure of simple stories using a grammar. For example, a fragment of his grammar might look as follows:

1.	STORY → SETTING EPISODES
2a.	EPISODES → EPISODE EPISODES
2b.	EPISODES → EPISODE
3a.	SETTING → STATE-DESC SETTING
3b.	SETTING → STATE-DESC
4.	EPISODE → EVENTS REACTIONS
5a.	EVENTS → EVENT-DESC EVENTS
5b.	EVENTS → EVENT-DESC

The terminals here correspond to sentences describing states (STATE-DESC) and events (EVENT-DESC). In addition, semantic constraints can be associated with each of the rules. For example, on rule 1 there would be a constraint that the setting must allow for Episode, whereas on rule 4 there would be a constraint that the event should cause the reaction. In some cases, of course, these constraints would be obviously satisfied. In other cases, where there potentially could be ambiguity, the constraints can be used to select the appropriate reading. While this formalism produces an analysis for some simple stories, it does not seem directly extendable to discourse in general. In particular it has no mechanism for explaining how interruptions and digressions can occur and how the original discourse can then be later resumed.

The discourse grammar fragment described in Section 14.7 was an example of the second approach, where the emphasis is on modeling the topic flow. That example is a simplified version of a model proposed by Polanyi and Scha (forthcoming). In addition, Polanyi and Scha present a good argument on the distinction between true (discourse) returns and semantic returns.

In linguistics Halliday and Hasan (1976) claim that structure of discourse is primarily a result of certain linguistic devices that make sentences **cohere** to each other. Two sentences cohere because of:

1. reference -- the use of pronouns and definite descriptions to refer back to objects mentioned in other sentences (this includes deep and surface forms, one-anaphora, and so on);

2. ellipsis -- using the structure of one sentence to "fill in" another;

3. conjunction -- connecting sentences by *and*, *further*, *but*, and so on; and

4. lexical connections -- the use of words that are related to each other, such as opposites, paraphrase, repetition, and so on.

This approach is dramatically different from the computational theories presented in this chapter. The authors say these phenomena cause cohesion, whereas the computational approaches say that the content and topic flow of the discourse make it coherent and that the phenomena just listed are simply artifacts of this coherence. In other words, using reference doesn't make a text coherent, but a coherent text will generally involve a lot of reference since those objects are being talked about.

Linde (1979) and Grosz (1974) both observed that the flow of the topic of conversation in task-oriented conversations could be explained in terms of the hierarchical structure of the task being discussed. Studying descriptions of apartments, Linde showed that rooms are not randomly chosen, and that the discourse topics progressed according to a hypothetical "walk" through the apartment. Grosz studied dialogs in which an expert aids an apprentice in assembling a water pump. Again, she found that the flow of topics followed the actual execution of the plan to assemble the pump. She defined the notion of **global focus** for reference, which is realized in this chapter by having the plan reasoner constrained by the segment stack mechanism. She used a mechanism called **focus spaces**, which identified the parts of the plan that were under discussion. These focus spaces were maintained in a stack structure, which gave the appropriate objects for determining the referents of definite descriptions. This corresponds to the organization of the history list by segments that was discussed earlier. She showed that after the focus stack is "popped," objects in the resumed focus space could be immediately pronominalized without explicit reintroduction.

Exercises for Chapter 14

1. *(easy)* Draw the sequence of stack states for a discourse that could be boxed as follows (each number represents a sentence):

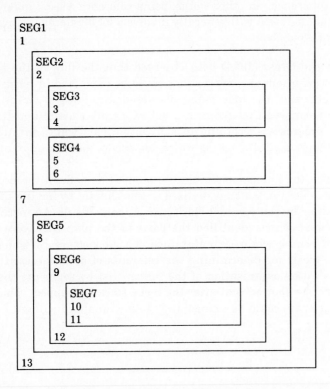

2. *(medium)* Find about a half-page of text somewhere and use the techniques described in this chapter, and your intuitions, to produce a segmentation of it. For each segment boundary, explicitly identify the method for detecting the shift.

3. *(medium)* Trace the algorithm in Figure 14.5 as the following sentences are analyzed, showing the details of every call to the reference filter.

> An old lawnmower is next to a TV set in the garage.
> Even though the engine stalls frequently, we still hope to sell it.

Your answer should not be the intuitively correct one. What was wrong? Outline an extension to the algorithm so that it produces the correct answer.

4. *(medium)* Modify the definitions given in Chapter 13 for the actions GET-TICKET and GIVE so that the story fragment in Section 14.6 can be analyzed as described. Give a detailed trace of the three filters as they analyze the fragment. In particular, show the logical form of each sentence, and describe what each filter returns in the analysis of each sentence. Show in detail when each action parameter is set and how the referent is determined for each noun phrase.

Chapter 15

Belief Models and Speech Acts

This chapter explores the issues involved in representing and reasoning about the beliefs and intentions of individuals, and it describes how this information affects the understanding of sentences. Such an ability is useful in two related problem areas. The first area is the understanding of a narrative where some of the actions described may involve communication, as in *Jack warned Sue about the elephant*. To understand such a sentence and connect it to the rest of the narrative requires a model of the action of warning, which is a **speech act**. The second problem area concerns man-machine dialogs, where the system must first recognize what the person is trying to accomplish and then be able to plan speech acts in response.

Section 15.1 introduces the notions of beliefs and speech acts and explains their use in narrative understanding. Section 15.2 describes some computational techniques for representing beliefs. A simple computational model of speech acts is then developed in Section 15.3 and extended in Section 15.4. Section 15.5 examines the relationship between speech act models and discourse structure. Finally, Section 15.6 looks at some of the more formal issues in representing beliefs in a logic.

15.1 Beliefs, Speech Acts, and Language

Consider a system that must understand the connections between the following pairs of sentences and draw the appropriate conclusions.

1.1   Jack believes the owner of the house is in the kitchen.
1.2   Sue is the owner of the house.

2.1   Jack told Sue that Sam stole the car.
2.2   Sue believes Sam will go to jail.

If the verb *believe* maps to a predicate (or frame structure) BELIEVE, the final meaning of sentence 1.1 could be

BELIEVE(JACK1, INSIDE(Owner(H1), Kitchen(H1)))

where H1 is the referent for *the house*. The final representation of sentence 1.2 would be

Owner(H1) = SUE1

The first reasoning ability provided by any frame-based or logic-based representation is the setting of role values. Thus, given that the owner role of H1 is SUE1, any system could now conclude

BELIEVE(JACK1, INSIDE(SUE1, Kitchen(H1)))

But this conclusion is not necessarily true. In fact Jack may not know who the owner of the house is, or he may be mistaken and think the owner is Sam. If *believe* is represented by a simple predicate or frame, these facts could not be represented. This property is often called **failure of substitutivity**, because one term cannot be substituted for a term to which it is equal. An operator that does not allow substitution is called a **referentially opaque operator**--a term that draws on a metaphor between substitution and visibility. Substitution is allowed with **transparent operators** (which include ordinary predicates).

To make matters more complicated, substitution sometimes appears to be allowed. For example, given the sentences

3.1   Jack believes Sam stole the car.
3.2   Jack believes Sam is poor.

the system should be able to conclude that Jack believes that a poor man stole the car. A representation that handles both of these cases is introduced in the next section.

The second pair of sentences (2.1 and 2.2) demonstrates how verbs describing communication may interact with beliefs. In particular, in order to relate sentences 2.1 and 2.2, the system would have to know that an effect of sentence 2.1 is that Sue now believes that Sam stole the car and, as a result, believes that he will be caught and punished. Apparently the verb *tell* should be mapped to an action that has the appropriate belief defined as an effect.

In this example, the speech act was explicitly mentioned in the sentence. Another, more common source of speech acts arises in dialogs. Namely, each time a person speaks to another person, the first person is performing a speech act. In general, identifying what speech act was performed is a complex reasoning task depending heavily on the context. For example, consider the sentence:

4.   Do you know the time?

In its most common use sentence 4 is a request that the hearer tell the speaker what the time is. If you were to describe this act later (where Jack was the speaker), you might say

Jack asked Sam what the time was.

On the other hand, sentence 4 could also be used in other settings as an offer. If Jack knows the time and Sam doesn't, sentence 4 might be described later as

Jack offered to tell Sam the time.

Of course, neither of these interpretations is the **literal interpretation**. Literally speaking, sentence 4 is a yes-no question that might be described as

Jack asked Sam whether he knew the time.

In some contexts this would be the intended speech act, but these occasions are rare, because just knowing that someone else knows the time is not very useful in most situations.

If a computer system is going to be able to communicate with a person in a dialog, it must be able to recognize and distinguish between the different **intended meanings** of sentences like sentence 4. The most crucial information needed to distinguish these cases is information about what the speaker believes. For example, if the speaker already knows the time, the offer interpretation is likely. If the speaker doesn't know the time, the offer interpretation is impossible, but the request interpretation is likely. The rest of this chapter introduces enough mechanisms that simple situations like this can be represented and the intended speech act can be recognized.

15.2 Simple Belief Models

All the preceding examples point out a need to be able to represent the beliefs of different agents explicitly. This section examines some of the more practically oriented belief representations used in current systems. While these representations have known problems that are the subject of current research, they are rich enough to represent a good range of examples. The discussion will be restricted to representing the beliefs of two agents, Jack and Sue. The techniques, however, can be generalized to include additional agents. In addition, in man-machine dialog systems, one of the agents may be the system itself, and all beliefs will be relative to what the system believes.

The simplest representation that allows multiple agents' beliefs involves labeling each fact in the knowledge base with the agents that believe that fact. Although this technique is useful in some limited settings, it is very weak, because it does not allow agents to have erroneous beliefs or allow different agents to hold beliefs that contradict each other. A generalization of this technique, however, can avoid these difficulties.

In particular the knowledge base could be divided into separate data bases, called **belief spaces**, each one representing a particular agent's set of beliefs. All reasoning done by the knowledge representation would be relative to a particular belief space. For example, assume that the knowledge representation uses a Horn clause prover as an inference engine. Then if a certain belief space contains the facts that Fido is dog and that all dogs bark, the system would be able to conclude that Fido barks relative to this belief space. This is valid even if another belief space contains the fact that Fido doesn't bark. A distinction can be made between the facts explicitly asserted in a belief space, called the **explicit beliefs,** and those that can be derived in that belief space, called the **implicit beliefs.** Figure 15.1 shows a knowledge base consisting of two belief spaces with differing explicit beliefs and implicit beliefs. In that situation both Jack and Sue believe that Fido is a dog and that all dogs bark. Sue, in addition, believes that all things that bark are hostile. Thus Sue has an implicit belief that Jack doesn't have--namely, that Fido is hostile.

Similarly, you could encode different action and plan structures in each belief space and thus represent the individual plans of the agents. There are still some major holes, however, in constructing rich belief models. Thus the following discussion considers these areas: (1) representing nested beliefs; (2) representing shared beliefs; and (3) representing beliefs about others' knowledge and abilities. For the moment the discussion will not make any distinction between the terms *knowledge* and *belief* but will use the words interchangeably. In this sense both terms correspond to your intuitions of what it means to believe something.

Nested Beliefs

A large number of any agent's beliefs are actually about the beliefs of other agents. For instance, consider Jack as he reasons about Sue's beliefs. He does not have any access directly to Sue's actual beliefs. Rather, he has only what he believes Sue believes. Thus, if Jack recognizes Sue's plan from what she says, this plan will need to be constructed using Jack's beliefs about what Sue believes. In particular, Jack should be able to recognize such a plan even if he knows that the plan is faulty for some reason. For example, suppose he believes that he has a combination lock on his locker but believes that Sue believes that he has a key lock. Then when she asks for his key, he should be able to recognize that Sue's plan is to open the locker, even though opening his locker with a key is an incoherent plan from his point of view.

Also, when you try to determine the intended referent of a noun phrase, these belief models come into play. Again, suppose Jack knows that a certain book--say, *The Revenge of Mrs. Smith*--is in his office, but he believes that Sue believes it is on a table in the lounge. Then if Sue asks, *Have you read the book on the table in the lounge?* Jack should recognize that Sue means *The Revenge of Mrs. Smith*, even though the description used to refer to it is inaccurate (from his viewpoint!).

Thus there are many cases where the one agent's beliefs about another's beliefs play an important role in language understanding. The natural question to ask is whether any deeper nesting is required in some cases. In fact examples can arise where such a distinction is necessary. For example, suppose Jack

	Jack's Beliefs	Sue's Beliefs
Explicit Beliefs	DOG(FIDO)	DOG(FIDO)
	BARKS(?x) < DOG(?x)	BARKS(?x) < DOG(?x)
		HOSTILE(?y) < BARKS(?y)
Derivable Beliefs	BARKS(FIDO)	BARKS(FIDO)
		HOSTILE(FIDO)

Figure 15.1 Representing beliefs as databases

believes that Sue thinks she just successfully lied about something, such as that it is raining outside. In this case the situation is as follows:

Jack believes: It is not raining.

Jack believes that Sue believes: It is not raining.

Jack believes that Sue believes that Jack believes: It is raining.

Both Jack and Sue believe it is not raining, but Jack now believes that Sue believes that he thinks it is raining, since she thinks her lie was successful.

Shared Knowledge

If you push matters, you can construct examples requiring arbitrarily deep nestings of beliefs. In practice, however, examples that go more than about three levels become incomprehensible. One particular problem, however, appears to force consideration of ever deeper nestings of belief. This problem gives rise to a new area known as **shared knowledge**, which is defined in this section.

As described earlier, to recognize another's plan, you should use what you believe are his or her beliefs about the world rather than your own beliefs. Likewise, when constructing a plan that you intend another agent to recognize, you should consider what he or she knows to ensure that he or she can recognize what is intended. But suppose an agent A is doing this in constructing a plan. When agent B tries to recognize the plan, shouldn't B use what B believes are A's beliefs about B's beliefs? This is the knowledge B has about what knowledge A used in constructing the plan. Such knowledge is three levels deep. But if A considers this, shouldn't A then construct a plan using what A knows about the knowledge B will use (which is four levels deep)? This argument can be pushed on indefinitely as an argument that an agent should consider an infinite nesting of beliefs whenever he or she wants a plan to be recognized.

A way out of this problem is to introduce the notion of shared knowledge, which is that knowledge that both agents know and know that the other knows.

Shared knowledge arises from the common background and situation that the agents find themselves in and includes most of our general knowledge about the world (such as how common actions are done, the standard type hierarchy classifications of objects, general facts about the society we live in, and so on). Agents that know each other or share a common profession will have considerable shared knowledge as a result of their previous interactions and their education in that field.

Shared knowledge plays a crucial role in successful communication. While individual beliefs may play a central role in the content of a conversation, most of the knowledge brought to bear to interpret the other's actions will be shared knowledge.

A Database Model of Belief

You can extend the knowledge representation to handle simple beliefs by using the database idea described earlier and introducing a new operator, BEL, which is recognized and treated specially by the knowledge representation. In particular, the knowledge base is partitioned into belief spaces linked by arcs labeled with one of the agents. Given any belief space, you can find what level of belief nesting is being represented by tracing back these inter-database arcs to the root node. The sequence of agent labels gives the belief nesting information. For example, Figure 15.2 shows a situation where Jack believes some book, BOOK1, is in his office. But he also believes that Sue believes the book is in the lounge, and that Sue in turn believes that Jack believes it was thrown out.

Shared knowledge is represented in one more database not in this hierarchy, called SHARED. A retrieval algorithm relative to a belief space is as follows:

> To retrieve a proposition P in belief space B:

> If P is of the form BEL(A, Q)
> then follow the link labeled A from B to a new belief space, say B'
>   and recursively call Retrieve(Q, B')
> else perform the retrieval operation using the facts in B and SHARED

For example, assume that the retriever is a simple Horn clause theorem prover. Also assume that the shared knowledge database contains the facts:

1.   LOC(GARBAGE, CITY-DUMP)
2.   LOC(?x, ?z) < LOC(?x, ?y), LOC(?y, ?z)

Consider trying to prove the proposition BEL(SUE1, BEL(JACK1, LOC(BOOK1, CITY-DUMP))) starting in belief space B1--namely, Jack's beliefs. The first pass through the algorithm finds the link labeled SUE1 from B1 to B2 and results in a call to retrieve the proposition BEL(JACK1, LOC(BOOK1, CITY-DUMP)) in belief space B2. The second pass through finds

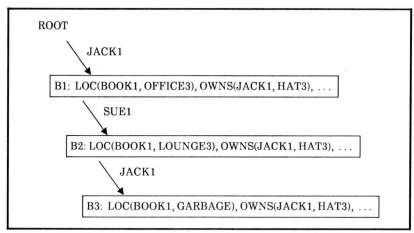

Figure 15.2 Representing three levels of nesting using separate belief spaces

the link labeled JACK1 from B2 to B3 and results in a call to retrieve the proposition LOC(BOOK1, CITY-DUMP) in belief space B3. The third pass invokes the theorem prover with the facts in the belief spaces B3 and SHARED, and is successful with the following proof. Rule 2 is instantiated to be

$$LOC(BOOK1, CITY\text{-}DUMP) < LOC(BOOK1, ?y), LOC(?y, CITY\text{-}DUMP)$$

The first literal on the right-hand side matches against the first fact in B3, binding the variable ?y to GARBAGE. The second conjunct, now LOC(GARBAGE, CITY-DUMP), is provable from a direct match in SHARED to fact 1. Thus the belief proposition is successfully proved. If the system had tried to prove BEL(SUE1, LOC(BOOK1, CITY-DUMP)) in B1, on the other hand, it would have failed.

You add facts to this belief representation in the same way. If the fact is a simple proposition (that is, no BEL operator), it is added to the current belief space; otherwise, the BEL operator is stripped off, and a link is followed to find the appropriate belief space in which to add the resulting proposition.

Knowledge About Others' Beliefs

Perhaps the most tricky problem in building a belief model is that much of your knowledge is of the form that some agent knows something, yet you do not know what they know. For instance, Jack probably believes that Sue knows her mother's name, yet Jack may not know the name himself. You cannot represent this situation simply by adding a fact into the appropriate belief space. There is no formula of the form NAMEOF(Mother(SUE1), xxx) that can be in the appropriate belief space since Jack does not know Sue's mother's name. If the system generated a skolem constant--say, name33--and added

NAMEOF(Mother(SUE1), name33) to the belief space B2, it simply has represented that Sue believes that her mother has a name. In FOPC, this would be

3.   *BEL(SUE1, ∃ x . NAMEOF(Mother(SUE1), x))*

One common solution to this problem is to use quantifier scoping over the belief operator to make this distinction. Thus formula 3 means that Sue believes that her mother has a name, whereas

4.   *∃ x . BEL(SUE1, NAMEOF(Mother(SUE1), x))*

means that she knows what the name actually is. Unfortunately, quantifier scoping with modal operators is not usually preserved by skolemization. The system can capture this scoping distinction, however, by making every skolem function dependent on the belief space in which it is created. Thus adding a fact corresponding to formula 3 to belief space B1 would create a skolem dependent on the belief space B2 (that is, what Jack1 believes Sue believes):

5.   B2: NAMEOF(Mother(SUE1), skol(B2))

Adding a fact corresponding to formula 4 would create a skolem dependent on B1 (that is, what Jack believes) and would add the following to B2:

6.   B2: NAMEOF(Mother(SUE1), skol(B1))

For convenience, define a new operator KNOWREF that means exactly the second interpretation. In other words, asserting KNOWREF(SUE1, x, NAMEOF(Mother(SUE1), x)) in B1 is formally defined to be equivalent to adding formula 4.

This method of retaining the scoping of existentials has to have a corresponding proof method for testing existential statements and be able to make a distinction between a query such as *Does Sue believe that her mother has a name?* and one such as *Does Sue know her mother's name?* To distinguish between these, the system needs to be able to restrict variables to match against objects defined in different belief spaces. Thus the first question might map to a query such as: find a value for ?x defined in B2 such that NAMEOF(Mother(SUE1), ?x) is provable in B2. To ensure that this succeeds given either formula 5 or 6, any object defined in B1 must also be defined in B2. In fact, this must be true in general: Any object defined in a belief space d is also defined in any belief space "reachable" from d. The second question, however, would map to a query such as: Find a value for ?x defined in B1 such that NAMEOF(Mother(SUE1), ?x) is provable in B2. This query should succeed given formula 6, but not formula 5. The algorithm would have to be clever enough to allow either of these queries to succeed if the fact in the belief space

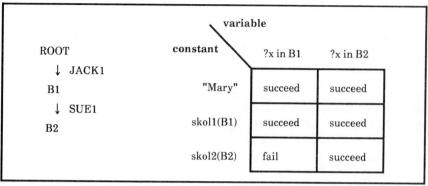

Figure 15.3 Matching variables and constants indexed by belief spaces

were NAMEOF(Mother(SUE1), "Mary")--that is, an actual value was known by Jack. You can implement this algorithm by defining all constants in the first belief space, so that all constants are defined in all belief spaces. A summary of the results of this algorithm is shown in Figure 15.3.

Another common form of knowledge is that someone knows whether a certain fact is true (yet the original agent doesn't know whether it's true or not). For example, Jack may believe that Sue knows whether she owns Fido or not. This might be represented as a disjunction of beliefs--that is, Jack believes that either Sue believes she owns Fido, or that Sue believes she doesn't own Fido. Thus a scoping distinction can be used to represent "knowing if." If a disjunction is within the belief operator

7. $BEL(SUE1, OWN(SUE1, FIDO2) \lor \neg OWN(SUE1, FIDO2))$

then Sue believes that either she owns Fido or she doesn't. This is almost certainly believed by Sue and by any other rational agent. The case with the disjunction outside the belief operator

8. $BEL(SUE1, OWN(SUE1, FIDO2)) \lor$
      $BEL(SUE1, \neg OWN(SUE1, FIDO2))$

represents that Sue knows whether she owns Fido or not. From now on, formula 8, and others like it, will be represented here using a special operator KNOWIF, as in KNOWIF(SUE1, OWN(SUE1, FIDO2)).

A possible approach to representing this in the belief space model would be to make two copies of the belief space representing Sue's belief and put one of the disjuncts in each. Anything that you then want to prove about Sue's beliefs would have to be proven in each. This approach is obviously impractical, since each time a disjunction is added, the number of belief spaces would need to be doubled.

You can deal with this limited case by turning to a new section of the knowledge base that includes the facts that an agent knows to be true or false. This section of the knowledge base is called the **knowif** database. It is not used during a regular retrieval, since it will not lead to any definite conclusion, but it can be used to prove facts about what an agent knows. The simplest proof method for showing that KNOWIF(A, P) holds would be first to try to prove BEL(A, P), and if that fails, try to prove BEL(A, ¬P), and finally, if that fails, to match P into the knowif database for A. While limited, this approach will allow you to pursue some interesting examples.

The final aspect is the most difficult to deal with, but ultimately it is far more important than the two forms of knowing discussed thus far. In fact the two preceding forms could be viewed as limited special cases of knowledge about what others know. In particular, what if your stereo is not working and you want to get help fixing it. You have knowledge that someone, such as Joe of Joe's Stereo Repair, can help you. Joe knows about fixing stereos and can tell you what you need to know. There are not necessarily any concrete propositions here for which you can assert that Joe knows if they are true or not. You may not even know the vocabulary to express these propositions. Yet you do have some belief about Joe's beliefs and knowledge that enable you to reason that Joe is the person to ask about your stereo.

Only very specialized and limited techniques have been developed so far to address this question. Typically this knowledge is embedded in heuristics that are hand-tailored to the expected user of the system. For example, for each action class, a system might explicitly represent what users know enough to be able to execute the action. Then the system could introduce action classes that are only partially described. For example, a (possibly partial) set of preconditions and effects could be defined for an action class FIX-STEREO, and yet the system may have no decomposition for such actions. It would then be asserted that Joe knows how to execute actions of the type FIX-STEREO. Thus, given a goal WORKING(S1), where S1 is a stereo, the system might find that FIX-STEREO is relevant since its effects match the goal, but it would not be able to decompose the action. It could then look up which agent it believes knows how to perform the action.

Even if such a technique could be made to work, there would still be problems in generalizing this type of reasoning to allow the system to infer such a fact from a conversation. For example, say the system does not know of any particular agent that knows how to fix stereos. But in a conversation Joe says *Last night I replaced a transistor in my amp*. The ideal system should be able to infer, or at least suspect, that Joe is likely to know how to fix stereos.

The action class INFORM(Speaker, Hearer, Proposition)
precondition: BEL(Speaker, Proposition)
effect: BEL(Hearer, Proposition)

Figure 15.4 A simple version of the INFORM speech act

15.3 Speech Acts and Plans

This section provides some concrete examples of how speech acts can be used in planning and plan recognition systems, producing a computational model of communication. Many of the difficult problems in speech act theory are left to be discussed in the next section.

Planning Speech Acts

Consider an example of Jack as he tries to execute a plan to buy a ticket for a train TR1 at the train station. Recall that the decomposition of the PURCHASE action involved three steps:

1.   GOTO(JACK1, CLERK)
2.   GIVE(JACK1, CLERK, Price(Ticket(TR1)))
3.   GIVE(CLERK, JACK1, Ticket(TR))

Jack may run into many potential problems as he tries to execute this plan. For example, he may not know the price of a ticket for TR1, and so he cannot execute step 2. This is an instance of a general constraint that has been ignored up until now. To execute any action, an agent must know the values of the parameters. One way of viewing this constraint is that there is a set of implicit preconditions on every action that the agent must know the value of the parameters. In many cases it is trivially satisfied in constructing the original plan. In this example, however, there is an implicit precondition

KNOWREF(JACK1, x, EQ(Price(Ticket(TR1)), x))

This then becomes a new goal for JACK1. Intuitively, he could achieve this goal in several ways. He could look up the price on a fare schedule, or he could ask someone who knows the price. This latter method involves language and so provides the example. The act that will achieve this goal is simply one where some agent who knows the price tells Jack. Call this speech act INFORM. An inform act might be defined as shown in Figure 15.4. As expected, there is a prerequisite that the speaker believes the proposition that is asserted, and the effect is that the hearer believes the proposition. In many cases a more complex definition of INFORM would be needed. In particular this definition forces the hearer to believe everything that is said, since there is no room for deliberation on the part of the hearer. Once an INFORM is done, the hearer's beliefs are automatically changed! But this simple version is quite adequate for the following examples.

All speech acts tend to have the same role structure--namely, the two conversants and the semantic content of the utterance, which is called the **propositional content**. The actual type of speech act is often referred to as the **illocutionary force**. The illocutionary force and the propositional content are independent of each other. For instance, Figure 15.5 shows three utterances with the same propositional content yet with differing illocutionary force.

Suppose Jack has reasoned that an INFORM act by the CLERK will achieve his goal. This problem is similar to the one discussed earlier with the BEL operator. In particular, since Jack doesn't know the price of the ticket yet, how can he describe the INFORM action that the CLERK should do? The answer is to introduce two additional inform acts used for planning that correspond to the KNOWREF and KNOWIF operators introduced earlier. These acts are defined in Figure 15.6.

Given the definitions stated earlier, Jack might have the following action in his plan to achieve the KNOWREF precondition of step 2:

INFORMREF(CLERK, JACK1, x, EQ(x, Price(Ticket(TR1))))

This, however, is an action by another agent. Thus Jack cannot execute this act but must wait for the clerk to execute it. But there is no reason why the clerk should know to execute this plan! Jack needs to do something to get the clerk to perform the appropriate act. The way this knowledge is incorporated into the plan reasoner is by using the implicit precondition trick again. On every action there is an implicit precondition, called the **want precondition**, which asserts that before any agent executes an action, he or she must intend to perform the act. When the planner is the agent of the action, this condition is trivially true since intending to do an act is defined as having that act in the plan that you are executing.

To incorporate this concept into the model, define a new operator WANT(Agent, Action) to mean that the Agent has the Action in his or her current plan. As you might expect, one way of causing another agent to want to do something is to request him or her to do it. A simple version of the REQUEST speech act is shown in Figure 15.7. As was also the case with the definition of INFORM earlier, a better definition of REQUEST would provide for the hearer to be able to decide whether to abide by the request or not. This definition, however, will be adequate to get across the major points.

If Jack then plans a request to accomplish the want precondition, his plan to enable step 2 in his plan looks as follows:

Utterance	Illocutionary Force
You ate my fish.	INFORM
Did you eat my fish?	QUESTION
Eat my fish!	REQUEST

Figure 15.5 Three utterances with the same propositional content

INFORMREF(Speaker, Hearer, x, P(x))
precondition: KNOWREF(Speaker, x, P(x))
effect: KNOWREF(Hearer, x, P(x))

INFORMIF(Speaker, Hearer, Proposition)
precondition: KNOWIF(Speaker, Proposition)
effect: KNOWIF(Hearer, Proposition)

Figure 15.6 The two variants of INFORM dealing with lack of knowledge

REQUEST(Speaker, Hearer, Action)
precondition: none
effect: WANT(Hearer, Action)

Figure 15.7 A simple definition of the REQUEST speech act

2.1   REQUEST(JACK1, CLERK,
          INFORMREF(CLERK, JACK1, x, EQ(x, Price(Ticket(TR1)))))

which has the effect

2.2   WANT(CLERK,
          INFORMREF(CLERK, JACK1, x, EQ(x, Price(Ticket(TR1)))))

which is an (implicit) precondition of

2.3   INFORMREF(CLERK, JACK1, x, EQ(x, Price(Ticket(TR1))))

which has the effect

2.4   KNOWREF(JACK1, x, Price(Ticket(TR1)))

which is an (implicit) precondition of

2.5   GIVE(JACK1, CLERK, Price(Ticket(TR1)))

Recognizing Speech Acts

Just as recognizing a plan from described actions was useful for modeling the structure of stories, recognizing the plan underlying another agent's utterances will be useful for identifying their intended meaning in conversation. For instance, suppose Jack had the plan described thus far. When executing the request (that is, step 2.1), he said, *How much is a ticket for the train to Rochester?* The system (say, playing the role of the clerk) could then use knowledge about the speech act definitions to recognize that Jack's plan was to take a trip to Rochester. As such, if there were other information relevant to the plan (say, all trains were cancelled today), this information could be included in the response to the question.

This plan recognition should be performed with respect to what (the system believes) are Jack's beliefs. Thus, suppose Jack believes there is a three o'clock train to Rochester, whereas in fact there isn't one until three-thirty. If Jack asks, *How much is a ticket for the three o'clock to Rochester?* the system could still recognize Jack's plan of taking the trip, even though it believes that no such train exists.

Thus the result of the plan recognition will be a plan that the system believes Jack has. To see this in a little more detail, consider the system as it recognizes the plan underlying the question *How much is a ticket for the train to Rochester?* The starting point is the observed speech act

> REQUEST(JACK1, CLERK,
>   INFORMREF(CLERK, JACK1, x, EQ(x, Price(Ticket(TR1)))))

together with additional beliefs implied by the sentence including

> BEL(JACK1, TO-LOC(TR1, ROC))

Using an algorithm based on the plan recognition methods introduced in the last chapter but relativized to Jack's beliefs, the system could construct an interpretation of Jack's plan analogous to the earlier plan in steps 2.2 to 2.5, and from 2.5 continue to recognize (via its decomposition) the act

> PURCHASE(JACK1, CLERK, Ticket(TR1))

and ultimately the act

> TAKE-TRIP(JACK1, TR1, ROC)

The final situation is shown in Figure 15.8.

TAKE-TRIP(JACK1, TR1, ROC)

↑ decomposition of

BUY(JACK1, CLERK, Ticket(TR1))

↑ decomposition of

GIVE(JACK1, CLERK, Price(Ticket(TR1)))

↑ enables

KNOWREF(JACK1, x, EQ(Price(Ticket(TR1)), x))

↑ effect

INFORMREF(CLERK, JACK1, x, EQ(Price(Ticket(TR1)), x))

↑ enables

WANT(JACK1, INFORMREF(CLERK, JACK1, x, EQ(Price(Ticket(TR1)), x)))

↑ effect

REQUEST(JACK1, CLERK, INFORMREF(JACK1, CLERK, x, EQ(Price(Ticket(TR1)), x)))

Figure 15.8 The plan recognized from *How much is a ticket on the train to Rochester?*

Selecting a Response

The benefit of this approach shows itself in the richer model it allows for selecting the appropriate answer. Rather than simply answering the question as asked, as a database query system might do, the system can generate an answer that it believes will best help Jack's overall goal. It could do this by anticipating his next actions--for instance, by executing some act that should occur next yet was not explicitly requested, or by inspecting the recognized plan for obstacles, such as parts of the plan that Jack will not be able to perform because of a lack of knowledge, or because of mistaken beliefs. This section will consider each class briefly in turn.

If the next action or actions to be executed in the plan are actions of the system, it could execute all of them rather than just the one explicitly requested. For example, in response to the earlier question about the ticket price, the clerk might not only perform the expected INFORM act (about the ticket price) but also might get out a ticket to give to Jack, since that is the next step in the plan that the clerk has to do. If the plan is defined such that a strict ordering of subactions is required (that is, Jack giving the money must proceed the clerk giving the ticket), then the clerk must wait for Jack's next act. If the plan is defined so that either order is acceptable, the clerk could give Jack the ticket immediately.

To find obstacles arising from lack of knowledge, the system checks each parameter of the upcoming actions in the plan to see if Jack knows their values. In particular, given a parameter p, it tests

BEL(CLERK, KNOWREF(JACK1, x, EQ(x, p)))

If this is false, then KNOWREF(JACK1, x, EQ(x, p)) is an obstacle. For example, the parameter Price(Ticket(TR1)) of the GIVE action would be found by this process. As another example, perhaps Jack, after getting the ticket, asks, *When does it leave?* In this case, giving the departure time of the train is one parameter explicitly indicated by the question. But another parameter might also be the train's departure location, which is needed to perform the GOTO step in the decomposition of the TAKE-TRIP plan. In this case the helpful answer might include both and the clerk might say, *At 6 PM from Gate 7.*

To find discrepancies between the two agents' beliefs, you can check each assumption underlying Jack's plan against the clerk's beliefs. For example, if p is an assumption underlying Jack's plan, you test BEL(CLERK, ¬p). If this is true, you mark the fact BEL(JACK1, p) as a discrepancy. What types of assumptions can be extracted from Jack's plan? These assumptions fall into two classes. Suppose in checking whether Jack knows the parameter values of the actions of the plan--that is, in checking KNOWREF(JACK1, x, EQ(p, x))--the system finds an explicit belief: Jack believes that p is equal to some value c. Then the system can check whether it believes p equals c as well. If not, this fact can be marked as a discrepancy. The other assumptions that are extractable are based on the assumption that Jack is a rational agent and thus has constructed a workable plan for good reason. In particular Jack should believe that the effects of the next action and its superactions up the decomposition hierarchy are not presently true. For example, given that the system recognized the plan in Figure 15.8, it could check the effects HAVE(JACK1, Ticket(TR1)) (the effect of the PURCHASE action) and IN(JACK1, ROC) (the effect of TAKE-TRIP). If it believes either of these to be true already, that would identify a discrepancy between its beliefs and Jack's beliefs.

Once the set of anticipated actions, obstacles, and discrepancies is derived, you can identify an appropriate answer. All possible responses, however, should not be considered equally. For example, if there is a discrepancy of beliefs between the system and the user, you should address these discrepancies rather than the other possibilities. Of course, if a discrepancy can be easily corrected, the answer might contain both the correction and other information. Within the possible responses found in the same class, you might also apply some relevance heuristic to select which ones are most appropriate. For example, you might address only those anticipated actions closest to the now point of the plan.

While only the simplest cases of this behavior are currently realizable, you can consider some interesting cases. For example, consider the example where Jack asks, *How much is a ticket for the three o'clock to Rochester?* in a situation where the next train to Rochester leaves at three-thirty. The following answers are possibilities:

1. Anticipated Actions:

   INFORMREF(CLERK, JACK1, y, EQ(Price(Ticket(TR1)), y))
   GIVE(CLERK, JACK1, Ticket(TR1))

2. KNOWREF Obstacles:

   KNOWREF(JACK1, x, EQ(Price(Ticket(TR1)), x))
       from the parameter of the action
   KNOWREF(JACK1, x, EQ(DepartLoc(TR1), x))
       from the GOTO step in the decomposition of the TAKE-TRIP act;

3. Discrepancies:

   BEL(JACK1, EQ(DepartTime(TR1), 3PM)), where no such train exists.

The system, as clerk, should select a response that corrects the discrepancy and then performs the anticipated action, such as: *There's no three o'clock train; the next one is at three-thirty. It costs twenty dollars.*

Much can be learned about Jack from the plan recognition process. Most obviously, Jack's goals and the method by which he is trying to achieve those goals are explicitly represented by the plan itself and can be retained as shared knowledge. In addition, many of his specific beliefs are reflected in the plan. For example, a method for detecting discrepancies between the system's and the user's beliefs was described earlier. Each assumption underlying the plan can be taken as a belief of the user. Furthermore, if such a belief is not contradicted by the system's beliefs and addressed in the response, it becomes part of the shared knowledge between the two agents. All this knowledge is then available for processing subsequent utterances.

Noun Phrase Sentence Fragments

Another area where this approach is useful is in dealing with utterances that consist of a single noun phrase. Actual dialogs collected in the train station setting showed that such fragments are quite common. For example, the clerk was asked, *The three-fifteen to Windsor?* He responded appropriately with the train's departure location. The intuition behind this is that the object described (the three-fifteen train) was sufficiently descriptive to identify the plan that the speaker had (take the train), and thus the clerk could respond on the basis of that plan using the same techniques described earlier. To actually handle such cases with the plan recognizer would require some extensions. In particular, the initial speech act analysis of this sentence would be that it is a request that the clerk do an INFORMREF of some property of the three-fifteen train to Windsor. To express this in the notation developed thus far, however, you would need to be able to quantify over "properties of objects." One approach is to allow quantification over the roles defined for an object class. Then the initial speech act is a request to do an INFORMREF of the value of some role value of the object described by *the three-fifteen train to Windsor*.

15.4 Speech Act Theory and Indirect Speech Acts

Speech act theory is a relatively recent development in the philosophy of language. It was developed to avoid some of the problems with the theories of semantics developed prior to the 1960s. At that time the prevailing theory was that the semantic content of a sentence was its truth value (just as is the semantics of a formula in FOPC). Thus a sentence such is *Snow is white* was said to be true or false depending on whether snow is actually white or not. While this presented at least a start of a theory for the semantics of assertions, it said nothing about requests or other acts such as warnings or promises, that cannot be said to be true or false. Rather you might say that a request or promise is sincere or insincere, or that it is successfully or unsuccessfully performed.

Consider an example of a sentence falling into the class of **explicit performatives**. These sentences explicitly name some act and, in doing so, perform the act. Thus, when an umpire says, *You're out*, you are out (by definition), or when the appropriate person at a ship-naming ceremony says, *I hereby name this ship the Beauregard*, the ship is named by this act. These utterances perform acts (such as calling out) because saying such sentences in the appropriate circumstances (such as being the umpire in an ongoing ball game) is defined to be the act. The performance of the utterance under the appropriate circumstances is said to **constitute** the performance of the act.

Note that there are potentially many actions that are performed when an utterance is made. The **locutionary** class of acts includes the acts of making a noise or saying words associated with the physical performance of the utterance. The **perlocutionary** class of acts includes acts that have effects beyond the speaker's control. For example, when saying something, a speaker might be overheard by Jack in the next room and thereby warn him that the speaker was nearby. In addition, Jack might be scared by this situation, since he is a fugitive from the law. Thus, while the utterance both warned and scared Jack, these acts are not the ones the speaker intended. The speech acts considered in this chapter, often called **illocutionary** acts, are the acts that the speaker intends to perform by making the utterance.

The earlier analysis of explicit performatives can be applied to more everyday speech acts such as requests and promises. Again, if the appropriate sentence is said (*I'll wash the dishes*) in the appropriate context (I intend to wash the dishes), the utterance constitutes the performance of a speech act (a promise). Defining speech acts then is reduced to defining the appropriate circumstances under which they are performed. This will consist of conditions on the speaker's beliefs and intentions, together with knowledge of the conventions of language.

For example, consider what the conditions might be to define the performance of a successful inform act that some proposition P is true. First, in order for P to be a sincere inform, the speaker must believe that P is true. Second, the speaker must say some utterance that could be expected to lead the hearer to believe P. You might think that these two conditions are enough, but simple counterexamples arise unless you add conditions on the intentions of the speaker. For example, Jack might lisp slightly, and thus when he introduces himself to Sue, she might come to believe that he lisps. Furthermore, Jack believes that he lisps, since he always has. Thus, if the preceding conditions were complete, whatever Jack said in this situation, he would have informed Sue that he lisped! You might object to this conclusion by pointing out that Jack didn't intend to get Sue to believe that he lisped. He merely intended to tell her his name. Thus there should be another condition on the inform act--that the speaker must intend that the utterance will lead the hearer to conclude P.

But even this is not a complete specification, since some counterexamples satisfy the preceding three conditions yet don't seem to be inform acts. For instance, Jack might believe that he knows very little about music and intends to say something that makes it obvious to Sue that he believes this. Thus he might ask, *What is a quarter note?* even though he actually does know about quarter notes. As a result of the question Sue may then believe that Jack knows little about music, just as Jack intended, but you would not say that Jack informed Sue that he knew little about music. What's missing here is that Jack didn't intend that Sue recognize his true purpose. Thus you must add a condition that the speaker must intend that the hearer recognize the utterance appropriately.

This can be summarized by the following: a speech act SA is successfully performed by a speaker S by saying an utterance U to a hearer H if and only if

1. The preconditions of SA hold (S believes P).

2. Saying U to H accomplishes the effects of SA (H believes P).

3. S intended that condition 2 would be the case (S intends to get H to believe P).

4. S intended that H would recognize S's intention in condition 3 (S intends that H recognize that S intends to get H to believe P).

You could construct further examples that show that condition 4 is not strong enough, and that you might have to add an indefinite number of conditions of the form (5) "S intends that H recognize S's intention in condition 4," and then

(6) "S intends that H recognize S's intention in condition 5," and so on. The way to avoid this annoying set of counterexamples is to recast conditions 1 to 4 so that a speech act is performed by an utterance U only if as a result of saying U, conditions 1 to 4 are shared knowledge between S and H.

Indirect Speech Acts and Helpful Responses

The last section described examples of helpful responses in which the hearer, after recognizing the speaker's plan, provided information that went beyond the response to the question taken literally. For example, in one case the clerk gave both the departure time and location rather than simply the departure time that was explicitly requested. In another case the speaker--say, Jack--might ask, *Do you know the departure gate of the train to Rochester?* and the clerk might recognize the plan shown in Figure 15.9.

This plan could be constructed using the plan recognition techniques discussed already with one exception. The plan recognizer would have to be able to consider the possible motivations behind a goal of the form KNOWIF(A, P). In general, an agent A may simply need to know whether P is true or not, or A has a plan that involves P as a precondition (that is, P must be true or must be false for their plan to succeed). The plan was constructed using the assumption that S wanted P to be true, or

$$KNOWREF(CLERK, x, EQ(DepartLoc(TR1), x))$$

Selecting the appropriate interpretation from these three choices can be aided by noting that S probably already knew the answer to the literal question when it was asked--that is, it is general background knowledge that the clerk knows the schedule information. Thus the literal interpretation doesn't lead to a reasonable plan (since its effects are already true).

When generating a response, the clerk might decide to tell Jack the gate number rather than simply state the literal response, which would be *yes*. Of course, in this setting that might be exactly the response Jack intended the clerk to give, and if Jack had intended the clerk to recognize that this was the desired response, then Jack's utterance would satisfy the conditions needed for a successful request for the departure location. In other words Jack performed one speech act (the request for the departure location) by performing an act that literally is only a question about whether the clerk knows the departure gate. This is called an **indirect speech act**.

In another setting, if Jack and Sue are fellow passengers in the station, and Jack has no idea whether Sue knows the information, then Jack might have intended the same question literally. Still, if Sue recognized the plan in Figure 15.9 as Jack's plan, she might still tell Jack the departure gate as the response.

TAKE-TRIP(JACK1, TR1, ROC)

↑ part of

GOTO(JACK1, DepartLoc(TR1))

↑ enables

KNOWREF(JACK1, EQ(DepartLoc(TR1), x))

↑ effect of

INFORMREF(CLERK, JACK1, x, EQ(DepartTime(TR1), x))

↑ enables

KNOWREF(CLERK, x, EQ(DepartLoc(TR1), x))

↑ enables (assuming *yes*)

KNOWIF(JACK1, KNOWREF(CLERK, x, EQ(DepartLoc(TR1), x)))

↑ effect of

INFORMIF(CLERK, JACK1, KNOWREF(CLERK, x, EQ(DepartLoc(TR1), x)))

↑ enables

WANT(CLERK, INFORMIF(CLERK, JACK1,
KNOWREF(CLERK, x, EQ(DepartLoc(TR1), x))))

↑ effect of

REQUEST(JACK1, CLERK, INFORMIF(CLERK, JACK1,
KNOWREF(CLERK, x, EQ(DepartLoc(TR1), x))))

Figure 15.9 The plan recognized from *Do you know the departure gate of the train to Rochester?*

In this case, however, it doesn't satisfy the conditions to be a request for the departure gate and is classified as a helpful response.

How can this difference be captured in the plan recognition model? The difference between the two cases depends on what the speaker intends and what the hearer recognizes as the speaker's intentions. This distinction is captured by using the following assumption:

> Any plan that the hearer can recognize using only shared knowledge, the speaker intends the hearer to recognize.

In other words, if the preceding plan was recognized using only shared knowledge, the utterance was an indirect speech act, and the hearer is obliged to give the departure location in the answer. On the other hand, if recognizing the plan used nonshared knowledge (such as particular beliefs of the hearer), the utterance is not an indirect speech act and the hearer may answer it literally, although he or she may also choose to perform the helpful response.

When constructing a system that always attempts to be helpful, you might conclude that it is not necessary to recognize that an indirect interpretation is intended. To some extent this is true, but making the distinction still remains important in cases where some action cannot be performed. If the action was requested via an indirect speech act, the hearer is obliged to give some reason why the action is not performed. If the action was merely suggested as a helpful response, the hearer can simply ignore it and answer the speaker's request literally.

15.5 Speech Acts and Discourse Structure

The last two sections described techniques for recognizing the intentions behind single utterances. Apparently such intentions could be generalized from single utterances to entire discourse segments, and from segments to an intention underlying an entire discourse. For instance, consider the intentions underlying the following short speech by a hypothetical politician:

5.1   I am an honest man.
5.2   I returned all the money that I received from organized crime,
5.3   and I refused money from people who wanted favors in return.
5.4   My opponent, on the other hand, is dishonest.
5.5   He stole money from the orphans' fund last year.
5.6   In conclusion, you should vote for me.

The immediate intention underlying all of these sentences is to get the hearer to believe the particular facts stated, but much more is going on. In particular the segment made up of clauses 5.2 and 5.3 (marked by the past tense) is a series of instances supporting the claim in sentence 5.1. In addition, utterance 5.5 is given as support for the claim in sentence 5.4. Finally, claims 5.1 and 5.4 are used as support for the overall intended conclusion of the speech, which is given explicitly in the last sentence, 5.6. Thus the segment hierarchy and a representation of the structure of the argument are very similar. A comparison is shown in Figure 15.10.

This suggests that the intentional structure and the segment structure can be closely related. They could not be made to be identical, however. In particular, the speech might contain digressions that do not serve the overall purpose or are only very indirectly related. While these segments would arise in the segment tree in the expected manner, they might have no correlate in the intentional structure. In fact, a single discourse might have several different intentional structures, each accounting for a subpart of the discourse. Thus, while the segment structure and the intentional structure are not identical, they are obviously closely related and may impose constraints on each other.

To explore this relationship, you must do two things. First, you have to generalize the notion of intention from a speech act representing the intention underlying a single utterance to some representation of the intention underlying a segment. Second, you have to identify any constraints between the segment stack and the discourse intentions.

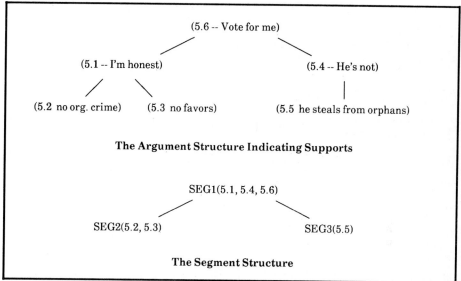

Figure 15.10 The argument and segment structure of the speech

On the first issue, each segment will be extended to have a **purpose**. For a segment consisting of a single speech act, this is the same as the effect of the speech act that produced the sentence. For larger segments, you must define larger discourse actions. For example, a segment might consist of a question-answering exchange to obtain some information. You could define a discourse act, such as ASKREF in Figure 15.11. A segment that realizes this act would involve a question (the REQUEST) followed by a reply (the INFORMREF). The purpose of the segment would be the effect--KNOWREF(S, x, P(x)). The purpose of the subsegment involving the REQUEST would be to get H to want to perform the INFORMREF, and so on.

With this in hand, you can state a constraint between the segment purpose and the stack structure. In particular if the purpose of a segment A is part of the purpose of a segment B, then segment B is said to **dominate** segment A. The main constraint is then as follows:

> If a segment B dominates a segment A, then B must be above A in the segment stack.

This means that when A is on the segment stack, B must also be on the stack below it. Such a constraint can be used in both directions. If the segment tracker identifies a dominance relationship between two segments, this information constrains the plan reasoner to find the relationship between the two using decomposition chaining. On the other hand, if the plan reasoner can recognize that the action that is the purpose of the new segment, NS, is part of

```
Action Class ASKREF(S, H, x, P(x))

precondition: KNOWREF(H, x, P(x))
effect: KNOWREF(S, x, P(x))
decomposition: REQUEST(S, H, INFORMREF(H, S, x, P(x))) →
                INFORMREF(S, H, x, P(x))
```

Figure 15.11 The discourse act ASKREF

the action described in the purpose of a preceding segment, PS, this information constrains the segment tracking to place NS above PS on the segment stack (that is, it cannot pop PS off the stack, but it may pop segments that are above PS on the stack).

How can the segment reasoner identify a dominance relationship? The most obvious way is by using certain cue phrases. As mentioned earlier, a cue phrase, in addition to signaling a sentence boundary, may also give information as to how two segments are related. The cue phrases *for example* and *first* both signal that the new segment is dominated by the immediately preceding segment, whereas *second, third, finally,* and *furthermore* all signal that the immediately preceding segment is ended but that the new segment is dominated by the segment lower on the stack that dominates the immediately preceding segment.

In addition, the segment reasoner can also identify situations where there is not going to be a dominance relationship with an existing segment on the stack. These cases are digressions, where some objects mentioned previously may become the focus of a new, otherwise unrelated, discussion, and interruptions, where there is no connection at all between the new segment and the preceding ones. In these cases it is important not to use the plan reasoner at all, lest you make unintended connections. Cue phrases that signal digressions include *by the way* and *did you hear about*, whereas a cue phrase signaling an interruption is the explicit sentence *Allow me to interrupt for a moment.*

Some of you may have noticed that in domains where the content of the discourse is modeled by a plan, there are now two plans involved in the analysis: the domain plan, as described in Chapter 13, and the discourse plan, as described here. The plans constructed during the speech act analysis earlier in this chapter would now be divided into two separate plans. For example, the information in the plan in Figure 15.8, underlying the question *How much is a ticket on the train to Rochester?* would now be represented as two plans, as shown in Figure 15.12. The clerk's reply will then be interpreted as being part of the same segment as the question, since it realizes the next step in the ASKREF plan.

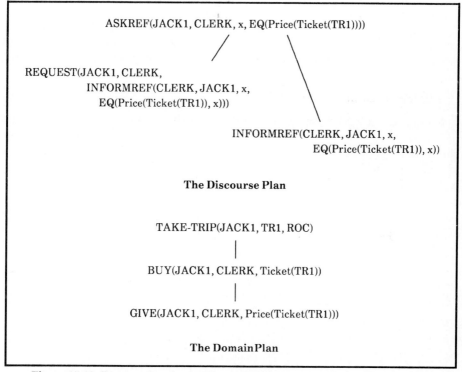

Figure 15.12 Representing the situation using a discourse plan and a domain plan

15.6 Formal Models of Belief and Knowledge

The formal properties of belief have been the subject of considerable investigation in philosophy. This section provides a quick overview of the most influential model, based on the possible worlds semantics. This theory can be used to define more formally the belief space model described earlier and to identify its weaknesses precisely. Some work has also been done in developing a computational model of belief directly based on the possible worlds semantics (see Box 15.1).

Belief as a Modal Operator

Incorporating a belief operator formally into a first-order logic is considerably more complex than you might first think. Consider what tools standard FOPC gives you. There are terms (such as functions, variables, and constants) that represent objects in some domain D and there are predicates that represent sets of objects over D (for example, the predicate name RED represents the set of all red objects in D). Formulas are made up of simple propositions, constructed by applying a predicate to a set of arguments, and complex propositions, built from the logical operators (such as &, ∨, ¬) that combine simple propositions and produce a new truth value. Finally, the quantifiers use propositions involving variables to make assertions about the objects in the domain. A more formal treatment of the semantics of FOPC is given in Appendix A and so is not repeated here.

Consider where the BEL construct might fit. It is not a term, since it is used to construct assertions that are true and false rather than denoting some object in the domain. Likewise, BEL is not a predicate name, since it does not take an object in the domain as an argument. Rather, BEL takes a proposition as an argument, which in turn denotes a truth value. The only option left is that BEL is like a logical operator. While both BEL and the logical operators take propositions as arguments, the logical operators have an important property called **truth functionality**. This means that their definition is strictly in terms of the truth value of their arguments. The BEL operator is not truth functional.

Consider an example. If propositions P and Q are true, any complex formula that also is true will remain true even if you replaced an occurrence of P with one of Q. Thus, if (P & R) is true, so must be (Q & R). This is simply because the logical operators are affected only by the truth values of their arguments. The BEL operator, however, doesn't behave this way at all. If the formula BEL(SAM1, P) is true--that is, Sam believes P--Jack need not believe Q--that is, BEL(SAM1, Q). Thus the BEL operator is not truth functional and is a completely different kind of operator than present in the FOPC. Such operators, which are called **modal operators**, are needed for many other constructs besides belief. Examples include the possibility operator (such as it is possible that P is true), the want operator (Jack wants to own a horse), and the future tense operator (P will be true).

Assume you can extend FOPC with modal operators. What axioms would you then consider for the BEL operator? The following is a set commonly used for belief (ignoring the quantifiers for the moment):

B1.   If an agent believes that P implies Q, and the agent believes P, then the agent believes Q:

$$(BEL(A, P \supset Q) \& BEL(A, P)) \supset BEL(A, Q)$$

B2.   If an agent believes ¬P, then he or she does not believe P:

$$BEL(A, \neg P) \supset \neg BEL(A, P)$$

B3.   If A believes P and Q, then A believes P and A believes Q, and vice versa:

$$BEL(A, P\&Q) \Leftrightarrow BEL(A, P) \& BEL(A, Q)$$

B4.   If A believes P or A believes Q, then A believes P or Q, but NOT
vice versa:

$$(BEL(A, P) \lor BEL(A, Q)) \supset BEL(A, P \lor Q)$$

Possible World Semantics

To assign a semantics to the belief operator you have to extend the standard
Tarskian semantics (see Appendix A) with a concept of possible worlds and
introduce truth relative to these worlds. A **possible world** is a complete
description of the way the world might be (or might have been). One of these
possible worlds is the actual world, and the others can be seen as variations from
that, starting from worlds where the changes are minor (I didn't eat pizza for
lunch), to those where the changes are major (The Roman Empire never
collapsed). The only constraint on what a world can be is that it must be
logically consistent.

You then define truth relative to a world. A proposition P is true in a world w
only if P holds in that world. Given any set of consistent propositions, there will
be a set of worlds that agree with that set on every count but vary in ways not
described by the propositions. The intuition for modeling beliefs is that there is a
(potentially infinite) set of possible worlds consistent with what an agent
actually believes about the actual world. If a proposition P is true in every one of
these worlds, you say that the agent believes P. All that is left to do now is
describe a mechanism for specifying the set of worlds consistent with some
agent's beliefs. Given that you want to model nested beliefs, this technique must
itself be relative to some possible world.

You define a relation between worlds called the **accessibility relation**. The
relation R(A, w1, w2) holds if relative to world w1, world w2 is consistent with
what A believes. You can now define the semantics for the BEL operator more
precisely. In particular,

A formula BEL(A, P) is true in a world w0, if for all worlds w
accessible from w0--that is, worlds such that R(A, w0, w)--P is true
in w.

Consider the conditions for a doubly nested formula BEL(A, BEL(B, P)) to be
true in a world w0. Essentially, it is true if for all worlds w1 such that
R(A, w0, w1) and for all worlds w2 such that R(B, w1, w2), P holds in w2. In
other words, starting at world w0, in all worlds that can be reached by following
an A accessibility relation followed by a B accessibility relation, P is true.

The possible world semantics can be used to define a wide range of modal
operators, as well as defining different possible versions of the same operator.

There is in fact a close correspondence to the properties of the R relation and to the axioms for the modal operator.

For example, if R is reflexive--that is, R(A, w, w) for any w--this has the consequence of validating the axiom that if A believes some proposition P, then P must be true:

BEL(A, P) ⊃ P

This is obviously inappropriate for a realistic model of belief, since you must allow cases where an agent might be mistaken, or change his or her mind. Such an axiom, together with the semantic constraint of reflexivity, does seem appropriate for the necessity operator (if P is necessarily true, then P is true) and has also been used for formal models of knowledge as opposed to belief (if A knows that P is true, then P is true).

If R is transitive (that is, if R(A, w0, w1) and R(A, w1, w2), then R(A, w0, w2)), it validates an axiom that if A believes that A believes P, then A believes P:

BEL(A, BEL(A, P)) ⊃ BEL(A, P)

This seems reasonable for a model of belief.

Quantification and Belief

The most tricky part of developing a formal semantics for belief is in dealing with the quantifiers. The semantics has to make sense of propositions such as $\exists x . BEL(A, P(x))$. Given the semantics sketched earlier, this formula is true in some world w, if there is an object O in w such that for all w' where R(A, w, w'), P(O) is true. For this to make sense at all, the object O, which exists in w, must also exist in all the worlds accessible from w. If you look at an example with a universal quantifier with scope wider than a belief operator, this same argument says that all objects in a world w must exist in all worlds accessible from w. This can be introduced as a constraint on the domains of all possible worlds. Thus, when accessibility links are followed, the domain of objects that exist can only get larger.

Is anything else needed to ensure that a formula such as $\exists x . BEL(A, AGE(A, x))$ represents the concept that A knows what A's age is? There is no restriction so far that an object in one world, such as the age 22, might not map to a different age in each world accessible from that world. To avoid this, you need to be able to fix the referent of certain terms no matter what world you are in. Such terms, called **rigid designators**, are essential for providing the intuition for knowing what an object is. That is, an agent A knows an object O in a world w, if in all worlds accessible from w, O denotes the same object.

Conversely, if O changes referent in some worlds compatible with A's beliefs, then A does not know O. For example, if in some worlds compatible with A's beliefs, A is 23, and in others A is 24, then A does not know his or her age.

The Problem of Deductive Closure

The preceding formal model has one serious flaw as a model of belief. It is unavoidable in such models that if some proposition P logically follows from an agent's beliefs, then that agent believes P. In other words, since most of mathematics can be derived from set theory, if an agent A knows the axioms of set theory, then A should then know all the theorems of mathematics. This is unavoidable given the possible world semantics, since each possible world is a complete, logically-consistent universe. Thus, if the axioms of set theory are true in each world consistent with an agent's beliefs, all the consequences of those axioms are also true in each world.

At best, then, these formal models capture what an ideal agent could potentially believe given its present state of belief. Thus if A believes the axioms of set theory, then potentially A could derive all of mathematics without having to be told any new facts! Another common way of describing this is that the model captures that set of propositions that the agent could be led to prove given the appropriate line of reasoning.

In practice, any implementation directly based on the possible world semantics would be inherently limited in the set of beliefs that it could actually prove. Thus you could claim that the system is a better model of human performance: if it can prove P from its explicit beliefs--that is, those in its database--then it believes P; otherwise it doesn't, even though it could potentially prove P if given enough time. This has led to a new area of work highly relevant to modeling beliefs: Given that you must work with incomplete reasoning systems, can you precisely define the set of inferences that the system will make?

Many suggestions have been made along these lines. One technique is to impose resource limitations of the inference process. For example, you might allow only proofs consisting of five steps or less. A problem with this is that it is hard to characterize semantically the set of consequences of a given set of facts. You could have two different sets of axioms that are formally equivalent--that is, they express exactly the same set of truths--thus the semantic models for each are identical. The set of derivable consequences, however, might differ drastically simply because of the syntactic differences in the axioms.

Another technique is to restrict the expressive power of the representation language so that all inferences can be efficiently computed. If you took this approach, however, you would not be able to express the meaning of all English sentences precisely, since such a language would be inherently less expressive than FOPC, which you already know is inadequate for some areas of meaning representation.

A promising approach is to weaken the set of inference rules so that the consequences are efficiently computed. To do this precisely, you need to give this weaker representation a correspondingly weaker semantics. The trick is, however, still to attach the full semantics to the individual facts in the database yet use the weakened semantics for describing what consequences can be computed.

Summary

This chapter introduced a technique for modeling the beliefs of different agents and then used this to develop a computational model of speech acts. Because speech acts can be defined using the same representation for actions as used in the previous chapters, it provides a richer model of the process of communication. An agent has a goal, and in pursuing that goal, plans some speech acts. The hearer, in the process of identifying the intended speech acts, may reconstruct at least some of the speaker's original goals. Such a model provides a promising start for recognizing indirection in language, and for producing an appropriate response.

Related Work and Further Readings

The database belief model described uses the techniques suggested by Moore (1973) and developed in detail by Cohen (1978). Cohen used the partitioned semantic networks framework of (Hendrix, 1975) to create separate belief spaces of semantic net structures representing beliefs. The belief spaces themselves were objects in the network, and thus the "belief" links between the belief spaces could be represented within the same formalism. He developed procedures from adding and testing beliefs similar to those described in Section 15.2. The resulting system was further refined and used in a system for recognizing speech acts by Allen and Perrault (1980).

The formal model of belief described in Section 15.6 is derived from that suggested by Hintikka and defined by him using a possible world semantics (Hintikka, 1969) based on that developed by Kripke (1963). A good text on modal logic and the possible world semantics is Hughes and Cresswell (1968). The necessity for mutual beliefs or shared knowledge is discussed in detail by Schiffer (1972) and Strawson (1971) in philosophy, and later used for problems of reference by Perrault and Cohen (1981) and Clark and Marshall (1981).

The distinction between explicit beliefs and implicit beliefs is made by Levesque (1984). He develops a logic of explicit belief (the propositions you actually believe) based on a weakened set of inference rules, where the implicit beliefs (the propositions you could consistently believe) would be the deductive

BOX 15.1   Implementations of Belief Based on Formal Models

Moore (1977) produced an implementable theory of knowledge by axiomatizing its possible world semantics as a first-order theory and implementing a theorem prover using that logic.   To prove some assertion--say, KNOW(JACK1, EQ(Mother(JACK1), SUE1))--he would first translate the statement into its equivalent statement in the possible world semantics, which would look like the following assertion, where W0 stands for the actual world, the variable w ranges over possible worlds, the predicate TRUE(p, w) asserts that proposition p is true in world w, and K is the accessibility relation between worlds (that is, K(A, w, w') means that world w' is compatible with what agent A knows in world w):

$$\forall\, w \,.\, K(JACK1, W0, w) \supset TRUE(EQ(Mother(JACK1), SUE1), w)$$

This, together with his axiomatization of the possible world semantics, would be the set of facts that a standard first-order theorem prover would use. After the proof was completed, the result would be retranslated back into the original language containing the KNOW operator. Moore's framework is also notable for its integration of the preceding logic of knowledge with a logic of action based on the situation calculus (McCarthy and Hayes, 1969), creating a framework in which the rich interaction between knowledge and action could be explored. For example, he could construct plans that involved acquiring knowledge during the execution of the plan and prove that they would work.

Other formalizations of knowledge and belief have defined the belief operator as a normal first-order predicate in a logic extended to allow quotation. Thus the fact that Jack believes that his mother is Sue might be expressed as:

$$BEL(JACK1, \text{"}EQ(Mother(JACK1), SUE1)\text{"})$$

where "EQ(Mother(JACK1), SUE1)" is a legal term in the logic that denotes the expression *EQ(Mother(JACK1), SUE1)*. Defining such a logic is not without its problems, however, since you can easily construct a language that is inherently inconsistent--that is, there are formulas that deny their own truthhood. Such a formula could be true only if it was in fact false, and vice versa. Perlis (1985) showed how to avoid this problem, however, and Haas (1986) used this approach for modeling beliefs. A similar approach is used by Konolige (1985), who investigates ways in which deductive closure of beliefs can be formally avoided.

closure of the beliefs given their normal first-order semantics. Frisch (1985) and Patel-Schneider (1986) have developed more powerful logics that still remain computationally tractable. In addition, they develop techniques for allowing certain forms of inference (such as inheritance of properties) to be retained in the weakened logic.

Austin (1962) introduced the concept of speech acts. He considered only explicit performatives for the most part. Searle started from this work and used a theory of communication developed by Grice (1957) to develop a speech act theory for everyday acts such as informs, requests, and promises. Grice argued that the essential requirement for communication to occur is the speaker's intention to communicate and the hearer's recognition of that intention. Grice (1975) also introduced a set of guiding principles that underlie all communication. These principles, while not specific enough to be directly used in a computational model of communication, provide motivation and justification for a wide range of phenomena in language, especially in the area of implicature.

A plan-based model of speech acts was suggested by Bruce (1975) and developed in a series of papers, starting with (Cohen and Perrault, 1979). This paper lays out the general principles of the approach and shows how speech acts can be planned in order to achieve goals using standard planning techniques. Allen and Perrault (1980) used the same model and applied it to question answering. They showed how to generate helpful responses to questions and how to reason about NP fragment questions.

Pollack (forthcoming) has relaxed some of the assumptions that underlie the earlier models and allows misconceptions to be recognized. For example, the earlier approaches all assumed that the action definitions were shared knowledge, so there could be no disagreement or uncertainty about how actions could be performed. Pollack's model explicitly handles such misconceptions.

Perrault and Allen (1980) develop the computational model of indirect speech acts described in this chapter, drawing on the work by Searle (1975). Note that in this framework the indirect speech act is actually recognized as part of the speaker's plan. More recently, other authors have argued that an actual act representing the indirect speech act need not be present in the recognized plan at all. If the plan otherwise satisfies the requirements in the definition of the speech act, the speaker performed that act whether or not it is physically present in the plan. This approach solves some technical problems relating to how a single utterance may realize multiple speech acts, and how multiple utterances might realize a single speech act. This approach is described in detail in Cohen and Levesque (1985).

The generalization of speech acts to discourse structure is based on work by Litman and Allen (1987) and Grosz and Sidner (1986). Litman and Allen describe a representation with separate discourse plans and domain plans. Grosz and Sidner investigate the relationship between the intentional structure of discourse and the segment stack.

Exercises for Chapter 15

1. *(easy)* Give an English statement or question corresponding to each of the following formulas. What is the answer to each question?

    Add BEL(JACK1, HAPPY(SUE1))
            BEL(JACK1, BEL(SUE1, $\neg$HAPPY(SUE1)))
            BEL(JACK1, $\exists$ x . BEL(SUE1, AGE(SUE1, x)))
            BEL(JACK1, BEL(SUE1, $\exists$ x . OWNS(JACK1, x)))

    Test BEL(JACK1, $\exists$ x . HAPPY(x))
            BEL(JACK1, $\exists$ x . BEL(SUE1, $\neg$HAPPY(x)))
            $\exists$ x . BEL(JACK1, BEL(SUE1, AGE(SUE1, x)))
            BEL(JACK1, BEL(SUE1, $\exists$ x . AGE(SUE1, x)))
            BEL(JACK1, $\exists$ x . BEL(SUE1, OWNS(JACK1, x)))

2. *(hard)* Write a program for adding and testing simple beliefs (such as literals), based on the algorithm descriptions in Section 15.2. Trace its operation in adding and testing the formulas corresponding to the facts in Exercise 1.

PART IV

RESPONSE GENERATION

Chapter 16

Question-Answering Systems

Chapter 17

Generating Natural Language

Chapter 16

Question-Answering Systems

In Chapter 15, one of the main motivations for the speech act model was that it allowed the system to produce more natural responses. The principal technique used there was to reason explicitly about the speaker's intentions and then to select a response that was helpful with respect to these intentions. These techniques have been developed in experimental systems and so far have proved to be too computationally expensive for use in practical systems. This chapter examines some of the techniques used in practical question-answering systems. Current question-answering systems use many of the techniques for syntactic and semantic processing described in the first two parts of this book, so this chapter will concentrate on the process of finding appropriate answers to questions.

One of the most influential techniques, based on a procedural semantics, is described in Section 16.1. The next two sections provide case studies of two actual systems. The first, LUNAR, is based on the procedural semantics approach, and the second, CHAT-80, uses an extended Horn clause proof method.

Sections 16.4 and 16.5 then address some issues in making such systems more useful. In particular some simple techniques for recognizing misconceptions underlying a question are examined. While a full analysis of these problems requires the use of belief models and plan recognition, some simpler techniques can be useful in the simple data base applications.

16.1 Procedural Semantics

The most common application of natural language systems today is in the construction of interfaces to database systems. These systems offer the simplest view of context: There is a fixed database of knowledge that does not change, and the interpretation of any given sentence is virtually independent of the interpretation of preceding sentences. In other words the system does not acquire any information from the input in order to maintain a "conversational context." As such the natural language is viewed simply as a convenient query language for the database, and the system's only task is to map sentences into an actual database query.

In these systems there has to be some way of mapping the results of parsing a question into a possibly complex series of database queries. One influential technique is based on an intermediate representation that is close to a logical form yet in fact can be interpreted as a program. This method is generally called a **procedural semantics**. This section develops one example of such a representation and shows how it can be used in question answering.

A Procedural Representation of Queries

The intermediate language looks like a variant of FOPC with typed variables. Consisting of relations, types, terms, and quantifiers, it uses the nesting of quantifiers to indicate scope. Any quantified formula is of the form

>   *(FOR quantifier var type restrictions; formula)*

Both the restrictions and the formula may be other quantified formulas or may be simple relations. The procedural representation of the question *What flight arriving in Chicago before 10 AM serves breakfast?* would be

>   (FOR SOME t TIME (BEFORE t 10AM);
>   (FOR WH f FLIGHT (ATIME f CHI t);
>   (BREAKFAST f)))

Here, the relation (BEFORE t 10AM) asserts that the time t is before 10 AM, (ATIME f CHI t) asserts that flight f arrives in Chicago at time t, and (BREAKFAST f) asserts that f serves breakfast.

Such a representation could be generated from the logical form using techniques described earlier in the book. The constraints on quantifier ordering described in Chapter 10 could be used to determine the allowable quantifier nestings, and mapping tables could relate the word sense/case role representation into database relations. In addition, proper names could be mapped to the appropriate constants in the database. All other reference issues, however, are left for the procedural interpretation to handle. For example, the question *When does the flight arrive in Chicago?* would map to a procedure such as

>   (FOR THE f FLIGHT;
>   (FOR WH t TIME;
>   (ATIME f CHI t)))

The referent for *the flight* will be determined when the quantified statement involving the quantifier THE is executed.

Before the details of executing this language are described, a simple database system needs to be defined. The one here represents flight information and provides a very simple interface based on pattern matching. The database of facts is shown in Figure 16.1. This database system provides a simple interface for retrieving relations using a simple pattern matching. The query

>   *(Retrieve varname formula₁ ... formulaₙ)*

```
(TYPE F1 FLIGHT), (TYPE F2 FLIGHT)
(TYPE CHI AIRPORT), (TYPE BOS AIRPORT)
(TYPE 4PM TIME), (TYPE 5PM TIME), ...
(ATIME F1 CHI 5PM) -              arrival time of flight F1 in Chicago is 5 PM
(ATIME F2 CHI 10 AM)
(ATIME F3 CHI 9AM)
(DTIME F1 BOS 4PM) -              departure time of F1 from Boston is 4 PM
(DTIME F2 BOS 9AM)
(DTIME F3 BOS 8AM)
(CONNECT F1 BOS CHI) -            flight F1 goes from Boston to Chicago
(CONNECT F2 BOS CHI)
(RUN-BY F1 SLOTH-AIR) -           flight F1 is run by SLOTH airways
(RUN-BY F2 SLOTH-AIR)
(RUN-BY F3 SLOTH-AIR)
(BEFORE 10AM 11AM) -              10 AM is before 11 AM
```

Figure 16.1 A simple database for an airline schedule

Query	Response
What flights arrive in Chicago? (Retrieve ?v (ATIME ?v CHI ?t))	(F1 F2)
What flight arrives in Chicago at 10 PM? (Retrieve ?f (ATIME ?f CHI 10AM))	(F2)
What flights leave at 4 from any airport? (Retrieve ?x (DTIME ?x ?y 4PM))	(F1)
What flight arrives in Chicago before 11 AM? (Retrieve ?y (ATIME ?y CHI ?t) (BEFORE ?t 11AM))	(F2)

Figure 16.2 Sample queries

returns all the possible bindings for the variable such that all the formulas listed are present in the database. Sample queries and the resulting answers, given the database in Figure 16.1, are shown in Figure 16.2. The only other basic operation on the database is a simple test for a relation, which is essentially a retrieve without any variable. Thus the query

(*Test formula$_1$ ... formula$_n$*)

returns true only if the specified formulas are all present in the database.

The Interpretation of Quantifiers

The real power of this approach arises from the procedural interpretation of the natural language quantifiers, which are compiled into more complex retrieval programs. For example,

(FOR DEF/SING f FLIGHT (ATIME f CHI 10AM);
    statement)

is executed by the following procedure:

1. Find all flights f that arrive in Chicago at 10 AM (that is, (Retrieve ?x (TYPE ?x FLIGHT) & (ATIME ?x CHI 10AM))).

2. If there was a single flight f found in step 1, then execute the statement with symbol f replaced by the value found in 1.

3. If there was no value found in step 1, or more than one, then fail.

For instance, the query *Is the flight arriving in Chicago at 10 AM late?* might map to the form

(FOR DEF/SING f FLIGHT (ATIME f CHI 10AM); (LATE f))

As this query is executed in step 1, the database is queried to find all flights that arrive in Chicago at 10 AM:

(Retrieve ?x (TYPE ?x FLIGHT) (ATIME ?x CHI 10AM))

This query returns the answer (F2). Since this is a single answer, step 2 involves testing for the formula

(LATE F2)

which would succeed (and possibly print out the answer *yes*).

The standard quantifiers are treated in a similar way. The program for ALL performs a retrieval to find all objects in the database satisfying the description and then executes the embedded statement multiple times, once for each value found. For example, the query *Are all flights arriving in Chicago at 10 AM late?* would be represented by

(FOR ALL f FLIGHT (ATIME f CHI 10AM);
    (LATE f))

This can be executed in much the same way as the previous example. Only in this case the query succeeds even if there is more than one answer found in step

To execute (FOR DEF/SING x T (R x); (P x)):   To execute (FOR ALL x T (R x); (P x)):

  1. Refs ← Gather (T, (R x))   1. Refs ← Gather (T, R x))
  2. **If** number of Refs ≠ 1   2. **If** Refs = nil
      then return failure   **then** return failure
      else For the r ∈ Refs   **else** For each r ∈ Refs
         If execute (P r) succeeds   **If** execute (P r) fails
            then return success   **then** return failure
            else return failure   3. Return success

To execute (FOR SOME x T (R x); (P x)):   The procedure Gather collects all objects
                                   satisfying a given description:
  1. Refs ← Gather (T, (R x))
  2. **If** Refs = nil   Gather (T, (R x))
      then return failure
      else For each r ∈ Refs   1. List ← (Retrieve ?x (TYPE ?x T))
         If execute (P r) succeeds   2. For each l ∈ List
            then return success   **If** (Test (R l)) succeeds
  3. Return failure   **then** add l to FinalList
                                3. Return FinalList

Figure 16.3 The procedures for three quantified formulas

1. The program for ALL repeatedly performs the test (LATE f) for each answer found in step 1 and succeeds only if all the individual tests succeed.

Details on these quantifiers are found in the algorithm shown in Figure 16.3. As expected, the procedure of DEF/SING succeeds only if there is a single referent found and the referent satisfies the predication P. The procedure for ALL succeeds if any number of referents are found, all of which satisfy P, while the procedure for SOME succeeds if any number of referents are found, and at least one of them satisfies P.

Nested quantifiers behave in the expected manner. For example, consider executing the following query:

    (FOR SOME f FLIGHT (CONNECT f BOS CHI);
      (FOR DEF/SING t TIME (DTIME f BOS t);
        (EQUAL t 9AM)))

To execute the SOME structure, the system gathers all flights from Boston to Chicago, returning the flights (F1 F2). In step 2 of the procedure for SOME, the remainder of the expression is executed for each flight in turn until one succeeds. The first expression, after substituting F1 for f, is

    (FOR DEF/SING t TIME (DTIME F1 BOS t);
      (EQUAL t 9AM))

This checks whether the departure time of F1 (4PM) is equal to 9AM, and fails. Next the form

    (FOR DEF/SING t TIME (DTIME F2 BOS t);
        (EQUAL t 9AM))

is executed and succeeds, yielding an answer of *yes* to the query.

Now consider how wh-questions are handled. The procedure for a form such as

    (FOR WH x T (R x) ; (P x))

could be

1. Refs ← Gather (T, (R x) & (P x))

2. Printout Refs

Essentially, the system simply finds all objects in the database that satisfy both the restrictions and the predication, and prints them out as the answer.

Consider the query *When does each flight for Chicago leave Boston?* It might have the procedural representation

    (FOR EACH f FLIGHT (CONNECT f BOS CHI);
        (FOR WH t TIME;
            (DTIME f BOS t)))

The execution of this query (assuming the procedure for EACH is identical to the one for ALL) begins by retrieving all flights that connect Boston to Chicago, returning the list (F1 F2 F3). For each of these the system then executes the wh-quantified expression. The first of these is

    (FOR WH t TIME;
        (DTIME F1 BOS t))

Executing this will retrieve all values of t such that (TYPE t TIME) and (DTIME F1 BOS t) hold. Any time found is then printed out. Thus the answer printed for this query might be "4PM, 9AM, 8AM" after the system has considered each of flights F1, F2, and F3.

The Limits of Procedural Semantics

A system based on a procedural semantics can be quite useful in database query applications. However, the success of the approach depends on several important limitations on the type of knowledge that can be represented and on the interactions in which the user can partake. In particular the database cannot represent general facts (such as all flights serve meals) or uncertainty (such as either flight F1 serves breakfast or it serves dinner). Consider this in a little more detail.

The database cannot represent any general facts such as all flights serve meals. The only way such information could be present in the system would be to assert, for every flight known, a fact that that particular flight serves a meal. Likewise, the only way to answer such a question would be to find every instance of a flight and check if it serves a meal, and this is exactly what the procedural interpretation for ALL does. Thus the restriction on the form of knowledge that can be represented allows the limited query technique to work as desired.

The database also cannot represent disjunction information such as flight F1 serves either breakfast or dinner, or negated information such as flight F1 does not serve breakfast. Of course, given these two facts, it would be true that flight F1 serves dinner. In the query language, however, the only way to show that F1 serves dinner is to find that exact relation in the database. While this appears limited, it is adequate given that disjunctive facts cannot be represented. If there are no disjunctions or universally quantified statements allowed, the only way that a fact can be proven is for it to be explicitly present in the database.

16.2 LUNAR: A Case Study

The LUNAR system was a natural language front end to a database of moon rock samples brought back by the Apollo space program. The system consisted of an ATN parser with a wide range of coverage for English questions and a semantic interpreter based on pattern-action rules that produced a logical form that was directly executed on the database using a procedural semantics. As such, the techniques to construct a system like LUNAR have already been introduced in some detail. This section describes a few points where the approach in LUNAR has not been adequately covered.

Interpreting Commands

Many of the queries to the LUNAR system were imperative commands such as *List all samples that contain silicon* or *Print the two samples that contain the most silicon*. To handle these, the logical form allowed actions as well as database formulas in the logical form. The action (PRINTOUT *term*) could be used in place of some assertion. The procedure for this action simply printed out the value of its argument. Thus the representation for *List all samples that contain silicon* would be

```
(FOR ALL s SAMPLE (CONTAIN s SI);
    (PRINTOUT s))
```

BOX 16.1   Quantifier Collars and Ordering

The LUNAR system supported a logical form in which quantifier scoping was not yet determined by maintaining a representation that consisted of two parts, the SEM and the QUANT. In the semantic interpretation of a noun phrase the SEM corresponds to the name assigned to represent the object denoted, whereas the QUANT structure would contain the quantifier, type, and restriction information. A sentence interpretation has a SEM built out of the SEMs of the NPs, and a QUANT consisting of the QUANTs of the NPs. For example, the NP *every sample containing silicon* might be analyzed as having a SEM value s1 and a QUANT value, called a **collar** (FOR EVERY s1 SAMPLE (CONTAINS s1 SI); Δ). The constant "Δ" in the QUANT is a placeholder to be used later. The question *Is every sample containing silicon heavy?* has an interpretation that builds from the NP interpretation. Its SEM might be (HEAVY s1), using the SEM from the NP interpretation to fill in an argument position, and its QUANT would be the QUANT from the NP, i.e., (FOR EVERY s1 SAMPLE (CONTAINS s1 SI); Δ). The final interpretation would be constructed by replacing the Δ term with the SEM, yielding

(FOR EVERY s1 SAMPLE (CONTAINS s1 SI); (HEAVY s1))

With a sentence with multiple quantifiers, the different scopings are generated by the different order in which a collar is picked from the QUANT structure to add around the SEM value. For instance, the final representation for *Every boy loves a dog* would be something like

        SEM: (LOVES b1 d1)
        QUANT: ((FOR EVERY b1 BOY; Δ),
                    (FOR INDEF/SING d1 DOG; Δ))

If the system picks the indefinite first, it would produce

        SEM: (FOR INDEF/SING d1 DOG; (LOVES b1 d1))
        QUANT: ((FOR EVERY b1 BOY; Δ))

Then picking the universal, the final representation would be

        (FOR EVERY b1 BOY;
            (FOR INDEF/SING d1 DOG; (LOVES b1 d1)))

The LUNAR system utilized a simple algorithm for quantifier ordering: The quantifiers were ordered in the left-to-right order in which they appeared in the sentence, with the exception of PP modifiers of NPs, where the PP modifier was placed outside the scope of the NP.

Numeric Quantifiers and Sets

Besides providing a semantics for SOME, EVERY, THE, and so on, as discussed in the last section, the LUNAR system gave a procedural semantics to many nonstandard quantifiers such as *three, more than four*, and *less than six*, as well as set operations important in database applications such as average, sum, and cardinality.

The numeric quantifiers are easily handled procedurally. For instance, the logical form

(FOR (GREATER-THAN n) x T (Rx); (Px))

will be successfully queried by the procedure that gathers all objects x of type T that satisfy both (Rx) and (Px) and returning true if more than n were found. The quantifiers (LESS-THAN n) and (EXACTLY n) can be similarly defined. In the actual system, queries are optimized so that not all the objects satisfying a description are necessarily retrieved. For example, with the preceding example of the (GREATER-THAN n) quantifiers, as soon as the $n+1$st object is found, the procedure can return true. Thus the entire set need not be generated.

The operators AVERAGE, NUMBER, and SUM are very important in database domains and are treated as operators on sets. Consider the approach for dealing with averages. The first thing to consider is its interaction with the generic (INDEF/PL) quantifier. This quantifier is sensitive to the context in which it arises. In some contexts it behaves like a universal quantifier, as in the sentence

Students enrolled in CS247 will take a final exam.

where it is meant that all students will take the exam, whereas in other cases, such as in

the average grade of students enrolled in CS247

it behaves more like an existential quantifier (what is wanted is the average of the set of all grades such that some student in CS247 received that grade). If you use an operator *(SET-OF var type restriction)* that returns the set of all objects of the indicated type that satisfy the restrictions, the semantic interpretation of this NP would be

(FOR THE a (AVERAGE
    (SET-OF g GRADE
       (FOR GEN s STUDENT (ENROLLED-IN s CS247)
          (GRADE s g)))); ...)

The procedural definition for SET-OF will find all the objects in the database satisfying the restriction that some student enrolled in CS247 obtained that grade, and the procedure for AVERAGE will compute the average value for that set and assign it to the variable "a."

An operator such as AVERAGE introduces possible scoping ambiguity with the quantifiers. In particular, while in the NP *the average grade of students in CS247*, the average is taken over all grades of students in CS247, in the NP *the average of the grades of each student in CS247*, the average apparently refers to a set of grades, each one being the grade average of a student in CS247. The LUNAR system handled this in the semantic interpretation phase, forcing the EACH quantifier to take wider scope than AVERAGE, and forcing the GEN quantifier to take narrow scope. In actual fact it transformed the GEN quantifier into a set union operation, but that is not important for the discussion here.

Informative Answers

The basic approach to wh-quantifiers in LUNAR is similar to what was described in the previous section, but uses the PRINTOUT action. A query such as *What is the weight of each sample?* would have a logical form such as

> (FOR EACH s SAMPLE;
>   (FOR THE w WEIGHT (WEIGHS s w);
>   (PRINTOUT w)))

If executed as it stood, this would print out a long list of weights with no identification of the samples involved. In most cases this would be an uninformative answer. LUNAR dealt with this problem by making PRINTOUT a fairly complex procedure that inspected the entire query to find other variables on which the variable to be printed was dependent. In the preceding case w is dependent on the value of s, and so the system would print a table listing the name of each sample and its weight, such as

SI001	1.3 oz
SI002	2.5 oz
SI004	1 oz

16.3 Logic-Based Question Answering

Some of the restrictions on expressibility of a database representation can be removed by moving to languages based on logic. The database is then a set of logical assertions, and querying the database is a theorem-proving process. A yes-no question concerning whether some proposition P is true, for instance, would be answered by trying to prove that P is true (or is false). Unless some restrictions are put on this process, you cannot build a general theorem prover that is guaranteed to terminate. Restricted forms of logic, however, can support limited forms of theorem proving that can be guaranteed to halt under appropriate circumstances. One of the best studied of these is the Horn clause logic as realized in languages such as PROLOG and used in systems such as CHAT-80.

CHAT-80 uses PROLOG for all phases of the analysis, which is divided into three distinct parts: syntactic parsing, semantic interpretation, and quantifier scoping. The parsing is done using the logic grammar techniques described in Chapters 4 and 5. The syntactic structure is then transformed to a logical form using techniques like those described in Section 9.6. Finally, a quantifier scoping algorithm is applied using simple heuristics along the lines of those described in Section 10.1. The final result is a fully-scoped logical form expressed in a notation called definite closed world (DCW) clauses. This section introduces this notation and shows how it can then be used to drive the question-answering process.

The DCW notation was designed to overcome some of the difficulties in capturing natural language quantification in a logic-based representation. It explicitly utilizes certain assumptions about the domain that allow the efficiency of Horn-clause-based provers to be used to advantage. In particular Horn clause systems cannot support full reasoning about negation. In such a framework, rather than proving that some formula ($\neg P$) is true, the system can only try to prove that P is true and fail to do so. While failing to prove P does not guarantee that ($\neg P$) is true in general, in certain domains this assumption can be made. This assumption is called the **closed world assumption**. An important consequence of making this assumption is that ignorance about whether a proposition P is true or false is not representable. Either P is provably true, or it is not provably true, in which case, using the closed world assumption, it is false.

Assume an operator *unless*, where *(unless P)* is true only if the theorem prover recursively attempts to prove P and fails. This operator can be used in place of the negation operator, as long as the formula P does not contain any variables. To simplify matters for the present discussion, assume that all facts in the database contain no variables--that is, are **ground**. In other words you may assert that (P A) is true, but you cannot assert that (P ?x) is true. This is called the **groundness assumption**.

For question answering, Horn clauses are limited in that only existentially quantified variables are provided in queries. For example, the query

(SERVE-BREAKFAST ?x)

will succeed if a binding for ?x can be found making the formula true. Thus the ?x acts like an existentially quantified variable.

The DCW language introduces several mechanisms that extend the expressibility of the language over straight Horn clauses. In addition, by exploiting the closed world assumption, DCW clauses can then be compiled (or interpreted) into standard Horn clause programs for execution in order to answer a query.

A DCW clause is of the form

   literal ⇐ *condition*

where *literal* is any simple formula containing no connectives or quantifiers. Any variables in the literal will act like universally-quantified variables, as will be seen later. The condition is a formula built out of operators including the following:

P & Q - holds only if both P and Q hold

exists (x, Px) - holds only if there is an instance of x such that if you substituted this instance for x in the formula Px, then the resulting formula would be true

unless (P) - holds only if the prover fails to prove P

For example, to find all dogs that have an owner, the corresponding DCW clause would be

   answer (?x) ⇐ (DOG ?x) & exists (?o, (OWNS ?x ?o))

That is, ?x is an answer if it is of type DOG and there is a substitution for ?o such that (OWNS ?x ?o) can be proven. The interpreter attempts to find all proofs of (answer ?x). Thus it will find all instances of ?x such that the condition is true.

DCW also has a facility for reasoning about finite sets. In particular the following operators are defined:

setof (s, x, Px) - holds only if s is a finite nonempty set of all x such that Px holds

card (s, n) - holds if s is a finite set of cardinality n

member (x, s) - holds only if x is a member of set s

The operator setof is well defined only because of the restriction on the domain. Since a formula of form Px can hold only for a ground term substitution for x (the

DCW Operator	Theorem Prover Call
exists (x, Px)	($\neq$ nil (FindAll x Px))
setof (s, x, Px)	(= s (FindAll x Px))

Figure 16.4 Defining exists and setof

groundness assumption), and Px is false for every other term (the closed world assumption), that set of ground terms defines the finite set.

A statement in the DCW language can be "executed" as a data query by interpreting it using a Horn clause theorem prover. A simple way to do this is to extend the Horn clause interpreter with an ability to call itself recursively using a function

(FindAll x Px)

that finds all proofs of Px and returns the list of bindings for x that made Px succeed. If this list is empty, Px cannot be proven. The operators defined earlier can now be defined as shown in Figure 16.4.

An interpreter for DCW clauses can easily be built using the equivalences in Figure 16.4 and a logic programming system with an ability to call itself recursively to implement the function FindAll. The CHAT-80 system actually optimizes the query beyond the obvious interpretation, but this is not relevant to our present purposes.

The Interpretation of Quantifiers

The natural language quantifiers are now treated as shown in Figure 16.5. The expressions T, R, and P in the translation refer to the type, restrictions, and the proposition in the quantified formula, respectively.

Universal quantifiers outside the scope of a wh-term, as in *Which employees of each company attended AAAI-84?* are treated specially. Like the wh-quantified variable, these variables are inserted in the ANSWER literal on the left-hand side of the DCW clause. Thus the preferred reading of the preceding question is

(ANSWER ?e ?c) $\Leftarrow$ (attend ?e AAAI-84) & (employee-of ?e ?c)

The nonpreferred reading, in which the question is asking about a single person employed by all companies, would be

(ANSWER ?e) $\Leftarrow$ (attend ?e AAAI-84) &
        unless (exists (?c,(TYPE ?c COMPANY) &
                unless (employee-of ?e ?c)))

Quantifier	Translation
SOME, INDEF/SING, DEF/SING	exists (?x, (TYPE ?x T) & $R_{?x}$ & $P_{?x}$)
NO	unless (exists (?x, (TYPE ?x T) & $R_{?x}$ & $P_{?x}$))
EVERY, ALL, EACH (inside scope of WH)	unless (exists (?x, (TYPE ?x T) & $R_{?x}$ & (unless $P_{?x}$)))
DEF/PL	exists (?s, (setof ?s ?x (TYPE ?x T) & $R_{?x}$) & $P_{?s}$)
ONE, TWO, ..., n, ...	exists (?s, (setof ?s ?x (TYPE ?x T) & $R_{?x}$) & (Card ?s n) & $P_{?s}$)
WH	(answer ?x) $\Leftarrow$ (TYPE ?x T) & $R_{?x}$ & $P_{?x}$
HOW MANY	(answer ?n) $\Leftarrow$ exists (?s, (setof ?s ?x $R_{?x}$ & $P_{?x}$) & (Card ?s ?n))

Figure 16.5 The meaning of some natural language quantifiers

This latter query would usually fail, since it would normally be impossible to find an employee employed by every company. The answer to the preferred interpretation would be a list of employee-company pairs, which would probably be the answer desired.

Consider a very simple example of how a DCW formulation of the query *When does each flight leave Boston for Chicago?* would be executed on the airline database (reformulated as a Horn clause database). After parsing, semantic interpretation, and quantifier scoping, the following DCW form would be generated:

$$\text{(ANSWER ?f ?t)} \Leftarrow \text{(TYPE ?f FLIGHT) \& (TYPE ?t TIME) \&}$$
$$\text{(DTIME ?f BOS ?t) \& (CONNECT ?f BOS CHI)}$$

The appropriate translation of this would be added to the logic database, and then the prover would be called to prove all instances of (ANSWER ?f1 ?t1). The list of answers returned--(ANSWER F1 4PM), (ANSWER F2 9AM), and (ANSWER F3 8AM)--gives all the information needed to provide an informative answer.

As a more complicated example, consider the query *Which airlines have three flights to Chicago from Boston?* which has the DCW form

$$\text{(ANSWER ?a)} \Leftarrow \text{(TYPE ?a AIRLINE) \&}$$
$$\text{exists (?s,}$$
$$\text{setof (?s, ?f, (TYPE ?f FLIGHT) \&}$$
$$\text{(RUN-BY ?f ?a) \&}$$
$$\text{(CONNECT ?f BOS CHI)) \&}$$
$$\text{card (?s, 3))}$$

To execute this query, you construct for each airline the set of flights from Boston to Chicago. For example, for SLOTH-AIR, the expression

    setof (?s, ?f, (TYPE ?f FLIGHT) &
           (RUN-BY ?f SLOTH-AIR) &
           (CONNECT ?f BOS CHI))

will be evaluated by recursively calling the prover to find all instances of ?f such that the three listed conditions hold:

    (FindAll ?f (TYPE ?f FLIGHT) & (RUN-BY ?f SLOTH-AIR) &
             (CONNECT ?f BOS CHI))

Given the present database (in Figure 16.1), this will return and thus bind ?s to the list (F1 F2 F3). Since the cardinality of this set is 3, the right-hand side of the query will succeed for ?a bound to SLOTH-AIR, and thus this will be recorded as one of the answers.

16.4 Providing Useful Answers

The techniques for soliciting responses have so far dealt only with simple database worlds. Even within such restricted domains, a system still faces difficult problems in order to generate intelligent answers. This section considers several additional issues needed to answer questions adequately.

In many systems such as the two described previously, definite descriptions are handled by retrieving from the database objects that satisfy the descriptions. For example, the query *Does the plane from Shady Bend to Rochester arrive at three?* might map to a final form such that answering the question requires the retrieval

    (Test (TYPE ?x FLIGHT) & (CONNECT ?x SHADY-BEND ROC) &
          (ATIME ?x ROC 3PM))

An answer of *no* might arise from the fact that no such flight arrives at three, or that there are no flights from Shady Bend to Rochester at all, or that there are no flights to anywhere. Only in the first case is a straight answer of *no* appropriate (and even in this case, a better one may be given). If there are no flights from Shady Bend to Rochester, an answer of *no* is misleading, since it allows the questioner to continue to believe (incorrectly) that such flights exist.

Other cases similar to this are equally important for question answering. For example, if person A asks B *Did you pass the exam?* A must be assuming that B took the exam; otherwise A would know the answer to his own question!

The main observation is that these problematic cases all arise when the answer to the question is negative. One useful strategy for handling these situations is the following: If a query fails, then retry the query after deleting some part of it--say, the main proposition--leaving the restrictions and type information in the logical form. For example, the question *Is there a flight from Shady Bend to Rochester arriving at three?* might result in the query

1.   (Retrieve ?f (TYPE ?f FLIGHT) & (CONNECT ?f SHADY-BEND ROC)
            & (ATIME ?f ROC 3PM))

If there are no such flights, this query will fail. The strategy outlined here indicates to delete the literal (ATIME ?f ROC 3PM) and retry, using the new query

2.   (Retrieve ?f (TYPE ?f FLIGHT) & (CONNECT ?f SHADY-BEND ROC))

This query will also fail if there are no such flights, indicating that the answer should be *There are no flights from Shady Bend to Rochester* rather than a simple *no*. Of course, since this query failed, the system can retry again by deleting another literal. This time it might try the query

3.   (Retrieve ?f (TYPE ?f FLIGHT))

If this failed (which it won't, in this case), the most appropriate answer would be a more shocking revelation: *There are no flights!* This simple method of deleting literals until a query is successful can be effective in producing useful responses.

Other techniques may be useful in finding relevant information on why an answer is *no* rather than simply deleting a literal. For instance, the system might replace a constant in the query with an existentially quantified variable. For example, a generalization of query 2 would produce the query

4.   (Retrieve ?f (TYPE ?f FLIGHT) & (CONNECT ?f SHADY-BEND ?a))

If this failed, the system could give the useful response: *There are no flights from Shady Bend.* Of course, with this technique, there needs to be some metric determining which constants to replace. For example, if the system replaced SHADY-BEND in query 1 with a variable, it would produce query 5:

5.   (Retrieve ?f (TYPE ?f FLIGHT) & (CONNECT ?f ?a ROC) &
            (ATIME ?f ROC 3PM))

If this failed, a reply such as *There are no flights arriving in Rochester at three PM* might be generated, which is unlikely to be appropriate. Determining the constants of main interest to the questioner is a difficult problem, but for any given database application, this information might be able to be precoded.

BOX 16.2   Presupposition

The failure of definite reference is actually just one instance of a more general phenomena of failed presuppositions. A **presupposition** of an assertion is a proposition that is implied by both the assertion and its negation. Likewise the presupposition of a question is a proposition that is implied by the question irrespective of whether the answer is affirmative or negative. For example, if I answer the question *Have you stopped beating your dog?* either affirmatively or negatively, I am admitting that I once beat my dog. The question does not make sense if this was never the case. We say that this sentence presupposes the fact that I beat my dog. If faced with such a question in an actual conversation, I wouldn't answer either *yes* or *no* but would respond with a denial of the presupposition, such as *I never beat my dog.*

This presupposition is a result of the verb *stop*, which, as the main verb of a sentence, presupposes that the event in its complement occurred. Other verbs that introduce presuppositions are *know* and *realize.* For example, both these sentences presuppose that I beat my dog:

> Jack knows I beat my dog.
> Jack doesn't know that I beat my dog.

From another perspective the presuppositions of a sentence are the facts that the speaker must be committed to believing if he or she is speaking sincerely. This view provides another tool for disambiguating the meaning of sentences. Given two interpretations of a sentence, if one involves a violated presupposition, the other would be preferred.

Questions also often introduce a form of presupposition. For example, the question *Was it John who stole the money?* presupposes that someone stole the money, and it is asking whether that person was John. A *no* response denies that John committed the theft, but allows that the money was stolen. This is also why the response *No, it was Bill who stole the money* is more appropriate than *No, it was John who stole the cake.* McCawley (1981) discusses presupposition in general, and Weischedel (1979) describes a method for computing presuppositions while parsing.

16.5 Responses to Questions in More Complex Domains

As the domain of application becomes more general, answering a question appropriately becomes significantly more complicated. For example, consider a system that maintains a large knowledge base of actions and must advise a user on how to perform simple tasks. In such an application the system must be able to answer questions such as *How do I open this box?* and *Why do I need the hammer?* as well as anticipate problems that might arise and give unsolicited advice. None of this can be done without a user model that draws on the belief representations discussed in the last chapter.

For example, consider *how* questions. In general these questions are asking about the method by which a certain action is performed or a state achieved. The question might be answered in several ways depending on what the system thinks the questioner knows and needs to know. For example, the answer to the question *How do I pull the nail out?* might be something like *Pick up a hammer and lever the nail out using its claw*--that is, a decomposition sequence for the action of pulling out a nail. In most settings, however, this answer would be inappropriate, because the questioner would normally know how to pull out nails with a hammer. In such cases an answer such as *With a hammer* would be more appropriate, since it identifies the method (vs. other possibilities, such as using pliers or getting Jack to do it) without providing a lot of redundant information. In other *how* questions, a fuller description of the method might be the appropriate answer as opposed to describing what instrument to use. Consider another example: The appropriate answer to the question *How do I connect the tape recorder up to the amp?* will vary depending on the context. If the questioner does not know much about electronics, an answer like *Plug one end of the wire into the "out" connector on the tape recorder and the other into the "tape in" connector on the amp* is likely to be appropriate. If the questioner does know a lot about electronics, the question may be interpreted in other ways. For instance, if the wire is missing, the answer might be *The wire is in the top drawer.* Thus the appropriateness of a certain answer in these examples depends crucially on what prior knowledge is attributed to the questioner. In the nail example, you can assume that virtually everyone knows how to use a hammer to pull out a nail, so just identifying this method by mentioning the instrument is best. In the case of connecting electronic components, the answer will vary according to the questioner's knowledge about basic electronics.

Questions involving *why* present similar problems. In general a *why* question is asking about the desired effect of some action. It may be answered by stating the effect explicitly, but it usually is better answered by describing the action that the effect enables, or by stating the action of which the queried action is a decomposition. These two techniques can be seen in alternate answers to the question *Why did you pull the nail out?* An answer based on the enablement relation would be *So I can use it to attach these two boards*, while an answer based on decomposition would be *To loosen the board.* Again the situations where each answer is appropriate can be classified by considering what the hearer already knows and what he or she needs to know.

Helpful Responses

In the last section some problems in dealing with *no* answers to questions were discussed briefly. Reconsider this problem and examine its relation to user models. Assume that a question such as *Did Jack go to the grocery store?* can be answered by *no*. In many cases a much better answer would be to address some related question instead. For example, the answer *No, Sam did* is appropriate if the questioner is interested in who went to the store, and the answer *No, he went to the hardware store* is appropriate if the questioner is interested in where Jack went.

Helpful responses arise even when a question can be answered affirmatively. For instance, suppose Jack has asked Sue to go to his house to pick up some records that he forgot, and Sue asks *Will I be able to get in?* Jack couldn't really answer with a simple *yes* if he knows that all the doors are locked except for the basement door at the back of the house. Rather a response such as *Yes, the back basement door is unlocked* is required. Again, to supply this information, Jack has to know why Sue asked the question and what information she needs to accomplish her plan.

Questions may also reveal that the questioner is operating under mistaken assumptions, and a useful system should be able to recognize these assumptions and provide corrections as necessary. It should also be able to recognize that the answers it gives may also cause certain assumptions to be made by the questioner. If these are inappropriate, they need to be explicitly cancelled in the answer.

For example, return to the situation where Jack is asking Sue to get his records. Suppose he has recently reorganized his house, and the records are now in a cupboard upstairs, rather than in the living room where they used to be. Sue may still believe they are in the living room. The dialog may go as follows:

SUE: Will I be able to get in?
JACK: Yes, the back basement door is unlocked.
SUE: The front basement steps lead up to the living room, right?

Even though the answer to Sue's second question is *yes*, Jack should realize that it is irrelevant to the task of getting the records (say the back steps go up to the second floor) and reflects a mistaken assumption that the records are in the living room. Thus his best reply is along the lines of *Yes, but the records are in a cupboard upstairs, so take the back steps*. This reply corrects the mistaken assumption that Jack inferred from his previous knowledge of Sue together with her second question.

Assumptions like this that underlie sentences are often called **implicatures**. An implicature is not a logical consequence of the sentence, because it can be explicitly cancelled, but it is an assumption made in the absence of evidence to the contrary. For example, if someone approaches you on the side of a road carrying an empty gas can and asks, *Is there a gas station down this way?* it would be inappropriate to answer *yes* if you knew that the gas station was closed.

Systems that can handle situations like the ones described in this section await future research. At present there are results on isolated parts of the problem. For example, the techniques described in the last chapter for representing beliefs and actions can be used for some of these situations. Current work is aimed at generalizing these techniques and investigating other sources of information needed to handle more complex domains.

Summary

This chapter has examined the techniques used in question-answering systems and presented two case studies of systems that have influenced the current generation of commercial natural language interface systems. All practical systems are currently limited to comparatively simple database representations and cannot be directly extended to handle richer domains involving ongoing actions by one or more agents.

Related Work and Further Readings

The procedural semantics representation was developed by Woods (1968) and used in the LUNAR system (Woods, 1977). The CHAT-80 system was developed by Warren and Pereira (1982). There is a fair-sized literature on natural language interfaces to databases. A good collection of recent papers on the subject can be found in the Proceedings of the 1983 ACL Conference on Applied Natural Language Processing.

The TEAM system (Grosz et al., 1987) is a good example of the current state of the art in natural language interfaces. It is aimed at being transportable, which means it can be readily adapted to a different database without having to rewrite the grammar and semantic interpreter. To do this, it uses a logical form independent of the application, which is then translated into the particular database application. It also contains an extensive facility that allows a user to define new vocabulary for the system.

Kaplan (1983) addressed the issue of generating helpful responses to database queries when the answer to be given was *no*. For example, if the answer to the question *How many boys at the party drank some beer?* is *no* because there were no boys at the party, then it is misleading to say simply *no*, because it leads the questioner to believe that the question was well formed, and thus that there were boys at the party. Kaplan detected such cases by computing the sets referred to by all subparts of the query. If some set smaller than the one directly queried (the set of boys at the party who drank beer) is null, the helpful answer is computed and given. This technique is efficiently implementable and can greatly improve the quality of simple database query applications. It fails as a general model of helpful behavior, however, because the response is based only on the structure of the question and involves no user model.

An excellent brief survey of the work on generating useful responses is Webber (1987b).

Exercises for Chapter 16

1. *(medium)* Consider a question-answering system on a fixed database restricted to ground literals as shown below and using the closed world assumption:

> TYPE(FORD, MANUFACTURER), TYPE(GM, MANUFACTURER)
> TYPE(CAR1, AUTO), ..., TYPE(CAR9, AUTO)
> MADE-BY(CAR1, FORD), COLOR(CAR1, WHITE)
> MADE-BY(CAR2, FORD), COLOR(CAR2, WHITE)
> MADE-BY(CAR3, FORD), COLOR(CAR3, BLACK)
> MADE-BY(CAR4, FORD), COLOR(CAR4, WHITE)
> MADE-BY(CAR5, GM), COLOR(CAR5, RED)
> MADE-BY(CAR6, GM), COLOR(CAR6, WHITE)
> MADE-BY(CAR7, GM), COLOR(CAR7, BLUE)
> MADE-BY(CAR8, GM), COLOR(CAR8, RED)
> MADE-BY(CAR9, GM), COLOR(CAR9, BLUE)

a) In a representation used in this chapter give a "semantics" for the English quantifier *most* appropriate for database queries. Discuss any complications that arise, and any assumptions that you need to make.

b) Give the two different interpretations, due to quantifier scoping, of the sentence *Most cars made by some manufacturer are white.* Give an informal trace of the question-answering process in each of the interpretations. What is the answer in each case?

c) What knowledge of the domain could be brought to bear to select the most likely interpretation in part b? Informally describe a disambiguation process that would select the appropriate interpretation in such cases, using the analysis in part b as an example.

Chapter 17

Natural Language Generation

Natural language generation is the inverse of natural language understanding. Generation systems accept a representation of some set of linguistic goals and have to produce a set of natural language sentences that realize those goals. The problem can be divided into two main areas:

1. selecting from the knowledge representation the particular semantic content of the sentences

2. transforming the semantic content into actual natural language sentences

Much of what has already been discussed in this book is directly relevant to these issues. The area of planning and plan-based representations of linguistic goals is relevant to the first problem, and the mappings between the final representation, the logical form, and the syntactic structure are relevant to the second. Many issues that become crucial to the generation process could, however, be largely ignored in understanding systems. These issues have to do with the relevance of certain pieces of information and the functional properties of linguistic structures. The following paragraphs examine these issues in turn.

Consider a situation where an agent Jack sold a car to another agent Sam. If this is represented in a frame-based system, the information immediately available would include all the properties of Jack, all the properties of Sam, whatever is known about the car Jack is selling, plus information about selling events in general, and this selling event in particular. How is a generation system to choose the information that is relevant and should be included in a description of what happened? The decision must be based in part on what the system thinks is necessary to identify the key objects involved (for example, possibly the hearer doesn't know Sam by name, so the system might describe Sam in terms of his relationship to Jack, say as Jack's boss), and what aspects of the situation are important to convey (for example, possibly Jack asked a price that is much more than the car is worth). This question, of course, cannot be decided independently of some description of what linguistic goals the speaker has (for example, maybe the speaker wants to convince the hearer that Jack is a swindler, or maybe the speaker wants to show that Jack didn't like his car, and so on).

Once the content has been decided, it must then by realized in a set of sentences. This requires significant knowledge about how different linguistic structures have different linguistic effects. Even when the content can be realized in a single sentence, the situation is very complex. For example, the following sentences say nearly the same thing, and most understanding systems would abstract away the differences between them during syntactic and semantic processing.

1.   The man in the top hat dropped the cane made of bamboo.
2.   The man in the top hat dropped the bamboo cane.
3.   The man wearing the top hat dropped the bamboo cane.
4.   The cane that the man wearing the top hat dropped was made of
      bamboo.
5.   The bamboo cane was dropped by the man who was wearing the top
      hat.
6.   The man who dropped the bamboo cane was wearing a top hat.

All of these sentences have approximately the same meaning, and if one
sentence is true, then they all are true. They each have slightly different effects,
however. Sentences 2 and 6, for example, use different information to identify
the man (the man in the top hat versus the man who dropped the bamboo cane)
and thus would have different effects when processed by the referential analysis.
A generation program would have to know which one of these is the appropriate
description. Sentences 3 and 5, on the other hand, differ in voice. While this
might be ignored by the understanding program, a generation program must
decide which voice should be used. If you assume that voice is not random, you
need some theory of language that examines how voice is used to make a
reasonable decision. These two examples are the more easy cases. A
well-motivated theory of generation would have to produce criteria that
distinguish between each of the variations.

Section 17.1 examines the issues involved in selecting the appropriate
content from a knowledge base and in planning an extended discourse if the
content cannot be realized in a single sentence. Then Section 17.2 examines the
mapping between the knowledge representation and actual words and phrases.
Section 17.3 examines some simple techniques that can produce natural
language output from a selected part of a representation. Finally, Section 17.4
examines the role of large grammars in the generation process and discusses
some current research in the area.

17.1 Deciding What to Say

You have already seen several simple examples of how a system might decide
what to say. In the last chapter you saw question-answering systems that used
deductive techniques to find an answer to a question. The answer returned was
the content for the system's response. More complicated question-answering
systems may generate helpful responses as well, as described in that chapter.
Another example was in Chapter 13, where knowledge about actions was used to
understand stories. With that representation, questions again can be answered
in a fairly straightforward manner by defining particular search strategies for
answering each type of question.

Action Class OPEN(Agent, Door, Key)
precondition: LOCKED(Door)
                FITS(Key, Door)
effect: OPENED(Door)
decomposition: GOTO(Agent, Loc(Key)) → PICKUP(Agent, Key) →
                GOTO(Agent, Loc(Door)) →
                UNLOCK(Agent, Door, Key) → PUSH(Agent, Door)

Action Class PICKUP(Agent, Object)
precondition: AT(Agent, Loc(Object))
effect: HAS(Agent, Object)

Action Class GOTO(Agent, Loc)
effect: AT(Agent, Loc)

Figure 17.1 Actions defined for requesting that the door be opened

In both those examples the response selection is built into the system and works because the situation in which the system must respond is predictable in advance. Each system has to answer the questions given in a more or less direct manner. In more complex situations, however, such as those described in Chapter 15 where the system was an expert advising a user as the user performed some task, the situation cannot be predetermined. Rather, depending on the situation, the system may have to take the initiative and generate instructions and other information that is not explicitly asked for. In addition, it must take into account some knowledge of what the user already knows in order to be helpful. In essence the system needs to be able to vary its behavior based on its current goals and what it believes are the user's goals and beliefs.

The basic techniques for a first attempt at such a system have already been described. With a representation of speech acts as operators in a planning system, deciding on the content of what to say can be modeled as a planning algorithm. In particular, remember the example in Section 15.3, where Jack planned a question in order to perform his task of buying a ticket. These techniques need to be elaborated on, however, before this can be used to generate actual language.

For example, consider a simple situation where the system wants to get the user to open a certain door, and it knows that the door is locked and the key is under the doormat. The definition of the relevant actions for this setting is shown in Figure 17.1. Using the techniques from Chapter 15, the system could plan to do a request that the user open the door, with the intended effect that the user actually does the action. The situation becomes interesting as the system reasons about what the user knows. If the system believes that the user does not know that the door is locked, it should also plan to tell the user that it is locked. Assume that the user already knows it is locked but doesn't know where the key is. The system must then plan to tell the user the key's location. The final plan of the system in this situation might look as shown in Figure 17.2.

The two speech acts in this plan indicate the content of the system's utterance. A simple generation scheme, such as one described later in Section 17.3, could take these two speech acts and generate a sequence of sentences such as *Please open the door with the key that fits the door. The key that fits the door is under the doormat.* The remainder of this section examines several techniques needed to improve on this output. For instance, a better response would take into account the context created by the first sentence and generate something like *Please use the key under the doormat to open the door.*

The first issue raised by the preceding examples involves finding appropriate descriptions for the objects in the planned utterance. This requires both a model of the hearer and a model of the conversation's context. The system must find a description of each object that will allow the hearer to identify it. For instance, suppose the current situation is represented as a set of assertions describing the room that the agents are in, and that there is only one door. If this is the case, the system, knowing that the layout of the room is shared knowledge, can decide that the simple predication of the form DOOR(x) is sufficient for the user to identify DOOR4 uniquely. Using knowledge of the situation, the system might also decide that a predication of the form KEY(x) is not sufficient to identify the key for DOOR4 (say there are two keys in the room). Thus it might expand this to a complex formula such as KEY(x) & FITS(x, DOOR4), which would be realized by an NP such as *the key to the door.* While this description may uniquely specify the key, it still might not identify the key to the hearer. In fact, a much more useful description in this setting identifies the key by its location.

Realizing more than one speech act in a single utterance requires further analysis of the contents of each act. For example, if the planning of each definite description in a sentence is treated as an action in the decomposition of the speech act, an extended plan reasoning system might be able to conclude that the INFORM act (saying that the key is under the doormat) could be eliminated if the description of the key in the REQUEST were something like *the key under the doormat.* Thus the request *Please use the key under the doormat to open the door* would make a separate INFORM act unnecessary. Planning complex sets of sentences remains an open problem, but simple referential cases like this one can be handled.

If the information needed cannot be given in a single sentence or two, there is a significant problem of planning how to construct a coherent text. Everyone who has ever had to write an essay has been faced with the difficult problem of determining the best way to present the information. Solutions to some simple cases of this can be found using scriptlike structures to organize information in situations that are predictable in advance. For example, a script to identify a

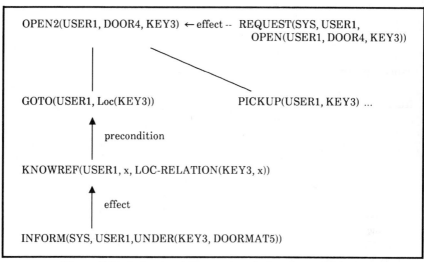

Figure 17.2 A plan to get the user to unlock and open the door

> The Action Class IDENTIFY(Class):
> decomposition: IDENTIFY-CLASS (Class, SuperClass) →
>   IDENTIFY-PROPS(Class, SuperClass) →
>   GIVE-EXAMPLE(Class)

Figure 17.3 The script to identify object classes

particular class of objects--say, from a large database that contains information about various objects--might be as shown in Figure 17.3. This action, IDENTIFY, might be used to answer questions such as *What is a dog?* Each action in the decomposition might be defined by script structures as well. Eventually, however, each of these actions would reduce to a set of speech acts. For example, the action IDENTIFY-CLASS might decompose into an INFORM that the object class is a subtype of some superclass, the action IDENTIFY-PROPS might decompose into INFORM acts of properties of the class that are not properties of the superclass, and the action GIVE-EXAMPLE might decompose into an INFORM naming an instance of the class.

With these definitions, and the knowledge base in Figure 17.4, the action IDENTIFY(DOG) might produce the following speech acts: from the IDENTIFY-CLASS action, INFORM(SYS, USER, SUBTYPE(DOG, ANIMAL)); from the IDENTIFY-PROPS action, INFORM(SYS, USER, $\forall$ x . DOG(x) $\supset$ BARKS(x)) and INFORM(SYS, USER, $\forall$ x . DOG(x) $\supset$ COMMON-PET(x)); from the GIVE-EXAMPLE action, INFORM(SYS, USER, DOG(FIDO1)). Using the techniques described in the following sections, generating these speech acts might produce the text

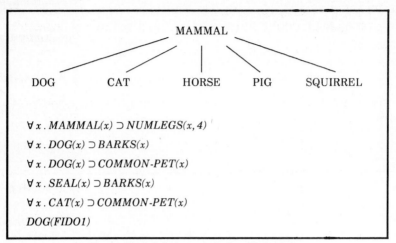

Figure 17.4 A fragment of a knowledge base

> Dogs are animals. They bark. They are common pets. Fido is a dog.

To be useful, even in the limited application of defining classes of objects, such generation scripts would have to contain more possibilities for extracting information from the knowledge base. For instance, some classes might be best identified by some contrast or comparison with another class, and so on.

17.2 Selecting Words and Phrases

Given some set of propositions, perhaps in the form of partially filled frame structures, how can these predicates be described in natural language? There are often many different ways in which the same content can be expressed, governed by two interrelated issues: lexical choice and syntactic choice. For example, consider a proposition FITS(KEY3, DOOR4) with the intended meaning that key KEY3 fits door DOOR4. This proposition could be realized as a sentence by *The key fits the door* or as a noun phrase by *the key for the door*. The difference between these two depends on a syntactic choice: Either use a sentence or a noun phrase. On the other hand, consider the action P1 of type PURCHASE, with the Seller role set to JACK1, the Object role set to a book, and the Buyer role set to SUE3. If *sell* is chosen as the main verb, this action can be realized by a sentence such as *Jack sold a book to Sue*, whereas if the verb *buy* is chosen, it can be realized by a sentence such as *Sue bought a book from Jack*. The difference between these two depends on a lexical choice: Either use *sell* or *buy* as the main verb. This section examines the important issues in lexical choice and looks at some techniques for mapping a representation into lexical form, such as a semantic network. Later sections will then consider syntactic choices involved in generating language from the semantic network.

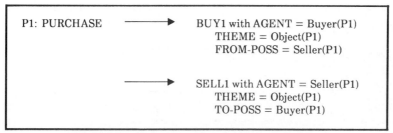

Figure 17.5 Two realization rules for PURCHASE

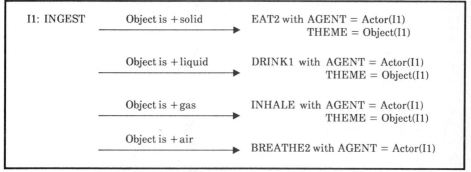

Figure 17.6 Four realization rules for INGEST

The simplest idea is to use a mapping function similar to the mapping function from word senses to frames used to interpret logical forms. For example, the information needed for the frame PURCHASE might be expressed as a choice between two **realization rules**, shown in Figure 17.5.

The outstanding question is how the system might make the decision between the two possible realizations. A last resort would be a selection at random. In many cases, however, there are better techniques. For example, if the system maintains a model of focus as described in Chapter 14, it might select the choice that makes the focused object the AGENT of the sentence, thereby giving it a prominent position in the final sentence. This can become complicated, however, since it might interact with syntactic decisions such as whether the sentence should be active or passive voice.

Other cases are more straightforward. Consider a representation where all action verbs involving some agent consuming some substance are mapped to a single action INGEST. Then, this action may be realized by many different verbs depending on the properties of the object consumed. For example, if the Object role is a food, the verb *eat* is appropriate, whereas if the Object role is a liquid, the verb *drink* is appropriate. Four different realizations of INGEST are shown in Figure 17.6. The tests on each choice are shown above the choice lines.

BOX 17.1 Canned Text

Several techniques are used in current systems for generating text directly from an internal representation. This works well only in situations where single sentences need to be generated and the context is predictable in advance. As a consequence, they are useful in some limited situations where very simple natural language output is useful. An extreme case of this is a compiler that uses natural language text in its error messages. This **canned text** is the output of a program that has no knowledge of natural language at all, and yet the error message can be very useful to the user. Slightly more sophisticated techniques were seen in the ELIZA program described in the introduction. It reused the user's input for constructing parts of the output. But again this program has no knowledge of the language itself and is not very reliable. Even though these techniques are limited, they can be used quite successfully in particular systems. But they do not contribute anything to your knowledge of natural language generation.

More complex examples arise when more than one action can be described by a single lexical structure. For example, the action GIVE might map simply to the verb sense GIVE2 (realized as *give*). A combination of two GIVE actions, however, might be realized in many ways by single verb senses such as TRADE1, SELL1, DONATE1, LOAN1, and so on. Figure 17.7 shows a notation for selecting verbs from two arbitrary giving actions, G1 and G2.

Given a set of propositions to realize, one good lexical strategy would be to find the lexical realizations that have the most specific matches. In other words, choose the realizations that convey the greatest number of propositions in the fewest lexical choices. For example, given two events, GIVE(JACK1, SUE1, BOOK3) and GIVE(SUE1, JACK1, PEN2), this strategy would generate the semantic network shown in Figure 17.8 rather than two networks involving the verb sense GIVE1. This means that the sentence *Jack traded Sue a book for a pen* would be preferred over the sentence *Jack gave Sue a book and Sue gave Jack a pen*.

Once a lexical choice for the main verb is made, the remaining propositions that have not yet been accounted for must then be considered. For example, if the proposition WEIGHT(BOOK3, WGT33) was to be realized with the two GIVE actions, this proposition might be mapped to a word sense HEAVY1 with BOOK3 as the THEME argument, which would be added to the network in Figure 17.8. Note that even though lexical choices have been made, many different sentences could be generated. If the node T1 is used for the main verb,

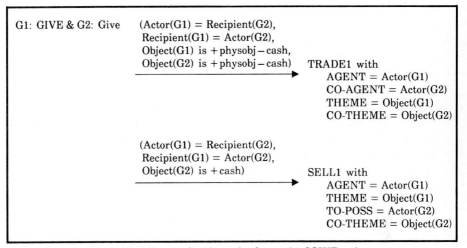

Figure 17.7 Two realization rules for a pair of GIVE actions

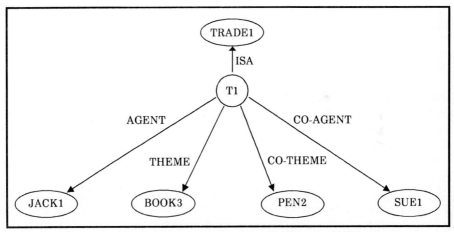

Figure 17.8 The semantic network constructed from two GIVE actions

a sentence like *Jack traded a heavy book to Sue for a pen* might be generated. If the node HEAVY1 is used for the main verb, a sentence like *The book that Jack traded to Sue for a pen was heavy* might be generated.

There is considerable lexical choice in specifying descriptions as well. For example, a constant P23 might be an instance of the class PERSON with a SEX role set to the value MALE. This object could be identified using a MAN1 as the type of P23, or by using HUMAN1 as the type and adding another predication based on the adjective sense MALE1. Of course, unless some other factors are at play, the system should probably always pick the former, because it is more concise. In any event the final output of this stage would be a semantic network structure that specifies the lexical content of the sentences to be generated.

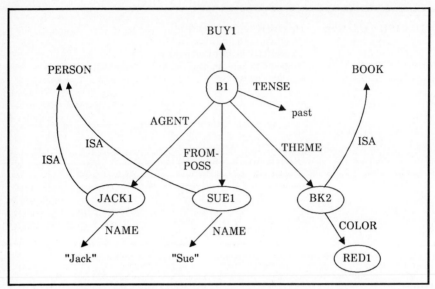

Figure 17.9 The input semantic network to the generator

17.3 Producing Sentences Directly from a Representation

The most direct technique for generating text from a representation is to associate one phrase structure with each proposition type and always to use that phrasing when generating a sentence from such a proposition. This technique is most effective on representations that are close to lexical forms, like the semantic networks generated earlier. It also can be used with other representations as well. For instance, a frame could have a phrasing associated with it for generating a description of the frame. Or, each frame could have a set of lexical decision choices, as described in the last section, and could use these choices to select from a set of phrasings predefined for that frame.

Consider an example of the generation of language from the semantic network shown in Figure 17.9. This process can be specified using a realization function **G** that maps network fragments to phrases, as shown in Figure 17.10. The notation should be fairly clear. Symbols like >AGENT indicate the node that is found by following the arc labeled AGENT, and so on. Curly brackets indicate optional elements that are generated only if the appropriate roles have values. Each rule is defined on a class of objects. Thus rule gen.1 will be used to determine the value of **G**(B1), since node B1 is an instance of BUY1.

A sentence realizing the network in Figure 17.9 can be generated by computing the value of **G**(B1). Using rule gen.1, you can generate the following form (note that the optional phrase for the FROM-POSS role is present, but the one for the CO-THEME, which is not in the initial network, is omitted):

gen.1   **G**(BUY1) = **G**(>AGENT) bought **G**(>THEME) {from **G**(>FROM-POSS)}
{for **G**(>CO-THEME)}

gen.2   **G**(PERSON) = **G**(>NAME) if node >NAME exists

gen.3   **G**(BOOK) = the **G**(>COLOR) book {by **G**(>AUTHOR)}

gen.4   **G**(RED2) = red

Figure 17.10 Some generation rules

gen.1   **G**(BUY1, S) = **G**(AGENT, NP) **G**(BUY1, (VERB **TENSE** >TENSE))
G(>THEME, NP)
{from **G**(>FROM-POSS, NP)}
{for **G**(>CO-THEME, NP)}

gen.5   **G**(BUY1, (VERB **TENSE** pres)) = buy

gen.6   **G**(BUY1, (VERB **TENSE** past)) = bought

Figure 17.11 Some generation rules extended with syntactic features

G(JACK1) bought **G**(BK2) from **G**(SUE1)

Using the rules gen.2 and gen.3 for the three **G** function applications, you produce the following:

Jack bought the **G**(RED2) book from Sue

Finally, using the rule gen.4, you rewrite the form as follows:

Jack bought the red book from Sue.

Of course, to produce better text, the rules need to be more complicated to account for complexities such as tense and agreement. In most applications where a technique as simple as this is useful, the tense can be predicted in advance from the setting. For example, all sentences generated by these rules would be in the simple past. One way to extend this method is to allow extra arguments on the **G** function that can record syntactic constraints on the generator. For example, G(n, S) might generate node n as a sentence, while G(n, NP) might generate the same node as a noun phrase. The extra argument position can then be used to pass in the features necessary to generate words in the appropriate forms. For example, rule gen.1 might be recast as shown in Figure 17.11. The tense of the sentence is passed on to the verb generation rule, which then generates the appropriate form. Of course, a useful system would need to be extended to extract the number of the subject NP and pass that on to the verb generation rule as well.

Another way to generalize this process further is to allow a full programming language to specify the **G** function. This gives the power for the generator to interact with other components of the system as required. For example, to generate appropriate definite descriptions in a multisentence text, you need a reference component to maintain a history list and a focus, as described in Chapter 14. The **G** function could then be defined to access this information and act appropriately. For example, a simple version of the **G** function for generating definite descriptions might be as follows:

> **G**(n, NP):
>> **If** n is the focused element,
>>> **then** return the value **G**(n, PRO)
>>> **else if** >NAME is defined
>>>> **then** return the value **G**(>NAME, NAME)
>>>> **else if** n is the first object on the history list of type >ISA
>>>>> **then** return the words *the* **G**(n, NOUN)
>>>>> **else** find properties of n that uniquely identify it
>>>>>   and generate them

The final technique to be discussed in this section involves the use of an explicit grammar that directs the generation process. In this case there is no further need for a **G** function because its role is subsumed by the grammar. Consider using an ATN, shown as Grammar 17.12, that can generate simple active and passive sentences. If this grammar is to be used for generation, the treatment of the registers and arcs must be different:

- The value of register * will be a node or arc in the semantic network rather than the next word in the sentence.

- A class of presetting actions are executed before the arc is followed. Presetting registers affects the operation of the arc but does not permanently change any register values in the original network.

- To follow a CAT arc, such as arc VERBS/1 labeled "verb," there must be a verb defined in the lexicon for the node or arc in *. In addition, other special registers affecting the lexicon might also be preset. For instance, if the FORM register is set to past, then following the arc should generate the appropriate verb in the form for the past tense.

The annotations use the simple language for traversing the semantic network, as well as the register testing and setting introduced in Chapter 4. A special action is provided to mark nodes to keep track of what parts of the network have already been generated. There are two different annotations on arc S/1 that perform different actions depending on the value of the **VOICE** register.

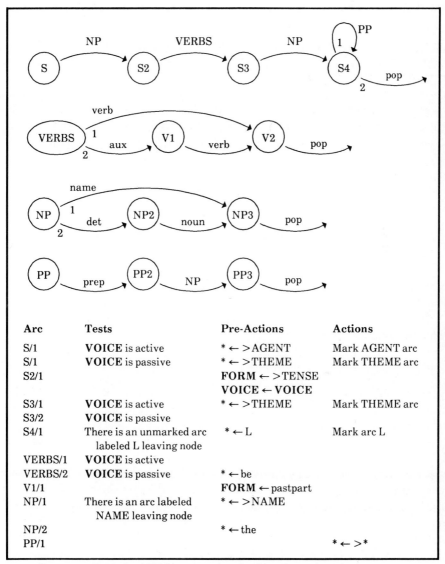

Arc

Arc	Tests	Pre-Actions	Actions
S/1	**VOICE** is active	* ← >AGENT	Mark AGENT arc
S/1	**VOICE** is passive	* ← >THEME	Mark THEME arc
S2/1		**FORM** ← >TENSE **VOICE** ← **VOICE**	
S3/1	**VOICE** is active	* ← >THEME	Mark THEME arc
S3/2	**VOICE** is passive		
S4/1	There is an unmarked arc labeled L leaving node	* ← L	Mark arc L
VERBS/1	**VOICE** is active		
VERBS/2	**VOICE** is passive	* ← be	
V1/1		**FORM** ← pastpart	
NP/1	There is an arc labeled NAME leaving node	* ← >NAME	
NP/2		* ← the	
PP/1			* ← >*

Grammar 17.12 An ATN for generating simple active and passive sentences

Consider this ATN operating from node B1 with the decision already made to generate an active sentence. In other words, the register * is set to B1, and **VOICE** is set to active. To follow arc S/1, its test for the active voice succeeds, and the NP network is called with * preset to node JACK1. When arc NP/1 is followed, * is preset to "Jack" and *Jack* is generated as the first word of the sentence. The system is now at node NP3, and following the pop arc, returns to the S network at arc S/1. Remember that the value of * in the S network was not changed when * was preset to the value for the NP network; thus it is still set to node B1. The actions on arc S/1 are performed, and the AGENT role is marked as generated. Arc S2/1 is tried next. The register **FORM** is preset to PAST, **VOICE** (in the VERBS network) is preset to active, and when arc VERBS/1 is followed, the verb *bought* is generated. After the pop arc, the system is at node S3. The test on arc S3/1 is tried and succeeds; * is preset to the THEME node, BK2; and the NP network is called. The test on arc NP/1 fails, so NP/2 is followed with register * preset to *the*. Next arc NP2/1 is tried and the word *book* is generated interpreting node BK2. Following the pop arc from node NP3, the interpreter returns to the S network ready to perform the action for arc S3/1. This marks the THEME role as generated.

The test on arc S4/1 succeeds in finding the FROM-POSS arc, and the PP network is called with * preset to that arc. Arc PP/1 is followed, generating the preposition *from* interpreting the arc FROM-POSS, and * is updated to >FROM-POSS, which is node SUE1. When the NP network is called, the name *Sue* is generated by arc NP/1. Thus a correct realization of the logical form has been generated from this modified ATN grammar. The final sentence is *Jack bought the book from Sue*. If the **VOICE** register had been set to passive, this same ATN would have generated the sentence *The book was bought from Sue by Jack*, given node B1.

17.4 Grammars and Generation

The techniques discussed in the last section can be used quite successfully in situations where the processes of deciding what to say, of choosing the lexical realizations, and of generating a sentence can be handled as separate phases. It is difficult, however, to deal with situations where planning the content of what to say might depend on the way that the content is realized. For instance, a speaker might give quite different utterances as requests to do some task, such as borrowing some money, depending on how well he or she knows the hearer, and depending on what has been said already. In other words the way the sentence is phrased can be important to the planning process. The earlier organization did not allow such interactions, because the processes of selecting the content and of generating the actual sentence were completely independent.

There are different ways to organize a generation system to gain more flexibility. The ideal organization lets each module contribute the choices to do with its area of concern, without having to make other decisions that would be better made by some other module. There are two main approaches addressing this goal. The first approach involves a more general notion of grammar than you've seen so far and uses the grammar to drive the generation process. Systems using this approach tend to use some variant of the systemic grammar framework (see Box 17.2). The other approach involves a more distributed control, where the syntactic component is only one of many components that contribute to the design of the sentence. This section considers one example of each of these two approaches.

You have already seen a generator driven by a syntactic component--the ATN system that interpreted semantic networks. The problem with using this approach to drive the entire generation process is that it forces a certain ordering of decisions about the surface structure of the sentence that must be followed by the system. For example, the active-passive decision must be made at the start, even though more important decisions regarding the overall form of the content and the lexical choices might seem more appropriate to consider first. In fact, the active-passive decision many times may be a result of some other module: The planning module might want to avoid attributing responsibility by using the passive, or a discourse component might choose a certain subject NP for coherency reasons. A better order would be for the syntactic module to make the active-passive decision near the end so that it can accommodate the decisions made by the other components of the generation system. Thus a syntax-driven generator might be awkward to design or would involve considerable backtracking to redesign the sentence structure when new constraints are found.

Another type of grammar, however, is much better suited for controlling the generation process. Systemic grammars are organized as sets of loosely related choice systems, where each choice adds some constraint to the final sentence form, but the final structure of the sentence is determined only by the combination of all the different choices made. Thus the decisions about the mood of the sentence can be made either before or after decisions about what the new content of the sentence will be, or decisions about what objects should be in focus. The generator can then be driven by these choice systems: It simply picks one of the systems and then proceeds to call whatever modules in the system can best make the decision.

For example, most of the choices in the mood system can best be made by the utterance content planner. If the system uses a speech act planner for this purpose, the decisions about the mood can be made by that module. Assume the system is planning to realize an inform act, such as INFORM(SYS, USER, LOVES(JACK1, FIDO1)). The mood system in Box 17.2 can be used to control the decisions; then the first decision is to realize this by an indicative or imperative clause. Since this is an INFORM, the planner chooses an indicative clause and then chooses a declarative. Finally, the planner may decide whether to put this information into a sentence by itself, or to incorporate it into another as a relative clause. Assume that the planner chooses a bound clause, generating the INFORM by a separate sentence. These are all decisions that it is reasonable for the planner to make. As a result of each of these decisions, the following constraints have now been placed on the final sentence to be generated:

BOX 17.2 Systemic Grammar

One of the primary influences on work in natural language processing is **systemic grammar** (Halliday, 1985). This is a theory of language as a social activity, rather than a theory of abstract linguistic structure. It emphasizes the functional role of different linguistic constructs and the way they affect communication. This theory has had a significant impact on computational models, especially natural language generation systems. The grammar is organized as a set of choices that mirror the types of decisions that must be made when a generation system is attempting to choose a particular syntactic form. The choices in systemic grammar are organized into groups called **systems**, which represent the different interdependencies between choices.

For example, the mood system, which would represent all the choices that can affect the mood of a sentence, is written as follows:

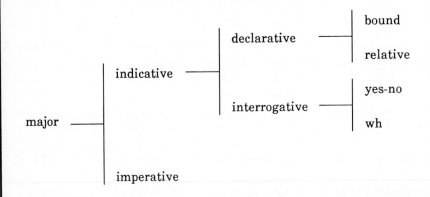

Once you make a certain choice, such as that the clause is indicative (in contrast to imperative), then you can make a decision as to whether the clause is declarative or interrogative, and so on. Each of these choices imposes some syntactic constraints on the final sentence. For instance, when an indicative clause is chosen, the sentence must have a subject NP; when an interrogative is chosen, the subject must be inverted with the first auxiliary; and so on.

In addition, complex interactions can be represented using an extended notation. In a sense the straight bars here represent a disjunction. Thus an indicative clause may be a declarative clause or an interrogative clause. Brackets can be used to represent conjunctions. For example, in a system to determine the proper form for pronouns, each pronoun is determined by both a choice of number and a choice of person.

In addition, the gender of the referent only is a relevant choice when the pronoun is third-person singular. The pronoun system would look as follows:

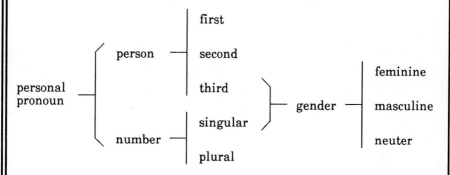

Attaching syntactic features to each of these choices, such systems can guide the formation of a particular sentence structure by providing a well-organized set of choices. A brief overview of systemic grammar can be found in Winograd (1983).

- The sentence will contain a subject NP, the verb group will carry tense, and the subject and first verb will agree (an indicative clause).

- The subject will precede the first verb (declarative).

- It will be realized as a complete sentence (bound).

The power of this framework is that the grammar translates decisions that the planner makes into constraints of the syntactic form of the sentence. The planner itself need have no knowledge of the syntactic consequences of its decisions. Other modules make decisions based on other choice systems and add additional constraints. For example, another choice system would include a choice between the active and passive voice. If the passive is chosen, it would include a choice between including or omitting the agent of the action. If a discourse module decided on a passive voice sentence with an explicit agent, the following syntactic constraints would be added to the preceding ones:

- The referent of the subject is FIDO1, there is an auxiliary *be*, the main verb is a past participle, and the auxiliary precedes the main verb (passive voice).

- There is a PP with preposition *by* and an NP with referent JACK1, which follows the main verb (explicit).

As each choice system is traversed, more syntactic constraints are added until the final sentence is completely specified.

In the alternative organization the grammar is not used to control the generation process. Rather, other techniques are used to produce partial semantic and syntactic strutures, which are then processed by the grammar to fill in the remaining details. If not enough information has been specified to identify a single sentence uniquely, the syntactic component might pass back additional decisions that need to be made, leading to the successive specification of the complete sentence structure. To make this possible, you need some uniform representation for the content, structure, and lexical items in the sentence. A framework that is useful for this purpose is called **functional unification grammar** (FUG), which is essentially the same framework as the unification grammar described in Chapter 5, except that there are no context-free rules associated with it. Rather, the syntactic ordering restrictions are given by patterns in the structures. The syntactic part of a very simple functional unification grammar is shown in Grammar 17.13.

Each structure roughly represents a rule in a grammar. Constructing a full sentence involves unifying structures together as described in Chapter 5. The only addition is the **PATTERN** slot that determines the order of constituents. A list of constituents indicates that they must appear in that order in the final sentence. If the pattern contains dots (...), this means that other constituents can be inserted there, but the ordering of the named constituents must be preserved. For example, the pattern (**FIRST-NP MAIN-V OBJ**) unifies with (... **MODS**) to produce (**FIRST-NP MAIN-V OBJ MODS**). The pattern (**DET ... NOUN**), on the other hand, could unify with (... **ADJ HEAD**) to produce (**DET ADJ HEAD**).

The power of this approach for generation arises from the fact that semantic and discourse information can be encoded in the same notation as well. This requires introducing a simple notational variant of the logical form as follows. The case roles become slots, and new slots are introduced for the tense, type, and specifiers as needed. For example, node B1 in Figure 17.9 would be represented as structure 1.

1. (S **TENSE** past
        TYPE BUY1
        AGENT JACK1
        THEME BOOK23
        FROM-POSS SUE1)

```
(S  FIRST-NP (NP)
    MAIN-V (VERB)
    NUM = NUM_FIRST-NP = NUM_MAIN-V
    OBJ (NP)
    PATTERN (FIRST-NP MAIN-V OBJ))

(S  MODS (PP)
    PATTERN (... MODS))

(NP DET (ART)
    HEAD (NOUN)
    PATTERN (DET ... HEAD))

(NP PRO (PRO)
    PATTERN (PRO))

(NP NAME (NAME)
    PATTERN (NAME))

(PP PREP (PREP)
    POBJ (NP)
    PATTERN (PREP POBJ))
```

Grammar 17.13 A simple functional unification grammar

```
(S  FIRST-NP = (NP REF = ^AGENT)
    OBJ = (NP REF = ^THEME)
    VOICE active)

(S  FIRST-NP = (NP REF = ^THEME)
    AUX be
    MODS (PP PREP by
                POBJ = (NP REF = ^AGENT))
    VOICE passive)

(S  FIRST-NP = (NP REF = ^THEME)
    AUX be
    VOICE passive)
```

Figure 17.14 Three rules for the active/passive choice

With this representation, the mapping to the syntactic form can be done by unification operations that equate roles like **AGENT** with syntactic slots like **FIRST-NP**. For example, assume there is a discourse module that chooses between active and passive sentence forms. To record its decision, it simply has to pick one of the S forms in Figure 17.14 that map the case roles to the syntactic positions desired. The "^" symbol in the structures indicate that the register following the symbol is part of the constituent containing the current constituent. Thus (NP **REF** = **^AGENT**) unifies the **REF** role of the NP with the **AGENT** role of structure 1 that contains the NP. By unifying one of these into structure 1, the final structure is constrained to the desired form. For example, unifying the first of the structures in Figure 17.14 with structure 1 produces structure 2.

2.   (S **TENSE** past
          TYPE BUY1
          AGENT JACK1
          THEME BOOK23
          FROM-POSS SUE1
          FIRST-NP (NP **REF** JACK1)
          OBJ (NP **REF** BOOK23)
          VOICE active)

If there is no reason to make a choice between active and passive at this stage, the S structure may be left unconstrained, and a decision can be made later when the sentence is generated. By then, however, some other choice may have been made that eliminates one or more of these choices because of some other criteria. For example, the planning module may want to avoid attributing responsibility to the **AGENT** and thus constrain S to forms where the **AGENT** role is not realized. Only the third structure in Figure 17.14 could unify with this S structure.

The tense analysis can be done by a separate module that then simply unifies its results back into the S form being constructed. For example, if it chooses the simple past tense, it would unify the structure (S **MAIN-V** (VERB **TENSE** past)) into the result.

So far the basic overall structure of the sentence has been determined. None of the subconstituents of the S structure have yet been planned, except that both JACK1 and SUE1 will be referred to by noun phrases. A lexical analyzer could take this and plan how to realize each slot-value pair in the structure. For instance, the pair **TYPE**/BUY1 can be realized using a main verb with root *buy*. This is recorded by unifying in the structure (S **MAIN-V** (VERB **ROOT** BUY)). Note that this structure will be unified with the result of the tense analysis producing an almost complete lexical entry (the **NUM** register is not yet set).

It is already decided that the **AGENT**/JACK1 pair will be realized as an NP, so far specified as (NP **REF** JACK1) in the **FIRST-NP** slot. A referential analyzer (along the lines described in Section 17.3) might choose to realize this as a pronoun, unifying in the structure (NP **PRO** he). Similarly, the **THEME**/BK1 pair must be realized as an NP in the **OBJ** slot. The reference module might reason that this object has not been mentioned before and choose to introduce with an indefinite NP--namely, (NP **DET** a **HEAD** book). Unifying this with the first NP rule in Figure 17.13 produces the final NP specification:

```
(S  TENSE past
    TYPE BUY1
    AGENT JACK1
    NUM = NUM_{FIRST-NP} = NUM_{MAIN-V}
    THEME BOOK23
    FROM-POSS SUE1
    MAIN-V (VERB ROOT BUY
                 TENSE past
                 NUM {3s})
    FIRST-NP (NP PRO he
                 NUM {3s}
                 REF JACK1)
    OBJ (NP DET a
            HEAD book
            PATTERN (DET HEAD)
            REF BOOK23)
    MODS (PP PREP from
             POBJ (NP NAME Sue
                      REF SUE1)
             PATTERN (PREP POBJ))
    PATTERN (FIRST-NP MAIN-V OBJ MODS))
```

Figure 17.15 The final representation of the sentence

```
(NP DET a
    HEAD book
    PATTERN (DET HEAD))
```

The realization of the pair **FROM-POSS/SUE1** is planned as a prepositional phrase by adding the following structure

```
(S MODS (PP PREP from
            POBJ (NP REF = ^FROM-POSS)))
```

Finally, the NP in this structure might be planned as a proper name.

Once you have made all these choices, you determine the remaining details of the sentence structure by unifications with rules from the grammar itself, part of which was shown in Figure 17.13. In particular, unifying the current structure with the two S structures in Figure 17.13 would produce the final form shown in Figure 17.15, having constrained the PATTERN register for the S structure, and enforcing the subject-verb agreement. The sentence can then be trivially generated from this structure, as all ordering and word choice decisions have been determined, and the output would be *He bought a book from Sue.*

This example introduced a lot of mechanisms that may seem like overkill for such a simple sentence. The important point is that this method generalizes to more complex cases and, because of the loose independencies of many of the decisions made by the different components, it can be used to support the complex types of reasoning needed to generate coherent text. Each component needs to specify only the information relevant to its choice, be that a syntactic decision, a semantic decision, a lexical decision, or a combination of these. Also, because of the property of the unification operation, there is no particular order in which decisions have to be made. For example, the decisions about how to realize lexically the slot-value pairs (such as **FROM-POSS/SUE1**) could be done before the active-passive decision was made, and so on.

Summary

Natural language generation raises a set of problems different from natural language understanding. A system must have much more knowledge about the effects of different ways of phrasing sentences and must explicitly reason about how to organize the content of the sentences. There are two main problem areas, which are not wholly independent: planning the content of what to say and deciding how to say it. Some of the plan-based methods developed earlier were a useful starting point for the former problem. The role of syntax in generation systems must be different because the decisions about the actual structure of the sentence are best made last after the more functional properties of the structure have been considered. Systemic grammar and functional unification grammar may be suitable frameworks for this type of processing.

Related Work and Further Readings

A good survey of work in generation by McDonald appears in Shapiro (1987) under the heading "Natural Language Generation."

The section on deciding what to say is based on work by Cohen and Perrault (1979), Appelt (1985), and McKeown (1985). Cohen and Perrault showed how to use speech acts in a planning system and thus connected the goals of a system to the language that it generated. They did not consider the details of generating actual text, however, and simply produced a list of speech acts that would accomplish the goal. Appelt took this work and examined how to generate actual text from speech act descriptions. He developed techniques for eliminating unnecessary sentences by combining INFORM acts into other sentences and gave an explicit planning model for deciding on the appropriate way to generate descriptions for objects. McKeown considered the issues in planning extended text. She used a scriptlike representation to organize the discourse and used a reference module, similar to that described in Chapter 14, to determine appropriate descriptions for objects in discourse. McDonald and Conklin (1982), who looked at the problem of deciding what to say from a different perspective, developed a model based on what was most relevant in a given situation.

One of the earliest computation works on lexical choice was by Goldman (1975) who, using a primitive-based representation, used discrimination networks to select words that captured the situations described. Hovy (1985) has recently done work in this area, concentrating on the way that having different conversational goals can influence the choice of words and the phrasing of the sentences. There is at best a fine line between choosing single words and choosing entire phrases. Becker (1975) argued that phrases must be included in the lexicon to handle idioms, metaphors, and other colloquial uses of language. Many of these phrases cannot be analyzed in terms of their subparts and must be selected and generated as complete units. Jacobs (1985) has built a generator using the lexicon as the primary organizing tool.

Most generation systems in actual use today utilize techniques similar to those described in Section 17.3. The output is generated from a direct traversal of the representation and, in most cases, there is only one way to express any structure in the representation. This technique works only because the context is fixed in advance, so the programmer can predict how each part of the representation would be realized in a sentence. Winograd (1972) is a good example of this approach. Early systems that relied on explicit grammars often used an ATN to drive the generation of text, as in Simmons and Slocum (1972) and Goldman (1975). The material on ATNs in this chapter is derived from work by Shapiro (1982).

A paper by McDonald (1983) is a good example of how far the techniques in Section 17.3 can be pushed. His system starts with some representation and then interprets it using highly-specialized programs that progressively refine the representation into a syntactic description of the text, which is then interpreted by a syntactic component to generate the actual output.

Davey (1979) produced an early generation system using a systemic grammar. This system took advantage of a highly-restricted domain (describing tic-tac-toe games) to produce quite sophisticated descriptions of the content of the output, which then was mapped to language using a component based on a systemic grammar. More recently, Mann (1983) and Mann and Mathiesson (1985) have developed a large systemic grammar for English that is used to drive their generator. The discussion in Section 17.4 is derived from their work.

Functional unification grammars (Kay (1985)) have been used by Appelt (1985) and McKeown (1985). Both of these research projects concentrated on the planning of the content of the text (as described in Section 17.4), and they found this grammatical formalism well-suited for investigating the interaction between the grammatical issues and the content-planning issues.

Exercise for Chapter 17

1. *(medium)* Trace in detail the generation of the sentence *The book was bought from Sue by Jack* using the ATN grammar in Figure 17.12. Show the state of the system at the end of each arc traversal.

Appendix A

Logic and Rules of Inference

Logic has a long history, going back to before Aristotle. Modern logic, however, takes its form from the work of Frege in the late nineteenth century. The set-theoretic semantics for logic was developed by Tarski (1944). It is important to keep in mind here that there are many possible different notations for a logic, but the principles remain the same. In particular many of the notations used in AI can be shown to be notational variants, or subsets, of the first-order predicate calculus (henceforth called FOPC).

A.1 Logic and Natural Language

Logic was developed as a formal notation to capture the essential properties of natural language and reasoning. As a consequence, many of the structural properties have a parallel in natural language. For instance, an important distinction that can be made is between expressions that identify objects and expressions that assert properties of objects and identify relationships between objects. Noun phrases perform the first task in language, while sentences and clauses perform the second. In FOPC this same distinction is made between **terms**, which denote individuals or objects in the world, and **propositions**, which make claims about objects in the world.

There are two major classes of terms: **constants** and **functions.** The constants, which correspond most closely to proper names in language, will be written in uppercase italic letters with one or more digits following. For example, the name John might correspond to constants *JOHN1*, *JOHN2*, and so on, depending on how many individuals are named John. There is an important difference demonstrated here between natural language and FOPC: While natural language is ambiguous, each symbol in FOPC has a single meaning. The name *John* can be used in natural language to refer to many different people, whereas each one of those people would be represented by a distinct constant in FOPC.

Functions in FOPC correspond to noun phrases that refer to an object in terms of some property or relationship to other objects, such as *John's father* or *the king of Prussia*. They are written in FOPC as an expression consisting of a function name, written in lowercase italics, followed by a list of arguments (other terms) enclosed in parentheses. For example, the function corresponding to *John's father* might be *father(JOHN1)*.

Simple propositions in FOPC consist of a predicate name, written in uppercase italics, usually without any following digits, and a list of arguments, which are terms, enclosed in parentheses. These correspond to simple sentences in natural language, where the predicate names correspond to the verbs. For example, the sentence *John likes his father* might correspond to the formula *LIKES(JOHN1, father(JOHN1))*. More complex propositions are built out of simple ones using a set of logical operators, which have correlates in natural language. The simplest one of these is the negation operator (written as ¬), which corresponds to one common use of negation in natural language. For example, the sentence *John doesn't like his father* would correspond to the following formula:

$\quad$ ¬*LIKES(JOHN1, father(JOHN1))*

Other logical operators correspond to some of the connectives found in language. For example, the connective *and* in language corresponds to a conjunction operator (written as &) in FOPC. The connective *or* in language is ambiguous between two logical operators. The first, called disjunction, and written as ∨, corresponds to the interpretation of the sentence *John likes Sue or Mary*, where it is allowed that he might like both of them. The second, called exclusive-or, and written as ⊕, corresponds to the interpretation where he may like only one or the other, not both. Another important logical operator is the implication operator, written as ⊃, which corresponds roughly to the language connective *implies* in sentences such as *The fact that John has no money implies that he will not be able to buy a car.* Finally, the logical equivalence operator, written as ⇔, corresponds to the phrase *if and only if* in sentences such as *John will come to the party if and only if Sue comes.* In other words, they are either both at the party, or neither of them is at the party.

The final construct in FOPC is the quantified variable. A new term, known as a **logical variable**, is allowed in the logic, and two new operators are introduced to identify the way the variable is to be interpreted. The **existential quantifier**, written as ∃, is used for variables in sentences such as *There is a man who likes John*, which could be represented by the following formula:

$\quad$ ∃ *x . MAN(x) & LIKES(x, JOHN1)*

The **universal quantifier**, written as ∀, is used for variables in sentences such as *All men like John*, which could be represented by the following formula:

$\quad$ ∀ *y . MAN(y) ⊃ LIKES(y, JOHN1)*

Since logical operators can be nested within each other, a potential ambiguity arises in formulas depending on what operator is within the scope of what other operator. For example, the formula

$\quad$ ¬*P & Q*

could be read as the conjunction of two formulas (¬*P* and *Q*), or as the negation of the formula *P&Q*. To eliminate this possible ambiguity, you use the convention that the negation operators always take the smallest possible scope. If a wider scope is desired, then parentheses can be introduced. Thus the

Phrase	FOPC Equivalents
John	*JOHN1*
John's father, the father of John	*father(JOHN1)*
John likes his father	*LIKES(JOHN1, father(JOHN1))*
John doesn't like his father	$\neg$*LIKES(JOHN1, father(JOHN1))*
Either John is happy, or he is rich (or both)	*HAPPY(JOHN1)* $\vee$ *RICH(JOHN1)*
Either John is rich, or he is poor	*RICH(JOHN1)* $\oplus$ *POOR(JOHN1)*
John is happy and rich	*HAPPY(JOHN1)* & *RICH(JOHN1)*
That John is rich implies that he is happy	*RICH(JOHN1)* $\supset$ *HAPPY(JOHN1)*
John will go to the party if and only if Sue does	*GOTO(JOHN1, P5)* $\Leftrightarrow$ *GOTO(SUE1, P5)*
There is a fish in the pond	$\exists f$. *FISH(f)* & *IN(f, POND44)*
All fish are in the pond	$\forall f$. *FISH(f)* $\supset$ *IN(f, POND44)*

Figure A.1 The FOPC equivalents of natural language phrases

preceding formula takes the first interpretation described, whereas the second would be written as

$$\neg(P \,\&\, Q)$$

One other convenient notation was introduced earlier with the logical quantifiers. A dot (.) in a formula is used to indicate that the scope of the preceding operator extends to the end of the entire formula. This is a convenient way to eliminate deep nestings of parentheses. For example, consider the following formula, which corresponds to a reading of the sentence *Every boy likes some girl*:

$$\forall b \,.\, BOY(b) \supset \exists g \,.\, GIRL(g) \,\&\, LIKES(b, g)$$

Without the dot convention this would be written as follows:

$$\forall b \,(BOY(b) \supset \exists g \,(GIRL(g) \,\&\, LIKES(b, g)))$$

This notation is summarized in Figure A.1.

Inference: Logic as a Model of Thought

The primary motivation for developing such a notation is that it then allows a precise formulation of the notion of inference as well as of a valid argument or proof. For instance, as a speaker of the language, you recognize the following as an acceptable line of reasoning:

All dogs love bones and Fido is a dog. Thus Fido loves bones.

On the other hand, you probably find the following argument faulty:

Some dogs have fleas and Fido is a dog. Thus Fido must have fleas.

Acceptable lines of reasoning can be stated in an abstract form called an inference rule. For example, the first argument just cited could be stated in FOPC as the following rule, where D is a predicate true only of dogs, and LB is a predicate true only of objects that like bones:

$\forall x . D(x) \supset LB(x)$
$\underline{D(FIDO1)}$
$LB(FIDO1)$

This is read as follows: If the formula $\forall x . D(x) \supset LB(x)$ and the formula $D(FIDO1)$ are true, then the formula $LB(FIDO1)$ must also be true. Alternatively, if you think of this in computational terms, if the first two formulas are asserted to be true in a database, you can add that $LB(FIDO1)$ is also true.

In practice, inference rules are not specific to a particular predicate name; they are expressed using schemas where parameters of the form p, q, r, s stand for arbitrary propositions, and a, b, c stand for arbitrary terms, and x, y, z stand for arbitrary logical variables. If an index is added, as in p_x, then the parameter stands for an arbitrary proposition involving a term x. Given this, two inference rules of FOPC that account for the earlier argument are shown in Figure A.2.

Multiple inference rules may be combined to derive conclusions by constructing a proof. A proof consists of a set of premises and then a sequence of formulas, each derived from the previous formulas and the premises using some inference rule. For example, the simple argument about Fido loving bones can now be formally justified by the proof in Figure A.3.

In general, two inference rules--the **elimination rules** and the **introduction rules**--are defined for every logical operator defined in the logic. The former takes a formula that contains the connective as a premise and has a conclusion that does not contain the operator, while the latter takes one or more premises that do not contain the operator and has a conclusion that does contain the operator. While many of the rules can be expressed in the notation developed so far, some require an extension. For example, the rule of neg-introduction intuitively is as follows: To prove $\neg p$, assume p is true and show this results in a contradiction. For example, suppose you are given that Jack does not love bones and you want to prove that Jack is not a dog, given that all dogs love bones. You assume that Jack is a dog and show that this allows you to conclude that Jack loves bones, which contradicts your original premises. This proof is shown in

Implication-elimination Rule (or "Modus Ponens")	**Universal-elimination Rule**
$p \supset q$	$\forall x . px$
$\underline{p}$	$\overline{}$
q	pa

Figure A.2 Two inference rules

Step	Formula	Justification
1.	$\forall x . D(x) \supset LB(x)$	*premise*
2.	$D(FIDO1)$	*premise*
3.	$D(FIDO1) \supset LB(FIDO1)$	*univ-elim from step 1 (x replaced by FIDO1)*
4.	$LB(FIDO1)$	*implication-elim from steps 2 and 3*

Figure A.3 A proof that Fido likes bones

Step	Formula	Justification
1.	$\neg LB(JACK1)$	*premise*
2.	$\forall x . D(x) \supset LB(x)$	*premise*
2.1	$D(JACK1)$	*assumption for subproof*
2.2	$D(JACK1) \supset LB(JACK1)$	*univ-elim from step 2*
2.3	$LB(JACK1)$	*modus ponens from steps 2.1, 2.2*
2.4	$\neg LB(JACK1)$	*reiterating step 1*
3.	$\neg D(JACK1)$	*neg-introduction, steps 2.1, 2.3, 2.4*

Figure A.4 A proof deriving a negation via a contradiction

Figure A.4, where subproofs based on assumptions are indented to separate them from the main proof. In step 2.1, the assumption is made, and a contradiction is derived in steps 2.3 and 2.4. Step 2.4 is simply copied from step 1 using a new inference rule called **reiteration**, which allows a formula previously derived to be copied into a later position in an "assumption" subproof.

Similar inference rules based on making assumptions are needed to formulate implication-introduction (that is, assume p, then if you can derive q in the subproof, conclude $p \supset q$ in the main proof) and for universal introduction. For details, consult a text on introductory logic such as McCawley (1981) or Thomason (1970). A sample set of inference rules is shown in Figure A.5. Given

And-introduction Rule	And-elimination Rules
p	$p \ \& \ q$ $\qquad$ $p \ \& \ q$
q	———— $\qquad$ ————
$p \ \& \ q$	p $\qquad\qquad$ q
Or-introduction Rule	**∃-introduction Rule**
p	Pa
————	————
$p \lor q$	$\exists \, x \, . \, Px$
Neg-elimination Rule	**Neg-introduction Rule**
$\neg \, \neg p$	*assume p*
————	*derive q and $\neg q$*
p	$\neg p$

Figure A.5 Some additional inference rules

a set of inference rules, there will be a set of formulas that can be proven starting with no premises. These are called **tautologies** or, more simply, **theorems**, and reflect inherent properties of the logic itself. One theorem of great significance is the law of the excluded middle, which states that every proposition is either true or false (it can't be "undetermined"). The law states that any formula of the form

$$p \lor \neg p$$

must be true. In computational models, however, this law does not say that a particular reasoning system must know whether a particular proposition is true or not; it might not be able to prove p or prove $\neg p$. All this theorem says is that p is either true or false in actual fact; it does not comment on whether a particular reasoning system or proof method can show it to be true or false. A proof of this theorem is shown in Figure A.6, which proves it by assuming its negation and deriving a contradiction.

Two important theorems are called De Morgan's Laws:

1. $\neg(p \ \& \ q) \Leftrightarrow \neg p \lor \neg q$
2. $\neg(p \lor q) \Leftrightarrow \neg p \ \& \ \neg q$

Note that by combining the first of these laws with the law of the excluded middle you obtain another important theorem: $p \lor \neg p$ is equivalent to $\neg(p \ \& \ \neg p)$ (that is, let q be $\neg p$ in theorem 1). Since you just proved that $p \lor \neg p$ must be true (Figure A.6), this means that $\neg(p \ \& \ \neg p)$ must always be true as well. This says that no formula can be both true and false.

Step	Formula	Justification
1.1	$\neg(p \vee \neg p)$	*assumption*
1.2.1	p	*assumption*
1.2.2	$p \vee \neg p$	*or-introduction from 1.2.1*
1.2.3	$\neg(p \vee \neg p)$	*reiteration of 1.1*
1.3	$\neg p$	*neg-introduction using 1.2.1 to 1.2.3*
1.4.1	$\neg p$	*assumption*
1.4.2	$p \vee \neg p$	*or-introduction from 1.4.1*
1.4.3	$\neg(p \vee \neg p)$	*reiteration of 1.1*
1.5	$\neg \neg p$	*neg-introduction using 1.4.1 to 1.4.3*
1.6	p	*neg-elimination from 1.5*
2.	$\neg \neg(p \vee \neg p)$	*neg-introduction from 1.1, 1.3, 1.6*
3.	$p \vee \neg p$	*neg-elimination from 2*

Figure A.6 A proof of the law of the excluded middle

The syntactic description of legal formulas and the set of inference rules defines a rich framework in which many things can be proven. But this is not the most important point of logic for present purposes. For these applications the most important aspect of logic is that you can independently specify a notion of truth and assign a "meaning" to arbitrary formulas. This is the role of logical semantics, and it is the topic of the rest of this appendix.

A.2 Semantics

The aim of a formal semantics for logic is to be able to answer the following sorts of questions. Is there a definition of truth independent of what is provable from a set of axioms? How can you tell if a system contains enough inference rules? How can you tell if the set of inference rules proposed is reasonable--they can't be used to "prove" things that are false? How can you tell if a set of axioms is coherent and could describe some actual situation? These questions can be answered by formalizing the notion of what an actual situation could be and showing how formulas in the logic map to assertions about that situation. Such situations will be called **models of the logic**, and the approach to semantics described here is called **model theory**.

Consider a subset of FOPC consisting solely of propositions and the logical connectives. In other words there are no terms, no variables, and no quantifiers. This subset is usually called the **propositional calculus**. A model for the propositional calculus is simply a mapping from formulas to the values T (for true) and F (for false). Such a model is constructed by specifying the mapping for all atomic propositions and then deriving the values for compound formulas using definitions of the logical operators as functions from truth values to a single truth value. As such, this method embodies the assumption that the meaning of the logical operators can be defined solely in terms of the truth values of their arguments and is independent of the actual propositions themselves. For example, suppose the propositions P and Q are true (both are mapped to T). Thus if $P \& R$ is true for some proposition R, then $Q \& R$ must be true as well. The operator & is not affected by whether P or Q is its first argument, since both have identical truth values.

Specifically, define a function V, called the **valuation function**, that maps formulas to the values T or F. This function can be defined recursively using the following rules:

V.1 $V(p \& q) = T$ if $V(p) = T$ and $V(q) = T$, and is F otherwise;
V.2 $V(\neg p) = T$ if $V(p) = F$, and is F otherwise;
V.3 $V(p \lor q) = T$ if $V(p) = T$ or if $V(q) = T$, and is F otherwise;
V.4 $V(p \supset q) = T$ if $V(p) = F$, or if $V(q) = T$, and is F otherwise;
V.5 $V(p \Leftrightarrow q) = T$ if $V(p) = V(q)$, and is F otherwise.

The definitions V.1 through V.3 should agree readily with your initial intuitions when the operators were first defined using their natural language analogues. The definition for implication, however, requires some explanation. If you say a sentence such as *John being in the room implies that he saw the murder*, you are actually claiming not only that there is some logical connection between *John being in the room* and *John seeing the murder* but also that John was in the room. This second assumption is not included in the logical implication operator. The question then arises as to what the truth value of a formula such as $p \supset q$ is when p is false. While there are several options available, each one producing a possible operator, the interpretation in common use, and the one assumed in constructing the inference rules for implication, is that the formula is simply true in such cases. This definition is embodied in rule V.4.

Using these rules, you can construct a complete set of models for the propositional logic containing only two propositions--P and Q. There are exactly four possible models, each one capturing one of the possible ways to assign T or F to each of the propositions. These models are summarized in tabular form in Figure A.7, where each row of truth values represents a single model. The truth values for simple formulas built from a single application of a logical connective are shown as well. All of these values are derived using rules V.1 to V.5. Inspecting this table, you can see a new way in which to demonstrate logical equivalence between formulas. For example, rather than constructing a proof that the formula $P \supset Q$ is equivalent to the formula $\neg P \lor Q$, you can show that in all possible models the formula $(P \supset Q) \Leftrightarrow (\neg P \lor Q)$ has the value T. To see this, consider building up the truth value for this formula in model 2. Using rule

Model	P	Q	¬P	P&Q	P∨Q	P⊃Q	P⇔Q	¬P∨Q	(P⊃Q) ⇔ (¬P∨Q)
1.	T	T	F	T	T	T	T	T	T
2.	T	F	F	F	T	F	F	F	T
3.	F	T	T	F	T	T	F	T	T
4.	F	F	T	F	F	T	T	T	T

Figure A.7 The possible models for P and Q

V.4 you see that the value for $P \supset Q$ is F. Using rule V.2 you see that the value of $\neg P$ is F, and via V.3 you see that the value of $\neg P \vee Q$ is F. Combining these two results, you see that the value for $(P \supset Q) \Leftrightarrow (\neg P \vee Q)$ is T. Similarly, in all the other models, the value is T as well.

So you now have two independent definitions of the logical operators--one by inference rule, and the other by the valuation function. Can you show that both methods agree on all formulas? If so, you have gone a long way toward answering the questions at the beginning of this section.

The Relationship Between Logics and Semantics

Start by examining whether the inference rules are **sound**--that is, they can never be used to prove something to be true when in actual fact it is not. For example, consider the rule of modus ponens (implication-elimination):

$$p \supset q$$
$$\underline{p \qquad\qquad}$$
$$q$$

While the inference rule is stated in terms of parameters ranging over propositions, you can instead consider the single case involving the propositions P and Q, since you are considering all possible combinations of truth values anyway. To show that this inference rule is sound you need to show that in any possible model where the premises are true, the conclusion must hold as well. In this case, using P and Q for p and q, respectively, you see that $P \supset Q$ and P are true only in model 1 in Figure A.7, in which Q is also assigned T as well. Similarly, for the or-introduction rule, you see that models 1 and 2 satisfy the premise P, and in both models the formula $P \vee Q$ is assigned to be T.

Another problem described earlier can now be solved. You can show that a given set of formulas is **consistent**: They could describe an actual situation by finding a model that assigns every formula in the set to T. Such a model is said to **satisfy** the set of formulas. For example, you can show that the set of formulas

$\{\neg P,\ P \vee Q,\ Q\}$

is consistent because model 3 in Figure A.7 assigns each one of them to T. Conversely, you can show that the set of formulas

$\{P \supset (Q\ \&\ R),\ P,\ \neg Q\}$

is inconsistent by showing that no model exists that assigns each of them to T simultaneously. The complete truth table for this example is shown in Figure A.8.

With the proof theory there was a notion of formulas being provable and no notion of formulas actually being true. With the model theory you can now define a notion of truth as follows:

> A formula f is true if and only if f is assigned to T in all possible models.

It is not difficult to see that all tautologies should satisfy this definition. Since a tautology is provable using the inference rules and no premises, if you can show that all your inference rules are sound, the tautology must be true in all possible models. As a simple example, consider the truth table for a propositional logic involving a single predicate P. There are two models, one in which P is assigned T, and the other where it is assigned F. In either model the formula $P \vee \neg P$ is assigned T: if P is assigned T, then by rule V.3, $P \vee \neg P$ is assigned T; if, on the other hand, P is assigned F, then $\neg P$ is assigned T and hence by rule V.3, $P \vee \neg P$ is assigned T.

A more general form of this, called **entailment**, is defined as follows, where s stands for a set of formulas:

> s entails p (written as $s \vdash p$) if and only if p is assigned T in all models that satisfy s.

The final question to consider is whether you can show that a given set of inference rules is sufficient to allow all true formulas to be proven. In other words, if by using the model theory, you can show that some formula p is true in all models, then you want to show that p is provable using the inference rules defined for the logic. Completeness can be shown for a wide variety of different inference rules. Of most importance to computational approaches, the resolution method specifies a single inference rule that can be proven to be complete. That is, every true formula can be proven using repeated applications of the resolution rule.

Model	P	Q	R	$\neg Q$	$Q \& R$	$P \supset (Q \& R)$
1.	T	T	T	F	T	T
2.	T	T	F	F	F	F
3.	T	F	T	T	F	F
4.	T	F	F	T	F	F
5.	F	T	T	F	T	T
6.	F	T	F	F	F	T
7.	F	F	T	T	F	T
8.	F	F	F	T	F	T

Figure A.8 The possible models for P, Q, and R

A.3 A Semantics for FOPC: Set-Theoretic Models

A semantics for the first-order predicate calculus requires an extension of the truth table method and is most conveniently expressed in terms of set theory. This is because other expressions besides propositions need to be defined. The terms in FOPC represent not truth values but rather physical objects, events, times, locations, and so on. All these objects are considered to be members of a set of objects called the **domain**. If this set is divided into subclasses, such as physical object, event, time, and so on, the semantics would describe a logic called a **sorted logic**, where terms are classified according to what subclass they describe. For present purposes, however, assume a single set of elements in a domain called Σ. Given this, the valuation function for terms defines an element of Σ that the term refers to (often called the element that the term **denotes**).

In FOPC there is also a distinction between the predicate names and the propositions, which are constructed from a predicate name and a list of arguments. The valuation function maps unary predicate names to subsets of the domain. For example, the predicate name *RED* might map to the set of all elements of Σ that can be described as being red. The semantics for a simple proposition built from an unary predicate name can now be defined as follows (where P is any unary predicate name, and t is any term):

$V(P(t)) = $ T if $V(t)$ is a member of $V(P)$, and F otherwise

Predicate names that take more than one argument are treated similarly. The valuation function maps a predicate name P that takes n arguments to a set of lists of elements of length n, and the semantics for simple propositions can be defined as follows (where P is any n-argument predicate name, and a_1, ..., a_n are any terms):

$V(P(a_1, ..., a_n)) = $ T if $(V(a_1), ..., V(a_n))$ is a member of $V(P)$,
    and F otherwise

For example, consider a domain Σ consisting of elements σ, δ, and ϕ and a model in which the valuation function is defined as follows for the terms:

$V(A1) = \sigma;\ \ V(B1) = \sigma;\ \ V(C1) = \delta;$ and $V(D1) = \phi$

Then let the valuation of the predicate name *LIKES* be the set $\{(\sigma, \delta), (\delta, \phi)\}$. Given this, the valuation of the proposition *LIKES(A1, C1)* is T since $V(LIKES(A1, C1)) = $ T if $(V(A1), V(C1))$ is a member of $V(LIKES)$. That is, if (σ, δ) is a member of $\{(\sigma, \delta), (\delta, \phi)\}$, which is the case. Similarly, in this model $V(LIKES(B1, C1)) = $ T and $V(LIKES(A1, B1)) = $ F.

The Semantics for Quantifiers

The quantifiers can now be given a semantics. All that is needed is an ability to make substitutions for variables in formulas. Rather than define this formally here, proceed on an intuitive basis. Letting P_x be any formula involving the term x (as defined earlier), the semantics for the quantifiers is as follows:

$V(\forall x . Px) = $ T if for every element α in Σ, $V(P_\alpha) = $ T

$V(\exists x . Px) = $ T if there is at least one α in Σ such that $V(P_\alpha) = $ T

Note that there is a problem with this definition since the elements of Σ are not legal terms in the logic, and thus an expression like P_α is not really a well-formed formula in the logic. This difficulty can be avoided in a more complicated definition, but that will not be pursued here since the essence of the approach is captured well here.

All of the preceding definitions of soundness, consistency, completeness, and so on carry over to the semantics for FOPC without change. For instance, you can show that a set of formulas is consistent by constructing a model that makes each one true. For example, consider the following set of formulas:

$\{\forall x . Q(x) \supset R(x), Q(A1),\ Q(B1),\ \neg Q(C1)\}$

A model can be constructed for these formulas as follows: Let Σ be the set $\{\sigma, \delta, \phi\}$ where $V(A1) = \sigma$, $V(B1) = \delta$, and $V(C1) = \phi$. Let $V(Q) = \{\sigma, \delta\}$ and $V(R) = \{\sigma, \delta, \phi\}$. Now you see that each of the preceding formulas evaluates to T given this model. In fact, there is another equally simple model that also satisfies these formulas where $V(R) = \{\sigma, \delta\}$. These two models could be summarized in an extended truth table format as shown in Figure A.9. As you can see, the extended truth table requires an entry for every possible predicate/argument combination and so rapidly becomes unwieldy as the number of terms grows.

Model	$Q(A1)$	$Q(B1)$	$Q(C1)$	$R(A1)$	$R(B1)$	$R(C1)$	$\neg Q(C1)$	$\forall x . Q(x) \supset R(x)$
1.	T	T	F	T	T	T	T	T
2.	T	T	F	T	T	F	T	T

Figure A.9 Two models for $\{\forall x . Q(x) \supset R(x), Q(A1), Q(B1), \neg Q(C1)\}$

That is why the set-theoretic formulation is commonly used. Presenting the small example in truth table form, however, shows the relationship between the semantics for propositional logic and that for FOPC.

Related Work and Further Readings

A good text on logic and its relevance to linguistics is McCawley (1981). Otherwise, there are many good introductory texts (for example, Thomason (1970)).

Exercises for Appendix A

1. *(easy)* Represent "Sam is Bill's father" by FATHER(BILL, SAM), and "Harry is one of Bill's ancestors" by ANCESTOR(BILL, HARRY). Write a formula to represent "Every ancestor of Bill is either his father, his mother, or one of their ancestors."

2. *(easy)* Construct two sentences that seem difficult to express in predicate calculus and discuss why you think this is so.

3. *(easy)* Define the valuation function that defines the semantics of the exclusive-or operator as defined in this appendix, and then show that the following rules of inference are sound.

$$\frac{\begin{array}{c} p \oplus q \\ p \end{array}}{\neg q} \qquad \frac{\begin{array}{c} p \oplus q \\ \neg p \end{array}}{q}$$

4. *(easy)* For each of the following sets of formulas, determine whether or not it is consistent by constructing a truth table.

   $S1 = \{P, \neg P\}$
   $S2 = \{P \supset Q, \neg P, \neg Q\}$
   $S3 = \{P \supset Q, Q \supset R, \neg P, R, \neg Q\}$
   $S4 = \{P \vee Q, \neg P \& \neg Q]$

5. *(medium)* Express the following facts in FOPC and give a proof of the conclusion. If necessary, add common-sense axioms so that the conclusion follows from the given assumptions.

a) Assumptions:

   Tomorrow it will either be warm and sunny or cold and rainy.
   Tomorrow it will be sunny.
   Conclusion: Tomorrow it will be warm.

b) Assumptions:

   Tweety is a bird.
   Tweety eats all good food.
   Sunflower seeds are good food.
   Conclusion: There is a bird that eats sunflower seeds.

6. *(hard)* Define the valuation function for unary function terms as follows
   (hint: this development will mirror the valuation of predicates):

   a) To what should the valuation function map a unary function-name?

   b) Define the general rule that defines the valuation of a unary function term
      (that is, a function-name applied to its argument).

   c) Extend the following definition of the valuation function V by defining it for
      the function-name *father* so that the following set of formulas is satisfied.

      $S = \{HAPPY(father(JOHN1)), \neg HAPPY(father(SUE2)),$
      $\qquad HAPPY(JACK2)\}$

   The valuation function is partially defined by

   $V(JOHN1) = \sigma;\ V(SUE2) = \delta,\ V(JACK2) = \phi;\ V(HAPPY) = \{\phi\}$

Appendix B

Symbolic Computation

This appendix introduces some of the basic techniques of symbolic computation. The text assumes some familiarity with a programming language but not necessarily one that deals with symbolic data. If you are familiar with the languages LISP or PROLOG, Section B.1 may be safely skipped. If, in addition, you have some background in artificial intelligence and know the unification algorithm, Section B.2, which deals with matching and unification, may be skipped. Section B.3 describes the basic ideas underlying Horn-clause-based theorem proving, and finally Section B.4 presents the unification algorithm in detail.

B.1 Symbolic Data Structures

Lists

This text uses many different data structures to represent the results of different forms of analyses. All of these structures will be built from a simple data structure upon which the programming language LISP is based, which is called a **list**. A simple list is constructed out of a sequence of terms called **atoms**, which are simply strings of characters that do not begin with a number. For example,

(A Happy TOAD)

is a list consisting of three atoms--A, Happy, and TOAD. Atoms do not have to be English words; the following is also a valid list of five atoms:

(R3 forty XX3Y7 AAA1 ?X3)

A list in general may contain not only atoms but other lists as well. The following is a valid list consisting of four **elements**--the atom NP, the list (DET the), the list (ADJ happy), and the list (HEAD toad):

(NP (DET the) (ADJ happy) (HEAD toad))

You shall see many structures like this later on. This one could be a syntactic representation of the English noun phrase *the happy toad*. How it is interpreted will be discussed later.

There is no limit to how many times a list may be embedded in another list. Thus

(((A TWO) (B THREE)) (((D)) E))

is a valid list. Taking it apart, you see that it is a list consisting of two elements: the list ((A TWO) (B THREE)) and the list (((D)) E). The second element itself is a list consisting of two elements: the list ((D)) and the atom E. The element ((D)) is a list consisting of one element, the list (D), which itself consists of one element--the atom D.

The list containing one atom, such as (D), is very different from the atom--that is, D. These might have completely different interpretations by a program.

Finally, a list containing no elements, written as ( ), is a valid list and may itself be an element of another list. It is called the null, or **empty** list, and is often written as NIL or nil.

The following are not valid lists:

((A B)--The parentheses are not balanced.

((1A B))--1A is not a valid atom.

A few operations on lists are important to know. These operations take lists apart or construct new lists out of other lists and atoms. There are two basic functions for taking a list apart:

First(<list>) - takes any list and returns its first element. It is undefined on the empty list and on atoms.

Rest(<list>) - takes a list and produces the list consisting of all elements but the first one. It is also not defined on atoms or the empty list.

Figure B.1 shows the results of applying these functions to various lists.

To construct lists, you can use two functions: Insert and Append. Figure B.2 shows these functions used in various situations.

Insert(<atom>, <list>) - returns a new list with the <atom> as the first element, followed by the elements in <list>.

Append(<atom>, <list>) - returns a new list with the <atom> added onto the end of the <list>.

Finally, some tests on lists are useful for examining lists. These tests return a value of TRUE or FALSE depending on the structure of their arguments, and are usable in **if-then-else** type statements:

Null(<list>) - is TRUE only if the <list> is the empty list.

Member(<atom>, <list>) - is TRUE only if the <atom> is an element of the <list>.

```
First((A B C))        equals    A
First(((A B) C))      equals    (A B)
First(((A B C)))      equals    (A B C)

Rest((A B C))         equals    (B C)
Rest(((A B) C))       equals    (C)
Rest(((A B C)))       equals    ( ), the empty list
```

Figure B.1 Examples of list operations

```
Insert(A, (B C))      equals    (A B C)
Insert((A B), (C))    equals    ((A B) C)
Insert((A B C), ( ))  equals    ((A B C))

Append(A, (B C))      equals    (B C A)
Append((A B), (C))    equals    (C (A B))
Append((A B C), ( ))  equals    ((A B C))
```

Figure B.2 Examples of list constructors

```
Member(A, (A B C))       is      TRUE
Member(A, ((A) B C))     is      FALSE
Member((A), (A B C))     is      FALSE
Member((A), ((A) B C))   is      TRUE
Member(B, (A B C))       is      TRUE
Member(B, (A B C B))     is      TRUE
Member(B, ((A B) C))     is      FALSE
```

Figure B.3 Examples of the Member predicate

Multiple occurrences of the atom in a list are allowed, and the Member predicate will return TRUE in such situations. Member succeeds only if the atom is an element of the list, not if the atom occurs within a sublist element. Figure B.3 shows some examples of this.

While this book can be understood without a knowledge of the LISP language, the LISP equivalents to these functions and predicates are shown in Figure B.4 for those who are interested. Further details on LISP can be found in textbooks such as Wilensky (1986) and Winston and Horn (1984).

Stacks and Queues

In the algorithms outlined in this text you will often use data structures named **stacks** and **queues**. These can be built simply from list structures but are important enough to consider separately.

Operation	LISP Equivalent
First((A B C))	(CAR '(A B C))
Rest((A B C))	(CDR '(A B C))
Insert(A, (B C))	(CONS 'A '(B C))
Append(A, (B C))	(APPEND '(B C) (LIST 'A))
Null((A))	(NULL '(A))
Member(A, (A B C))	(MEMBER 'A '(A B C))

Figure B.4 LISP equivalents

A **stack** is a list where all adding and removing of elements takes place at one end, called the **top** of the stack. This is analogous to a stack of trays in a cafeteria: When a tray is returned, it is put on the top; when a tray is taken, it is removed from the top. So at any time the tray just removed is always the last one that was added. For this reason, stacks are also often called LIFO (last in/first out) lists.

Stacks will be used in algorithms to keep track of items that need considering by the program. The general organization of such a program looks as follows:

1. Initialize the stack with one or more items.

2. Repeat the following until the answer is found:
    2.1 Remove the top item of stack.
    2.2 Consider the item.
    2.3 Add any new items to be considered onto the stack.

In general, the operation of adding an item to the stack is called **pushing** the item onto the stack, while removing an item is called **popping** the stack.

A more concrete example of a stack organization is the "in" tray in an office. The person in the office might operate as follows:

1. Letters are added to tray overnight.

2. Repeat until no letters:
    2.1 Remove top letter.
    2.2 Read it and reply.
    2.3 If new letters arrive in the meantime, add them to the tray.

Of course, if there are more letters arriving than the person can read, some letters that arrived overnight might never get read! Thus sometimes a different data organization must be used.

A **queue** is a list where all adding is done at one end, and removing is done at the other end. This is analogous to a queue in a bank. People enter at the end of the line, while the people at the front get served. This scheme is often called a

List 1	List 2	Match Result	Bindings
(A ?x C)	(A B C)	success	?x ← B
(A ?x C)	(A (B C) C)	success	?x ← (B C)
(A ?x C)	(A ?z C)	success	?x ← ?z
(A ?x C)	(A B D C)	fails	-----

Figure B.5 Some simple examples of matching with variables

FIFO queue (first in/first out), since the first person to arrive is the first one served.

If the harried office worker used a queue instead of a stack, he or she would eventually get to all the letters that arrived overnight, even though new letters arrived at an ever-increasing rate. Similar considerations will arise later in algorithms when you have to decide whether to use a stack or a queue structure.

B.2 Matching

Most of the techniques discussed throughout will involve some notion of matching lists together. The simplest match between two lists is whether they are identical. To obtain more general forms of matching, you need to allow **variables** in lists, which can match any element. Variables will be indicated by atoms with a prefix "?".

A variable may match any atom, sublist, or another variable. Thus a list with a variable, such as (A ?x C), could match (A B C), (A (B C) C), or (A ?z C) but could not match (A B D C), since ?x can take the place only of a single element.

It is often useful to know what a variable matched against. A variable is **bound** to a value if that variable matched against that value in the match. Thus, in the preceding examples, ?x would have been bound to B, (B C), and ?z, respectively, on the three successful matches. These results are summarized in Figure B.5.

Given this background, you can now define the concept of matching more precisely as follows:

> Two lists are said to **unify** if there is a set of bindings for the variables in the lists such that, if you replace the variables with their bindings, the two lists are identical.

Given that two lists unify, there may be many possible bindings that make them identical. For example, in unifying (A ?x C) with (A ?z C), there are many possible bindings for ?x and ?z, as shown in Figure B.6. When this arises, there is always one set of bindings that produces a new list that could unify with all the other solutions. This one is called the **most general unifier**. In Figure B.6,

	Bindings	Common Value
1.	?x ← ?z	(A ?z C)
2.	?x ← B, ?z ← B	(A B C)
3.	?x ← C, ?z ← C	(A C C)

Figure B.6 Three possible unifications of (A ?x C) and (A ?z C)

result 1 is the most general unifier, since it could unify with results 2 and 3. Neither 2 nor 3 can be most general, because they do not match with each other. If two lists unify, there is always a most general unifier, and it can be found reasonably efficiently using an algorithm called the **unification algorithm**.

Consider some more complex situations of unification. These arise when the same variable is used more than once in a list. In such cases some possible matches that look like they might succeed don't, because there is no single value for the variable that will make the two lists identical. For example, the list (A ?x ?x) does not unify with (A B C) because ?x would have to match both B and C. If ?x was bound to B, the first list would become (A B B), which is not identical to (A B C). Similarly, if ?x was bound to C, the first list would become (A C C), which is not identical to (A B C).

More complex examples can occur with sublists. For example, (A ?x C) will match (A (f ?y) C), since you can bind ?x to (f ?y) and the lists are identical. Furthermore, (A ?x C) would match (A (f ?y) ?y), since if you let ?x ← (f C) and ?y ← C, both lists become (A (f C) C).

Informally, you can match two lists by going through each list, element by element. Every time a variable must be bound, you rewrite each formula with every occurrence of the variable replaced by its new binding and then continue matching. If you are careful not to bind a variable unnecessarily, you will produce a most general unifier. Figures B.7 and B.8 contain a trace of this process on two situations--one a success and one a failure. The unification algorithm is presented in detail in Section B.4.

B.3 Horn Clause Theorem Proving

An important computational method is based on a specialized theorem prover called a **Horn clause theorem prover**. Such techniques are used in the programming language PROLOG.

A **Horn clause** can be viewed as a logical implication in which the left-hand side of the implication is a single, simple proposition. Thus

(FRIENDLY FIDO1) < (DOG FIDO1) (WELL-FED FIDO1)

To match (A ?x C ?x) with (A (f ?y) ?y ?z):

1. First Elements are: A and A

2. Second Elements are: ?x and (f ?y)

   Bind ?x to (f ?y), rewrite the two formulas to
   (A (f ?y) C (f ?y)) and (A (f ?y) ?y ?z)

3. Continue with Third Elements: C and ?y

   Bind ?y to C, rewrite the two formulas to
   (A (f C) C (f C)) and (A (f C) C ?z)

4. Continue with Fourth Elements: (f C) and ?z

   Bind ?z to (f C), rewrite the two formulas to
   (A (f C) C (f C)) and (A (f C) C (f C))

The lists are identical, so they unify.

Figure B.7 An informal trace of a unification procedure

To match (A ?x C ?x) with (A (f ?y) ?y ?y):

1. First Elements are: A and A

2. Second Elements are: ?x and (f ?y)

   Rewrite the formulas to
   (A (f ?y) C (f ?y)) and (A (f ?y) ?y ?y)

3. Third Elements are: C and ?y

   Rewrite the formulas to
   (A (f C) C (f C)) and (A (f C) C C)

4. Fourth Elements are: (f C) and C

Failure, since these cannot be made identical.

Figure B.8 An informal trace of a failure to unify

is a Horn clause interpreted as: FIDO is friendly if he is a dog and is well fed. That is, this would be expressed in FOPC as

$$(DOG\,(FIDO1)\ \&\ WELL\text{-}FED\,(FIDO1))\supset FRIENDLY(FIDO)$$

Horn clauses can also be viewed procedurally using the following interpretation of the Horn clause: To prove FIDO is friendly, prove that he is a dog, and then prove he is well fed.

You can use variables in Horn clauses, which are interpreted as universally quantified variables. Variables are prefixed by a "?". Thus

1.   (FRIENDLY ?x) < (DOG ?x) (WELL-FED ?x)

can be interpreted as all dogs that are well fed are friendly (that is, $\forall x (DOG (x)$ & $WELL\text{-}FED (x)) \supset FRIENDLY (x))$, or alternately, for any object x, to prove x is friendly, prove that x is a dog and that x is well fed.

Facts are Horn clauses without a right-hand side. Thus to assert that Fifi is a dog that is well fed, you add the facts

2.   (DOG FIFI) <
3.   (WELL-FED FIFI) <

Using clauses 1, 2, and 3, the system can prove that Fifi is friendly as follows:

    Goal: (FRIENDLY FIFI)

Matching the goal against clause 1, it finds the rule (letting ?x be FIFI)

4.   (FRIENDLY FIFI) < (DOG FIFI) (WELL-FED FIFI)

It would use the unification algorithm to instantiate the variable ?x in clause 1 to FIFI to produce clause 4. Continuing, to prove the goal in light of 4, it must prove the subgoals

5.   Goal: (DOG FIFI)
6.   Goal: (WELL-FED FIFI)

Since these are asserted in clauses 2 and 3, the proof of each of these subgoals is trivial, and the original goal is proved.

In general, many different rules might apply to a goal. In these cases they will be tried in turn until one succeeds. As another example, consider the following axioms:

        All fish live in the sea.
7.   (LIVE-IN-SEA ?x) < (FISH ?x)
        All cod are fish.
8.   (FISH ?x) < (COD ?x)
        All mackerel are fish.
9.   (FISH ?x) < (MACKEREL ?x)
        Whales live in the sea.
10.   (LIVE-IN-SEA ?y) < (WHALE ?y)
        Homer is a cod.

```
14.  (FISH WILLIE)
     Rule 8 applies, giving
         (FISH WILLIE) < (COD WILLIE),
         so there is a new subgoal
         15.  (COD WILLIE)
         ×  No rule applies, try other ways to prove 14
     Rule 9 applies, giving
         (FISH WILLIE) < (MACKEREL WILLIE)
         So there is a new subgoal
         16.  (MACKEREL WILLIE)
         ×  No rule applies, try 14 again, no more ways to prove 14
     ×  No rule applies, try other ways to prove 13
 Rule 10 applies giving
     (LIVE-IN-SEA WILLIE) < (WHALE WILLIE)
     So there is a new subgoal
     17.  (WHALE WILLIE)
     Rule 12 asserts 17 as a fact
     √  Goal 17 is Proved.
 √  Goal 13 is Proved.
```

Figure B.9 Trace of a Horn clause proof

11.   (COD HOMER) <
       Willie is a whale.
12.   (WHALE WILLIE) <

Given these axioms, a system can prove Willie lives in the sea as follows, using what is called a **backtracking** search. It starts with the goal:

13.   (LIVE-IN-SEA WILLIE)

Rule 7 appears applicable: unifying the left-hand side of 7 with 13, it obtains the rule

       (LIVE-IN-SEA WILLIE) < (FISH WILLIE)

It replaces the original goal with the new subgoal (FISH WILLIE) and continues as shown in Figure B.9.

B.4 The Unification Algorithm

This section presents the unification algorithm in detail. Remember that two arbitrary lists containing constants and variables unify if there is a set of **bindings** (that is, values) for the variables in the lists so that they become identical.

To MATCH T1 and T2

1. **If** T1 is a variable,
    then replace T1 with value of GET-VALUE(T1)

2. **If** T2 is a variable
    then replace T2 with value of GET-VALUE(T2)

3. **If** T1 = T2
    then return SUCCESS
    else if T1 is a variable
        then ADD-TO-ST(T1, T2) and **return** SUCCESS
        else if T2 is a variable
            then ADD-TO-ST(T2, T1) and **return** SUCCESS
            else if T1 and T2 are both lists
                then if MATCH (First(T1), First(T2)) succeeds
                    then return result from MATCH(Rest(T1), Rest(T2))
                    else return FAIL
                else return FAIL

Figure B.10 A preliminary matching algorithm

The values of variables can be stored in a data structure called the **symbol table**, or ST. Suppose you have an ST as follows:

variable	value
?x	A
?y	?z
?z	B

This would mean that ?x has the value A and ?y has the value ?z, which has the value B (thus ?y has the value B). Two functions need to be defined:

ADD-TO-ST(varname, value) - adds a new entry onto the ST.

GET-VALUE(varname) - returns the value for a variable.

GET-VALUE should check the symbol table repeatedly to find the most specific value for a variable. For example, GET-VALUE(?y) with the preceding ST should return B. If the variable has no entry on the ST, the variable name is returned. Thus GET-VALUE(?t) should return ?t given the preceding table.

With these tools the match algorithm between two formulas T1 and T2 is defined in Figure B.10. Rather than rewriting the formulas each time a variable binding is found, the information is stored in the symbol table. If MATCH succeeds, it returns SUCCESS and the symbol table will have been set to the variable values.

```
MATCHING (A ?y ?z) with (?x (B ?x) ?x)

Both are lists, so
      MATCHING A with ?x
      ← returns SUCCESS, and the ST now has the value A for ?x
      MATCHING (?y ?z) with ((B ?x) ?x)
            Both are lists, so
                  MATCHING ?y with (B ?x)
                  ← returns SUCCESS, and ST now has value (B ?x) for ?y
                  MATCHING (?z) with (?x)
                        Both are lists, so
                              MATCHING ?z with ?x
                                    Step 2: ?x has value A
                              ← returns SUCCESS, and ST now has value A for ?z
                  ← returns SUCCESS
      ← returns SUCCESS
```

Figure B.11   Trace of the matching algorithm

Steps 1 and 2 in Figure B.10 simply find the values of variables if they are already known. Step 3 does the actual matching. If one of the formulas is still a variable, that variable can be bound to the value of the other formula. Finally, if T1 and T2 are both list structures, it checks each element one by one to make sure each list matches. As an example, consider the trace of the algorithm in Figure B.11, matching the formula (A ?y ?z) with the formula (?x (B ?x) ?x), starting with an empty ST.

The final result is SUCCESS, and the ST is set to the following:

variable	value
?x	A
?y	(B ?x)
?z	A

If you **instantiate** the variables in one of the formulas with the values in the ST, you will get the answer, which is (A (B A) A). Note that while ?y is bound to (B ?x), ?x is bound to A, so ?y is actually bound to the value (B A).

One minor problem is left to resolve. If you tried to match the formula (P ?x ?x) with (P (f ?y) ?y) with the present algorithm, it would succeed with the ST

variable	value
?x	(f ?y)
?y	(f ?y)

To MATCH T1 and T2

1. **If** T1 is a variable,
   then replace T1 with value of GET-VALUE(T1)

2. **If** T2 is a variable
   then replace T1 with value of GET-VALUE(T2)

3. **If** T1 = T2
   then return SUCCESS
   else if T1 is a variable and T2 does not contain T1
       then ADD-TO-ST(T1, T2) and **return** SUCCESS
       else if T2 is a variable and T1 does not contain T2
           then ADD-TO-ST(T2, T1) and **return** SUCCESS
           else if both T1 and T2 are lists
               then if MATCH (First(T1), First(T2)) succeeds
                   then return the result from MATCH(Rest(T1), Rest(T2))
                   else return FAIL
               else return FAIL

Figure B.12 The unification algorithm

The problem is that now there is no instantiation of the variables that makes the two formulas identical. This is because ?y has the value (f ?y), which is actually (f (f ?y)), which is actually (f (f (f ?y))), and so on. Each time you replace ?y with its value, another ?y is introduced that needs replacing. These cases can be eliminated by checking that a variable is not being bound to a value that contains the same variable within it. In these cases the match should simply fail. Thus the final algorithm is as shown in Figure B.12. In practice, however, most PROLOG systems use the simpler version of unification for efficiency reasons.

Related Work and Further Readings

The best sources for additional reading in this area are textbooks on programming techniques in artificial intelligence, including sections on pattern matching, such as Winston and Horn (1984) and Wilensky (1986).

Exercises for Appendix B

1. *(easy)* Using the list functions First, Rest, Insert, and Append, generate

   a) (B A) from (A B)
   b) (A B) from (A B C)
   c) (D B C) from (A B C) and D

2. *(easy)* Unify the following pairs of lists, if possible. If not, show why they cannot be unified. Show the final symbol table and the most general unifier.

   a) ((A ?X) ?X), (?Y (B c))
   b) (?X ?Y), ((A ?Y) (B ?X))
   c) ((A ?X) ?X), (?Y ?Z)

3. *(easy)* Find the most general unifier for the following clauses, or explain why they do not unify (x, y, and z are variables):

   a) P(f(x), y), P(z, g(z))
   b) P(f(x, x), A), P(f(y, f(y, A)), A)
   c) P(f(A), x), P(x, A)

Bibliography

Abbreviations

Abbreviations are used for many of the references from conference proceedings and journals. In particular, AAAI is the American Association for Artificial Intelligence, and IJCAI is the International Joint Conference on Artificial Intelligence. Proceedings of the conferences for both of these organizations can be obtained from Morgan Kaufmann Publishers, Inc., 95 First Street, Los Altos, California, USA, 94022.

ACL is the Association of Computational Linguistics, COLING is the International Conference on Computational Linguistics, and AJCL is the *American Journal of Computational Linguistics*, the old name of the journal currently named *Computational Linguistics*. These conference proceedings and the journal can be obtained from Dr. Donald Walker (ACL), Bell Communications Research, 445 South Street, MRE 2A379, Morristown, New Jersey, USA, 07960.

An excellent collection of papers in the area is *Readings in Natural Language Processing*, edited by B. Grosz, K. Jones, and B. Webber and published by Morgan Kaufmann Publishers, Inc., in 1986. Papers reprinted in that volume are indicated here by the abbreviation RNLP.

Aho, A., R. Sethi, and J. Ullman. *Compilers: Principles, Techniques, and Tools*. Reading, MA: Addison-Wesley, 1986.

Aho, A.V. and J.D. Ullman. *The Theory of Parsing, Translation and Compiling*. Englewood Cliffs, NJ: Prentice-Hall, 1972.

Allen, J.F. "Recognizing intentions from natural language utterances," in M. Brady and R.C. Berwick (eds.), 107-166. *Computational Models of Discourse*. Cambridge, MA: MIT Press, 1983.

Allen, J.F. "Towards a general theory of action and time," *Artificial Intelligence* 23, 2, 123-154, 1984.

Allen, J.F. and C.R. Perrault. "Analyzing intention in utterances," *Artificial Intelligence 15*, 3, 143-178, 1980 (reprinted in RNLP).

Appelt, D.E. *Studies in Natural Language Processing: Planning English Sentences*. Cambridge, England: Cambridge U. Press, 1985.

Austin, J.L. *How to Do Things with Words.* New York: Oxford U. Press, 1962.

Bates, M. "The theory and practice of augmented transition networks," in L. Bloc (ed.). *Natural Language Communication with Computers.* New York: Springer, 1978.

Bates, M., M.G. Moser, and D. Stallard. "The IRUS transportable natural language database interface," in L. Kerschberg (ed.). *Expert Database Systems.* Menlo Park, CA: Benjamin/Cummings, 1986.

Becker, J. "The phrasal lexicon," *Proc. Theoretical Issues in Natural Language Processing (TINLAP-1),* 60-64, 1975.

Berwick, B. *The Acquisition of Syntactic Knowledge.* Cambridge, MA: MIT Press, 1985.

Birnbaum, L. and M. Selfridge. "Conceptual analysis of natural language," in R. Schank and C. Riesbeck (eds.). *Inside Computer Understanding.* Hillsdale, NJ: Lawrence Erlbaum, 1981.

Bobrow, D.G., R. Kaplan, D. Norman, H. Thompson, and T. Winograd. "GUS: A frame-driven dialog system," *Artificial Intelligence 8,* 155-173, 1977.

Bobrow, D.G. and T. Winograd. "An overview of KRL, a knowledge representation language," *Cognitive Science 1,* 3, 3-46, 1977.

Bobrow, R.J. and B.L. Webber. "Knowledge representation for syntactic/semantic processing," *Proc. AAAI,* 316-323, 1980.

Bobrow, R.J. and B.L. Webber. "PSI-KLONE: Parsing and semantic interpretation in the BBN Natural Language Understanding System," *Proc. Canadian Society for Computational Studies of Intelligence Conf.,* 1982.

Brachman, R.J. "On the epistemological status of semantic networks," in N.V. Findler (ed.). *Associative Networks.* New York: Academic Press, 1979.

Brachman, R.J. and H. Levesque (eds.). *Readings in Knowledge Representation.* Palo Alto, CA: Morgan Kaufmann, 1985.

Brown, J.S. and R.R. Burton. "Multiple representations of knowledge for tutorial reasoning," in D.G. Bobrow and A. Collins (eds.). *Representation and Understanding.* New York: Academic Press, 1975.

Brown, J.S. and R.R. Burton. "A paradigmatic example of an artificially intelligent instructional system," *Int'l. J. of Man-Machine Studies 10,* 323-339, 1978.

Bruce, B.C. "A model for temporal references and its application in a question-answering program," *Artificial Intelligence 3,* 1, 1-25, 1972.

Bruce, B.C. "Case systems for natural language," *Artificial Intelligence 6,* 327-360, 1975a.

Bruce, B.C. "Generation as a social action," *Proc. Theoretical Issues in Natural Language Processing* (ACL), 64-67, 1975b (reprinted in RNLP).

Carbonell, J. "POLITICS: Automated ideological reasoning," *Cognitive Science* 2, 27-51, 1978.

Carlson, G. "Generic terms and generic sentences," *J. Philosophical Logic 11*, 145-181, 1982.

Chafe, W.L. "Givenness, contrastiveness, definiteness, subjects, topics, and points of view," in C.N. Li (ed.). *Subject and Topic*. New York: Academic Press, 1976.

Charniak, E. "Context and the reference problem," in R. Rustin (ed.). *Natural Language Processing*. New York: Algorithmics Press, 1972.

Charniak, E. "A framed painting: The representation of a common sense knowledge fragment," *Cognitive Science 1*, 4, 1977.

Charniak, E. "The case-slot identity theory," *Cognitive Science 5*, 3, 285-292, 1981.

Charniak, E. "A parser with something for everyone," in M. King (ed.). *Parsing Natural Language*. New York, NY: Academic Press, 1983a.

Charniak, E. "Passing markers: A theory of contextual influence in language comprehension," *Cognitive Science 7*, 2, 171-190, 1983b.

Charniak, E. and D. McDermott. *An Introduction to Artificial Intelligence*. Reading, MA: Addison-Wesley, 1985.

Chomsky, N. "Three models for the description of language," *IRE Transactions PGIT*, 2, 113-124, 1956.

Chomsky, N. *Aspects of the Theory of Syntax*. Cambridge, MA: MIT Press, 1965.

Clark, H.H. and C.R. Marshall. "Definite reference and mutual knowledge," in A. Joshi, B. Webber, and I. Sag (eds.). *Elements of Discourse Understanding*. New York: Cambridge U. Press, 1981.

Clocksin, W. and C. Mellish. *Programming in PROLOG*. New York: Springer-Verlag, 1981.

Cohen, P.R. "On knowing what to say: Planning speech acts," Ph.D. thesis and TR 118, Computer Science Dept., U. Toronto, 1978.

Cohen, P.R. and H.J. Levesque. "Speech acts and rationality," *Proc. ACL*, 49-59, 1985.

Cohen, P.R. and C.R. Perrault. "Elements of a plan-based theory of speech acts," *Cognitive Science 3*, 177-212, 1979 (reprinted in RNLP).

Cohen, R. "Analyzing the structure of argumentative discourse," *Computational Linguistics 13*, 1-2, 11-24, 1987.

Colmerauer, A. "Metamorphosis grammars," in L. Bloc (ed.). *Natural Language Communication with Computers*. Berlin: Springer-Verlag, 1978.

Computational Linguistics 9, 3-4, (Special Issue on Ill-Formed Input), July-December 1983.

Cooper, R. *Quantification and Syntactic Theory*. Dordrecht: D. Rudel, 1983.

Cottrell, G.W. and S.L. Small. "A connectionist scheme for modelling word sense disambiguation," *Cognition and Brain Theory 6*, 89-120, 1983.

Cullingford, R. "SAM," in R. Schank and C. Riesbeck (eds.). *Inside Computer Understanding*. Hillsdale, NJ: Lawrence Erlbaum, 75-119, 1981.

Davidson, D. "The logical form of action sentences," in N. Rescher (ed.). *The Logic of Decision and Action*. Pittsburgh, PA: U. Pittsburgh Press, 1967.

Davy, A. *Discourse Production*. Edinburgh: Edinburgh U. Press, 1979.

DeJong, G. "Prediction and substantiation: A new approach to natural language processing," *Cognitive Science 3*, 251-273, 1979.

Donnellan, K. "Reference and definite descriptions," *Philosophical Review 75*, 281-304, 1966; reprinted in S. Schwartz (ed.). *Naming, Necessity, and Natural Kinds*. Ithaca, NY: Cornell U. Press, 1977.

Dowty, D.R (ed.). *Tense and Aspect in Discourse*, Special Issue, *Linguistics and Philosophy 9*, 1, 1986.

Dowty, D.R., L. Karttunen, and A. Zwicky (eds.). *Natural Language Parsing*. New York: Cambridge U. Press, 1985.

Dowty, D.R., R.E. Wall, and S. Peters. *Introduction to Montague Semantics*. Dordrecht, Holland: D. Reidel, 1981.

Dyer, M. *In-depth Understanding: A Computer Model of Integrated Processing for Narrative Comprehension*. Cambridge, MA: MIT Press, 1983.

Early, J. "An efficient context-free parsing algorithm," *Commun. of the ACM, 13*, 2, 94-102, 1970 (reprinted in RNLP).

Edwards, P. *The Encyclopedia of Philosophy*. New York: Macmillan, 1967.

Etherington, D. and R. Reiter. "On inheritance hierarchies with exceptions," *Proc. AAAI*, 104-108, 1983.

Fass, D. and Y. Wilks. "Preference semantics, ill-formedness, and metaphor," *Computational Linguistics 9*, 3-4 (Special Issue on Ill-Formed Input), 178-187, July-December 1983.

Feldman, J.A. and D.H. Ballard. "Connectionist models and their properties," *Cognitive Science 6*, 205-254, 1982.

Fikes, R.E. and N.J. Nilsson. "STRIPS: A new approach to the application of theorem proving to problem solving," *Artificial Intelligence 2*, 3/4, 189-208, 1971.

Fillmore, C.J. "The case for case," in E. Bach and R. Harms (eds.). *Universals in Linguistic Theory*. New York: Holt, Rinehart, and Winston, 1-90, 1968.

Fillmore, C.J. "The case for case reopened," in P. Cole and J. Sadock (eds.), 59-81. *Syntax and Semantics 8: Grammatical Relations*. New York: Academic Press, 1977.

Findler, N. *Associative Networks*. New York: Academic Press, 1979.

Finin, T. "The semantic interpretation of nominal compounds," *Proc. AAAI*, 310-312, 1980.

Flickinger, D., C. Pollard, and T. Wasow. "Structure-sharing in lexical representation," *Proc. ACL*, 262-267, 1985.

Fodor, J.D. *Semantics*. Cambridge, MA: Harvard U. Press, 1977.

Ford, M., J.W. Bresnan, and R.M. Kaplan. "A competence based theory of syntactic closure," in J.W. Bresnan (ed.). *The Mental Representation of Grammatical Relations*. Cambridge, MA: MIT Press, 1982.

Frazier, L. and J.D. Fodor. "The sausage machine: A new two-stage parsing model," *Cognition 6*, 291-295, 1978.

Frisch, A.M. "Using model theory to specify AI programs," *Proc. IJCAI*, 148-154, 1985.

Gazdar, G. "Phrase structure grammar," in P. Jacobson and G.K. Pullum (eds.). *The Nature of Syntactic Representation*. Dordrecht: D. Reidel, 131-186, 1982.

Gazdar, G., E. Klein, G.K. Pullum, and I. Sag. *Generalized Phrase Structure Grammar*. Oxford: Basil Blackwell, 1985.

Goldman, N.M. "Conceptual generation," in R.C. Schank (ed.). *Conceptual Information Processing*. Amsterdam: North-Holland, 1975.

Goodman, B. "Reference identification and reference identification failures," *Computational Linguistics 12*, 4, 1986.

Grice, H.P. "Meaning," *Philosophical Review 66*, 377-388, 1957; reprinted in D. Steinburg and L. Jakobovits (eds.). *Semantics*. New York: Cambridge U. Press, 1971.

Grice, H.P. "Logic and conversation," in P. Cole and J. Morgan (eds.), 41-58. *Syntax and Semantics 3: Speech Acts*. New York: Academic Press, 1975.

Grimes, J.E. *The Thread of Discourse*. The Hague: Moulton Press, 1975.

Grosz, B.J. "The representation and use of focus in a system for understanding dialogs," *Proc. IJCAI*, 67-76, 1977 (reprinted in RNLP).

Grosz, B.J. "The structure of task oriented dialog," *IEEE Symposium on Speech Recognition*, 1974; reprinted in L. Polanyi (ed.). *The Structure of Discourse*. Norwood, NJ: Ablex, 1986.

Grosz, B.J., D. Appelt, P. Martin, and F. Pereira. "TEAM: An experiment in the design of transportable natural-language interfaces," *Artificial Intelligence 32*, 2, 173-244, 1987.

Grosz, B.J., A.K. Joshi, and S. Weinstein. "Providing a unified account of definite noun phrases in discourse," *Proc. ACL*, 44-50, 1983.

Grosz, B.J. and C. Sidner. "Attention, intention, and the structure of discourse," *Computational Linguistics 12*, 3, 1986.

Gruber, J.S. "Look and see," *Language 43*, 937-947, 1967.

Haas, A.R. "A syntactic theory of belief and action," *Artificial Intelligence 28*, 3, 245-292, May 1986.

Halliday, M.A.K. "Notes on transitivity and theme in English," *Journal of Linguistics 3*, 199-244, 1967.

Halliday, M.A.K. *A Short Introduction to Functional Grammar*. London: Arnold, 1985.

Halliday, M.A.K. and R. Hasan. *Cohesion in English*. London: Longman, 1976.

Hankamer, J. and I. Sag. "Deep and surface anaphora," *Linguistic Inquiry 7*, 3, 391-426, 1976.

Hayes, P.J. "In defense of logic," *Proc. IJCAI*, 559-565, 1977.

Hayes, P.J. "The logic of frames," in D. Metzing (ed.). *Frame Conceptions and Text Understanding*. New York: de Gruyter, 1979.

Hendler, J. *Integrating Marker Passing and Problem Solving*. Hillsdale, NJ: Lawrence Erlbaum, 1987.

Hendrix, G.G. "Expanding the utility of semantic networks through partitioning," *Proc. IJCAI*, 115-121, 1975.

Hendrix, G.G., E. Sacerdoti, D. Sagalowicz, and J. Slocum. "Developing a natural language interface to complex data," *ACM Trans. on Database Systems 3*, 2, 105-147, 1978.

Herskovits, A. *Language and Spatial Cognition*. New York: Cambridge U. Press, 1986.

Hewitt, C. "PLANNER: A language for proving theorems in robots," *Proc. IJCAI*, 1971.

Hintikka, J. "Semantics for propositional attitudes," in J.W. Davis, D.J. Hockney, and K.W. Wilson (eds.). *Philosophical Logic*. Dordrecht: Reidel, 1969;

also appeared in L. Linsky (ed.). *Reference and Modality*. New York: Oxford U. Press, 1971.

Hirst, G. *Anaphora in Natural Language Understanding*. Berlin: Springer-Verlag, 1981a.

Hirst, G. "Discourse oriented anaphora resolution in natural language understanding: A review," *AJCL 7*, 2, 85-98, 1981b.

Hirst, G. *Semantic Interpretation Against Ambiguity*. New York: Cambridge U. Press, 1987.

Hobbs, J.R. "Resolving pronoun references," *Lingua 44*, B11-338, 1978 (reprinted in RNLP).

Hobbs, J.R. "Coherence and co-reference," *Cognitive Science 3*, 1, 67-82, 1979.

Hobbs, J.R. and S.M. Shieber. "An algorithm for generating quantifier scopings," *Computational Linguistics 13*, 1-2, 1987.

Hovy, E. "Integrating text planning and production in generation," *Proc. IJCAI*, 848-851, 1985.

Hughes, G. and M.J. Cresswell. *Introduction to Modal Logic*. London: Methuen, 1968.

Jackendoff, R.S. *Semantic Interpretation in Generative Grammar*. Cambridge, MA: MIT Press, 1972.

Jacobs, P. "PHRED: A generator for natural language interfaces," *Computational Linguistics 11*, 4, 219-242, 1985.

Jensen, K. and J. Binot. "Disambiguating prepositional phrase attachments by using on-line dictionary definitions," *Computational Linguistics 13*, 3-4, 1987.

Joshi, A. "Tree-adjoining grammars: How much context sensitivity is required to provide reasonable structural descriptions," in D.R. Dowty, L. Karttunen, and A. Zwicky (eds.). *Natural Language Parsing*. New York: Cambridge U. Press, 1985.

Kahn, K.M. and A.G. Gorry. "Mechanizing temporal knowledge," *Artificial Intelligence 9*, 2, 87-108, 1977.

Kamp, H. "A theory of truth and semantic representation," in J. Groenedijk, J. Janssen, and M. Stokhof (eds.), 277-322. *Formal Methods in the Study of Language*. Dordrecht: Foris Publications, 1984.

Kaplan, R.M. "A general syntactic processor," in R. Rustin (ed.). *Natural Language Processing*. New York: Algorithmics Press, 1973.

Kaplan, R.M. and J. Bresnan. "Lexical-functional grammar: A formal system for grammatical representation," in J. Bresnan (ed.). *The Mental Representation of Grammatical Relations*. Cambridge, MA: MIT Press, 1982.

Kaplan, S.J. "Co-operative response from a portable natural language system," in M. Brady and B. Berwick (eds.), 167-208. *Computational Models of Discourse.* Cambridge, MA: MIT Press, 1983.

Katz, J.J. and J.A. Fodor. "The structure of semantic theory," *Language 39*, 170-210, 1963; also in J.A. Fodor et al. (eds.). *The Structure of Language: Readings in the Philosophy of Language.* Englewood Cliffs, NJ: Prentice-Hall, 1984.

Kay, M. "The MIND system," in R. Rustin (ed.), 155-188. *Natural Language Processing.* New York: Algorithmics Press, 1973.

Kay, M. "Parsing in functional unification grammar," in D.R. Dowty, L. Karttunen and A. Zwicky (eds.), 251-278. *Natural Language Parsing.* New York: Cambridge U. Press, 1985 (reprinted in RNLP).

Kimball, J. "Seven principles of surface structure parsing in natural language," *Cognition 2*, 1, 15-47, 1973.

Konolige, K. "A computational theory of belief introspection," *Proc. IJCAI*, 502-508, 1985.

Kowalski, R.A. *Logic for Problem Solving.* Amsterdam: Elsevier North-Holland, 1979.

Knuth, D.E. "Semantics for context-free languages," *Mathematical Systems Theory 2*, 127-145, 1968.

Kripke, S. "Semantical consideration on modal logic," *Acta Philosophica Fennica 16*, 83-94, 1963.

Lehnert, W.G. *The Process of Question Answering.* Hillsdale, NJ: Lawrence Erlbaum, 1978.

Levesque, H.J. "A logic of implicit and explicit belief," *Proc. AAAI*, 1984.

Levin, J. and J. Moore. "Dialogue-games: Metacommunication structures for natural language interaction," *Cognitive Science 1*, 4, 395-421, 1977.

Lewis, D.K. *Counterfactuals.* Oxford: Basil Blackwell, 1973.

Linde, C. "Focus of attention and the choice of pronouns in discourse," in T. Given (ed.). *Syntax and Semantics* (vol. 12). New York: Academic Press, 1979.

Litman, D.J. and J.F. Allen. "A plan recognition model for subdialogues in conversations," *Cognitive Science 11*, 2, 163-200, 1987.

Lyons, J. *Semantics* (vols. 1 and 2). London: Cambridge U. Press, 1977.

Lytinen, S.L. "Dynamically combining syntax and semantics in natural language processing," *Proc. AAAI*, 574-578, 1986.

Mann, W.C. "An overview of the Penman text generation system," *Proc. AAAI*, 261-265, 1983.

Mann, W.C. and C. Mathiesson. "Nigel: A systemic grammar for text generation," in O. Freedle (ed.). *Systemic Perspectives on Discourse.* Norwood, NJ: Ablex, 1985.

Marcus, M. *A Theory of Syntactic Recognition for Natural Language.* Cambridge, MA: MIT Press, 1980.

Mays, E. "Failures in natural language systems: Applications to data base query systems," *Proc. AAAI,* 327-330, 1980.

McCarthy, J. "Circumscription: A form of non-monotonic reasoning," *Artificial Intelligence 13,* 27-39, 1980.

McCarthy, J. and P.J. Hayes. "Some philosophical problems from the standpoint of artificial intelligence," in B. Meltzer and D. Michie (eds.). *Machine Intelligence 4.* Edinburgh: Edinburgh U. Press, 1969.

McCawley, J.D. *Everything That Linguists Have Always Wanted to Know about Logic.* Chicago: U. Chicago Press, 1981.

McCord, M.C. "Slot grammars," *AJCL 6,* 1, 31-43, 1980.

McCord, M.C. "Modular logic grammars," *Proc. ACL,* 104-117, 1985.

McCord, M.C. "Focalizers, the scoping problem, and semantic interpretation rules in logic grammars," in D.H. Warren and M. van Caneghem (eds.). *Logic Programming and its Applications.* Norwood, NJ: Ablex, 1986.

McCord, M.C. "Natural language processing in Prolog," in A. Walker (ed.). *Knowledge Systems and Prolog: A Logical Approach to Expert Systems and Natural Language Processing.* Reading, MA: Addison-Wesley, 1987.

McDermott, D.V. "Tarskian semantics, or No notation without denotation!" *Cognitive Science 2,* 3, 1978 (reprinted in RNLP).

McDermott, D.V. "A temporal logic for reasoning about processes and plans," *Cognitive Science 6,* 101-155, 1982.

McDonald, D.D. "Natural language generation as a computational problem," in M. Brady and B. Berwick (eds.), 209-266. *Computational Models of Discourse.* Cambridge, MA: MIT Press, 1983.

McDonald, D.D. "Description directed control," *Computers and Mathematics 9,* 1, 1-33, 1985 (reprinted in RNLP).

McDonald, D.D. and E.J. Conklin. "Salience as a simplifying metaphor for natural language generation," *Proc. AAAI,* 75-78, 1982.

McKeown, K.R. *Text Generation.* New York: Cambridge U. Press, 1985.

Milne, R. "Resolving lexical ambiguity in a deterministic parser," *Computational Linguistics 12,* 1, 1-12, 1986.

Minsky, M. "A framework for representing knowledge," in P. Winston (ed.). *The Psychology of Computer Vision*. New York: McGraw-Hill, 211-277, 1975.

Moore, R.C. "D-SCRIPT: a computational theory of description," *Proc. IJCAI*, 223-229, 1973.

Moore, R.C. "Problems in logical form," *Proc. ACL*, 117-124, 1981 (reprinted in RNLP).

Moore, R.C. "Reasoning about knowledge and action," *Proc. IJCAI*, 223-227, 1977; extended version in J.R. Hobbs and J. Moore (eds.). *Formal Theories of the Common Sense World* (vol. 1). Norwood, NJ: Ablex, 1985.

Nilsson, N.J. *Principles of Artificial Intelligence*. Los Altos, CA: Morgan Kaufmann, 1980.

Palmer, M. "A case for rule-driven semantic processing," *Proc. ACL*, 125-151, 1981.

Patel-Schneider, P. "A four-valued semantics for frame-based description languages," *Proc. AAAI*, 344-348, 1986.

Pereira, F.C.N. "Extraposition grammars," *AJCL 7*, 4, 243-256, 1981.

Pereira, F.C.N. "Logic for natural language analysis," SRI Technical Note 275, SRI International, Menlo Park, California, 1983.

Pereira, F.C.N. "Characterization of attachment preferences," in D.R. Dowty, L. Karttunen, and A. Zwicky (eds.), 307-319. *Natural Language Parsing*. New York: Cambridge U. Press, 1985a.

Pereira, F.C.N. "Structure-sharing representation for unification-based grammar formalisms," *Proc. ACL*, 137-144, 1985b.

Pereira, F.C.N. and D.H.D. Warren. "Definite clause grammars for language analysis--A survey of the formalism and a comparison with augmented transition networks," *Artificial Intelligence 13*, 3, 231-278, 1980 (reprinted in RNLP).

Perlis, D. "Languages with Self-Reference I: Foundations," *Artificial Intelligence 25*, 3, 301-322, March 1985.

Perlmutter, D.M. and S. Soames. *Syntactic Argumentation and the Structure of English*. Berkeley, CA: U. California Press, 1979.

Perrault, C.R. "On the mathematical properties of linguistic theories," *Computational Linguistics 10*, 3-4, 165-176, 1984 (reprinted in RNLP).

Perrault, C.R. and J.F. Allen. "A plan-based analysis of indirect speech acts," *AJCL 6*, 3-4, 167-182, 1980.

Perrault, C.R. and P.R. Cohen. "It's for your own good: A note on inaccurate reference," in A. Joshi, B. Webber, and I. Sag (eds.). *Elements of Discourse Understanding*. New York: Cambridge U. Press, 1981.

Perrault, C.R. and B.J. Grosz. "Natural language interfaces," *Annual Review of Computer Science 1*, 47-82, 1986.

Polanyi, L. and R.J.H. Scha. "Discourse syntax and semantics," in L. Polanyi (ed.). *The Structure of Discourse*. New Jersey: Ablex, forthcoming.

Pollack, J. and D. Waltz. "Massively parallel parsing: A strongly interactive model of natural language interpretation," *Cognitive Science 9*, 51-74, 1985.

Pollack, M. "Plans as complex mental attitudes," in P. Cohen, J. Morgan, and M. Pollack (eds.). *The Role of Intentions and Plans in Communication and Discourse*. Cambridge, MA: MIT Press, forthcoming.

Pollard, C. *Generalized Phrase Structure Grammars, Head Grammars, and Natural Languages*. New York: Cambridge U. Press, forthcoming.

Pollard, C. and I. Sag. *Information-Based Syntax and Semantics, Vol. I: Fundamentals*. CSLI Lecture Note Series. Chicago, IL: Chicago U. Press, forthcoming.

Prior, A.N. *Past, Present, and Future*. Oxford, England: Oxford U. Press, 1967.

Proudian, D. and C. Pollard. "Parsing head-driven phrase structure grammar," *Proc. ACL*, 167-171, 1985.

Quillian, M.R. "Semantic memory," in M. Minsky (ed.). *Semantic Information Processing*. Cambridge, MA: MIT Press, 1968.

Quirk, R., S. Greenbaum, G. Leech, and J. Svartik. *A Grammar of Contemporary English*. New York: Seminar Press, 1972.

Radford, A. *Transformational Syntax*. New York: Cambridge U. Press, 1981.

Reichenbach, H. *Elements of Symbolic Logic*. New York: Macmillan, 1947.

Reichman, R. "Conversational coherency," *Cognitive Science 2*, 4, 283-328, 1978.

Reichman, R. *Getting Computers to Talk Like You and Me*. Cambridge, MA: MIT Press, 1985.

Reinhart, T. *Anaphora and Semantic Interpretation*. London: Croom Helm, 1983.

Reiter, R. "A logic for default reasoning," *Artificial Intelligence 13*, 81-132, 1980.

Rich, E. *Artificial Intelligence*. New York: McGraw-Hill, 1983.

Riesbeck, C. and R.C. Schank. "Comprehension by computer," in W. Levelt and G.B. Flores d'Arcais (eds.). *Studies in the Perception of Language*. Chichester, England: Wiley, 1978.

Ritchie, G.D. *Computational Grammar*. New York: Barnes and Noble, 1980.

Robinson, A.E. "Determining verb phrase referents in dialogs," *AJCL 7*, 1, 1-16, 1981.

Robinson, J.A. "A machine-oriented logic based on the resolution principle," *Journal of the ACM 12*, 1, 1965.

Robinson, J.J. "DIAGRAM: A grammar for dialogues," *Commun. of the ACM 25*, 1, 27-47, January 1982 (reprinted in RNLP).

Rosenschein, S.J. and S.M. Shieber. "Translating English into logical form," *Proc. ACL*, 1-8, 1982.

Rumelhart, D.E. "Notes on schema for stories," in D. Bobrow and A. Collins (eds.). *Representation and Understanding*. New York: Academic Press, 1975.

Rumelhart, D.E. and J. McClelland. *Parallel Distributive Processing*. Cambridge, MA: MIT Press, 1986.

Russell, B. and A.N. Whitehead. *Principia Mathematica* (vol. 1, 2nd edition). New York: Cambridge U. Press, 1925.

Sacerdoti, E. *A Structure for Plans and Behavior*. New York: Elsevier North-Holland, 1977.

Sager, N. *Natural Language Information Processing: A Computer Grammar of English and its Applications*. Reading, MA: Addison-Wesley, 1981.

Schank, R.C. (ed.). *Conceptual Information Processing*. Amsterdam: North-Holland, 1975.

Schank, R.C. "Language and memory," *Cognitive Science 4*, 243-284, 1980 (reprinted in RNLP).

Schank, R.C. and R. Abelson. *Scripts, Plans, Goals and Understanding*. Hillsdale, NJ: Lawrence Erlbaum, 1977.

Schank, R.C. and K.M. Colby. *Computer Models of Thought and Language*. San Francisco, CA: Freeman, 1973.

Schank R.C., and C.J. Rieger. "Inference and the computer understanding of natural language," *Artificial Intelligence 5*, 373-412, 1974.

Schank, R.C. and C.K. Riesbeck. *Inside Computer Understanding* (chap. 2). Hillsdale, NJ: Lawrence Erlbaum, 1981.

Schiffer, S.R. *Meaning*. London: Oxford U. Press, 1972.

Schubert, L.K. "Are there preference tradeoffs in attachment decison?" *Proc. AAAI*, 601-605, 1986.

Schubert, L.K., M.A. Papalaskaris, and J. Taugher. "Accelerating deductive inference: Special methods for taxonomies, colours, and times," in N. Cercone and G. McCalla (eds.). *Knowledge Representation*. New York: Springer-Verlag, 1986.

Schubert, L.K. and F.J. Pelletier. "From English to logic: Context-free computation of conventional logical translation," *AJCL 8*, 1, 165-176, 1982 (reprinted in RNLP).

Searle, J.R. "Indirect speech acts," in P. Cole and J. Morgan (eds.), 59-82. *Syntax and Semantics 3: Speech Acts.* New York: Academic Press, 1975.

Shapiro, S.C. "Generalized augmented transition network grammars for generation from semantic networks," *AJCL 8*, 1, 12-25, 1982.

Shapiro, S.C. (ed.). *Encyclopedia of Artificial Intelligence.* New York: Wiley, 1987.

Shieber, S. "The design of a computer language for linguistic information," *Proc. COLING*, 362-366, 1984.

Shieber, S. "An introduction to unification-based approaches to grammar," CSLI Lecture Notes 4, Chicago U. Press, 1986.

Sidner, C. "Focusing in the comprehension of definite anaphora," in M. Brady and R.C. Berwick (eds.), 267-330. *Computational Models of Discourse.* Cambridge, MA: MIT Press, 1983 (reprinted in RNLP).

Simmons, R. and J. Slocum. "Generating English discourse from semantic networks," *Commun. of the ACM 15*, 10, 891-905, 1972.

Slocum, J. "A survey of machine translation," *Computational Linguistics 11*, 1, 1-17, 1985.

Sowa, J. *Conceptual Structures.* Reading, MA: Addison-Wesley, 1984.

Steedman, M. "Reference to past time," in R.J. Jarvella and W. Klein (eds.). *Speech, Place and Action.* New York: Wiley, 1982.

Strawson, P.F. "Intention and convention in speech acts," *Philosophical Review 73*, 4, 439-460, 1964; reprinted in J.R. Searle (ed.). *The Philosophy of Language.* London: Oxford U. Press, 1971.

Tarski, A. "The semantic conception of truth and the foundations of semantics," *Philosophy and Phenomenological Research 4*, 341-375, 1944.

Tedesci, P and A. Zaenen (eds.). *Syntax and Semantics. Vol. 14: Tense and Aspect.* New York: Academic Press, 1981.

Thomason, R. *Symbolic Logic.* New York: Macmillan, 1970.

Thompson, F. and B. Thompson. "Practical natural language processing: The REL system as prototype," in M. Rubinoff and B. Yovits (eds.), 109-168. *Advances in Computers 13.* New York: Academic Press, 1975.

Tomita, M. *Efficient Parsing for Natural Language.* Boston: Kluwer Academic Publishers, 1986.

Touretzky, D. *The Mathematics of Inheritance Systems.* Los Altos, CA: Morgan Kaufmann, 1986.

Wahlster, W., H. Marburger, A. Jameson, and S. Buseman. "Over-answering yes-no questions," *Proc. IJCAI*, 643-646, 1983.

Walker, D.E. (ed.). *Understanding Spoken Language.* New York: Elsevier North-Holland, 1978.

Waltz, D.L. and B.A. Goodman. "Writing a natural language data base system," *Proc. IJCAI*, 144-150, 1977.

Wanner, E. "The ATN and the sausage machine: Which one is baloney?", *Cognition 8*, 209-225, 1980.

Warren, D.H.D. and F.C.N. Pereira. "An efficient easily adaptable system for interpreting natural language queries," *Computational Linguistics 8*, 3-4, 110-122, 1982.

Webber, B.L. "So what can we talk about now," in M. Brady and B. Berwick (eds.), 331-370. *Computational Models of Discourse.* Cambridge, MA: MIT Press, 1983 (reprinted in RNLP).

Webber, B.L. "The interpretation of tense in discourse," *Proc. ACL*, 147-154, 1987a.

Webber, B.L. "Question Answering," in S.C. Shapiro (ed.), 814-822. *Encyclopedia of Artificial Intelligence.* New York: Wiley, 1987b.

Weischedel, R.M. "A new semantic computation while parsing: Presupposition and entailment," in C. Oh and D. Dineen (eds.), 155-182. *Syntax and Semantics II: Presupposition.* New York: Academic Press, 1979 (reprinted in RNLP).

Weischedel, R.M. and N.K. Sondheimer. "Meta-rules as a basis for processing ill-formed output," *Computational Linguistics 9*, 3-4 (Special Issue on Ill-Formed Input), 161-177, July-December 1983.

Weizenbaum, J. "ELIZA," *Commun. of the ACM 9*, 36-45, 1966.

Wilensky, R. *Planning and Understanding.* Reading, MA: Addison-Wesley, 1983.

Wilensky, R. *Common LISPcraft.* New York: W.W. Norton, 1986.

Wilks, Y. "An intelligent analyzer and understander of English," *Commun. of the ACM 18*, 5, 264-274, 1975 (reprinted in RNLP).

Winograd, T. *Understanding Natural Language.* New York: Academic Press, 1972.

Winograd, T. *Language as a Cognitive Process. Vol. 1: Syntax.* Reading, MA: Addison-Wesley, 1983.

Winston, P.H.   *Artificial Intelligence* (2nd edition).   Reading, MA: Addison-Wesley, 1984.

Winston, P.H. and B.K.P. Horn.   *LISP* (2nd edition).   Reading, MA: Addison-Wesley, 1984.

Woods, W.A. "Procedural semantics for question answering," *Proc. AFIPS Conf. 33*, 457-471, 1968.

Woods, W.A. "Transition network grammars for natural language analysis," *Commun. of the ACM 13*, 591-606, 1970 (reprinted in RNLP).

Woods, W.A. "An experimental parsing system for transition network grammars," in R. Rustin (ed.). *Natural Language Processing*. New York: Algorithmics Press, 1973.

Woods, W.A. "What's in a link: Foundations for semantic networks," in D.G. Bobrow and A. Collins (eds.). *Representation and Understanding: Studies in Cognitive Science*. New York: Academic Press, 1975.

Woods, W.A. "Lunar rocks in natural English: Explorations in natural language question answering," in A. Zampoli (ed.). *Linguistic Structures Processing*. New York: Elsevier North-Holland, 1977.

Woods, W.A. "Semantics and quantification in natural language question answering," in M. Yovitz (ed.). *Advances in Computers* (vol. 17). New York: Academic Press, 1978 (reprinted in RNLP).

Woods, W.A. "Cascaded ATN grammars," *AJCL 6*, 1, 1-12, 1980.

Index